The Back Door Guide to
Short Term
Job Adventures

PIECE TOGETHER YOUR FUTUR
• GET INVOLVED • TAKE THE NEX
STEP • FANTASTIC CHALLENGE
• YOU CAN MAKE A DIFFERENC
• THE WORLD IS YOUR CLASS
ROOM • ENDLESS OPTIONS • EAR
AS YOU LEARN • A WORLD OF DIS
COVERY • LOOK AT THE POSSIBIL
ITIES • DO IT ALL • PIEC
TOGETHER YOUR FUTURE • GE
INVOLVED • TAKE THE NEXT STE
• FANTASTIC CHALLENGES • YO
CAN MAKE A DIFFERENCE • TH
WORLD IS YOUR CLASSROO

The Back Door Guide to
Short Term
Job Adventures

INTERNSHIPS · EXTRAORDINARY EXPERIENCES
SEASONAL JOBS · VOLUNTEERING · WORK ABROAD

BY MICHAEL LANDES

Ten Speed Press
Berkeley, California

To my mom and dad, who not only opened my eyes to so many things while growing up, but also provided me with the tools needed to develop into the person I am today. I feel very fortunate: it's comforting to know that someone encourages and has faith in your abilities no matter what.

Ten Speed Press
P.O. Box 7123
Berkeley, CA 94707
www.tenspeed.com

Distributed in Canada by Ten Speed Press Canada; in Australia by Simon & Schuster Australia; in New Zealand by Tandem Press; in South Africa by Real Books; in the United Kingdom and Europe by Airlift Books; and in Southeast Asia by Berkeley Books.

Cover design and interior design by Toni Tajima
Cover illustration by Tony D'Agostino
Printed in Canada

Library of Congress Cataloging-in-Publication Data
Landes, Michael.
The back door guide to short-term job adventures : internships, extraordinary experiences, seasonal jobs, volunteering, work abroad / by Michael Landes.
        p. cm.
Includes index.
ISBN 0-89815-954-7 (pbk.)
1. Job hunting. 2. Interns. 3. Volunteers. 4. Overseas employees. I. Title.
HF5382.7.L352 1997
650. 14—dc21   97-9441
                                                        CIP

2 3 4 5 — 02 01 00 99 98

Stumbling Upon a New Path . . .

These were the college years—the good years, they say. For most, it's a time where we happily plod along, enjoying life without thinking too much about it. You study a little, go to class, play with your friends, and become involved in almost anything imaginable. However, these years go by quickly and the next thing you know, you've got your diploma in your hand and a worried look on your face. You see, many of us forget to ask (let alone answer) the simple question, "What the heck am I going to do when I graduate?"

I, too, almost succeeded in graduating without a vision for the future. It's easy to end up being unprepared for life after college. You see, since age four (or so), most of our lives have revolved around our education. Year after year after year as we progress through the education system, no one really teaches us about or prepares us for this thing called life.

I thought about the possibilities: I could move onward in the education world and get a master's. I could become a bum and travel around until I ran out of money. I could stay in my waiting job and enjoy the good life of living in a college town. I could be like some of my older friends who moved back home with their folks and found thankless and mindless jobs. None of these choices really sounded good. I knew that the world had to offer more than these few options I could come up with.

One day, as I wandered aimlessly on campus pondering my life's path, I chanced upon an internship flyer posted on a kiosk: "Come join the Gallo team this summer, helping us market our new line of Bartles and Jaymes wine coolers!" An internship—what was this all about?

Well, for the next three months, my life revolved around internships. Every waking moment I visualized getting an internship, and each day I prepared myself for the process, researching and applying to any programs that sounded interesting to me (a *Back Door Guide* sure would have been nice to have back then). At that point in my life, any internship with any program sounded good to me (I was still trying to overcome the feeling of being a lost soul).

Then, the day came when I opened my mailbox and found a letter from Gallo Winery. Ripping it open, I discovered I had

Preface

been asked to become a part of "the Gallo Team" as their summer intern. "Hmmm, free wine and a summer with Frank and Ed? When do I start?" So I ventured into my first internship (and my first business cards, great salary, expense account, full benefits, sales training classes, wine-tasting seminars, a company car, and a sampler case of Gallo's "finest" wine). Not only that, I found myself living in San Francisco—a place I had always wanted to explore.

From that point on, my whole life changed. Actually, I may want to step back just a little and explain what happened in more detail.

OK, I may have made it sound like I sent off a letter to the Gallo recruiters one day, and the next, they offered me the job. No, it wasn't quite like that. In fact, it was a tremendously grueling process. I had to learn everything from A to Z about getting a real job. It was a little different from my past jobs, when friends and family recommended me to their supervisors and the next day I was working. This was a whole new ball game. This meant creating a resume; writing a creative cover letter for the first time; learning how to interview (I practiced in my closet); writing thank-you letters; following up with letters and phone calls; tracking down Gallo sales reps out in the field to get their insights on the company; having a second interview, on-site, during my spring break (the last spring break of my college career, which was supposed to take me to Mexico); following up again; and then receiving the letter. Many of you have already gone through this process, but if you haven't, you're in for a real big treat. Before you know it, you'll be an expert in getting any job you set your mind to. It means getting to know yourself, inside and out, and then figuring out how your God-given talents and abilities can be put to good use somewhere in our society.

After my first internship with Gallo, I had an overwhelming dose of the internship bug and couldn't get it out of my system. I took the next semester off from school to do another internship with another company. I became aggressive and wanted the best internship in the United States (at least in my mind). My goal was a computer company that was blossoming back in 1987—Apple Computer. They were offering one hundred students the chance to travel around the United States (all expenses paid) and teach people the magic of what Apple computers could do. This was it. I focused entirely on getting this internship (and although it's great to be focused and go after a dream, I now can look back at the situation and realize how unbalanced my life became—all that mattered to me was Apple).

As you probably guessed, I got my job with Apple. My initial phone call with an Apple recruiter became an on-site interview, that very same day (just a short 200-mile drive from where I lived). I impressed her with my background (the fact I had a previous internship), and I think she really liked that I drove so far at a moment's notice—and the clincher was the handwritten thank-you note I left on her car, making sure she knew I would make a difference. My point here is, if you want something bad enough, go after your dream with everything you've got and be creative. Organizations are looking for good people who have that "fire in their belly" and who want to make a difference in the company. I always asked myself, "If I were the president of this company, would I want to hire myself?"

Working for Apple provided me with an experience of a lifetime—one that provided both a career direction and a developing passion for travel and adventure. I learned how to be an explorer, and most importantly, how essential it is to put yourself out there and meet (and learn from) people you encounter daily. A chance meeting with someone can change your entire life, but you have to be receptive to these encounters and learn to take risks.

As my college career came to an end, I had two internships under my belt and an offer from Apple upon graduation. They wanted me to represent them in another traveling trade show, MTV's Museum of UnNatural History. Of course, I accepted this position and started what I thought would be my career path to becoming the CEO of Apple (and the lifestyle that came from that position).

Then, while on the road with Apple and MTV's promotional tour, an event happened that would completely change my thinking on where my life was headed. I got smushed by a car. I guess there's not a really pleasant way to describe a car hitting your body, so I'll spare you the gruesome details. The car did a number on my legs, forcing me to stop working and move back home, as I couldn't do the "daily rituals" without help from my family. Now, I guessed, I was like all my friends who moved back home....

The next six months were dedicated to rehabilitating my legs so I could walk again (a miracle in itself). And in this time, my whole thinking about the meaning of life changed (lying in bed with a couple of broken legs gives you ample time to think about this stuff). I was thankful for so many things and for so many people who had provided a helping hand in this unique experience. Even though this was a challenging time in my life, I look back on it with fond memories because of all the growing I did. Tough times don't last, tough people do!

I had a new perspective on and appreciation for life. I wanted to make a difference in the world, with the talents that were beckoning me to pursue them. Although I eventually went back to Apple, I knew the corporate world was not for me. I continued to ask myself tough questions and to search, and eventually I began to help coordinate a university internship program. I did this for almost five years and loved it, but I still questioned my path. Was this my calling—making a daily impact on the lives of students and helping them to figure out what they wanted to be when they grew up? Yes, but I also knew there was more in store for me.

I looked at my work experience. In addition to the experiences I've described, I had worked at a tennis club, tossed luggage in 747s at an airport, participated in a Burger King commercial, backpacked and cycled in Europe, had several food-server jobs, performed in an outdoor theatre production, coordinated a recreation program at Yellowstone National Park, done various consulting work (including work for a nonprofit started by Julia Child and Robert Mondavi), worked numerous odd jobs (from getting paid to spy on someone to installing computer systems for the U.S. Forest Service), and put in thousands of hours of volunteer work. My whole life seemed to revolve around varied experiences, experiences which helped me open doors I never knew existed and gave me the confidence to get any job I set my mind to getting.

OK, so what provoked me to write this guidebook? What you're looking at today was created out of a void I saw of help for those who were transitioning and needed a little push to actively pursue something different, something that would bring more meaning to life than their current situation provided. Some of you may have found that it's too easy to get settled into a nice-paying job with benefits—one that neither gives you any tangible gratification nor taps into your God-given skills and talents or does much for society.

Look at your current situation in life and take a hard look at what you are doing and where you are going. Do you like what you see? What do you really want to be when you grow up? (Even if you're seventy-two, you can still ask this question.) How will you realistically change your whole life around to accommodate your dreams? What programs, resources, and people are out there to help you? What will it take to make this change happen? Yes, there are many questions to consider: some of which you've answered, others that still need attention. Once you do some soul-searching, you'll find that the answers lay deep inside and that it's up to you to bring these answers out.

Most of my writing comes from my own struggles and accomplishments and from the wisdom they've brought me. This guidebook will provide you with new information and fresh ideas—with the underlying message that there is room for every person in our world to work at a job they love: one that will offer personal satisfaction and growth and a good dose of adventure! As you dive into your guide, you'll find that it will provide you with the information and inspiration to better understand yourself, instill confidence in your own abilities, help you to work, travel, and learn somewhere new, and to take a nontraditional route to finding your vocational passion in life!

Acknowledgments . . . .

Great things don't happen without great people. I thank those graciously who have helped me inspire Back Door readers all over the world. I couldn't have done it without these folks: Scott Lewis for his computer wizardry, support, and inspiration since day one; Dorrie and Mike Williams for their creativity, great stories, and for housing and putting up with me; Craig Dunkin, my "lawyer," who is on the road to fulfilling his own passion in life; Richard Ramsey from Disneyland Resort for his valuable encouragement and help; Lucy Izon, Barbara Winter, Jim Williams, Patrick Combs, and Dick Bolles for helping me get the word out; Professor Borrie for his drollery and for bringing the guide into his classroom; all the college campuses across the nation who believe in my work and have provided super feedback; the Association for Experiential Education for their initial backbone; all the great musical artists who kept me going when I was glued to my computer; my family, who inspired me with this message (which I read every day): "Entrepreneur...he casts aside his assurance of forty-hour weeks, leaves the safe cover of tenure and security...and charges across the perilous fields of change and opportunity. If he succeeds, his profits will come not from what he takes from his fellow citizens, but from the value they freely place on the gift of his imagination"; my "new family" at Ten Speed Press, especially Kirsty for dragging my manuscript out of the slush, Clancy for her whacky style, spirit, and dedication to this project, Wade for his keen and thoughtful copyedit, Toni for her inspired design, Tony for his wonderful illustrations, and Rebecca for her careful proofread; and—finally—to Back Door readers, who have written me with their reactions, success stories, great quotes, and fun postcards. Thank you to all!

The Splatter Effect . . . .

Beware! Reading through your guidebook is an experience. In addition to your back door listings, you'll find quotes, hot tips, Back Door Tales, insights to tweak your brain, and other great resources, including reviews of books, magazines, newsletters, brochures, and Web sites "splattered" from cover to cover!

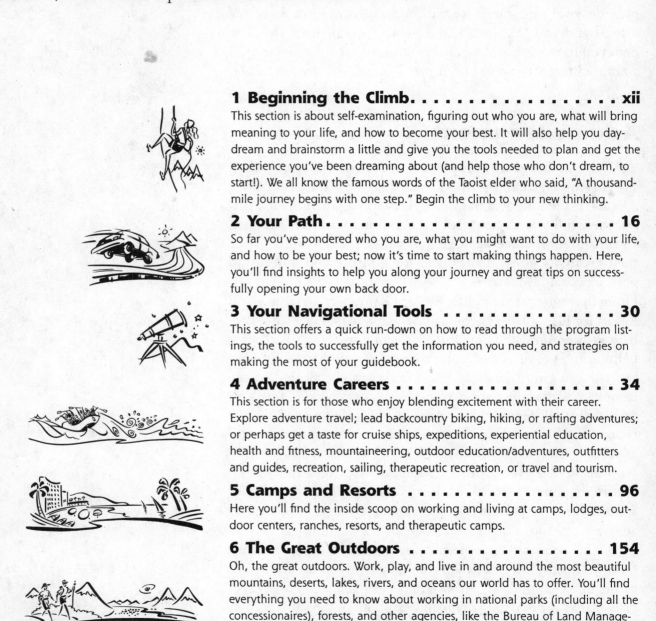

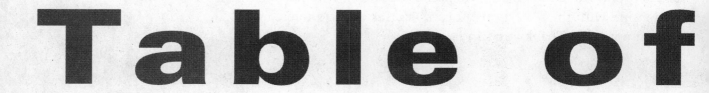

Table of

I made a big decision a little while ago. I don't remember what it was, which prob'ly goes to show. That many times a simple choice can prove to be essential even though it often might appear inconsequential.

I must have been distracted when I left my home because left or right I'm sure I went. (I wonder which it was!) Anyway, I never veered: I walked in that direction utterly absorbed, it seems, in quiet introspection.

For no reason I can think of, I've wandered far astray. And that is how I got to where I find myself today.

—BILL WATTERSON, *Calvin and Hobbes*

Contents

1

THE CLIMB

A small boy heard the mountain speak
"there are secrets on my highest peak;
but beware, my boy, the passing of time.
Wait not too long to start the climb."

So quickly come and go the years,
and a young man stands below—with fears.
"Come on—come on," the mountain cussed.
"Time presses on—on, climb you must."

Now he's busied in middle-aged prime,
and maybe tomorrow he'll take the climb.
Now is too soon—it's raining today;
Gone all gone—years are eaten way.

An old man looks up—still feeling the lure.
Yet, he'll suffer the pain—not climb for the cure.
The hair is white—the step is slow.
And it's safer and warmer to stay here below.

So all too soon the secrets are buried,
along with him and regrets he carried.
And it's not for loss of secrets he'd cried,
But rather because he'd never tried.

—PHYLLIS TRUSSIER

Beginning

Your Back Door Approach to Life . . . .

A back door approach is not a conventional one. But the career environment is changing, and long-term job security—with its focus on putting in your forty hours, living for the weekends, collecting a paycheck, and remaining in a possibly thankless job for life—seems to be a thing of the past. Instead, an increasingly viable approach centers around the development of a unique career path that promotes your personal interests and convictions and brings out your undiscovered talents. This means leaping headfirst into a long and incredible journey of self-discovery, expanding your vision and understanding of your life, your mission, and the world in which you live. Even though society is just learning to accept, support, and encourage those of us who are on this path, the rewards of your back door approach can be as great as they are unexpected.

By thinking (and acting) with a back door approach to life and work, you will begin to pay more attention to your career path—and it will not become a random process that never adds up to real personal fulfillment. You'll break free from your current mold, meet new people, learn new skills, and find out where you can make a difference in our world (no matter how small). The process of personal discovery should be a daily part of your life. The place where you fit in is not so much something you find as it is something that you make. It's your daily actions that shape and guide you in new directions. Challenge yourself each and every day and think of your career—and moreover, your life—as an adventure through a world of opportunities.

If this idea of a back door approach appeals to you, but seems impossible, or if you're really not sure what you might want to do, read on. Tough questions will be asked; my hope is to share ideas toward a new way of looking at your life, so you can answer these questions yourself. Too often, we look for easy answers through books, friends, family, and counselors—all of which can be very helpful; however, you are the only one who can actively engage in your life and find the answers to what you want from it.

Whatever you are from nature, keep to it; never desert your own line of talent. Be what nature intended you for, and you will succeed; be anything else, and you will be ten thousand times worse than nothing.

—SYDNEY SMITH

The way we choose to see the world creates the world we see.

—BARRY NEIL KAUFMAN

Many things are clarified only with the passage of time.

—ANSEL ADAMS

the Climb

Fall in love with what you're going to do for a living. It's very important. To be able to get out of bed and do what you love for the rest of the day is beyond words. It's just great. It'll keep you around for a long time.

—GEORGE BURNS

■▪■▪■■▪■■▪■■▪■■▪■■

Often in life we sell ourselves short and never reach our dreams or become truly happy. By taking that first step we certainly delve into a world of truth about ourselves—that is the sole foundation of education. And this is my way of fulfilling life…taking the risk!

—JOSEPH OVERBERGER, *BACK DOOR* READER

■▪■■▪■■▪■■▪■■▪■■▪■

We are all unique and have something to offer that no one else can!

Everyone has his own specific vocation or mission in life…therein he cannot be replaced, nor can his life be repeated. Thus, everyone's task is as unique as is his specific opportunity to implement it.

—VIKTOR FRANKL

For those who have already started their back door approach (and already know they want to excavate an archaeological dig in Peru or guide folks down the white waters of the Snake River or teach kids about the wonders of the ocean) and don't need to do extensive soul-searching, taking a peek at this section can't hurt. So, hold onto your shorts. Finding yourself, deciding what brings meaning to your life, and determining your destiny all take time. This section will give you some creative ideas about the bigger picture in life and start your climb off on the right foot.

Who Are You? . . . .

It really is an exciting world out there. But with so many choices, so many people, so many jobs, so many places, and so many organizations to choose from, how do you actually fit into the scheme of it all? What makes one person a pilot, the next a basketball player, and another the director of a nonprofit? And once you figure out what you might want to do, how and where should you do it? Should you grow in your own backyard or be open to the possibility of blooming anywhere in the world? Should you follow your heart, doing something you love (and possibly struggling financially), or find a nice-paying job so you can live a comfortable lifestyle?

First you have to figure out who you are before you can go after what you want in life. You especially lose out when you are unable to promote your unique qualities and abilities to others when the time arises. Now is the time to think about your skills, your personal quirks, and what you really like doing. Then you can promote your uniqueness with passion and vigor.

Think of your life as a long, never-ending pathway stretching out ahead of you, with many pathways leading off to either side. The path you are on now represents the lifestyle you are now living (whether it be good or bad); the offshoots from this pathway represent new directions you might take—new jobs, new places to live, new relationships, and new activities. However, in giving yourself many options, you'll always come to a signpost on the road presenting you with two (or three or four or…) attractive possibilities. Which one should you take? Which one will help you in your long-term goals? Of course, some of these paths might have huge doors in front of them, and to get through these doors, you must do certain things before they swing open for you. A particular door might need a certain skill, a degree, a well-connected friend or family member, a unique personal characteristic, or a past experience as a key. So, let's start from the beginning and take a look at what makes you tick. Who are you?

Setting the Stage. . . . .

Have you ever been to a play? If not, put your guide down and go to a play for the sheer enjoyment of it. Now, take a few seconds and ponder all the things that went into the play's production: the directors, producers, writers, the cast, set designers and scenery construction, costuming, acting, rehearsals, development, fund-raising, program design, publicity, and so forth. It's amazing to think of all the steps necessary to create one production. Have you thought about what will make your very own "production" incredible? Have you thought about the gifts, abilities, and strengths you currently possess? How about the things you want to (or may want to) accomplish to create an incredible story for yourself? Do you feel like you're not tapping into your potential? Do you feel like you're on a raft just drifting through life? Think of all the players who are involved in your story, the scenery, the things that happen on a daily basis, the decisions that are made, the highs, the lows, and so forth. Are you the director and author of your story, or are you letting society or others dictate your story? Are you actively taking the time to develop your plot and making the things you want most happen in your life? (Wow, I'm even overwhelmed by all these questions.)

The best way to start answering these questions is to become aware of what's happening in your life right now, but it will take some doing on your part. You need to take an active role in the exploration, writing out your dreams and aspirations. Sure, there are readers and there are writers. However, you'll find that, once you write this important stuff down, it gives you something to work with, and you're more apt to act upon it. Start making lists, just like a list you would make for your weekly trip to the supermarket. These lists will work in the same way. You put bananas on the list, and you buy them. Pickles aren't on your list, so you don't buy them (unless, of course, it's an impulse buy). Get the picture? Easy stuff. So, let the fun begin. Get out a paper of any size, your favorite writing tools, and maybe put on your favorite sweatshirt and beat-up shorts. This is brainstorming time and anything goes. And don't edit or censor yourself—just write, doodle, type or crayon away, jotting down everything you feel and know.

How can you get very far,
If you don't know who you are?
How can you do what you ought,
If you don't know what you've got?
And if you don't know which to do
Of all the things in front of you,
Then what you'll have when you
 are through
Is just a mess without a clue
Of all the best that can come true
If you know what and which and who.

—A.A. MILNE, *WINNIE THE POOH*

I believe one of the hardest things about growing up is finding our place in the world. Where do we belong? Where can we make a difference? It is important to find a path with heart. Be open, vulnerable, and embrace challenges; you will grow from every experience!

—ALONA JASIK, *BACK DOOR* READER

If you always do what you've always done, you'll always get what you've always got.

—LARRY WILSON

I can play the piano. I speak two languages. I can juggle. I love teaching kids about the wonders of the world. I hate snakes. I love frogs. I'm a so-so painter. I love thunderstorms, I'm afraid of not having enough money/going into debt/being dependent on my parents or another person. I'm a pretty good baker. I'm a rotten city driver and really don't care for big cities. I really want to be a writer, photographer, teacher and speaker! I love Italian music and food. A lot of money is not important to me. I want to travel in my work. I want to be settled somewhere. I just want to goof off for a couple of months. I'd like to try living on a boat or on a remote island. One day I'd like to have my own business. I like a lot of change and stimulation.

List 1. Your Story . . . .

This list answers questions about who you are as a person. Reflect on some or all of the questions (or make up some of your own). If the question moves you to answer it from your heart, go for it; if not, move on to the next. The goal is to get a better perspective on you—the good, the bad, and the ugly of your story.

What's unique about yourself?
What do you gravitate towards naturally?
What are your likes and dislikes?
What are your strengths and weaknesses?
What do your friends say you are good at?
What are your skills?
What are your dreams and fears?
What are your long-term goals? medium-term goals? short-term goals?

Being good at something doesn't necessarily translate into its being your dream career. You may be great at playing dominoes, but as far as hitting the domino circuit as a career....

List 2. Imagine This! . . . .

Stop and take the time to dream. This is your ongoing list of possibilities in your life—practical or not. If you want to fly to the moon or learn how to make your own batch of beer, put it down. If you've always wanted to participate in a workcamp in Poland or play in the Caribbean, jot it down. Maybe you've always wanted to own a tandem bicycle or buy an old VW van to travel around the United States (and visit each national park)—add these ideas to your list. This is your *ongoing* record of things you might want to accomplish in life. And since it's ongoing, when you actually do something, you can check it off and see the strides you are making. You'll be amazed that, by writing a dream down, you're telling your innards that this stuff is important, and in a week, a year, five years, or maybe thirty, you'll eventually have checked it off your list.

LIST 3. The Good Stuff in My Life . . . .

Start making a list of all your accomplishments. When you do something great, complete a project, make a friend, add it to your list. Now you have some history to look at. Not only that, you'll find that this list will help keep you motivated. We need to be given praise to keep us going, and more often than not, you won't receive the praise you were hoping for when you finish a project. You need to become your own cheerleader and pat yourself on the back when you deserve it. Reward yourself by taking yourself out to dinner or buying that CD you've wanted for a long time. This small reward will compel you to stay on top of your world. For starters, when you finish this section of the book, put it on your list—you have to begin somewhere! Later, your accomplishment list can also double as your resume.

These lists are simply to get you to know yourself better and to help you see when you're making some progress. By making them, you might find some very interesting facts about yourself. But don't be alarmed if you don't. You might just need to think, explore, and do more. Always keep these lists nearby and where you can see them. Then, whenever an idea comes to mind, you can add to them (or cross them off) and create more adventures to explore in your story.

Don't spend a lifetime exploring possibilities and doing nothing. Have the courage to take action.

EXCELLENCE can be attained if you:
CARE more than others think is wise,
RISK more than others think is safe,
DREAM more than others think is practical,
EXPECT more than others think is possible.

Feeling Groovy: Staying Your Best . . . .

Have you noticed that when you overexert yourself in one area of your life, other areas might suffer? For instance, now that you have this guide, your attention may be completely focused on making a change in your life. However, with all this mental stimulation going on, other areas in your life may begin to suffer. Have you stopped making time for writing in your journal, eating well, exercising, having friends over for dinner? Conversely, maybe all this mental stimulation has jump-started your balancing engine, and you are engaged in all areas of your life! You'll find that when you strive to reach a balance in your life (in all areas), you become a happier, more energetic, and more productive person.

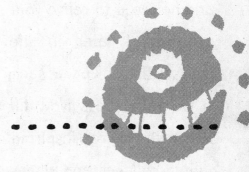

When you are doing what is true, what is honest to your nature, you'll feel right. When you're false, you'll feel wrong.

KEEPING A JOURNAL

Make time in your life to reflect upon your experiences. You don't have to start a new job or partake in a new experience to begin. Start today! Journals (or creating another list) can help you discover and uncover yourself, encourage yourself, sort out difficulties with others, invent new ways of seeing things, plan new adventures, and help you to relive your experiences later in life. Books with blank pages seem to work the best. Now fill them with pictures, inspiring quotes, collages, and whatever is on your mind. You might just find the answers you were looking for.

MENTALLY

When was the last time you read a good book? Good literature can expand your mind in ways that are life changing (hopefully your guide is helping to change your life). How about keeping a personal journal of your life—your thoughts, insights, experiences, or lessons from others? Instead of sitting on the couch watching mindless television (unless, of course, you are watching *Seinfeld*), stay mentally active by reading, taking courses/workshops, and exposing yourself to others who can give you new perspectives. Maybe do something fun that you've been meaning to do, like planting that row of flowers in your front yard, going to see a play, exploring a hiking trail you've never taken, asking a friend out for coffee, or filling up your bulletin board with pictures of inspirational scenes. And if all this mental activity is bringing you down, let it go! Life is a learning experience. Learn to forgive yourself and get on the right path again. If you seem to be on a roller coaster with your thinking, focus on making lists, writing on calendars, and making reminders of the things that are important to you. Daily reminders help to keep you on track. It's also good to be around people that not only support and bring positive influence to your life, but who will also challenge you.

PHYSICALLY

All right, put the book down and give me fifty. That's right, do your body some good and pump out fifty sit-ups. Being physically balanced means making a commitment to taking care of your body. For one, this means exercising on a daily basis. I recommend at least thirty minutes a day (and more if you can). You'll find that when you look great, you tend to be a happier person, with more confidence in everything you do. For some it will take breaking old habits and starting out fresh. Just do it. Today, get up in the morning (or at any time of the day) to go jogging, pump some iron at the gym, or go for a bike ride in the park with your mate. Make exercise a ritual and vary it every day so you don't get bored with your newfound love of activity. The key is making time for it, but most importantly, listen to your body. It will tell you if you've had too much or too little, so don't overdo. Sometimes, lounging on the couch all day reading a good book is all you really need to recharge your batteries. So listen. Getting sufficient sleep and relaxation is just as important as pushing your body.

With all this exercise you'll be doing, you'll be changing your eating habits as well. If you're eating balanced meals, great!

For some, you'll have to learn to cook meals that are healthy. It is so easy to become "unbalanced" throughout the day by not eating at all, not eating enough, eating too much, or by overdoing items such as processed food, caffeine, and alcohol. Pick up a good book on nutrition or share food ideas with friends, who can help keep you motivated. Now, instead of being fatigued or sluggish throughout your day, you'll find, if you keep a proper diet, daily exercise, and proper relaxation, you'll have an energy that will invigorate everything you do. Really!

SPIRITUALLY

Close your eyes. Be still. Daydream. Practice yoga or some sort of meditation. Do affirmations. Listen to your favorite Italian sonata. Clear the chatter going on in your mind.

Although spirituality has a religious connotation, it isn't synonymous with going to church once a week for spiritual fulfillment (although it may be for some). Spirituality is what affects your soul—that intangible area that yearns to know why we are here and what our mission is in life. Each of us is given certain gifts, which are revealed to us the more we become aware.

Whatever you do to get in touch with your core, it's very important to make time for this very private area of your life. Some pray regularly or read the Bible; others may immerse themselves in nature or listen to the sounds or rhythms of a particular song to tap into their innermost thoughts and passions. Religious leader David McKay taught, "The greatest battles of life are fought out daily in the silent chambers of the soul." Once you deal with these inward battles (or challenges) you can reach out to others and be genuinely concerned with and happy with their successes. Set aside a small part of your day to get in touch with who you are and where you are going. With the world spinning faster and faster these days, you'll find peace in slowing it down just a bit.

EMOTIONALLY

The reason many of you have picked up this book is because you want some sort of change in your life. You've been grappling with how, where, and when to change. Life, not to mention every minute of the day, is filled with emotions tied to change. What happens in every situation

Remember taking naps as a child? Incorporate a few into your life. They do wonders.

Slow me down God, and inspire me to send my roots down deep into the soil of life's enduring values, so I may grow toward the stars and unfold my destiny.

—Wilfred Peterson

DREAMS

Listen to yourself and listen through your dreams. Dreams can help you understand your inner workings, solve life's problems, and see what your unconscious mind is working on at the moment. Dreams can point you in the right direction, whether you are lost or on the right track, and our unconscious loves to guide us and answer questions we're not ready to ask our conscious mind.

The grand essentials to happiness in this life are something to do, something to love, and something to hope for. —Joseph Addison

7

What's the first thing you say to yourself when you wake up in the morning? Try this out: "I wonder what exciting thing is going to happen to me today?!"

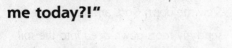

Happiness is like a butterfly. The more you chase it, the more it will elude you. But if you turn your attention to other things, it comes and softly sits on your shoulder.

It's not the clever mind that's responsible when things work out. It's the mind that has a vision, sees what's ahead, and follows the nature of things.

throughout your day can affect the way you feel. Staying emotionally balanced is the ability to be secure enough within yourself that you can handle life's roller-coaster ride in every situation presented to you and not let "them" control your life.

Emotional balance also allows you to build rich and productive relationships with others. Really listen to others. If you are making time for them, at least give them the time of day by listening. Talk to others about the way you feel about things: don't bottle these emotions inside or they may get the best of you. Balance your emotions and enjoy life's simple pleasures. Compliment a stranger, hug a friend, laugh hysterically, scream at the top of your lungs, cry until the tears run dry. Remember you're human; do what you need to feel groovy.

PUTTING IT ALL TOGETHER

Ahhh—this is the tricky part. It's easy to psyche yourself up to become balanced, but actually doing it is another thing, if you don't have the energy and drive within. Remember, what you do once in a while doesn't shape your life, it's what you do consistently. Working on balance on a daily basis will help you hit the curve balls that life can throw your way. But what about when all this balancing is not enough? What about the feeling you need more to bring a fresh perspective and vitality to your life? Well, you may have lapsed into a rut, which can happen even when you think you are doing everything right. The solution to this is easy: Just change your usual focus and *do the opposite!* If you don't exercise regularly, exercise twice a day; if you haven't read a good book, start; if you're always indoors, try going outside. Learn a new skill that you don't think you really need. Start eating completely differently. Volunteer for a good cause for an extended period of time. By making a change in your life you will keep your vitality level high. Even if you're on the right path, a detour sometimes does you some good.

Beginning the Decision-Making Process. . . . .

Making choices and developing your personal plan is of great importance in your journey. By choosing, you learn to be responsible; however, more times than not, you will struggle with your choices. By paying the price of your choices, you also learn to make better choices. When you face the difficulties of making conscious choices, you will grow stronger, more capable, and more responsible to yourself. All of us are meant to work in ways that draw from our natural talents and abilities to express ourselves and contribute to others. This work, when you find it and do it, is a key to your true happiness.

An important part of arriving at your goals is figuring out what you want and what you need, and finding a way to meet both. Most basic needs are the same—food, shelter, health, personal relationships, mental/physical stimulation, spiritual fulfillment, financial responsibility—but everyone will have different levels of each need as well as different ways to meet them. Wants are, well, anything. If you can figure out what you really want to do and what your basic needs are, you can be creative and resourceful about meeting both of them.

THE UNIQUE YOU
Maslow's Hierarchy of Needs

A musician must make his music, an artist must paint, a poet must write if he is to ultimately be at peace with himself. —ABRAHAM MASLOW

Beauty, Truth, Goodness, Aliveness, Individuality, Perfection, Necessity, Completion, Creativity, Simplicity, Playfulness, Self-sufficiency, Significance	STEP 5	SELF-ACTUALIZATION
Self-esteem, Status, Ego	STEP 4	GROWTH NEEDS
Belonging, Love	STEP 3	
Safety, Security, Risk-Avoidance	STEP 2	
Basic Survival Needs, Air and Water, Food, Shelter, Sleep, Sex, Clothing	STEP 1	BASIC NEEDS

Have the ability to make a decision and stick with it, riding out the storms that may follow.

The tragedy is not failing to reach your goal. The tragedy is not having one.

● ● ● ● ● ● ● ● ● ●

Hot tips on keeping a positive mental attitude to reach your goals:

- *Memorize your favorite motivating phrases in this guide and say them everyday!*

- *Make little signs (or huge obnoxious ones that demand your attention) that point towards what you want in your life and put them all over your home. These will serve as tiny reminders of where you want your life to go. Don't take them down until you have actually succeeded in your efforts.*

● ● ● ● ● ● ● ● ● ●

If you can verbalize your top goals without having to sit down and think about them, you're closer to reaching them than you realize.

Action may not always bring happiness, but there is no happiness without action.

One of the main reasons wealth makes people unhappy is that it gives them too much control over what they experience. They try to translate their own fantasies into reality instead of tasting what reality itself has to offer.

—PHILIP SLATER

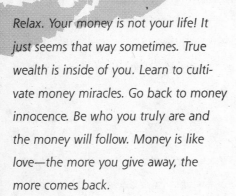

Relax. Your money is not your life! It just seems that way sometimes. True wealth is inside of you. Learn to cultivate money miracles. Go back to money innocence. Be who you truly are and the money will follow. Money is like love—the more you give away, the more comes back.

—SARK

Planning will help you reach your current choices in life and lay out a tentative course of action. Sometimes your plans will turn out, and other times they won't. By realizing that either a positive or a negative outcome may result, you'll save yourself a lot of grief when things don't work out.

Then There's Money . . . .

It's easy to become very motivated by money. Let's face it: it's nice to have money to buy the things we think we need or, perhaps, to use for extended travels and to live fat. However, money is also destructive when it lures you into a job that is unsatisfying or if you only participate in the daily grind for the dough. For some, it's also hard to move on because they've created a comfortable lifestyle that's hard to give up. Additionally, some are so in debt that breaking out of the mold presents a challenge. But you can either be unhappy with a big chunk of your life, or you can become a little creative and go after what is important to you (and shake your life up for the better). You'll find that when you do what you love, you are 110 percent committed to it, and doors open that you would never dream were there. You may even find that living a simple life, by being frugal and resourceful, is an attractive lifestyle once you experience it.

So how do you survive when you're off searching for your passion in life, with no money? How do you pay for rent? for food? for a good book? What about saving for the goal you've set for yourself?

- **Chop your living expenses in half.**
  Can you cut your rent in half by moving in with a friend or by living in a more affordable place? This is a tough one, especially if you're used to a certain standard of living, and you have to go backward. Remember your goal. Shaking up your current situation is key to that goal. Sharing living expenses, utilities, food, and basic necessities is a great way to get started in your money-saving journey.

- **Got skills? Sell and Barter!**
  What skill do you have that could benefit others? Are you a closet artist? Maybe a local business in town might need your help designing a few brochures for a few bucks, or— perhaps the business is a health club—barter your creativity for a membership in the club. This is a great way to get just about anything that is important to you. Show off your stuff. Talk to everybody. Before you know it, the word will get out that you have unique skills.

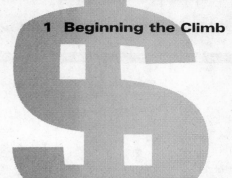

- **Temp Jobs.**

That's all they are—temporary work that could last anywhere from a day or two to a few months or even more. Some temp jobs even turn into permanent positions—especially great if you love the work. Although the work sometimes isn't all that glamorous, you'll at least have a somewhat steady stream of money and a sense of structure to your life while you search out what really matters. You'll also meet some unique people and be exposed to different work environments that just might give you insights on new paths to consider.

- **Sparklett's Jug Theory.**

This is the only way I can save money. Maybe not the smartest way, but it does the job. Find yourself an old Sparklett's jug at your local junk store (you usually can find one for about a buck). Bring it home, set it in your house somewhere, and start dropping. That is, any time you have spare change, drop them babies in. You'll be amazed at how much you can save. But—be forewarned—be sure to attach a goal to your newly saved money (as it is easy to dip into the jug for quick cash). Personally, my Sparklett's fund is dedicated to a travel spot I pick at the beginning of each year. Though I'll spend an entire day rolling all these coins for the bank, the anticipation of finding out how much I've saved is overwhelmingly satisfying. By having a goal attached to your jug, you'll be more motivated in saving. Maybe also hang a sign on it—you know—for friends who stop by and have a "heavy pocket."

- **Sell everything.**

Or, for those that don't have the courage to release themselves from their possessions, at least go straight to your garage, your closet, or wherever you leave your clutter, and make a pile of this stuff that's been sitting around for years. Now, put an ad in the paper and have yourself a garage sale. It's also best to tell friends, neighbors, your mailman (and so forth) a few days ahead of time and invite these folks over the evening before for a VIP, pre-garage-sale hoopla. It's amazing, but most people can sell most of their loot the night before.

- **Do without.**

The next time you go shopping, ask yourself, "Do I really need this?" More than likely you don't, so do without.

Do What You Love, the Money Will Follow by Marsha Sinetar. Filled with inspirational examples of people who have pursued what they love, rather than just the making of money. A must for those who are in jobs for the wrong reason or need a push in the right direction. (Dell, $10.95)

How to Survive Without Your Parents' Money by Geoff Martz. Your parents may love you, but now that you've graduated the free ride is over. You will receive first-person accounts from people who got the job they wanted. Perhaps you are destined to be a musician, artist, or writer, or you simply have an allergy to panty hose and neckties. This book is a practical and slightly humorous guide to finding your first job after college. (Princeton Review, $10)

Be a lamp to yourself. Be your own confidence. Hold to the truth within yourself.
—THE BUDDHA

- **Personal savings or loans from family.**
  This might be the time to dip into your savings to contribute to your cause, and if it is a worthy cause, you may want to think about looking for individual grants or raising money through the local community. This might include philanthropic groups (like Kiwanis), campus/alumni groups, community organizations, civic/religious groups, local businesses, colleagues, or even your current co-workers. In addition, don't be afraid to ask your family for help. A small loan might be the helping hand you need until you get on your feet. But, if you're borrowing just to goof around for the summer to "find yourself," don't bother asking.

- **Credit cards.**
  Don't use credit if at all possible, because it's hard to dig yourself out once you're in deep. However, if you know money will be trickling in soon, this might be the way to start out, especially with all the credit card companies offering low percentage rates to get you on board (just learn how to shuffle your money around). Again, the best rule of thumb is live within your means.

- **You're holding the answer.**
  Yes, this book. That's right. Go after one of the short-term experiences listed here in your guide, and you're home free. You'll find that most offer room, board, and some sort of compensation. You can't go wrong. You'll walk away from every experience with a new perspective.

We are very short on people who know how to do anything. So please don't set out to make money. Set out to make something and hope you get rich in the process.

—ANDY ROONEY

Without exploration there are no discoveries.

—DENG MING-DAO

Don't Travel Down That Big River in Egypt... . . . .

It's the start of the college years for Craig Dunkin, and like many of us during college, he is a little clueless about making big decisions on what to study. At that age, most of us are unaware of what we really want and allow the hand of society to push us in certain directions, instead of making the big decisions for ourselves. Craig was really interested in sports broadcasting; however, smart people go to law school, so that's what he did.

Twelve years later, Craig sits in his office at a very reputable law firm in Los Angeles. He's very successful and makes good money, but on this day, mindless lawyer tasks are par for the course. Then, the epiphany hit: "There is more to life than what I'm doing." This thought consumed him for the rest of the day, with the "Inner-Craig" whispering, "What are you doing practicing law? What are you working toward?" This day changed his life.

While still acting as a lawyer, Craig took a class at a local community college on sports broadcasting, with the professor becoming his mentor and helping him feed his passion. From that point on, Craig dedicated himself to becoming a sports broadcaster. He spent the next few years revitalizing his inborn talents. He would go see the Angels, Dodgers, Lakers, Clippers, Kings—any games he had time to see—and this is the best part—he would take out his microphone and tape recorder and start announcing the games. Yes, right there at the game! Most of the time he would be in the centerfield bleachers or away from the crowds, but occasionally he received curious looks from sports fans wondering what this "nut" was doing. Yes, he had that fire in the belly.

He would purchase a program so he would have enough stats on the players to sit there and call games, to have the action pass through his eyes and brain and out his mouth. He practiced until he got good—good enough that these "demo tapes" doubled as his first broadcasting resume. "I called every minor-league baseball team across the nation and asked if they needed a broadcaster. If they said 'yes' or 'maybe,' I sent the tapes."

Months went by (which seemed like years) until he finally got a break in the South: a team thought he had potential and a deal was made. So this ex-California lawyer made his way to the small town of Clarksville, Tennessee.

Although he would spend extra time on weekends and at night figuring out the small details that make a ball game exciting, the extra work became a labor of love, rather than just laboring (as he felt as a lawyer). "That's what drew me to it all. It is my chance to be really good at something." He looks back at all his lawyer years as "floating down that big river in Egypt." When people stare at him, wondering what he's talking about, he continues, "You know, *the Nile.*" Yes, he lived in a world of **denial**—denial of what he really felt and wanted to do with his life.

Breaking into the field is one thing, but now the real work begins. Craig has to juggle a wife (who has a successful and grounded career) with the season-to-season lifestyle he'll be living. "You really earn your stripes doing games in the bush leagues." This means going from job to job, working your way up the ladder, and making next to nothing. Craig's next goal is to get a home base and to balance out the other aspects in his life. Patience, my friend, patience.

So what advice does Craig have to offer to help you break out of your mold?

"If you don't like being a lawyer, but it allows you to have season tickets to the opera or a beautiful home on five acres—and that's what brings meaning to your life—then so be it. But if that's not enough for you, then why do it? You have to figure out what's important and then fill that aspect in your life. No matter how difficult it is to get into something, don't let that stop you. If you feel you are a talented actor, go do that. But, most importantly, just don't visit that river out in Egypt."

The 7 Habits of Highly Effective People by Stephen R. Covey. This motivating book provides a step-by-step pathway for living, principles that give us the security to adapt to change, and the wisdom and power to take advantage of the opportunities that change creates. (Fireside, $12)

Ask For The Moon—And Get It! by Percy Ross. Most people don't fully appreciate the fact that no matter who you are, if you want something in life, you've got to learn to ask for it. This book focuses on this most neglected secret to success and happiness. (Berkeley Books)

Bus 9 to Paradise by Leo Buscaglia. An investment in life is an investment in change. We're constantly changing, which means we must continue to adjust to change and overcome new obstacles. That's the joy of living. Once you're involved in the process of becoming, there is no stopping. Join the author on this mythical bus. He will help guide you to new levels of happiness on this fantastic journey we're all on. If you like this book, Dr. Buscaglia has a wonderful collection of other books devoted to getting the most out of life through love. (Fawcett, $10)

first you have to row a little boat by Richard Bode. To tack a boat, to sail a zigzag course is not to deny our destination or our destiny—despite how it may appear to those who never dare to take the tiller in their hand. Tacking recognizes the obstacles that stand between ourselves and where we want to go and that we must maneuver with patience and fortitude, making the most of each leg of our journey until we reach our landfall. (Warner Books, $14.95)

Illusions by Richard Bach. I command that you be happy in the world, as long as you live! What if someone demanded that of you? And is it really possible? A wonderful story (and quick read), Richard Bach's book takes you on a journey that explores your unique life and, possibly, answers the question of why we exist. This classic can be found at any used bookstore across the country. (Dell, $4.99)

Inspiration Sandwich by SARK. This guide is written to inspire our creative freedom. Stroll down the path of life with SARK and learn about her 250 jobs, how to relax about money, making friends with freedom and uncertainty, living juicy, drawing on the walls, and making your life an adventure. To receive SARK's free catalog or to find out about her **Magic Museletter,** call (800) 374-5505 or write Camp SARK, P.O. Box 330039, San Francisco, CA 94133; www.campsark.com. And if you need a good dose of inspiration, call SARK's Inspiration Hotline at (415) 546-3742 for a three-minute recorded message by SARK. (Celestial Arts, $14.95)

It's All in the Face by Naomi Tickle. Is there a correlation between your face and the disposition of your life? Naomi Tickle's interesting guide helps you make in-depth character assessments by understanding facial features and what they reveal about you. Take the guessing out of deciding which direction to take in your life. Call Naomi at (415) 965-9540 to receive more information. (Daniels Publishing, $9.95)

Life Types by Sandra Hirsh and Jean Kummerow. Understand yourself and make the most of who you are in life. This book helps you develop a thorough self-portrait. It also helps you to know your strengths and tendencies, overcome your weaknesses, and understand the people in your life better. (Warner Books, $9.99)

Oh, the Places You'll Go! by Dr. Seuss. This joyous ode to personal fulfillment is Dr. Seuss at his best. You'll find this is the perfect send-off for your new adventure. Dr. Seuss addresses the Great Balancing Act (life itself and the ups and downs it presents) while encouraging you to find the success that lies within. "And will you succeed? Yes! You will indeed! (98 and ³/₄ percent guaranteed)." (Random House, $12.95)

Roger von Oechs' Creative Whack Pack. Do you need a whack on the side of the head…or maybe just a kick in the pants? This deck of cards will give you the "kick" you need to get your ideas in action and "whack" you out of habitual thought patterns, allowing you to look at what you're doing in a fresh way. Each card in the deck is designed to provide a brief story, hint, or insight that can help you when you are spinning your problem-solving wheels. Don't get the idea that this is just another one of those granola-brained yuppie trends that you will buy into today and throw into your drawer next week when the fun wears off. This is something to keep in your backpack, so the next time you or a friend are having a creative or mental block, you can pull one out. To get your own pack, check out your local bookstore or call Roger at (415) 321-6775. (U.S. Games Systems, $12.95)

The Tao of Pooh by Benjamin Hoff. See life through the eyes of Winnie the Pooh. What's his secret? "Just take the path to nothing and go nowhere till you reach it." This playful book will get you moving in the right direction. But, remember, "a thousand-mile journey starts with one step." Take your time along the way. (Penguin Books, $10.95)

Give Yourself a Kick in the Seat of the Pants

58 Many of our personal goals are stranded on a little island called the "Someday I'll." Don't wait for your idea to happen. Give yourself a kick in the seat of the pants to make it happen. As adman Carl Ally put it, "Either you let your life slip away by not doing the things you want to do, or you get up and do them." What are three things you can do to reach your goal?

Reprinted with the permission of Roger von Oechs

Each day comes to me with both hands full of possibilities, and in its brief course I discern all the verities and realities of my existence; the bliss of growth, the glory of action, the spirit of beauty. —HELEN KELLER

15

So far, you've pondered who you are, what you might want to do with your life, and how to be your best; now it's time to take action and make things happen. Yes, it is possible for you to end up in the career of your dreams. Make your work your dream (or work that at least leads to your dream). Affirm to others the vision of the world you want. Affirm it, spread it, radiate it. Think day and night about it, and you will see a miracle bloom.

THE TOP TEN SECRETS TO ACHIEVING YOUR DREAM CAREER

10. What would you attempt to do if you knew you could not fail?

9. "Whatever you can do, or dream you can, begin it. Boldness has genius, power, and magic in it. Begin it now."—Johann von Goethe

8. Plan ahead! It wasn't raining when Noah built the ark.

7. Don't spend a lifetime exploring possibilities and do nothing. Action requires courage.

6. Don't put all your eggs in one basket. Always have an alternate plan.

5. To get what you want in life, you've got to ask others for help.

4. The shortest route to your life's work is not necessarily a straight line.

3. "Never let the fear of striking out get in your way." —Babe Ruth

2. "Perseverance is a great element of success. If you only knock long enough and loud enough at the gate, you are sure to wake up somebody." —Henry Wadsworth Longfellow

1. "Never, never, never give up!"—Winston Churchill

Each path is only one of a million paths. Therefore, you must always keep in mind that a path is only a path. If you feel that you must now follow it, you need not stay with it under any circumstances. Any path is only a path. There is no affront to yourself or others in dropping it if that is what your heart tells you to do. But your decision to keep on the path or to leave it must be free of fear and ambition. I warn you— look at every path closely and deliberately. Try it as many times as you think necessary. Then ask yourself and yourself alone one question. It is this— does this path have a heart? If it does, then the path is good. If it doesn't, it is of no use.

—THE TEACHINGS OF DON JUAN

Your Path

The Windows of Opportunity . . .

Is there a right time to make changes in your life? Too often we wait until we are comfortable with a new step or career before launching, thinking that the fear of beginning makes it the "wrong path" or the "wrong time." Fear is a natural part of anything new we do in life—beginning a new relationship, learning a new program on our computer, making new friends, starting a new job, whatever. We are nervous about making a good impression, doing a good job. Everything in life becomes more comfortable with practice and experience. Nobody starts off experienced.

Then what's the best time to participate in a program? As Gray Dean suggests, "Yesterday is history. Tomorrow is a mystery. Today is the gift. That's why it's called the present." That's right. You'll find that the present is your best bet. Why put it off any longer? Make things happen in your life today. If it's October and you're interested in participating in a summer program, you'll have some waiting to do; however, this is the perfect time to start the whole planning process. Most summer programs begin their hiring in January (if not earlier), and sometimes many of the best positions are filled in the first three months of the year. You'll also find that the summer is the most competitive time. If you don't feel you're a strong candidate for a job you really want, it might be in your best interest to apply during a season other than summer. So get off your buns and make things happen now.

Never look down to test the ground before taking your next step. Only he who keeps his eye fixed on the far horizon will find the right road.

—DAG HAMMARSKJÖLD

The right time is anytime one is so lucky as to be alive.

—HENRY JAMES

Are You a Gatherer? . . . .

Now that you have a pretty good idea what path you've decided to take, it's time to gather as much information as you can. Your guide provides a pretty good start, but there is so much more out there. Write, E-mail, call, surf the net, go to the library—do whatever it takes to get more information on your newfound passion.

Whatever method you use in gathering, you'll find that people will become the key to your success. Build relationships and reach out to others who can help you in your cause! Besides the

During your life, everything you do and everyone you meet rubs off in some way. Some bit of everything you experience stays with everyone you've ever known, and nothing is lost. That's what's eternal, these little specks of experience in a great and enormous river that has no end.

—HARRIET DOERR

The people I consider successful are so because of how they handle their responsibilities to other people, how they approach the future—people that have a full sense of the value of their lives and what they want to do with it.

—RALPH FIENNES

Never be scared to ask. Ask and keep asking. Communicate your needs to others. Call people out of the blue. Take people to lunch. Open yourself up to others. You'll find success is usually a team effort. Asking is powerful. It can work magic. It sure isn't easy, and it doesn't work every time. It will, however, if you persist. So ask, and it shall be given to you.

If you want help while you move toward your goals, be sure to also help those around you with their goals. People will treat you as well as you treat them.

Send short, handwritten thank-you notes to all who help you in your quest. You'll realize at a later point how important these people were in getting you where you are today.

support group you're creating, you're also gathering important bits of information about your goal. If you're having trouble figuring out who to start talking with, begin with family connections and friends, university career/internship programs, professors or colleagues in the field, or anyone that you feel comfortable with. This will build your confidence to reach out to strangers.

I found the best way to get the information you need is by talking with someone who is working in the job you want. If you want to write a book, talk to other authors. If you want to be a raft guide, talk to raft guides. Find role models who are acting in ways you might like to act. You might even go on an informational interview. Go to the raft-guide business, introduce yourself, and ask if you can pick their brains about the industry. You'll find that, often, people love to talk about themselves, especially if they love what they are doing. The more information you have, the more apt you are to make a great decision. By talking and gathering, you are opening new doors without realizing it.

Staying Organized . . . .

What works best for you? Each of us has a different style of staying on top of things. Whether it be with index cards, file folders, a three-ring binder, or your computer, you need to keep track of all this information you've been collecting. For starters, create a "Notes Log" of your correspondence. Write down everything, from the date of your initial phone calls to the details of your conversation. Especially if you are applying to a handful of programs, your log will keep you focused on the needs of each. Make notes of important dates: deadlines, when you followed up with a phone call, your interview date, or when you need to send off a thank-you letter.

Thank You!

Make a Move and Pick Up the Phone . . . .

After doing all your research, narrow down the first round of prospective programs to ten (so you don't get overwhelmed at first). Out of this ten, pick the one program that interests you the *least* and make your call. Call your least favorite as a practice call. This way, you can get all the "phone-talk" kinks worked out before you talk to the program that is on top of your list.

Your guide has contact names for most of the programs listed, so be sure to ask for this person; however, sometimes the contact has changed. Don't let that throw you off. Generally, someone will just transfer you to the right person; other times you'll have to explain what you're after. Eventually, you will talk to the right person.

The initial contact is your first impression on the organization, so make it a good one. Something that happens in this conversation just may be the link that gets you the job. Some program contacts are receptive to talk; others don't have the time. Basically, what you are after is to be sent more information and an application. This call is also a great time to promote your enthusiasm for their program.

Half the time you won't be speaking to a real person. You'll be talking to a digitized "virtual" person. Be prepared. If you stumble here, there's no way to erase what you've said. Before you call, it is a good idea to write out exactly what you want to say:

- Who you are
- How you heard about their program (don't forget to plug your guide)
- What you want (send me your application packet)
- Your address/telephone number
- Your enthusiasm for possibly working for them

When leaving messages, speak slowly and clearly, and spell out any words that are difficult to understand. Remember someone is writing down your message to get you the information you need.

Then there is E-mail. For those who have modernized their lifestyle, this is the easiest way to get the information you need. Though E-mail is easy, it's important that you "professionally" write an E-mail note to the program (addressing the points above). This could be considered your first cover letter to the organization.

THE APPLICATION PACKAGE CHECKLIST

- Resume
- Cover letter
- Letters of recommendation
- Reference names and addresses
- Employment history
- College transcripts
- Writing samples
- Portfolio (slides, photos, video clips, tapes, artwork, etc.)
- A completed employment application

God has an overall plan for people's lives and the details get worked out along the way, even though we usually have no idea what's going on.

The Program Application Package . . . .

Once you get the application in your hands, don't let it sit. Act upon it right away. This will assure that you make any deadlines, and the earlier you get your application in, the better your chances are. You'll also find that everything takes longer than you anticipate. Each organization wants you to take time out of your day, to see how serious you are about their program. This might mean filling out a four-page application, writing five short essay questions, getting official transcripts from your college, finding three people to write letters of recommendation for you, and finally, sending it all with a personalized cover letter and resume (that you also have to create). Some programs may ask a lot from you, but just remember your payoff—getting in with a program that will forever change your life!

The Resume . . . .

This is a very important step in your journey. Your resume is your selling tool, the informational brochure about you. What kind of person are you? What kind of skills do you have? What are some of your life's experiences? What do you do in your spare time? What hobbies do you have? What are some major things that you have accomplished? If you're having trouble answering these questions, read the first chapter again and work on your lists.

The best resumes are those that are filled with the whole you, not just your past work experiences and education but what makes you tick as a person. Include your skills, accomplishments, volunteer service, and unique attributes:

- You were a volunteer at a homeless shelter.
- You're certified in CPR and first aid.
- You can speak and write fluently in French.
- You play the guitar.
- You've climbed to the top of Mount Lassen.
- You cycled and backpacked throughout Europe.
- You studied on exchange in England.
- You tutor at the local elementary school.

Paint a picture of what you're really like, in all capacities. I even put my favorite quote on my resume.

The most important thing to remember when applying is to be yourself and to make sure your skills and interests are very apparent in your application.

Before sending off your completed application, make a copy of it. In case it gets lost in the mail or at the organization, you'll have a spare copy. This copy can also serve as your master for doing other applications.

The Cover Letter . . . .

Many people think that cover letters are the same as a Post-It note that says: "Hey, check this out—I'd really like to work for you!" You'll find these cover letters lying in the bottom of recycle bins. Your cover letter is the icing on the cake and is just possibly as important as the resume itself. It is an expansion of your resume and brings out:

- Why you are writing to the program

- Why you want to work for them and your passion for the job

- That you have a good understanding of their program

- Your skills and experiences (with supporting examples) that you want them to know about

- What you are currently working on that relates to what they are doing

- What you can bring to the program if they hire you

Your cover letter also describes your potential to the employer. Let your personality show in your writing. You might not have all the necessary skills, but your cover letter might demonstrate that you're trainable for the job. Remember, many applicants aren't necessarily hired based on skill, but more for enthusiasm and energy. Job-specific skills and responsibilities can be taught!

Do your own resume (or get help from a friend). Getting a job is a learning process, and you need to participate in every step along the way.

Letters of Recommendation . . . .

If the organization needs letters of recommendation, put these on top of your priority list because getting them generally takes a long time. When asking someone to write your letter, it's always best to pick someone who knows your abilities—maybe one letter from your favorite boss and another from a professor. Recruiters can get a better perspective on you if you provide them with views of different aspects of your life which demonstrate your varied strengths.

The best way to get people to write your letter is to actually write it for them—well, not the letter itself, but any information that will assist them in writing their letter. Your letter to your recommender should address **Even though a program might not ask for letters of recommendation, include them anyway. They will make your application packet stand out.** what types of positions you are applying to, what the organization is looking for in a candidate, and what strengths you think your recommender should highlight. You'll get a quicker response rate and a better recommendation by doing the initial work. Another nice touch is to provide them with a postage-paid envelope, so they can get it back to you right away, and do thank the people that take time out of their lives to do this for you with a handwritten letter (or in whatever way you feel is generous). You'll find that their recommendation will play a big part in getting you your dream job.

Follow-Up . . . .

Although each step in getting your dream job is important in itself, follow-up might make the difference in who gets the job. Sending off your application materials to a program and waiting for their phone call is generally not enough these days. More often than not, your application will sit in a stack with others until someone calls (that's you) and the program director takes action.

One to three weeks after sending in your application, pleasantly surprise your contact with a phone call. In this phone call, make sure they have received your application, ask if there is anything else you can provide, and ask any specific questions you might have for them.

Then, **promote your enthusiasm.** If this job is what you want in your life right now, let them know how badly you want it (in a playful but professional way). You'll find that this phone call can make all the difference in the world.

Your Interview . . . .

Congratulations! If you made it this far, all your preliminary hard work has paid off (and impressed the hiring team). This final step of landing the job is where you get to show off what you're all about and how you'll make a difference in their program. Whether it is in-person or over the phone, your interview will also seem like the longest hour (or so) of your life. To grapple with your uneasiness, the best way to approach your interview is to take a deep breath and **be yourself**. Your goal is to paint a very real and sincere picture of who you are, what skills you have obtained over the years, and your potential for future growth. Know your resume inside and out and have specific examples for everything you mention in it. Those who have successful interviews are those who have done

That which we persist in doing becomes easier—not that the nature of the task has changed, but our ability to do has increased.

—RALPH WALDO EMERSON

Be persistent without being a pest.

plenty of preparation and anticipate what questions the interviewer might ask. Try to treat your interview as a conversation with someone you just met, but also as a chance to knock 'em out with all your talents and abilities. In addition, you should be doing most of the talking and asking just as many questions as your interviewer asks you. Just like anything, the more you interview, the better you'll become at answering any question they present to you.

Thank-You Letters . . . .

Even though a follow-up thank-you letter makes a nice impression on the recruiter after an interview, many times interviewers have made up their minds on who they want to hire long before a thank-you note arrives on their desk. However, you'll find that recruiters generally interview a handful of super applicants for only one position. Help influence their decision-making process by sending a sincere note that reiterates your excitement and your sense of how you'll make an impact on their program. This letter will make a difference.

Rejection Shock . . . .

After all your hard work, the reality is that you might not get the job you wanted (at least this time around). However, sometimes it's out of your hands: organizations sometimes receive hundreds of applications for just a few positions. No matter if you apply to one organization or many, your application will eventually get thrown into the rejection pile, and the mailman will bring you that really thin envelope containing the words, "…thanks for applying…you sounded like a great candidate…unfortunately we've chosen another candidate that we liked a lot better…." OK, so you got a rejection letter. Big deal! It's not the end of the world. Who knows? It might be a blessing in disguise. Everything happens for a reason. So you try again and again and again, until, one day, you receive the magical "Welcome Aboard" letter (and it will come).

If you're not rejected ten times a day, you're not trying hard enough.

—Anthony Coleman

If you really wanted to work for a particular organization and got rejected, don't give up. Apply again for next term. This will knock their socks off and let them know you mean business.

Just as anything in life, we can't have it all. We sure can try, but we can't possibly get everything we want all the time. If

DON'T QUIT

When things go wrong, as they some-times will; when the road you're trudging seems all uphill; when the funds are low and the debts are high, and you want to smile, but you have to sigh; when care is pressing you down a bit—rest if you must but don't you quit.

Life is queer with its twists and turns, as every one of us sometimes learns; and many a fellow turns about when he might have won had he stuck it out. Don't give up though the pace seems slow—you may succeed with another blow.

Often the goal is nearer than it seems to a faint and faltering man; often the struggler has given up when he might have captured the victor's cup; and he learned too late when the night came down. How close he was to the golden crown.

Success is failure turned inside out—the silver tint of the clouds of doubt; and you never can tell how close you are. It may be near when it seems afar; so stick to the fight when you're hardest hit—it's when things seem worst that you mustn't quit.

you're not getting what you want, the key is to keep trying. The more programs you apply to, the more apt you are to get rejected. But, conversely, the more you apply to, the more apt you are to receive an offer. It's just how you look at it which makes all the difference in the world.

Is your search dragging? More often than not, this process of searching for what will make you happy in life or figuring out what doors to knock on can be a difficult experience. Being human, we like to avoid the struggles and look for the path that will bring us the most happiness. Going through the struggle is not fun and can affect everything you do. You must remember that just around the corner something good could come your way. You must have faith and keep a positive and productive out-look.

Is there a "time-out" activity (like napping, watching TV, playing on the swings at the park, listening to your favorite music, running in the hills, daydreaming, writing in your jour-nal) that will give your search efforts renewed vigor? Maybe the answer is getting into some sort of daily routine. For example, wake up each morning with the sun (don't get into the habit of sleeping in), plan your schedule for the day (making a list and setting priorities), read the paper while eating a hearty breakfast, make strides in your job hunt (make phone calls, write letters, move forward in job leads, revise your resume for the hundredth time), read a good book, meet with friends, exercise, write in your journal, and so forth. If you're having trouble finding bal-ance in your life, you may just want to go back and reread the balancing section. The more active and organized you are, the better off you'll become in the long run. Remember the old adage, "Idle hands are the devil's playground." Get busy, have a productive day, don't become stagnant, and reward yourself when you accomplish something.

Back to Patience . . . .

As you are well aware, it takes time for things to happen in your life—just as when you learned to talk or ride a bike, or when you develop a friendship. There is a process to everything you do. To reach any goal, you must take small strides. With each step, you will feel more comfortable with taking a risk for the next one, until you feel comfortable in the goal you've set for yourself.

Try to think of what you are doing right now as your never-ending journey. The things you do now affect the things in your future—this is the long-haul mentality. Overnight success is rare (and is usually because of the hard work that led up to that point). Don't rush the process. Each step in your journey takes time. If you're impatient, go hang out with a farmer, who can offer you one of the best perspectives on "the wait." The farmer knows there are certain steps you need to take to get from seed to harvest (despite Mother Nature's late freezes or flood rains)—all of which add up over the long haul. Treat your life the same way. Enjoy every good and challenging step along the way.

Only those who have the patience to do simple things perfectly will acquire the skill to do difficult things easily.

Life is not easy for any of us. But what of that? We must have perseverance and above all confidence in ourselves. We must believe that we are gifted for something, and that this thing, at whatever cost, must be attained.

—MARIE CURIE

SKEPTICS

Watch out for skeptics who want to divert you from your destiny.

"If I had thought about it, I wouldn't have done the experiment. The literature was full of examples that said you can't do this."

—SPENCER SILVER, ORIGINATOR OF POST-IT NOTEPADS

"Guitar music is on the way out."

—DECCA RECORDS, TURNING DOWN THE BEATLES IN 1962

"You can do a lot of things if you don't know you can't."

—SAM BROWNBACK, CONGRESSMAN, 1995

"Everything that can be invented has been invented."

—CHARLES DUELL, OFFICE OF PATENTS COMMISSIONER, 1899

"Louis Pasteur's theory of germs is ridiculous fiction."

—PIERRE PACHET, PROFESSOR OF PHYSIOLOGY, 1872

Don't forget Columbus, who was looking for India, or the fact that Edison knew 1,800 ways not to build a light bulb. It was Mark Twain who once said, "Let us be thankful for the fools—but for them the rest of us could not succeed!" Although many will like you to fail (misery loves company), don't you ever give up. Success is generally just around the corner.

The greater the number of job-hunting avenues you use, the greater the likelihood that you will find a job. —RICHARD BOLLES

25

Finding a job is a job in itself. There aren't any quick fixes in life. Through perseverance, patience, and hard work, you'll find yourself in a position that will change your entire life. Good things come to people who work hard to get what they're after. You might not see the results today or next week or even a month from now, but they'll hit you when you least expect it, and you'll be very happy to know that all your hard work has paid off.

Take Time

Take time to work.
It is the price of success.

Take time to think.
It is the source of power.

Take time to play.
It is the secret of perpetual youth.

Take time to read.
It is the foundation of wisdom.

Take time to be friendly.
It is the road to happiness.

Take time to dream.
It is hitching your wagon to a star.

Take time to love and to be loved.
It is the privilege of the gods.

Take time to look around.
The day is too short to be selfish.

Take time to laugh.
It is the music of the soul.

Open Yourself Up to the Possibilities . . . .

Mike and Dorrie Williams were living the "American Dream"—well-paying corporate jobs, benefits, a beautiful two-story home, security, and all the nice things that a lifestyle like this can bring. Yet, there was a downside to the world Mike and Dorrie Williams created for themselves. They were married to their jobs, Uncle Sam was taking most of their loot, and living through another Philadelphia winter wasn't helping. All they could think of was a week's vacation that would recharge their batteries.

However, their plan for a one-week vacation soon turned into two weeks, which kept escalating the more they talked about it. "We got to thinking. Why are we living this sort of lifestyle? What were we really working toward? What would we do if we put all our responsibilities aside?" Finally, it was an overnight decision. An overwhelming realization consumed them. Now was the time for them to walk away from the things that society dictated as being the right things to do. Their decision? To adventure around the United States on their bikes for not a week or two, not a month—but a whole year.

That night they talked about their trip. The next morning they worked out the details. Just like that. They broke the news of the new direction in their life to co-workers, family, and friends. At the same time, they started sifting through the material possessions in their home, soon to be peddled off and turned into funds for their trip. "It was the biggest garage sale we ever had. We sold everything except for the things that meant the world to us (and a couple bikes)."

What about security? What about money? What about the future? "That's why a lot of people don't want to make a change. They're scared about starting over, that they're not going to find a job again." Quite the contrary for Mike and Dorrie—"There will always be jobs out there. If you want something bad enough, you'll get it eventually."

And the adventure began! They hopped on their bikes and took off across America—from the hills of Kentucky, through the flatlands of the Midwest (milking a few cows along the way), across the perilous Rockies (conquering the tops of three passes), all the way to the Pacific Ocean. To help them on their 3,700 mile journey, they used maps and guides purchased through Adventure Cycling, which provided information on hostels, campgrounds, bike shops, where to get food, and distances between landmarks on the Trans-America Bike Trail.

The trip wasn't about covering a certain distance each day for the Williamses. Their philosophy: Open yourself up to the experience and other people, and let anything happen; then deal with it, learn from it, and experience it as it comes to you. "We knew nothing about what to expect, and that's why we had such a great time. Without setting up a structure or any restrictions, you won't set yourself up for a letdown. Some days we rode just a few miles because we loved where we were or the company we were with." The key—the more risk they took, the more they opened themselves up to new adventures.

This doesn't mean that each day was full of high times. Mother Nature dished out her fair share of ugly weather. Then, there were days when the next place to lay their weary bodies was further than they had anticipated. "You learn to adapt to these situations and try to keep a positive attitude." And so they did.

They challenged their bodies and their minds, and they made their dreams a reality. Not only did they enrich their own lives with this new experience, they now have the opportunity to enrich others by sharing with them the tales of their trip. For Mike and Dorrie, you can either lead a path of mediocrity and let life decide your path, or you can open yourself up and see what happens. "It's those who take the risk and make that left-hand turn in the road—opening themselves up to the opportunity—who get the most from life."

What do you do when you finish a trip like this? Mike and Dorrie found themselves back in the small college town where they first met. Their trappings are fewer, and they live on less; but they live more happily and at a better pace. "It's nice to plant some roots, have a circle of friends, and balance adventure with the grounding we've created."

Enjoy your achievements as well as your plans. Keep interested in your own career, however humble; it is a real possession in the changing fortunes of time.—*DESIDERATA*

The Career Guide for Creative and Unconventional People by Carol Eikleberry. Your dream job doesn't have to be just a dream. There are millions of fulfilling and interesting jobs out there for folks that don't seem to fit the "norm." Being different, unconventional, and hard-to-categorize can be a big asset if you know how to use it. After all, do you really want to do what everybody else does? This book gives you a boost to make your dreams a reality! (Ten Speed Press, $11.95)

Don't wait 'til you graduate: The Canadian job search guide for the real world by Stephen Kaplan. This comprehensive job search guide is written from a recruiter's perspective and is specifically tailored for Canadian college and university students. The guide covers a broad range of topics, information that will give you a different perspective on searching for a "real" job. I particularly enjoyed the great quotes and advice from Canadian employers and recruiters scattered throughout the book. It's published by the Canadian Association of Career Educators and Employers (CACEE) for $17.95. Get in touch with them for a complete catalog of job resources (416) 535-8126; cacee@inforamp.net; www.cacee.com

Dynamic Cover Letters by Kathy and Randall Hansen. This indispensable and reasonably priced guide for job seekers contains everything you need to create a stunningly effective cover letter, providing step-by-step instructions and copious examples (Ten Speed Press, $7.95). Also check out the authors' web site at www.stetson.edu/~hansen/ dcl.html, which includes some great resources and a fairly inclusive list of the best job-hunting and career resources links on the Web.

Major in Success by Patrick Combs. Loaded with tons of energy and great quotes, this book is a must for every college student. Patrick Combs walks you through an inspirational journey, explaining how to find your dream job while you're in school. Even if you have finished your schooling (at least, for now), this book will still give you a fresh look at who you are and how to get where you want to go. Not only is his book a hit, his web site is just as good: www.goodthink.com (Ten Speed Press, $9.95)

Got the urge to throw in the towel at what you're currently doing and become joyfully jobless? **Make a Living Without a Job** ($11.95, Bantam Books) provides you with inspiration, support, and practical information on your road to self-discovery, helping you integrate the things you like to do with the things you're good at doing. Author Barbara Winter also self-publishes a brilliant newsletter called Winning Ways (six issues per year for $31), which is designed to share creative ideas about successful self-employment, along with thoughts on personal development. Contact Barbara Winter, Winning Ways, P.O. Box 39412, Minneapolis, MN 55439, (612) 835-5647; BABS WIN@aol.com

Six Months Off by Hope Dlugozima, James Scott, and David Sharp. If you've been dreaming of embarking on a life-transforming journey, one that will take you away from the office for a while, *Six Months Off* can help you take your fantasies off the shelf and transform them into reality. The authors talked to more than 200 people who'd actually gathered the gumption to take time off of work and make their vagabond dreams come true. These stories will help you overcome any self-doubt that all too often can derail your great escape before you even suggest it to your boss. (Henry Holt, $12.95)

Taking Time Off by Colin Hall and Ron Lieber. In this practical and inspirational collection of profiles, more than thirty students from all over the country demonstrate how taking time off gives you a chance to explore career interests, gain practical experience, and develop a new perspective on your studies. (Noonday Press, $12.00)

Un-Jobbing, The Adult Learning Handbook by Michael Fogler. This handbook gives you the ideas, information, and inspiration to free yourself from a life of merely earning a paycheck and to do things based on your personal values. Michael shares the tools needed to achieve a life doing what you really want to do—and still make ends meet. For more information, drop Michael an E-mail note at mfogler@igc.apc.org (Free Choice Press, $9.95)

What Color Is Your Parachute? by Richard Bolles. This book should be required reading for all. Revised and updated annually, this career guide is about taking chances, gaining confidence, and making changes in your career and life. Complete with exercises on self-assessment and career planning, it will give you the tools to carve out your own career niche. You'll find that it's not just for the those who are out of work and is perhaps most valuable to those who are securely employed but unhappy with what they're doing. You can also find Richard Bolles online at www.washingtonpost.com/parachute, which includes the newest section of his book—"The Net Guide"— which explains how and where to use the Internet in your job search. (Ten Speed Press, $16.95)

For a look at almost every career-related book available, call for a copy of the ***Whole Work Catalog.*** The catalog's goal is to help you find "whole" work—work that is personally satisfying as well as financially rewarding (and each book is backed by a one-year guarantee). Tom and Sue Ellison, The New Careers Center, 1515 23rd St., Box 339, Boulder, CO 80306; (800) 634-9024; (303) 447-1087.

> *To put one's thoughts into actions is the most difficult thing in the world.*
>
> —JOHANN VON GOETHE

Your Compass . . . .

With over 1,000 programs and resources listed in your guide, the task of finding "the program for you" might seem a bit overwhelming. To ease this feeling, you'll find a quick overview for each program listed, allowing you to scan for the things that are most important to you. The indexes (in the final pages of your guide) also serve as a great starting point to quickly get the information you need. Although each program has been given a home in a particular section, some of these programs cover such a wide spectrum of opportunities that they could be listed in each. So, even though your focus might be on "The Great Outdoors," you may find the information you're looking for in other sections. Here's a quick look at making the most of each listing:

Program Overview: . . . .

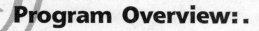

COMPENSATION: Over 75 percent of the programs listed offer a salary or stipend; others are either volunteer positions or you might have to pay a fee for their services. If a program provides compensation, this icon ⚡ appears beside the program's name.

HOUSING: As an extra perk, many programs also provide room and board or offer housing when you join their team! If a program provides housing, this icon 🏠 appears beside the program's name.

REGION/HQ: Listings are broken down by a specific region and where the main office of the program is located. Here's how the world is broken down:

- **Pacific Northwest:** Alaska, California, Hawaii, Idaho, Nevada, Oregon, and Washington

- **Rocky Mountains:** Colorado, Montana, North Dakota, South Dakota, Utah, and Wyoming

Your Naviga

- **South/Midwest:** Arizona, Arkansas, Iowa, Kansas, Louisiana, Missouri, Nebraska, New Mexico, Oklahoma, and Texas
- **Great Lakes:** Illinois, Indiana, Michigan, Minnesota, Ohio, and Wisconsin
- **Northeast:** Connecticut, Delaware, Maine, Maryland, Massachusetts, New Hampshire, New Jersey, New York, Pennsylvania, Rhode Island, and Vermont
- **Nation's Capital:** Washington, D.C. and nearby areas in Maryland, Virginia, and West Virginia
- **Southeast:** Alabama, Florida, Georgia, Kentucky, Mississippi, North Carolina, South Carolina, Tennessee, Virginia, and West Virginia
- **Nationwide:** Programs offered in more than one state
- **Worldwide:** Programs offered in more than one country
- **Specific Country:** Programs offered in a specific country

CATEGORY: From Adventure Travel to Zoos (and everything in between), this provides you with a "buzz word" associated with this organization, all of which can be found in the Category index.

POSITION TYPE: Each program is grouped under one of six "work/learn" types: Internship, Seasonal Job, Work/Learn Adventure, Unique Experience, or Association.

DURATION: A quick look at when the program is offered.

IDEAL CANDIDATE: Who does this program appeal to most? Broken down by five broad categories, including High School Students, College Students, Career Changers, Retired Folks, and Foreigners.

APPLICANT POOL AND APPLICANTS ACCEPTED: A realistic look at how many applications each program receives and how many are accepted into the program.

Each section is set up with fuller and shorter listings, and finishes up with additional contacts in the field. The main difference between the three types of listings is the amount of information presented. Sometimes the essence of the program only needs a shorter listing; however, all should be looked at equally. Also tucked away in each section are other great goodies that are pertinent to this field, so be sure to read through the entire chapter!

Sample Listing

Adventure Connection, Inc.

REGION/HQ: Pacific Northwest/California • **CATEGORY:** Outfitter • **POSITION TYPE:** Seasonal • **DURATION:** Spring & Summer • **IDEAL CANDIDATE:** High School Students, College Students, Career Changers, Retired Folks, Foreigners • **APPLICANT POOL:** Varies • **APPLICANTS ACCEPTED:** Varies

ADVENTURE CONNECTION was created by a dedicated group of river enthusiasts who saw how river trips had the power to change lives. After working for, and with, some of California's finest professional river outfitters, they knew they could offer something different—a little more luxury, a tastier menu, a slightly higher-class trip—and still have competitive prices. They are now one of California's largest outfitters in the Mother Lode area.

Work/Learn Program Specifics: They offer an annual white-water rafting workshop each spring and hire guides from among its best students (the course costs $750). A low student-to-instructor ratio is maintained in order to provide each participant with the best opportunity to develop his or her skills. As Adventure Connection's hiring varies year to year, the course also helps workshop participants apply to all outfitters in the area. They also provide canoe and kayak instruction.

Duration: Seasonal positions are available from March/April through October.

Compensation and Perks: Pay varies by the river and the experience of the guide. Trip guides are paid by the day, generally $60 to $100 per day. Guides also receive generous tips, free meals and camping facilities, use of equipment for private trips, and a chance to work in the great outdoors.

The Ideal Candidate: They hire people with great attitudes and good social skills. Applicants for guide positions with no prior experience should enroll in the company's annual river-guide school.

Making It Happen: Call for application materials. Prospective candidates should attend the white-water rafting workshop, generally held in early April of each year. Application deadline: March 1.

INSIDER TIPS: *...tough for first-year guides to get full-time work.*

Contact Information: Nate Rangel, President • Adventure Connection, Inc. • P.O. Box 475 • Coloma, CA 95613 • Phone: (916) 626-7385 • Fax: (916) 626-9268 • Toll Free: (800) 556-6060

I have been anchored in a safe, pleasant harbor for most of my life. However, even good ropes fray after a while (as they are meant to be contorted into a variety of twistings which prove their usefulness). Putting out to sea will involve risk, a general sense of panic at times, and possible hardships during storms. The treasure is the gold of growth, testing, and courage—creative action taken in spite of fear.

—ALEXANDRIA BEGET,
BACK DOOR READER

Breaking Down the Listings—Even Further.

Once you've found a program that piques your interest, check out the detailed overview of the program provided. Details of the "fuller" listings include: organization highlights, your area and working environment, work/learn program specifics, duration specifics, compensation and perks, the ideal candidate specifics, and how to make it happen. Many listings also provide "insider tips" straight from the program coordinators (who you'll be talking with), providing insights on how you actually get in the "back door" and what they're really looking for in a candidate. Finally, each listing provides specific contact information, including contact name, address, phone/fax/toll-free numbers, and on-line information. Although every effort is taken to ensure the most up-to-date contact information is provided, our world constantly changes, and so does contact and program information. However, once you make the initial contact with a program, you'll be provided with their most current information.

So what are you waiting for? Dig in!

Full listing

Short listing

Addresses

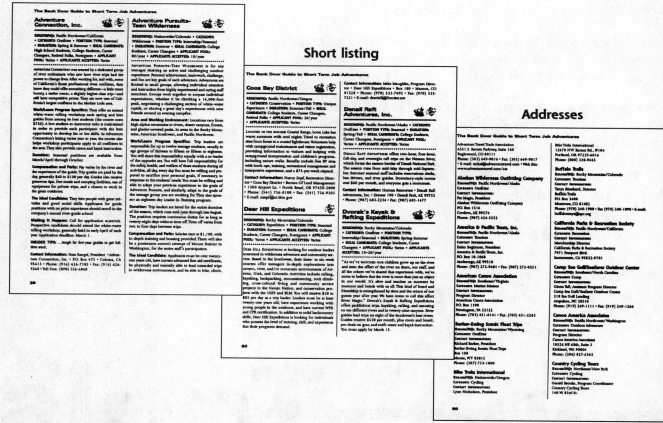

JobWeb and its companion online careers magazine, *Job Choices Online*, form a very comprehensive web site for college students and graduates seeking information on employment, including short-term work or internship experiences. Visit *JobWeb* at www.jobweb.org and link to other sites that detail summer work, internships, and fieldwork opportunities, in addition to a broader jobs database for persons seeking permanent employment.

The National Directory of Internships, published by the **National Society of Experiential Education,** has a comprehensive listing of internship opportunities accessible through its web site. You can find internship opportunities tailored to your needs by region, field of study, or both. www.tripod.com/work/internships

The Riley Guide is one of the most comprehensive indexes of job-listing sites on the internet. You can also purchase *The Guide to Internet Job Searching* by Margaret Riley—(301) 946-1917; mfriley@erols.com; www.jobtrak.com/jobguide

The Student Center site offers in-depth information that helps students and recent graduates identify their personal strengths, define career goals, and learn about those companies that best match their interests. www.studentcenter.com

Resources

Chance favors the prepared mind.

4

How often do you find yourself taking extravagant pleasure in being alive? Hiking over the crest of a snowy ridge in the heart of the vast wilderness, the world seemingly unfolds in front of us. At once, we can embrace endless miles of ridges, peaks, and valleys. An inner joy bubbles up within each of us. Overtaken with the beauty of the moment, one of us spontaneously shouts out, *"Nuanaarpuq!"*

Later, passing through a mountain meadow, we come upon a patch of small wildflowers. Their crimson beauty shows us the first signs of summer after many days of traveling on snow. The group gasps in awe. All that is heard is a subtle *"Nuanaarpuq!"*

Is it possible to express the feelings of such special moments in words? Mere words? We used to be skeptical, purists really, who felt that the joy of the moment alone would suffice. That was until we learned of *"Nuanaarpuq."* *"Nuanaarpuq"* is an Alaskan Inuit expression. Those who live by this expression live with a deep respect for the natural world and have learned to appreciate and celebrate all the wonders of nature. They use the word *"Nuanaarpuq"* to express their reverence and pleasure.

Photo by Jake Mills

Are you aware of such moments of extravagant pleasure? Do you share this with others? *"Nuanaarpuq"* is about awareness, about finding and celebrating beauty in the simple things in life. It is the key word for opening up eyes and creating an excitement for life. It is a way to express our celebration of the present moment and for expressing deep joy.

Begin making this newfound awareness a daily part of your life and extend your joy to others. After all, excitement for life is contagious. *Nuanaarpuq!*

—Contributed by Christian Bisson and Julie Gabert who work as outdoor educators at Hollins College in Virgina during the academic year and teach seasonally for the National Outdoor Leadership School in Wyoming. Through these experiences, they find many moments of *Nuanaarpuq!*

Adventure

The Adventure Center at Pretty Lake

REGION/HQ: Great Lakes/Michigan • **CATEGORY:** Experiential Education • **POSITION TYPE:** Internship/Seasonal • **DURATION:** Spring/Fall • **IDEAL CANDIDATE:** College Students, Career Changers • **APPLICANT POOL:** 70–80/year • **APPLICANTS ACCEPTED:** 6+/year

THE ADVENTURE CENTER provides exposure to the many facets of adventure education, offering a realistic framework of actual experience in this field. Their clients include middle schools, high schools, colleges, universities, community agencies, courts, alternative schools, professional facilitators, social groups, and corporations. Their site offers five challenge ropes courses and seven low initiative areas. They also offer two fifty-foot climbing towers and facilities for groups to camp out or stay indoors.

Area and Working Environment: The Center is located on 213 acres of forested property overlooking a small but beautiful lake, just twenty minutes from downtown Kalamazoo and about one hour from Lake Michigan.

Work/Learn Program Specifics: Internships are designed to offer interns a wide range of experiences, across as many aspects of experiential programming as possible. Responsibilities may include group facilitation, maintenance of equipment and sites, preparation for incoming groups, overnight supervision, and taking an active role as part of the staff by being open to giving and receiving feedback. The first phase of an internship may include participation in a five-day personal-exploration workshop and three-day logistical workshops. Interns will have the opportunity for observations, instructions from highly experienced facilitators, first-hand experience facilitating groups, working with equipment, and an opportunity for certification at the Adventure Center. Longer internships may also include participation in program design, development, and marketing.

Duration: Because of the pace and number of clients that they program within their busiest seasons, things can get hectic. As a result, they rely heavily on seasonal staff to help out wherever necessary. Rarely will you work 9 to 5, sometimes you will work overnight, and your work experience can become emotionally and physically demanding.

Compensation and Perks: Housing is available if needed. Interns receive an extensive amount of training and experience. Opportunities for personal and professional growth are extraordinary and are dependent upon your willingness to explore the dynamics between you and your groups and the other members of the staff. As a staff member, you may be included in such staff opportunities as off-site rock climbing and spelunking.

The Ideal Candidate: Must be at least twenty-one years of age, with a background in psychology, social work, counseling, or other human services; experience in experiential/adventure education; a high level of maturity; and energy, flexibility, and enthusiasm for intensive work.

Making It Happen: Call, write, or E-mail for application materials. Upon receiving and reviewing your application, they will be in touch with you to discuss a possible interview. Rolling deadlines.

INSIDER TIPS: *The two most important requirements for prospective employees are a dedication to learning and a willingness to commit yourself to your own and others' personal growth. We are a process-focused experiential education organization. Because of this, in order to have a meaningful impact on the growth of our clients, we are looking for people who are ready to explore their personal issues and take a look at how their lives impact the facilitation of a group.*

Contact Information: Margie West, Staff Supervisor • The Adventure Center at Pretty Lake • 9310 W. "R" Ave. • Kalamazoo, MI 49009 • Phone: (616) 375-1664 • Fax: (616) 375-0735 • E-mail: tcentre@aol.com • Web Site: www.net-link.net/ACPL

Careers

Adventure Connection, Inc.

REGION/HQ: Pacific Northwest/California
• **CATEGORY:** Outfitter • **POSITION TYPE:** Seasonal
• **DURATION:** Spring & Summer • **IDEAL CANDIDATE:** High School Students, College Students, Career Changers, Retired Folks, Foreigners • **APPLICANT POOL:** Varies • **APPLICANTS ACCEPTED:** Varies

ADVENTURE CONNECTION was created by a dedicated group of river enthusiasts who saw how river trips had the power to change lives. After working for, and with, some of California's finest professional river outfitters, they knew they could offer something different—a little more luxury, a tastier menu, a slightly higher-class trip—and still have competitive prices. They are now one of California's largest outfitters in the Mother Lode area.

Work/Learn Program Specifics: They offer an annual white-water rafting workshop each spring and hire guides from among its best students (the course costs $750). A low student-to-instructor ratio is maintained in order to provide each participant with the best opportunity to develop his or her skills. As Adventure Connection's hiring varies year to year, the course also helps workshop participants apply to all outfitters in the area. They also provide canoe and kayak instruction.

Duration: Seasonal positions are available from March/April through October.

Compensation and Perks: Pay varies by the river and the experience of the guide. Trip guides are paid by the day, generally $60 to $100 per day. Guides also receive generous tips, free meals and camping facilities, use of equipment for private trips, and a chance to work in the great outdoors.

The Ideal Candidate: They hire people with great attitudes and good social skills. Applicants for guide positions with no prior experience should enroll in the company's annual river-guide school.

Making It Happen: Call for application materials. Prospective candidates should attend the white-water rafting workshop, generally held in early April of each year. Application deadline: March 1.

INSIDER TIPS: *...tough for first-year guides to get full-time work.*

Contact Information: Nate Rangel, President • Adventure Connection, Inc. • P.O. Box 475 • Coloma, CA 95613 • Phone: (916) 626-7385 • Fax: (916) 626-9268 • Toll Free: (800) 556-6060

Adventure Pursuits– Teen Wilderness

REGION/HQ: Nationwide/Colorado • **CATEGORY:** Wilderness • **POSITION TYPE:** Internship/Seasonal
• **DURATION:** Summer • **IDEAL CANDIDATE:** College Students, Career Changers • **APPLICANT POOL:** 80/year • **APPLICANTS ACCEPTED:** 10/year

ADVENTURE PURSUITS—TEEN WILDERNESS is for any teenager desiring an active and challenging outdoor experience. Personal achievement, teamwork, challenge, and fun are key goals of each adventure. Adventures are limited to small groups, allowing individual attention and instruction from highly experienced and caring staff members. Groups work together to surpass individual expectations, whether it be climbing a 14,000-foot peak, negotiating a challenging section of white-water rapids, or sharing a great day's experiences with new friends around an evening campfire.

Area and Working Environment: Locations vary from high alpine mountains to rivers, desert canyons, forests, and glacier-covered peaks, in areas in the Rocky Mountains, American Southwest, and Pacific Northwest.

Work/Learn Program Specifics: Trip leaders are responsible for up to twelve teenage students, usually in age groups of thirteen to fifteen or fifteen to eighteen. You will share this responsibility equally with a co-leader of the opposite sex. You will have full responsibility for the safety, health, and welfare of these students during all activities, all day, every day. You must be willing and prepared to sacrifice your personal goals, if necessary, in response to the students' needs. You must be willing and able to adapt your previous experience to the goals of Adventure Pursuits, and similarly, adapt to the goals of the teenage group you are working for. They also sponsor an eighteen-day Leader-In-Training program.

Duration: Trip leaders are hired for the entire duration of the season, which runs mid-June through late August. The position requires continuous duties for as long as twenty-eight days without time off. Time off varies from two to four days between trips.

Compensation and Perks: Salaries start at $1,100, with in-depth training and housing provided. There will also be a postseason summit attempt of Mount Rainier in Washington, for the entire staff's participation.

The Ideal Candidate: Applicants must be over twenty-one years old, have current advanced first aid certificates, be physically and mentally able to lead extended trips in wilderness environments, and be able to hike, climb, bike, raft, kayak, and participate in and/or lead all activities on assigned trips.

Making It Happen: Write or call for a trip leader application. Qualified applicants will be contacted for phone interviews.

INSIDER TIPS: *We are looking for mature, young adults with a proven ability to combine backcountry and teaching skills, with solid experience working with teenagers.*

Contact Information: Farley Kautz, Program Director • Adventure Pursuits—Teen Wilderness • 31160 Broken Talon Trail • Oak Creek, CO 80467 • Phone: (970) 226-4543 • Fax: (970) 226-4543 • Toll Free: (800) 651-8336 • E-mail: info@apadventures.com • Web Site: www.apadventures.com

Adventures Cross-Country

REGION/HQ: Worldwide/California • **CATEGORY:** Adventure Travel • **POSITION TYPE:** Seasonal • **DURATION:** Summer • **IDEAL CANDIDATE:** College Students, Career Changers • **APPLICANT POOL:** 700/year • **APPLICANTS ACCEPTED:** 35–40/year

ADVENTURES CROSS-COUNTRY provides adventure travel programs for teenagers who are excited to participate in the program, experience new environments, and try new activities (not youth-at-risk teenagers). Students from all over the world join their program to travel in small groups.

Area and Working Environment: Groups travel to Australia, Costa Rica, British Columbia, the western United States, Alaska, and Hawaii.

Work/Learn Program Specifics: Lead a group of twelve teenagers, with a co-leader of the opposite sex, through a rigorous wilderness trip. Outdoor wilderness activities include backpacking, rock climbing, mountain biking, rafting, kayaking, mountaineering, and scuba diving.

Duration: Tours are from June 15 to August 15. Guides normally lead two trips for three weeks.

Compensation and Perks: You will receive $25 to $35 per day and transportation to trip destinations.

The Ideal Candidate: Must be at least twenty-one years of age and have a clean driving record, teaching experience with teenagers, formal wilderness training, and advanced wilderness first aid certification. Technical rafting and rock-climbing skills not required.

Making It Happen: Send cover letter and resume by May 15.

INSIDER TIPS: *We're looking for guides with fun* sonalities who are able to leap over tall buildings in a s bound!

Contact Information: Kent Grady, Program Director • Adventures Cross-Country • 3030 Bridgeway • Sausalito, CA 94965 • Phone: (415) 332-5075 • Fax: (415) 332-2130 • Toll Free: (800) 767-2722

Alaska Sightseeing/ Cruise West

REGION/HQ: Pacific Northwest/Washington • **CATEGORY:** Cruise Ship • **POSITION TYPE:** Seasonal • **DURATION:** Spring/Fall • **IDEAL CANDIDATE:** College Students, Career Changers, Retired Folks • **APPLICANT POOL:** Varies • **APPLICANTS ACCEPTED:** Varies

ALASKA SIGHTSEEING/CRUISE WEST (AS/CW) is a soft adventure cruise and tour company, operating eight cruise vessels as well as land tours throughout southeast and south-central Alaska. They pride themselves on their up-close and personal cruising style, which focuses on learning about and experiencing the area outside the vessel rather than on shipboard entertainment and amenities. They offer guests unique destinations and a casual, intimate atmosphere that is difficult to achieve on larger vessels.

Area and Working Environment: They operate throughout Alaska, the Pacific Northwest, the Columbia and Snake Rivers, and the Sacramento River Delta.

Work/Learn Program Specifics: Because of the high rate of return among crew members, and the commitment towards promoting from within, most of the available opportunities exist in entry-level positions. These positions include customer service representative (dining room/stateroom steward), galley prep, deckhand, and driver/guide. Supervisory openings may become available as cruise coordinator, hotel manager, customer service supervisor, or chef. All positions are multifunctional and involve guest interaction, participation in onboard guest programs, cleaning, and lifting.

Duration: Applicants must be available from March through November, and some positions may require availability outside these dates. You will be scheduled to work onboard your vessel for six weeks at a time. While onboard, you will work every day in shifts of approximately twelve hours. At the end of this six-week period, you will receive two full weeks of time off the vessel.

Compensation and Perks: Employees working aboard vessels are paid on a daily rate. Nonmanagement positions participate in a tip pool and receive gratuities at the end of each voyage. Land-based employees are paid at an hourly rate and can receive gratuities. Bonus programs are offered for all qualified candidates. While working onboard, crew members receive meals free of charge and share a stateroom with other crew members. While on scheduled time off the vessel, crew members pay their own room and board. Housing is not provided for land-based positions.

The Ideal Candidate: They hire outgoing, enthusiastic individuals with a personal commitment towards providing the best possible service and experience to their guests. If you honestly enjoy serving others, are not afraid of hard work, and are looking for an employment experience far away from the regular nine-to-five routine, this is it. Minimum age of twenty-one is required.

Making It Happen: Send cover letter and resume.

INSIDER TIPS: *We are looking for people who are not afraid of hard work, able to smile all-the-while, are dependable, willing to work long hours, and who enjoy constant interaction with all kinds of people.*

Contact Information: Personnel Director • Alaska Sightseeing/Cruise West • 4th & Battery Bldg., Suite 700 • Seattle, WA 98121 • Phone: (206) 441-8687

Alaska Wildland Adventures

REGION/HQ: Pacific Northwest/Alaska • **CATEGORY:** Outdoor Adventure • **POSITION TYPE:** Internship/Seasonal • **DURATION:** Summer • **IDEAL CANDIDATE:** College Students, Career Changers, Foreigners • **APPLICANT POOL:** Varies • **APPLICANTS ACCEPTED:** Varies

• •

ALASKA WILDLAND ADVENTURES runs five- to twelve-day natural-history-focused "safaris" for adults and families, along with fishing and rafting programs. Alaska Wildland Adventures also operates Denali Backcountry Lodge, located in the Kantishna region of Denali National Park.

Area and Working Environment: Programs operate in the Kenai Peninsula and Denali regions of Alaska.

Work/Learn Program Specifics: Positions include: outdoor leadership (natural history trip leader, natural history guide, apprentice guide, rafting guide, and fish-

ing guide), professional drivers (safari driver and shuttle driver), hospitality (assistant hospitality manager, cook, assistant cook, housekeeper, and dishwasher), administrative (assistant safari manager, head raft guide, and maintenance coordinator), and office (office assistant).

Duration: Positions run from mid-May through mid-September.

Compensation and Perks: Salaries range from $800 to $1,600 per month (plus gratuities) and depend on experience. Tent housing provided with deduction for meals.

The Ideal Candidate: They are seeking experienced, high-energy, people-oriented outdoor leaders. Applicants must possess adult CPR and standard first aid certifications. Eligibility requirements vary with each position; however, natural-history teaching experience, rafting competence, and commercially licensed drivers are preferred.

Making It Happen: Send a resume and cover letter requesting an application. Deadline: April 30.

Contact Information: Scott Thomas, Program Director • Alaska Wildland Adventures • P.O. Box 389 • Girdwood, AK 99587 • Phone: (907) 783-2928 • Fax: (907) 783-2130 • Toll Free: (800) 334-8730 • E-mail: coopland @alaska.net

Alaska Women of the Wilderness

REGION/HQ: Pacific Northwest/Alaska • **CATEGORY:** Wilderness • **POSITION TYPE:** Internship • **DURATION:** 3 to 6 months • **IDEAL CANDIDATE:** College Students, Career Changers, Foreigners • **APPLICANT POOL:** Varies • **APPLICANTS ACCEPTED:** Varies

• •

ALASKA WOMEN OF THE WILDERNESS is a nonprofit year-round wilderness and spiritual empowerment program for girls and women who want to explore and deepen their relationships with themselves, with others, and with the Earth. They promote a safe, nurturing atmosphere for each woman to "believe in herself; learn new skills; develop newfound strengths; journey beyond previous limitations; celebrate the wild and playful spirit of women; honor her connection with the rhythms of the Earth; listen to her voice, seek her truth, speak from her heart, and awaken her passion."

Area and Working Environment: Their homestead is located thirty miles north of Anchorage on twenty-two acres.

Work/Learn Program Specifics: Grant researcher/writer and fundraising coordinators assist the director in areas of research, planning, organizing, drafting, and writing of grant proposals. You will be responsible for researching available grant resources, evaluating potential new programs, assisting in the development of grant proposals, and providing follow-up. You will also design, develop, and organize a fund-raising event to create a scholarship fund. Assistant wilderness instructors assist the course instructor and director in the planning, organizing, packing, and evaluating of each outdoor course. The Women and Wilderness Leadership practicum is limited to students who will live on their homestead and attend courses in wilderness leadership for women, navigation, backpacking skills, mountaineering, menu and trip planning, environmental ethics, safety and judgment, and curriculum and program planning.

Duration: Positions are three to six months, offered year-round.

Compensation and Perks: A monthly stipend of $100 and a rustic 10' x 10' cabin are provided. The cabin has electricity, but no running water (there is no running water on the land), and is heated by wood. Laundry and shower facilities are within three miles. Interns will be reimbursed for gas expenses incurred.

The Ideal Candidate: Candidates should have a degree in or be currently studying English, women's studies, outdoor education, environmental education, or a related field in the humanities. Macintosh computer experience preferred, as is a genuine love for women and their empowerment.

Making It Happen: Call or write for program information, application, and their *Alternate Trails* newsletter. Rolling deadlines.

INSIDER TIPS: *Please do not underestimate what you will need to financially support yourself during your internship, and have a passion for wanting to be here.*

Contact Information: Roschele Wagoner, Program Coordinator • Alaska Women of the Wilderness • P.O. Box 773556 • Eagle River, AK 99577 • Phone: (907) 688-2226 • Fax: (907) 696-3297 • E-mail: akwow@alaska.net

AmeriCan Adventures

REGION/HQ: Nationwide/California • **CATEGORY:** Adventure Travel • **POSITION TYPE:** Seasonal • **DURATION:** Summer • **IDEAL CANDIDATE:** College Students, Career Changers, Foreigners • **APPLICANT**

POOL: 200/year • **APPLICANTS ACCEPTED:** 60–70/year

BE PAID TO TRAVEL NORTH AMERICA and share your culture with visitors from all over the world. AmeriCan passengers are mostly between eighteen and thirty-five years old and are interested in experiencing the "real" North America, on and off the beaten track. Leading camping and hostelling tours is challenging, exciting, and rewarding. They also coordinate a program called Road Runner which focuses on hostelling adventures all over the world.

Area and Working Environment: With approximately thirty different itineraries, their adventures cover most of North America, including Canada, Alaska, and Mexico. Tours visit national parks, cities, small towns, and everything in between.

Work/Learn Program Specifics: AmeriCan Adventures offers active small-group camping and hostelling tours to foreign travelers. Each summer they hire outgoing tour leaders/drivers to lead tours throughout North America in fifteen-passenger vehicles. Tour leaders/drivers must be prepared for daily driving, organizing each day's activities, providing daily briefings and commentary, and leading a safe and enjoyable holiday for all passengers.

Duration: Schedules are very flexible, but first-year tour leaders/drivers can normally expect to work from June through September. Longer seasons are possible in subsequent years. Each tour lasts from two to six weeks, and there are normally one to five days off between assignments.

Compensation and Perks: Base pay is $240 to $295 per week, plus tips, commissions, and possible bonus. All en route and between trip accommodation is provided, and most meals are covered while on tour. Meet interesting people from around the world and participate in a variety of adventure activities, such as horseback riding, jeep tours, flightseeing, and watersports on a complimentary basis.

The Ideal Candidate: Applicants must be at least twenty-one with a clean driving record. They should have strong organizational and leadership skills and must be able to work well with minimal supervision. The best applicants are outgoing, adventurous, and flexible. Knowledge of a foreign language is helpful, but not required. All tour leaders/drivers must participate in a two- to three-week training process before leading any tours. Training is unpaid, but most accommodation is covered during the training period.

The luckiest people in the world are those who get to do all year round what they most like to do during their summer vacation. —MARK TWAIN

39

Making It Happen: Call for application materials. Applications are accepted throughout the spring and early summer. Training usually takes place sometime in June, at all three of their bases in the Northeast, Northwest, and Southwest.

INSIDER TIPS: *Have an open, flexible attitude and an interest in meeting people of diverse backgrounds. Have a considerable knowledge of North American history, geography, and culture, and the ability to share that information in an interesting and coherent fashion. Possess leadership abilities, with an emphasis on safety. Be organized and speak a foreign language. For a fantastic summer and a great learning experience, become a tour leader/driver for AmeriCan Adventures.*

Contact Information: Rhonda Anisman, Operations Manager • AmeriCan Adventures • 6762A Centinela Ave. • Culver City, CA 90230-6304 • Phone: (310) 390-7495 • Fax: (310) 390-1446 • Toll Free: (800) 873-5872

Appalachian Mountain Teen Project, Inc.

REGION/HQ: Northeast/New Hampshire
• **CATEGORY:** Experiential Education • **POSITION TYPE:** Internship • **DURATION:** Year-Round • **IDEAL CANDIDATE:** College Students, Career Changers, Foreigners • **APPLICANT POOL:** Varies • **APPLICANTS ACCEPTED:** Varies

THE PURPOSE OF the Appalachian Mountain Teen Project is to offer support to children and their families as they face critical life transitions. The AMTP was initiated in the spring of 1984 as a response to the problems of rural, low-income, and/or victimized children and youth, and for the development of youth leadership. Activities include a wide range of outdoor adventure programs, community service, and cross-cultural experiences. Parents are involved through home visits, family days, and parenting courses.

Work/Learn Program Specifics: Duties include assisting with program planning, trip leadership, administration, and fund-raising. Interns will plan and execute projects of their own, and counseling opportunities and classroom experiences are possible. Most of the experience involves working directly with youths aged ten to eighteen.

Duration: One academic year, one semester, or during the summer.

Compensation and Perks: A $100-per-week stipend has been offered in the past, but depends upon funding. They will assist in locating housing, and all outdoor clothing and equipment may be borrowed from the program.

The Ideal Candidate: Candidates must have previous experience working with youths, be capable of strenuous physical activity, be conscious of class, race, and gender stereotyping and the effects on children, and able to work both independently and as part of a team. First aid/CPR certifications helpful.

Making It Happen: Send resume and cover letter stating interests, professional goals, education, counseling experience, a statement of philosophy, and the names and numbers of three references.

Contact Information: Program Director • Appalachian Mountain Teen Project, Inc. • P.O. Box 1597 • Wolfeboro, NH 03894 • Phone: (603) 569-5510

Association for Experiential Education

REGION/HQ: Rocky Mountains/Colorado
• **CATEGORY:** Experiential Education • **POSITION TYPE:** Internship • **DURATION:** Year-Round • **IDEAL CANDIDATE:** College Students, Career Changers, Foreigners • **APPLICANT POOL:** 100–150/year • **APPLICANTS ACCEPTED:** 10–15/year

THE ASSOCIATION FOR EXPERIENTIAL EDUCATION (AEE) is a nonprofit, international, professional organization with roots in adventure education, committed to the development, practice, and evaluation of experiential learning in all settings. AEE sponsors local, regional, and international conferences, and publishes the *Journal of Experiential Education, Jobs Clearinghouse*, directories of programs and services, and a wide variety of books and periodicals to support educators, trainers, practitioners, students, and advocates. AEE's diverse membership consists of 2,300 individuals and organizations with affiliations in education, recreation, outdoor adventure programming, mental health, youth service, physical education, management development training, corrections, programming for people with disabilities, and environmental education.

Area and Working Environment: Boulder is uniquely located at the base of the scenic foothills of the Rocky Mountains, just thirty minutes from Denver. With 80,000 residents (20,000 of which are college students), Boulder is positioned to provide everything but surfing. Some of the world's best athletes make their homes in Boulder.

Work/Learn Program Specifics: Administrative Internship. This program is threefold in process and participation. First, you will be deeply involved with a project that will be both challenging and experiential to you and relevant to the association's current needs. Examples might include designing a brochure, compiling new material for publications, conducting surveys, assisting one of the Association's six directors/managers, or helping with the development and stewardship of the membership. The second aspect is administrative in nature. Interns are asked to assist with everything from processing credit card orders to answering the telephones. The third part is educational. Interns are encouraged, with the staff's assistance, to seek out information about the many forms of experiential education that exist today. This will give you opportunities to explore those areas of experiential education that interest you. Interns might attend a regional conference, visit a local ropes course, or meet teachers who use experiential learning techniques. The staff tries in every way possible to support you in fulfilling your goals.

Duration: Scheduling is very flexible. Some weeks may require the full 20 hours, while others may only require you to be in the office for a couple of hours for a few days. AEE staff realizes that you are giving of yourself and sincerely appreciate that fact.

Compensation and Perks: Life experience, creative support, and free access to all of AEE's publications and services—including the *Jobs Clearinghouse*. Interns enjoy significant discounts on outdoor gear and services. AEE staff has had great success in terms of "introducing interns to the local social atmosphere" of Boulder.

The Ideal Candidate: Prefer applicants with a sense of humor, experiential education background, self-starters with good organizational abilities and attention to detail, good telephone skills, Macintosh computer background, and basic office skills.

Making It Happen: Call for application packet. This contains information about the organization and internship. Once your application has been received, they will set up a telephone interview and chat with you further about the opportunities available. Rolling deadlines.

INSIDER TIPS: *Be very clear about your needs and goals; have a good sense of humor; Macintosh computer experience is extremely helpful; request an application before sending your resume.*

Contact Information: Sky Gray, Membership Services Manager • Association for Experiential Education • 2305 Canyon Blvd., Suite 100 • Boulder, CO 80302-5651 • Phone: (303) 440-8844 • Fax: (303) 440-9581 • E-mail: Info@aee.org • Web Site: www.princeton.edu/~recurtis/aee.html

Athletic Club Boca Raton

REGION/HQ: Southeast/Florida • **CATEGORY:** Fitness • **POSITION TYPE:** Internship • **DURATION:** Year-Round • **IDEAL CANDIDATE:** College Students, Career Changers, Foreigners • **APPLICANT POOL:** 30/term • **APPLICANTS ACCEPTED:** 4/term

EXPERIENCE THE FINEST and most complete club in south Florida. You'll find a wide variety of activities, programs, equipment, and amenities. In the center at Athletic Club Boca Raton, a devotion to physical fitness and athletics comes naturally. Their facility provides members with a spectacular 72,000-square-foot tri-level athletic complex.

Area and Working Environment: Positions are currently in Boca Raton; however, positions will soon be offered in thirty-nine clubs throughout the nation.

Work/Learn Program Specifics: Their comprehensive internship program will prepare the student for every aspect of the club industry: exercise testing and prescription, developing and administering individualized fitness programs, membership retention programming, working side-by-side with their physical therapy technicians, aerobic class instruction, professional networking, interviewing, budgeting, and much more.

Duration: Internships are fourteen to sixteen weeks, offered year-round.

Compensation and Perks: A stipend is paid upon successful completion of program. Housing is not provided, although they will make every attempt to assist in your search. Perks include membership at the club, working with a great staff, and living in Florida. Athletic Club Boca Raton is part of Club Sports International, which owns thirty-nine clubs nationwide and believes in promoting from within. If a student does a great job, the opportunity for permanent placement at one of these clubs is excellent.

The Ideal Candidate: Candidates must have a background in exercise science, health education, adult fitness, or a related health field.

Making It Happen: Send cover letter and resume requesting application. Once they receive your completed application, they will schedule a telephone interview. Deadlines: spring—November 15; summer—March 15; and fall—July 15.

INSIDER TIPS: *I take interns with energy and enthusiasm... I can train skill and technique. If you apply early, appear energetic, organized, and driven to get the best possible experience from your internship, your chances are excellent.*

Contact Information: Christopher Young, Athletic Director • Athletic Club Boca Raton • 1499 Yamato Rd. • Boca Raton, FL 33431 • Phone: (407) 241-5088 • Fax: (407) 241-8358 • E-mail: salsacy@aol.com

Avon/Beaver Creek Transit

REGION/HQ: Rocky Mountains/Colorado • **CATEGORY:** Transportation • **POSITION TYPE:** Seasonal • **DURATION:** Fall/Winter • **IDEAL CANDIDATE:** College Students, Career Changers, Retired Folks, Foreigners • **APPLICANT POOL:** 75–100/year • **APPLICANTS ACCEPTED:** 75/year

AVON/BEAVER CREEK TRANSIT is the only inter-valley connection for transportation in the Vail Valley. Each year they carry over a million riders to their assorted destinations, with a goal to provide safe and dependable travel.

Area and Working Environment: The town of Avon has a population of 3,000 and is located in the heart of the Colorado Rockies, at the base of Beaver Creek Ski Resort. If your goal is to work at a ski resort, you'll be ten miles from Vail and within a half hour of seven major Colorado ski resorts.

Work/Learn Program Specifics: Drivers operate buses and vans. Office clerks are the primary connection between the general public and the drivers, and work in the transportation office answering schedule questions and general information. Guest attendants spend their shifts outside, helping passengers load skis, making change, selling tokens, and giving directions. This position is great for a skier or snowboarder, as it has a split shift with a couple of hours free at lunch.

Duration: All staff will work forty or more hours per week, on a flexible schedule.

Compensation and Perks: Staff members earn $10 per hour and either a Vail Associates (Vail, Beaver Creek, and Arrowhead) season ski pass or a $1,000 end-of-

season bonus. They also receive a deeply discounted Avon Recreation Center pass and Columbia winter uniforms.

The Ideal Candidate: The most desired employees are those who possess good people skills. Driver applicants must be at least twenty-one years of age, with a clean driving record, and office clerk job applicants must possess data-entry skills and cash-handling abilities. Training is provided for guest attendants, so experience is not necessary.

Making It Happen: Call for application materials.

Contact Information: Michelle Frongillo, Marketing Specialist • Avon/Beaver Creek Transit • P.O. Box 1726 • Avon, CO 81620 • Phone: (970) 949-6121 • Fax: (970) 845-8589 • Web Site: www.vail.net/avon

AYF–Cedar Lake Education Center

REGION/HQ: Pacific Northwest/California • **CATEGORY:** Experiential Education • **POSITION TYPE:** Internship/Seasonal • **DURATION:** Year-Round • **IDEAL CANDIDATE:** College Students, Career Changers, Retired Folks, Foreigners • **APPLICANT POOL:** 20 per term • **APPLICANTS ACCEPTED:** 3–4/term

THE PROGRAMS AT CEDAR LAKE are designed to enhance personal development and group dynamics. Whether a program focuses on school children or corporate executives, whether it lasts a day or a week, you learn to set goals, build teams, take risks, and solve problems. Programs are designed and conducted by the American Youth Foundation, a preeminent national organization that has taught leadership development for over seventy years. The organization's philosophy challenges participants to achieve their personal best, live balanced lives, and lead through service. The climbing wall, and high- and low-challenge courses, are learning labs where you test real-life situations without real-life consequences. Imagine a curriculum where you learn by doing and where the lessons last a lifetime.

Area and Working Environment: Cedar Lake is located on 270 spectacular acres high in the San Bernardino mountains. Hiking, skiing, and nature trails lace through ponderosa pine forests, and a pristine five-acre lake beckons one to fish, boat, or jump in for a swim.

Work/Learn Program Specifics: Interns will select one of the following areas in which to spend most of

Justin says the San Bernardino area can be quite nasty + smoggy. Just below LA

their time, but can expect to assist in most of these areas during the course of their fieldwork: program development/implementation, conference hospitality, site/facility management, administration, and marketing/public relations.

Duration: Typical duration is three to nine months, with a flexible schedule.

Compensation and Perks: Stipends range from $50 to $200 per week—including room, board, and health insurance—dependent on time commitment.

The Ideal Candidate: Some knowledge of teaching or adventure education helps; but the key is getting a kick out of helping people reach peak performance.

Making It Happen: Send resume and cover letter stating general educational goals for the internship. Rolling deadlines.

INSIDER TIPS: *If it excites you to work hard in a beautiful outdoor setting and that you're part of the solution, you're a candidate.*

Contact Information: Mark Rowland, Program Director • AYF–Cedar Lake Education Center • 1100 Mill Creek Rd. • P.O. Box 1568 • Big Bear Lake, CA 92315-1568 • Phone: (909) 866-5724 • Fax: (909) 866-5715 • E-mail: cedarlake@bigbear.net • Web Site: www.castlepoint.com/cedarlake

AYF—STREAM

REGION/HQ: South/Midwest/Missouri • **CATEGORY:** Experiential Education • **POSITION TYPE:** Internship • **DURATION:** Year-Round • **IDEAL CANDIDATE:** College Students, Career Changers, Foreigners • **APPLICANT POOL:** Varies • **APPLICANTS ACCEPTED:** Varies

STREAM, A PROGRAM OF the American Youth Foundation, provides leadership education through experiential adventure programs to a wide variety of clients throughout the St. Louis area. They combine hands-on participation and outdoor adventure, which results in challenge, education, and fun.

Work/Learn Program Specifics: Interns gain a wide variety of experiences, ranging from program coordination and logistics to group facilitation and hard-skills training. All interns will be certified by STREAM in low and high ropes, and can expect to assist as well as lead programs from one-day events to five-day adventures.

Duration: Internships usually run February through October; however, exceptions may be made.

Compensation and Perks: Interns receive a $575-per-month stipend, plus room and board.

The Ideal Candidate: Candidates must be self-motivated, have the ability to listen and work well with others, and have good written/oral communication skills. Candidates must also possess first aid and CPR certification, as well as some outdoor leadership experience.

Making It Happen: Send resume and cover letter before October 1.

Contact Information: Berita Weight, Program Manager • AYF–STREAM • 1315 Ann Ave. • St. Louis, MO 63104 • Phone: (314) 772-9002 • Fax: (314) 772-7542

AYF–Miniwanca

REGION/HQ: Great Lakes/Michigan • **CATEGORY:** Experiential Education • **POSITION TYPE:** Internship • **DURATION:** Year-Round • **IDEAL CANDIDATE:** College Students, Career Changers, Foreigners • **APPLICANT POOL:** 10–15/term • **APPLICANTS ACCEPTED:** 3–4/term

THE AMERICAN YOUTH FOUNDATION (AYF) is a nonprofit organization founded in 1925 to help young people and those who serve young people achieve their personal best, lead balanced lives, and serve others. Programmatically, their roots are in running a residential summer camp, a four-trails program, and a high school leadership conference. AYF also provides year-round outreach programs to serve the communities which house their sites and programs. These services include designing and implementing programs tailored to specific needs, collaborating with organizations and staff to facilitate programs, facilitating programs at other sites, and hosting conferences, camps, or retreats.

Area and Working Environment: Located on Stony Lake, thirty miles north of Muskegon, Michigan, their 360 acres of wooded sand dunes extend for a mile along the shore of Lake Michigan. Secluded trails, Stony Creek, distinctive buildings, and beautiful sunsets all combine to make this an ideal setting

Work/Learn Program Specifics: Interns assist in program development and implementation for a variety of populations; facilitate programs, with a curriculum based around outdoor education, team building, leadership development, and service-learning; assist in support services for all programs; assist in administration, marketing, public relations, and evaluation of programs; and host retreat/rental groups. Interns will gain training and experience facilitating the low ropes course, initiatives, the AYF's Framework for Facilitation and Team Formula for Effecting Change. Interns will be given the opportunity to create and complete an individual project and will work closely with the outreach program director to design an experience that will serve individual goals and expectations.

Duration: Minimum fifteen-week commitment.

Compensation and Perks: Interns receive a $375-per-month stipend, room, partial board, and staff training. Many opportunities exist to create a meaningful experience by exploring particular individual areas of interest.

The Ideal Candidate: Candidates must have current first aid and CPR certification (lifeguarding is also preferred) and experience facilitating low and high ropes is very helpful. Applicants must possess an interest in fostering personal development of people of all ages and furthering the AYF mission.

Making It Happen: Send cover letter and resume. Rolling deadlines.

INSIDER TIPS: *Candidates must be ready to learn, have experience working with youth programs, an ability to laugh easily, have a positive attitude, an interest in experientially-based programs, and a willingness to put 110 percent energy into the program.*

Contact Information: "Poppy" Elizabeth Potter, Outreach Program Director • AYF—Miniwanca • 8845 W. Garfield Rd. • Shelby, MI 49455 • Phone: (616) 861-2262 • Fax: (616) 861-5244

Backroads

REGION/HQ: Worldwide/California • **CATEGORY:** Cycling • **POSITION TYPE:** Seasonal • **DURATION:** Year-Round • **IDEAL CANDIDATE:** College Students, Career Changers, Retired Folks • **APPLICANT POOL:** Varies • **APPLICANTS ACCEPTED:** Varies

BACKROADS IS THE world's number one active-travel company, offering bicycling, walking, hiking, and cross-country skiing vacations in more than eighty-five destinations worldwide.

Work/Learn Program Specifics: Leaders are involved in all aspects of trips: ensuring that all equipment is in optimal working condition; buying and preparing food; offering support to guests en route; delivering luggage at each night's accommodations; acting as a representative at hotels, restaurants, campgrounds, and with the general public; and keeping accurate financial records and complete written reports.

Compensation and Perks: First-year leaders receive $55 per day for hotel trips and $73 per day for camping trips, plus meals, lodging, and transportation costs. The pay scale and benefits increase in recognition of each year's experience.

The Ideal Candidate: Leader candidates must relate well to people of varied ages and backgrounds, have excellent driving records, be over twenty-one, have good public speaking skills, and be capable of solving problems independently and professionally.

Making It Happen: Write for application (no phone calls, please).

Contact Information: Leader Applications—BDG • Backroads • 801 Cedar St. • Berkeley, CA 94710-1800 • Phone: (510) 527-1555 • Fax: (510) 527-1789 • Toll Free: (800) 462-2848 • E-mail: goactive@backroads.com • Web Site: www.backroads.com

BCTel Employee Fitness Program

REGION/HQ: Canada/British Columbia • **CATEGORY:** Fitness • **POSITION TYPE:** Internship • **DURATION:** Year-Round • **IDEAL CANDIDATE:** College Students, Career Changers, Foreigners • **APPLICANT POOL:** 25–30/term • **APPLICANTS ACCEPTED:** 15–20/term

SINCE ITS INCEPTION IN 1977, the BCTel (British Columbia Telephone) Employee Fitness Program has developed into one of the largest and most comprehensive programs of its kind in North America, with twelve fitness centers. Its mission is to provide all employees with an opportunity to adapt their living habits towards a state of optimal health through the provision of quality fitness and related lifestyle services.

Work/Learn Program Specifics: Fitness specialist interns provide fitness assessment, exercise prescription, fitness class instruction, facility supervision, special event planning, sports programming, and general administrative duties.

Duration: Duration is twelve to fifteen weeks, corresponding to your school schedule.

Compensation and Perks: There is a small honorarium of $300. Benefits include a free fitness membership, fitness apparel, professional library access, and training opportunities.

The Ideal Candidate: Looking for students (or recent graduates) who are studying health/fitness/recreation at a university or college. CPR and first aid certification is mandatory (they can help you get them) and fitness leader certification is helpful. Since you get thrown right into your position (which can be quite hectic), you must be outgoing, a self-starter, and adaptable.

Making It Happen: Send cover letter and resume. Deadlines: spring—December 1; summer—April 1; and fall—August 1. Informal interview process.

Contact Information: Susan Hui, Student Internship Coordinator • BCTel Employee Fitness Program • 7000 Lougheed Highway • Burnaby, British Columbia V5A 4K4 • Canada • Phone: (604) 444-8858 • Fax: (604) 444-8848

Boojum Institute for Experiential Education

REGION/HQ: Pacific Northwest/California • **CATEGORY:** Experiential Education • **POSITION TYPE:** Internship • **DURATION:** Year-Round • **IDEAL CANDIDATE:** College Students, Career Changers • **APPLICANT POOL:** 12/term • **APPLICANTS ACCEPTED:** 1–2/term

BOOJUM INSTITUTE IS A nonprofit educational organization whose mission is to promote self-discovery, constructive interaction with others, and a deeper understanding of nature through experiential, adventure, and environmental education. Their clients are primarily students, from sixth grade through college, and courses include such components as backpacking, ropes courses, rock climbing, canoeing, and hiking.

Area and Working Environment: Idyllwild is situated in a yellow pine forest at an elevation of 5,500 feet. Clean air, beautiful views, and a friendly community of 2,500 all contribute to creating a healthy environment. Joshua Tree National Park, the Sierra Nevada, and Lake Mead National Recreational Area all serve as the Boojum Institute's outdoor classroom.

Work/Learn Program Specifics: Interns must have clear goals of what they want to learn at Boojum. Then, during the internship, they "build in" formal training or other opportunities for each intern. This training could include accompanying an instructor in the field, or one of their administrative staff taking the time to explain new employee application, selection, and staffing procedures. Logistics lessons include menu planning, food buying, some food preparation, the movement of gear and people to course sites, and gear inventories and ordering. Administrative tasks include a hodgepodge of office duties and special projects in the areas of curricula development, risk management, and staff coordination.

Duration: Positions are available from February through November. Interns can expect to work weekends and some holidays depending on course load. The busiest time is mid-August through mid-November.

Compensation and Perks: A $100-per-month stipend and comfortable housing are provided.

The Ideal Candidate: Applicants must be at least twenty years old, hold current first aid and CPR certification, have an excellent driving record, a genuine interest in learning more about the outdoor experiential education field, and be able and willing to work hard.

Making It Happen: Call for application materials. A resume and cover letter are required (including your goals for the internship), along with your completed application and three reference forms you have sent to past supervisors, employers, or teachers. Rolling deadlines.

INSIDER TIPS: *This is an entry-level position for someone who is interested in the experiential field. We are looking for folks who are open and honest and have good self-assessment skills. A good sense of humor and initiative are definitely helpful.*

Contact Information: Pete Stocks, Operations Manager • Boojum Institute for Experiential Education • P.O. Box 687 • Idyllwild, CA 92549 • Phone: (909) 659-6250 • Fax: (909) 659-6251 • E-mail: BoojumInst@aol.com

Bradley Wellness Center

REGION/HQ: Southeast/Georgia • **CATEGORY:** Fitness • **POSITION TYPE:** Internship • **DURATION:** Year-Round • **IDEAL CANDIDATE:** College Students, Career Changers, Foreigners • **APPLICANT POOL:** 20/term • **APPLICANTS ACCEPTED:** 6/term

BRADLEY WELLNESS CENTER, a 54,000-square-foot multipurpose facility, offers experience in adult fitness, cardiac and pulmonary rehabilitation, aquatics, recreational sports, and educational programming. Wellness is a dynamic process that has as its foundation the concept of personal responsibility for one's health. Bradley Wellness Center's comprehensive approach of assessment, education, and fitness strives to represent this ideal. Health is not merely the absence of disease; it is the achievement of optimal well-being.

Area and Working Environment: Dalton is located in northern Georgia, near Chattanooga, Tennessee, and is known as the "carpet capital" of the world.

Work/Learn Program Specifics: Intern's responsibilities include assessment, exercise supervision and leadership, exercise prescription, program development, and health/lifestyle education. The internship experience is geared to the individual goals and qualifications of each intern in this supervised program.

Duration: Positions are open year-round, for a minimum duration of three months, forty hours per week.

Compensation and Perks: Interns receive a $75-per-month stipend. Housing is provided at Hamilton Medical Center (adjacent to facility) and interns will receive a 50 percent discount in the hospital cafeteria.

The Ideal Candidate: A background in exercise science or other health-related field is required. Current CPR certification is required.

Making It Happen: Call for more information, then send resume, cover letter, and transcripts.

Contact Information: Laura Poe, Intern Supervisor • Bradley Wellness Center • 1225 Broadrick • P.O. Box 2514 • Dalton, GA 30722-2514 • Phone: (706) 278-9355 • Fax: (706) 226-6872

Breckenridge Outdoor Education Center

REGION/HQ: Rocky Mountains/Colorado • **CATEGORY:** Therapeutic Recreation • **POSITION TYPE:** Internship • **DURATION:** Year-Round • **IDEAL CANDIDATE:** College Students, Career Changers • **APPLICANT POOL:** 100/year • **APPLICANTS ACCEPTED:** 10/term

SINCE 1976, the Breckenridge Outdoor Education Center (BOEC) has been dedicated to its mission of providing empowering outdoor experiences for people with a wide variety of physical and mental disabilities, serious illnesses, and other "at-risk" populations. The center's goal is to provide participants with the opportunity to learn new skills, experience pristine natural areas, challenge themselves, and work together to enhance the health and self-confidence necessary to expand human potential. BOEC offers wilderness/adventure programs in: downhill and cross-country skiing, ropes course, rafting, rock climbing, camping, fishing, and other activities.

Area and Working Environment: BOEC's Griffith Lodge is nestled amidst the pines overlooking an alpine lake and the peaks of the Ten Mile Range. This beautiful facility is the temporary home for participants and guests of the BOEC. Just two miles from the center of Breckenridge, the Griffith Lodge is also a ski-in/ski-out facility.

Work/Learn Program Specifics: Interns are the lifeblood of the center and are "where the rubber meets the road." Time and time again, BOEC's clients comment that the energy, professionalism, and expertise of the staff is the center's greatest asset. The bottom line on all intern work, whether in the Wilderness Program, ski office, Professional Challenge Program, administration office, or maintenance around the program site, is that it can be very difficult and very rewarding. Winter interns focus on teaching lessons in the Adaptive Ski Program for people with disabilities and assist the course directors in leading multi-day programs in the great outdoors. Summer interns focus on the Wilderness Program, where they have the opportunity to develop the full range of skills necessary to become a top-notch wilderness instructor.

Duration: BOEC interns must commit to working full-time for an entire season. The winter season runs from early November to May 1; and the summer, May 15 to September 15. The initial training phase lasts three weeks, with few days off and many long days.

Compensation and Perks: Interns receive a $50-per-month stipend, plus room and board. The cabins are lovely, rustic, and peaceful, but remember you are living on a program site, where you also do your job. Perks include a ski pass in the winter, workmen's compensation, and of course, the invaluable training and great experience that come from participation in the internship. Interns are able to trade some of their time and wilderness expertise for a membership at the Breckenridge Recreation Center, which has hot showers, hot tubs, swimming pools, and workout equipment.

The Ideal Candidate: Group facilitation and strong supervisory skills are important. Other qualities, such as flexibility, willingness to work long hours, and the ability to live harmoniously with others in a community setting are just as important. However, they have hired interns with a limited experiential education background, basing their decisions largely on the applicant's commitment, good attitude, and enthusiasm for the BOEC and mission. Applicants must be over twenty-one years of age and have advanced first aid certification, current CPR certification, and outdoor skills.

Making It Happen: Call for application. Send completed application with cover letter and resume. Deadlines: summer—March 20; winter—September 15. Your application will be reviewed and either a phone or in-person interview will be conducted with the strongest applicants. If you have not heard from them within two weeks of the application deadlines, feel free to call the office.

Contact Information: Earl Richmond, Asst. Wilderness Program Director • Breckenridge Outdoor Education Center • P.O. Box 697 • Breckenridge, CO 80424 • Phone: (970) 453-6422 • Fax: (970) 453-4676 • Toll Free: (800) 383-2632 • E-mail: boec@colorado.net • Web Site: www.brecknet.com/boec

Challenge Alaska

REGION/HQ: Pacific Northwest/Alaska • **CATEGORY:** Therapeutic Recreation • **POSITION TYPE:** Internship • **DURATION:** Summer • **IDEAL CANDIDATE:** College Students, Career Changers, Foreigners • **APPLICANT POOL:** Varies • **APPLICANTS ACCEPTED:** Varies

• •

CHALLENGE ALASKA IS A nonprofit organization that provides sports and recreational therapy opportunities to Alaskans with disabilities. Challenge Alaska believes that everyone, regardless of physical ability, should have an equal opportunity to engage in diverse recreational activities. Exhilarating physical recreation is a crucial aspect of early rehabilitation and lifelong well-being, an important track to improved mobility, increased self-confidence, and development of specific skills. These benefits, in turn, promote employment opportunities, social integration, spiritual peace, and physical independence. Activities include sea kayaking, sailing, fishing, camping, rafting, skiing, waterskiing, wheelchair racing, and a variety of other events.

Area and Working Environment: Anchorage and Girdwood, Alaska.

Work/Learn Program Specifics: Interns will be involved in recreation, special events, fund-raising, vol-

unteer coordination, administration, resource development, newsline production, and database operations.

Duration: Internships last for at least three months, with a possible start date some time in June and a possible end date some time in October. Interns will work full- or part-time and a ten- to twelve-week commitment is asked for.

Compensation and Perks: Interns receive a $50 per week stipend, housing, and some assistance with food.

The Ideal Candidate: Students majoring in recreation, social services, outdoor education, recreation therapy, or the human services fields are encouraged to apply.

Making It Happen: Submit cover letter and resume. Deadline is one month prior to start date of internship.

Contact Information: Program Director • Challenge Alaska • 1132 E. 74, Suite 107 • Anchorage, AK 99511 • Phone: (907) 344-7399 • Fax: (907) 344-7349

City of Eugene

REGION/HQ: Pacific Northwest/Oregon • **CATEGORY:** Recreation • **POSITION TYPE:** Internship • **DURATION:** Year-Round • **IDEAL CANDIDATE:** College Students, Career Changers, Retired Folks, Foreigners • **APPLICANT POOL:** Varies • **APPLICANTS ACCEPTED:** Varies

• •

THE CITY OF EUGENE LIBRARY, Recreation, and Cultural Services Department is an innovative leader in a unique partnership between community recreation programs, library, and cultural services. The department's operating budget is in excess of $10 million and the department consists of three divisions and ten major facilities. The department's mission is to provide access to lifelong learning, recreational, and cultural experiences. They have nationally recognized programs in aquatic fitness, working with specialized populations and seniors.

Area and Working Environment: Located at the southern end of the lush Willamette Valley, Eugene is ideally situated for persons who enjoy the outdoor lifestyle. It is the home of the University of Oregon, international sporting events, a world-class performing arts center, and hundreds of restaurants, cafes, and shops.

Work/Learn Program Specifics: Interns can focus on athletics, aquatics, community centers, marketing/special events, senior centers, specialized recreation programs, outdoor programs, or youth-at-risk, and interns may take on special assignments. Examples of special projects include facility enhancement, youth outreach programs, coordination of fund-raising efforts, revenue generating concepts, marketing, and an automation training program. The internship will provide you with experiences, skills, and challenges to help you make a successful transition into the professional world.

Duration: Duration is flexible to accommodate university requirements. The summer and fall are their busiest seasons.

Compensation and Perks: All internships provide a stipend or single payment ranging from $600 to $1,200 per term. There is assistance in helping interns find adequate and affordable housing. You also receive free access to their fitness and swim facilities.

The Ideal Candidate: All interns need to be motivated to have fun and work hard. First aid and CPR certifications are required for some internships, and specific training or certifications may be required in other program areas. You should also be comfortable with Microsoft Windows.

Making It Happen: Call for application form. Submit completed application, cover letter, resume, and three references with phone numbers. The summer program deadline is March 30; other deadlines are rolling. Telephone interviews are acceptable if all appropriate paperwork is completed. Be sure to phone their office after you submit all your application material.

INSIDER TIPS: *Pinpoint a specific internship job. Describe knowledge, skills, or abilities that best suit you for achieving success in that position. Describe how this internship will help meet your career goals and how you are going to contribute something positive to our organization.*

Contact Information: Andre Briggs, Resource Development Manager • City of Eugene • Library, Recreation, & Cultural Services • 22 W. 7th Ave. • Eugene, OR 97401 • Phone: (503) 682-5306 • Fax: (503) 683-6834 • E-mail: andre.c.briggs@ci.eugene.or.us

Coconino County Parks

REGION/HQ: South/Midwest/Arizona • **CATEGORY:** Recreation • **POSITION TYPE:** Internship • **DURATION:** Summer • **IDEAL CANDIDATE:** College Students • **APPLICANT POOL:** Varies • **APPLICANTS ACCEPTED:** 2/year

THE PARKS AND RECREATION DEPARTMENT provides park

facilities, including a campground, stables, a racetrack, and fairgrounds. The summer's main events include the Coconino County Horse Races and the County Fair.

Area and Working Environment: Flagstaff is situated in the beautiful mountains of northern Arizona at an elevation of 7,500 feet. Fort Tuthill County Park is approximately 70 miles from the Grand Canyon and 125 miles north of Phoenix.

Work/Learn Program Specifics: Interns will work in many areas, including administration, special-event planning, scheduling and setup, public relations, and contracting fair entertainment/concessionaires. Interns may also be required to perform some light maintenance, campground management, and/or security.

Duration: Interns will work from May 1 to September 30 (the exact time frame is negotiable). You must be willing to work weekends, holidays, and irregular hours as the needs arise.

Compensation and Perks: $100-per-week stipend, plus furnished housing.

The Ideal Candidate: Recent graduates or junior/senior undergraduates from a four-year university with a major in parks and recreation or related field are preferred. Applicants should be able to communicate effectively (both orally and in writing); have skills in public relations; be able to operate maintenance equipment; handle record keeping; and have knowledge of first aid, fire protection, and boating safety.

Making It Happen: Call for application materials. Applications must be received by March 1.

Contact Information: Jon Baker, Parks, Fair and Racing Director • Coconino County Parks • Fort Tuthill County Park • HCR-30, Box 3A • Flagstaff, AZ 86001 • Phone: (520) 774-5139 • Fax: (520) 774-2572

Contiki Holidays

REGION/HQ: Nationwide/California • **CATEGORY:** Tourism • **POSITION TYPE:** Seasonal • **DURATION:** Year-Round • **IDEAL CANDIDATE:** Career Changers, Retired Folks • **APPLICANT POOL:** Varies • **APPLICANTS ACCEPTED:** Varies

CONTIKI IS THE WORLD's largest tour operator specializing in travel for eighteen to thirty-five year olds. Because of this age category, they offer exciting and fun-filled holidays with action-packed optional excursions, such as helicopter rides, bungee jumping, white-water rafting, and much more!

Area and Working Environment: Contiki travels throughout North America—including Canada, Mexico, Alaska, and Hawaii—and gives its workers the opportunity to experience and explore these beautiful places.

Work/Learn Program Specifics: Tour managers conduct city tours, give historical and practical information talks, and deal with clients and suppliers in a professional manner. They also organize each day of a tour, including stops en route, meals, and excursions. Coach drivers work with a tour manager on every tour and are responsible for driving forty-foot motorcoaches with up to forty-seven passengers.

Duration: Tours run year-round and depart from Anaheim, California. Tours range in duration from four to twenty-three days and generally are conducted May through October. You are responsible for your clients twenty-four hours per day. Mandatory training begins mid-April.

Compensation and Perks: Pay is $80 to $100 per day. Accommodations, food, and expenses are covered while on tour. The biggest perk working for Contiki is travel. Tour managers and drivers travel around the country and show their clients a great time—and they get paid for doing it!

The Ideal Candidate: It's preferred that tour manager applicants have a college degree, a couple years of work experience, and knowledge of U.S. history and geography. Driver applicants should possess a commercial driver's license with passenger endorsement and air brakes certification. Coach driving experience is not required, as driving school will be made available to qualified candidates. The cost of driving school will be reimbursed to the driver after successfully completing the tour season. This particular office runs North American tours only and legal U.S. working status is required.

Making It Happen: Call for application materials and most current deadlines. Interviews are generally conducted in February and March.

Contact Information: Susan Charlton, Operations Manager • Contiki Holidays • 300 Plaza Alicante, Suite 900 • Garden Grove, CA 92640 • Phone: (714) 740-0808 • Fax: (714) 740-0818 • E-mail: contikiusa@aol.com • Web Site: www.contiki-tours.com

Environmental Traveling Companions

REGION/HQ: Pacific Northwest/California • **CATEGORY:** Outdoor Adventure • **POSITION TYPE:** Internship/Seasonal • **DURATION:** Winter/Summer • **IDEAL CANDIDATE:** College Students, Career Changers, Retired Folks, Foreigners • **APPLICANT POOL:** Varies • **APPLICANTS ACCEPTED:** Varies

FOUNDED IN 1971, Environmental Traveling Companions is a nonprofit organization which provides outdoor adventure and environmental education experiences for people of all abilities, including people with special needs. The populations they serve are diverse—many of their participants have visual and hearing impairments, physical and/or developmental disabilities, and some are disadvantaged, inner-city youths. Their work involves many school groups and employee groups. ETC's primary goal is to provide access to the wilderness to people of all abilities and to promote self-esteem, self-sufficiency, and a greater appreciation for the environment. Annually, they serve over 1,800 participants in their three outdoor programs, which include white-water rafting, sea kayaking, and Nordic skiing.

Area and Working Environment: Sea Kayaking: Trips are conducted from Sausalito to Angel Island and to other sites in San Francisco and Tomales Bays. White-water Rafting: ETC runs the American, Carson, Klamath, Trinity, Deschuttes, Yampa, and Green Rivers. Nordic Skiing: Trips are located in the high Sierras, at Bear Valley.

Work/Learn Program Specifics: White-water rafting field interns will assist and/or guide white-water rafting trips and outdoor activities and games, aid in logistical planning, coordination of volunteers, program development, maintenance of the site, and repair of equipment. White-water guide school takes place in early spring and is mandatory for prospective interns without solid class three rafting skills. Training will include white-water guiding, outdoor-leadership skills, working with special populations, and running an outdoor program (the work is often hard and the hours long). Nordic ski guide interns will lead and guide ski trips for groups of people with varying needs. They will also help with logistics, course planning, and maintenance of site and equipment. ETC also has salaried, short-term management and administration positions. Call for details on these.

Duration: Seasonal positions offered summer or winter, thirty to forty hours per week.

Compensation and Perks: Interns receive a small stipend of $100 per month, room and partial board, rafting/skiing privileges, training as a white-water raft guide or cross-country ski guide, leadership experience, and training in disability awareness. Management positions receive $700 to $1,500 per month, depending on experience (including room and partial board).

The Ideal Candidate: Applicants must have a desire to develop leadership skills; have experience working with special populations (preferred but not necessary); be enthusiastic about wilderness adventure; comfortable in the outdoors; a self-starter and able to work independently; clear communicator; enjoy working with people; and CPR/first aid certified. Some rafting/Nordic ski experience (depending on position) and wilderness/environmental education skills are preferred. ETC Guides represent a diversity of cultures, abilities, and backgrounds. Many guides are teachers, engineers, counselors, carpenters, lawyers, and university interns.

Making It Happen: Write or call for application details. Deadlines: winter—November 10; summer—February 20.

INSIDER TIPS: *The over 400 volunteer guidepool makes up an incredibly enthusiastic, eclectic, and fun community. Once introduced, most folks get sucked into the ETC whirlpool and stay involved for years to come!*

Contact Information: Jennifer Talbot, Program Coordinator • Environmental Traveling Companions • Fort Mason Center, Building C • San Francisco, CA 94123 • Phone: (415) 474-7662 • Fax: (415) 474-3919

Four Corners Rafting

REGION/HQ: Rocky Mountains/Colorado
• **CATEGORY:** Outfitter • **POSITION TYPE:** Seasonal
• **DURATION:** Spring/Summer • **IDEAL CANDIDATE:** College Students, Career Changers, Foreigners
• **APPLICANT POOL:** 15–25/year • **APPLICANTS ACCEPTED:** 3–10/year

COLORADO'S ARKANSAS RIVER is home to the most popular mild to wild raft trips in the country. Since 1976, Four Corners has been operating white-water rafting and float-fishing trips with the utmost concern for safety, customer service, and quality staff.

Area and Working Environment: In the Buena Vista area you can climb numerous 14,000-foot mountain peaks; take leisurely day hikes; venture into several wilderness areas to backpack, kayak, and fish lakes and streams; visit ghost towns; bike miles of dirt roads and trails; camp; or visit several unique art galleries and hot springs.

Work/Learn Program Specifics: Guides run mostly half- and one-day trips on various stretches of the Arkansas (primarily class three and some class four and five white-water). Learn to operate paddle and oar rafts and meet many interesting people.

Duration: You must be able to come to guide training, which starts mid-May, followed by additional training on a local river until competent. Some guides are ready in late May; most, the first week of June. You will work six days a week, but some days there aren't any trips or only a half-day trip. A full day is from 7:30 A.M. until 4:00 P.M.

Compensation and Perks: Pay is $26 per half-day trip for first year, more for experienced guides. Benefits include workmen's compensation, use of equipment on days off and for extended river trips, easy access to other outdoor activities, the opportunity to learn to kayak, discounts on river gear and clothing, and cost sharing when upgrading emergency skills. Housing can be difficult to find, although they keep an eye out for you. Four Corners leases campsites or spaces in large, lockable tents for a very reasonable fee.

The Ideal Candidate: Applicants must be at least eighteen and have first aid and CPR certification. Must be comfortable in water, a good swimmer, personable, well-groomed, and able to work in hot, wet, or cold weather. Any river training or experience you can get on your own or in other guide schools, a higher level first aid certification, and ability to stay past mid-August helps. Show initiative and be willing to do whatever is asked. Want to learn and don't push instructors to check you out until you are ready by their standards. Want to learn local history, geology, plants, and animals.

Making It Happen: Call for application. They screen and let you know if you are being considered. They check references, then decide who to invite for their training trip (usually six days on the Dolores River in southwestern Colorado). Training is $250, with half refunded if you stay the whole season. Hiring is done after the six-day training trip. There is no guarantee you will be hired if you are selected to go on the training trip.

INSIDER TIPS: *Get on a river with an outdoor club or check out nearby guide-training schools. Contact us early and do your paperwork correctly and neatly. Be complete and make sure your references have current contact information.*

Contact Information: Karen and Reed Dils, Owners • Four Corners Rafting • Box 569—BDE • Buena Vista, CO 81211-1032 • Phone: (719) 395-8949 • Fax: (719)

395-8949 • Toll Free: (800) 332-7238 • E-mail: dils@usa.net • Web Site: www.pikes-peak.com/fourcorners

Glacier Park Boat Company

REGION/HQ: Rocky Mountains/Montana
• **CATEGORY:** Outfitter • **POSITION TYPE:** Seasonal
• **DURATION:** Summer • **IDEAL CANDIDATE:** College Students, Career Changers, Foreigners • **APPLICANT POOL:** 45/year • **APPLICANTS ACCEPTED:** 15/year

YOU WILL HAVE THE CHANCE to work in one of the most beautiful places in the world, with regular days off to hike, fish, and explore the scenery.

Work/Learn Program Specifics: Employees are expected to pilot tour boats carrying from forty-five to ninety passengers, while giving commentaries on the historic and natural aspects of Glacier National Park. In addition, they do have a few employees who work at renting small boats only. Being a boat captain in Glacier is the best summer job in the world for a college person.

Duration: Employees generally work five days per week from June 1 through September 15. It is preferable that you work the entire season, but they can make some modifications depending on the availability of the entire crew.

Compensation and Perks: Pay is $4.55 per hour, plus family-style housing and board (for $5 per day). Employees live with other employees and the location manager.

The Ideal Candidate: Applicants must be at least eighteen years of age, possess current CPR/first aid certificates, pass the Boat Captain Certification Exam, successfully complete a physical exam, enjoy working with the public, and have good communication skills—especially public speaking. The setting is gorgeous but it is a long way from civilization. If pizza and a movie is your favorite form of relaxation, this is probably not for you.

Making It Happen: An interview is mandatory due to the high degree of responsibility the position entails. They can provide a telephone interview or substitute an interview with a former boat captain.

INSIDER TIPS: *Apply early (December through February)! We are a small company. The person who opens your request for an application probably writes your check. All impressions count. We don't like laconic applications; we want to see your best effort. You need to like people, be mechanically apt, and not mind less privacy.*

Contact Information: Susan Burch, Administration Officer • Glacier Park Boat Company • P.O. Box 5262 • Kalispell, MT 59903 • Phone: (406) 257-2426 • Fax: (406) 756-1437 • Alternate: (406) 756-1439 • Web Site: www.glaciercountry.com

Gray Line of Alaska

REGION/HQ: Pacific Northwest/Washington
• **CATEGORY:** Adventure Travel • **POSITION TYPE:** Internship/Seasonal • **DURATION:** Spring/Summer • **IDEAL CANDIDATE:** College Students, Career Changers, Retired Folks, Foreigners • **APPLICANT POOL:** Varies • **APPLICANTS ACCEPTED:** Varies

GRAY LINE OF ALASKA IS a subsidiary of Holland American Line-Westours, a complete cruise and tour company. Currently they have ten cruise ships, two day-boats, and approximately sixteen Westmark hotels throughout Alaska and the Yukon. They also have McKinley Explorer railcars on the Alaska Railroad, which run between Anchorage and Fairbanks through Denali National Park, and a fleet of over 250 motorcoaches in Alaska.

Area and Working Environment: Alaska is definitely the last frontier—it's beautiful and filled with amazing wildlife (including bears, eagles, and whales). It's an outdoor enthusiast's paradise, where one can hike, bike, fish, and kayak.

Work/Learn Program Specifics: A driver/guide is not just a "chauffeur." Drivers must also learn and develop tour narratives in order to provide an enjoyable vacation experience for customers through informative and entertaining narration. This position is customer service-oriented and you must be willing to go that "extra mile" to meet the needs of their passengers.

Duration: You must be able to relocate to Washington or Alaska for the thirteen-week training program which starts in early February. After training is complete, you must be able to commit to a three-month contract working in Alaska during the summer. Guides average fifty to fifty-five hours per week, with daily work loads varying between six and thirteen hours depending on the tour assignment.

Compensation and Perks: During the training period you will receive minimum wage. First-year drivers generally make $6,000 to $8,000, plus gratuities. Gray Line also has a bonus program in which drivers can earn up to 12 percent of their total wages for the season. Housing varies with each location. All employees receive discounted or "comp" fares for travel on company "products," including McKinley Rail, Gray Line motorcoaches, Westmark Hotels, and dayboats, and a free cruise of up to fourteen days on a Holland America line ship (for you and a guest).

The Ideal Candidate: Driver/Guides must be self-confident, have the ability to speak well, present a professional image, and maintain a responsible attitude. Must be twenty-one years of age, with no more than one moving violation on driving records in the last three years.

Making It Happen: Call for additional information and application. Deadline: February 28.

INSIDER TIPS: *You must love working with and around people, be flexible, able to go with the flow, and have a work hard/play hard mentality.*

Contact Information: Jeanie Fillingim, Program Manager • Gray Line of Alaska • 300 Elliott Ave., West • Seattle, WA 98119 • Phone: (206) 281-0559 • Fax: (206) 281-0621 • Toll Free: (800) 544-2206

Green Valley Recreation

REGION/HQ: South/Midwest/Arizona • **CATEGORY:** Recreation • **POSITION TYPE:** Internship • **DURATION:** Year-Round • **IDEAL CANDIDATE:** College Students, Foreigners • **APPLICANT POOL:** Varies • **APPLICANTS ACCEPTED:** 1/term

GREEN VALLEY RECREATION (GVR) is a nonprofit membership organization which operates twelve recreation centers in active retirement communities. The mild winter months, with temperatures averaging in the 70s during the day and above freezing at night, are what bring most visitors to the Green Valley area. But, finding that the supposedly unbearably hot summer months aren't all that bad either, has kept residents in the Greater Green Valley area.

Area and Working Environment: Situated in the Santa Cruz Valley, the Greater Green Valley area consists of a core age-restricted retirement community surrounded by numerous family-oriented subdivisions with a total population of over 22,000. Green Valley is only a hop, skip, and a jump from all that Tucson has to offer, as well.

Work/Learn Program Specifics: Recreation interns will assist with coordination of all details needed to implement recreation department activities, which may

include special-interest classes, dances, lectures, movies, concerts, parties, special events, and Senior Olympics.

Duration: Twelve- to sixteen-week programs offered year-round. The typical workweek is forty or more hours long, with work on the evenings and weekends.

Compensation and Perks: Interns receive a $3,000 stipend per season, plus housing. Interns also have access to Green Valley's facilities and programs.

Making It Happen: Send a cover letter and resume. Deadlines: winter—November 15; and fall—April 30. Telephone interviews will be conducted with selected applicants.

Contact Information: Jeff Ziegler, Executive Director • Green Valley Recreation • P.O. Box 586 • Green Valley, AZ 85622-0586 • Phone: (602) 625-3440 • Fax: (602) 625-2352

Greenbrier River Outdoor Adventures

REGION/HQ: Southeast/West Virginia • **CATEGORY:** Experiential Education • **POSITION TYPE:** Internship/Seasonal • **DURATION:** Summer • **IDEAL CANDIDATE:** College Students, Career Changers • **APPLICANT POOL:** 300/year • **APPLICANTS ACCEPTED:** 20/year

GREENBRIER RIVER OUTDOOR ADVENTURES offers a wide variety of programs for young people between the ages of ten and seventeen. Programs are based on the development of self-esteem and leadership through adventure, challenge, and small-group experiences—through adventure-based activities and community service projects. Everything (sleep, eat, cook, and play) is done in the outdoors. While not a survival program, a large part of the program is learning how to live comfortably in the outdoors while taking time to enjoy the experience.

Area and Working Environment: The base camp is located on a 250-acre site, nestled in the mountains of the Monongahela National Forest, an excellent place for rock climbing, white-water rafting, mountain biking, caving, and backpacking.

Work/Learn Program Specifics: Summer staff (group leaders and specialists) and interns will provide for the general safety and supervision of students, oversee program logistics and itinerary, teach outdoor living skills, and facilitate and develop group dynamics. Staff members participate in a week-long intensive training session to kick off the summer.

Duration: Positions are available mid-June through mid-August.

Compensation and Perks: Staff receives an hourly wage or stipend, plus room and board. Pro deals are available on outdoor clothing and equipment.

The Ideal Candidate: Applicants must have a sincere interest in working with youth in the outdoors and should have experience in the field, competency in outdoor living, and related program skills. Must be at least nineteen years old and have certificates in CPR, first aid, and water safety.

Making It Happen: Send resume and cover letter requesting application. Applications are accepted year-round.

Contact Information: Rachel Bryant, Program Director • Greenbrier River Outdoor Adventures • P.O. Box 160 • Bartow, WV 24920-0160 • Phone: (304) 456-5191 • Fax: (304) 456-3121 • Web Site: www.camp.org/greenbrier

Hostelling International—Alaska

REGION/HQ: Pacific Northwest/Alaska • **CATEGORY:** Hostel • **POSITION TYPE:** Internship/Seasonal • **DURATION:** Year-Round • **IDEAL CANDIDATE:** College Students, Career Changers, Foreigners • **APPLICANT POOL:** Varies • **APPLICANTS ACCEPTED:** Varies

HOSTELLING INTERNATIONAL—ALASKA is a ninety-five-bed hostel with ten bathrooms and four kitchens. They have common areas on each of the three floors and even have a small TV on one floor. Their office is open daily from 7:30 A.M. until midnight, and their lodging areas are open from 5 P.M. until noon the following day. They have limited storage, including bicycle and backpack storage (they have bus-station-type lockers for seventy-five cents per use). During the summer, several shuttle services pick up and drop off hostellers at the door, with most services heading to Mt. McKinley. Besides offering overnight lodging for world travelers at inexpensive rates ($15 for members/$18 for non-members), they also provide many educational opportunities for hostellers. Programs include slide presentations by individuals and organizations, covering a range of topics from "What I did on my summer vacation" to cultural dissertations. Interpretive tours and excursions are organized and launched from the hostel (e.g., eagle-release field trips, fair attendance, wetlands, and bird rookery trips).

Area and Working Environment: Anchorage is located on Cook Inlet, which rolls in about 100 miles from the open ocean. Because Anchorage is surrounded by mountains, you can drive, fly, or take rail transit into some of the most breathtaking scenery you will ever see. Alaska is blessed with an abundance of fine musicians and artists, and Anchorage is the cultural arts center within the state.

Work/Learn Program Specifics: Positions include house parents and generalists that take on multiple tasks of running the hostel. Projects and tasks will be assigned, depending on your interests.

Duration: Alaska's busy season begins in April and ends in September, although the hostel operates year-round. In the winter months, educational groups and students are also housed at the hostel. Six- to eight-hour shifts are usually utilized at the hostel and teams generally will work a shift. You will typically not work over eight hours a day or forty hours per week.

Compensation and Perks: Once the initial scope of the project is established, a stipend is discussed case by case. Housing is supplied for house parents and other essential employees. The hostel is located downtown, across from the public transit station, two blocks from the Performing Arts Theatre, one block from the Park Strip, and four blocks from a coastal/bicycle trail which extends 100 miles, throughout Anchorage and its outlying districts (meaning easy access to cultural activities for those without a car!).

The Ideal Candidate: Applicants must be willing to work and willing to dedicate (during the working period) to the HI–AYH philosophy. Ideally, applicants should be students on an internship program or independent studies program or students looking for seasonal employment, although other candidates are also considered.

Making It Happen: Send cover letter, resume, and three references. After review of application materials, you will be notified of available opportunities. Rolling deadlines.

INSIDER TIPS: *We have piles of tasks and projects that need attention and a board with committees that always need more bodies. Involvement in our hostel goes a long way in becoming part of what we are. Talk is cheap, action gets you everywhere.*

Contact Information: Pat Wendt, Executive Director • Hostelling International—Alaska • 700 H St. • Anchorage, AK 99501 • Phone: (907) 276-3635 • Fax: (907) 276-7772 • E-mail: hi_anchorage@surfcafe.com

Hostelling International— National Office

REGION/HQ: Nationwide/Washington, D.C.
• **CATEGORY:** Hostel • **POSITION TYPE:** Internship
• **DURATION:** Year-Round • **IDEAL CANDIDATE:** College Students, Career Changers, Foreigners
• **APPLICANT POOL:** Varies • **APPLICANTS ACCEPTED:** Varies

• •

HOSTELLING INTERNATIONAL–AMERICAN YOUTH HOSTELS (HI–AYH), a nonprofit organization founded in 1934, promotes international understanding among peoples of all ages through educational travel. As a member of the International Youth Hostel Federation (IYHF), HI–AYH provides 200,000 members with access to 150 U.S. hostels and 5,000 hostels in seventy countries worldwide. The national office staff is responsible for the overall growth of the organization, developing hostels, and promoting HI–AYH memberships. The national office, in conjunction with forty regional offices (councils), provides programming and hostel development at the local, state, and regional levels.

Area and Working Environment: Washington, D.C. is the home of HI–AYH's national office, although various other hostels throughout the United States sometimes have positions available.

Work/Learn Program Specifics: HI–AYH's relatively small professional staff relies upon interns to complete purposeful and responsible tasks. Intern responsibilities include special projects as well as routine office duties. Marketing interns implement ongoing market research at the hostel level on a national basis, develop and implement domestic membership marketing plans, and assist in direct mail member-acquisition programs. Hostel service interns support the management of a national network of hostels, develop training courses for hostel managers, and assist in production of publications to support hostel operations and marketing. Hostel development interns provide direct technical support for nationwide hostel-development projects. Programs and education interns assist with managing and operating the HI–AYH "Discovery Tours" program and develop materials to support programming throughout the national hostel network.

Duration: Positions are available year-round, with a minimum duration of ten weeks. More positions are offered in the summer months, an extremely busy time for HI–AYH.

Compensation and Perks: Interns receive free housing at the Washington, D.C. International AYH Hostel (or a similar housing arrangement), a stipend of $100 per week for undergraduates, $150 per week for graduate students, and $200 for relocation assistance (paid upon completion of internship).

The Ideal Candidate: Must have a genuine interest in Hostelling International and the specific internship you are applying for.

Making It Happen: Send resume, transcript, three letters of recommendation, and a cover letter highlighting your personal interest in Hostelling International, your department preference, and the dates of availability. Deadlines: winter—December 1; spring—February 1; summer—May 1; and fall—August 15.

Contact Information: Demetria Robinson, Office Manager • Hostelling International—National Office • 733 15th St., NW, Suite 840 • Washington, DC 20005 • Phone: (202) 783-6161 • Fax: (202) 783-6171 • E-mail: hiayhserv@hiayh.org • Web Site: www.hiayh.org

Hostelling International— San Francisco

REGION/HQ: Pacific Northwest/California
• **CATEGORY:** Hostel • **POSITION TYPE:** Internship
• **DURATION:** Year-Round • **IDEAL CANDIDATE:** College Students, Career Changers, Foreigners
• **APPLICANT POOL:** Varies •**APPLICANTS ACCEPTED:** Varies

• •

THE GOLDEN GATE COUNCIL OF HI–AYH offers a wide variety of educational and recreational programs to hostellers and to the community, including a travel center, travel seminars, walking tours, information services, special events, art events, videos, sports and games, and interpretive programs.

Work/Learn Program Specifics: Program interns assist in creating, planning, and overseeing hostel programs, create promotional materials for programs, develop resources for use in programs and information services, and initiate community outreach. Environmental education interns assist with curriculum development, trip orientations, community outreach, and program administration. Marketing interns assist with the member newsletter; write and target press releases and public announcements; follow up with media; represent HI–AYH at travel fairs and seminars; write, design, and distribute all HI–AYH promotional literature; and maintain media files and contacts.

Duration: Interns must commit fifteen to twenty hours per week for two to six months.

Compensation and Perks: Possibility of free board at San Francisco youth hostels.

The Ideal Candidate: Applicants must have a strong interest or experience in the position they are applying for, as well as enthusiasm for goals of HI–AYH and the ability to follow through on projects.

Making It Happen: Send cover letter and resume. Rolling deadlines.

Contact Information: Patrick Kinney, Volunteer/Intern Coordinator • Hostelling International—San Francisco • Golden Gate Council • 425 Divisadero, #307 • San Francisco, CA 94117• Phone: (415) 863-1444 • Fax: (415) 863-3865 • E-mail: hiayh@norcalhostels.org • Web Site: www.norcalhostels.org

Hulbert Outdoor Center

REGION/HQ: Northeast/Vermont • **CATEGORY:** Experiential Education • **POSITION TYPE:** Seasonal • **DURATION:** Year-Round • **IDEAL CANDIDATE:** College Students, Career Changers • **APPLICANT POOL:** 50/term • **APPLICANTS ACCEPTED:** 15/term

ESTABLISHED IN 1978, the Hulbert Outdoor Center is a nonprofit educational institution that serves 6,000 participants annually through programs designed to foster personal growth, self-reliance, cooperation, confidence, and a sense of community in people of all ages.

Area and Working Environment: The center is located in Vermont's Upper Connecticut River Valley on the shores of Lake Morey, surrounded by over 500 acres of young forests, bluffs, and rolling countryside.

Work/Learn Program Specifics: Hulbert provides unique opportunities that combine elements of wilderness travel, outdoor skill development, teamwork, sensitivity to the environment, and personal growth experiences. School program instructors work with participants in programs emphasizing team-building, ropes course, natural history, and other curriculum areas. Trip leaders (and assistants) lead extended wilderness experiences for groups of eight to ten participants. Support staff is responsible for setting up, running, and assisting with the ropes course; driving, dropping off, picking up, and restocking supplies; and assisting the pack-out equipment manager. The food and equipment manager is responsible for organizing all of the food and equipment necessary for every trip.

Duration: Programs are offered year-round.

Compensation and Perks: Your salary is dependent on experience. Room and board are provided.

The Ideal Candidate: Applicants should be energetic, talented, and dedicated, and have the desire to live, learn, and work in an intense and positive environment. CPR and wilderness first responder certification is required for leadership positions.

Making It Happen: Call for application materials. Rolling deadlines.

Contact Information: Meredyth Morley, Wilderness Trips Director • Hulbert Outdoor Center • The Aloha Foundation, Inc. • RR 1, Box 91A • Fairlee, VT 05045-9719 • Phone: (802) 333-3405 • Fax: (802) 333-3404 • Toll Free: (888) 333-3405

Inner Quest, Inc.

REGION/HQ: Southeast/Virginia • **CATEGORY:** Experiential Education • **POSITION TYPE:** Work/Learn Adventure • **DURATION:** Year-Round • **IDEAL CANDIDATE:** College Students, Career Changers, Retired Folks, Foreigners • **APPLICANT POOL:** 60/year • **APPLICANTS ACCEPTED:** 10–20/year

INNER QUEST IS AN experiential educational organization encouraging holistic growth through safe, challenging adventure. Through demanding and exhilarating outdoor adventure activities, Inner Quest challenges all participants to become more fully themselves. Inner Quest experiences are designed to enhance self-awareness, strengthen self-confidence, deepen interpersonal responsibility and compassion, and heighten sensitivity to the natural environment. These educational benefits are available to all ages, interest groups, and special populations through Inner Quest's unique adaptive programming capabilities.

Area and Working Environment: They operate in the Washington, D.C. metro area and near Harper's Ferry, West Virginia; both of which are full of historical and educational sites and information.

Work/Learn Program Specifics: The apprentice program is designed to provide training and work experience in safety, instructional methods, ropes and initiatives, rock climbing, map and compass use, general knowledge, rope management, expedition leadership, emergency care, spelunking, canoeing, kayaking, water safety, physical fitness, and logistics. The apprentice receives twenty or more days of formal training and is expected to show interest, concern, initiative, enthusiasm, and a desire to learn. All training and testing must be completed with a high degree of competence. The apprentice also participates in thirty-five or more days of supervised work experience. Within three to four weeks, the apprentice begins acting in the capacity of assistant instructor, exercising leadership, technical skills, and group dynamics with small groups of eight to twelve students while assisting a regular staff instructor. Eventually, the apprentice is given the opportunity to act as a primary instructor, with full responsibility for safety and course objectives for their own group, under the supervision of the course director. This phase will begin with short one-day programs, but can progress based entirely on the apprentice's capabilities.

Duration: Internships are offered in March, May (limited positions available), and August, for a total of twelve weeks. They also have part-time positions in the winter.

Compensation and Perks: Apprentices will receive a stipend of $800 for a three-month duration; however, the apprentices are responsible for housing, transportation, and food while at Inner Quest. The apprenticeship is a high quality training program for those trying to get started in the field. You'll find that the more popular instructor-training courses in the field will run close to $2,000. Many participants complete the program just for training and experience; others are interested in working for Inner Quest after the program is completed. They only hire apprentices when there are openings—so chances look good.

The Ideal Candidate: Applicants should be eighteen years of age or older, have an intense desire to learn, work hard, and develop into a professional member of the Inner Quest staff during their tenure of the apprenticeship. Although the program provides the training necessary to become an instructor, Inner Quest prefers that applicants have current Red Cross qualifications in first aid, canoeing, and water safety. Experience in backpacking, rock climbing, and spelunking is desirable, but not necessary. Applicants who have or are pursuing a college degree are preferred. The primary prerequisites are maturity, interest, and stamina.

Making It Happen: Call for more information and an application. Selections are made forty-five to sixty days prior to the beginning of each program.

INSIDER TIPS: *We are looking for people who are mature, interested in working with people in the outdoors,* *and have stamina. It helps to have some experience working with groups of people.*

Contact Information: Sara Smith, Assistant Director • Inner Quest, Inc. • 34752 Charles Town Pike • Purcellville, VA 22132 • Phone: (540) 478-1078 • Fax: (540) 668-6253 • Alternate: (540) 668-6699

Interlocken International

REGION/HQ: Worldwide/New Hampshire • **CATEGORY:** Outdoor Adventure • **POSITION TYPE:** Unique Experience • **DURATION:** Summer • **IDEAL CANDIDATE:** College Students, Career Changers, Retired Folks, Foreigners • **APPLICANT POOL:** 700/year • **APPLICANTS ACCEPTED:** 80/year

SINCE 1961, MORE THAN 10,000 young people have explored the world, Interlocken-style. Whether you join the residential summer camp in New Hampshire or a travel or community service program, Interlocken campers and students "learn by doing" and enrich their lives with lasting friendships, new skills, self-discoveries, and increased environmental and cross-cultural awareness.

Area and Working Environment: Interlocken is situated on a 1,000-acre lakeside preserve in Hillsboro, New Hampshire, just two hours from Boston. Travel programs are available in the United States, Canada, Europe, the Caribbean, Africa, and Asia.

Work/Learn Program Specifics: The International Summer Camp is a caring, creative community of 160 boys and girls (ages nine to fifteen) and 60 staff members from all over the world. All summer campers choose their own activity programs, and counselors are encouraged to offer activities beyond their program-area responsibilities. Counselors are needed for the following areas: sports (tennis, archery, soccer, basketball, and mountain biking), waterfront (canoeing, sailing, windsurfing, kayaking, and swimming instruction), music (guitar, folk singing, and song leading), visual arts (ceramics, woodworking, photography, and ethnic art), theatre, environmental studies, and wilderness (mountaineering, rock climbing, and ropes course). Crossroads travel leaders take to the road with small groups of twelve to sixteen students and explore new and unusual environments, learn new skills, and challenge themselves physically and intellectually. Leaders are needed for the following areas: performing arts (traveling theatre in New England and Europe), wilderness adventure, cycling, environmental studies, and leadership training.

Duration: Summer Camp has a nine-week commitment starting mid-June; Crossroads travel is three to six weeks in length.

Compensation and Perks: Summer camp positions start at $1,200 for nine weeks; Crossroads travel positions start at $200 per week. All staff members receive room, board, and great training.

The Ideal Candidate: Summer camp applicants must be at least twenty years of age and have finished one year of college. Applicants should have experience teaching children and skill/expertise in wilderness/adventure, sports, theatre, music, applied arts, or waterfront. Crossroads travel applicants must be at least twenty-four years of age, with expertise in teaching theatre, visual arts, outdoor adventure, language (French or Spanish), or environmental education, with the ability to work with small groups of teenagers.

Making It Happen: Send cover letter and resume requesting staff application packet. It's best to apply by January.

Contact Information: Judi Wisch, Staffing Director • Interlocken International • RR 2, Box 165 • Hillsboro, NH 03244 • Phone: (603) 478-3166 • Fax: (603) 478-5260 • E-mail: interlocken@conknet.com • Web Site: www.interlocken.org

Legacy International

REGION/HQ: Southeast/Virginia • **CATEGORY:** Experiential Education • **POSITION TYPE:** Internship • **DURATION:** Summer • **IDEAL CANDIDATE:** College Students, Career Changers, Foreigners • **APPLICANT POOL:** 175/year • **APPLICANTS ACCEPTED:** 25–30/year

SINCE 1979 LEGACY HAS hosted young people in their Global Youth Village from more than seventy-eight different countries. Each person contributes their own thread of education, thought, personality, and dreams to Legacy. Legacy's aim is to transform the legacy of prejudice, fear, confusion, and misunderstanding into a legacy of hope and to help future generations realize their capabilities. Legacy promotes peaceful resolution to ethnic, social, and religious conflicts; comprehensive education; experiential leadership training; and environmentally sound development.

Area and Working Environment: Legacy is located in the foothills of Virginia's Blue Ridge Mountains, including seventy-five acres of clearings, woodlands, ponds, and streams. It's also 225 miles southwest of Washington, D.C.

Work/Learn Program Specifics: Practicum intercultural relations: You will be living and working with people from all over the world, developing a deeper understanding of community development issues; discovering the broader implications of daily actions and choices; and exploring the complexity of political and social situations. Very different from an academic environment, the practicum is an intensive and fulfilling learning opportunity which requires active, responsible participation. This experiential program includes a two week pre-program training, the field experience, supplemental training and personal advisement, and your practicum project.

Legacy also offers various other summer staff positions. Program staff participates in programs in youth for environment and service, dialogue, global issues, leadership training, performing arts for social change, English as a second language, art studio, sports and recreation, and outdoor living skills; administrative staff jobs include special programs coordinator, world awareness program coordinator, program assistant, summer office manager, bookkeeper, health care coordinator, pool director, and videographer. Counseling and support service staff positions are also available.

Duration: Legacy has a nine-week program during the summer. Many positions involve a 6 1/2-day work week with twenty-four-hour on-site responsibility as live-in cabin counselors.

Compensation and Perks: The practicum program is unpaid; other positions offer a stipend. Perks include housing, meals, medical benefits, and laundry service. Accommodations are in cabins with youths and/or other staff. In addition, Legacy offers a healthful rural environment with a whole-foods, vegetarian diet, and clean air and water.

The Ideal Candidate: The Practicum in International Relations is carefully designed for college students and recent graduates, ages twenty to twenty-four, who seek professional youth work or teaching experience. People with professional skills are welcome and encouraged to apply. Smoking and alcohol are not allowed during term of employment.

Making It Happen: Call or write for more information and an application. Telephone interviews are set up when an in-person interview is not possible. Rolling deadlines and positions open until filled. It is suggested you contact them by April 1 at the very latest.

INSIDER TIPS: *We look for people who are really excited about the program and show the flexibility and maturity to work in an intense, multicultural setting with lots of challenges. With these qualities, we'll sometimes overlook a person's lack of experience just because of their openness and excitement, and we'll train them.*

Contact Information: Leila Baz, Summer Program Co-Director • Legacy International • Route 4, Box 265 • Bedford, VA 24523 • Phone: (540) 297-5982 • Fax: (540) 297-1860 • E-mail: mail@legacyintl.org • Web Site: www.legacyintl.org

Leo Burnett—Revisions Fitness Center

REGION/HQ: Great Lakes/Illinois • **CATEGORY:** Fitness • **POSITION TYPE:** Internship • **DURATION:** Year-Round • **IDEAL CANDIDATE:** College Students, Career Changers • **APPLICANT POOL:** Varies • **APPLICANTS ACCEPTED:** 1–2/term

THE LEO BURNETT FITNESS CENTER is a 14,250-square-foot facility, providing a variety of cardiovascular and muscle toning equipment, group exercise classes, wellness programs, an indoor running track, laundry service, and full locker rooms. The facility is available to 2,000 employees.

Area and Working Environment: Leo Burnett is located in exciting downtown Chicago, near mass transit.

Work/Learn Program Specifics: While fitness interns become familiar with the day-to-day operation of the facility, they will gain experience with fitness evaluations, exercise prescription, equipment orientation, group exercise instruction, client interaction, computer skills, and wellness and incentive program development. The center also provides students with introductions to a variety of wellness activities including CPR training for employees, nutrition seminars, and stress management. The staff is made up of professionals who have at least a bachelor's degree in a fitness-related field. Their solid backgrounds in anatomy and exercise physiology, physical therapy, cardiac rehabilitation, nutrition, and physical education help make the internship experience both worthwhile and enjoyable.

Duration: Positions are available year-round.

Compensation and Perks: Interns receive a $250 per month stipend and the chance to work in an excellent

learning environment, with a very team-oriented staff and progressive company.

The Ideal Candidate: They are searching for enthusiastic students who are willing to take initiative and get involved, have first aid and CPR certifications, and have group exercise instruction experience.

Making It Happen: Send cover letter and resume. Rolling deadlines.

INSIDER TIPS: *We are looking for high-energy candidates, who have a passion for helping others.*

Contact Information: Laura Barney, Assistant Program Director • Leo Burnett—Revisions Fitness Center • 55 W. Wacker Dr., 2nd Floor • Chicago, IL 60601 • Phone: (312) 220-5346 • Fax: (312) 220-0794

Longacre Expeditions

REGION/HQ: North/South America/Pennsylvania • **CATEGORY:** Adventure Travel • **POSITION TYPE:** Internship • **DURATION:** Summer • **IDEAL CANDIDATE:** College Students, Career Changers, Retired Folks, Foreigners • **APPLICANT POOL:** Varies • **APPLICANTS ACCEPTED:** Varies

LONGACRE EXPEDITIONS IS ONE OF the most respected outdoor travel programs in the United States. They offer programs for young outdoor enthusiasts with skills ranging from novice to advanced. Each summer, coed groups of ten to sixteen teenagers and their leaders bicycle, backpack, rock climb, kayak, mountaineer, whitewater raft, snowboard, snorkel, scuba dive, explore caves, and canoe across miles of the most beautiful territory in North and Central America. Trips focus on group living, wilderness skills, cooperation, independence, and fun.

Area and Working Environment: You will work in one of five different course areas throughout North and Central America, including the Mid-Atlantic, New England/Nova Scotia, Colorado, Pacific Northwest, and Belize, Central America.

Work/Learn Program Specifics: Become a trip leader or assistant trip leader. Different trips emphasize different ability levels. Entry Level: Kids spend more time on skills and the physical challenges are appropriate for the age and ability level. Most of the camping is done in established campgrounds that are equipped with showers, latrines, and other creature comforts. Intermediate Level: Courses are geared to enthusiastic beginners or kids with some experience. Advanced

Level: Leaders for these programs must have extensive experience leading trips of teenagers, have very good hard skills, advanced first aid certification, and must have participated in a significant number of wilderness expeditions. Besides leadership positions, there are other jobs that are just as essential, including base camp cook, kitchen assistant, nurse trip support, and various specialists. All staffers are required to attend an eight- to nine-day staff training period, which begins around June 15.

Duration: There are many options available for your summer. Many staffers choose to lead a trip for four weeks and act as support staff for two to five additional weeks. Individuals can also be employed for a two- to six-week trip only. Staff can come a few weeks early to help open the base camp before staff week. Equipment inventory and repair, building construction and maintenance, and lighter office work are all likely tasks during this period. Staff may also scout new routes and campsites in program areas.

Compensation and Perks: Field staff is paid on a per diem basis and will make anywhere from $25 to $50 per day. Base camp staff is paid $1,050 to $2,500 depending on position. Staffers who hold current certificates in EMT, WEMT, WSI, and lifeguard training will be compensated at higher levels. There is no compensation for the staff training period, but room and board are supplied. Perks include pro-deal packages with outdoor manufacturers.

The Ideal Candidate: Applicants must be twenty-one years of age, have a good driving record, and have certification in first aid, a water safety course, and CPR. Qualities they look for in a potential staffer include the ability to communicate and be comfortable with teenagers, competence in a variety of outdoor activities, great physical condition, the ability to embrace Longacre's trip-leading philosophy, and commitment to the group. Staffers come from all over the country and are often graduate students or college juniors/seniors who have taken a few years off to take a job or tour the world. Others are teachers who see the summer as an opportunity to be with kids in a non-classroom setting. Still, others join Longacre each year, coming from seasonal positions at ski resorts, environmental centers, and other wilderness programs.

Making It Happen: Call for application materials; applications must be received by June 15. A personal interview is highly recommended.

INSIDER TIPS: *Hard skills, advanced first aid certifications, and a sense of humor are highly valued by the organization.*

Contact Information: Meredith Schuler, Owner/Director • Longacre Expeditions • RD 3, Box 106 • Newport, PA 17074 • Phone: (717) 567-6790 • Fax: (717) 567-3955 • Toll Free: (800) 433-0127 • E-mail: longacre@pa.net

Maine Sport Outdoor School

REGION/HQ: Northeast/Maine • **CATEGORY:** Outfitter • **POSITION TYPE:** Internship • **DURATION:** Summer • **IDEAL CANDIDATE:** College Students • **APPLICANT POOL:** 30–40/year • **APPLICANTS ACCEPTED:** 4/year

SINCE 1976, MAINE SPORT OUTFITTERS has been introducing people to the outdoors. Their outdoor school is nationally recognized as a leader in sea kayak tours and instruction for people of all ages and abilities—they offer a wide variety of quality outdoor-adventure programs for individuals, families, and groups.

Work/Learn Program Specifics: Interns will assist senior sea kayak guides and instructors in all aspects of trip and course preparation, instruction, leadership, group facilitation, and program evaluation; assist ropes course facilitators with custom program setup, facilitation, safety, and debriefing; assist with daily enrollment procedures, administrative tasks, and special projects; and assist with maintenance and upkeep of the outdoor school and island base facilities and equipment. Interns will have the opportunity to take steps towards becoming a registered Maine guide, an American Canoe Association certified instructor in coastal kayaking, and certified in wilderness marine medicine.

Duration: A minimum of eight weeks during the summer is required. Your work hours will not follow a normal nine-to-five workweek.

Compensation and Perks: Interns receive a $100-per-week stipend, plus comfortable and private living accommodations and meals. You will also have limited gear discounts at their retail shop.

The Ideal Candidate: Applicants must be college junior or senior students who seek employment experience in the fields of outdoor and environmental education, recreation management, sea kayak guiding and instruction, or marine science.

Making It Happen: Send a cover letter and resume by April 1.

INSIDER TIPS: *Successful applicants should possess a willingness to be challenged, excellent communication skills,* *strong leadership and teaching skills, a love and respect for the natural world, a desire to learn, wilderness experience, strong interpersonal skills, and paddling experience.*

Contact Information: Matthew Levin, Director • Maine Sport Outdoor School • P.O. Box 956, Route 1 • Rockport, ME 04856 • Phone: (207) 236-8797 • Fax: (207) 236-7123 • Toll Free: (800) 722-0826 • E-mail: mainespt@midcoast.com • Web Site: www.midcoast.com/~mainespt

Metropolitan Park District of Tacoma

REGION/HQ: Pacific Northwest/Washington • **CATEGORY:** Recreation • **POSITION TYPE:** Internship • **DURATION:** Year-Round • **IDEAL CANDIDATE:** College Students, Career Changers, Foreigners • **APPLICANT POOL:** Varies • **APPLICANTS ACCEPTED:** Varies

THE METROPOLITAN PARK DISTRICT, created in 1907, administers services and facilities in more than seventy-five park sites ranging from the 698-acre Point Defiance Park to small neighboring parks. Other facilities include three athletic fields, six community recreation centers, fitness trails, nature preserves, more than thirty neighborhood parks and playgrounds, twenty-two wading pools, two outdoor/indoor swimming pools, tennis courts, waterfront parks, fishing piers, several lakes, and some of the most beautiful gardens on the West Coast.

Work/Learn Program Specifics: Recreation and Parks Intern: Each intern selects one or more of the following major areas of interest: Administrative Services, Park Police, Planning and Development, Recreation and Leisure, Park Maintenance and Operations, Wildlife Park, Zoo and Aquarium. Interns will spend the majority of their time within their selected area, but will gain broad experience of the entire department. Other areas of exposure may include the following: finance, aquatics, athletics, recreation programs/community centers, specialized recreation (for special populations), Snake Lake Nature Center, Fort Nisqually Historic Site, Never Never Land, youth outreach, general service shops, horticulture and nursery, Seymour Conservatory, Meadow Park Golf Course, boathouse/marina park bait shop, food service operation, zoo and aquarium education and maintenance, comprehensive system planning, facility planning and design, project construction, and marketing/public relations.

Duration: Duration is flexible, depending upon university requirements.

Compensation and Perks: Though the stipend varies with each intern, it usually consists of $500 for a ten-week period. However, work outside of internship responsibilities (with pay) is also offered. Assistance is also given in locating inexpensive housing.

The Ideal Candidate: Desire applicants with a background in recreation or leisure studies.

Making It Happen: Call for application. Send completed application, cover letter, and resume. Applications are accepted on a continual basis.

Contact Information: Recreation Manager • Metropolitan Park District of Tacoma • 4702 S. 19th St. • Tacoma, WA 98405-1175 • Phone: (206) 305-1034 • Fax: (206) 305-1014 • E-mail: info@tacomaparks.com

National Institute for Fitness & Sport

REGION/HQ: Great Lakes/Indiana • **CATEGORY:** Fitness • **POSITION TYPE:** Internship • **DURATION:** Year-Round • **IDEAL CANDIDATE:** College Students, Foreigners • **APPLICANT POOL:** Varies • **APPLICANTS ACCEPTED:** 10/term

THE NATIONAL INSTITUTE FOR FITNESS & SPORT is a nonprofit organization which manages five operating centers, including The Center for Health & Fitness Services, The Fitness Center, The Center for Athletic Development, The Center for Educational Services, and The Center for Corporate Fitness Management. The institute's fitness, wellness, and athletic programs are designed to benefit all, from the ranks of the professional and amateur, to the fitness enthusiast, to children and adults of all ages and abilities.

Area and Working Environment: The building is situated on land owned by Indiana University and leased to the National Institute for Fitness & Sport.

Work/Learn Program Specifics: They offer internships in seven different areas: aerobics, athletic department, corporate fitness management, educational services, fitness center, health and fitness services, and marketing/public relations. Additional activities you may be involved with include health screenings, health fairs, athletic development camps, preschool motor-development programs, field trips, workshops, presentations, nutrition and weight management programs, special events, and incentive-program development. Interns will be expected to complete the following educational requirements: deliver a twenty-minute oral presentation, conduct a fifty- to sixty-minute fitness lesson, pass fitness assessments, complete weekly evaluations, become proficient in weight-training methods, write a lay article, update your resume, and submit an evaluation of your internship experience.

Duration: Interns work fifteen to sixteen weeks, for approximately forty hours per week, year-round.

Compensation and Perks: Interns receive a $250-per-month stipend. Interns are responsible for securing their own housing during their internship. Benefits include membership in the fitness center, a parking permit, and free attendance to educational workshops.

The Ideal Candidate: The institute desires an undergraduate college student within twelve to fifteen credit-hours of graduation, or graduate students currently enrolled in academic programs in exercise science, exercise physiology, sports science, wellness/health promotion, or other related fields. CPR certification is required (they offer free CPR classes to employees and interns who need to update their certifications).

Making It Happen: Call for application. Submit cover letter, completed application, resume, and a copy of your transcript. They will not start reviewing your application packet until all materials are received. Positions will be filled on an ongoing basis beginning on these selection dates: spring—September 1 through October 15; summer—January 1 through March 1; and fall—May 1 through July 1. Positions will be determined based on experience, achievement, professional recommendations, and a phone interview. If you are in the Indianapolis area, you are welcome to call and arrange an interview on-site.

Contact Information: Jill Dempsey, Intern Director • National Institute for Fitness & Sport • 250 University Blvd. • Indianapolis, IN 46202-5192 • Phone: (317) 274-3432 • Fax: (317) 274-7408

National Outdoor Leadership School

REGION/HQ: Worldwide/Wyoming • **CATEGORY:** Wilderness • **POSITION TYPE:** Unique Experience • **DURATION:** Year-Round • **IDEAL CANDIDATE:** High School Students, College Students, Career Changers, Retired Folks, Foreigners • **APPLICANT POOL:** 3,000/year • **APPLICANTS ACCEPTED:** 2,700/year

NOLS IS AN EDUCATIONAL ORGANIZATION with its roots in extended wilderness expeditions. They believe that long stays in wild places are vital to understanding both the natural world and ourselves. Courses take students away from the distractions of civilization and into the mountains, deserts, and oceans to learn the skills they need to run their own expeditions. NOLS graduates are leaders who have an understanding of environmental ethics, a sense of teamwork, an appreciation of natural history, and overall competence and good judgment.

Area and Working Environment: NOLS operates eight branch schools all over the world, including the Southwest, Pacific Northwest, Rocky Mountains, Alaska, British Columbia, Kenya, Patagonia (Chile), and Mexico.

Work/Learn Program Specifics: Most folks select their NOLS course by either concentrating on location or skills. Terrain, weather, expedition length, and specialized skills vary, but every course includes a core curriculum emphasizing leadership through the development of judgment and decision-making skills. Your choice will depend on your interests, experience, and time constraints. Course types include mountaineering, wilderness backpacking, ocean (sea kayaking and sailing), river (kayaking, rafting, and canoeing), winter (backcountry skiing and dog sledding), semester (a variety of skills over three months), outdoor educators (for practicing or potential outdoor educators), and twenty-five years and older (shorter courses for people twenty-five years and older).

Duration: Courses are generally thirty days in length; however, semester courses run ninety days in length and ten-day courses are also offered.

Compensation and Perks: Fees range from $750 to $8,300 depending on the location and the length of the educational expedition.

The Ideal Candidate: Successful students come willing to learn and develop leadership skills and wilderness ethics. Prior outdoor experience is not a prerequisite for most NOLS courses; although being in good shape, a positive attitude, and the desire to learn wilderness skills in locations of incredible beauty are musts.

Making It Happen: Call for application materials. Rolling admissions.

Contact Information: Admissions Dept. • National Outdoor Leadership School • 288 Main St. • Lander, WY 82520 • Phone: (307) 332-6973 • Fax: (307) 332-1220 • E-mail: admissions@nols.edu • Web Site: www.nols.edu

National Sports Center for the Disabled

REGION/HQ: Rocky Mountains/Colorado • **CATEGORY:** Therapeutic Recreation • **POSITION TYPE:** Internship • **DURATION:** Summer/Winter • **IDEAL CANDIDATE:** College Students, Career Changers, Foreigners • **APPLICANT POOL:** 15–20/year • **APPLICANTS ACCEPTED:** 10/year

THE NATIONAL SPORTS CENTER FOR THE DISABLED is the world's largest and most comprehensive program in disabled recreation. They provide very dynamic programming, host a full competition for disabled ski racers, and serve children and adults with disabilities from all over the United States and the world. They publish the only teaching manual on disabled skiing: *Bold Tracks*, by Hal O'Leary.

Area and Working Environment: Located in Winter Park, just sixty-five miles west of Denver, they operate the program at the Winter Park Resort, a "top fifteen" rated ski and summer resort.

Work/Learn Program Specifics: Interns will work with individuals and groups from schools, hospitals, group homes, and rehabilitation centers. More specifically, winter interns provide alpine skiing, snowboarding, snowshoeing, and Nordic skiing for children and adults with disabilities. Summer interns provide white-water rafting, mountain biking, hiking, sailing, therapeutic horseback riding, camping, and fishing for the disabled.

Duration: Winter interns work mid-November through mid-April, four or five days per week. Summer interns work the first week of June through the last week of August, four ten-hour days per week.

Compensation and Perks: The internships are volunteer positions; however, you will receive a season pass to Winter Park Resort, 50 percent off all cafeteria food in the winter (20 percent in the summer), free employee shuttle, a uniform, and a locker. Interns are eligible for employee housing at $200 to $250 per month.

The Ideal Candidate: University students must have completed their junior year in therapeutic recreation, special education, adaptive physical education, occupational therapy, physical therapy, or a related field. It's also preferred that you've had at least one year of experience working with the disabled. Winter interns must be advanced intermediate skiers and have their own ski equipment; summer interns must have experience with cycling and outdoor activities.

Making It Happen: Write or call for application materials. Deadlines: winter—August 1; summer—March 1. Phone or personal interviews required.

INSIDER TIPS: *An applicant must have the desire to work with the disabled, be educated in a related field, and be an avid outdoor person in good physical condition.*

Contact Information: Gigi Glass Dominguez, Assistant Director • National Sports Center for the Disabled • P.O. Box 36 • Winter Park, CO 80482 • Phone: (970) 726-1542 • Fax: (970) 726-4112

National Tour Foundation

REGION/HQ: Southeast/Kentucky • **CATEGORY:** Tourism • **POSITION TYPE:** Internship • **DURATION:** Fall • **IDEAL CANDIDATE:** College Students, Career Changers • **APPLICANT POOL:** Varies • **APPLICANTS ACCEPTED:** Varies

THE NATIONAL TOUR FOUNDATION is the nonprofit education and research arm of the National Tour Association (NTA). The NTA is the premier leisure travel association in North America. The foundation maintains a list of more than 100 internship opportunities with tour operators, hotels, attractions, restaurants, and convention and visitors bureaus.

Work/Learn Program Specifics: Tourism interns meet and correspond with the tourism industry's leading professionals and gain experience in convention and special event planning and execution. The internship also includes the chance to work behind the scenes as a part of the NTA staff.

Duration: Positions begin in August and continue through December.

Compensation and Perks: A $3,000 stipend is given to offset travel and lodging expenses while in Lexington, Kentucky. The biggest perk includes travel and participation in the week-long National Tour Association's annual convention (held at a different locations each year), all expenses paid. This element of the internship package is valued at $2,000.

The Ideal Candidate: Seeking a student pursuing a tourism/travel-related degree who has excellent written, oral, and interpersonal skills.

Making It Happen: Call for application. Submit completed application, cover letter, and resume by the end of April. For more information about their free internships listing, call their 800 number, using extension 4251.

Contact Information: Stephani Ashly, Program Director • National Tour Foundation • 546 East Main St. • Lexington, KY 40508 • Phone: (606) 226-4851 • Fax: (606) 226-4414 • Toll Free: (800) 682-8886

Nature Expeditions International

REGION/HQ: South/Midwest/Arizona • **CATEGORY:** Adventure Travel • **POSITION TYPE:** Internship • **DURATION:** Year-Round • **IDEAL CANDIDATE:** College Students, Career Changers, Foreigners • **APPLICANT POOL:** 3/term • **APPLICANTS ACCEPTED:** 2/term

FOUNDED IN 1973 AS AN outgrowth of a college field trip and lecture series, Nature Expeditions International (NEI) has been a pioneer in the field of ecotourism. NEI expeditions emphasize adventure, learning, and discovery in a broad range of programs throughout the world. These trips are active vacations, focusing on direct experience of the wildlife, culture, and natural history of exotic lands.

Work/Learn Program Specifics: NEI's internship program provides participants with a hands-on experience encompassing all facets of the adventure travel business, including marketing/public relations, trip coordination, customer relations, inquiry fulfillment, and travel research. Typical responsibilities include working with NEI staff in trip preparation; assisting in writing and editing marketing materials, including travel guides, newsletters, and brochures; researching and developing new trip itineraries; and assisting in daily office procedures.

Duration: The average internship period is six months at fifteen to twenty hours per week (although the minimum requirement is three months at twenty-five to forty hours per week). Positions are offered continually throughout the year.

Compensation and Perks: Interns receive hands-on, multifaceted experience in a small, but dynamic adventure travel/ecotourism company. In addition, the internship is a direct route into full-time employment with the company.

The Ideal Candidate: Applicants must have an interest or a background in foreign travel, ecotourism, natural/cultural history, or wildlife/animal sciences. Writing, organizational, and phone skills are a plus.

Making It Happen: Send resume and cover letter addressing your time frame and hours available. Interviews are conducted in person, if possible; or if not, by phone. Rolling deadlines.

INSIDER TIPS: *Have the love of travel and the desire to learn about the world, combined with excellent writing and computer skills, and you're almost assured a spot as an intern.*

Contact Information: Christopher Kyle, President • Nature Expeditions International • 6400 E. El Dorado Cir., Suite 210 • Tucson, AZ 85715-4602 • Phone: (520) 721-6712 • Fax: (520) 721-6712 • Toll Free: (800) 869-0639 • E-mail: naturexp@aol.com

The Outdoor Network

REGION/HQ: Rocky Mountains/Colorado • **CATEGORY:** Outdoor Adventure • **POSITION TYPE:** Internship/Seasonal • **DURATION:** Year-Round • **IDEAL CANDIDATE:** College Students, Career Changers • **APPLICANT POOL:** Varies • **APPLICANTS ACCEPTED:** Varies

THE OUTDOOR NETWORK is the industry's only international networking forum for professionals. The mission is not limited to job placement; rather, it's to keep the professional members of the outdoor community in touch with each other to promote growth and development in the industry.

Work/Learn Program Specifics: This is an ideal environment for self-starters and people who handle delegation well. There is always something worthwhile to do if you have the energy. Most jobs will offer the opportunity to attend trade shows and conferences and learn the intricacies of a publishing/direct-mail business. The Outdoor Network shares their office suite with Boulder Outdoor Survival School (BOSS), so a wide variety of administrative/learning opportunities exist.

Duration: A workweek may be anything from six hours per week up to twenty hours per week.

Compensation and Perks: Salary is based on experience.

The Ideal Candidate: An undergraduate degree in outdoor education, marketing, or psychology is a plus. You should be presentable and clear-spoken, as you will attend outdoor conferences, and excellent phone skills are important. Internet savvy and familiarity with Macintosh computers (including FileMaker Pro, QuarkXpress, and PhotoShop) are suggested.

Making It Happen: Send your resume and cover letter explaining why you want to work for The Outdoor

Network. Successful phone interviews will lead to a local interview. Rolling deadlines.

INSIDER TIPS: *We serve the professionals in the industry. Therefore, it helps if you have an understanding of the big picture. Think about the needs of small outfitters and how we can help them. Then compare that with large nonprofits or university recreation managers. Our newsletters, Web site, and benefits packages are all designed to offer something to everyone. Most important, applicants should express sincerity, professionalism, and intent. A bulk-mailed cover letter saying "Dear _____, I really want to work for you" will not be read.*

Contact Information: Josh Bernstein, President • The Outdoor Network • P.O. Box 4129 • Boulder, CO 80306 • Phone: (303) 444-7117 • Fax: (303) 442-7425 • Toll Free: (800) 688-6387 • E-mail: editor@ outdoornetwork.com • Web Site: www.outdoornetwork.com

Outdoors Wisconsin Leadership School

REGION/HQ: Great Lakes/Wisconsin • **CATEGORY:** Outdoor Adventure • **POSITION TYPE:** Internship • **DURATION:** Year-Round • **IDEAL CANDIDATE:** College Students, Career Changers, Foreigners • **APPLICANT POOL:** 200/year • **APPLICANTS ACCEPTED:** 75/year

THE LAKE GENEVA CAMPUS provides conference services, experiential education, and recreational programs for more than 35,000 guests each year.

Area and Working Environment: The campus is located about eighty miles northwest of Chicago, in southeastern Wisconsin, and consists of 150 acres of rolling, glacial terrain on the north shore. It is also within easy driving distance of rock climbing, canoeing, backpacking areas, and other outdoor recreational sites.

Work/Learn Program Specifics: Adventure education interns facilitate team-building and leadership-development programs for adolescents, colleges, and adult groups. The curriculum includes trust building, group initiatives, high- and low-ropes courses, team and individual climbing elements, and off-campus rock climbing. Outdoor/environmental education interns teach classes in natural awareness, wetlands, lake study, astronomy, and the weather, and coordinate school groups. Outdoor/guest recreation interns

lead activities, including sports, games, natural awareness, and orienteering, and coordinate conference groups. Seasonal positions include arts and crafts supervisor, preschool supervisor, assistant waterfront director, swim area supervisor, lifeguard, recreation coordinator, sailing instructor, small craft instructor, summer nurse, front desk clerk, summer cook, dining room attendant, housekeeping, grounds, college inn/campus shop, golf maintenance, baker's help, dish crew, service, painters, golf clubhouse, and summer security.

Duration: Adventure education internships and seasonal positions are available from March through November of each year. Outdoor/environmental education positions are available September through May, and outdoor/guest recreation positions are available summer and winter.

Compensation and Perks: Wages vary from $125 to $195 per week (depending on experience and position), plus room and board and a supplemental medical policy. Staff members live on the campus in comfortable, rustic cabins which include showers, toilet facilities, and single beds with linens. No more than two people share a room, and single rooms are assigned whenever possible. Wholesome and nutritious meals are served family- or buffet-style in their spacious dining room. Recreational facilities include a waterfront, tennis courts, and a golf course.

The Ideal Candidate: For instructor positions, applicants should be college graduates with degrees in education, recreation, or a related field, and experience teaching in the outdoors. Interns should have at least college senior status, with coursework in related areas and experience working with people. Requirements for seasonal positions vary with the position.

Making It Happen: Send a cover letter, resume, and names and addresses of three references. Apply within four to six months of start date. No phone calls, please.

INSIDER TIPS: *A high energy level, good communication skills, and a strong commitment to creating powerful recreational and learning experiences for others are the most important qualifications for all positions.*

Contact Information: Cathy Coster, Associate Director • Outdoors Wisconsin Leadership School • George Williams College Educational Centers • P.O. Box 210 • Williams Bay, WI 53191-0210 • Phone: (414) 245-5531 • Fax: (414) 245-9068 • E-mail: lkgencam@ idcnet.com • Web Site: www.camping.org/gwc1.htm

Overland Travel

REGION/HQ: Nationwide/Massachusetts
• **CATEGORY:** Adventure Travel • **POSITION TYPE:**
Work/Learn Adventure • **DURATION:** Summer
• **IDEAL CANDIDATE:** College Students • **APPLICANT
POOL:** 500/year • **APPLICANTS ACCEPTED:** 45/year

OVERLAND TRAVEL PROVIDES a variety of adventure programs, with a focus on bicycling, hiking, or mountain biking (and canoeing, rafting, and rock climbing to complement the main focus). Each itinerary also includes conservation-based volunteer work and a conservation ethic. Participants might spend a day rebuilding a trail, refurbishing a hut, or cleaning a backcountry camping area. In this way, groups are educated and sensitized to the importance of caring for the environment.

Area and Working Environment: Trips are held in New England, the Northern Rockies, Colorado, California, France, and East Africa.

Work/Learn Program Specifics: Former participant and leader, Lisee Goodykoontz, says this about her experience: "Overland first showed me the outdoors, and how great it could be. Leading for Overland has given me the opportunity to share the gift I received as a teenager and to create for my Overland students the kind of positive, wholesome, and group-focused experience that was important to me growing up." Leaders go through extensive training prior to the start of their trips, including intensive sessions on safety, first aid, group dynamics, conservation, and fostering a community spirit.

Compensation and Perks: Leaders receive a $125-per-week stipend, plus the benefit of traveling, working, and learning in some of the most spectacular places.

The Ideal Candidate: Applicants are college graduates, have leadership experience, especially with thirteen- to eighteen-year-olds, and have excellent people skills.

Making It Happen: Rolling deadlines, however most leaders are hired during the months of November through March. Finalists are invited out to Overland for a series of in-person interviews.

Contact Information: Lew Fisher, Assistant Director • Overland Travel • P.O. Box 31 • Williamstown, MA 01267 • Phone: (413) 458-9672 • Fax: (413) 458-9672 • Toll Free: (800) 458-0588 • E-mail: overland@ berkshire.net

Phillips Cruises & Tours

REGION/HQ: Pacific Northwest/Alaska • **CATEGORY:** Cruise Ship • **POSITION TYPE:** Seasonal • **DURATION:** Spring-Fall • **IDEAL CANDIDATE:** College Students, Career Changers, Retired Folks • **APPLICANT POOL:** Varies • **APPLICANTS ACCEPTED:** Varies

PHILLIPS OPERATES THE POPULAR "26 Glacier Cruise," giving thousands of people an opportunity to experience spectacular fjords, ice-blue glaciers, and the amazing wildlife of Prince William Sound.

Work/Learn Program Specifics: Passenger service crew members prepare and serve meals, bartend, and provide cruise narration, line handling, and other services to passengers. Reservation/sales agents work at their main office in Anchorage and are responsible for sales of Alaskan tour products, as well as providing communication between the cruise ship and sales office.

Duration: The season runs May through September, with a week of pre-season training. Your work schedule will be based on three weeks working a six-day workweek—the fourth week being a four-day workweek with three days off.

Compensation and Perks: Salaries start at $1,600 per month. The only way to get to Whittier is via the Alaska Railroad. Because of Whittier's remoteness and the shortage of accommodations, Phillips Cruises rents housing facilities which crew members may live in at a small expense. Cable TV and all utilities are provided by the company.

The Ideal Candidate: Applicants should be dynamic, enthusiastic, and have a service background. Candidates also must be at least twenty-one years of age, committed to working a full season, and be comfortable sharing accommodations in a remote location.

Making It Happen: Send a resume and request for employment information via E-mail, fax, or mail.

Contact Information: Carol Hugh, Personnel Officer • Phillips Cruises & Tours • 519 W. 4th Ave., Suite 100 • Anchorage, AK 99501 • Phone: (907) 274-2723 • Fax: (907) 276-5315 • Toll Free: (800) 544-0529 • E-mail: phillips@alaskanet.com • Web Site: www. alaskanet.com/glacier

Sailing the Seven Seas . .

Do you see yourself traveling to exotic ports of call? Do you like the thrill of seeing new places and constantly meeting new people from around the world? Are you comfortable with being in the public eye? Do you have the type of enthusiasm it takes to lead activities while making sure everyone is having a good time?

If so, then working for a cruise line might be for you. However, keep in mind that the pace is fast, the work is hard, the hours are long, and, unfortunately, you can't go home at the end of the day. Although cruise-ship work is a dream for many, the long days of repetitive tasks and the challenges of working and living in the same environment and with the same people for extended periods of time, can become disheartening and frustrating for some. On the other hand, for those who enjoy the challenge, the people, and the places, working on a ship is often the most rewarding adventure job they'll ever have.

A couple of cruise lines you might want to check out include: Carnival Cruise Line (800) 438-6744; Odyssey Cruises (202) 488-6010; and Premier Cruise Line (800) DREAM 54, www.bigredboat.com. There is also a book entitled *How to Get a Job with a Cruise Line*, by Mary Fallon Miller, that may be of some assistance to you in your search. To get more information call (813) 544-0066.

Or maybe you'd like to learn how to become your own skipper: contact the American Sailing Association, 13922 Marquesas Way, Marina del Rey, CA 90292, (310) 822-7171; or U.S. Sailing, Box 1260, Portsmouth, RI 02871, (401) 683-0800, for a list of accredited schools to get the training you need.

Pine Ridge Adventure Center

REGION/HQ: Northeast/Vermont • **CATEGORY:** Wilderness • **POSITION TYPE:** Seasonal • **DURATION:** Summer • **IDEAL CANDIDATE:** College Students, Career Changers • **APPLICANT POOL:** 50/year • **APPLICANTS ACCEPTED:** 3/year

PINE RIDGE ADVENTURE CENTER is a nonprofit educational organization committed to providing experiential opportunities for personal growth and team development. Participants learn to take care of themselves and to share the responsibility for meeting the group's needs in an exciting and challenging environment.

Area and Working Environment: The wilderness areas of Vermont, Maine, New Hampshire, New York, Ontario, and Quebec serve as the classroom.

Work/Learn Program Specifics: Trip leaders work as part of a gender-balanced leadership team on wilderness trips, building a sense of community on the ropes course, raising awareness, and developing new skills for the participants.

Compensation and Perks: Leaders receive a stipend, plus room and board.

The Ideal Candidate: At minimum, each candidate is a certified provider of first aid and CPR, while many draw experiences from such trainings as wilderness first responder, water safety instruction, and swift water rescue.

Making It Happen: Send cover letter and resume by February 15.

Contact Information: Skip Dewhirst, Director • Pine Ridge Adventure Center • 1079 Williston Rd. • Williston, VT 05495 • Phone: (802) 434-5294 • Fax: (802) 434-5512 • E-mail: prschool@together.net

The Princeton-Blairstown Center

REGION/HQ: Northeast/New Jersey • **CATEGORY:** Experiential Education • **POSITION TYPE:** Seasonal • **DURATION:** Spring-Fall • **IDEAL CANDIDATE:** College Students, Career Changers • **APPLICANT POOL:** Varies • **APPLICANTS ACCEPTED:** Varies

THE PRINCETON-BLAIRSTOWN CENTER (PBC) is located on 280 acres in northwestern New Jersey and conducts year-round experiential programming for a wide variety of populations. Activities include group problem-solving initiatives, rappelling, high and low ropes courses, backpacking, rock climbing, and canoeing. They use adventure programming to direct clients towards specific goals determined by the contracting agency.

Work/Learn Program Specifics: Resident instructors facilitate groups of ten to twelve clients in all program activities and assist with logistical support and routine equipment and facilities maintenance. Summer counselors co-facilitate all aspects of camp life for one of six groups. Summer support staff develops and delivers programming to support the counselors' work with their groups.

Compensation and Perks: Weekly salaries begin at $140 for resident instructors. Summer staff wages start at $1,175 for the season. All receive room, board, and extensive training.

The Ideal Candidate: Experience and/or certification in child-care, outdoor skills, ropes courses, ALS/lifeguard, EMT, or first responder preferred but not required. Current certification in first aid and CPR is required.

Making It Happen: Call for application materials. Rolling deadlines.

Contact Information: Kate Thielbar, Program Coordinator • The Princeton-Blairstown Center • 158 Millbrook Rd. • Blairstown, NJ 07825-9627 • Phone: (908) 362-6765 • Fax: (908) 362-7699

Putney Student Travel

REGION/HQ: Worldwide/Vermont • **CATEGORY:** Educational Travel • **POSITION TYPE:** Seasonal • **DURATION:** Summer • **IDEAL CANDIDATE:** College Students, Career Changers • **APPLICANT POOL:** 200–300/year • **APPLICANTS ACCEPTED:** 50/year

PUTNEY STUDENT TRAVEL PROVIDES unusual opportunities for small groups of students to share an exciting educational summer. They emphasize doing, having fun, getting off the beaten path, making friends, and being involved rather than just touring or sightseeing, participating actively rather than passively, working together, helping build a sense of community—this is part of the Putney way.

Area and Working Environment: Programs are located in the United States (Alaska and Montana), China, Australia/New Zealand/Fiji, Latin America (Costa Rica and Ecuador), Europe (Czech Republic,

Italy, Switzerland, France, Holland, and England), and Africa (Tanzania).

Work/Learn Program Specifics: Leaders will lead groups of high school students to various places around the world, with a focus on travel, language learning, and community service. You are given a high degree of independence and responsibility, and a three-day orientation in Vermont precedes the program.

Duration: The program is four to six weeks long during the summer.

Compensation and Perks: You will receive $400 per week, and all expenses will be covered.

The Ideal Candidate: Applicants must be energetic, fun, creative, active, knowledgeable about the area they are visiting, and excited about spending time with high school students. In countries where English is not the primary language, applicants must speak the country's language.

Making It Happen: Send cover letter and resume.

Contact Information: Ellen Stein, Director • Putney Student Travel • 345 Hickory Ridge Rd. • Putney, VT 05346 • Phone: (802) 387-5885 • Fax: (802) 387-4276 • E-mail: pst@sover.net • Web Site: www.sover.net/~pst

Roads Less Traveled, Inc.

REGION/HQ: Rocky Mountains/Colorado • **CATEGORY:** Adventure Travel • **POSITION TYPE:** Internship/Seasonal • **DURATION:** Year-Round • **IDEAL CANDIDATE:** High School Students, College Students, Career Changers, Retired Folks, Foreigners • **APPLICANT POOL:** 200/year • **APPLICANTS ACCEPTED:** 10/year

ROADS LESS TRAVELED (RLT) was founded in 1988 with the objective of offering high-quality services to individuals seeking adventure from the outdoors and teaching the skills needed to enjoy these activities. RLT is based in Colorado and operates in the Rockies, Southwest, and Canyon Country. The location of RLT and the backgrounds of the original staff have led to an emphasis on backcountry biking and hiking adventures. They include white-water rafting and/or horseback riding on their sampler trips and offer international travel adventures.

Work/Learn Program Specifics: Lead backcountry biking and hiking adventures. Trips run six to eight weeks and feature both inn-to-inn and camping retreats. Other areas of operations include office and reservations, bike mechanics, marketing, transportation, and maintenance. They also offer internships for those who are interested in the adventure travel industry.

Duration: Tour season runs from late March to late October. In-depth guide training is held in April. A normal schedule for a guide is two to four weeks per month on tour, with time off in between trips.

Compensation and Perks: All staff will receive opportunities for personal and professional growth, as well as fair wages and fringe benefits. The beginning wage for guide positions is $40 per day, and tips from guests can be expected and will range from $200 to $400 per trip. Though room and board are provided for guides during each trip, all RLT staff are expected to find their own living arrangements in the greater Boulder, Colorado area.

The Ideal Candidate: Guides must be at least twenty-five years old, and at a minimum, have current CPR and Red Cross standard first aid. Guides provide their own mountain bikes, helmets, first aid kits, bike racks, panniers, and other personal gear. Equipment to be used for guiding may be purchased directly from RLT at a discount. Other positions don't have an age requirement.

Making It Happen: Call for application materials. Once you've sent in your complete application, they will contact you. Note that it is essential that they meet you in person and that you attend their guide training in April.

INSIDER TIPS: *Applicants should be self-motivated, self-disciplined, work with a minimum of direction, and be flexible in meeting our work schedule. Our staff members work hard and, sometimes, long hours because they enjoy what they are doing, want to do the job well, and believe in RLT. Persons who cannot work well under such expectations are unlikely to fit into our community.*

Contact Information: Brian Mullis, Operations Director • Roads Less Traveled, Inc. • P.O. Box 8187 • Longmont, CO 80501 • Phone: (303) 678-8750 • Fax: (303) 678-5568 • Web Site: www.roadslesstraveled.com

Royal Palm Tours, Inc.

REGION/HQ: Southeast/Florida • **CATEGORY:** Tourism • **POSITION TYPE:** Internship • **DURATION:** Year-Round • **IDEAL CANDIDATE:** College Students • **APPLICANT POOL:** 4/year • **APPLICANTS ACCEPTED:** 1/term

SINCE 1980, ROYAL PALM TOURS has been providing customized tours for groups coming to Florida from both domestic and international origins. They also plan and operate local tours for convention, conference, and incentive groups. In 1993, Royal Palm began wildlife/nature-based outbound tours, customized for upscale, special interest groups.

Area and Working Environment: You will work in subtropical, southwest Florida, close to the Gulf of Mexico, in an area known as the Lee Island Coast. Tour operations cover most of the state.

Work/Learn Program Specifics: Tourism interns will gain hands-on experience in tour program research, destination development, copy writing, pricing, marketing, and operations. Visits to other tourism and recreation agencies will be provided, and a major project is assigned based on an intern's strengths and the agency's current needs. In a single word, they offer students a diverse internship experience.

Duration: Internships are offered year-round, with length conforming to students' curriculum requirements, usually ten to sixteen weeks for 400+ hours.

Compensation and Perks: Royal Palms locates affordable housing (under $50 per week) in a private home. Flexible internship hours accommodate an agency-secured part-time job in a resort recreation department paying $100, or more, per week. Your internship compensation is a wealth of "real-world" experience. Office attire is casual; most of the time you will be wearing shorts and Ts! Other benefits include working with a member of the National Tour Association and the American Bus Association: access to their membership provides travel, tourism/recreation, and leisure career opportunities, with over 5,000 fellow members.

The Ideal Candidate: Royal Palm prefers students studying commercial recreation, leisure studies, tourism marketing, and destination development. Helpful skills include typing/computer proficiency, attention to detail, friendly/professional telephone manner, and excellent grammar/spelling. A car is necessary.

Making It Happen: Send cover letter (with preferred start and finish date) and resume. Rolling deadlines. Interviews are conducted by telephone.

INSIDER TIPS: *Creative abilities to color outside the lines, attention to detail, compassion and sensitivity for the client's needs, and interest in exceeding client's expectations make the best interns.*

Contact Information: Ron Drake, President • Royal Palm Tours, Inc. • P.O. Box 60079 • Fort Myers, FL

33906-0079 • Phone: (941) 368-0760 • Fax: (941) 368-7141 • Toll Free: (800) 296-0249

Southern Land Programs

REGION/HQ: Southeast/Florida • **CATEGORY:** Experiential Education • **POSITION TYPE:** Internship • **DURATION:** Year-Round • **IDEAL CANDIDATE:** College Students, Career Changers, Foreigners • **APPLICANT POOL:** 70/term • **APPLICANTS ACCEPTED:** 8–16/term

THE HURRICANE ISLAND OUTWARD BOUND school's (HIOBS) Southern Land Programs offers the Outward Bound experience and philosophy to both delinquent and at-risk youth throughout Florida. In 1994, the U.S. Department of Justice reported HIOBS as one of the top five most successful programs in the nation. The program serves over 1,000 youths per year and is a leader in community service.

Area and Working Environment: Paddle in a variety of rivers throughout Florida, with alligators, heron, and a plethora of other animals.

Work/Learn Program Specifics: The Southern Land Programs has seven programs located throughout Florida. Each program teaches the pillars of Outward Bound (self-reliance, craftsmanship, physical fitness, and compassion) to young adults between the ages of twelve and eighteen. Programs are either exclusively wilderness based or are a combination of wilderness and residential programming. Courses range from 10 to 180 days, and all programs work with teams of instructors and teachers. Your internship experience includes a ten-day orientation/expedition and then 2 1/2 months of experiential work in two program areas. All interns will act as a third instructor on wilderness courses.

Duration: You will receive lots of draining, exhausting, feel-good work, which is their training ground for wilderness instructors. Positions are available throughout the year.

Compensation and Perks: There is a cost of $250 per participant for the orientation, which includes all food and lodging for ten days. During the internship, you will receive a $10-per-day stipend, plus food, lodging, and travel between bases. You will also have access to HIOBS staff trainings and pro purchase deals.

The Ideal Candidate: Candidates must be at least twenty-one years of age, pass a State of Florida clear-

ance, have current CPR and first aid certification, and have energy and an interest in becoming a part of a unique community.

Making It Happen: Call for application materials. Rolling deadlines.

INSIDER TIPS: *We're looking for those who have participated in an Outward Bound course as a student and/or have worked with teenagers; have an enthusiasm and interest to impact young adults; and are CPR/first aid certified.*

Contact Information: Alyse Ostreicher, Staff Developer/Recruiter • Southern Land Programs • Hurricane Island Outward Bound School • 907 N. Gadsden St. •Tallahassee, FL 32303 • Phone: (904) 414-8816 • Fax: (904) 922-6721 •Alternate: (904) 224-2752 • E-mail: AlyseO@aol.com

The Outward Bound Experience . . . .

Outward Bound is a growing federation of Outward Bound schools and centers in twenty-six countries. In the United States, five wilderness schools and several urban centers make up the Outward Bound USA system. Since the first U.S. school was established in 1961, over 400,000 people have participated in their programs. Well over a million people of all ages and backgrounds have benefited from Outward Bound around the world.

Outward Bound courses are designed to help people develop confidence, compassion, an appreciation for service to others, and a lasting relationship with the natural environment. Outward Bound is not a survival school. They do offer, however, a rugged adventure in the wilderness during which you will receive unparalleled training in wilderness skills. They provide a unique, rigorous curriculum, in which you will learn by doing, and put your learning to the test daily. Personal growth is central to the Outward Bound experience.

Outward Bound will challenge you, both individually and as a member of a team, by taking you into unfamiliar territory and allowing you to apply your newfound knowledge and skills. Sometimes you may fail in your efforts. Facing failure and learning to overcome it through reasonable, responsible action is an essential part of the Outward Bound experience. Teammates and instructors provide the emotional support for you to try and, if you fail, to try again. Perseverance is the basis for the Outward Bound motto, "to serve, to strive and not to yield."

Photo © Terry Moore

WORKING FOR OUTWARD BOUND

Many factors influence the quality and success of a group's Outward Bound experience, but none is more important than the quality of the staff. Staff members are sensitive, highly skilled, energetic outdoor leaders who are committed to the Outward Bound philosophy. The majority of staff are educators who are also mountaineers, climbers, and paddlers with solid life experience. Some work year-round; others only work two or three courses per year and work the rest of the year in education or other professions. Above all, staff members possess one important outdoor skill—good judgment and the ability to make sound, safe decisions under challenging circumstances.

Positions include instructional staff, support staff, and volunteer positions. All staff receive room and board and are paid on a per diem basis. The pay ranges from $40 to $125 per day (not to mention great discounts on outdoor equipment and clothing).

Please note that Outward Bound **does not** offer a formal internship program. Occasionally an internship position is created for the "right" person who applies for the assistant instructor position and doesn't have all the necessary skills to assume the responsibilities of the position. Taking a course prior to working for Outward Bound is strongly encouraged and may be required, depending on the program to which you are applying.

OUTWARD BOUND FIELD OFFICES:
Outward Bound USA
Barry Rosen, Vice President
Route 9D
R2, Box 280
Garrison, NY 10524-9757
Phone: (914) 424-4000 • Fax: (914) 424-4280
• Toll Free: (888) 882-6863 • E-mail: national@ outwardbound.org

Colorado Outward Bound School
Staffing Coordinator
945 Pennsylvania St.
Denver, CO 80203-3198
Phone: (303) 837-0880 • Toll Free: (800) 477-2627

Course areas include Alaska, Arizona, Colorado, Utah, Nepal, and Sweden.

Hurricane Island Outward Bound School

Staffing Coordinator
P.O. Box 429
Rockland, ME 04841
Phone: (207) 594-5548 • Fax: (207) 594-9425
• Toll Free: (800) 643-4462 • E-mail: hiobs@ .
outwardbound.org

Course areas include Florida, Maryland, Maine, New Hampshire, and Canada.

New York City Outward Bound Center

140 West St., Suite 2626
New York, NY 10007
Phone: (212) 608-8899

North Carolina Outward Bound School

Stephen Streufert, Staffing Director
2582 Riceville Rd.
Asheville, NC 28805
Phone: (704) 299-3366 • Toll Free: (800) 841-0186

Course areas include North Carolina, Florida, Georgia, Costa Rica, and Mexico.

Pacific Crest Outward Bound School

Richard Dickinson, Staffing Coordinator
0110 SW Bancroft St.
Portland, OR 97201-4050
Phone: (503) 243-1993 • Fax: (503) 274-7722 • Toll Free: (800) 547-3312

Course areas include California, Oregon, Washington, and Idaho.

Thompson Island Outward Bound Education Center

P.O. Box 127
Boston, MA 02127-0002
Phone: (617) 328-3900 • Fax: (617) 328-3710

Voyageur Outward Bound School

Suite 120, Mill Place
111 Third Ave., South
Minneapolis, MN 55401-2551
Phone: (612) 338-0565 • Fax: (612) 338-3540 • Toll Free: (800) 328-2943

Course areas include Arizona, Minnesota, Montana, New Mexico, Texas, Canada, and Mexico.

On the web: www.outwardbound.org

Student Hostelling Program

REGION/HQ: Worldwide/Massachusetts
• **CATEGORY:** Cycling • **POSITION TYPE:** Seasonal
• **DURATION:** Summer • **IDEAL CANDIDATE:** College Students, Career Changers, Foreigners • **APPLICANT POOL:** Varies • **APPLICANTS ACCEPTED:** Varies

••

SINCE 1969, THE STUDENT HOSTELLING PROGRAM (SHP) has been offering one- to nine-week teenage bicycle touring trips through the countrysides and cultural centers of the world. SHP trips provide adventure, fun, outdoor education, and the opportunity for emotional growth, while providing one of the safest and most wholesome youth environments available. Their groups are small, usually eight to twelve trippers and two to three leaders, making possible a close and rewarding group experience. SHP groups travel by bicycle, at their own pace and close to the land, using public and private transportation when necessary. Groups live simply, using campsites, hostels, and other modest facilities. In the countryside, groups buy food at local markets and cook their own meals.

Area and Working Environment: Tours are available in and across the United States, Canada, and Europe.

Work/Learn Program Specifics: Senior leaders and assistant leaders will conduct bicycling tours for students, grades seven through twelve. Before becoming a leader, you will complete a five-day training course to find out which age groups and types of trips best fit you. In addition, leaders receive further training for their particular trip during a five-day preparation and orientation period just before their trip departure date. Leaders also return to SHP for three days after their trips end for trip evaluation and organizational work. Leaders are not meant to be tour guides—each has extensive SHP notes and guides about the area in which the group is traveling. Leaders are firm in matters of safety, respect for others, and the SHP rule structure, but they also have the warmth, the humor, and the enthusiasm to provide a rewarding group experience.

Duration: The minimum leadership time commitment is four weeks. Employment begins in late June for part or all of the summer.

Compensation and Perks: Senior leaders make $728 to $1,932 depending upon the length of the work period; assistant leaders make from $520 to $1,380. All expenses are paid, as well.

There are only two ways to live your life—one is as if everything is a miracle, the other is as though nothing is a miracle. —ALBERT EINSTEIN

The Ideal Candidate: Senior leaders must be at least twenty-one years of age (the average is about twenty-five) and are typically teachers, graduate students, and college seniors. Assistants must be at least eighteen years old and are usually college sophomores and juniors. Many are former SHP trip participants. All leaders must hold a valid Red Cross first aid certificate and many have advanced first aid training as well. Most importantly, the leader's personality is the most critical element in making a trip work.

Making It Happen: Call for application materials and to set up a time to interview. No phone interviews are conducted. After a lengthy screening process, leaders are selected to complete one of the five-day training courses in Massachusetts before being assigned a trip. After this, SHP can make a better judgment of what age groups/tours you'll work best with.

Contact Information: Ted Lefkowitz, Program Director • Student Hostelling Program • Ashfield Rd. • Conway, MA 01341 • Phone: (413) 369-4275 • Fax: (413) 369-4257 • Toll Free: (800) 343-6132 • E-mail: shpbike@aol.com

Tahoma Outdoor Pursuits

REGION/HQ: Pacific Northwest/Washington • **CATEGORY:** Outfitter • **POSITION TYPE:** Internship • **DURATION:** Year-Round • **IDEAL CANDIDATE:** College Students • **APPLICANT POOL:** Varies • **APPLICANTS ACCEPTED:** 5/term

TAHOMA OUTDOOR PURSUITS is the region's single best source for outdoor activities. They offer classes and tours at all skill levels throughout the year in kayaking and canoeing, rock and alpine climbing, skiing and snowshoeing, as well as exciting kid's adventure camps in the summer. They currently offer tours through eighteen local parks departments and colleges, along with various corporate programs for businesses.

Area and Working Environment: Located in the middle of one of the most beautiful places to kayak in the world—the South Puget Sound!

Work/Learn Program Specifics: Interns will be put through training to be a sea kayak guide and will participate in other classes and tours, such as rock climbing and canoeing, and skiing and snowshoeing in the winter. Eventually interns will assist with these classes. Interns are also responsible for office work, assisting with registration and other office duties, including marketing tours, assisting with inventories, and developing new programs.

Duration: Internships are offered for three to four months, throughout the year. Applicants must have flexible schedules.

Compensation and Perks: Interns receive a $600 stipend upon completion of the program.

The Ideal Candidate: Applicants must be fast learners, hardworking, have a good sense of humor and common sense, and be CPR/first aid certified.

Making It Happen: Send cover letter and resume. Rolling deadlines.

Contact Information: Mary Rink, Manager • Tahoma Outdoor Pursuits • 5206 S. Tacoma Way • Tacoma, WA 98409 • Phone: (206) 474-8155 • Fax: (206) 475-6575

United States Water Fitness Association

REGION/HQ: Southeast/Florida • **CATEGORY:** Fitness • **POSITION TYPE:** Internship • **DURATION:** Year-Round • **IDEAL CANDIDATE:** College Students, Career Changers, Foreigners • **APPLICANT POOL:** Varies • **APPLICANTS ACCEPTED:** Varies

THE UNITED STATES WATER FITNESS ASSOCIATION (USWFA) is a nonprofit, educational organization formed to unite people and organizations throughout the country. They promote the benefits of water exercise and aquatics and offer a wide variety of programs and services. Their motto is "The health and safety of our participants (including instructors) is our top priority." Their national headquarters consists of office space only. They do not have a swimming pool or other facilities.

Area and Working Environment: Located ten minutes south of West Palm Beach and twenty-five minutes north of Ft. Lauderdale, Boynton Beach is on the ocean and has beautiful beaches.

Work/Learn Program Specifics: Interns will receive a well-rounded experience in the organization and administration of physical education, recreation, and sports. Interns will work on the annual international water-fitness and aquatic-therapy conference, national aquatics newsletter (published six times per year), a wide variety of national certification courses, and a book/video order department.

Duration: Interns usually work four to six months, full-time.

Compensation and Perks: Interns will receive a stipend of $300 per month. Room and board is not included. It is usually not hard to find housing for $300 to 400 per month, including utilities. Benefits include working at the national headquarters of an organization which is involved in water fitness and a wide variety of other aquatic activities.

The Ideal Candidate: Candidates must have a positive mental attitude and also want to make a difference in the program.

Making It Happen: Send a resume and cover letter indicating your area of interest, suggested length of service, and starting dates. Interviews are conducted by telephone or in-person.

INSIDER TIPS: *We are not looking for normal people. We are looking for creative, excited, enthusiastic, hardworking people who are honest and sincere and have a positive attitude. We want interns who want to play a major role in helping our organization be the best national organization possible!*

Contact Information: John Spannuth, President/CEO • United States Water Fitness Association • P.O. Box 3279 • Boynton Beach, FL 33424-3279 • Phone: (561) 732-9908 • Fax: (561) 732-0950

Woodswomen, Inc.

REGION/HQ: Worldwide/Minnesota • **CATEGORY:** Adventure Travel • **POSITION TYPE:** Internship/Seasonal • **DURATION:** Year-Round • **IDEAL CANDIDATE:** College Students, Career Changers, Foreigners • **APPLICANT POOL:** 20–30/year • **APPLICANTS ACCEPTED:** 4 at any one time

SINCE 1978, WOODSWOMEN has created a variety of adventure travel programs for women, and women and children together, which have allowed them to reach places only the most rugged individualists have seen. Woodswomen's annual trip calendar features more than seventy different activities in ten countries and around the United States. From wilderness journeys to exotic vacations to cultural odysseys—they help women experience the world. Trips are adventurous, enjoyable, safe, educational, empowering, environmentally sensitive, and provide fun challenges.

Area and Working Environment: Internships are in Minneapolis, Minnesota. Guide positions vary in location around the world.

Work/Learn Program Specifics: The structure and content of the internship is based on the participant's strengths, interest, experience, and the needs of Woodswomen. You can concentrate on one area or combine several. Possible areas include: learning about small business operations (financial aspects, office management, volunteer recruiting, public relations), trip logistics and equipment organization, and research topics of your interest on women and outdoor adventure. In addition, you can choose to also develop leadership skills through Woodswomen's support guide program. This primarily involves assisting with the leadership of their service projects for special populations. Woodswomen guides are women who love people, love being with them, and who are committed to providing healthy, instructive, fun, and challenging outdoor trips for women, and women and children.

Duration: Internships last one to four months, with the specific schedule tailored to your needs and office needs.

Compensation and Perks: Interns who work 160 hours or longer will receive a one-year free membership with Woodswomen, free participation in any Woodswomen day trip or weekend trip, and a 15 percent discount on all general store items. If you work over 360 hours, you also receive a $50-per-month stipend. If you work longer, you receive additional benefits, including seminars, discounts on equipment, and free or reduced prices on trips.

The Ideal Candidate: Sorry guys, applicants must be women who are highly self-motivated, able to work independently, and are good-humored. All interns must attend a Woodswomen two-day leadership workshop (free of charge) if one is offered during the internship. Since an internship experience doesn't include guiding trips, applicants should desire an office experience.

Making It Happen: Potential interns can call Woodswomen's office and they will send out a packet of materials which fully explains the options and application procedure. Send your completed application, resume, and two letters of reference. Rolling deadlines.

INSIDER TIPS: *The support guide program is fun and interesting, but requires a significant investment of time and money. We call it a college for guides, and it takes that kind of commitment to complete. We are very excited to get women involved in our various programs—if you have the intention and desire, we are likely to find a place for you and your skills.*

Contact Information: Peggy Willens, Administrative Manager • Woodswomen, Inc. • 25 West Diamond Lake

Rd. • Minneapolis, MN 55419-1926 • Phone: (612) 822-3809 • Fax: (612) 822-3814 • Toll Free: (800) 279-0555

Short Listings

Adventure Cycling Association

REGION/HQ: Nationwide/Montana • **CATEGORY:** Cycling • **POSITION TYPE:** Association • **DURATION:** Year-Round • **IDEAL CANDIDATE:** High School Students, College Students, Career Changers, Retired Folks, Foreigners • **APPLICANT POOL:** Varies • **APPLICANTS ACCEPTED:** Varies

THE ADVENTURE CYCLING ASSOCIATION is America's largest nonprofit recreational bicycling organization. Since 1973 they have been helping their members use their bicycles for adventure, exploration, and discovery. They publish detailed bike maps for over 21,000 miles of scenic backroads and trails in the United States which allow you to travel cross-country without ever seeing an interstate highway. The maps include information on bicycling conditions, local history, and services that cyclists need (such as location of bike shops, campgrounds, motels, and grocery stores). Memberships give you discounts on all sorts of resources, plus you'll receive *Adventure Cyclist*, their member-only magazine and *The Cyclist's Yellow Pages*, the complete guide to bicycle maps, books, routes, and organizations—updated each year.

Contact Information: Membership Director • Adventure Cycling Association • 150 E. Pine St. • P.O. Box 8308 • Missoula, MT 59807-8308 • Phone: (406) 721-1776 • Fax: (406) 721-8754 • E-mail: acabike@aol.com

Adventure Learning Center at Eagle Village

REGION/HQ: Great Lakes/Michigan • **CATEGORY:** Experiential Education • **POSITION TYPE:** Internship/Seasonal • **DURATION:** Year-Round • **IDEAL CANDIDATE:** College Students, Career

Changers, Foreigners • **APPLICANT POOL:** 60/year • **APPLICANTS ACCEPTED:** 8/year

THE ADVENTURE LEARNING CENTER has delivered quality relationship-focused adventure programs since 1979. The staff reach out from basic Christian principles in a practical, positive manner, sharing by being living examples of their faith. Interns will assist the full-time team with all aspects of program design, delivery, and follow-up. Activities are designed to detect abilities and build on strengths and successes, increase self-confidence, and provide opportunities for growth. Experiences include climbing tower and ropes courses, recreational activities, and a blend of traditional and innovative camp activities designed to teach and promote growth. Interns receive a $100-per-month stipend, plus room and board.

Contact Information: Denise Mitten, Director • Adventure Learning Center at Eagle Village • 5044 175th Ave. • Hersey, MI 49639 • Phone: (616) 832-1424 • Fax: (616) 832-1468 • Toll Free: (800) 748-0061 • E-mail: alc@eaglevillage.org • Web Site: www.eaglevillage.org

All Aboard America

REGION/HQ: South/Midwest/Arizona • **CATEGORY:** Tourism • **POSITION TYPE:** Internship • **DURATION:** Year-Round • **IDEAL CANDIDATE:** College Students, Career Changers, Retired Folks, Foreigners • **APPLICANT POOL:** Varies • **APPLICANTS ACCEPTED:** Varies

ALL ABOARD AMERICA ACTS as a liaison between the vacation destination and the room accommodations for guests. They organize tour packages for vacationing guests that include the finest hotels, casinos, and required transportation. Interns will provide research on tour visits, take tours periodically, and be involved in sales calls/meetings.

Contact Information: Staci Blunt, Sales Director • All Aboard America • 230 S. Country Club Dr. • Mesa, AZ 85210 • Phone: (602) 962-6202 • Fax: (602) 962-5727 • Web Site: www.pcslink.com/~swigley

AMC Health Promotion

REGION/HQ: Southeast/Virginia • **CATEGORY:** Fitness • **POSITION TYPE:** Internship • **DURATION:** Year-Round • **IDEAL CANDIDATE:** College Students, Career Changers • **APPLICANT POOL:** Varies • **APPLICANTS ACCEPTED:** Varies

THE AMC HEALTH PROMOTION PROGRAM is a comprehensive worksite wellness program and cost-effectiveness study for the Headquarters U.S. Army Materiel Command. It is operated by American University's National Center of Health Fitness. The philosophy of the program is based on a broad definition of health which includes physical, social, and psychological dimensions. Participants take part in a thorough screening process, health education programs, materials provided at the fitness center, and in a variety of activities and staff interactions. Duties for fitness interns include clinical data collection, fitness assessments, health-risk appraisal, exercise prescription, primary cardiovascular screening, secondary cardiovascular screening, and strength training instruction.

Contact Information: Internship Coordinator • AMC Health Promotion • 4940 B Eisenhower Ave. • Alexandria, VA 22304 • Phone: (703) 751-7330 • Fax: (703) 751-0230 • E-mail: amcfit@pop.erols.com • Web Site: www.healthydc.american.edu/amc.html

America by Bicycle

REGION/HQ: Nationwide/New Hampshire • **CATEGORY:** Cycling • **POSITION TYPE:** Seasonal • **DURATION:** Summer • **IDEAL CANDIDATE:** College Students, Career Changers, Foreigners • **APPLICANT POOL:** Varies • **APPLICANTS ACCEPTED:** Varies

AMERICA BY BICYCLE IS A unique outdoor adventure organization, hosting fully supported bicycle tours. They have a number of touring options ranging from one week up to a seven-week coast to coast tour. All America by Bicycle tours are fully supported events featuring motel accommodations, meals, ride leaders on the road, sag wagons and scheduled sag stops throughout the day, a mechanic in a "rolling bike shop," luggage transportation, daily maps, and so much more. As the cyclist, you come out and ride your bicycle every day, for the time of your life, as they take care of all your needs. Their events are not races. Participants ride their own pace and stop and do the things they want. If you would like to work for America by Bicycle, they have positions available as support truck and sag wagon drivers.

Contact Information: Douglas Torosian, Director • America by Bicycle • P.O. Box 805 • Atkinson, NH 03811-0805 • Phone: (603) 382-1662 • Fax: (603) 382-1697 • E-mail: AbBike@aol.com • Web Site: www.abbike.com

American Alpine Club

REGION/HQ: Rocky Mountains/Colorado • **CATEGORY:** Mountaineering • **POSITION TYPE:** Association • **DURATION:** Year-Round • **IDEAL CANDIDATE:** College Students, Career Changers, Foreigners • **APPLICANT POOL:** Varies • **APPLICANTS ACCEPTED:** Varies

THE AMERICAN ALPINE CLUB (AAC) is the oldest and largest national mountaineering organization in America. AAC maintains the largest mountaineering library in the Western Hemisphere, including rare books dating to the fifteenth century and historical photographs from the past century. They publish the world renowned American Alpine Journal, sponsor and endorse climbing expeditions to foreign countries, and provide grants to young climbers. Positions vary due to season and immediate program activities. Internships may involve work on the AAC annual meeting, the *American Alpine Journal*, or other special events. Interns will receive pro purchase discounts from various outdoor gear manufacturers.

Contact Information: Program Director • American Alpine Club • 710 Tenth St., Suite 100 • Golden, CO 80401 • Phone: (303) 384-0110 • Fax: (303) 384-0111 • E-mail: amalpine@ix.netcom.com

American Alpine Institute

REGION/HQ: Nationwide/Washington • **CATEGORY:** Mountaineering • **POSITION TYPE:** Seasonal • **DURATION:** Summer • **IDEAL CANDIDATE:** College Students, Career Changers • **APPLICANT POOL:** 25/year • **APPLICANTS ACCEPTED:** 3/year

AAI CONDUCTS BASIC CLIMBING courses of six, twelve, or twenty-four days which cover alpine mountaineering skills and glacier travel techniques. The programs operate in the Cascades of Washington, the Sierras of California, and in the Alaska and St. Elias ranges. Courses are presented in a full range of skill levels. Rock climbing is taught in Baja, the Sierras, Washington, and British Columbia. A number of summit expeditions, suitable for novice mountaineers, are run to 20,000'+ peaks in Ecuador, Argentina, Bolivia, and on the three high-altitude volcanoes in Mexico. Summer staff is needed to outfit clients with rental gear and for general assistance with the program. The salary is $6 per hour, and discounts of 35 percent off equipment and clothing at the institute's retail mountain shop are provided.

Pray as though everything depended on God; then work as though everything depended on you.

75

Contact Information: Dave Pilar, Program Director • American Alpine Institute • 1515 12th St. • Bellingham, WA 98225 • Phone: (360) 671-1505 • E-mail: aai@az.com • Web Site: www.az.com/~aai

American Orient Express

REGION/HQ: Nationwide/Missouri • **CATEGORY:** Train • **POSITION TYPE:** Unique Experience • **DURATION:** Summer • **IDEAL CANDIDATE:** College Students, Career Changers, Retired Folks, Foreigners • **APPLICANT POOL:** Varies • **APPLICANTS ACCEPTED:** Varies

•••••••••••••••••••••••••••••••••••••••

BE PART OF THE AMERICAN ORIENT EXPRESS or Clipper Cruise Line crew! The American Orient Express is a deluxe private train in the tradition of the legendary trains of Europe. The thirteen vintage carriages of the express were built in the 1940s and 1950s and have been completely restored. The express carries up to 100 passengers per voyage on six specially designed itineraries, through some of the most beautiful landscapes on the North American continent. On-board crew positions include dining room servers and porters. All positions require a three- to four-month contract based on the train schedule, and you'll work ten hours or more per day, seven days per week. You are paid on a per diem basis, plus tips (which are pooled with your fellow crew members). Additionally, you will receive room, board, and transportation to the train. Clipper Cruise Line provides employment opportunities on board their ships, the Yorktown Clipper and the Nantucket Clipper. All on-board crew begin their employment in an entry-level position, as either a steward/stewardess or a deckhand.

Contact Information: Personnel • American Orient Express • Clipper Cruise Line • 7711 Bonhomme Ave. • St. Louis, MO 63105-1956 • Phone: (314) 727-2929 • Fax: (314) 727-5246 • Toll Free: (800) 325-0010 • E-mail: ClipperHR@aol.com

Amethyst Lake Pack Trips, Ltd.

REGION/HQ: Canada/Alberta • **CATEGORY:** Outfitter • **POSITION TYPE:** Seasonal • **DURATION:** Summer • **IDEAL CANDIDATE:** College Students, Career Changers, Foreigners • **APPLICANT POOL:** 20/year • **APPLICANTS ACCEPTED:** 8/year

•••••••••••••••••••••••••••••••••••••••

AMETHYST LAKE PACK TRIPS, located in Jasper National Park, provides horseback treks which are ideal for horse lovers, fishermen, nature photographers, and outdoor enthusiasts. Cabins, or a mountain chalet, are available. The company provides all meals and supplies boats for guests to use on the Amethyst Lakes. They have openings for cooks, chambermaids, and wranglers. Wages range from CAN$800 to $1,500 per month, depending on job and experience, plus room and board.

Contact Information: Owner • Amethyst Lake Pack Trips, Ltd. • Box 23 • Brule, Alberta T0E 0C0 • Canada • Phone: (403) 865-4417 • Fax: (403) 865-4415

Apache Rescue Team

REGION/HQ: South/Midwest/Arizona • **CATEGORY:** Therapeutic Recreation • **POSITION TYPE:** Unique Experience • **DURATION:** Year-Round • **IDEAL CANDIDATE:** High School Students, College Students • **APPLICANT POOL:** 25/term • **APPLICANTS ACCEPTED:** 2/term

•••••••••••••••••••••••••••••••••••••••

THE APACHE RESCUE TEAM is an outdoor program funded by the Arizona Supreme Court, with much support from national industry leaders. They provide a youth-oriented rescue team with a focus on medical and technical issues. Team leaders teach three basic courses and co-teach three advanced courses per week.

Contact Information: David Line Denali, Outdoor Program Coordinator • Apache Rescue Team • P.O. Box 2012 • Springville, AZ 85938 • Phone: (520) 333-5867 • Fax: (520) 333-5907 • Alternate: (520) 333-2898

Appalachian Mountain Club

REGION/HQ: Northeast/New Hampshire • **CATEGORY:** Conservation • **POSITION TYPE:** Work/Learn Adventure • **DURATION:** Year-Round • **IDEAL CANDIDATE:** High School Students, College Students, Career Changers, Retired Folks, Foreigners • **APPLICANT POOL:** Varies • **APPLICANTS ACCEPTED:** 700/year

•••••••••••••••••••••••••••••••••••••••

APPALACHIAN MOUNTAIN CLUB, the nation's oldest and largest recreation and conservation organization, offers a smorgasbord of projects for volunteers who are sixteen years of age or older. These include numerous weekend projects (Trails Day, Adopt-A-Trail, and chapter events) in the Northeast, and five unique volunteer base camps (White Mountains in New Hampshire, Delaware Water Gap in New Jersey, the Berkshires in Massachusetts, the Catskills in New York, Baxter State Park and Acadia National Park in Maine) that offer week-long experiences in the summer and fall. More than 700 volunteers participate annually. AMC also offers a series of trail-skills workshops and publishes the widely used book, *Trail Building and Maintenance*. The AMC is responsible for maintaining more than 1,200 miles of trail in the northeast, including 350 miles of the Appalachian Trail. In addition to the hundreds of volunteers involved, AMC also hires seasonal staff for professional trail crews, shelter caretakers, and volunteer program leaders.

Contact Information: Volunteer Program Coordinator • Appalachian Mountain Club • P.O. Box 298 • Gorham, NH 03581 • Phone: (603) 466-2721 • Fax: (603) 466-2822

Bicycle Africa Tours

REGION/HQ: Africa/Washington • **CATEGORY:** Cycling • **POSITION TYPE:** Unique Experience • **DURATION:** Year-Round • **IDEAL CANDIDATE:** High School Students, College Students, Career Changers, Retired Folks, Foreigners • **APPLICANT POOL:** Varies • **APPLICANTS ACCEPTED:** Varies

BICYCLE AFRICA TOURS PROMOTES environmental conservation, economic development, and cultural diversity through bicycle touring. The program is for the good-natured realist who can appreciate the challenges and the rewards of travel in a foreign culture by bicycle. Africa is beautiful, friendly, complex, and diverse. Programs are two and four weeks long, and costs range from $900 to $1,290, not including airfare. David Mozer is also director of the International Bicycle Fund, which promotes bicycles in transportation planning, economic development, and safety education. Call to receive a free newsletter, *IBF News*, which includes great information on grassroots cycling programs all over the world.

Contact Information: David Mozer, Director • Bicycle Africa Tours • 4887 Columbia Dr., South • Seattle, WA 98108-1919 • Phone: (206) 767-0848 • E-mail: intlbike@scn.org • Web Site: www.halcyon.com/fkroger/bike/bikeafr.htm

The Biking Expedition

REGION/HQ: Nationwide/New Hampshire • **CATEGORY:** Cycling • **POSITION TYPE:** Work/Learn Adventure • **DURATION:** Summer • **IDEAL CANDIDATE:** College Students, Career Changers • **APPLICANT POOL:** 450/year • **APPLICANTS ACCEPTED:** 22/year

THE BIKING EXPEDITION provides mountain bike and road tours through the United States and Canada for students, ages eleven to eighteen. More than just a travel organization, they seek to build community, heighten self-esteem, and foster independence, while having tons of fun playing in the outdoors. Each summer they hire bike trip leaders. Interns work as volunteers; leaders receive $235 per week while on a trip; and veteran leaders receive $315 per week while on a trip, plus bonuses and trip preference. All receive complimentary room, board, and travel to the best road biking and mountain biking areas in North America. You must be at least twenty-one years of age (the staff average is twenty-six), wilderness first responder certified, and it's preferred you have a history of working for reputable outdoor education programs.

Contact Information: Brent Bell, Program Director • The Biking Expedition • P.O. Box 547 • Henniker, NH 03242 • Phone: (603) 428-7500 • Fax: (603) 428-3414 • Toll Free: (800) 245-4649 • E-mail: bjb@nec1.nec.edu

Boy Scouts of America

REGION/HQ: Northeast/New Hampshire • **CATEGORY:** Experiential Education • **POSITION TYPE:** Internship • **DURATION:** Academic year • **IDEAL CANDIDATE:** College Students, Career Changers, Foreigners • **APPLICANT POOL:** Varies • **APPLICANTS ACCEPTED:** Varies

THE BOY SCOUTS OF AMERICA uses experiential education, with small groups, to build leadership skills and self-esteem. Counseling interns will be responsible for co-leading in-school group meetings and for assisting in adventure trips which consist of hiking, canoeing, cross-country skiing, rock climbing, ropes courses, and overnight camping trips.

Contact Information: Sharon Fogarty, Learning For Life Director • Boy Scouts of America • Daniel Webster Council • 571 Holt Ave. • Manchester, NH 03109-

It's not the clever mind that's responsible when things work out. It's the mind that sees what's in front of it, and follows the nature of things.

77

5214 • Phone: (603) 625-6431 • Fax: (603) 625-2467 • E-mail: SFogs@aol.com

California Handicapped Skiers

REGION/HQ: Pacific Northwest/California • **CATEGORY:** Therapeutic Recreation • **POSITION TYPE:** Work/Learn Adventure • **DURATION:** Summer/Winter • **IDEAL CANDIDATE:** College Students, Career Changers, Foreigners • **APPLICANT POOL:** Varies • **APPLICANTS ACCEPTED:** Varies

CALIFORNIA HANDICAPPED SKIERS provides outdoor recreational opportunities to physically and cognitively challenged individuals. People with disabilities can now learn how to snow ski and waterski safely and well. Adaptive teaching techniques and equipment can overcome almost any disability—physical or mental. Adaptive ski instruction is available all season, with the summer program (Alpine Challenge) focusing on waterskiing, sailing, fishing, canoeing, and kayaking. Volunteers may work as instructors or support staff, or participate in fund-raising activities. You will be trained by staff members certified by the Professional Ski Instructors of America. Alpine Challenge volunteers are trained in adaptive waterskiing and water safety procedures, adaptive camping, fishing, canoeing, and kayaking. In addition, all volunteers receive a complimentary ski pass.

Contact Information: KelLe Malkewitz, Ski School Director • California Handicapped Skiers • P.O. Box 2897 • Big Bear Lake, CA 92315-2897 • Phone: (909) 585-2519 • Fax: (909) 585-6805

Camp Manito-wish

REGION/HQ: Great Lakes/Wisconsin • **CATEGORY:** Experiential Education • **POSITION TYPE:** Seasonal • **DURATION:** Year-Round • **IDEAL CANDIDATE:** College Students, Career Changers • **APPLICANT POOL:** Varies • **APPLICANTS ACCEPTED:** Varies

SINCE 1919, MANITO-WISH has offered wilderness programs for youth throughout North America.

Contact Information: Caroline Bone, Program Director • Camp Manito-wish • N14 W24200 Tower Place, Suite 205 • Waukesha, WI 53188 • Phone: (414) 523-1623 • Fax: (414) 523-1626

Canadian Border Outfitters

REGION/HQ: Great Lakes/Minnesota • **CATEGORY:** Outfitter • **POSITION TYPE:** Seasonal • **DURATION:** Summer • **IDEAL CANDIDATE:** College Students, Career Changers, Foreigners • **APPLICANT POOL:** Varies • **APPLICANTS ACCEPTED:** Varies

CANADIAN BORDER OUTFITTERS is a full service wilderness canoe trip outfitter located in the northeast corner of Minnesota, just a few miles from the Ontario border. Most staff are hired to work in an "area" of their business, not one specific job. Areas you may work in include pack house, store clerk, restaurant, cleaning/maintenance, dock/canoe handling, or wilderness instruction. Limited lodging is available for staff at their base on Moose Lake. Some choose to rent apartments in the Ely area, share expenses, and commute to Moose Lake. You may purchase meals at the base at a discount and use the employee kitchen if desired.

Contact Information: Patrick and Chickie Harristhal, Owners • Canadian Border Outfitters • P.O. Box 117 • Ely, MN 55731 • Phone: (218) 365-5847 • Fax: (218) 365-5847 • Toll Free: (800) 247-7530 • E-mail: paddle@northernnet.com • Web Site: www.canoetrip.com

Canyonlands Field Institute

REGION/HQ: Rocky Mountains/Utah • **CATEGORY:** Outdoor Education • **POSITION TYPE:** Internship • **DURATION:** Winter/Summer • **IDEAL CANDIDATE:** College Students, Career Changers, Foreigners • **APPLICANT POOL:** 50/year • **APPLICANTS ACCEPTED:** 1–3/year

CANYONLANDS FIELD INSTITUTE is an educational nonprofit organization. Their main offices are in Moab, with a field camp near the Colorado River and adjacent to Professor Valley Ranch. The goal of their internship program is to provide opportunities for professional development in outdoor education/interpretation and nonprofit management, particularly program planning and implementation aspects. Interns receive a $400-per-month stipend, plus housing.

Contact Information: Field Director • Canyonlands Field Institute • P.O. Box 68 • Moab, UT 84532 • Phone: (801) 259-7750

Catherine Freer Wilderness Therapy Expeditions

REGION/HQ: Pacific Northwest/Oregon
• **CATEGORY:** Experiential Education • **POSITION TYPE:** Unique Experience • **DURATION:** Year-Round • **IDEAL CANDIDATE:** College Students, Career Changers • **APPLICANT POOL:** Varies • **APPLICANTS ACCEPTED:** Varies

• •

CATHERINE FREER WILDERNESS THERAPY EXPEDITIONS is a unique treatment program for troubled adolescents which combines twenty-one-day wilderness backpacking expeditions with intensive group and individual therapy provided by a master's-level clinician or chemical dependency counselor. The White-water Camp is intended for adolescents who are not in need of the clinical intensity of a Freer Expedition, but would benefit from a structured summer program. They also host clinically-focused practitioner training and wilderness first responder medical training.

Contact Information: Brooke Anderson, Program Director • Catherine Freer Wilderness Therapy Expeditions • P.O. Box 1064 • Albany, OR 97321 • Phone: (541) 926-7252 • Fax: (541) 967-8701 • E-mail: cfwte@proaxis.com

Chuck Richards' Whitewater, Inc.

REGION/HQ: Pacific Northwest/California
• **CATEGORY:** Outfitter • **POSITION TYPE:** Seasonal • **DURATION:** Summer • **IDEAL CANDIDATE:** College Students, Career Changers • **APPLICANT POOL:** 25/year • **APPLICANTS ACCEPTED:** 20/year

• •

GRAB THAT SUNSCREEN YOU thrill seekers. Here's rafting Southern California–style—blazing hot days, balmy starlit evenings, sizzling barbecues, great grins, no bugs, and no goosebumps. You will become a raft guide on the Kern River (with class three to five rapids), east of Bakersfield, California, and just three hours from Los Angeles. You will receive $40 to $60 per day (plus tips) for your efforts. The company provides lodging in its bunkhouse for all employees.

Contact Information: Chuck Richards, President • Chuck Richards' Whitewater, Inc. • Box W.W. • Lake Isabella, CA 93240 • Phone: (619) 379-4444 • Fax: (619) 379-4685

Classic Adventures

REGION/HQ: Worldwide/New York • **CATEGORY:** Cycling • **POSITION TYPE:** Unique Experience • **DURATION:** Spring-Fall • **IDEAL CANDIDATE:** College Students, Career Changers, Retired Folks, Foreigners • **APPLICANT POOL:** Varies • **APPLICANTS ACCEPTED:** Varies

• •

CLASSIC ADVENTURES ARE DESIGNED for married and single adults of varied ages, interests, lifestyles, and abilities. Cycling trips, walks, and hikes are offered in North America and Europe. Call for details about becoming a guide.

Contact Information: Dale Hart, Director • Classic Adventures • P.O. Box 153 • Hamlin, NY 14464-0153 • Phone: (716) 964-8488 • Fax: (716) 964-7297 • Toll Free: (800) 777-8090 • E-mail: classadv@frontiernet.net • Web Site: www.travelsource.com/cycling/classic.html

Colorado Mountain School

REGION/HQ: Worldwide/Colorado • **CATEGORY:** Mountaineering • **POSITION TYPE:** Unique Experience • **DURATION:** Year-Round • **IDEAL CANDIDATE:** High School Students, College Students, Career Changers, Retired Folks, Foreigners • **APPLICANT POOL:** Varies • **APPLICANTS ACCEPTED:** Varies

• •

COLORADO MOUNTAIN SCHOOL does a great job with novices, yet also offers challenging multi-pitch climbs for intermediates looking to become advanced climbers with the ability to lead. In addition to its rock courses, CMS conducts expeditions to major peaks around the world, including the Mt. McKinley Range in Alaska, the Mexican volcanoes, Huascaran and Aconcagua in Latin America, and Kilimanjaro in Africa. At $1,495, CMS's three-volcanoes trip is a bargain-priced introduction to high-altitude climbing. CMS has drawn high praise from past participants, particularly for its attention to individual student needs and its great Rocky Mountain climbing sites.

Contact Information: Program Director • Colorado Mountain School • P.O. Box 2062 • Estes Park, CO 80517 • Phone: (970) 586-5758 • Fax: (970) 586-5798 • Toll Free: (800) 444-0730 • Web Site: http://www.sni.net/homepage/cms

Knowledge and experience do not necessarily speak the same language. But isn't the knowledge that comes from experience more valuable than the knowledge that doesn't?

Coos Bay District

REGION/HQ: Pacific Northwest/Oregon
• **CATEGORY:** Conservation • **POSITION TYPE:** Unique Experience • **DURATION:** Summer/Fall • **IDEAL CANDIDATE:** College Students, Career Changers, Retired Folks • **APPLICANT POOL:** 20/year
• **APPLICANTS ACCEPTED:** Varies

LOCATED IN THE RUGGED Coastal Range, Loon Lake has warm summers with cool nights. Travel to recreation sites from forest to a coastal lighthouse. Volunteers help with campground maintenance and visitor registration, providing information to visitors and helping with campground interpretation and children's programs, including nature walks. Benefits include free RV sites with hook-ups, training, recreational management and interpretive experience, and a $75-per-week stipend.

Contact Information: Nancy Zepf, Recreation Director • Coos Bay District • Bureau Of Land Management • 1300 Airport Ln. • North Bend, OR 97459-2000 • Phone: (541) 756-0100 • Fax: (541) 756-9303 • E-mail: nzepf@or.blm.gov

Deer Hill Expeditions

REGION/HQ: Rocky Mountains/Colorado
• **CATEGORY:** Expedition • **POSITION TYPE:** Seasonal
• **DURATION:** Summer • **IDEAL CANDIDATE:** College Students, Career Changers, Foreigners • **APPLICANT POOL:** Varies • **APPLICANTS ACCEPTED:** Varies

DEER HILL EXPEDITIONS IS looking for outdoor leaders interested in wilderness adventure and community service. Based in the Southwest, their three- to six-week courses offer teenagers in-depth explorations into canyon, river, and/or mountain environments of Arizona, Utah, and Colorado. Activities include rafting, kayaking, backpacking, mountaineering, rock climbing, cross-cultural living and community service projects in the Navajo Nation, and conservation projects with the USFS and BLM. You will receive $30 to $85 per day as a trip leader. Leaders must be at least twenty-one years old, have experience working with young people in the outdoors, and have current WFR and CPR certification. In addition to solid backcountry skills, Deer Hill Expeditions is looking for individuals who possess the level of training, skill, and experience that their programs demand.

Contact Information: Mike Maughlin, Program Director • Deer Hill Expeditions • Box 180 • Mancos, CO 81328 • Phone: (970) 533-7492 • Fax: (970) 533-7221 • E-mail: deerhill@frontier.net

Denali Raft Adventures, Inc.

REGION/HQ: Pacific Northwest/Alaska • **CATEGORY:** Outfitter • **POSITION TYPE:** Seasonal • **DURATION:** Spring/Fall • **IDEAL CANDIDATE:** College Students, Career Changers, Foreigners • **APPLICANT POOL:** Varies • **APPLICANTS ACCEPTED:** Varies

DENALI RAFT ADVENTURES offers two-hour, four-hour, full-day, and overnight raft trips on the Nenana River, which forms the eastern border of Denali National Park. The season runs from mid-May through mid-September. Summer seasonal staff includes reservations clerks, bus drivers, and river guides. Dormitory-style rooms cost $60 per month, and everyone gets a roommate.

Contact Information: Human Resources • Denali Raft Adventures, Inc. • Drawer 190 • Denali Park, AK 99755 • Phone: (907) 683-2234 • Fax: (907) 683-1477

Dvorak's Kayak & Rafting Expeditions

REGION/HQ: Rocky Mountains/Colorado
• **CATEGORY:** Outfitter • **POSITION TYPE:** Internship/Seasonal • **DURATION:** Spring-Summer
• **IDEAL CANDIDATE:** College Students, Career Changers • **APPLICANT POOL:** Varies • **APPLICANTS ACCEPTED:** 10–20/year

"AS WE'VE WATCHED OUR children grow up on the river and seen the effect of the river on them, our staff, and all the others we've shared that experience with, we've come to believe that the river is more than just an object in our world. It's alive and teaches us moment by moment and bonds with us all. This kind of bond and friendship is strengthened by time and the return of our guests year after year. We have come to call this effect River Magic." Dvorak's Kayak & Rafting Expeditions offers paddleboat trips, kayaking, rafting, and canoeing on ten different rivers and in twenty-nine canyons. River guides lead trips on eight of the Southwest's best rivers. Guides receive $530 per month, plus room and board, pro deals on gear, and swift-water and kayak instruction. You must apply by March 15.

Contact Information: Bill Dvorak, President • Dvorak's Kayak & Rafting Expeditions • 17921 U.S. Highway 285 • Nathrop, CO 81236 • Phone: (719) 539-6851 • Fax: (719) 539-3378 • Toll Free: (800) 824-3795 • E-mail: dvorakex@rmii.com • Web Site: www.vtinet.com/dvorak

Dynamy— Education in Action

REGION/HQ: Northeast/Massachusetts • **CATEGORY:** Experiential Education • **POSITION TYPE:** Work/Learn Adventure • **DURATION:** Academic year • **IDEAL CANDIDATE:** High School Students, College Students • **APPLICANT POOL:** 60/year • **APPLICANTS ACCEPTED:** 40/year

• •

COME TAKE PART IN THE DYNAMY internship year, and you will discover learning can happen in some unexpected places—on mountain trails and lakes, at a newspaper's city desk, in a glassblowing studio, or just possibly a hospital emergency room. Education leaves the classroom and enters the workplace and the wilderness as you explore choices for the future, learn valuable new skills, and discover more about making the most of opportunities. The program begins with an outdoor challenge at Maine's Hurricane Island Outward Bound School. Then the focus changes to learning through a series of three nine-week internships in career fields of your choice. You'll also participate in weekly workshops, meetings with your advisor, service projects, retreats, and life with others in Dynamy apartments. Tuition is $9,950, and housing is $3,500 for the academic year. Financial aid is available.

Contact Information: Priscilla Bradway, Admissions Director • Dynamy—Education in Action • 27 Sever St. • Worcester, MA 01609-2129 • Phone: (508) 755-2571 • Fax: (508) 755-4692 • E-mail: dynamy@nesc.org • Web Site: www.nesc.org/~dynamy

Earth Treks

REGION/HQ: Northeast/Maryland • **CATEGORY:** Mountaineering • **POSITION TYPE:** Internship/Seasonal • **DURATION:** 9 months • **IDEAL CANDIDATE:** College Students, Career Changers • **APPLICANT POOL:** 30/term • **APPLICANTS ACCEPTED:** 1/term

• •

EARTH TREKS IS A FULL-SERVICE rock-climbing school, mountaineering guide service, and indoor climbing gym. Each year, Earth Treks teaches over 1,000 people to climb and guides a dozen national and international expeditions. Climbing guide interns teach indoor and outdoor rock climbing, supervise the gym floor, and provide maintenance of all equipment. Working directly with the climbing school director and gym manager, interns will participate fully in the overall operations of Earth Treks, from teaching to the marketing/sales of expeditions. This is a nine-month position, and you will receive a $1,000 monthly stipend.

Contact Information: J. Daniel Jenkins, Climbing School Director • Earth Treks • 7125-C Columbia Gateway Dr. • Columbia, MD 21046 • Phone: (410) 465-5492 • Fax: (410) 465-9527 • Toll Free: (800) 254-6287 • E-mail: earthtreks@aol.com

Epley's Whitewater Adventures

REGION/HQ: Pacific Northwest/Idaho • **CATEGORY:** Outfitter • **POSITION TYPE:** Seasonal • **DURATION:** Summer • **IDEAL CANDIDATE:** College Students, Career Changers, Foreigners • **APPLICANT POOL:** Varies • **APPLICANTS ACCEPTED:** 10/term

• •

LEADING GREAT ADVENTURES since 1962, Epley's provides half- to five-day river float trips on the lower Salmon River. Although your principle job will be guiding, you will be involved in many other types of work, including maintenance of equipment, buildings, and grounds, food preparation, and kitchen cleanup. You will start your training period around June 1 (when you will secure a license and become first aid certified) and finish up about August 31, working a six-day work-week. Beginning pay starts at $700 per month, after you complete training (although all your expenses are covered during the training period), and may be higher, depending on your experience. Perks include room and board, free laundry service, worker's compensation, and medical benefits. Guides live in group quarters with a bathroom, beds, refrigerator, and living room. They also have a VCR, trampoline, and a basketball hoop for your after-work entertainment. Upon your proper certification, Epley's will obtain a guide license for you at a cost of $85, and if you complete your work agreement, the cost will be refunded to you. Completed applications must be turned in by April 1. "We are looking for guides who have high morals, a willing-to-learn attitude, who work well with people, and don't drink alcohol or smoke."

If you don't pay the price day in and day out, you never achieve true mastery of the subjects you study or develop an educated mind.

81

Contact Information: Ted Epley, Owner/Operator • Epley's Whitewater Adventures • P.O. Box 987 • McCall, ID 83638 • Phone: (208) 634-5173 • Toll Free: (800) 233-1813

Exum Mountain Guides

REGION/HQ: Rocky Mountains/Wyoming • **CATEGORY:** Mountaineering • **POSITION TYPE:** Unique Experience • **DURATION:** Year-Round • **IDEAL CANDIDATE:** High School Students, College Students, Career Changers, Retired Folks, Foreigners • **APPLICANT POOL:** Varies • **APPLICANTS ACCEPTED:** Varies

EXUM PROVIDES THE MOST experienced and versatile alpine guide service in the northern Rockies. Exum is one of the oldest climbing schools in North America, having operated in the Tetons since 1935. Exum's former and current guides include many of America's most famous climbers. Customized training programs for all levels can be arranged, and Exum can put together a guided ascent to Grand Teton, as well as dozens of local peaks. Exum also offers a full range of winter programs, from ice climbing to ski touring.

Contact Information: Program Director • Exum Mountain Guides • Grand Teton National Park • Box 56 • Moose, WY 83012 • Phone: (307) 733-2297

Eye of the Whale

REGION/HQ: Pacific Northwest/Hawaii • **CATEGORY:** Natural Resources • **POSITION TYPE:** Learning Adventure • **DURATION:** Year-Round • **IDEAL CANDIDATE:** High School Students, College Students, Career Changers, Retired Folks, Foreigners • **APPLICANT POOL:** Varies • **APPLICANTS ACCEPTED:** Varies

A UNIQUE BLEND OF NATURE STUDY, adventure, play, and relaxation allows you to explore the most exotic natural areas in the Hawaiian Islands. Through a combination of sailing, snorkeling, and hiking, seasoned naturalists introduce you to the natural history of Hawaii, emphasizing the origin and identification of tropical flora, the development and exploration of coral reef ecosystems, and the biology and observation of marine mammals. Programs are designed for all ages and levels of experience. These one-week adventures cost $950 per person.

If I could have my way about it, I would go back there and remain the rest of my days. It is paradise! If a man is rich he can live expensively and his grandeur will be respected as in other parts of the earth. If he is poor he can herd with the natives and live on next to nothing; he can sun himself all day long under the palm trees, and be no more troubled by his conscience than a butterfly would. When you are in that blessed retreat, you are safe from the turmoil of life. The past is a forgotten thing, the present is forever, the future you leave to take care of itself.

—MARK TWAIN, ON HAWAII

Contact Information: Mark and Beth Goodoni, Owners • Eye of the Whale • Hawaiian Outdoor Adventures • P.O. Box 1269 • Kapa'au, HI 96755 • Phone: (808) 889-0227 • Toll Free: (800) 659-3544 • E-mail: e-whale @aloha.net • Web Site: www.gorp.com/ewhale

Great Northern Whitewater Resort

REGION/HQ: Rocky Mountains/Montana • **CATEGORY:** Outfitter • **POSITION TYPE:** Seasonal • **DURATION:** Summer • **IDEAL CANDIDATE:** College Students • **APPLICANT POOL:** 100/year • **APPLICANTS ACCEPTED:** 15/year

GREAT NORTHERN WHITEWATER RESORT takes pride in helping guests enjoy a unique outdoor adventure. Seasonal positions include raft guides (half- to three-day trips), reservationists, retail shop, photography, kitchen, and housekeeping. They make sure everyone has as much work as they want and, also, time to enjoy the beautiful surroundings. "We're looking for people who have a love for the river, enjoy the outdoors, and want to share that love with visitors to the area."

Contact Information: Reno Baldwin, Program Director • Great Northern Whitewater Resort • P.O. Box 278 • West Glacier, MT 59936 • Phone: (406) 387-5340 • Fax: (406) 387-9007 • E-mail: whiteh2o@digisys.net

The Green Mountain Club

REGION/HQ: Northeast/Vermont • **CATEGORY:** Recreation • **POSITION TYPE:** Internship/Seasonal • **DURATION:** Spring/Fall • **IDEAL CANDIDATE:** College Students, Retired Folks • **APPLICANT POOL:** 150/year • **APPLICANTS ACCEPTED:** 20–30/year

THE GREEN MOUNTAIN CLUB is a nonprofit, volunteer organization founded in 1910 to establish Vermont's 440-mile-long trail system, the oldest long-distance hiking trail in the United States. The club is responsible for leadership in developing policies and coordinating efforts of its members and similar organizations in the preservation, maintenance, and proper use of hiking trails in Vermont. Internships and seasonal positions include long trail patrol/trail crew, backcountry site caretaker, and summit caretaker. They offer $50 to $180 per week, and some positions include meals and/or rustic housing.

Contact Information: Lars Botzojorns, Field Programs Director • The Green Mountain Club • RR 1, Box 650 • Waterbury Center, VT 05677 • Phone: (802) 244-7037 • Fax: (802) 244-5867 • E-mail: gmclars@sover.net

Harrah's Lake Tahoe Casino

REGION/HQ: Pacific Northwest/Nevada • **CATEGORY:** Casino • **POSITION TYPE:** Seasonal • **DURATION:** Spring-Summer • **IDEAL CANDIDATE:** College Students • **APPLICANT POOL:** Varies • **APPLICANTS ACCEPTED:** Varies

HARRAH'S INTERNSHIP PROGRAM IS designed to provide students with educational, culturally diverse, practical work experience, in an atmosphere of fun and excitement, that will enhance the intern's understanding of the hotel, restaurant, and gaming entertainment industry. Positions are available in hotel (guest services, housekeeping, parking, and health club), food and beverage, human resources, finance, and casino (keno writer, racebook writer, sportsbook, slot host, security officer, and dealer). You will receive an hourly wage and one free meal per day on days worked. Housing in the Tahoe area ranges from $200 to $500 per person, depending on your roommate situation.

Contact Information: Lydia Zuniga, Human Resources Representative • Harrah's Lake Tahoe Casino • P.O. Box 8

• Stateline, NV 89449 • Phone: (702) 588-6611 • Fax: (702) 586-6605

Henry Crown Sports & Aquatic Center

REGION/HQ: Great Lakes/Illinois • **CATEGORY:** Fitness • **POSITION TYPE:** Internship • **DURATION:** Year-Round • **IDEAL CANDIDATE:** College Students, Career Changers • **APPLICANT POOL:** 10–15/term • **APPLICANTS ACCEPTED:** 2–3/term

THE HENRY CROWN SPORTS & AQUATIC CENTER is one of the finest health/fitness facilities in the nation and successfully serves a variety of individuals varying in age, fitness level, and overall needs. The center is uniquely designed to take advantage of its prime location on beautiful Lake Michigan. The east end of the jogging track has a glass rotunda which enables walkers and joggers to view the lake while they walk or jog. Windows along the swimming pool allow early morning swimmers to watch the sunrise. The second floor, containing the fitness/conditioning equipment and lounge area, has glass windows which allow one to view the beautiful beachfront area. Fitness/wellness interns receive hands-on experience in each of the following areas: program development, facility/program management, facility and program marketing/promotion, exercise testing/prescription, health/fitness screening, personal training, weight conditioning instruction and supervision, and health education.

Contact Information: Nancy Tierney, Fitness/Wellness Director • Henry Crown Sports & Aquatic Center • Northwestern University • 2379 Sheridan Rd. • Evanston, IL 60208-3600 • Phone: (847) 491-4300 • Fax: (847) 467-1405 • E-mail: n-tierney@nwu.edu

High Sierra Adventure Center

REGION/HQ: Great Lakes/Illinois • **CATEGORY:** Experiential Education • **POSITION TYPE:** Internship • **DURATION:** Year-Round • **IDEAL CANDIDATE:** College Students, Career Changers • **APPLICANT POOL:** Varies • **APPLICANTS ACCEPTED:** Varies

HIGH SIERRA ADVENTURE CENTER is a nonprofit dedicated to community service and outreach, working with populations ranging from corporate offices to high school groups, elementary schools, and populations with special needs. The facility includes a ropes course and an

180-acre year-round camp. Interns have the opportunity to assist in all areas of program development and implementation. Your primary responsibilities include ropes course facilitation and environmental/outdoor education. Interns receive a $100-per-week stipend, plus housing and an opportunity for ropes course certification.

Contact Information: Kenley Perry, Program Director • High Sierra Adventure Center • P.O. Box 297 • Ingleside, IL 60041-0297 • Phone: (847) 740-5010 • Fax: (847) 740-5010

Holiday Expeditions

REGION/HQ: Rocky Mountains/Utah • **CATEGORY:** Expedition • **POSITION TYPE:** Seasonal • **DURATION:** Spring-Fall • **IDEAL CANDIDATE:** College Students, Career Changers • **APPLICANT POOL:** 100/year • **APPLICANTS ACCEPTED:** 10–15/year

HOLIDAY EXPEDITIONS HAS BEEN in the backcountry outfitting business for over thirty years. They take pride in providing low-impact backcountry expeditions, which include one- to six-day rafting and mountain bike trips in some of the most spectacular areas of Utah. Guides lead day trips and longer trips on various rivers in Utah. During time away from the river, responsibilities may include warehouse work and shuttle drives. Guides receive $40 to $100 per day, and room and board are provided when not on trips. "We are looking for motivated guides with good people skills and a desire to learn. Must be willing to work with and in a structured program."

Contact Information: Tim Gaylord, Operations Manager • Holiday Expeditions • 544 E. 3900 S. • Salt Lake City, UT 84107 • Phone: (801) 266-2087 • Fax: (801) 266-1448 • Toll Free: (800) 624-6323

Hostelling International—Boston

REGION/HQ: Northeast/Massachusetts • **CATEGORY:** Hostel • **POSITION TYPE:** Internship • **DURATION:** Year-Round • **IDEAL CANDIDATE:** High School Students, College Students, Career Changers, Retired Folks, Foreigners • **APPLICANT POOL:** 30/year • **APPLICANTS ACCEPTED:** 5/year

THE EASTERN NEW ENGLAND COUNCIL, a regional office of HI–AYH, operates a travel service center, organizes educational and recreational activities, and supports a local network of thirteen hostels. Internship positions are available in curricula and program development, public relations, organizational development, resource development, and college development and marketing. You must commit to a minimum of twelve hours per week for a full semester. Perks include a year-long membership in Hostelling International and possible accommodations at the Boston International Hostel for full-time interns. "Energy and enthusiasm go a long way with us. Before you apply, find out what we're all about and be sure to visit one of our hostels and/or call a hostel manager. Also follow up on your application with a phone call."

Contact Information: Mark Gesner, Director of Hostels • Hostelling International—Boston • Eastern New England Council • 1020 Commonwealth Ave. • Boston, MA 02215 • Phone: (617) 731-6692 • Fax: (617) 734-7614 • E-mail: mgesner@juno.com • Web Site: www.tiac.net/users/hienec

Inner Harbour Adventure Camp

REGION/HQ: Southeast/Georgia • **CATEGORY:** Experiential Education • **POSITION TYPE:** Internship • **DURATION:** Year-Round • **IDEAL CANDIDATE:** College Students • **APPLICANT POOL:** Varies • **APPLICANTS ACCEPTED:** Varies

INNER HARBOUR HAS BEEN IN the business of helping troubled youth for over thirty years. They have created an environment where experiential processes are the foundation for the education and counseling of young people. Internships can be in either the counseling component or under the guidance of licensed educators. Ropes course, backcountry trip, and on-site group facilitation are also available.

Contact Information: Jay McLeod, Experiential Therapies Director • Inner Harbour Adventure Camp • 4685 Dorsett Shoals Rd. • Douglasville, GA 30135 • Phone: (770) 942-2391 • Fax: (770) 489-0406 • Toll Free: (800) 255-8657 • E-mail: JMcLeod007@aol.com

InnerAction Adventures

REGION/HQ: Pacific Northwest/California • **CATEGORY:** Ecotourism • **POSITION TYPE:** Unique Experience • **DURATION:** Year-Round • **IDEAL CANDIDATE:** High School Students, College Students,

Career Changers, Retired Folks, Foreigners
• **APPLICANT POOL:** Varies • **APPLICANTS ACCEPTED:** Varies

• •

AT THIS POINT THIS PROGRAM IS offered through the Athenian School (a private high school in Danville, California) as a three-week summer program for young adults from the ages of fourteen to seventeen. The program hopes to grow over the next couple of years, with the hopes of being available to people of all ages, throughout the year. The program is based on principles that have come out of the deep ecology movement. The first week you'll work side by side a professional field scientist so that you will learn the principles of in-depth observation and data collection, while studying hawks, salmon, a plant community, or something else involving ecology, conservation, and biology. The second week you actively explore the outdoor world through a week-long wilderness excursion in the Sierra Nevada. The third week you'll return to the Bay Area to use the knowledge and skills you have learned (hopefully) to focus on bettering the human ecology. You will spend some time exploring the expressive arts in the area—including museums, theater, and music—as well as being engaged in some kind of community service activity, such as restoring a part of a house for Habitat for Humanity or planting trees for the Urban Habitat project. Essentially you will join forces to further an existing project that has a similar and appropriate mission to that of Inner-Action Adventures. There is a fee of $950.

Contact Information: Summer Programs Director • InnerAction Adventures • Athenian School • 2100 Mt. Diablo Blvd. • Danville, CA 94526 • Phone: (510) 837-5375

International Field Studies

REGION/HQ: The Bahamas/Ohio • **CATEGORY:** Natural Resources • **POSITION TYPE:** Internship
• **DURATION:** Year-Round • **IDEAL CANDIDATE:** College Students, Career Changers, Retired Folks
• **APPLICANT POOL:** 50/year • **APPLICANTS ACCEPTED:** 10/year

• •

INTERNS WILL LEAD A high school- and college-age group in natural science activities, including diving and snorkeling in the Bahamas. A one-year commitment is required, and the ideal candidate is a college graduate with a natural sciences background and a sense of adventure. You will receive a $200 to $800-per-month stipend, plus board, rustic housing on the beach, travel from Florida to the Bahamas, educational courses, permits, training, and licenses in scuba and outboards. Interviews are in the Bahamas for a week. The cost is $495, which is refunded after working one year.

Contact Information: Walter Bohl, Executive Director • International Field Studies • 709 College Ave. • Columbus, OH 43209 • Phone: (614) 235-4646 • Fax: (614) 235-9744 • Toll Free: (800) 962-3805 • E-mail: ifsoffice@aol.com

International Guide Academy

REGION/HQ: Rocky Mountains/Colorado
• **CATEGORY:** Tourism • **POSITION TYPE:** Unique Experience • **DURATION:** Year-Round • **IDEAL CANDIDATE:** College Students, Career Changers, Foreigners • **APPLICANT POOL:** 18/term
• **APPLICANTS ACCEPTED:** 18/term

• •

THE INTERNATIONAL GUIDE ACADEMY is a national training center specializing in training and certifying professional tour managers and tour guides. The program teaches you about public speaking, tour management, group psychology, leadership, the tourism industry, and networking and hiring. The tuition is $755. Tour managers are paid to travel the world, and many earn $50 to $150 per day, plus commissions. Tour guides lead groups of people around various locales and act as local experts and ambassadors. Guides can earn anywhere from $8 to $25 per hour.

Contact Information: Lynette Hinings-Marshall, President • International Guide Academy • Foote Hall, Suite 313 • 7150 Montview Blvd. • Denver, CO 80220 • Phone: (303) 794-3048 • Fax: (303) 730-2365 • E-mail: hinings@ix.netcom.com

Interventions

REGION/HQ: Great Lakes/Illinois • **CATEGORY:** Experiential Education • **POSITION TYPE:** Internship
• **DURATION:** Year-Round • **IDEAL CANDIDATE:** College Students • **APPLICANT POOL:** Varies
• **APPLICANTS ACCEPTED:** Varies

• •

INTERVENTIONS OFFERS A VARIETY OF experiences, from creative expressions to three-day adventure camping trips. Interns will assist in planning, implementing, and documenting experiential and expressive therapy activities, outings, and special events.

We are cups, constantly and quietly being filled. The trick is knowing how to
tip ourselves over and let the beautiful stuff out. —RAY BRADBURY

85

Contact Information: Christine Evans, Adventure Therapist • Interventions • 2221 64th St. • Woodbridge, IL 60517 • Phone: (630) 968-6477 • Fax: (630) 968-6670

Iron Oaks Adventure Center

REGION/HQ: Great Lakes/Illinois • **CATEGORY:** Experiential Education • **POSITION TYPE:** Internship • **DURATION:** Year-Round • **IDEAL CANDIDATE:** College Students, Career Changers • **APPLICANT POOL:** Varies • **APPLICANTS ACCEPTED:** Varies

INTERNSHIPS ARE AVAILABLE IN teams/ropes course training and facilitation, logistical support for adventure trips, environmental education, park maintenance, marketing, and administration. Interns receive a $125-per-week stipend, plus a complimentary health club membership.

Contact Information: Ryan Furer, Program Director • Iron Oaks Adventure Center • 2453 Vollmer Rd. • Olympia Fields, IL 60461 • Phone: (708) 481-2330

Jackson Hole Mountain Guides

REGION/HQ: Rocky Mountains/Wyoming • **CATEGORY:** Mountaineering • **POSITION TYPE:** Unique Experience • **DURATION:** Year-Round • **IDEAL CANDIDATE:** High School Students, College Students, Career Changers, Retired Folks, Foreigners • **APPLICANT POOL:** Varies • **APPLICANTS ACCEPTED:** Varies

THE JACKSON HOLE MOUNTAIN GUIDES and Climbing School, the only year-round climbing service in the Tetons, is widely acknowledged as one of the very best in the business. The school offers a wide variety of programs, with small classes and very skilled guides. Patagonia's company founder, Yvon Chouinard, has stated that "Jackson Hole Mountain Guides is one of the few really serious mountain guide services in the States. They not only offer excellent instruction for the beginning climber but their guides are qualified to take you on any level climb, whether rock, ice, or ski mountaineering."

Contact Information: Program Director • Jackson Hole Mountain Guides • 165 N. Glenwood • P.O. Box 7477 • Jackson, WY 83001 • Phone: (307) 733-4979

Kitty Hawk Kites, Inc.

REGION/HQ: Southeast/North Carolina • **CATEGORY:** Outfitter • **POSITION TYPE:** Unique Experience • **DURATION:** Summer • **IDEAL CANDIDATE:** College Students, Career Changers • **APPLICANT POOL:** Varies • **APPLICANTS ACCEPTED:** Varies

KITTY HAWK KITES IS THE OLDEST hang gliding school on the east coast of the United States and the largest school of its kind in the world. They provide hang gliding and paragliding instruction, guided kayak ecotours, sport wall climbing, sailing and windsurfing instruction and certification, guided bicycle tours, and kids' programs. Full- and part-time positions include hang gliding, kayaking, and sport wall climbing instructors, and retail, reservations, accounting, and warehouse staff.

Contact Information: Program Director • Kitty Hawk Kites, Inc. • P.O. Box 1839 • Nags Head, NC 27959 • E-mail: ucanfly@outer-banks.com • Web Site: www.kittyhawk.com

Mountain Trail Outdoor School

REGION/HQ: Southeast/North Carolina • **CATEGORY:** Experiential Education • **POSITION TYPE:** Internship/Seasonal • **DURATION:** Spring/Fall • **IDEAL CANDIDATE:** College Students, Foreigners • **APPLICANT POOL:** 20/term • **APPLICANTS ACCEPTED:** 6–8/term

KANUGA IS A YEAR-ROUND conference center affiliated with the Episcopal Church and sponsors the Mountain Trail Outdoor School. Kanuga also offers residential summer camp programs for youth and adults. The school is set among a 1,400-acre area of the beautiful Blue Ridge Mountains that contains two endangered species. After a training period, interns are responsible for teaching natural history classes, environmental awareness, new games and initiatives, adventure activities, low and high ropes, and rock climbing. Interns receive $150 per week plus room and board. A jack-of-all-trades attitude and flexibility are key assets for prospective interns.

Contact Information: Paul Bockoven, Outdoor Education Director • Mountain Trail Outdoor School • P.O. Drawer 250 • Hendersonville, NC 28793 • Phone: (704) 692-9136 • Fax: (704) 696-3589

National Ocean Access Process

REGION/HQ: Northeast/Maryland • **CATEGORY:** Sailing • **POSITION TYPE:** Unique Experience • **DURATION:** Year-Round • **IDEAL CANDIDATE:** High School Students, College Students, Career Changers, Retired Folks, Foreigners • **APPLICANT POOL:** Varies • **APPLICANTS ACCEPTED:** Varies

NATIONAL OCEAN ACCESS PROCESS, in conjunction with the American Friends of the Jubilee Sailing Trust, holds week-long sailing expeditions in the Bahamas on the *Lord Nelson*, a "tall ship" custom built to be accessible to sailors with disabilities. Adaptations in the design allow up to half the crew to be people with various physical impairments. No sailing experience is necessary, but paying crew members are expected to take part in all aspects of operating the ship. Crew members must be between the ages of sixteen and seventy years old. NOAP stresses integration of disabled and nondisabled people working together.

Contact Information: Program Director • National Ocean Access Process • Annapolis City Marina, Suite 306 • 410 Severn Ave. • Annapolis, MD 21403

North Beach Sailing, Inc.

REGION/HQ: Southeast/North Carolina • **CATEGORY:** Sailing • **POSITION TYPE:** Learning Adventure • **DURATION:** Summer • **IDEAL CANDIDATE:** High School Students, College Students, Retired Folks, Foreigners • **APPLICANT POOL:** 200/year • **APPLICANTS ACCEPTED:** 20/year

NORTH BEACH SAILING staff includes sailing, windsurfing, and kayak instructors, kayak guides, parasail captains and mates, reservationists, and retail and watersports rental help. The season runs mid-May to mid-October. You'll make $6 per hour plus housing in beach resort area (for most of the staff), have use of watersports equipment, and receive discounts in the retail store.

Contact Information: Bill Miles, Program Director • North Beach Sailing, Inc. • P.O. Box 8279 • Duck, NC 27949 • Phone: (919) 261-6262 • Fax: (919) 261-1494 • E-mail: nbsail@interpath.com

Offshore Sailing School

REGION/HQ: Southeast/Florida • **CATEGORY:** Sailing • **POSITION TYPE:** Learning Adventure • **DURATION:** Year-Round • **IDEAL CANDIDATE:** High School Students, College Students, Career Changers, Retired Folks, Foreigners • **APPLICANT POOL:** Varies • **APPLICANTS ACCEPTED:** Varies

IF YOU'RE ON A STARBOARD TACK and the wind veers, will you get lifted or headed? You'll learn the answer to this question, plus much more, by enrolling in Offshore's Learn to Sail program. This program offers some invaluable experiences and unexpected lessons on the ABCs of sailing. When you finish this course, you should be able to daysail a sailboat of up to 30 feet without an instructor or paid skipper. The curriculum is based on seeing it, hearing it, and then going out and doing it.

Contact Information: Kirk Williams, Director • Offshore Sailing School • 16731 McGregor Blvd. • Fort Myers, FL 33908 • Phone: (941) 454-1700 • Fax: (941) 454-1191 • Toll Free: (800) 221-4326 • E-mail: offshore@coco.net

Organizers, Etc./ Any Season Travel

REGION/HQ: Rocky Mountains/Colorado • **CATEGORY:** Tourism • **POSITION TYPE:** Internship • **DURATION:** Spring/Fall • **IDEAL CANDIDATE:** College Students, Career Changers, Foreigners • **APPLICANT POOL:** Varies • **APPLICANTS ACCEPTED:** Varies

ORGANIZERS, ETC./ANY SEASON TRAVEL is one of Colorado's largest tour and travel operators specializing in active-sports travel packages. The company sells to travel agents, individuals, and groups around the world. Some of its major clients include IBM, Hewlett Packard, and U.S. West. Interns will assist with all aspects of the operation and work with the account coordinators, sales representatives, and suppliers—ski areas, properties, airlines, and other transportation companies—to insure every detail for their client's trip is properly performed. Plus, interns will participate in on-site coordination at resorts during client trips. Interns receive a $50 per week stipend.

Contact Information: Yola Martin, Operations Director • Organizers, Etc./Any Season Travel • 7373 S. Alton Way

glewood, CO 80112 • Phone: (303) 771-1178
x: (303) 771-1157 • Toll Free: (800) 283-2754

Outdoor Adventure River Specialists

REGION/HQ: Pacific Northwest/California
• **CATEGORY:** Outfitter • **POSITION TYPE:** Internship
• **DURATION:** Year-Round • **IDEAL CANDIDATE:**
College Students • **APPLICANT POOL:** Varies
• **APPLICANTS ACCEPTED:** Varies

OUTDOOR ADVENTURE RIVER SPECIALISTS, commonly known as OARS, has been recognized worldwide as the industry model for river outfitters. They operate river trips on over 25 rivers, including Canadian and international waters. Internships are available in marketing, customer service, interpretation, and Internet development. Pay is $200 per week, with basic housing. Free trips are also available as a perk during days off.

Contact Information: Russell Walters, Director • Outdoor Adventure River Specialists • P.O. Box 67 • Angels Camp, CA 95222 • Phone: (209) 736-4677 • Fax: (209) 736-2902 • E-mail: russell@oars.com • Web Site: www.oars.com

Project Adventure

REGION/HQ: Northeast/Massachusetts • **CATEGORY:** Experiential Education • **POSITION TYPE:** Seasonal
• **DURATION:** Year-Round • **IDEAL CANDIDATE:**
College Students, Career Changers, Foreigners
• **APPLICANT POOL:** Varies • **APPLICANTS ACCEPTED:** Varies

PROJECT ADVENTURE OFFERS experiential-based activities for people of all ages and abilities.

Contact Information: Program Director • Project Adventure • P.O. Box 100 • Hamilton, MA 01936 • Phone: (508) 468-7981

Rainbow Adventures, Inc.

REGION/HQ: Rocky Mountains/Montana
• **CATEGORY:** Adventure Travel • **POSITION TYPE:**
Unique Experience • **DURATION:** Year-Round
• **IDEAL CANDIDATE:** College Students, Career Changers, Retired Folks • **APPLICANT POOL:** Varies
• **APPLICANTS ACCEPTED:** Varies

RAINBOW ADVENTURES IS ONE of the nation's most successful and popular adventure travel companies, tailored exclusively for women over thirty years of age, with headquarters in the heart of the Yellowstone ecosystem. Trips range from the Montana Cowgirl Sampler, a multi-activity trip where participants "sample" rafting, hiking, canoeing, horseback riding, and trips into Yellowstone National Park, all from the comfort of a Big Sky guest ranch, to a once-in-a-lifetime Nepal/Annapurna Lodge to Lodge Trek in the Himalayas, a low altitude, lodge-based trek in one of the most dramatic and scenic areas found anywhere in the world. Gourmet helicopter hiking in British Columbia, sailing and snorkeling in the Caribbean on a 130-foot tall ship, and a special fifteenth anniversary trip, Classic Greece/Hiking and Sailing the Greek Islands, are just a few of the activities which keep women returning year after year.

Contact Information: Susan Eckert, Program Director • Rainbow Adventures, Inc. • 15033 Kelly Canyon Rd. • Bozeman, MT 59715 • Phone: (406) 587-3883 • Fax: (406) 587-9449 • Toll Free: (800) 804-8686 • E-mail: RainbowAdv@aol.com

River Odysseys West

REGION/HQ: Pacific Northwest/Idaho • **CATEGORY:** Outfitter • **POSITION TYPE:** Seasonal • **DURATION:** Summer • **IDEAL CANDIDATE:** College Students, Career Changers • **APPLICANT POOL:** Varies
• **APPLICANTS ACCEPTED:** Varies

RIVER ODYSSEYS WEST, commonly known as ROW, leads wilderness rafting or walking trips in Idaho, adventures in the rainforests of the Amazon basin, a yachting trip along the coast of Turkey, and barge trips in France. Guides lead one- to six-day white-water trips on the rivers of northern and central Idaho. Some trips paddle through deep gorges; others through beautiful valleys. Guides receive food, housing, and a weekly wage. The ideal candidate has great people and boating skills and a musical background.

Contact Information: Peter Grubb, Owner • River Odysseys West • P.O. Box 579 • Coeur D'Alene, ID 83816-0579 • Phone: (208) 765-0841 • Fax: (208) 667-6506 • Toll Free: (800) 451-6034 • E-mail: rowinc@aol.com • Web Site: www.rowinc.com

Sports Leisure Travel

REGION/HQ: Pacific Northwest/California
• **CATEGORY:** Tourism • **POSITION TYPE:** Internship

• **DURATION:** Year-Round • **IDEAL CANDIDATE:** High School Students, College Students, Career Changers, Retired Folks, Foreigners • **APPLICANT POOL:** Varies • **APPLICANTS ACCEPTED:** Varies

. . . .

SPORTS LEISURE TRAVEL IS a tour operator specializing in sightseeing tours for seniors. They are also a full-service travel agency with some sports-oriented tours available. The agency has a large gay and lesbian clientele, in addition to seniors and the general public. The intern will be a general office assistant, entry-level tour director (one-day tours only), and will also answer phones, take reservations, and perform filing and clerical duties. Interns receive $5.50 per hour, plus tips when escorting tours. Tour directing pays $63 per day.

Contact Information: Mark Hoffmann, Owner • Sports Leisure Travel • 9527-A Folsom Blvd. • Sacramento, CA 95827 • Phone: (916) 361-2051 • Fax: (916) 361-7995

Trailmark Outdoor Adventures

REGION/HQ: Nationwide/New York • **CATEGORY:** Outdoor Adventure • **POSITION TYPE:** Seasonal • **DURATION:** Year-Round • **IDEAL CANDIDATE:** College Students, Career Changers • **APPLICANT POOL:** Varies • **APPLICANTS ACCEPTED:** Varies

. . . .

TRAILMARK IS A SUMMER adventure travel program for teenagers aged twelve to seventeen. Trips are offered all over the United States, with activities encompassing rafting, biking, backpacking, horse packing, climbing, mountaineering, windsurfing, sea kayaking, and canoeing. Group leaders and activity specialists are needed. You will receive a salary plus room and board.

Contact Information: Rusty Pedersen, Director • Trailmark Outdoor Adventures • 16 Schuyler Rd. • Nyack, NY 10960 • Phone: (914) 358-0262 • Fax: (914) 358-2488 • Toll Free: (800) 229-0262 • E-mail: rusty@trailmark.com • Web Site: www.trailmark.com

Wilderness Way Experiential Learning Program

REGION/HQ: Northeast/New York • **CATEGORY:** Experiential Education • **POSITION TYPE:** Seasonal • **DURATION:** Summer • **IDEAL CANDIDATE:** College

Students • **APPLICANT POOL:** 20–30/year • **APPLICANTS ACCEPTED:** 6–9/year

. . . .

WILDERNESS WAY EXPERIENTIAL LEARNING PROGRAM is committed to offering challenging activities for groups wishing to learn and grow in the outdoors. The non-competitive "learn by doing" approach sparks excitement about the self, the group, and the environment. Staff will work with youth, ages three to fifteen, focusing on cooperative learning and experiential education through on-site activities (initiative games courses, low/high ropes courses, and zip lines) and off-site activities (rock climbing, rappelling, and backpacking). Staff receives extensive training and $225 to $400 per week.

Contact Information: Bruce Matrisciani, Program Director • Wilderness Way Experiential Learning Program • 115 Post Rd. • Slate Hill, NY 10973 • Phone: (914) 355-2624

● ● ● ● ● ● ● ● ● ● ● ● ● ● ● ● ●

Addresses

Adventure Discovery Tours
REGION/HQ: Rocky Mountains/Utah
CATEGORY: Adventure Travel
CONTACT INFORMATION:
Myke Hughes, Program Director
Adventure Discovery Tours
P.O. Box 577
Moab, UT 84532
Phone: (801) 259-8594

Adventure Travel Trade Association
REGION/HQ: Rocky Mountains/Colorado
CATEGORY: Adventure Travel
CONTACT INFORMATION:
Mikal Belicove, Executive Director
Adventure Travel Trade Association
6551 S. Revere Parkway, Suite 160
Englewood, CO 80111
Phone: (303) 649-9016 • Fax: (303) 649-9017
• E-mail: mikal@adventuretravel.com • Web Site: www.adventuretravel.com/ats

The reason a lot of people do not recognize opportunity is because it usually goes around wearing overalls looking like hard work. —THOMAS EDISON

Alaskan Wilderness Outfitting Company

REGION/HQ: Pacific Northwest/Alaska
CATEGORY: Outfitter
CONTACT INFORMATION:
Pat Magie, President
Alaskan Wilderness Outfitting Company
P.O. Box 1516
Cordova, AK 99574
Phone: (907) 424-5552

America & Pacific Tours, Inc.

REGION/HQ: Pacific Northwest/Alaska
CATEGORY: Tourism
CONTACT INFORMATION:
Keizo Sugimoto, President
America & Pacific Tours, Inc.
P.O. Box 10-1068
Anchorage, AK 99510
Phone: (907) 272-9401 • Fax: (907) 272-0251

American Canoe Association

REGION/HQ: Southeast/Virginia
CATEGORY: Marine Science
CONTACT INFORMATION:
Program Director
American Canoe Association
P.O. Box 1190
Newington, VA 22122
Phone: (703) 451-0141 • Fax: (703) 451-2245

Barker-Ewing Scenic Float Trips

REGION/HQ: Rocky Mountains/Wyoming
CATEGORY: Outfitter
CONTACT INFORMATION:
Richard Barker, President
Barker-Ewing Scenic Float Trips
Box 100
Moose, WY 83012
Phone: (307) 733-1800

Bike Treks International

REGION/HQ: Nationwide/Oregon
CATEGORY: Cycling
CONTACT INFORMATION:
Lynn Nicholson, President
Bike Treks International
12670 NW Barnes Rd., #104
Portland, OR 97229-6016
Phone: (800) 338-9445

Buffalo Trails

REGION/HQ: Rocky Mountains/Colorado
CATEGORY: Tourism
CONTACT INFORMATION:
Tanya Rinehard, Director
Buffalo Trails
P.O. Box 3400
Montrose, CO 81402
Phone: (970) 240-1900 • Fax (970) 240-1890 • E-mail:
buffalotanya@apc.org

California Parks & Recreation Society

REGION/HQ: Pacific Northwest/California
CATEGORY: Recreation
CONTACT INFORMATION:
Membership Director
California Parks & Recreation Society
7971 Freeport Blvd.
Sacramento, CA 95832-9701

Camp Sea Gull/Seafarer Outdoor Center

REGION/HQ: Southeast/North Carolina
CATEGORY: Camp
CONTACT INFORMATION:
Ginna Taft, Assistant Program Director
Camp Sea Gull/Seafarer Outdoor Center
218 Sea Gull Landing
Arapahoe, NC 28510
Phone: (919) 249-1111 • Fax: (919) 249-1266

Canoe America Associates

REGION/HQ: Pacific Northwest/Washington
CATEGORY: Outdoor Adventure
CONTACT INFORMATION:
Program Director
Canoe America Associates
10526 NE 68th, Suite 3
Kirkland, WA 98004
Phone: (206) 827-6363

Country Cycling Tours

REGION/HQ: Northeast/New York
CATEGORY: Cycling
CONTACT INFORMATION:
Gerald Brooks, Program Coordinator
Country Cycling Tours
140 W. 83rd St.
New York, NY 10024
Phone: (212) 874-5151

Four Seasons Cycling

REGION/HQ: Southeast/Virginia
CATEGORY: Cycling
CONTACT INFORMATION:
Jorn Ake, Program Coordinator
Four Seasons Cycling
P.O. Box 203
Williamsburg, VA 23187-0203
Phone: (804) 253-2985

Glacier Raft Company

REGION/HQ: Rocky Mountains/Montana
CATEGORY: Outfitter
CONTACT INFORMATION:
Personnel Director
Glacier Raft Company
P.O. Box 264B
West Glacier, MT 59936
Phone: (406) 888-5454

Glacier Wilderness Guides

REGION/HQ: Rocky Mountains/Montana
CATEGORY: Outfitter
CONTACT INFORMATION:
Personnel Director
Glacier Wilderness Guides
P.O. Box 535
West Glacier, MT 59936
Phone: (406) 387-5555 • Fax: (406) 387-5656
• Toll Free: (800) 521-7238
• E-mail: glguides@cyberport.net
• Web Site: www.gorp.com/glacierwg

Grand Canyon Expedition Company

REGION/HQ: Rocky Mountains/Utah
CATEGORY: Expedition
CONTACT INFORMATION:
Marc Smith, Vice President of Operations
Grand Canyon Expedition Company
P.O. Box O
Kanab, UT 84741
Phone: (801) 644-2691

Hells Canyon Adventures

REGION/HQ: Pacific Northwest/Oregon
CATEGORY: Outfitter
CONTACT INFORMATION:
Doris, Manager
Hells Canyon Adventures
P.O. Box 159
Oxbow, OR 97840
Phone: (541) 785-3352 • Fax: (541) 785-3353
• Toll Free: (800) 422-3568

IMBA

REGION/HQ: Rocky Mountains/Colorado
CATEGORY: Cycling
CONTACT INFORMATION:
Program Director
IMBA
P.O. Box 7578
Boulder, CO 80306-7578
Phone: (303) 545-9011 • Fax: (303) 545-9026

International Bicycle Tours

REGION/HQ: Worldwide/Connecticut
CATEGORY: Cycling
CONTACT INFORMATION:
Frank Behrendt, Director
International Bicycle Tours
7 Champlain Square
P.O. Box 754
Essex, CT 06426
Phone: (203) 767-7005 • Fax: (203) 767-3090

Keewaydin Wilderness Canoe Trips

REGION/HQ: Northeast/Vermont
CATEGORY: Wilderness
CONTACT INFORMATION:
Seth Gibson, Wilderness Trip Director
Keewaydin Wilderness Canoe Trips
P.O. Box 626
Middlebury, VT 05753-0626
Phone: (802) 388-2556 • Fax: (802) 388-7522

Mile Mark Watersports, Inc./Dive St. Croix

REGION/HQ: Southeast/Virgin Islands
CATEGORY: Outdoor Adventure
CONTACT INFORMATION:
Personnel Director
Mile Mark Watersports, Inc./Dive St. Croix
P.O. Box 3045
Christiansted, St. Croix 00822
Virgin Islands, U.S.A.
Phone: (809) 773-2628 • Toll Free: (800) 523-3483

National Recreation & Parks Association

REGION/HQ: Washington, D.C./Virginia
CATEGORY: Recreation
CONTACT INFORMATION:
Program Director
National Recreation & Parks Association
2775 S. Quincy, Suite 300
Arlington, VA 22206
Phone: (703) 820-4940

The ultimate measure of a man is not where he stands in moments of comfort and convenience, but where he stands at times of challenge and controversy. —MARTIN LUTHER KING, JR.

91

Onshore Offshore Explorations

REGION/HQ: South/Midwest/Colorado
CATEGORY: Outdoor Adventure
CONTACT INFORMATION:
Karen McCarthy, Director
Onshore Offshore Explorations
P.O. Box 178
Durango, CO 81302
Phone: (970) 947-4673 • Fax: (970) 247-0565
• Toll Free: (800) 947-4673

Oregon Trail Wagon Trail

REGION/HQ: South/Midwest/Nebraska
CATEGORY: Outdoor Adventure
CONTACT INFORMATION:
Gordon Howard, Wagon Master/Manager
Oregon Trail Wagon Trail
Rt. 2, Box 502
Bayard, NE 69334
Phone: (308) 586-1850

Sierra Outfitters & Guides

REGION/HQ: South/Midwest/New Mexico
CATEGORY: Outfitter
CONTACT INFORMATION:
Peter Hanson, Hiring/Training Manager
Sierra Outfitters & Guides
Box 2756
Taos, NM 87571
Phone: (505) 758-1247

SOAR

REGION/HQ: Nationwide/North Carolina
CATEGORY: Therapeutic Recreation
CONTACT INFORMATION:
John Willson, Director
SOAR
1984 Rosemount Rd.
P.O. Box 388
Balsam, NC 28707
Phone: (704) 456-3435

Timberline

REGION/HQ: Rocky Mountains/Colorado
CATEGORY: Cycling
CONTACT INFORMATION:
Dick Gottsegen, Program Director
Timberline
7975 E. Harvard
Denver, CO 80231
Phone: (303) 759-3804 • Fax: (303) 368-1651
• Toll Free: (800) 417-2453

Triangle X Float Trips

REGION/HQ: Rocky Mountains/Wyoming
CATEGORY: Outfitter
CONTACT INFORMATION:
John Turner, Float Trip Manager
Triangle X Float Trips
Moose, WY 83012
Phone: (307) 733-5500

Vermont Bicycle Touring

REGION/HQ: Northeast/Vermont
CATEGORY: Cycling
CONTACT INFORMATION:
William Perry, President
Vermont Bicycle Touring
P.O. Box 711
Bristol, VT 05445
Phone: (800) 245-3868

VisionQuest National

REGION/HQ: South/Midwest/Texas
CATEGORY: Experiential Education
CONTACT INFORMATION:
Program Director
VisionQuest National
P.O. Box 92874
Austin, TX 78709-2894

Wild River Adventures

REGION/HQ: Rocky Mountains/Montana
CATEGORY: Outfitter
CONTACT INFORMATION:
Program Director
Wild River Adventures
P.O. Box 272B
West Glacier, MT 59936

Wilderness Hawaii

REGION/HQ: Pacific Northwest/Hawaii
CATEGORY: Wilderness
CONTACT INFORMATION:
Shena Sandler, Program Director
Wilderness Hawaii
P.O. Box 61692
Honolulu, HI 96839
Phone: (808) 737-4697

Wildland Adventures, Inc.

REGION/HQ: Pacific Northwest/Washington
CATEGORY: Outdoor Adventure
CONTACT INFORMATION:
Program Director
Wildland Adventures, Inc.
3516 NE 155th St.
Seattle, WA 98155
Phone: (206) 365-0686 • Fax: (206) 363-6615 • Toll Free: (800) 345-4453

World Leisure & Recreation Association

REGION/HQ: Canada/Ontario
CATEGORY: Recreation
CONTACT INFORMATION:
Secretariat
World Leisure & Recreation Association
P.O. Box 309
Sharbot Lake, Ontario K0H 2P0
Canada
Phone: (613) 279-3172

The way I see it, if you want the rainbow, you gotta put up with the rain.
—DOLLY PARTON

The Adventures of Tom Sawyer by Mark Twain. This book takes us back to a dreamlike world of summertime and pleasantly reminds us that we were once boys and girls ourselves, and to remember to carry our childlike qualities into adulthood.

If your roots are embedded in adventure education, check out the **Association for Experiential Education's** *Jobs Clearinghouse Newsletter.* Hot off the presses each month, this newsletter provides contacts and job descriptions of seasonal jobs and internship opportunities in the experiential/adventure education field. You can pick up a single copy for $9, three issues for $24, or a monthly subscription ($40/year if you're a member; $80/year if you're not). (303) 440-8844; info@aee.org; www.princeton.edu/~rcurtis/aee.html. You can also subscribe to the AEEList, an E-mail hub for issues related to experiential education. To subscribe, send a message to: listproc@lists.princeton.edu. In the body of the message write: Subscribe aeelist (your name).

Cool Works on-line provides up-to-date listings of seasonal jobs in great places, including employment in national or state parks, cruise ships, dude ranches, ski/summer resorts, or at summer camps. www.coolworks.com/showme

The International Bicycle Fund publishes a free newsletter called *IBF News,* which includes great information on grassroots cycling programs all over the world. This nonprofit is dedicated to promoting bicycles in transportation planning, economic development, and bicycle safety. Contact David Mozer, International Bicycle Fund, 4887 Columbia Dr. South, Seattle, WA 98108-1919; (206) 628-9314; intlbike@scn.org; www.halcyon.com/fkroger/bike/homepage.html

Intern-NET on-line provides up-to-date listings to students interested in commercial recreation and tourism, parks and outdoor recreation, environmental interpretation/education, therapeutic recreation, military recreation, municipal/nonprofit recreation, sports, health and fitness. www.vicon.net/~internnet

The **National Tour Foundation** maintains a list of more than 100 internship opportunities with tour operators, hotels, attractions, restaurants, and convention and visitors bureaus. To receive this free publication, call (800) 682-8886, extension 4251.

Looking for a job with an outdoor organization or work in the outdoors? Add your free one-paragraph bio in the jobs wanted area on the **Outdoor Network's Web site** at www.outdoornetwork.com

Perpetual Press publishes a unique series called **Now Hiring!** Current editions include *Outdoor Jobs, Destination Resort Jobs, Ski Resort Jobs, Jobs In Asia,* and *Jobs in Eastern Europe.* Each guide hopes to inspire and prepare you for your work adventures. To get the scoop on these guides and more, call Perpetual at (800) 807-3030.

To the full-time RVer, home is where you park it. In years past, RVers were synonymous with retired folks, but there is a growing trend of people of all ages who have taken to the road seeking recreation, friendships, new opportunities, and exciting jobs, while traveling around in motor homes and travel trailers. **Workamper News,** published bimonthly, provides you with information on jobs and opportunities all around the country. Yearly subscriptions run $23. Greg and Debbie Robus, *Workamper News,* 201 Hiram Rd., Heber Springs, AR 72543-8747; (800) 446-5627, (501) 362-2637; workamp@arkansas.net; www.workamper.com

I learned early that the richness of life is adventure. Adventure calls on all faculties of mind and spirit. It develops self-reliance and independence. Life then teems with excitement. But you are not ready for adventure unless you are rid of fear. For fear confines you and limits your scope. You stay tethered by strings of doubt and indecision and have only a small and narrow world to explore.

—William O. Douglas

Security is mostly superstition. It does not exist in nature, nor do the children of men as whole experience it. Avoiding danger is no safer in the long run than outright exposure. Life is either a daring adventure or nothing.

—Helen Keller

All you need in life is ignorance and confidence, and then success is sure.
—Mark Twain

5

Dude and guest ranching is more than a vacation; it is a
spirit, a tradition of Western hospitality, warmth, honesty, family and natural beauty. It is, indeed, a ministry
that touches lives and helps to make this a better world in which
to live.

—GENE KILGORE,
IN PREFACE TO *KILGORE'S RANCH VACATIONS*

Fresh Air Fund. Photo © Jerry Speier

Camps and

Amelia Island Plantation

REGION/HQ: Southeast/Florida • **CATEGORY:** Resort • **POSITION TYPE:** Internship • **DURATION:** Year-Round • **IDEAL CANDIDATE:** College Students, Foreigners • **APPLICANT POOL:** Varies • **APPLICANTS ACCEPTED:** 25–30/term

NOTED FOR THEIR ENVIRONMENTALLY conscious development, Amelia Island Plantation is Florida's greenest resort. This 1,250-acre resort features four miles of wide, white sand beaches, forty-five holes of golf, tennis facilities, fine dining, shopping, conference facilities, and an on-property complimentary transportation system. They cater to guests of all ages, conference groups, club members, and their property owners. Lodging opportunities include seventeen varying types of accommodations, ranging from deluxe hotel rooms and penthouses to three-bedroom beach townhouses and villas.

Area and Working Environment: The historic city of Fernandina Beach is nestled on the island and hosts the annual Shrimp Festival in May.

Work/Learn Program Specifics: Floral/Horticulture: greenhouse production, floral design, and sales. Culinary: food preparation, presentation for fine and casual dining, and purchasing. Recreation: program planning/implementation/evaluation, facility maintenance, and holiday/special program theme design. Areas of emphasis include social-guest programming, conference group recreation, equipment rental, and aquatic programming. Health and Fitness: guest relations, exercise prescription, health and wellness programming, budgeting, and marketing. Special Events: planning and implementation of holiday and special events including design, layout, supervision, and evaluation of each party set. Internships are also available in promotions, public relations, graphics, marketing, retail, and golf/tennis/turf management. All interns participate in seminars and workshops to gain a working knowledge of their department.

Duration: All internships are based upon a sixteen-week duration, and a twelve-week minimum is required. Interns will be expected to work an average of forty to fifty hours per week, with one or two days off.

Compensation and Perks: Interns receive a "housing stipend" of $150 per week. Uniforms are provided for most internships, as is one meal per working day in the employee cafeteria. Limited housing is available, in lieu of a partial stipend; otherwise interns are encouraged to live with one another, lessening the financial burden of housing. Interns are also encouraged to use the Amelia Island Plantation's outlets, including the health and fitness center, golf course, tennis courts, and shops, and eat in the restaurants (at a discount).

The Ideal Candidate: The plantation desires students majoring in horticultural studies, culinary studies, marketing, recreation, resort and lodging management, health and fitness, public relations, theater, graphic design, or related fields.

Making It Happen: Submit cover letter, resume, and the names and telephone numbers of five references (three past employers and two academic advisors). It's best to apply at least two months prior to start date.

Contact Information: Barbara Ross, Intern Training Coordinator • Amelia Island Plantation • P.O. Box 3000 • Amelia Island, FL 32035-3000 • Phone: (904) 277-5904 • Fax: (904) 277-5994

Resorts

Aspen Skiing Company

REGION/HQ: Rocky Mountains/Colorado
• **CATEGORY:** Ski Resort • **POSITION TYPE:** Seasonal
• **DURATION:** Year-Round • **IDEAL CANDIDATE:**
College Students, Career Changers, Foreigners
• **APPLICANT POOL:** Varies • **APPLICANTS ACCEPTED:**
2,000/year
••

THE ASPEN SKIING COMPANY operates four ski areas (Snowmass Ski Area, Aspen Mountain, Buttermilk, and Aspen Highlands) that operate during the winter season, with summer activities during the summer, and three hotels (the Little Nell, the Snowmass Lodge and Club, and the Aspen Meadows) which are open year-round.

Work/Learn Program Specifics: Winter season positions include lift attendants, childcare attendants, ticket sellers, snowcat operators, rental shop attendants, and skier services staff. In addition, year-round positions are available in hotel operations, such as room attendants, food and beverage, front desk staff, valet/bell, and athletic club staff.

Duration: Most positions are seasonal, beginning in early November and lasting through early April; although there are year-round positions available.

Compensation and Perks: Entry-level positions start at $8 per hour. Benefits include a free, unrestricted four-mountain ski pass, dependent ski passes, complimentary ski lessons, affordable health plan, paid personal days, comp and discount lift tickets for family and friends, and discounts on bus transportation (to get you to and from work), health club memberships, company ski shops, and on-mountain restaurants.

The Ideal Candidate: Applicants must have excellent guest service skills.

Making It Happen: Call for brochure. In order to be considered for employment opportunities, make plans to visit the Aspen area because they require personal interviews. Please be aware that housing in the Aspen area is limited, and it is best to arrive prior to the beginning of the summer or winter seasons to begin your search. Community bulletin boards, local newspapers, property management companies, and networking with locals are the best ways to find housing. Here are some key contacts to help you out: Classic Properties (970) 925-1110, Coates Reid & Waldron (970) 925-1400, Carol Jacobson Rentals (970) 925-2811, and Pitkin County Housing Authority (970)

920-5050. Or pick up one of their two newspapers—the *Aspen Times*: (970) 925-3414 or the *Aspen Daily News* (970) 925-2220.

INSIDER TIPS: *A majority of our winter hiring is done at our job fairs in October and continues as needed throughout the season. Summer hiring usually begins in early May.*

Contact Information: Eva Zimmerman, Human Resources • Aspen Skiing Company • P.O. Box 1248 • Aspen, CO 81612-1248 • Phone: (970) 920-0945 • Fax: (970) 920-0771 • Job Hotline: (970) 923-0499 • E-mail: eva@rof.net • Web Site: www.skiaspen.com

The Big Mountain Ski & Summer Resort

REGION/HQ: Rocky Mountains/Montana
• **CATEGORY:** Ski Resort • **POSITION TYPE:** Internship
• **DURATION:** Winter/Summer • **IDEAL CANDIDATE:**
College Students, Career Changers, Retired Folks, Foreigners • **APPLICANT POOL:** Varies • **APPLICANTS ACCEPTED:** 250/year
••

THINGS ARE VERY DIFFERENT up at Big Mountain. For fifty years the Big Mountain has been the secret winter getaway of skiers, and now snowboarders, who like to have fun—real fun—big, healthy, frolicking, feel-like-a-kid-on-recess kind of fun. The Big Mountain is one of the largest resorts in North America, famous for bold beautiful terrain.

Area and Working Environment: Located in the beautiful Flathead Valley on the Canadian border next to Glacier National Park, the resort is surrounded by vast wilderness. It's often described as the way Vail, Colorado, was twenty years ago.

Work/Learn Program Specifics: Big Mountain offers seasonal positions in all areas of hospitality management and food service, and two very unique internships. Summer recreation interns rotate through these areas: guided nature hikes, mountain bike rentals and trail maintenance, activity service and information center staffing, coordinating activity reservations for customers, and helping with ticket sales and special events. Opportunities will be available to learn about advertising, creative programming, budgeting, coordinating multiple activities, and complete resort interdepartmental exposure. Winter recreation interns are in charge of production and coordination of forty-five special events throughout the winter season, and ski racing events and other activities. Other responsibilities include budgeting, advertising, sponsorship, staffing, marketing, and complete coordination for various special events. Complete interdepartmental exposure to ski patrol, ski school, purchasing, lift operations, accounting, marketing, security, and reservations.

Duration: Summer positions run from late May through mid-October. Winter positions run from mid-November through mid-April.

Compensation and Perks: Interns are paid $300 per month; seasonals range from $4.25 to $8.50 per hour. There will be assistance in finding housing arrangements, but employee housing is not available. Perks include 20 percent discounts at all facilities and group reception parties. Winter employees receive a free season ski pass.

The Ideal Candidate: Big Mountain desires friendly, helpful, and outgoing individuals who enjoy interacting with customers. For recreation internships, they seek individuals who are in good physical shape and carry a current CPR certification; and for the winter, skiing ability should be intermediate to advanced.

Making It Happen: Submit cover letter and resume. Rolling deadlines. They are accepting resumes up to one year in advance due to the popularity of the program.

Contact Information: Dave Harrison, Events Coordinator • The Big Mountain Ski & Summer Resort • P.O. Box 1400 • Whitefish, MT 59937 • Phone: (406) 862-2911 • Fax: (406) 862-2955 • Toll Free: (800) 858-5439 • Web Site: www.bigmtn.com/resort

Bluewater Bay Resort

REGION/HQ: Southeast/Florida • **CATEGORY:** Resort • **POSITION TYPE:** Internship • **DURATION:** Summer • **IDEAL CANDIDATE:** College Students, Foreigners • **APPLICANT POOL:** 20/year • **APPLICANTS ACCEPTED:** 4/year

BLUEWATER BAY RESORT HAS something for everyone, from the young to the young at heart, including sailing, fishing, biking, swimming, walking/jogging, golfing, and tennis.

Area and Working Environment: Bluewater is in 2,000 acres of natural beauty on the shore of Choctawatchee Bay in northwest Florida, just minutes away from the sugar-white beaches of Destin.

Work/Learn Program Specifics: Recreation interns lead youth and teen programs and will take an active role throughout all aspects of the recreation department. This includes planning, leading, and evaluating youth pro-

grams (ages three to five and six to twelve), special holiday events, office administration, bicycle and sports equipment rental, and checking facilities for cleanliness and neatness. Each intern will be required to develop and present a special project for Bluewater before the completion of the internship.

Duration: The program is from May 15 to September 15. Interns will work an average of forty hours per week, although there will be occasions when interns are required to work over forty hours per week.

Compensation and Perks: Interns will receive a stipend of $50. Housing is provided on the resort property, and the facilities are fully equipped (although meals are not provided). Interns will be furnished with Bluewater Bay T-shirts to be worn at all times on the job. Interns receive up to 30 percent discounts on golf and tennis clothing, accessories, and meals at the Clubhouse Restaurant. Employees have free use of all pools and tennis courts and participate in many socials.

The Ideal Candidate: The prospective intern must have completed their junior year and be enrolled in a college or university recreation program.

Making It Happen: Submit cover letter (outlining your interests, experiences, talents, and other information which qualifies you for the position), resume, and three work references with current phone numbers by March 31.

INSIDER TIPS: *To get into our organization, you must have previous recreation experience, be very outgoing, work well with the public, and be persistent.*

Contact Information: Recreation Program Manager • Bluewater Bay Resort • 1950 Bluewater Blvd. • Niceville, FL 32578 • Phone: (904) 897-3664 • Fax: (904) 897-2424 • Toll Free: (800) 874-2128

Camp Chatuga

REGION/HQ: Southeast/South Carolina • **CATEGORY:** Camp • **POSITION TYPE:** Internship/Seasonal • **DURATION:** Summer • **IDEAL CANDIDATE:** College Students, Career Changers, Foreigners • **APPLICANT POOL:** 150/year • **APPLICANTS ACCEPTED:** 40/year

CAMP CHATUGA IS A SMALL, independent camp for boys and girls from six to sixteen. They seek to inspire campers and staff to develop their best individual potentials intellectually, emotionally, spiritually, and physically in a fun and relaxed natural environment.

Area and Working Environment: The camp is located on the foothills of the Blue Ridge Mountains, near the Chattooga River.

Work/Learn Program Specifics: A job at Chatuga is not a summer vacation—it is work. It is mentally and physically exhausting, but unbelievably rewarding. Can you live without alcohol, tobacco, perfect hair, privacy, a Walkman, air-conditioning, a VCR, a predictable schedule, and lots of money? Then this may be the job for you. Positions include: program director, head counselors, counselors, junior counselors, nanny, dining hall supervisor, waterfront supervisor, horseback supervisor, outdoor program supervisor, health supervisor, health lodge counselor, mechanic, and maintenance crew.

Duration: Eight-week season during the summer.

Compensation and Perks: Staff members receive $125 per week, plus free room and board. Your salary goes up based on education, experience, and certifications. Perks include free trips, laundry, and staff T-shirt. Pre-camp training helps you earn or renew certifications that will benefit you the rest of your life.

The Ideal Candidate: Staff are hired for their character, maturity, love of the outdoors, and enjoyment of children and teens.

Making It Happen: Call for a staff application packet.

Contact Information: Kelly Moxley, Personnel Director • Camp Chatuga • 291 Camp Chatuga Rd. • Mountain Rest, SC 29664 • Phone: (864) 638-3728 • Fax: (864) 638-0898

Camp Courage

REGION/HQ: Great Lakes/Minnesota • **CATEGORY:** Therapeutic Camp • **POSITION TYPE:** Internship/ Seasonal • **DURATION:** Year-Round • **IDEAL CANDIDATE:** College Students, Career Changers • **APPLICANT POOL:** Varies • **APPLICANTS ACCEPTED:** Varies

CAMP COURAGE, A NONPROFIT United Way organization, provides rehabilitation, enrichment, vocational, independent living, and educational services to empower children and adults with physical disabilities and sensory impairments to achieve their full potential.

Area and Working Environment: Maple Lake is a rural area, just one hour from the Twin Cities. The site includes two lakes, numerous wetlands, forests, fields, and miles of hiking and skiing trails.

Work/Learn Program Specifics: Environmental education/generalist staff prepares the camp and provides teaching and hosting for Camp Courage environmental education and retreat groups. You will attend all scheduled training events, workshops, and staff meetings; teach outdoor and environmental education programs in a style attractive to and consistent with formal school educators; and host groups one evening per week, including opening the pool and gym, setting up campfires, and leading night hikes. Cleaning, food service, maintenance, and other tasks necessary for the camp to run smoothly will also be assigned.

Duration: Staff can expect to work thirty to forty hours per week, which will include some weekends.

Compensation and Perks: You will receive $4.75 to $5.50 per hour (if working September through May) or a $140-per-week stipend (during the summer), plus room, board, holiday breaks, and work in a beautiful setting.

The Ideal Candidate: Applicants must have at least two years of college, with classes in the natural sciences, recreation, or education fields. Consistent and appropriate leadership of children is vital, as are good communication skills. A qualified individual must be able to enthusiastically lead outdoor education activities one day, then clean cabins or help in the kitchen the next.

Making It Happen: Call for application form. Deadlines: summer—March 15; September through May—August 15.

INSIDER TIPS: *Proven ability to work with school-age children and applying early will help those who apply.*

Contact Information: Kurt Marple, Environmental Education Coordinator • Camp Courage • 8046 83rd St., NW • Maple Lake, MN 55358-9774 • Phone: (320) 963-3121 • Fax: (320) 963-3698 • E-mail: ccourage@ lkdllink.net • Web Site: www.lkdllink.net/~ccourage

Camp Courageous of Iowa

REGION/HQ: South/Midwest/Iowa • **CATEGORY:** Therapeutic Camp • **POSITION TYPE:** Internship • **DURATION:** Year-Round • **IDEAL CANDIDATE:** College Students, Career Changers, Foreigners • **APPLICANT POOL:** 50–100/year • **APPLICANTS ACCEPTED:** 25/year

CAMP COURAGEOUS OF IOWA is a year-round camp founded on the belief that individuals with disabilities have the right to opportunities found in the world around them. The curriculum challenges those individuals with recreational and educational activities.

Area and Working Environment: Located in eastern Iowa, Camp Courageous is surrounded by 1,000 acres of state and county lands. Caves, limestone bluffs, and the Maquoketa River are a few of the nearby natural resources.

Work/Learn Program Specifics: Counselors supervise the health, well-being, and personal care of groups of campers and ensure that they have a successful and enjoyable time. Activity specialists develop and implement activities for campers, including canoeing, swimming, adventure, outdoor living skills, recreation, nature, and crafts activities.

Duration: Full-time positions are offered three to nineteen weeks, year-round.

Compensation and Perks: Interns receive a salary of $80 per month; seasonal staff receives $500 to $600 per month; and year-round staff receives $700 to $750. All receive room and board.

The Ideal Candidate: Candidates should have flexibility and patience. A genuine desire to give your time, energy, and enthusiasm to others is required.

Making It Happen: Call for application. Rolling deadlines.

INSIDER TIPS: *Working with children and adults with disabilities is an experience you will never forget.*

Contact Information: Jeanne Muellerleile, Camp Director • Camp Courageous of Iowa • P.O. Box 418 • Monticello, IA 52310-0418 • Phone: (319) 465-5916 • Fax: (319) 465-5919 • Web Site: www.campcourageous

Camp Easter Seal–East

REGION/HQ: Southeast/Virginia • **CATEGORY:** Therapeutic Camp • **POSITION TYPE:** Internship • **DURATION:** Year-Round • **IDEAL CANDIDATE:** College Students, Career Changers, Foreigners • **APPLICANT POOL:** Varies • **APPLICANTS ACCEPTED:** Varies

CAMP EASTER SEAL–EAST is a fun residential camp for children and adults with physical or cognitive disabilities. The summer program serves about forty-five campers a session. During the non-summer months, the camp runs various weekend retreats as well as community swim and recreation programs. The campsite

is composed of fully-winterized and air-conditioned dormitory and lodge-style buildings.

Area and Working Environment: The camp is located in rural Caroline County, about an hour north of Richmond.

Work/Learn Program Specifics: The majority of staff opportunities are during the summer session. During this time, interns will serve as general counselors or activity specialists. During non-summer months, interns will have roles consisting of administrative, maintenance, and programming tasks.

Duration: Summer positions run from late May to mid-late-August. The duration of non-summer positions are negotiable, though it is generally twelve weeks.

Compensation and Perks: Interns will be paid $110 per week, plus room and board. The camp food is well known for being the best around (YUM!).

The Ideal Candidate: Applicants should have at least one year of college experience and have a positive attitude. Preference given to those who have previous successful experience with persons with disabilities.

Making It Happen: Call or write for application materials. Personal interviews are preferred; however, phone interviews are an option.

INSIDER TIPS: *We're a fun place to work. The days are long and the work is hard, but if you keep a positive attitude, you are in for the experience of a lifetime.*

Contact Information: Devin Brown, Resident Director • Camp Easter Seal—East • 20500 Easter Seal Dr. • Milford, VA 22514-9730 • Phone: (804) 633-9855 • Fax: (804) 633-6203

Camp Echo Lake

REGION/HQ: Northeast/New York • **CATEGORY:** Camp • **POSITION TYPE:** Seasonal • **DURATION:** Summer • **IDEAL CANDIDATE:** College Students • **APPLICANT POOL:** 60/term • **APPLICANTS ACCEPTED:** 12/term

TREK IS ECHO LAKE'S wilderness outreach program. From simple nature walks to overnight adventures, a variety of programs at Echo Lake open, up the wonders of nature to campers of all ages and experience. Through TREK, campers make direct connections with the outdoors. Ecology and the environment become more than abstract concepts; campers acquire personal knowledge and experience of natural systems as realities.

Area and Working Environment: Camp Echo Lake's location provides access to white-water rafting trips on the Sacandaga River, overnight backpacking trips to the High Peaks, exploration of Knox Cave, technical climbing at King Phillips Ledge, or basking under the fresh waters of Split Rock Falls.

Work/Learn Program Specifics: Activity specialists teach skills in a particular sport or activity, offering group and individual attention. Cabin specialists live with the campers and are essential in helping children adjust successfully to camp and in maintaining the campers' quality of life.

Duration: You'll work two intense weeks during the summer.

Compensation and Perks: Salary is commensurate with experience. Room, board, and laundry service are also provided.

The Ideal Candidate: "They rush down the hill every morning with the same exuberance, wearing funny noses, and cracking jokes. They're always there with a hug. They take the time to listen and adjust their leadership to their campers' needs. They like sharing a cabin with half a dozen ten-year-olds!" Does this sound like someone like you?

Making It Happen: Call for application materials. Applications must be received by May 15.

Contact Information: Dawn Ewing, Associate Director • Camp Echo Lake • 3 W. Main St. • Elmsford, NY 10523 • Phone: (914) 345-9099 • Fax: (914) 345-2120 • Toll Free: (800) 544-5448 • E-mail: echolake@campecholake.com • Web Site: www.campecholake.com

Camp Friendship

REGION/HQ: Southeast/Virginia • **CATEGORY:** Environmental Education • **POSITION TYPE:** Internship/Seasonal • **DURATION:** Year-Round • **IDEAL CANDIDATE:** College Students, Career Changers, Foreigners • **APPLICANT POOL:** 400/year • **APPLICANTS ACCEPTED:** 40/year

CAMP FRIENDSHIP IS LOCATED ON 733 acres of woodlands, with the Rivanna on three sides and a small lake in the center. The Summer Camp Program serves nearly 1,700 children—coming from twenty-seven states and twenty countries—each year. Facilities include a stable for eighty horses, gym, swimming pool, archery and riflery ranges, tennis courts, theater, ropes course (over sixty elements), and an environmental education center.

Area and Working Environment: The camp is located in the foothills of the Blue Ridge Mountains of central Virginia. Driving distance to Washington, D.C. is about 2 1/2 hours; to the beach, three hours; and to the mountains, forty-five minutes from Skyline Drive.

Work/Learn Program Specifics: Summer camp offers a diverse selection of elective activities: swimming, canoeing, gymnastics, riding, sports, crafts, pottery, photography, ropes course, drama, archery, riflery—over thirty choices. A specialized equestrian camp for girls is offered, as well as thirteen different challenge trips for teenagers, which include hang gliding, rafting, caving, rock climbing, kayaking, bicycling, and waterskiing. Counselors with instructional skills are hired for this season. The environmental education program is offered to school groups in the spring and fall, with weekend conferences and special program weekends for children. Program staff teach environmental education, orienteering, and ropes courses; lead canoe trips and campfires; and lifeguard for swimming. When program groups are not in camp, staff may be asked to assist with basic maintenance or recruitment assignments.

Duration: During the summer, most positions involve being on-duty twenty-four hours each day. Each staff member is scheduled for a twenty-four-hour period off each week and two hours free from responsibilities each day. During the school year, staff usually work 5 1/2 days per week, averaging eight to ten hours per day.

Compensation and Perks: Staff will receive a salary, housing, meals, and use of the camp's recreational facilities when they are not scheduled for use by guests.

The Ideal Candidate: Applicants should be at least nineteen, with one year of college completed. Preference is given to those with previous successful, documented work experience with children. Some positions may have additional requirements of age and certifications. A criminal record and driver's license check will be required.

Making It Happen: Call for application. Interviews in person are preferred, although telephone interviews are possible.

INSIDER TIPS: *Preference for positions during the school year is given to summer staff. A strong commitment to the environment and to the importance of each individual child is essential.*

Contact Information: Linda Grier, Director • Camp Friendship • P.O. Box 145 • Palmyra, VA 22963 • Phone:

(800) 873-3223 • Fax: (804) 589-5880 • E-mail: 103075.531@compuserve.com

Camp Horizons

REGION/HQ: Southeast/Virginia • **CATEGORY:** Camp • **POSITION TYPE:** Seasonal • **DURATION:** Year-Round • **IDEAL CANDIDATE:** College Students, Career Changers, Foreigners • **APPLICANT POOL:** Varies • **APPLICANTS ACCEPTED:** Varies

CAMP HORIZONS IS A summer residential camp for children, ages seven to eighteen, and serves as a corporate training center and retreat center for schools, churches, and universities during the fall and spring.

Area and Working Environment: The 240 acres of Camp Horizons are located in the Shenandoah Valley of Virginia, bordering the George Washington National Forest, just a two-hour drive from our nation's capital.

Work/Learn Program Specifics: Summer positions include waterfront counselors, general activities counselors, general riding counselors, kitchen staff, and adventure coordinators (who teach teens white-water rafting, caving, rock climbing, mountain biking, rappelling, scuba diving, hang gliding, backpacking, canoeing, and kayaking). Spring and fall positions include ropes course facilitators, school groups hosts, and maintenance.

Duration: In the summer staff get twenty-four hours off per week and are on duty twenty-four hours per day; in the fall and spring they get one day off per week and work eight to five when no groups are in camp. Staff members are on duty as long as a group needs a staff person.

Compensation and Perks: Staff receive a salary of $1,200 to $1,500 per season, plus room and board.

The Ideal Candidate: First aid and CPR certifications are required and many candidates have lifeguard certification as well. A knowledge of ropes course, rock climbing, adventure skills, and a foreign language (French, Spanish, Russian, or Japanese) is also very helpful.

Making It Happen: Call for application materials. It's best to apply by February for summer positions.

Contact Information: Rajan Bajumpna, Director • Camp Horizons • Route 3, Box 374 • Harrisonburg, VA 22801 • Phone: (540) 896-7600 • Fax: (540) 896-5455 • Toll Free: (800) 729-9230 • E-mail: camphorizons@rica.net • Web Site: www.kidscamps.com/traditional/horizons

Camp Scherman

REGION/HQ: Pacific Northwest/California • **CATEGORY:** Camp • **POSITION TYPE:** Seasonal • **DURATION:** **Summer** • **IDEAL CANDIDATE:** College Students, Career Changers, Foreigners • **APPLICANT POOL:** 250/year • **APPLICANTS ACCEPTED:** 100/year

CAMP SCHERMAN OFFERS AN outdoor camping experience for girls, ages seven to seventeen. Their program revolves around developing a sound Girl Scout program. While girls spend the day involved in swimming, canoeing, and the like, there are also plenty of opportunities to develop leadership skills, become more independent, live in a diverse environment, and learn about living responsibly in the outdoors.

Area and Working Environment: The camp is located on 700 acres in the San Jacinto Mountains, in Southern California. It's a high desert setting surrounded by a number of mountain peaks that are a part of the Pacific Crest Trail. There are two small lakes on the property that supply ample opportunity to canoe, sail, and windsurf.

Work/Learn Program Specifics: Camp counselors have a wide range of program possibilities: canoeing, swimming, nature activities, sailing, windsurfing, arts and crafts, pottery, horseback riding, rock climbing, archery, drama, backpacking, and more.

Duration: The camp season runs from mid-June to late August. There are three, three-day breaks during the summer, when camp closes down, as well as daily and weekly time off. Typically a camp counselor works for $2\frac{1}{2}$ weeks, takes a short break, then is back for two weeks.

Compensation and Perks: Staff members receive a $200-per-week salary, plus room and board.

The Ideal Candidate: It's beneficial that applicants have experience working with children; knowledge of girl scouting; lifeguard certification; sailing, horseback riding, or rock climbing experience; and a love for the outdoors. You also must be able to work the entire camp season.

Making It Happen: Call for application packet. The application period is January through May, although it's best to apply in January/February, especially if you are interested in pursuing a position that has limited openings.

Contact Information: Patty Thomas, Camp Administrator • Camp Scherman • Girl Scout Council Of Orange

County • P.O. Box 3739 • Costa Mesa, CA 92628-3739 • Phone: (714) 979-7900 • Fax: (714) 850-1299

Camp Woodson

REGION/HQ: Southeast/North Carolina • **CATEGORY:** Camp • **POSITION TYPE:** Internship • **DURATION:** Year-Round • **IDEAL CANDIDATE:** College Students, Career Changers, Foreigners • **APPLICANT POOL:** Varies • **APPLICANTS ACCEPTED:** Varies
....

CAMP WOODSON IS A THERAPEUTIC, adventure-oriented camping program operated by the North Carolina Division of Youth Services. Camp Woodson believes that the wilderness provides a unique environment for learning, change, and personal growth. Activities such as hiking, rock climbing, canoeing, urban exploring, and horseback riding are used to address issues of troubled youth. Their approach is to challenge individuals and provide opportunities for success. The camp's students are from diverse backgrounds, but all have been through the court system and are in training school.

Area and Working Environment: Camp Woodson's offices are located on the campus of the Juvenile Evaluation Center in Swannanoa, North Carolina. They operate in and around western North Carolina, using everything from the city streets of Asheville to remote wilderness areas as locations for activities.

Work/Learn Program Specifics: Interns will conduct and process games and perform both individual and group counseling for students, aged thirteen to seventeen, who have come from unstable family situations and have failed in the traditional school system (their range of offenses might include breaking and entering, assault, substance abuse and drug violation, auto theft, or sexual offenses, and their attendance at the camp is voluntary). Interns become role models and friends, with their goal to capture the magic from difficult and challenging situations and make that magic real for the students.

Duration: Working three sessions (five-week sessions, plus one training week between each session) is recommended. This gives the intern an opportunity to experience one session of each shift—activity, hiking, and the weekend shift. Each shift lasts two to three days. Camp Woodson is willing to consider other scheduling options for interns.

Compensation and Perks: Although no compensation is provided, housing and food may be available. Perks include living in the beautiful western North Car-

olina mountains, where there are many opportunities for climbing, hiking, canoeing, and mountain biking.

The Ideal Candidate: Interns typically have backgrounds in human service fields and have experience in leading and facilitating outdoor adventure activities.

Making It Happen: Submit cover letter and resume, then call to arrange an interview. Rolling deadlines.

Contact Information: Marilyn Kaylor, Internship Director • Camp Woodson • 741 Old U.S. Highway 70 • Swannanoa, NC 28778 • Phone: (704) 686-5411 • Fax: (704) 686-8189

Casa Ybel Resort

REGION/HQ: Southeast/Florida • **CATEGORY:** Resort • **POSITION TYPE:** Internship • **DURATION:** Year-Round • **IDEAL CANDIDATE:** College Students, Career Changers, Foreigners • **APPLICANT POOL:** Varies • **APPLICANTS ACCEPTED:** 1–3/term
....

CASA YBEL IS A FAMILY RESORT that offers its guests the full beauty of the island. Casa Ybel Resort includes comprehensive recreation programming for all ages: tennis, beach and watercraft operations, swimming pools, restaurant, pool bar, a souvenir store, and other amenities.

Area and Working Environment: The resort is spread out over thirty acres of beachfront property on the Gulf of Mexico.

Work/Learn Program Specifics: Recreation interns provide quality recreation programs to resort guests by planning and implementing all resort social activities with hands-on attention to pertinent administrative functions. As an intern, you will become part of Casa Ybel's family. They work as a team, expecting 100 percent from each player. Their goal is to offer all guests an atmosphere that allows them the opportunity to relax, play, and—most of all—have fun. With this as their focus, the recreation department uses its enthusiasm and creativity to develop programs that exceed the guests' expectations.

Duration: Duration is negotiable, though it is generally fifteen weeks, full-time. Positions are offered year-round. Must be flexible and willing to work a variety of shifts including evenings, weekends, and some holidays.

Compensation and Perks: Interns receive $105 every two weeks. Housing is provided. Perks include use of on-site facilities (pool, restaurant, and store).

The Ideal Candidate: Applicant must be at least a junior in college, majoring in recreation or a related field. Must present a healthy appearance, a sense of humor, a pleasing personality, and the ability to work well with every age group. CPR and first aid certification is required.

Making It Happen: Submit cover letter indicating specific goals, resume, and list of references.

INSIDER TIPS: *The most important factor in getting involved with our organization is to have that spirit, enthusiasm, creativity, and drive that all recreation professionals want to see. You must remember in your interview to get across these characteristics. Professionals want to let in those who can show that they really want to get in.*

Contact Information: Recreation Director • Casa Ybel Resort • P.O. Box 167 • Sanibel Island, FL 33957 • Phone: (813) 472-3145 • Fax: (813) 472-2109

Celio Outdoor Center

REGION/HQ: Pacific Northwest/California
• **CATEGORY:** Camp • **POSITION TYPE:** Internship/ Seasonal • **DURATION:** Spring/Summer • **IDEAL CANDIDATE:** College Students, Career Changers
• **APPLICANT POOL:** Varies • **APPLICANTS ACCEPTED:** 4/term

CELIO OUTDOOR CENTER IS owned and operated by Camp Fire Boys and Girls, Bay Area Council, and is accredited and an approved site of the American Camping Association. They are dedicated to helping children and teens (ages six to seventeen) to develop into confident, self-directed individuals able to cope with the world around them. In addition to their environmental education programs, Celio Outdoor Center provides a variety of activities. Campers can canoe, swim, sail, and fish in and around beautiful Lake Vera. An archery range and teams course make up part of their 140 acres of woodlands, which provide an excellent area for backpacking and many other adventures.

Area and Working Environment: Nestled beneath tall pine trees, the Celio Outdoor Center is located around a private lake, a few miles outside of Nevada City (in Northern California), at an elevation of 2,500 feet.

Work/Learn Program Specifics: The responsibilities of an intern will include working in all areas of the outdoor center. Interns will be involved with the environmental education programs, camp maintenance, camp management, and weekend programs.

Duration: Positions are available during the spring/ summer.

Compensation and Perks: Interns receive a $125-per-week stipend, with free housing and board.

The Ideal Candidate: They desire individuals with a background in recreation, education, child development, psychology, or related fields, who have had prior experience in working with children. First aid and CPR certifications are required.

Making It Happen: Send a cover letter, resume, and references. You will be called for an interview.

INSIDER TIPS: *Our internship program is new, so the competition is not that great; however, we feel we have an excellent program, which provides a variety of opportunities and makes for a wonderful learning experience. Enthusiasm, motivation to work hard, and assertiveness are the key.*

Contact Information: Dawn Chandler, Environmental Education Director • Celio Outdoor Center • 20864 Rector Rd. • Nevada City, CA 95959 • Phone: (916) 265-4498 • Fax: (916) 265-0876 • E-mail: celioducky @aol.com

Coffee Creek Ranch, Inc.

REGION/HQ: Pacific Northwest/California
• **CATEGORY:** Ranch • **POSITION TYPE:** Internship
• **DURATION:** Year-Round • **IDEAL CANDIDATE:** College Students, Career Changers, Foreigners
• **APPLICANT POOL:** 100/year • **APPLICANTS ACCEPTED:** 8/year

AT COFFEE CREEK RANCH, guests may experience trout fishing, hiking, riding, kayaking, wilderness pack trips, Nordic skiing, health spa use, gold-panning, and use of the rifle range. Coffee Creek Ranch was nominated for *Family Circle's* Family Resort of the Year and received Honorable Mention in 1990–1991.

Area and Working Environment: Their ranch is located on 127 acres in Trinity Center, surrounded by national forest and the Trinity Alps Wilderness Area in Northern California.

Work/Learn Program Specifics: Office, Front Desk, and Accounting: Duties include office cleaning, general bookkeeping, mailings, phone answering, and running of the gift shop. Other responsibilities include loaning out equipment, typing letters, computer work, and helping guests check in and out. They also have a need for kitchen help, including prep chefs and bakers.

Duration: Positions generally last ten to sixteen weeks, depending upon academic requirements. Internships are offered year-round.

Compensation and Perks: Pay depends upon the position and season chosen, generally $700 per month. Room and board are also provided as well as use of the facilities at the ranch, including the exercise room and hot tub.

The Ideal Candidate: Applicants must be flexible and willing to work hard, and computer knowledge is a must for office-related positions.

Making It Happen: Call for application. Rolling deadlines, although, for the summer, candidates who apply by March 1 receive first consideration.

INSIDER TIPS: *The more versatile you are the better. We are looking for a person that never says, "not my job!"*

Contact Information: Ruth Hartman, Owner • Coffee Creek Ranch, Inc. • HC2, Box 4940 • Trinity Center, CA 96091-9502 • Phone: (916) 266-3343 • Fax: (916) 266-3597 • Toll Free: (800) 624-4480

College Settlement/ Kuhn Day Camps

REGION/HQ: Northeast/Pennsylvania • **CATEGORY:** Camp • **POSITION TYPE:** Seasonal • **DURATION:** Year-Round • **IDEAL CANDIDATE:** College Students, Career Changers, Foreigners • **APPLICANT POOL:** 170/year • **APPLICANTS ACCEPTED:** 50/year

THE COLLEGE SETTLEMENT OF PHILADELPHIA operates a day and resident summer camp and residential outdoor school, mostly for seven- to fourteen-year-olds from economically disadvantaged families. Many of these children live in difficult situations and face challenging problems in their daily lives. There are about thirty buildings, including two nature centers, a dining hall, several pavilions, and cabins which serve as living quarters. The resident camp also owns and operates a seventy-five-acre outpost in the central Pennsylvania mountains amidst 6,000 acres of state gamelands.

Area and Working Environment: The camp is situated in the suburban town of Horsham, fifteen miles north of Philadelphia. The camp was originally farmland before it became a children's camp. There are 265 acres of fields, forest, trails, and streams that are used as

classrooms, as well as a three-acre lake full of frogs, fish, and turtles.

Work/Learn Program Specifics: The Teen Adventure program offers a once in a lifetime chance for urban youth to experience the thrill of camping, hiking, and adventuring on the east coast. Trip leaders plan custom trips and activities and take their groups by van to Maine, West Virginia, and New England. Summer camp staff teach and share experiences with children in a fun and caring environment, with positions varying from counselor to lifeguard.

Duration: Positions offered year-round.

Compensation and Perks: Starting salary for all positions is $1,600, with adjustments made relative to experience and qualifications. All housing and meals are provided.

The Ideal Candidate: Teen Adventure applicants should have experience in outdoor pursuits (climbing, backpacking, rafting, or kayaking preferred), be enthusiastic, work well with others, and have a sense of fun mixed with a great dose of common sense. Base camp applicants should have experience with children and a general understanding of and respect for the natural environment. People who are open-minded and enjoy making a difference in others' lives are strongly encouraged to apply.

Making It Happen: Call for application materials.

Contact Information: Karyn Mcgee, Program Director • College Settlement/Kuhn Day Camps • 600 Witmer Rd. • Horsham, PA 19044 • Phone: (215) 542-7974 • Fax: (215) 542-7457 • E-mail: camps2@aol.com

Colorado Mountain Ranch

REGION/HQ: Rocky Mountains/Colorado • **CATEGORY:** Camp • **POSITION TYPE:** Seasonal • **DURATION:** Summer • **IDEAL CANDIDATE:** College Students, Career Changers, Foreigners • **APPLICANT POOL:** 300/year • **APPLICANTS ACCEPTED:** 75/year

COLORADO MOUNTAIN RANCH offers a residential leadership-training program for teens, ages fifteen to seventeen, and a separate day-camp program for local children.

Area and Working Environment: Nestled in the pine and aspen forests and wildflower meadows of Colorado's Rocky Mountains, the ranch encompasses 180

acres at an elevation of 8,500 feet. The camp is bordered on the east by the Gold Hill Mining District; and to the west, Roosevelt National Forest rises to the magnificent snowcapped peaks of the Continental Divide.

Work/Learn Program Specifics: The Activity Program abounds in outdoor fun and adventure. They also have their own horses for Western riding on beautiful Rocky Mountain trails. Those who like may help with horse care, training, and overnight horseback trips. Other regular highlights include challenge ropes course for problem solving and team building, swimming in their heated pool, gymnastics and trampolining, archery and riflery, arts and crafts, Native American lore, natural ecology, environmental awareness, organic gardening, gold mining, history, drama, the camp newspaper, games and sports, rowing, canoeing, sailing, low-impact camp crafts and wilderness ethics, high-country camping, hiking, and backpacking.

Duration: Full-time, summer position.

Compensation and Perks: Staff members receive a stipend of $900 per season, plus room and board. The mountain climate and setting are perfect for a full range of healthful, outdoor activities, from swimming and riding to playing in the high-country snow fields. Days are generally sunny and warm, nights cool, and the air is usually crisp and clear. Living with others and working together as a team, staff members grow in love and understanding of themselves, each other, and life.

The Ideal Candidate: Counselors are selected on the basis of abilities, enthusiasm, creativity, sincerity, sensitivity, and commitment to guiding children toward their full potential.

Making It Happen: Call for application and brochure. Open deadline.

The ranch is a song; it is a song of happiness, of love, of peace and of understanding. It is a song which had a beginning, but which can never die, for too many people have heard this song. The intertwining of the melodies will continue until the song has become a part of everyone who has come here. That song will go out from here in the hearts and minds of those who know it and spread itself and become a part of all it touches. Let your song reflect that which you are and will become here, and carry it with you when you leave.

Contact Information: Mike Walker, Owner • Colorado Mountain Ranch • 10063 Gold Hill Rd. • Boulder, CO 80302-9770 • Phone: (303) 442-4557 • Fax: (303) 442-4873

Colvig Silver Camps

REGION/HQ: Rocky Mountains/Colorado
• **CATEGORY:** Camp • **POSITION TYPE:** Internship/Seasonal • **DURATION:** Summer • **IDEAL CANDIDATE:** College Students, Career Changers, Foreigners
• **APPLICANT POOL:** 300–350/year • **APPLICANTS ACCEPTED:** Varies
··

COLVIG SILVER CAMPS IS A residential, wilderness-oriented summer camp serving children seven to seventeen years of age. Their program is unique in that they have a mix of traditional summer activities and backcountry wilderness trips. In-camp activities include (but are not limited to) swimming, games, sports, arts and crafts, campfires, skits, fishing, boating, target sports, ropes course, climbing wall, mountain biking, and horseback riding. Backcountry wilderness trips include alpine backpacking, mountain climbing, rock climbing, desert backpacking/Indian ruins, mountain biking, windsurfing, flatwater canoeing and rafting, white-water tubing, badlands, survival skills, and horse packing.

Area and Working Environment: Located in the San Juan Mountains of southwest Colorado, the camp is a short drive/hike from high alpine regions (14,000-foot peaks), desert canyon areas (including Anasazi ruins), low alpine regions, mountain lakes and streams, raging rivers, and ponderosa pine forests.

Work/Learn Program Specifics: Program coordinators organize and implement their camp's daily schedule, with input from both staff and campers. Head counselors and assistant counselors are responsible for planning and leading in-camp activities and wilderness trips and living with a group of four to six campers. Arts and crafts coordinators develop crafts programs for all age levels and supervise the craft shop when campers are involved in craft projects. Wranglers/assistant wranglers are responsible for planning and teaching western-style riding and tack care. The expedition coordinator packs food and equipment for all expedition trips leaving camp.

Duration: Campers are with you for three, four, and five weeks at a time between early June and late August. Mandatory staff training begins in early June.

Compensation and Perks: Staff members receive $700 to $1,000 per summer and room, board, laundry, and worker's compensation.

The Ideal Candidate: All applicants must be over eighteen, with one year beyond high school. Current lifeguarding certificate is very beneficial.

Making It Happen: Call for application materials. After your application is received, they follow up on your references, then schedule an on-site or phone interview. Positions are filled on a first-come, first-served basis.

Contact Information: Scott Kelley, Program Director • Colvig Silver Camps • 9665 Florida Rd. • Durango, CO 81301 • Phone: (970) 247-2564 • Fax: (970) 247-2547 • E-mail: 76601.2705@compuserve.com • Web Site: www.kidscamps.com/traditional/colvig-silver

Costa Azul Adventure Resort

REGION/HQ: Mexico/California • **CATEGORY:** Resort • **POSITION TYPE:** Unique Experience • **DURATION:** Year-Round • **IDEAL CANDIDATE:** College Students, Career Changers, Foreigners • **APPLICANT POOL:** Varies • **APPLICANTS ACCEPTED:** Varies

Costa Azul's resort atmosphere is relaxing and casual. To preserve the natural feel of the resort, there are no phones or faxes at Costa Azul. The resort has twenty-eight units, a pool with swim-up bar, an open air restaurant, a sand volleyball court, and a poolside barefoot bar. Costa Azul specializes in running ecology and adventure trips out of the resort. Trips include sea kayaking, whale watching, surfing, horseback riding, bird watching, and snorkeling. Their goal is to continue to bring educational and academic value to the trips and the entire vacation experience.

Area and Working Environment: Located thirty minutes north of Puerto Vallarta, Mexico, Costa Azul sits on its own white, sandy beach in the tiny fishing village of San Francisco.

Work/Learn Program Specifics: Adventure, Guide/Guest Services: Staff are required to lead some of the following trips: kayaking, snorkeling, hiking, bird watching, botany, horseback riding, biking, surfing, and boating. Other responsibilities include attending to guests, activity and trip planning, on-site promotion of activities, working with several employees, and implementing recommendations for their tour program.

Duration: Applicants must be able to relocate to Mexico for at least six months. Start dates begin every month.

Compensation and Perks: You will receive $200 per month for living expenses, on-site housing, all meals and beverages, a round-trip plane ticket or $300 (whichever is less) upon completion of six months of work, and complimentary hotel rooms for visiting family or friends.

The Ideal Candidate: Applicants must have an outgoing personality, enjoy working and serving the public, current CPR certification, the ability to relocate to Mexico for at least six months, and been enrolled in Spanish courses or have a working knowledge of the language. Other qualifications and experiences that would make the applicant stand out include a background in environmental studies; knowledge of or interest in plants and wildlife; service-industry background; mountain biking, snorkeling, or scuba diving skills; first aid/life-saving training; prior resort experience; ocean kayaking experience; knowledge of horses; and recreation management experience.

Making It Happen: Send resume and cover letter. If you would like additional information about the positions, please call. Rolling deadlines.

Contact Information: Personnel Director • Costa Azul Adventure Resort • 224 Avenida Del Mar, #D • San Clemente, CA 92672-4011 • Phone: (714) 498-3223 • Fax: (714) 498-6300 • Toll Free: (800) 365-7613

Coulter Lake Guest Ranch

REGION/HQ: Rocky Mountains/Colorado • **CATEGORY:** Ranch • **POSITION TYPE:** Seasonal • **DURATION:** Winter/Summer • **IDEAL CANDIDATE:** College Students, Career Changers, Foreigners • **APPLICANT POOL:** 200/year • **APPLICANTS ACCEPTED:** 8/year

Located on the scenic western slopes of the Rockies, with a sparkling blue lake for swimming, fishing, and boating, Coulter Lake Guest Ranch has eight cabins scattered along the lakefront, among the aspen trees. The owners were annual guests at this ranch for eight years before finally buying it. Twenty-eight hours of horseback riding are offered each week, along with square dances, bonfires, and sing-alongs. The trout-stocked lake has rowboats available to guests. Any trout you catch you can eat for dinner. The ranch is also open for snow sports during the winter months.

Area and Working Environment: The ranch is nestled in a small mountain valley at 8,100 feet, just 21 miles northeast of Rifle.

Work/Learn Program Specifics: Positions available: inside staff (housekeepers, servers, bussers, cleaners, dishwashers, and others), wranglers/trail guides, and maintenance staff.

Duration: Positions are offered year-round. Work schedules vary throughout the week.

Compensation and Perks: Staff members receive $100 or more per week, plus tip pool. Housing, meals, necessities, laundry, and horseback riding are provided. The staff is also encouraged to "play guest" on days off.

The Ideal Candidate: They prefer a healthy, active, organized, responsible, and tactful person. Applicants must also have a wholesome attitude, good people skills, and a clean vocabulary. The ability to play the guitar is also a plus.

Making It Happen: Send resume and a cover letter describing job desired and a brief rundown on experience, if any. A snapshot is appreciated. Rolling deadlines. Phone interviews are conducted after your application is received.

Contact Information: Sue Benzinger, Owner • Coulter Lake Guest Ranch • P.O. Box 906 • Rifle, CO 81650 • Phone: (970) 625-1473 • Toll Free: (800) 858-3046

Crested Butte Mountain Resort

REGION/HQ: Rocky Mountains/Colorado • **CATEGORY:** Ski Resort • **POSITION TYPE:** Seasonal • **DURATION:** Winter/Spring • **IDEAL CANDIDATE:** College Students, Career Changers, Foreigners • **APPLICANT POOL:** 250/year • **APPLICANTS ACCEPTED:** 60/year

CRESTED BUTTE MOUNTAIN RESORT is the fifth largest ski area in the state. Known for its awesome extreme skiing and its funky Victorian architecture, Crested Butte remains one of the last undiscovered ski towns in the west—"The way Aspen used to be and the way Vail never was." Crested Butte is the site of the U.S. Extreme Skiing and the U.S. Extreme Snowboarding Championships.

Area and Working Environment: The resort is located in the south-central mountains of Colorado.

Work/Learn Program Specifics: How would you like to experience a winter ski season working at one of Colorado's premier ski resorts? Then participate in Crested Butte's College Student Employee Program. Your winter will be spent having fun while learning about resort operations. You'll ski like crazy and live in a resort community with about sixty other college students from around the United States and other parts of the world. Meanwhile, you will be earning a scholarship to return to school, competitive wages, and an unlimited ski pass valued at $800. Seasonal employment is offered in many different departments, including lift operations, children's ski school, hotel operations, and guest services.

Duration: Positions are available from mid-November through mid-April, full-time (thirty to forty hours per week).

Compensation and Perks: Besides providing a guaranteed job with competitive wages ($5.50/hour), they also provide affordably priced, pre-arranged housing, an unlimited ski pass (valued at over $800), and by working the entire season, you also earn a $500 scholarship. With this scholarship you may return to the accredited college or university of your choice within a year of completing this program. The student employees live in a beautiful resort area called Three Rivers Resort, about twenty minutes from the town of Crested Butte. The accommodations are cozy log cabins, many with wood stoves to make the cabin feel rustic but comfortable. Wildlife such as bighorn sheep, mule deer, elk, and wintering bald eagles can be viewed from your cabin window. Other perks include discounted health club memberships, special events, and parties.

The Ideal Candidate: You must be a student or recent graduate with a passion for the snow and lots of enthusiasm.

Making It Happen: Call to receive an application packet and a recruiting schedule. Most interviews are done on various campuses during April, although applications are accepted as late as September.

INSIDER TIPS: *A personal interview really helps your chances of being accepted. Ask for a recruiting schedule, and if we are not visiting your school, try to meet us at a school that we are visiting. You can also arrange for an interview at the resort throughout the summer if positions are still available.*

Contact Information: Karen Robinson, Student Coordinator • Crested Butte Mountain Resort • 12 Snowmass Rd. • P.O. Box A • Mt. Crested Butte, CO 81225 • Phone: (970) 349-2312 • Fax: (970) 349-2250 • Job Hotline: (970) 349-4777 • Web Site: www.coolworks.com/showme/crested_butte

Custer State Park Resort Company

REGION/HQ: Rocky Mountains/South Dakota • **CATEGORY:** Resort • **POSITION TYPE:** Internship/Seasonal • **DURATION:** Spring-Fall • **IDEAL CANDIDATE:** High School Students, College Students, Career Changers, Retired Folks, Foreigners • **APPLICANT POOL:** Varies • **APPLICANTS ACCEPTED:** 250/year

IN THE SUMMER OF 1874, Major General George Custer led a scientific expedition through the Black Hills of South Dakota. When word spread that the expedition had discovered gold near the present-day city of Custer, prospectors and settlers soon followed. After the turn of the century, visionaries like South Dakota Governor Peter Norbeck realized that our environment was more precious than gold. In 1919, he urged the South Dakota State Legislature to preserve our natural resources and designate 48,000 acres near Custer as a permanent state park. Today, Custer State Park spreads across a total of 73,000 acres.

Area and Working Environment: Custer State Park is where the bison roam free, where granite spires tower over pristine lakes, where clear mountain streams flow through unspoiled forests.

Work/Learn Program Specifics: You may work in one of four resorts that are managed by Custer State Park Resort Company: the State Game Lodge and Resort, Blue Bell Lodge and Resort, Legion Lake Resort, or Sylvan Lake Resort. Positions are available in these departments: Food and Beverage, Rooms Division, Maintenance, Retail/Sales, Interpretive Guide Services (including jeep driver/interpretive guide and wrangler/interpretive guide), Accounting, Security, Entertainment, and Management. They offer a management trainee internship program, where interns will assist management staff in all areas of resort operations and receive training in all areas.

Compensation and Perks: All employees are paid a monthly salary. Meals are provided, as is housing, if needed. An end of season bonus is also available to all who finish their agreements.

The Ideal Candidate: All employees must be at least sixteen years of age.

Making It Happen: Call for application materials.

Contact Information: Phil Lampert, President • Custer State Park Resort Company • HC 83, Box 74 • Custer, SD 57730 • Phone: (605) 255-4541 • Fax: (605) 255-4706 • Toll Free: (800) 658-3530 • E-mail: custer@iway1.iw.net

Diamond Peak Ski Resort

REGION/HQ: Pacific Northwest/Nevada • **CATEGORY:** Ski Resort • **POSITION TYPE:** Seasonal • **DURATION:** Winter/Summer • **IDEAL CANDIDATE:** College Students, Career Changers, Foreigners • **APPLICANT POOL:** 500/year • **APPLICANTS ACCEPTED:** 300/year

SUPERB! THAT'S WHAT GUESTS think about Lake Tahoe's premier family ski resort, and that's what Diamond Peak strives for—excellence in everything that they do. At Diamond Peak, you will find spectacular views, incredible skiing, service that is second to none, and value-priced programs guaranteed to make every ski day worthwhile.

Area and Working Environment: The resort is located in Lake Tahoe's showcase community—Incline Village. You will experience spectacular alpine and cross-country skiing, with incomparable views of Lake Tahoe.

Work/Learn Program Specifics: Winter seasonal positions include lift operator, ticket checker, ski instructor, child ski center instructor, ticket cashier, groomer/snowmaker, ski patrol, receptionist/snow reporter, rental shop, ski technician, food and beverage (server, bartender, cook, busperson, and dishwasher), property maintenance, shuttle driver, and parking lot attendant. Summer job opportunities with their parent company are available in these departments: golf, tennis complex, and parks and recreation.

Duration: Most winter positions commence in the beginning of December and continue through mid-April (depending on the snow conditions). Inquire about summer terms. Full- and part-time positions are available.

Compensation and Perks: Hourly wage dependent on position, but wages range from $5.00 to $13.50 per hour. Perks include free skiing/snowboarding, free basic ski equipment rental, free lessons, food and beverage discounts, and access to the Incline Village Recreation Center.

Making It Happen: Call for application and details. It's best to attend their job fair held mid-October each year.

INSIDER TIPS: *Attending the job fair is a great way to learn more about employment opportunities.*

Contact Information: Elizabeth Coffey, Business Office Manager • Diamond Peak Ski Resort • 1210 Ski Way • Incline Village, NV 89451 • Phone: (702) 832-1126 • Fax: (702) 832-1281 • Toll Free: (800) 468-2463 • E-mail: IVGID@sierra.net

Drowsy Water Ranch

REGION/HQ: Rocky Mountains/Colorado • **CATEGORY:** Ranch • **POSITION TYPE:** Internship/ Seasonal • **DURATION:** Summer • **IDEAL CANDIDATE:** High School Students, College Students, Career Changers, Retired Folks, Foreigners • **APPLICANT POOL:** 300/year • **APPLICANTS ACCEPTED:** 20/year

DROWSY WATER RANCH IS A genuine Western ranch on 640 acres in Colorado's beautiful Rocky Mountains. They have a complete program of horseback riding, swimming, horseshoes, steak fries, trout fishing, square dancing, wilderness jeep trips, song fests, campfires, hayrides, movies, pack trips, staff entertainment, gymkhana rodeos, raft trips, children's programs, and much more!

Area and Working Environment: The ranch, at 8,300 feet, borders thousands of acres of backcountry and the Arapahoe National Forest. They are close to Rocky Mountain National Park, near the Colorado River, and in the famous ranch country of the Middle Park of Colorado. It is a short drive to Granby, Shadow Mountain, and Grand Lakes.

Work/Learn Program Specifics: Positions include cooks, horse wranglers/trail guides, maintenance, counselors, housekeepers, and waitstaff. Jobs require guest interaction at all levels, including country dancing and staff shows.

Duration: Applicants must be able to stay, at least, from late May through the end of August to be considered. The ranch stays open until September 15.

Compensation and Perks: Staff members receive $475 per month, plus room and board. Many staff members make $3,000 or more in tips per summer! Perks—the staff can participate in all Dude Ranch activities and facilities; this is a great people-oriented experience.

Making It Happen: Call after January 1 for application. Telephone interviews are conducted with viable candidates.

INSIDER TIPS: *Dates of availability, many times, determine if a person can get hired.*

Contact Information: Ken and Randy Sue Fosha, Owners • Drowsy Water Ranch • P.O. Box 147-BD • Granby,

CO 80446 • Phone: (970) 725-3456 • Fax: (970) 725-3611 • Toll Free: (800) 845-2292

Ebner Camps

REGION/HQ: Northeast/Connecticut • **CATEGORY:** Camp • **POSITION TYPE:** Seasonal • **DURATION:** Summer • **IDEAL CANDIDATE:** College Students, Career Changers, Foreigners • **APPLICANT POOL:** Varies • **APPLICANTS ACCEPTED:** 25/year

EBNER CAMPS RUNS TWO children's resident summer camps: Awosting Camp (for boys), which is the oldest private boys' program in the country, and Chinqueka Camp (for girls). Campers range from age six to fifteen and are from all over the world, as is the staff.

Area and Working Environment: The camps are located in Litchfield Hills, in northwest Connecticut, which is 2 1/2 hours from Boston and two hours from New York City.

Work/Learn Program Specifics: Summer camp counselors will have the shared responsibility of running a group cabin as co-counselors as well as working as instructors in selected activity areas. Teaching positions include: go-carting, minibikes, woodshop, crafts, pottery/ceramics, tennis, archery, photography, computers, outdoor camping, waterfront activities, gymnastics, fencing, athletics/sports, golf, mountain biking, martial arts/wrestling/weightlifting, journalism, video/ film, drama, music, and dance. Other positions include kitchen aides and camp nurse.

Duration: Their camp season operates for eight weeks, usually the third week in June until the third week of August. Counselors report five days earlier than the campers for a five-day intensive orientation period covering the philosophy of the camp, ideals, objectives, program schedules, and material that may be helpful in making your summer at camp as successful as possible. You will receive one day and three or four nights off per week.

Compensation and Perks: Salaries range from $1,000 to $1,600 for the eight week camp season. Perks include free lodging, meals, a uniform shirt, laundry, a complimentary suntan, and a busload of memories. A bonus of 10 percent of contract salary is given for a "job well done!" Tipping is allowed, which could add up to an additional $300 to $500.

The Ideal Candidate: Candidates must have some basic skill in one of the camp's teaching positions, and a knowledge of other languages is helpful when dealing with campers and staff that originate from all over the world.

Making It Happen: Submit cover letter stating your interest and requesting an application, along with your resume. There is a late-April deadline, but it's best to apply in January or February.

Contact Information: Buzz Ebner, Director • Ebner Camps • 10 Breezy Hill Rd. • Harwinton, CT 06791 • Phone: (860) 485-9566 • Fax: (860) 485-1681 • Toll Free: (800) 662-2677 • E-mail: camps@netrax.net • Web Site: www.awosting.com

Fairview Lake YMCA Camps

REGION/HQ: Northeast/New Jersey • **CATEGORY:** Environmental Education • **POSITION TYPE:** Internship • **DURATION:** Year-Round • **IDEAL CANDIDATE:** College Students, Career Changers, Foreigners • **APPLICANT POOL:** 10–40/year • **APPLICANTS ACCEPTED:** 2–5/term

FAIRVIEW LAKE YMCA CAMPS provide environmental education and conference programming for students in first through twelfth grades, as well as adult groups. The camp's mission is to improve the quality of life in the community by fostering healthful living, developing responsible leaders and citizens, strengthening the family, promoting the equality of all persons, protecting the environment, and utilizing community members and organizations to solve contemporary problems.

Area and Working Environment: Located on 600 acres of mountains and forests, the center offers miles of trails for hiking, an indoor recreation room, athletic fields, a lighted tennis and basketball complex, cross-country skiing, boating, and canoeing.

Work/Learn Program Specifics: Intern responsibilities will include participation in staff training; preparation, planning, and teaching of environmental lessons on a variety of subjects, including aquatic ecology, forest/field ecology, orienteering, wildlife/tracking, geology, and survival skills; providing instruction on the Action Socialization Experience Course; completion of a project chosen in consultation with the director; leading or assisting in up to four evening activities a week; assisting at dining hall orientation and meal service when needed; assisting housekeeping and office staff; providing environmental education and

recreational programming and services to conference groups; and special assignments as designated.

Duration: Internships are available in two sessions: March through June and September through November.

Compensation and Perks: Interns are paid a stipend of $150 per week, plus room and board. Staff housing provides a semi-private room with kitchen/living room complex.

The Ideal Candidate: Students of sophomore status or above who are majoring in environmental science/studies, education, recreation, or a related field are desired. Lifeguard training, first aid, and CPR certifications preferred, but training may be provided by the camp.

Making It Happen: Submit resume and cover letter. Open deadline.

Contact Information: Christina Henriksen, Director • Fairview Lake YMCA Camps • 1035 Fairview Lake Rd. • Newton, NJ 07860 • Phone: (201) 383-9282 • Fax: (201) 383-6386

Fresh Air Fund

REGION/HQ: Northeast/New York • **CATEGORY:** Camp • **POSITION TYPE:** Seasonal • **DURATION:** Summer • **IDEAL CANDIDATE:** College Students, Career Changers, Foreigners • **APPLICANT POOL:** Varies • **APPLICANTS ACCEPTED:** 360/year

THE FRESH AIR FUND IS A nonprofit organization that provides New York City youngsters with completely free camping programs. The fund operates five camps, serving boys and girls between eight and fifteen years old. In natural and rustic surroundings, campers learn to respect the environment and its wildlife. The first priority of camp is to have fun away from the hot and noisy streets of New York City. In addition, all activities are designed to provide challenges, build self-esteem, develop leadership and social skills, stimulate sharing and trust, encourage openness and cooperation, and create a sense of community.

Area and Working Environment: The five camps are located on the Sharpe Reservation, sixty-five miles north of New York City. Sharpe is a 3,000-acre preserve, with forests, fields, lakes, and streams.

Work/Learn Program Specifics: Counselors are important people in the eyes of boys and girls who have just been introduced to a new and exciting world. Counselors teach new skills, answer questions about unfamiliar sights and sounds, and help plan days filled with fun and discovery. In addition to general camp counselors, the fund hires summer staff in supervisory positions and for jobs requiring special skills. These positions include village leaders, waterfront director and staff, program specialists, farm staff, and nutritionists.

Duration: The camp program is offered year-round; however most positions are offered during the summer.

Compensation and Perks: A competitive salary, plus room and board, is offered. A travel allowance is also provided for those who are traveling over 300 miles to the camp.

The Ideal Candidate: Applicants must be at least eighteen years of age, have completed their freshman year of college, and have previous experience with children. The most admirable quality is a sincere motivation to work with inner-city children. You will become a guide and role model to campers as they explore the beauty of nature and discover the fun of the great outdoors.

Making It Happen: Call for application materials. Rolling deadlines. Applicants not living in New York will be given phone interviews.

Contact Information: Thomas Karger, Associate Executive Director • Fresh Air Fund • 1040 Avenue of the Americas • New York, NY 10018 • Phone: (212) 221-0900 • Fax: (212) 302-7875 • Toll Free: (800) 367-0003 • E-mail: freshair@freshair.org • Web Site: www.freshair.org

Grand Targhee Ski & Summer Resort

REGION/HQ: Rocky Mountains/Wyoming • **CATEGORY:** Ski Resort • **POSITION TYPE:** Seasonal • **DURATION:** Winter/Summer • **IDEAL CANDIDATE:** High School Students, College Students, Career Changers, Retired Folks, Foreigners • **APPLICANT POOL:** 400/year • **APPLICANTS ACCEPTED:** 75/year

GRAND TARGHEE IS A SMALL, family-oriented resort nestled in the pines at 8,000 feet on the west side of the spectacular Teton Mountain range. Over 500 inches of annual snowfall provides some of the best skiing conditions during the winter, and you'll find miles of mountain-bike trails and terrain in the summer. For music lovers, Targhee is known for their great music festivals during the summer.

Work/Learn Program Specifics: Everyone at the resort works hard and is part of a professional team. You will also have the opportunity to become acquainted with a

large number of fellow employees from around the country. Targhee offers typical resort jobs in these departments: Mountain, Guest Services, Accounting/Administrative, Maintenance, Lodging, Food and Beverage, Retail, and Rental.

Duration: The summer season runs from June 1 to October 1; the winter season runs November 15 to April 15. You will work thirty to forty hours per week.

Compensation and Perks: Employees receive an hourly wage, a free season ski pass with reciprocal skiing privileges in Jackson Hole, Wyoming, and employee meal and retail discounts. Reasonable housing is available nearby, and the resort's free employee bus accommodates most work schedules.

The Ideal Candidate: They're looking for energetic, good-humored, and responsible people with great personalities.

Making It Happen: Call for application materials and ask about their job fair in late summer and fall. They begin hiring employees for the winter starting in August; for the summer, in March.

Contact Information: Dana Atkinson, Personnel • Grand Targhee Ski & Summer Resort • Ski Hill Rd. • Box SKI • Alta, WY 83422 • Phone: (307) 353-2300 • Fax: (307) 353-8148 • Toll Free: (800) 827-4433

Grand View Lodge, Golf & Tennis Club

REGION/HQ: Great Lakes/Minnesota • **CATEGORY:** Resort • **POSITION TYPE:** Seasonal • **DURATION:** Spring-Fall • **IDEAL CANDIDATE:** College Students, Career Changers, Foreigners • **APPLICANT POOL:** Varies • **APPLICANTS ACCEPTED:** 90/year

SPEND YOUR SUMMER ON the most beautiful lake in central Minnesota, playing golf on fifty-four holes or tennis on Grand View Lodge's eleven courts. Lay out on their 1,500-foot beach, or swim in their indoor pool and jacuzzi. Meet people your own age from all over the country and overseas (over half of their 200 employees are college students from the United States and abroad). In operation since 1919, Grand View Lodge, Golf & Tennis Club is an established site on the National Register of Historic Places. The facility has been owned and operated by the same family since 1940.

Area and Working Environment: The lodge is located fourteen miles north of Brainerd, Minnesota, on beautiful Gull Lake, 140 miles northwest of Minneapolis.

Work/Learn Program Specifics: Positions are available in these departments: Dining Room/Banquets (waitperson/busser), Kitchen (cooks/prep cooks), Housekeeping, Convention Services (setup staff and bartenders), Beach/Children's Program (attendants and counselors), and Golf Course. In addition, they have a number of supervisory positions available in each area, based on experience, responsibilities, and length of time available to work.

Duration: Grand View is open in late April and closes in late October. Many staff work the full season, others have shorter seasons, depending on their school schedules. The lodge especially needs people who can work April/May and September/October. Generally employees work up to forty hours per week, over six days. It is often necessary to work in more than one department to achieve your hours for the week.

Compensation and Perks: Wages start at $4.75 per hour. Employees can live at the resort in staff housing and eat meals in the employee cafeterias. The room charge is $90 per month, but does not include meals. A $30-per-month credit will be given back to you if you fulfill your contract. Perks include free golf and tennis, use of watersports equipment, beachfront, and great bike trails.

The Ideal Candidate: Grand View is interested in all outgoing people, and although hospitality experience is helpful, it is not necessary.

Making It Happen: Send cover letter and resume requesting an application. Rolling deadlines. The length of time an employee is able to work is a primary consideration when staff is chosen.

Contact Information: Paul Welch, Operations Manager • Grand View Lodge, Golf & Tennis Club • South 134 Nokomis Ave. • Nisswa, MN 56468 • Phone: (218) 963-2234 • Fax: (218) 963-2269

Harmel's Ranch Resort

REGION/HQ: Rocky Mountains/Colorado
• **CATEGORY:** Ranch • **POSITION TYPE:** Internship/ Seasonal • **DURATION:** Summer • **IDEAL CANDIDATE:** College Students, Career Changers, Foreigners • **APPLICANT POOL:** 300/year • **APPLICANTS ACCEPTED:** 35/year

HARMEL'S RANCH RESORT consists of approximately 300 acres of trees, water, and meadowland in a beautiful valley surrounded by the Gunnison National Forest. The ranch complex is composed of a variety of accommodations, including a poolside lodge, modern family cottages and suites, the main headquarters, and office buildings. Harmel's is of the finest guest ranches in America, due in part to the excellent service given to their guests for more than thirty years.

Area and Working Environment: The ranch is located in the Rocky Mountains, at the confluence of Spring Creek and Taylor River, halfway between Gunnison and Aspen, near the Crested Butte ski area.

Work/Learn Program Specifics: Harmel's generally does not hire people for a particular job, but instead hires the best people possible and puts them where they are best suited to help Harmel's obtain their goal of total guest satisfaction. Positions include kitchen help, waitstaff, housekeeping, store keepers, general maintenance, activity coordinators, and wranglers.

Duration: The staff works a five-day workweek of approximately forty-eight hours per week, mid-May through September 30. Harmel's needs employees to arrive prior to their opening, others who can stay through their closing, and students who can only work June through August. They try to accommodate individual schedules as much as possible.

Compensation and Perks: Staff members receive $450 per month (and pooled tips), plus room, board, and laundry. Tips generally net each staff member an additional $300 per month. Housing is in dormitory-style bunkhouses. On your days off (or spare time) enjoy horseback riding, mountain biking, white-water rafting, swimming, hiking, fishing, rock climbing, and the great outdoors.

The Ideal Candidate: They are looking for genuinely friendly people with high standards and outstanding personalities. They will consider only sincere and personable applicants who are not afraid to work, who can get along with a diverse group of people, and who are ready to help give the guests the best vacation they have ever had.

Making It Happen: Call for application. Send completed application, resume, a recent photograph, and a short letter by the end of February.

Contact Information: Brad Milner, General Manager • Harmel's Ranch Resort • P.O. Box 399 • Almont, CO 81210 • Phone: (970) 641-1740 • Fax: (970) 641-1944

Hilton Head Island Hilton Resort

REGION/HQ: Southeast/South Carolina • **CATEGORY:** Resort • **POSITION TYPE:** Internship • **DURATION:** Year-Round • **IDEAL CANDIDATE:** College Students • **APPLICANT POOL:** 50–60/term • **APPLICANTS ACCEPTED:** 25–30/year

••

THE RESORT IS A SHELTERED part of Palmetto Dunes Resort, a private, 2,000-acre retreat on the Atlantic Ocean. With three miles of Atlantic beach, tranquil lagoons, champion golf, a twenty-five-court tennis center, restaurants, nightclubs, shopping, and a deepwater marina, Palmetto Dunes offers a more rewarding spectrum of activities than any other resort on the island.

Area and Working Environment: Hilton Resort is an oasis of lush tranquillity overlooking three miles of white sand beach on Hilton Head Island, forty-five miles from Savannah.

Work/Learn Program Specifics: Recreation Interns: The Hilton Resort has one of the largest internship programs in the country. Interns will be involved with many different aspects of the operation, including school and daily reports, conference group recreation, cross-training, programming, health club operations, recreator-on-duty, sun touched attendant, bike rentals, and lucky loggerhead. Involvement will also include one or two of the following coordinator positions: convention, fitness, marketing/promotions, revenue and sales, special events, youth/teen/family, purchasing, equipment, historian, or administrative.

Duration: Internships are on a trimester system, each of which is sixteen weeks long. There is flexibility regarding exact dates.

Compensation and Perks: The salary is $5.15 per hour. Interns will be housed in fully furnished condominiums and will be given two meals in the employee cafeteria per day. The $200 rent will be deducted from each paycheck. For additional pay, interns can work part-time in other resort departments.

The Ideal Candidate: The program is designed for college students who are required to do an internship for their college degree. Interns should be energetic, service- and guest-oriented, thoughtful, dedicated, and self-motivated.

Making It Happen: Call or write for more information. Deadlines: spring—November 15; summer—April 1; and fall—July 1.

INSIDER TIPS: *We need interns who love to work with people and enjoy the resort industry.*

Contact Information: Meg Hooper, Recreation Director • Hilton Head Island Hilton Resort • P.O. Box 6165 • Hilton Head Island, SC 29938 • Phone: (803) 842-8000 • Fax: (803) 842-4988 • Toll Free: (800) 845-8001

Incline Village General Improvement District

REGION/HQ: Pacific Northwest/Nevada • **CATEGORY:** Resort • **POSITION TYPE:** Internship/Seasonal • **DURATION:** Year-Round • **IDEAL CANDIDATE:** College Students, Career Changers, Foreigners • **APPLICANT POOL:** Varies • **APPLICANTS ACCEPTED:** Varies

••

THE INCLINE VILLAGE GENERAL Improvement District (IVGID) has a great internship program, as well as wonderful facilities. Students are given many different opportunities to broaden their skills in the recreation field. The recreation center is a 37,200-square-foot, first-class complex offering a wide variety of activities for all ages and interests in a natural setting.

Area and Working Environment: Incline Village is located on the north side of beautiful Lake Tahoe. The recreation center is centrally located within the district.

Work/Learn Program Specifics: Recreation positions include sports leaders, who officiate, keep score, and provide site supervision for various sports programs; recreation hosts (at the recreation center) check in members, issue towels and equipment, collect daily fees, cashier, and assist members with their needs and requests; school leaders work with the youth program in scheduling and leading activities for youth five to twelve years old; day camp leaders organize, schedule, and lead activities for youth during the summer and school holiday breaks; child caregivers work with other childcare providers in the recreation center; park maintenance staff will work alongside the park's leadsman in maintaining and upgrading parks, beaches, sport fields, the tennis center, and the recreation center complex (summer only). Other positions include the executive and championship golf courses, Diamond Peak Ski Resort, food and beverage, administration and accounting, human resources, and information systems.

Duration: All internships are designed around twenty hours of paid work in various part-time positions within the department. Another twenty hours per week is on a volunteer basis and consists of administrative work for the department. Positions are offered year-round.

Compensation and Perks: The rate of pay varies, and benefits are dependent on your length of employment. However, you will receive full recreation privileges at district-owned facilities, which include two golf courses, Diamond Peak Ski Resort, the recreation center, and beaches.

Making It Happen: Call for application. Rolling deadlines.

INSIDER TIPS: *As a recruiter and a past intern with IVGID, I recommend that the applicant have a good work ethic, good personality, be a hard worker, and not be afraid to use their own ideas when creating projects. Be flexible, budget time wisely, have computer skills (a definite must), and be able to have fun. IVGID is a great place for an internship experience. I know. I got one!*

Contact Information: Laurie Gwinn, Human Resources Director • Incline Village General Improvement District • Parks & Recreation Dept. • 893 Southwood Blvd. • Incline Village, NV 89451 • Phone: (702) 832-1100 • Fax: (702) 832-1122 • E-mail: ivgid@sierra.net • Web Site: http://tahoe.ceres.ca.gov/ivgid

Indian River Plantation Resort

REGION/HQ: Southeast/Florida • **CATEGORY:** Resort • **POSITION TYPE:** Internship • **DURATION:** Year-Round • **IDEAL CANDIDATE:** College Students, Career Changers, Foreigners • **APPLICANT POOL:** 25/year • **APPLICANTS ACCEPTED:** 12/year

ORIGINALLY DEVELOPED AS A pineapple plantation, the island has become a paradise for vacationers and year-round residents alike. Guests enjoy resort living at its finest, with luxurious accommodations in over 200 rooms and suites at their main hotel, as well as 70 beachfront villas. The plantation offers a seventy-seven-slip marina, three swimming pools, a half-mile beach on the ocean, eighteen holes of golf, thirteen championship tennis courts, bicycling, dining facilities, conference center, and a fitness center.

Area and Working Environment: The 200-acre beach resort is bordered by the Intercoastal Waterway and the Atlantic Ocean. Stuart is known as the sailfish capital of the world and the fish are plentiful. Snorkelers, divers, and surfers all enjoy the ocean and the beauty it offers.

They are two hours from Orlando and forty-five minutes from the nightlife in West Palm Beach.

Work/Learn Program Specifics: The internship program provides experience in all areas of the resort recreation industry, assisting the intern in professional and personal growth. Interns will be responsible for working directly with guests in all areas of the resort. Possible duties include working with the children's camp or the beach rentals, running activities at the hotel pool, or planning special events, such as a theme party.

Duration: Internship lengths are twelve to sixteen weeks. Interns will work an average of forty-five to fifty-five hours per week, with one or two days off each week.

Compensation and Perks: A stipend of $100 per week is provided. Room and board are the responsibility of the intern. Interns will receive one meal per shift and free golf once per week.

The Ideal Candidate: Candidates must be working toward or have a degree in recreation, have program-planning skills, organizational and motivation skills, typing skills, previous experience with children, and public-speaking and program-leadership experience. A potential intern will be organized, motivated, possess leadership skills, and be personable. The position requires CPR and first aid certifications.

Making It Happen: Send cover letter, resume, and one letter of recommendation. Phone interviews will be conducted with qualified candidates. Rolling deadlines.

INSIDER TIPS: *We are motivated by helping our guests enjoy their time here, therefore we are looking for interns who love working with people. A positive attitude is a must, along with an open mind to learn and try.*

Contact Information: Stasha Worsena, Activities Director • Indian River Plantation Resort • Hutchinson Island • 555 NE Ocean Blvd. • Stuart, FL 34996 • Phone: (561) 225-6991 • Fax: (561) 225-0003

Kippewa For Girls

REGION/HQ: Northeast/Massachusetts • **CATEGORY:** Camp • **POSITION TYPE:** Internship/Seasonal • **DURATION:** Summer • **IDEAL CANDIDATE:** College Students, Career Changers, Retired Folks • **APPLICANT POOL:** Varies • **APPLICANTS ACCEPTED:** Varies

IT TAKES TREMENDOUS DISCIPLINE on the part of the staff to create Kippewa's relaxed ambiance. Kippewa teaches an extraordinary variety of activities to a very few girls (140 is small for a camp these days), principally through the vehicle of finding multiskilled teachers with solid work ethics.

Area and Working Environment: Kippewa enjoys a beautiful and private location on the shores of Lake Cobbosseecontee in Monmouth, Maine.

Work/Learn Program Specifics: Trip leaders/counselors assist or lead trips for girls on hiking or canoe trips in Maine and serve as activity specialists in their respective skill areas. Staff who accompany registered Maine guides will receive a superior education in the guides' work, and those leading trips of their own will have a significant job for their resumes. Four-day wilderness trips go to Mount Katadin, Grand Lake Stream, Rangeley Lakes, and other regions, and you might also accompany artists taking campers to paint pictures of ocean, marshes, and mountains. Go-getters with ideas thrive at Kippewa.

Compensation and Perks: Salaries begin at $1,200 for the season, plus room, board, and laundry.

The Ideal Candidate: Due to the nature of Kippewa's programming, they prefer multiskilled people and those who would be able and happy teaching in several areas. Counselors must have completed their sophomore year of college prior to starting work, and have the desire to live with and care for about a half dozen girls who might be as young as seven or as old as fifteen. Senior staff applicants generally have at least a decade's worth of experience in their respective fields. Canadians are also eligible to apply, as the camp can usually get the proper visas.

Making It Happen: Call for application materials. Rolling deadlines; however it's best to apply in January or February and most positions are filled by the end of March.

INSIDER TIPS: *Above all, Kippewa wants people who want to combine childcare and teaching work. We seek people of good values who will be good role models for our girls, the kinds of people the girls' parents would want them exposed to. The capacity to put the children before one's self is inherent in childcare. A solid work ethic is vital to not burning out and to keeping the perspective that allows one to feel affectionate towards the children in one's care amidst the demands of one's work. A relaxed humility helps in growing into the demands of the job, which always seem to increase with one's successes. Kippewa is an excellent place for people with initiative because of the leeway given to staff to run their own programs.*

Contact Information: Jon Silverman, Director • Kippewa For Girls • 60 Mill St., Box 307 • Westwood,

MA 02090-0307 • Phone: (781) 762-8291 • Fax: (781) 255-7167 • E-mail: kippewa@tiac.net • Web Site: www.kippewa.com/fun

Lake Powell Resorts & Marinas

REGION/HQ: South/Midwest/Arizona • **CATEGORY:** Resort • **POSITION TYPE:** Seasonal • **DURATION:** Summer • **IDEAL CANDIDATE:** College Students, Career Changers, Retired Folks, Foreigners • **APPLICANT POOL:** Varies • **APPLICANTS ACCEPTED:** 1,200/year

LAKE POWELL RESORTS & MARINAS, a subsidiary of ARAMARK Corporation, operates five marinas and resort properties, as well as Wilderness River Adventures, a river guide company. For those who want to enjoy Lake Powell in luxury, they offer quality accommodations, fine food, delightful shopping, great entertainment, marvelous scenic boat tours of Lake Powell, and unsurpassed service. For those who want the "roughing-it-easy" experience, they offer RV spaces with full hookups, mobile homes with full housekeeping facilities, fully-equipped houseboats that comfortably accommodate six to twelve people, and the rental of powerboats, fishing skiffs, and water toys. Those seeking a true wilderness experience can enjoy a tranquil day trip, floating from Glen Canyon Dam to Lee's Ferry on the Colorado River, or thrill to the excitement of a three- to fourteen-day white-water raft trip through the Grand Canyon.

Area and Working Environment: The vermilion ridges, towering mesas, long and twisting canyons, deep and clear mirrors of water, arching rainbows, and the play of light and shadow in Glen Canyon that inspired Zane Grey in 1915 will instill similar feelings of supernatural awe in you. With the added lure of Lake Powell's serene and sapphire waters, Glen Canyon National Recreation Area has become one of the most attractive vacation destinations anywhere, with visitation well over 3 million people a year. Though 186-mile-long Lake Powell, with its 1,960 miles of shoreline, only covers 13 percent of the 1,255,400 acres of the national recreation area, it naturally attracts the most activity. As one of the most beautiful desert oases in the world, the lake is both a sporting paradise and a glassy byway into the canyon backcountry.

Work/Learn Program Specifics: Positions are available in the Marina (marina utility, fuel attendant, boat rental attendant, boat instructor, marine mechanic, truck driver, maintenance, and rental clerk), Food and Beverage (food and cocktail servers, bus people, bartender, cook, cashier, dishwasher, and food and beverage utility), Hotel (front desk clerk, night auditor, housekeeper, bellhop, maintenance, utility, laundry, van driver, and bus driver), and Retail (sales clerk).

Duration: May through October.

Compensation and Perks: Most seasonal jobs pay $4.75 to $5 per hour, and employees can qualify for an additional 25¢ per hour completion bonus.

Making It Happen: Call for application materials.

Contact Information: Human Resources • Lake Powell Resorts & Marinas • Glen Canyon National Recreation Area • P.O. Box 1597 • Page, AZ 86040 • Phone: (520) 645-1081 • Fax: (520) 645-1016 • E-mail: lprmhr@ page.az.net • Web Site: www.coolworks.com/showme/ lkpowell

Life Adventure Camp

REGION/HQ: Southeast/Kentucky • **CATEGORY:** Therapeutic Camp • **POSITION TYPE:** Internship/ Seasonal • **DURATION:** Year-Round • **IDEAL CANDIDATE:** College Students, Career Changers, Retired Folks, Foreigners • **APPLICANT POOL:** 100/term • **APPLICANTS ACCEPTED:** 15/term

LIFE ADVENTURE CAMP is a primitive wilderness camp, concerned primarily with providing a successful and positive camping experience for children with emotional and behavioral problems. The program is designed around decentralized camping; campers and staff live in small groups in a primitive outdoor setting. Groups consist of eight to 10 campers and three counselors.

Area and Working Environment: Their campsite is located sixty miles southeast of Lexington on 500 acres of rugged, undeveloped land in Estill County. The land is densely forested and offers wildlife, creeks, caves, rock outcroppings, and other natural areas for exploring.

Work/Learn Program Specifics: Camp staff provide opportunities and activities that enhance a positive self-concept; provide a group living setting that encourages and teaches appropriate social-interaction skills among peers and adults; and teach basic and advanced low-impact camping skills, with the hope of increasing each camper's awareness and appreciation for the natural environment. There are no permanent facilities at the campsite; thus, campers and staff must build their

campsites, using natural materials and plastic tarps. Water is supplied by a well and must be carried by hand to all campsites. They provide extensive training for staff, perfect for anyone wanting to lead outdoor programs or work with children.

Duration: The season begins in mid-May and goes through early August.

Compensation and Perks: You will receive a stipend of $1,000 to $3,000, plus room and board. Housing is provided in Lexington during in-town staff training sessions and during time off between sessions for those staff members who do not live in the Lexington area. First aid and CPR certifications will be provided at no cost.

The Ideal Candidate: Must be nineteen and have either one year of college or work experience. Applicants must be interested in making social work, counseling, education, outdoor recreation, or other work with children their full-time career.

Making It Happen: Call or write for application materials. Applications must be received by March 30.

INSIDER TIPS: *We are looking for open-minded men and women who want to learn to live a simple lifestyle and share this with children. People who are excited about living in the woods, cooking meals over a fire, exploring caves and creeks, carrying water from a well, and being with children will thrive in our program.*

Contact Information: Kathleen Reese, Program Director • Life Adventure Camp • 1122 Oak Hill Dr. • Lexington, KY 40505 • Phone: (606) 252-4733 • E-mail: lifeadventurecamp@juno.com

Lost Creek Ranch

REGION/HQ: Rocky Mountains/Wyoming • **CATEGORY:** Ranch • **POSITION TYPE:** Seasonal • **DURATION:** Spring-Fall • **IDEAL CANDIDATE:** College Students, Career Changers, Retired Folks • **APPLICANT POOL:** Varies • **APPLICANTS ACCEPTED:** 35/year

LOST CREEK RANCH is a four-star guest ranch nestled between Grand Teton National Park and Bridger Teton National Forest (twenty-two miles from Jackson), at an elevation of 7,000 feet. Being an upscale ranch, Lost Creek's guests expect the very best from the ranch and staff.

Work/Learn Program Specifics: Positions are available in these departments: Administration (rotator and office assistant), Corral (wrangler/guide, vet/wrangler/guide, and head wrangler), Kitchen (chef, baker, cook/sous chef, and kitchen steward/dishwasher), Dining (server and dining supervisor), Facilities (attendant and supervisor), and Maintenance (ranch hand and maintenance supervisor). The dress at Lost Creek Ranch is Western—be prepared to dress in that style (meaning jeans, boots, and a Western shirt are a must).

Duration: The season runs mid-May through October 1.

Compensation and Perks: Room, board, and laundry facilities are provided at no charge. Employee housing is fairly rustic; however, they do provide the basic necessities. Most employees will have one or two roommates. Sorry, there is no housing for married couples or spaces for RVs/trailers, and pets are not allowed on the ranch. Those who complete their employment agreements receive a season-end bonus (consisting of $5 for each day worked during the non-guest season and $10 for each day worked during the guest season).

The Ideal Candidate: Preference is given to individuals who are twenty-one or older and can work the entire season. All applicants must be certified in CPR and first aid.

Making It Happen: To increase your chances of being hired, show the exact dates you are available and be realistic about your job choices.

Contact Information: Mike and Bev Halpin, Owners • Lost Creek Ranch • P.O. Box 95 • Moose, WY 83012 • Phone: (307) 733-3435 • Fax: (307) 733-1954 • E-mail: ranch@lostcreek.com • Web Site: www.lostcreek.com

Mt. Bachelor Ski & Summer Resort

REGION/HQ: Pacific Northwest/Oregon • **CATEGORY:** Ski Resort • **POSITION TYPE:** Internship/ Seasonal • **DURATION:** Year-Round • **IDEAL CANDIDATE:** High School Students, College Students, Career Changers, Retired Folks, Foreigners • **APPLICANT POOL:** 1,500/year • **APPLICANTS ACCEPTED:** 600/year

MT. BACHELOR IS A nationally known ski resort that caters to those skiers that enjoy little or no lift lines, being treated to excellent service, and skiing 100 percent natural snow. The ski area's base elevation is 6,000 feet, and the mountain top is at 9,000 feet. Mt. Bachelor's 3,100 vertical drop is served by eleven chair lifts, including four triples and six quads.

Area and Working Environment: Mt. Bachelor is located in beautiful central Oregon—the high desert of Oregon. Cold, crisp winter days abound, with plenty of natural, powder snow throughout the winter. The Bend-area economy is driven by recreational tourism and the timber industry.

Work/Learn Program Specifics: They primarily have seasonal, ski resort positions, including cooks, buspeople, cashiers, ski shop staff, lift operators, parking lot attendants, cocktail servers, bartenders, snow groomers, snowplow operators, and ski instructors. They also offer a marketing internship program.

Duration: Seasonal employment is offered mid-November through April. Internships are offered year-round.

Compensation and Perks: Seasonal employees receive $5.50 to $8.00 per hour. Perks include free transportation from Bend, ski passes, ski lessons, and mountain discounts offered for alpine and cross-country skiers. The intern program is non-paid, but you will receive all the above perks.

The Ideal Candidate: Seasonal applicants must be guest/customer-service-oriented with a desire to make a positive impact on the work environment. The intern program is open to recreation or marketing students with solid computer skills.

Making It Happen: Call for application and additional information. Interviews can be arranged over the phone. Deadlines: October for seasonal employment; rolling for interns.

Contact Information: Pat Gerhart, Human Resources Manager • Mt. Bachelor Ski & Summer Resort • P.O. Box 1031 • Bend, OR 97709-1031 • Phone: (541) 382-2442 • Fax: (541) 382-6536 • Toll Free: (800) 829-2442

Mt. Hood Meadows

REGION/HQ: Pacific Northwest/Oregon • **CATEGORY:** Ski Resort • **POSITION TYPE:** Seasonal • **DURATION:** Winter • **IDEAL CANDIDATE:** College Students, Career Changers, Foreigners • **APPLICANT POOL:** Varies • **APPLICANTS ACCEPTED:** 300/year

MT. HOOD MEADOWS is the premier ski resort on Mt. Hood, featuring 2,150 acres of terrain serviced by ten chair lifts. Its vertical drop of 2,777 feet offers steep and rugged terrain, complete with mogul-filled bowls, chutes, ridges, and outback skiing in Heather Canyon (quite an experience!).

Work/Learn Program Specifics: Positions include lift operators, ski patrol, snow groomers, rental technicians, cashiers, ticket checkers, bus drivers, and food service staff.

Duration: All jobs are for the winter season, lasting from early November to late April.

Compensation and Perks: Wages range from $4.25 to $5.50 per hour. Perks include a free season ski pass, lessons, and shuttle bus transportation. Discounts on food and ski shop purchases are also available.

The Ideal Candidate: Applicants should be gregarious, neat, and have previous service-oriented experience and the tenacity to work in a mountain environment.

Making It Happen: Call for application materials. They conduct a job fair the first week of October. It's highly recommended you attend this fair.

Contact Information: Human Resources Director • Mt. Hood Meadows • P.O. Box 470 • Mt. Hood, OR 97041 • Phone: (503) 337-2222

North Fork Guest Ranch

REGION/HQ: Rocky Mountains/Colorado • **CATEGORY:** Ranch • **POSITION TYPE:** Internship/Seasonal • **DURATION:** Spring-Fall • **IDEAL CANDIDATE:** High School Students, College Students, Career Changers, Retired Folks, Foreigners • **APPLICANT POOL:** 130/year • **APPLICANTS ACCEPTED:** 22/year

THE RANCH OFFERS EVERYTHING you could want, including great horseback riding, white-water rafting, overnight pack trips, hiking, trapshooting, terrific fishing, and the unique opportunity to meet and make friends from all over the world.

Area and Working Environment: Their facilities are on the gorgeous banks of the rushing north fork of the South Platte River. It's only an hour from Denver (yet very secluded) and adjoins the national wilderness area in the heart of the Rockies.

Work/Learn Program Specifics: Because the ranch is a people-serving business, they do not hire people merely to get a job done. You will be expected to give totally of yourself, sharing with and caring for their

guests. Positions include cook, kid's counselor, office/kitchen, wrangler, maintenance, and housekeeper/waitress.

Duration: The season starts in early May and does not end until the second week in September. They are primarily interested in those who can stay through the end of August or later.

Compensation and Perks: Staff members receive $375 to $425 per month, plus room and board. On your day off and after daily duties, you can enjoy all ranch activities.

The Ideal Candidate: Do you love people? Do you love to work? Are you willing to learn and do new things? Are you flexible and willing to help out anytime, anywhere, and do anything? Are you enthusiastic and excited about other people enjoying their vacation? Would you involve yourself in the basic ranch objective of making the guests' stay at North Fork Ranch a great experience? If you answered yes to these questions, you are the type of person they are looking for!

Making It Happen: Call for application materials. They begin their review of applications starting in January and try to have their entire staff hired by April 1.

Contact Information: Dean and Karen May, Owners • North Fork Guest Ranch • Box B • Shawnee, CO 80475 • Phone: (303) 838-9873 • Fax: (303) 838-1549 • Toll Free: (800) 843-7895

Northstar-at-Tahoe

REGION/HQ: Pacific Northwest/California **CATEGORY:** Ski Resort • **POSITION TYPE:** Seasonal • **DURATION:** Winter/Summer • **IDEAL CANDIDATE:** College Students, Career Changers, Foreigners • **APPLICANT POOL:** Thousands • **APPLICANTS ACCEPTED:** 250 summer, 1,000 winter

A SCENIC PLACE SPRINKLED with forests of evergreen and aspen beneath brilliant blue skies, Northstar offers first-class skiing and boarding, mountain bike action, and a par-72 golf course in summer.

Area and Working Environment: The Lake Tahoe area in the Sierra Nevada Mountains is a biker's, hiker's, skier's, and outdoor lover's paradise. Truckee, where Northstar is located, is six miles from the north shore of Lake Tahoe.

Work/Learn Program Specifics: Positions are available in lift operations, food and beverage operations, housekeeping, parking, ski school/instruction, childcare, retail, and ski rental. You'll have the chance to forge friendships that will last a lifetime, work side-by-side with other employees from around the world, and meet guests who come from all walks of life.

Duration: Northstar employs seasonal workers for both winter and summer, and openings exist throughout the year. Employees generally work between thirty to forty hours per week during normal business periods and forty to fifty hours during peak season. Most employees will work weekends and holidays, depending on the position.

Compensation and Perks: Wages range from $5.50 to $7.00 per hour for most seasonal positions, and $4.75 for tipped positions. Dormitory-style housing is available for a limited number of employees. In addition, a housing board helps match those with housing with those seeking housing. Perks include a free ski/snowboard pass, lessons and ski rental, and discounted snowboard rental. Employees also receive half-price food at resort locations, a 10 percent discount on gasoline, 20 percent retail discounts, generous incentive and recognition programs, and skiing privileges at their sister resorts, Sierra-at-Tahoe and Bear Mountain. Northstar sponsors great events for employees: employee ski races, great holiday events, some uniquely alternative downhill races, and dinners.

The Ideal Candidate: Northstar hires employees from all walks of life, and many have recently finished school or are looking for a lifestyle change. The best applicants are friendly, motivated, flexible, and hardworking individuals who want a fun and challenging work experience high in the Sierras.

Making It Happen: Applications for summer employment are usually reviewed during April/May. Application packets for winter employment are available starting in September. Most hiring for the winter season is done at job fairs at the end of October, which gives applicants the chance to meet managers in person. Applicants from the Western states are asked to attend this fair.

INSIDER TIPS: *Applicants are considered based on dates available, enthusiasm, customer-service skills, and specific job skills.*

Contact Information: Tom Dougherty, Recruiting Coordinator • Northstar-at-Tahoe • P.O. Box 129 • Truckee, CA 96160 • Phone: (916) 562-3510 • Fax: (916) 562-2214 • Job Hotline: (916) 562-2217 • E-mail: nstar@sierra.net • Web Site: www.skinorthstar.com

Oakland House Seaside Inn & Cottages

REGION/HQ: Northeast/Maine • **CATEGORY:** Hotel • **POSITION TYPE:** Seasonal • **DURATION:** Summer • **IDEAL CANDIDATE:** College Students, Career Changers, Foreigners • **APPLICANT POOL:** 75/year • **APPLICANTS ACCEPTED:** 15/year

OAKLAND HOUSE SEASIDE INN & COTTAGES first opened its doors in 1889. The first guests were the "Rusticators" who arrived on steamships from Boston, New York, and places beyond. They were writers, artists, and educators seeking respite from city bustle. Oakland House offers a half-mile of prime oceanfront, ocean and lakeside beaches, hiking trails, a dock, rowboats, and relaxation.

Area and Working Environment: This is spectacular coastal Maine at its best. You'll see beautiful vistas of water, islands, and distant hills, seals offshore and bald eagles in the air, windjammers sailing, and miles of rural, unpaved roads near this over 200-year-old farm. Acadia National Park, Deer Isle, and many quiet lobstering villages are nearby.

Work/Learn Program Specifics: No matter your position, the goal is to make guests feel welcome in this family atmosphere. Positions include waitstaff, office assistants, food prep and assistants, grounds people, cabin stewards, and housekeepers. Due to the general long-term nature of guest visits (one-week minimum in cottages), there are many opportunities for friendships and cordial staff relationships. Both guests and staff come from all over the world.

Duration: Positions are for eleven weeks during the summer, approximately forty hours per week, with many opportunities for more hours if desired.

Compensation and Perks: Pay varies per position. All staff members live in the 200-year-old hotel and are encouraged to the enjoy the surrounding area on days off.

The Ideal Candidate: You must be eighteen years or older. Staff members often return year after year as they work through college.

Making It Happen: Call for application materials.

Contact Information: Jim and Sally Littlefield, Innkeepers • Oakland House Seaside Inn & Cottages • RR1, Box 400 • Brooksville, ME 04617 • Phone: (207) 359-8521

The man who insists on seeing with perfect clearness before he decides, never decides. Accept life, and you must accept regret. —Henri Amiel

121

Palmer Gulch Resort

REGION/HQ: Rocky Mountains/South Dakota • **CATEGORY:** Camp • **POSITION TYPE:** Internship/ Seasonal • **DURATION:** Summer • **IDEAL CANDIDATE:** College Students • **APPLICANT POOL:** 200/year • **APPLICANTS ACCEPTED:** 60–80/year

PALMER GULCH RESORT/MT. RUSHMORE KOA is a full-service resort offering 500 campsites, a 62-room lodge, and 80 cabins. They are also the largest and most popular summer resort in South Dakota.

Area and Working Environment: Palmer Gulch is located five miles from Mount Rushmore National Memorial, at the foot of Harney Peak, in the heart of the Black Hills.

Work/Learn Program Specifics: Positions available include campground store/registration clerk, motel reservation/registration clerk, reservation clerks, housekeeping, shower cleaning, maintenance, waterslide, and food service.

Duration: Most positions start mid- to late May and continue through Labor Day, with some positions lasting into October. Positions are full-time, forty hours per week, with two days off per week.

Compensation and Perks: Staff is paid by the hour, plus a season-end bonus if you complete your contract. Dormitory housing and RV sites are available. Recreational opportunities at the resort include basketball, volleyball, swimming and hot tubs, horseback riding, miniature golf, and hiking.

The Ideal Candidate: Applicants must be customer service- and detail-oriented.

Making It Happen: Call for application materials.

Contact Information: Sharon Nilson, Assistant Manager • Palmer Gulch Resort • P.O. Box 295 • Hill City, SD 57745 • Phone: (605) 574-2525 • Fax: (605) 574-2574 • Toll Free: (800) 562-8503

Pathfinder Ranch

REGION/HQ: Pacific Northwest/California • **CATEGORY:** Camp • **POSITION TYPE:** Internship • **DURATION:** Spring/Fall • **IDEAL CANDIDATE:** High School Students, College Students, Career Changers, Retired Folks, Foreigners • **APPLICANT POOL:** Varies • **APPLICANTS ACCEPTED:** 2/year

PATHFINDER RANCH IS A PRIVATE, nonprofit organization affiliated with the Boy's Club of Palm Springs and governed by a board of directors. The ranch was founded in 1967, when the property was donated to the Boy's Club. The ranch has developed into a year-round facility able to house up to 150 campers.

Area and Working Environment: The Ranch is located in the foothills of the San Jacinto Mountains, at an elevation of 4,500 feet, about one hour southeast of Riverside, California. The ranch itself is located on thirty acres and borders the San Bernardino National Forest, which offers thousands of additional acres for hiking and exploration.

Work/Learn Program Specifics: The outdoor education instructor will teach educational and recreational classes to fifth- and sixth-grade students; take students on orientation hikes; set up, organize, and supervise all group activities; teach and supervise evening programs; develop lesson plans; provide weekly evaluations of schools and program; assist in the development of new classes and programs; and attend staff meetings. The outdoor education program director will administer programs; set up daily schedules for individual schools; give presentations to students and parents; schedule instructional staff; provide teacher and student orientations; teach classes; evaluate programs and instructors; and schedule and supervise support staff.

Duration: Spring session runs from January 15 to June 5, and the fall session runs from September 1 to December 15.

Compensation and Perks: Staff members receive $200 to 300 per week, plus room, board, and workers' compensation insurance.

The Ideal Candidate: A college degree is preferred (but not required) in outdoor education, outdoor recreation, or related fields. Experience in teaching/ instructing outdoor education and recreational classes; general knowledge of ecological, environmental, conservation concepts; specific knowledge in classes instructor will be teaching; self-motivation; a strong desire to teach children in the outdoors; and the ability and willingness to become part of a teaching team are also desirable. In addition, requirements for the director position include experience in programming and scheduling and good organizational, communication, and supervisory skills.

Making It Happen: Send resume and then call or write for an application packet. Deadlines: spring—December 1; fall—July 1.

Contact Information: Dave Keigan, Camp Director • Pathfinder Ranch • 35510 Pathfinder Rd., #104 • Mountain Center, CA 92561-9741 • Phone: (909) 659-2455 • Fax: (909) 659-0351

Pennsylvania Lions Beacon Lodge Camp

REGION/HQ: Northeast/Pennsylvania • **CATEGORY:** Therapeutic Camp • **POSITION TYPE:** Seasonal • **DURATION:** Summer • **IDEAL CANDIDATE:** High School Students, College Students, Foreigners • **APPLICANT POOL:** 100/term • **APPLICANTS ACCEPTED:** 50/term

PENNSYLVANIA LIONS BEACON LODGE CAMP is a nonprofit camp sponsored by the Lions Club of Pennsylvania. They focus on providing a positive outdoor camping experience for youth and adults who are visually, hearing, or mentally impaired, or who have other physical impairments.

Area and Working Environment: The camp is located in south-central Pennsylvania in a remote, wooded area covering 583 acres. Amish culture is prevalent in surrounding communities.

Work/Learn Program Specifics: Positions include directors, various specialty counselors/instructors, drivers, nurse, and outdoor adventure coordinators. You will have the opportunity to participate in (and share with campers) hiking, overnights, canoeing, kayaking, white-water rafting, arts and crafts, nature study, aquatics, bowling, dances, hayrides, trips, cookouts, games, and mountain biking. Training is provided in working with the various disabilities, including sign language, sighted-guide techniques, and seizure management. You will also be certified in CPR and first aid, if needed.

Duration: The season opens the beginning of June with a full week of staff orientation and training and concludes mid-August. For those that want to stay on after that time, you can participate in their new Diabetes Youth Camp.

Compensation and Perks: You will receive $125 to $145 per week. Room and board are provided, and you will live in cabins with the campers.

The Ideal Candidate: Applicants must be eighteen years of age, and they prefer those with previous camp experience and/or work experience with physically/mentally challenged individuals. Those with special skills, such as singing, guitar playing, gardening, photography, fishing, and other personal interests will find ample time to pursue these hobbies!

Making It Happen: Call for application packet, which must be received by March 31.

INSIDER TIPS: *We are looking for people who would like to share in the adventures of activities with persons with disabilities (who many times are denied the opportunity). A caring, good-natured person who accepts responsibilities and is hardworking, honest, dedicated, sincere, and willing to learn is highly regarded.*

Contact Information: Camp Director • Pennsylvania Lions Beacon Lodge Camp • 114 SR103 South • Mount Union, PA 17066-9601 • Phone: (814) 542-2511 • Fax: (814) 542-7437

Ramapo Anchorage Camp

REGION/HQ: Northeast/New York • **CATEGORY:** Therapeutic Camp • **POSITION TYPE:** Internship • **DURATION:** Summer • **IDEAL CANDIDATE:** College Students, Career Changers, Foreigners • **APPLICANT POOL:** Varies • **APPLICANTS ACCEPTED:** Varies

RAMAPO PROVIDES A SAFE, predictable, and highly structured environment which fosters the development of positive social and learning skills. Campers live in rustic bunks, with an average of six children in each group. An overall one-to-one staff-to-camper ratio helps children who have repeatedly met with failure experience success.

Work/Learn Program Specifics: During the months of May and June, Ramapo runs a program serving disadvantaged preschoolers aged four to six. Counselors work individually with each child, helping them to develop their school readiness and the communication skills necessary for healthy development. In July and August, the camp serves children aged six to fourteen with emotional or learning problems. During each of Ramapo's three-week summer sessions, 160 campers participate in creative projects, sports, and outdoor experiences. Adventures and friendships abound at Ramapo, providing opportunities for campers to learn to live within a group, form productive relationships, develop confidence, and recognize the benefits of good choices and the consequences of poor ones.

Compensation and Perks: Staff receive a stipend, plus room and board.

The Ideal Candidate: The Ramapo staff is mature, enthusiastic, and diverse. Most are college students studying education, psychology, or social work. They are selected for qualities of leadership, personal values, and caring, which enable them to relate to and motivate young people.

Making It Happen: Call for more information.

Contact Information: Camp Director • Ramapo Anchorage Camp • P.O. Box 266 • Rhinebeck, NY 12572 • Phone: (914) 876-8403 • Fax: (914) 876-8414

Resort Recreation & Tennis Management

REGION/HQ: Nationwide/South Carolina
• **CATEGORY:** Resort • **POSITION TYPE:** Internship/Seasonal • **DURATION:** Year-Round • **IDEAL CANDIDATE:** College Students, Career Changers, Foreigners • **APPLICANT POOL:** 1,000/year
• **APPLICANTS ACCEPTED:** 500/year

RESORT RECREATION & TENNIS MANAGEMENT (RRTM) is dedicated to providing excellent guest service to their resort clientele, while providing an exceptional learning experience to future recreation and hospitality professionals. They are contracted by over ninety resorts across the nation, including Marriott, Hilton, Sheraton, Holiday Inn, and Ramada, various cruise lines, and many other vacation resorts.

Area and Working Environment: Work locations include Palm Springs, Carlsbad, Capistrano Beach, and San Diego, California; Hutchison Island, Daytona Beach, the Florida Keys, Ft. Lauderdale, and Orlando, Florida; Hilton Head Island and Myrtle Beach, South Carolina; Las Vegas, Nevada; and various other locations throughout the United States.

Work/Learn Program Specifics: Activity coordinators lead and direct activities for guests of all ages; staff all activity centers including pools, marinas, activity offices, and all recreation centers; plan and implement special projects and events; and program for all holidays and convention groups. Hospitality hostesses provide tour coordination, ticket sales and collections, reservations, and group bookings; maintain friendly customer relations; assist captains as first mate; and distribute marketing materials. Front desk assistants train in all phases of front desk operations, while being exposed to additional experiences in the hotel, including guest services, reservations, PBX, and bell staff. Food and beverage assistants experience all aspects of food and beverage, including kitchen work, hosting, bartending, bookkeeping, server work, banquets, payroll, cashiering, inventory controls, purchasing/receiving, supervising, and working as banquet maître d's. Interns will be required to attend weekly training seminars and participate in various committees. Homework and special assignments will be assigned during these meetings. In addition, occasional guest speakers will share their expertise on the hospitality industry.

Duration: Each intern will be scheduled for a minimum of forty-five hours per week, six days per week. Each intern will receive one full day off and another half day.

Compensation and Perks: Wages are stipends of $150 per month for most positions (food and beverage positions receive $300 per month). Perks include a fully furnished townhouse, local phone, all utilities, and cable television. Some resort locations also provide complimentary meals. Intern socials are provided once a month and include beach olympics, sunset cruises, team-building events, beach bonfires, and intramural sports. Students who have completed a RRTM internship and have one or two semesters left of school are invited to become student ambassadors. You will receive a current list of resort locations and job opportunities available.

The Ideal Candidate: Majors in recreation, travel/tourism, public relations, hotel and restaurant management, or other majors in the hospitality field. Students must be receiving academic credit for their internship experience here.

Making It Happen: Call for application and details. Send completed application, cover letter, resume, and three references. Upon receipt of your completed application forms, you will be called for a telephone interview.

INSIDER TIPS: *Apply as early as possible to be able to secure the position and location you are most interested in.*

Contact Information: Personnel Director • Resort Recreation & Tennis Management • P.O. Box 7832 • Hilton Head Island, SC 29938 • Phone: (803) 785-7566 • Fax: (803) 785-4368 • Toll Free: (800) 864-6762

River Way Ranch Camp

REGION/HQ: Pacific Northwest/California
• **CATEGORY:** Camp • **POSITION TYPE:** Internship/Seasonal • **DURATION:** Year-Round • **IDEAL CANDIDATE:** College Students, Career Changers, Foreigners • **APPLICANT POOL:** Varies • **APPLICANTS ACCEPTED:** 130/term

RIVER WAY RANCH CAMP offers fun and excitement for children from all over the world. It offers over sixty different specialized activities, including archery, minibikes, photography, animal care, horse riding, waterskiing, journalism, golf, waverunners, ropes course, and a wide variety of other activities. Western Camps owns and operates River Way Ranch Camp, USC Alumni Family Camp, Alisa Ann Rousch Burn Foundation Camp (for burn victims), and Wonder Valley Ranch Resort. The resort caters to groups from several regions and offers many amenities, including a spa, horses, swimming, boating, and a lake.

Area and Working Environment: Located in the foothills of Sequoia/Kings Canyon National Parks.

Work/Learn Program Specifics: Western Camps offers an excellent opportunity for someone looking to work with the public or with children. They offer a challenge for those wanting to learn the camping or resort industry. Camp interns assist in marketing, evaluations, public relations, and behind the scenes; camp counselors supervise eight to twelve children during rest hour, evenings, meal time, and bunk activities. Counselors are also responsible for leading activities, providing the children with a positive role model, and seeing to the health and safety of their campers. Resort interns learn to work with the public as a programmer, activity leader, and in sales. And finally, the management team plans activities and trains the staff.

Duration: Internship duration is quite flexible.

Compensation and Perks: Staff receive a $1,300 to $2,000 stipend for the season, plus room and board. If employed full-time, year-round, medical benefits are provided after a minimum number of service years.

The Ideal Candidate: Open to all who would like to learn the resort and camp industry. Camp applicants must love children, and those who have lifeguard training and are CPR/first aid certified are preferred. Resort applicants must be outgoing, creative, and have a professional attitude. Management applicants must have excellent organizational skills. International applicants must speak English.

Making It Happen: Call for application materials. Rolling deadlines.

Contact Information: Nancy Oken Nighbert, Director • River Way Ranch Camp • 6450 Elwood Rd., "BD" • Sanger, CA 93657 • Phone: (209) 787-2551 • Fax: (209) 787-2556 • Toll Free: (800) 821-2801 • E-mail: rwrcamp@aol.com

Rose Resnick Lighthouse for the Blind

REGION/HQ: Pacific Northwest/California • **CATEGORY:** Therapeutic Recreation • **POSITION TYPE:** Internship/Seasonal • **DURATION:** Summer • **IDEAL CANDIDATE:** College Students, Career Changers, Foreigners • **APPLICANT POOL:** Varies • **APPLICANTS ACCEPTED:** Varies

ROSE RESNICK LIGHTHOUSE FOR THE BLIND serves blind, visually impaired, and deaf/blind persons of all ages by providing rehabilitation, social services, and recreational opportunities.

Area and Working Environment: Enchanted Hills Camp is located in the hills above Napa, one and a half hours from San Francisco.

Work/Learn Program Specifics: Enchanted Hills Camp is the only summer camp in northern California serving blind, visually impaired, deaf/blind, and blind children and adults with multiple disabilities. The sessions are designed to meet the special needs of different groups: preteens, teens, young adults, and adults. Campers enjoy horseback riding, swimming, arts and crafts, music and drama, recreation and sports, and outdoor education. Having fun is one goal, but the most important goal is for campers to achieve independence and develop confidence.

Duration: Mid-June to the end of August (each session is five to fourteen days long).

Compensation and Perks: Room and board are provided.

Making It Happen: Call by April/early May for more information.

Contact Information: Pam Spindler, Volunteer Services Director • Rose Resnick Lighthouse for the Blind • 214 Van Ness Ave. • San Francisco, CA 94102-4508 • Phone: (415) 431-1481 • Fax: (415) 863-7568 • E-mail: pspindler@lighthouse-sf.org

Seacamp

REGION/HQ: Southeast/Florida • **CATEGORY:** Camp • **POSITION TYPE:** Seasonal • **DURATION:** Summer • **IDEAL CANDIDATE:** College Students • **APPLICANT POOL:** 250/year • **APPLICANTS ACCEPTED:** 65/year

ESTABLISHED IN 1966, Seacamp is dedicated to the study of marine communities and island habitats.

There are only two things to aim for in life: first to get what you want and, after that, to enjoy it. Only the wisest of mankind achieve the second. —LOGAN PEARSALL SMITH

125

Courses are led by academically trained marine science instructors. Enhancing these science courses, basic and advanced scuba certifications are offered. Campers have an opportunity to develop skills in sailing, boardsailing, and kayaking, as well as photography, arts and crafts, and working on the camp newspaper to balance the camp experience. "For all the sea has to teach us—and for all the fun in learning it!"

Area and Working Environment: With its beautiful location at Newfound Harbor on Big Pine Key, Seacamp is minutes from the only living coral reef in North America. Opportunities abound to explore the exciting waters of the Florida Keys, both in the Atlantic Ocean and the Gulf of Mexico. Indians, pirates, and Flagler's Railroad all contribute to the heritage of this tropical area.

Work/Learn Program Specifics: A variety of instructor positions are available, including science, scuba, boardsailing, sailing, photography, arts and crafts, as well as positions as counselors, kitchen, and maintenance staff. Whatever your position, you will also participate in all camp activities. Camp is a unique learning environment that combines the living and working aspects of the staff member's life. Many times it becomes hard to distinguish between learning and teaching experiences. Working and living with staff and campers from all over the world allows one to develop not only job skills, but also teamwork and problem-solving skills. Learning a job and living with a group of campers who need supervision, while getting along with other staff and administrators in a residential community, can be the catalyst for great personal growth.

Duration: The season runs late May through late August.

Compensation and Perks: Staff receives a salary, health insurance, and room and board. All staff participate in a four-week pre-camp training program. This includes American Red Cross lifeguarding, first aid, and CPR certification, NAUI skin-diving instruction, a forty-hour workshop in seamanship and boat handling, and if scuba certified, rescue diver training.

The Ideal Candidate: The ideal candidate is an energetic, versatile, flexible college-age person, or graduate. The minimum age for employment is nineteen years. Applicants must possess strong aquatic skills, and scuba certification is desired, but not required.

Making It Happen: Phone interviews begin in March and last through April.

INSIDER TIPS: *With the heart of Seacamp's program being marine science education, the best applicants pos-* sess an interest in working with teenagers in a water-oriented setting. Experience in working with children or in a camp setting and environmental awareness are valuable assets.

Contact Information: Grace Upshaw, Camp Director • Seacamp • 1300 Big Pine Ave. • Big Pine Key, FL 33043 • Phone: (305) 872-2331 • Fax: (305) 872-2555 • Web Site: www.seacamp.org

Snow Mountain Ranch

REGION/HQ: Rocky Mountains/Colorado • **CATEGORY:** Ranch • **POSITION TYPE:** Seasonal • **DURATION:** Year-Round • **IDEAL CANDIDATE:** College Students, Career Changers, Foreigners • **APPLICANT POOL:** Varies • **APPLICANTS ACCEPTED:** Varies

SNOW MOUNTAIN RANCH is a conference center and family resort accommodating up to 1,700 guests per day. The facility offers hiking, horseback riding, mountain biking, snowshoeing, roller skating, an indoor pool, basketball/volleyball courts, and 100 km of groomed cross-country ski trails. Camp Chief Ouray, a summer resident youth camp, is located at Snow Mountain and serves youth from ages eight to sixteen. In addition to traditional camp activities, adventure-based and leadership programs are available for teens.

Area and Working Environment: Snow Mountain Ranch is a 5,000-acre facility located near Winter Park Ski Resort and Rocky Mountain National Park, 70 miles northwest of Denver.

Work/Learn Program Specifics: Seasonal positions include: lifeguards, crafts shop instructors, day-camp counselors, housekeeping, food service personnel, maintenance, retail sales, front desk clerks, resident camp counselors, adventure education instructors, and staff activities coordinators.

Duration: Year-round positions offered.

Compensation and Perks: Staff members receive a $120 to $140-per-week stipend, including room and board. Perks include formal ongoing training, free use of recreation facilities, and discounts in gift shops.

The Ideal Candidate: Instructors must have a degree in environmental education, environmental science, or related field, as well as a desire to work with children. First aid and CPR certificates are preferred.

Making It Happen: Call for application materials. Rolling deadlines.

Contact Information: Julie Watkins, Human Resources Director • Snow Mountain Ranch • YMCA Of the Rockies • P.O. Box 169 • Winter Park, CO 80482 • Phone: (970) 887-2152 • Fax: (303) 449-6781 • Web Site: www.ymcarockies.org

Sol Duc Hot Springs

REGION/HQ: Pacific Northwest/Washington • **CATEGORY:** Resort • **POSITION TYPE:** Seasonal • **DURATION:** Summer • **IDEAL CANDIDATE:** College Students • **APPLICANT POOL:** 300/year • **APPLICANTS ACCEPTED:** 70/year

THE QUILEUTE INDIANS called it *Sol Duc*—a land of sparkling water. The original resort was built in 1912 and was conceived as a health spa in the European tradition.

Area and Working Environment: The main attraction to the area is the three hot spring mineral pools. These soaking pools are man-made circular pools supplied with all natural, mineral rich, hot spring water. There is also a freshwater swimming pool which offers cool relief to hot bathers.

Work/Learn Program Specifics: Summer staff positions include front desk, gift/grocery, pool booth, grounds/janitor, massage therapist, housekeeping, lifeguard, espresso operator, and food and beverage. They also have one internship position available for someone who wants to learn the specifics of resort management.

Duration: The resort opens mid-May and closes the end of September.

Compensation and Perks: Pay starts out at $5.75 per hour. Housing is provided at a cost of $6.75 per day, which also includes three meals per day. Housing is coed dormitory style with gender-separate bedrooms. The rooms vary in size, with the largest housing up to six staff members at peak season. The employee lounge has games, books, a VCR, and over 200 videos to choose from. Room for married couples is limited. The biggest perk is a lively family atmosphere and work environment, not to mention free use of the hot spring mineral pools and swimming pool.

The Ideal Candidate: They employ those who are friendly and cheerful, can work as a team, and who are self-starters and hard workers.

Making It Happen: Call for application materials. Rolling deadlines. Few on-site interviews are conducted due to their isolated location.

INSIDER TIPS: *We seek out those who are dependable, flexible, and have a desire to work hard and do well. Previous hotel or restaurant experience is good, but positive energy and attitude, with a willingness to learn and put forward your best effort is better.*

Contact Information: Mark Wascher, Human Resources Manager • Sol Duc Hot Springs • Olympic National Park • P.O. Box 2169 • Port Angeles, WA 98362-0283 • Phone: (360) 327-3583 • Fax: (360) 327-3593 • E-mail: marksdr@aol.com

Stanford Sierra Camp

REGION/HQ: Pacific Northwest/California • **CATEGORY:** Resort • **POSITION TYPE:** Seasonal • **DURATION:** Spring/Fall • **IDEAL CANDIDATE:** College Students, Career Changers, Foreigners • **APPLICANT POOL:** 100+/term • **APPLICANTS ACCEPTED:** 35/term

STANFORD SIERRA CAMP provides full-service lodging and meeting facilities to conferences, business retreats, and social events of 30 to 200 people. Thankfully, they are not the Ritz-Carlton and do not offer valet parking or room service or wear uniforms or demand uniformity. However, they do provide their guests with four-star meals, comfortable lodging, a beautiful environment, and—above all—professional, efficient, and friendly service. They are in the service industry, whether they host a scientific conference or a wedding with a live band.

Area and Working Environment: The camp is located at Fallen Leaf Lake, a clear, deep lake with a breathtaking mountain backdrop, next to South Lake Tahoe, California. Behind the resort is Desolation Wilderness, a national wilderness area with some of the best hiking and scenery in the Sierras. The solitude of nature will be right outside your "back door."

Work/Learn Program Specifics: Conference staff positions include kitchen, fountain, office assistants, host/hostess, housekeeping, assistant head of housekeeping, evening manager, night watch, and accounting staff. Most staff members spend their time housekeeping and working in the dining room. Everyone shuttles guests to the airport, monitors the boat dock, washes dishes, and cleans the main lodge. You will gain valuable experience in resort management, work hard, play hard, make new friends, and help guests enjoy their stay.

Duration: The spring conference season begins mid-April and ends mid-June; while the fall conference season begins the first week in September and ends mid-November. The workload varies widely according to conference size and demands (anywhere from thirty to fifty hours per week, with shifts spread throughout the day). Staff members usually get two consecutive days off.

Compensation and Perks: The wages are $5.00 to $6.00 per hour, plus room and board, gratuities, and a season bonus. Housing is in rustic cabins (all have power; some have bathrooms; most staff have roommates; and all cabins are in an amazing locale), and the food is excellent, healthful, and plentiful, and vegetarian options are provided (you will often eat what the guests do: meaning salmon, prime rib, salads, and such). Perks include full use of the facilities (waterskiing, sailing, tennis, volleyball, and miles of hiking trails), fun fellow staff, and an opportunity to meet new people and make new friends.

The Ideal Candidate: They hire self-motivated, hardworking, and reliable people who have an excellent sense of professionalism, a warm personality, and a high level of maturity. Applicants also must be able to handle the responsibilities of living and working in a diverse community. Applicants must be friendly, courteous, and compatible with the service industry. The staff comes from all walks of life—college students, professionals between jobs, experienced workers in the service industry, travelers, or people taking time off. At a minimum, two years of college or more is preferred.

Making It Happen: Call for an application. Phone interviews and hiring will occur during the week following the application deadline (the spring deadline is mid-March and the fall is mid-August). Face-to-face interviews, if possible, usually work to the applicant's advantage.

INSIDER TIPS: *In general, the most successful staff members are team players who are compatible with the service industry, enjoy our unique natural setting, and take pride in a job well done (whatever that job may be).*

Contact Information: Bob McClure, Conference Staff Director • Stanford Sierra Camp • P.O. Box 10618 • South Lake Tahoe, CA 96158-3618 • Phone: (916) 541-1244 • Fax: (916) 541-2212 • E-mail: bmm@ leland.stanford.edu

Steamboat Ski & Resort Corporation

REGION/HQ: Rocky Mountains/Colorado
• **CATEGORY:** Ski Resort • **POSITION TYPE:** Seasonal
• **DURATION:** Year-Round • **IDEAL CANDIDATE:** College Students, Career Changers, Foreigners
• **APPLICANT POOL:** Varies • **APPLICANTS ACCEPTED:** 800/year

LOCATED IN STEAMBOAT SPRINGS, this is one of the world's top ski areas, with 2,700 permitted acres and 101 ski trails. Perched high atop Colorado's magnificent Rocky Mountains, this resort gets an average cumulative snowfall of more than twenty-seven feet each season.

Area and Working Environment: While the ski area has some of the best snow in the Rockies, the downtown area is much like any small ranching community, focusing on the daily business of the local residents. Two miles out of town in any direction puts you in the middle of underdeveloped Rocky Mountain beauty, from natural hot springs to miles of wilderness for cross-country skiing.

Work/Learn Program Specifics: The resort hires all typical ski area positions, including numerous openings in Lift Operations, Ski School, Kids' Vacation Center, Ticket Office, Food Service, and Mountain Maintenance departments. Summer operational needs include staffing in the areas of Kids' Activity Center, Food Service, trail maintenance, grounds maintenance, and mountain biking.

Duration: The ski season runs mid-November through mid-April. Summer operations for mountain biking and other activities runs from early June through Labor Day.

Compensation and Perks: Pay ranges from $4.70 to $5.50 per hour, plus an end of season cash bonus. Perks include a season ski pass, complimentary lift tickets, ski lessons, and discounts at shops, restaurants, and other Colorado ski areas. Housing opportunities within the community are usually best in early fall. As the ski season nears, the variety of choices diminish; however, there is typically a need for roommates throughout the ski season. While the resort does have employee housing, it is very limited and is generally offered on a first-come, first-served basis.

The Ideal Candidate: They look for friendly, energetic, and enthusiastic people to help them create a great vacation experience for their guests.

Making It Happen: Call for application materials. It's highly recommended you attend their job fair in late October. Rolling deadlines.

INSIDER TIPS: *A neat, well-groomed appearance and an outgoing attitude are a must.*

Contact Information: Bud Phillips, Human Resources Director • Steamboat Ski & Resort Corporation • 2305 Mt. Werner Circle • Steamboat Springs, CO 80487-9023 • Phone: (970) 879-6111 • Fax: (970) 879-7844 • E-mail: 102264.1024@compuserve.com • Web Site: www.steamboat-ski.com

Stowe Mountain Resort

REGION/HQ: Northeast/Vermont • **CATEGORY:** Ski Resort • **POSITION TYPE:** Seasonal • **DURATION:** Winter/Summer • **IDEAL CANDIDATE:** College Students, Career Changers, Foreigners • **APPLICANT POOL:** 1,500/year • **APPLICANTS ACCEPTED:** 600/year

MOST PEOPLE CAN ONLY dream of living and working in such a beautiful part of the country, known as the Ski Capital of the East. Their dream of providing a superior recreational experience is evidenced by the ongoing growth and continued improvements at Stowe. Stowe has over 480 skiable acres and eleven lifts, including the world's fastest eight-passenger gondola. Stowe's trails are the longest in the East and, on average, longer than every other mountain east of the Mississippi.

Area and Working Environment: Located on Vermont's highest peak, Stowe is steeped in history, tradition, and New England charm.

Work/Learn Program Specifics: Positions include Food and Beverage (cafeteria duties include food prep, line server, cashier and kitchen utility, cooks, waitstaff, buspersons, host/hostess, and bartenders), Hospitality (switchboard operators, information center, front desk clerks, and housekeeping), Retail (retail clerks, rent and repair shop, customer service representatives, and ticket sellers), Trail Maintenance (snowmakers and groomers), and Children's Center Staff (ski instructors and daycare providers). For staff with advanced skiing ability, positions include ski instructor and ski patrol.

Duration: Positions available during both the winter and summer. Their ski season begins mid-November, depending on snowfall and temperatures, and continues through mid-April (you are expected to be available through these dates, if hired).

Compensation and Perks: Pay ranges from $5.00 to $7.00 per hour. Perks include free skiing, rental ski equipment, and lessons. Discounts are available for food, daycare, retail shops, and the fitness center. You are encouraged to find housing in September or October, before the ski season begins. Most housing ranges from $400 to $700 per month.

The Ideal Candidate: Applicants must believe in teamwork and have a strong commitment to customer service. Advanced ski applicants must have current CPR and EMT certificates.

Making It Happen: Call for application. If selected you will interview first with Human Resources, then with your hiring manager.

INSIDER TIPS: *It's best to come to one of our job fairs, held October through December (call for a schedule). Appropriate dress is suggested.*

Contact Information: Nan Palmer, Human Resources Coordinator • Stowe Mountain Resort • 5781 Mountain Rd. • Stowe, VT 05672-4890 • Phone: (802) 253-3541 • Fax: (802) 253-3406 • Job Hotline: (802) 253-3543

Sunriver Resort

REGION/HQ: Pacific Northwest/Oregon • **CATEGORY:** Resort • **POSITION TYPE:** Seasonal • **DURATION:** Year-Round • **IDEAL CANDIDATE:** College Students, Career Changers, Foreigners • **APPLICANT POOL:** Varies • **APPLICANTS ACCEPTED:** 250/year

SUNRIVER RESORT IS THE MOST complete destination resort in the Northwest. With over 3,300 acres, the resort offers numerous recreational opportunities, including white-water rafting, canoeing, fishing, and swimming. The resort is surrounded by three 18-hole golf courses; 28 tennis courts; two pools; 30 miles of bike paths; a marina with canoe, kayak, raft, and fishing rentals; a bike shop with over 450 bikes; a complete stable operation; youth, teen, and family programs; and much more. Sunriver's facilities and programs have been repeatedly recognized by leading travel and recreational magazines.

Area and Working Environment: The Cascade mountain range and Mt. Bachelor offer unlimited recreation, including hiking, mountain biking, sightseeing, skiing, and snowmobiling.

Work/Learn Program Specifics: Resort internship positions include: social activities, youth programs, bike shop, and marina. Each intern will gain exposure to various departments to complete a well-rounded internship (such as sales and marketing, special events, recreation department, management, and tours, just to name a few). Each intern will also be responsible for completing and presenting a special project beneficial to both the intern and Sunriver. Seasonal positions: They have over 250 seasonal positions, including youth program leaders, lifeguards, bike shop mechanics/cashiers, marina program leaders/cashiers, restaurants, front office, service station, recreation, housekeeping, and golf.

Duration: Some year-round positions are available, and limited positions are available in May and June. Most positions are twelve weeks, mid-June through Labor Day, with work schedules varying.

Compensation and Perks: Interns will receive a stipend of $950 per month; seasonal employees receive $5.50 to $6.50 per hour (the pay rates in central Oregon are lower, but the cost of living and quality of life are very good). Housing is not provided; however, efforts are made to help employees find adequate housing. In addition to your wages, employees are welcome to take part in numerous free recreation amenities, such as golf, swimming, tennis, biking, canoeing, whitewater rafting, and movies. Discounts in all of their restaurants and resort shops are available, as is a 50 percent discount on accommodations for your immediate family. Your summer work attire is provided—Sunriver shirts and shorts. Oh, and don't forget your bike. It's the best way to get around.

The Ideal Candidate: Interested intern applicants should be juniors or seniors, majoring in a university recreation, physical education, elementary education, sports management, or hotel management program. First aid and CPR certifications are required for all recreation employees. Interns need to be devoted, caring, energetic, and self-motivated people. Seasonal employees need to be friendly and outgoing, enjoy working with people, and physically able to meet the demands of the job.

Making It Happen: Call for application and details of various positions. Submit completed application, cover letter, resume, and three references with phone numbers. A personal interview is a prerequisite to employment. The best time to apply is February and March.

INSIDER TIPS: *For those wanting a full-time job at Sunriver, get your foot in the door by working a summer seasonal job. The best employees get to stay on through winter.*

Contact Information: Personnel Department • Sunriver Resort • P.O. Box 3609 • Sunriver, OR 97707 • Phone: (503) 593-4600 • Fax: (503) 593-4411 • Web Site: www.sunriver-resort.com

SuperCamp

REGION/HQ: Nationwide/California • **CATEGORY:** Camp • **POSITION TYPE:** Seasonal • **DURATION:** Summer • **IDEAL CANDIDATE:** College Students, Career Changers • **APPLICANT POOL:** Varies • **APPLICANTS ACCEPTED:** 200/year

SUPERCAMP IS AN ACADEMIC and personal-growth camp for teenagers. Each program teaches academic skills that help campers succeed in any subject, at any level, and it also addresses life skills, to help develop friendships, resolve conflicts, and communicate more clearly.

Area and Working Environment: Camps are held on academic campuses across the country, including Claremont Colleges (Southern California), Stanford University (Northern California), Colorado College, University of Illinois, Urbana-Champaign, and Hampshire College (Massachusetts). They also have international programs in Malaysia, Singapore, Hong Kong, and England.

Work/Learn Program Specifics: Team leaders lead activities, supervise students, facilitate team meetings, and create camp spirit. This job also includes being a friend and role model to teens. A team usually consists of two or three team leaders, plus eleven to fourteen students. Facilitators set camp direction, inspiration, guidance, and tone, and are the most visible leaders at camp. Facilitators are responsible for presenting the life and academic skills curriculum. This consists of personal growth—communication, team building, relationships, and motivation—and academic growth—memory, creativity, power writing, quantum reading, and academic strategies. Medical personnel are responsible for the health maintenance and emergency care of both students and staff. Counselors are responsible for counseling, support, and leadership for both students and staff. Office managers perform the clerical functions of camp and support the site administrator.

Duration: Staff usually work three to six weeks during the summer; dates vary with each position and camp location. Most staff work two to four camp sessions.

Compensation and Perks: Staff receive an honorarium of $250 to $2,700 per camp session, depending on position, plus room and board. You will attend a five-day staff training session and learn accelerated learning philosophies and techniques, communication skills, and leadership skills, and gain experience working with teens.

The Ideal Candidate: Candidates must be at least eighteen years of age, physically fit and energetic, comfortable relating to teenagers, highly committed to others, self-motivated, enthusiastic, have high integrity, a positive attitude, strong communication skills, be full of playful energy, enjoy challenges, love learning, be willing to work long hours, and do whatever it takes to get the job done!

Making It Happen: Call for an application packet. Rolling deadlines.

Contact Information: Beth Talmon, Human Resources • SuperCamp • 1725 South Coast Highway • Oceanside, CA 92054-5319 • Phone: (619) 722-0072 • Fax: (619) 722-3507 • Toll Free: (800) 527-5321 • E-mail: supercamp@aol.com

Vernon Valley Great Gorge Ski Area

REGION/HQ: Northeast/New Jersey • **CATEGORY:** Ski Resort • **POSITION TYPE:** Internship/Seasonal • **DURATION:** Winter/Summer • **IDEAL CANDIDATE:** High School Students, College Students • **APPLICANT POOL:** Varies • **APPLICANTS ACCEPTED:** Varies

VERNON VALLEY GREAT GORGE SKI AREA is the closest major ski resort to New York City. Located in the picturesque Kitattinny mountains of northwest New Jersey, the resort has a vertical rise of more than one thousand feet, with fifty-two ski slopes spread across three huge mountains. The resort also features two complete base lodge facilities, a New England–style ski village with over 1,200 mountain villas, and a spectacular $12 million spa and fitness center, offering every imaginable recreation amenity.

Work/Learn Program Specifics: Various internships are available in marketing, food and beverage, recreation, operations, and human resources.

Duration: Individuals are hired for two seasons. The summer season beings Memorial Day and ends on Labor Day, and the winter season begins mid-December and ends in March. Employees must be available weekends (although hours are flexible) and a typical work schedule is six days per week.

Compensation and Perks: Besides the wage you'll be earning, you'll receive a free ski pass, lessons, and rentals

during the winter season. They also have an employee incentive program for employees of the week. As prizes, you might receive CDs, lunch for two, spa passes, and gift certificates.

The Ideal Candidate: Applicants must enjoy working with the public and customer-service experience is helpful. College students majoring in communications, marketing, English, hospitality, or recreation are ideal.

Making It Happen: Call for application materials.

Contact Information: Dina Vaccaro, Personnel Director • Vernon Valley Great Gorge Ski Area • P.O. Box 848 • McAfee, NJ 07428 • Phone: (201) 827-2000 • Fax: (201) 209-3342

Village at Breckenridge Resort

REGION/HQ: Rocky Mountains/Colorado • **CATEGORY:** Resort • **POSITION TYPE:** Internship/Seasonal • **DURATION:** Year-Round • **IDEAL CANDIDATE:** College Students, Career Changers, Foreigners • **APPLICANT POOL:** 250/season • **APPLICANTS ACCEPTED:** 175/season

THE VILLAGE AT BRECKENRIDGE RESORT hosts individuals, family groups, and conventions in seven hotel/lodge buildings with over 300 rooms. It has health-club facilities with a hot tub and pools, hiking and biking trails, a mall for convenient shopping, an alpine slide, a human maze, horseback riding, white-water rafting, and plenty of winter snow and skiing.

Area and Working Environment: The twenty-acre village is located steps from historic downtown and at the base of Peak Nine of the Breckenridge Ski Area. It is also just eighty miles west of Denver.

Work/Learn Program Specifics: Positions include front desk clerks, reservationists, PBX operators, cooks, kitchen stewards, waitstaff, buspeople, cashiers, hostesses, housekeepers, laundry personnel, grounds staff, health club attendants, and various winter positions.

Duration: Winter season is from mid-November through mid-April; summer season, from early June through early September.

Compensation and Perks: Wages are $4.75 to $12 per hour. Limited dormitory-style housing is available for $50 per week. Perks include free employee meals per shift worked and a 25 to 50 percent discount in their restaurants.

The Ideal Candidate: Applicants must be cheerful, articulate, and confident. Career-oriented individuals are especially encouraged to apply.

Making It Happen: Call for information packet. Rolling deadlines.

INSIDER TIPS: *Winter housing is very difficult to obtain in the area. It's usually necessary to come in September/October to secure housing; however, jobs usually don't start until mid-November.*

Contact Information: Cathy Radueg, Human Resources Specialist • Village at Breckenridge Resort • P.O. Box 8329 • Breckenridge, CO 80424 • Phone: (970) 453-3120 • Fax: (970) 453-1878 • Alternate: (970) 453-2000

Wilderness Canoe Base

REGION/HQ: Great Lakes/Minnesota • **CATEGORY:** Ministry • **POSITION TYPE:** Seasonal • **DURATION:** Year-Round • **IDEAL CANDIDATE:** College Students, Career Changers, Retired Folks, Foreigners • **APPLICANT POOL:** 130/year • **APPLICANTS ACCEPTED:** 100/year

WILDERNESS CANOE BASE serves youth-at-risk and church youth groups year-round. Off-season they serve young adults and are a retreat for adults. In addition, youth from inner-city schools visit several times per year. A youth hostel is located on the premises.

Area and Working Environment: Located in a rustic and remote wilderness setting on two islands.

Work/Learn Program Specifics: As a wilderness volunteer, you live in a vital, diverse community, helping young people to better know themselves, to live creatively with others, and to experience the greatness of God's love. Volunteers contribute energy and talents in all areas of camp ministry. Positions include nurse, cooks, trips assistant, naturalist, housekeeping, office intern, maintenance/construction, guest theologian, camp grandparent, composting gardener, recreational equipment repairer, logger, dishwasher, evaluation statistician, photographer, and sewing specialist.

Duration: Applicants should be able to commit to two weeks. Volunteers are especially needed in late April and the month of May.

Compensation and Perks: Room and board (great homemade meals), health and accident insurance, and a $10 credit per week of service from the camp store is provided.

The Ideal Candidate: Applicants must have a basic commitment to the Christian faith and its values and be willing to participate in the community process of work, worship, fellowship, affirmation, empowerment, and responsibility.

Making It Happen: Call for application packet. Deadline: one to two months prior to start date. When calling toll free, ask for extension 1388. You can also get ahold of the other director: Jim Wiinanen at 940 Gunflint Trail, Grand Marais, MN 55604, (208) 388-2241

Contact Information: Linda Thorson, Program Director • Wilderness Canoe Base • 2301 Oliver Ave., N • Minneapolis, MN 55411 • Phone: (612) 522-6501 • Fax: (612) 522-2519 • Toll Free: (800) 328-4827

Winter Park Resort

REGION/HQ: Rocky Mountains/Colorado • **CATEGORY:** Ski Resort • **POSITION TYPE:** Seasonal • **DURATION:** Winter/Summer • **IDEAL CANDIDATE:** College Students, Career Changers, Foreigners • **APPLICANT POOL:** Varies • **APPLICANTS ACCEPTED:** 500/year

WINTER PARK RESORT IS COLORADO'S favorite ski resort, using 20 lifts to carry skiers and boarders to 121 trails covering 1,414 skiable acres.

Area and Working Environment: Located sixty-seven miles west of Denver, in the Rocky Mountains.

Work/Learn Program Specifics: For applicants with a limited skiing or snowboarding background, positions available include food service, facilities team member, grounds crew and parking attendants, ticket and lesson sales clerks, reservationists, and children's center staff. For applicants with some basic skiing or snowboarding ability, there are numerous openings for lift attendants. Advanced skiers and snowboarders may apply for positions as race-crew members, ski and snowboard instructors, and ski patrol. Summer job opportunities include seasonal positions as lift attendants on the alpine slide, mini-golf attendants, and food service staff.

Duration: Winter positions begin mid-November and last through late April; summer positions last from mid-June through Labor Day weekend.

Compensation and Perks: Wages start at $6.25 per hour for entry-level positions, plus an end of season bonus. Perks include a free season pass, complimentary lift passes or dependent season passes, free ski and snowboard lessons, group health insurance, food and beverage discounts (food service employees receive a free shift meal), free employee shuttles, and many other on-mountain benefits. Their company store and on-site/low-cost laundry service are invaluable benefits to all. Employees can utilize the Sports Science Fitness Center or the Early Education Center (employee daycare) for a nominal fee. Winter Park also offers a limited amount of subsidized employee housing in nearby condos. As housing can be limited in this area, you are encouraged to come to the valley early in order to secure housing for the season.

The Ideal Candidate: Applicants must be responsible individuals with a neat appearance, a pleasant friendly personality, and an upbeat and positive attitude. Applicant references are checked. Having your own equipment (alpine, snowboard, telemark) is helpful, although local businesses have rental equipment available for all outdoor and winter sports.

Making It Happen: Call or write for application/employment materials. Most hiring takes place after the Labor Day weekend. A personal interview is generally required before a final hiring commitment is made.

INSIDER TIPS: *Come enjoy the year-round beauty of the Rockies—and don't forget to bring your adventurous spirit with you. Popular activities include skiing, snowboarding, snowshoeing, snow biking, ice-skating, snowmobiling, tubing, mountain biking, rafting, hiking, camping, fishing, stargazing, hunting, and more.*

Contact Information: Human Resources • Winter Park Resort • P.O. Box 36 • Winter Park, CO 80482 • Phone: (970) 726-1536 • Fax: (303) 892-5823 • Alternate: (970) 726-5514 • E-mail: hansonkj@csn.com • Web Site: www.skiwinterpark.com/wpmj

Woodhaven Lakes Association

REGION/HQ: Great Lakes/Illinois • **CATEGORY:** Resort • **POSITION TYPE:** Internship • **DURATION:** Year-Round • **IDEAL CANDIDATE:** College Students, Career Changers • **APPLICANT POOL:** Varies • **APPLICANTS ACCEPTED:** Varies

THE WOODHAVEN LAKES ASSOCIATION is a private camping resort. With over 6,000 property sites, Woodhaven is possibly the world's largest resort of its kind. A year-round calendar of programmed activities is complemented by the many amenities that Woodhaven offers to its property owners: two pools, a beach, sand volleyball, watercraft rentals, six tennis courts, eight basketball courts, roller-hockey court, five playgrounds, an outdoor pavilion, a family center, a recreation center, an activity center, a nature center, and an amphitheater.

Work/Learn Program Specifics: Recreation programmer interns will gain experience in a wide variety of activities, including family programs, youth activities, day camp, kids' camp, special event weekends, and numerous children's programs. The experience will also include exposure to other departments, including public relations and communications, finance, maintenance, public safety, and natural resources. Duties will include developing, organizing, and conducting programs; developing activity budgets; writing articles; developing brochures; and managing other projects.

Duration: Internships are ten to sixteen weeks and generally run May through September.

Compensation and Perks: An hourly wage will be paid based on the amount of tuition assistance required. Woodhaven shirts, sweatshirt, and coat will be provided. Assistance will also be given in finding suitable housing in the surrounding area.

The Ideal Candidate: Woodhaven desires applicants with a background in recreation administration or leisure studies.

Making It Happen: Submit cover letter, resume, and a list of three references with current phone numbers. Rolling deadlines.

Contact Information: Thomas Knuth, Recreation Manager • Woodhaven Lakes Association • 509 Lamoille Rd. • P.O. Box 110 • Sublette, IL 61367 • Phone: (815) 849-5209 • Fax: (815) 849-5116 • E-mail: ajbonnel@essex1.com

Y.O. Adventure Camp, Inc.

REGION/HQ: South/Midwest/Texas • **CATEGORY:** Environmental Education • **POSITION TYPE:** Internship/Seasonal • **DURATION:** Year-Round • **IDEAL CANDIDATE:** College Students, Career Changers, Foreigners • **APPLICANT POOL:** Varies • **APPLICANTS ACCEPTED:** 10–15/term

Y.O. ADVENTURE CAMP is an environmental education camp during the school year and a private residential camp during the summer. The ranch itself is home to the world's largest herd of registered longhorn cattle and also boasts one of the largest herds of free-roaming exotic animals.

Area and Working Environment: They are located on the historic 40,000-acre YO Ranch, 90 miles northwest of San Antonio.

Work/Learn Program Specifics: Staff will be trained to lead all activities conducted at the ranch, including YO safari, reptiles, insect study, orienteering, ropes course, group initiatives, climbing, overnight camp-outs, and more. School groups range from fourth to twelfth grade. They have a very comprehensive training program, which covers all of their activities, teaching techniques, child behavior, and more.

Duration: Positions available year-round; consecutive seasons are available.

Compensation and Perks: Pay is $350 to $650 per month, plus dorm-style housing and meals.

The Ideal Candidate: Applicants must be at least nineteen years of age, have completed one year of college, hold a valid driver's license, and must be first aid/CPR certified. Summer season applicants must be certified in lifeguard training.

Making It Happen: Call for application packet. Interviews are conducted over the telephone. Rolling deadlines.

Contact Information: Dan Reynolds, Director • Y.O. Adventure Camp, Inc. • HC-01, Box 555 • Mountain Home, TX 78058-9705 • Phone: (210) 640-3220 • Fax: (210) 640-3348 • E-mail: dreynold@ktc.com • Web Site: www.kidscamps.com/traditional/yo-adventure

● ● ● ● ● ● ● ● ● ● ● ● ● ● ●

Short Listings

Alta Ski Lifts

REGION/HQ: Rocky Mountains/Utah • **CATEGORY:** Ski Resort • **POSITION TYPE:** Seasonal • **DURATION:** Winter/Spring • **IDEAL CANDIDATE:** High School Students, College Students, Career Changers, Retired Folks, Foreigners • **APPLICANT POOL:** Varies • **APPLICANTS ACCEPTED:** 75/year

. . . .

ALTA SKI LIFTS BOASTS PLENTIFUL powder snow and a relaxed small-town atmosphere. The resort runs eight lifts and four tows. Positions include lift operators, ticket sales personnel, five ski instructors, ski patrol personnel, kitchen assistants, groomers, and parking assistants, with salaries starting at $5 per hour.

Contact Information: Program Director • Alta Ski Lifts • Alta, UT 84092 • Phone: (801) 742-3333

Angel Fire Resort

REGION/HQ: South/Midwest/New Mexico • **CATEGORY:** Ski Resort • **POSITION TYPE:** Seasonal • **DURATION:** Winter/Summer • **IDEAL CANDIDATE:** College Students, Career Changers, Foreigners • **APPLICANT POOL:** Varies • **APPLICANTS ACCEPTED:** 250/year

. . . .

ANGEL FIRE RESORT, during the winter season, operates a luxury hotel and a six-chair ski area, covering fifty-eight trails and catering to the high-intermediate/advanced skier. Positions are available for typical ski area and resort hotel line positions, including front desk, food and beverage, housekeepers, cashiers, lift operators, ticket takers, snowmakers, ski patrol staff, ski instructors, golf course personnel, and retail shop staff. Pay varies with your position and, although no employee housing is offered, there is affordable housing in town. All employees receive free skiing and golfing privileges.

Contact Information: Personnel Director • Angel Fire Resort • P.O. Drawer B • Angel Fire, NM 87710 • Phone: (505) 377-6401 • Fax: (505) 377-4240 • Toll Free: (800) 633-7463 • Web Site: www.angelfireresort.com

Aspen Lodge Ranch Resort

REGION/HQ: Rocky Mountains/Colorado • **CATEGORY:** Ranch • **POSITION TYPE:** Seasonal • **DURATION:** Year-Round • **IDEAL CANDIDATE:** College Students, Career Changers, Foreigners • **APPLICANT POOL:** Varies • **APPLICANTS ACCEPTED:** Varies

. . . .

ASPEN LODGE RANCH RESORT is a full recreation and sports facility bordering the Rocky Mountain National Park. Seasonal positions include sports center attendant, children's counselors, waitstaff, bartender, housekeepers, wranglers, groundskeepers, and conference attendants. Wages start at $4.25 per hour, and room and board are provided for $175 per month.

They also offer a 75¢-per-hour bonus at the end of each season.

Contact Information: Steve McFarland, Owner • Aspen Lodge Ranch Resort • 6120 Highway 7 • Estes Park, CO 80517 • Phone: (970) 586-8133 • Fax: (970) 586-8133 • Toll Free: (800) 332-6867

Beaver Run Resort

REGION/HQ: Rocky Mountains/Colorado
• **CATEGORY:** Ski Resort • **POSITION TYPE:** Seasonal
• **DURATION:** Year-Round • **IDEAL CANDIDATE:** College Students, Career Changers, Foreigners
• **APPLICANT POOL:** Varies • **APPLICANTS ACCEPTED:** 400/year

IN THE ROCKY MOUNTAINS, Breckenridge's Beaver Run Resort is a luxury year-round destination resort. Positions available include pool attendants, disc jockeys, housekeepers, snow shovel crew, groundskeepers, security officers, shuttle drivers, switchboard operators, bell staff, auditors, reservation agents, front desk clerks, sales clerks, food service personnel, and all areas of management.

Contact Information: Personnel Director • Beaver Run Resort • P.O. Box 2115 • Breckenridge, CO 80424 • Phone: (303) 453-6000

Best Western Buck's T-4 Lodge of Big Sky

REGION/HQ: Rocky Mountains/Montana
• **CATEGORY:** Lodge • **POSITION TYPE:** Seasonal
• **DURATION:** Winter/Summer • **IDEAL CANDIDATE:** College Students, Career Changers, Retired Folks, Foreigners • **APPLICANT POOL:** Varies • **APPLICANTS ACCEPTED:** 30/year

BEST WESTERN BUCK'S T-4 LODGE OF BIG SKY, located in the Gallatin Canyon and resting at the base of Lone Mountain Ski Hill, is a log-cabin-style lodge and a favorite rest stop for skiers, fishermen, hikers, and nature lovers. Seasonal work includes food service personnel, front desk clerks, auditors, bus drivers, and maintenance staff. Housing is available for a fee and discounts on dining are provided.

Contact Information: Operation Manager • Best Western Buck's T-4 Lodge of Big Sky • P.O. Box 279 • Big Sky, MT 59716 • Phone: (406) 995-4111

Big Sky of Montana

REGION/HQ: Rocky Mountains/Montana
• **CATEGORY:** Ski Resort • **POSITION TYPE:** Seasonal
• **DURATION:** Winter/Summer • **IDEAL CANDIDATE:** College Students, Career Changers, Foreigners
• **APPLICANT POOL:** Varies • **APPLICANTS ACCEPTED:** 350/year

BIG SKY IS ONE OF MONTANA'S premier ski and summer resorts. The resort's ski terrain includes more than fifty-five miles of skiing spread across two mountains. The resort also features the 200+ room Huntley Lodge, 94 condos, a conference center, restaurant, bar, sauna, and jacuzzi. Positions are available in reservations, front desk, accounting, housekeeping, lift operation staff, sales, food and beverage, and ski instruction. Salaries start at minimum wage. Perks include dormitory-style employee housing for $100 per month, a season ski pass, and discounts on meals in the cafeteria.

Contact Information: Hotel Manager • Big Sky of Montana • P.O. Box 160001 • Big Sky, MT 59716 • Phone: (406) 995-4211

Caesars Tahoe

REGION/HQ: Pacific Northwest/Nevada • **CATEGORY:** Casino • **POSITION TYPE:** Seasonal • **DURATION:** Summer • **IDEAL CANDIDATE:** College Students, Career Changers, Foreigners • **APPLICANT POOL:** Varies • **APPLICANTS ACCEPTED:** Varies

CAESARS IS A YEAR-ROUND RESORT and casino that blends in with Lake Tahoe's natural beauty and all-season recreation. Seasonal positions include Hotel (bell desk, front desk, health spa, housekeeping, PBX, reservations, and valet), Food and Beverage (barback, broiler cook, buffet supervisor, busperson, cocktail server, food cashier, food server, fry cook, host, and pantry person), Casino (cage cashier, change person, dealing school, pit clerk, race and sportsbook, retail sales, and security), Finance/Accounting, Special Events/Marketing, and Human Resources.

Contact Information: Human Resources Office • Caesars Tahoe • P.O. Box 5800 • Lake Tahoe, NV 89449 • Phone: (702) 588-3515 • Fax: (702) 586-2013

Camp High Rocks

REGION/HQ: Southeast/North Carolina
• **CATEGORY:** Camp • **POSITION TYPE:** Seasonal
• **DURATION:** Summer • **IDEAL CANDIDATE:** College Students • **APPLICANT POOL:** Varies • **APPLICANTS ACCEPTED:** 65/year

CAMP HIGH ROCKS IS A relatively small boy's camp with a staff-to-camper ratio of approximately one to three, insuring a high degree of individual attention for each boy. Activities emphasize mountaineering but include hiking, backpacking, mountain biking, rock climbing, riding programs, and water activities (from swimming to an extensive river canoeing and kayaking program). Counselors must have completed one year of college, be competent in their teaching field, and have an understanding of and interest in children. An extensive counselor training program is offered to staff before the camp begins. Counselor salaries range from $1,440 to $2,250 for the nine-week season, depending on experience and qualifications. Room, board, and laundry are included.

Contact Information: Hank Birdsong, Camp Director • Camp High Rocks • P.O. Box 127 • Cedar Mountain, NC 28718 • Phone: (704) 885-2153 • Fax: (704) 884-4612 • E-mail: mail@highrocks.com • Web Site: www. highrocks.com

Camp La Jolla

REGION/HQ: Pacific Northwest/California
• **CATEGORY:** Therapeutic Camp • **POSITION TYPE:** Internship/Seasonal • **DURATION:** Summer • **IDEAL CANDIDATE:** College Students, Career Changers, Foreigners • **APPLICANT POOL:** 500/year
• **APPLICANTS ACCEPTED:** 75–85/year

FEATURED ON *The Oprah Winfrey Show* and *Leeza*, Camp La Jolla is dedicated to providing children and young adult ladies with the best fitness and weight-loss program in the nation. Camp La Jolla's programs are held on the beautiful campus of UC, San Diego. Just a short walk from the sandy beaches of the Pacific Ocean, Camp La Jolla's site offers you boundless recreational and educational opportunities. Live-in resident counselors will provide sports and physical fitness activities in their $35 million complex, as well as nutrition education, behavior modification, field trips, and evening programs. Counselers receive $50 to $150 per week, plus

room and board. "Be persistent by calling and following up on your application several times."

Contact Information: Nancy Lenhart, Program Director • Camp La Jolla • 753 B Ave. • Coronado, CA 92118 • Phone: (619) 435-7990 • Fax: (619) 435-8188 • Toll Free: (800) 825-8746 • E-mail: camplj@aol.com • Web Site: www.camplajolla.com

Camp Mondamin/ Camp Green Cove

REGION/HQ: Southeast/North Carolina • **CATEGORY:** Camp • **POSITION TYPE:** Seasonal • **DURATION:** Year-Round • **IDEAL CANDIDATE:** College Students, Career Changers, Foreigners • **APPLICANT POOL:** Varies • **APPLICANTS ACCEPTED:** Varies

CAMP MONDAMIN (for boys) and Camp Green Cove (for girls) are brother/sister camps, located in the mountains of western North Carolina, on Lake Summit. They run a "traditional" program; it's not specialized in one area, but offers a broad spectrum of skills in the outdoor/ wilderness adventure arena for kids ages eight to seventeen. Staff must be at least eighteen (and finished with a year of college) and be adept at teaching at least one of the following skills: swimming (Water Safety Instruction needed), canoeing/kayaking (comfortable in class IV white-water), sailing (fifteen-foot to nineteen-foot sloop-rig boats), horseback riding (hunt seat), mountain biking, tennis, backpacking, and rock climbing.

Contact Information: Frank Bell, Jr., Camp Director • Camp Mondamin/Camp Green Cove • P.O. Box 8 • Tuxedo, NC 28784 • Phone: (888) 666-3264 • E-mail: mondamin@ioa.com • Web Site: www.mondamin.com

Camp Okizu

REGION/HQ: Pacific Northwest/California
• **CATEGORY:** Camp • **POSITION TYPE:** Seasonal
• **DURATION:** Summer • **IDEAL CANDIDATE:** College Students, Career Changers • **APPLICANT POOL:** Varies
• **APPLICANTS ACCEPTED:** Varies

CAMP OKIZU IS A BEAUTIFUL and heavily wooded facility located on Lake Vera, near Nevada City, with activities including swimming, boating, archery, arts and crafts, hiking, sports and games, and outdoor cooking and fishing. Every child should have the chance to experience the fun and excitement of summer camp. Camp Okizu is committed to providing these experiences for children with a chronic or life-threatening disease who do not have these opportunities. There is no charge to the campers, and all staff positions are voluntary.

Contact Information: Heather Ferrier, Executive Director • Camp Okizu • 16 Digital Dr., Suite 100 • P.O. Box 6115 • Novato, CA 94948-6115 • Phone: (415) 382-9083 • Fax: (415) 382-8334 • E-mail: okizu@aol.com

Camp Winnebago in Maine

REGION/HQ: Northeast/Virginia • **CATEGORY:** Camp • **POSITION TYPE:** Internship/Seasonal • **DURATION:** Summer • **IDEAL CANDIDATE:** College Students, Career Changers, Foreigners • **APPLICANT POOL:** Varies • **APPLICANTS ACCEPTED:** Varies

ESTABLISHED IN 1919, Camp Winnebago has been family-owned since day one. It is a summer community of 140 boys aged eight to fifteen, and a counselor staff of fifty adults in a superb Maine wilderness setting. Camp counselors will teach in Athletics (tennis, soccer, volleyball, baseball, basketball, hockey, rollerblading, sailing, canoeing, kayaking, waterskiing, and windsurfing), Individual Activities (photography, nature, arts and crafts, video, riflery, archery, and camping skills), and Outdoor Adventure (overnight, canoe, and mountain bike trips). You'll receive $500 to $1,000 per month, plus room and board.

Contact Information: Phil Lilienthal, Camp Director • Camp Winnebago in Maine • 1606 Washington Plaza • Reston, VA 20190 • Phone: (703) 437-0808 • Fax: (703) 437-8620 • Toll Free: (800) 932-1646 • E-mail: Philcwhv@aol.com • Web Site: www.iswest.net/~winnebago

Cherokee Park Dude Ranch

REGION/HQ: Rocky Mountains/Colorado • **CATEGORY:** Ranch • **POSITION TYPE:** Seasonal • **DURATION:** Spring-Fall • **IDEAL CANDIDATE:** College Students • **APPLICANT POOL:** 250/term • **APPLICANTS ACCEPTED:** 21/term

CHEROKEE PARK RANCH dates back to the late 1800s and is considered one of the oldest ranches in Colorado. When you begin work at Cherokee, you join a unique family and work in every conceivable part of operating a dude ranch. Your job is giving their guests the vacation of a lifetime. Thus, you must have a genuine interest in serving others. You will work six days per week, which includes evening activities with the guests, such as hayrides and square dances. You'll also eat, live, and work together with other staff members for a minimum of three months, between May and September. A weekly wage is offered, plus room and board.

Contact Information: Christine Prince, Owner • Cherokee Park Dude Ranch • 436 Cherokee Hills Dr. • Livermore, CO 80536 • Phone: (970) 493-6522 • Fax: (970) 493-5802 • Toll Free: (800) 628-0949

Cheyenne Mountain Conference Resort

REGION/HQ: Rocky Mountains/Colorado • **CATEGORY:** Resort • **POSITION TYPE:** Seasonal • **DURATION:** Year-Round • **IDEAL CANDIDATE:** College Students, Career Changers, Foreigners • **APPLICANT POOL:** Varies • **APPLICANTS ACCEPTED:** 200/year

THE CHEYENNE MOUNTAIN Conference Resort is located adjacent to the Country Club of Colorado, which features extensive outdoor activities, including fishing, boating, windsurfing, and canoeing on a private thirty-five-acre lake. Positions include food service, desk clerks, guest services, transportation, switchboard, housekeeping, maintenance, conference services, accounting, and personnel. Salaries range from $4.25 to $7.00 per hour.

Contact Information: Human Resources Director • Cheyenne Mountain Conference Resort • 3225 Broadmoor Valley Rd. • Colorado Springs, CO 80906 • Phone: (719) 576-4600

Clearwater Canoe Outfitters & Lodge

REGION/HQ: Great Lakes/Minnesota • **CATEGORY:** Lodge • **POSITION TYPE:** Seasonal • **DURATION:** Summer • **IDEAL CANDIDATE:** College Students, Career Changers, Foreigners • **APPLICANT POOL:** Varies • **APPLICANTS ACCEPTED:** Varies

THE MAIN LODGE OF Clearwater Canoe Outfitters & Lodge was completed in 1926 and is listed on the National Register of Historic Places. The largest remaining whole log structure in northeastern Minnesota, it has retained the look and feel of the pioneer days. A few secluded cabins, or bed and breakfast rooms upstairs in the lodge itself, offer an alternative to camping. The business is small, consisting of six to eight staff members, and prides itself on its wilderness preservation ethic. Positions are available in front desk/office/housekeeping, waterfront/maintenance, housekeeping/childcare, cook, naturalist, and outfitting packer/maintenance.

Contact Information: Owner • Clearwater Canoe Outfitters & Lodge • 355 Gunflint Trail • Grand Marais, MN 55604 • Phone: (218) 388-2254 • Fax: (218) 388-2254

Club Med Management Services, Inc.

REGION/HQ: Worldwide/Florida • **CATEGORY:** Resort • **POSITION TYPE:** Unique Experience • **DURATION:** Year-Round • **IDEAL CANDIDATE:** College Students, Career Changers, Retired Folks, Foreigners • **APPLICANT POOL:** Varies • **APPLICANTS ACCEPTED:** Varies

CLUB MED HAS JOB opportunities of varying lengths at their luxury resorts around the world. They hire year-round for positions ranging from snorkeling instructors to tour guides. You must be at least nineteen years old and willing to go anywhere in the world to work.

Contact Information: Human Resources Director • Club Med Management Services, Inc. • 4500 SE Pine Valley St. • Port St. Lucie, FL 34952 • Phone: (800) 258-2633 • Job Hotline: (407) 337-6660

Colorado Trails Ranch

REGION/HQ: Rocky Mountains/Colorado • **CATEGORY:** Ranch • **POSITION TYPE:** Seasonal • **DURATION:** Summer • **IDEAL CANDIDATE:** College Students • **APPLICANT POOL:** Varies • **APPLICANTS ACCEPTED:** Varies

BEAUTIFUL MOUNTAIN SCENERY, hard work, and lots of fun—these are just a few of the elements that guest ranch crew experiences every summer. If you have a ready smile, are willing to work hard, love the outdoors, and enjoy working with people, they may have a job for you. Colorado Trails Ranch is a full-service guest ranch located twelve miles northeast of Durango, Colorado. Summer positions include chef, riding guide,

housekeeping, server, floater, counselor, maintenance, and sports/utility. You will receive a salary, plus room and board.

Contact Information: Owner • Colorado Trails Ranch • 12161 CR 240 • Durango, CO 81031 • Phone: (970) 247-5055 • Toll Free: (800) 323-3833 • E-mail: CoTRanch@aol.com • Web Site: http://subee.com/colotrails/home.html

Copper Mountain Resort

REGION/HQ: Rocky Mountains/Colorado • **CATEGORY:** Ski Resort • **POSITION TYPE:** Seasonal • **DURATION:** Year-Round • **IDEAL CANDIDATE:** College Students, Career Changers, Foreigners • **APPLICANT POOL:** Varies • **APPLICANTS ACCEPTED:** 1,200/year

NESTLED IN THE COLORADO ROCKIES, Copper Mountain is repeatedly recognized as one of the top ski and resort areas in the United States. Area activities include skiing, golfing, tennis, and horseback riding. Seasonal positions include ski instructors, ski rental fitters, ski lift operators, ski repairmen, lift ticket checkers, ticket sellers, day-care teachers, bus drivers, parking attendants, phone operators, bellmen, cooks, food and beverage staff, front desk staff, lodging staff, shop sales, and base crew. Pay ranges from $5.00 to $7.50 per hour. Perks include a free season ski pass, complimentary ski tickets, and discounts for ski lessons/accessories and lodging.

Contact Information: Human Resources Department • Copper Mountain Resort • P.O. Box 3001 • Copper Mountain, CO 80443 • Phone: (970) 968-2318 • Job Hotline: (970) 968-6339 • E-mail: cmr-hr@skicopper.com • Web Site: www.ski-copper.com

Cross Bar X Youth Ranch

REGION/HQ: Rocky Mountains/Colorado • **CATEGORY:** Ministry • **POSITION TYPE:** Internship/Seasonal • **DURATION:** Summer • **IDEAL CANDIDATE:** College Students, Career Changers, Foreigners • **APPLICANT POOL:** Varies • **APPLICANTS ACCEPTED:** Varies

THE CAMP TAKES A maximum of twenty campers per session, lasting one to two weeks, with one counselor per five campers. Counselor responsibilities will include mountain biking, swimming, fishing, backpacking, horseback riding, archery, games, Bible lessons, and arts and crafts. Interns receive $50 per week, plus room and board. "We need a strong Christian commitment from our counselors."

Contact Information: Nick Brothers, Director • Cross Bar X Youth Ranch • 2111 County Rd. 222 • Durango, CO 81301 • Phone: (970) 259-2716

Double JJ Resort Ranch

REGION/HQ: Great Lakes/Michigan • **CATEGORY:** Ranch • **POSITION TYPE:** Seasonal • **DURATION:** Year-Round • **IDEAL CANDIDATE:** College Students, Foreigners • **APPLICANT POOL:** 700+/year • **APPLICANTS ACCEPTED:** 225/term

THIS IS A GREAT SITE for hospitality and recreation interns, as you will gain hands-on experience in a variety of positions, including office, sports, wrangler, golf course, food and beverage, and retail. You will receive a weekly salary, plus room and board.

Contact Information: Addie Trocano, Administrative Director • Double JJ Resort Ranch • P.O. Box 94 • Rothbury, MI 49452 • Phone: (616) 894-4444 • Fax: (616) 893-5355 • Toll Free: (800) 368-2535

Eckerd Family Youth Alternatives

REGION/HQ: Southeast/Northeast/Florida • **CATEGORY:** Therapeutic Recreation • **POSITION TYPE:** Internship • **DURATION:** Year-Round • **IDEAL CANDIDATE:** College Students, Career Changers • **APPLICANT POOL:** Varies • **APPLICANTS ACCEPTED:** Varies

ECKERD FAMILY YOUTH ALTERNATIVES provides a comprehensive, rehabilitative residential experience for at-risk youth, which includes adventure-based counseling, group peer counseling, and experiential education programs. The wilderness camps are spread out over Florida, Georgia, North Carolina, Tennessee, Vermont, Rhode Island, and New Hampshire. Counselor/teachers become role models and facilitators for self-healing for the campers (who come voluntarily in need of help). A competitive salary, plus room and board, is offered.

Contact Information: Wendy Douglas, Recruiting Administrator • Eckerd Family Youth Alternatives • 100 N. Starcrest Dr. • Clearwater, FL 34625 • Phone: (813) 461-2990 • Fax: (813) 442-5911 • Toll Free: (800) 222-1473 • E-mail: dsand332@mail.gte.net

Estes Park Center

REGION/HQ: Rocky Mountains/Colorado • **CATEGORY:** Camp • **POSITION TYPE:** Internship/Seasonal • **DURATION:** Year-Round • **IDEAL CANDIDATE:** College Students, Career Changers, Foreigners • **APPLICANT POOL:** Varies • **APPLICANTS ACCEPTED:** Varies

AN AFFILIATE OF THE International YMCA, the YMCA of the Rockies strives to maintain a Christian environment for its conferences, families, campers, and staff. Job opportunities are primarily available in food services, housekeeping, and buildings and grounds. Other positions include administrative personnel, front desk clerks, switchboard operators, craft shop instructors, pool guards (must have current certification), retail salesperson, hikemasters, camp counselors, and environmental education counselors.

Contact Information: Patrice Flauné, Human Resources Director • Estes Park Center • YMCA Of The Rockies • 2515 Tunnel Rd. • Estes Park, CO 80511-2550 • Phone: (970) 586-3341 • Fax: (970) 586-6078

Flagg Ranch Village

REGION/HQ: Rocky Mountains/Wyoming • **CATEGORY:** Ranch • **POSITION TYPE:** Seasonal • **DURATION:** Winter/Summer • **IDEAL CANDIDATE:** College Students, Career Changers • **APPLICANT POOL:** Varies • **APPLICANTS ACCEPTED:** Varies

FLAGG RANCH IS A privately-owned company that operates visitor services under a concession agreement with the National Park Service. They are located in the northwest corner of Wyoming, two miles south of Yellowstone National Park and three miles north of Grand Teton National Park. Positions are available in these areas: lodging, food and beverage, gift shop, front desk/reservations, auditor, campground, gas station, grocery store, maintenance, river guide, naturalist/ activities coordinator, security, dorm assistant, snowcoach driver, and management/supervisory positions. You will receive an hourly wage, and room and board are provided with the cost deducted from your paycheck. They also have a limited number of full hookup sites for those employees with their own trailers or motor homes.

Contact Information: Human Resources • Flagg Ranch Village • P.O. Box 187 • Moran, WY 83013 • Phone: (800) 443-2311

Food Service Management Internship

REGION/HQ: Nationwide/Utah • **CATEGORY:** Food Service • **POSITION TYPE:** Internship • **DURATION:** Summer • **IDEAL CANDIDATE:** College Students, Foreigners • **APPLICANT POOL:** 100–200/year • **APPLICANTS ACCEPTED:** 75/year

THE FOOD SERVICE Management Internship Program is co-sponsored by the National Association of College and University Food Services and the Association of College and University Housing Officers–International. Food service management interns participate in three phases, including orientation and introduction, participation, and the supervisory experience. Interns participate in all areas of kitchen production (meat cookery, baking), services (counter duties), testing and sampling new food products, quality control of food production and recipes, and purchasing procedures and ordering techniques. A stipend of $1,000—plus room, board, and uniforms (an approximate value of $1,600)—is provided.

Contact Information: Food Services Director • Food Service Management Internship • Brigham Young University Dining Services • 180 SASB, P.O. Box 21840 • Provo, UT 84602-1840 • Phone: (801) 378-2571 • Fax: (801) 378-7431

4-H Farley Outdoor Education Center

REGION/HQ: Northeast/Massachusetts • **CATEGORY:** Outdoor Education • **POSITION TYPE:** Seasonal • **DURATION:** Summer • **IDEAL CANDIDATE:** College Students • **APPLICANT POOL:** 200/year • **APPLICANTS ACCEPTED:** 50/year

4-H Farley, founded in 1934, is owned and operated by the Cape Cod 4-H Camp Corporation, a private nonprofit organization representing southeastern Massachusetts. In addition to the program staff, other positions include leadership/director, kitchen/food service, maintenance, and health/nurse/behavioral specialist. All staff receives a stipend plus room and board.

Contact Information: Michael Campbell, Executive Director • 4-H Farley Outdoor Education Center • 615 Route 130 • Mashpee, MA 02649 • Phone: (508) 477-0181 • Fax: (508) 539-0080

Four Winds * Westward Ho

REGION/HQ: Pacific Northwest/Washington • **CATEGORY:** Camp • **POSITION TYPE:** Internship/Seasonal • **DURATION:** Summer • **IDEAL CANDIDATE:** College Students, Career Changers, Foreigners • **APPLICANT POOL:** Varies • **APPLICANTS ACCEPTED:** Varies

FOUR WINDS * WESTWARD HO is a nonprofit, private, children's summer camp (located on 150 acres in the beautiful San Juan Islands) which emphasizes simplicity, community, respect for nature, and adventure. Diversity is a major highlight; their program is activity-based with arts and crafts, riding, canoeing, sailing, and sports. Their garden program is just getting off the ground and involves working closely with the head gardener, planning activities based in and around the garden, and helping campers understand aspects of gardening and natural environment around camp. Activities you may be involved with include making solar ovens and flower wreaths, drying flowers, making potpourri, preparing meals with fresh fruits and vegetables, building small animal houses, collecting seeds, painting signs, and much more. Housing, meals, and laundry are provided, as is an incredible working environment.

Contact Information: Katie Weinstein, Assistant Director • Four Winds * Westward Ho • P.O. Box 140 • Deer Harbor, WA 98243-0140 • Phone: (360) 376-2277

Golden Acres Farm & Ranch

REGION/HQ: Northeast/New York • **CATEGORY:** Ranch • **POSITION TYPE:** Seasonal • **DURATION:** Summer • **IDEAL CANDIDATE:** College Students, Foreigners • **APPLICANT POOL:** 500/year • **APPLICANTS ACCEPTED:** 90/year

LOCATED IN THE CATSKILL MOUNTAINS, this Kosher family resort offers summer jobs as counselors, administration staff, and food and beverage positions. European students make up 60 percent of the staff.

Contact Information: Patricia Gauthier, Program Director • Golden Acres Farm & Ranch • County Road 14 • Gilboa, NY 12076 • Phone: (607) 588-7329 • Fax: (607) 588-6911 • E-mail: PJG211@aol.com

Gunflint Lodge

REGION/HQ: Great Lakes/Minnesota • **CATEGORY:** Lodge • **POSITION TYPE:** Internship • **DURATION:** Year-Round • **IDEAL CANDIDATE:** College Students, Career Changers, Foreigners • **APPLICANT POOL:** Varies • **APPLICANTS ACCEPTED:** Varies

GUNFLINT LODGE IS A seasonal fishing resort and canoe outfitter and is surrounded by over one million acres of wilderness in the Superior National Forest. Guests come from all over the country to relax in the north woods atmosphere, fish, swim, canoe, and explore. Outfitting and hospitality interns are needed. You will receive $865 per month, plus a bonus. Recreational equipment is available for use in off hours. Bunkhouse-style accommodations are available for $110 per month.

Contact Information: Program Manager • Gunflint Lodge • 750 Gunflint Trail • Grand Marais, MN 55604 • Phone: (218) 388-2294 • Fax: (218) 388-9429

Harveys Resort Hotel/ Casino

REGION/HQ: Pacific Northwest/Nevada • **CATEGORY:** Casino • **POSITION TYPE:** Seasonal • **DURATION:** Year-Round • **IDEAL CANDIDATE:** College Students, Career Changers, Retired Folks, Foreigners • **APPLICANT POOL:** Varies • **APPLICANTS ACCEPTED:** Varies

OPPORTUNITIES ARE AVAILABLE in gaming, health club, hotel, housekeeping, food service, marketing, accounting, administration, cashiers, building maintenance, facilities, transportation, security, and human resources.

Contact Information: Human Resources Director • Harveys Resort Hotel/Casino • P.O. Box 128 • Stateline, NV 89449 • Phone: (702) 588-2411 • Fax: (702) 588-8084

Hidden Valley Camp

REGION/HQ: Northeast/Maine • **CATEGORY:** Camp • **POSITION TYPE:** Seasonal • **DURATION:** Summer • **IDEAL CANDIDATE:** College Students, Career Changers • **APPLICANT POOL:** Varies • **APPLICANTS ACCEPTED:** Varies

HIDDEN VALLEY IS SECLUDED in a 300-acre wooded glen with a mile-long private lake. Counselors teach or assist with four daily workshops, live in a cabin with one or two other counselors, and share in the responsibility of care of their campers. A competitive salary is offered, plus room and board.

Contact Information: Peter and Meg Kassen, Directors • Hidden Valley Camp • RR 1, Box 2360 • Freedom, ME 04941 • Phone: (207) 342-5177 • Fax: (207) 342-5685 • Toll Free: (800) 922-6737 • E-mail: hvcamp@aol.com

Holiday Inn & Conference Center of Estes Park

REGION/HQ: Rocky Mountains/Colorado • **CATEGORY:** Resort • **POSITION TYPE:** Internship/Seasonal • **DURATION:** Year-Round • **IDEAL CANDIDATE:** College Students, Career Changers, Retired Folks • **APPLICANT POOL:** Varies • **APPLICANTS ACCEPTED:** 80/year

OPERATED BY FOREVER RESORTS, Holiday Inn & Conference Center at Estes Park boasts a two-acre facility, which includes a conference center, fitness room, indoor pool/hot tub, restaurant, and banquet facilities. It sits at 7,500 feet and is five miles from the entrance to Rocky Mountain National Park. Year-round seasonal positions include guest services, food services, room attendants, and laundry personnel. Wages range from $2.50 to $8.00 per hour. Perks include on-site room and board for $21 per week (or off-site for $600 per month), half off on all meals in the restaurant, and discounts in the gift shop.

Contact Information: Paula Dunfee, Human Resources Director • Holiday Inn & Conference Center of Estes Park • P.O. Box 1468 • Estes Park, CO 80517 • Phone: (970) 586-2332 • Web Site: www.foreverresorts.com

The Home Ranch

REGION/HQ: Rocky Mountains/Colorado
• **CATEGORY:** Ranch • **POSITION TYPE:** Seasonal
• **DURATION:** Year-Round • **IDEAL CANDIDATE:** College Students, Career Changers, Foreigners
• **APPLICANT POOL:** Varies • **APPLICANTS ACCEPTED:** Varies

• •

THE CALL OF THE WEST has always been strong in the hearts of Americans. No matter if they were raised on the romantic tales of Zane Grey, thrilled to the heroics of matinee idols like Roy Rogers, or laughed at the antics depicted in *City Slickers*, it is a safe bet that members of every generation have longed for the opportunity to ride the range and conquer the mountains. Staying at the Home Ranch is a chance to heed the call of the West, if only for a little while. The 1,500-acre ranch accommodates over 42 guests per week and has wilderness trails, horseback riding trails, and fly-fishing on the Elk River in the summer; and cross-country skiing, snowshoeing, and downhill skiing in the winter. Staff positions include children's counselors, kitchen helpers, cooks, dishwashers, waitstaff, housekeepers, maintenance personnel, hiking guides, wranglers, and cross-country ski guides. All positions are offered with a graduated salary starting at $800 per month, plus room, board, and laundry facilities.

Contact Information: Will Hardly, Manager • The Home Ranch • P.O. Box 822 • Clark, CO 80428 • Phone: (970) 879-1780 • Fax: (970) 879-1795 • E-mail: hrclark@cmn.net • Web Site: www.homeranch.com

Hotel Washington

REGION/HQ: Washington, D.C./Washington, D.C.
• **CATEGORY:** Hotel • **POSITION TYPE:** Internship
• **DURATION:** Year-Round • **IDEAL CANDIDATE:** College Students, Career Changers, Foreigners
• **APPLICANT POOL:** Varies • **APPLICANTS ACCEPTED:** 1/term

• •

AS THE OLDEST CONTINUOUSLY operated hotel in D.C., Hotel Washington has been host to tour groups for over twenty years. Old, European-style, and newly remodeled, with the best location in Washington, D.C., this hotel is demanded by the domestic market. An intern is needed to help with everything from A to Z in tour and travel sales, including researching, prospecting, contracting, preparing final agreements, greeting escorts and guests, preparing for trade shows, and administrative duties. The intern will also accompany the tour and travel director on hotel sites for clients, lunches with other tour and travel sales managers, and local industry functions. The intern will receive complimentary lunches and the opportunity to work with the largest domestic-tour hotel in D.C.

Contact Information: Tour & Travel Director • Hotel Washington • Pennsylvania Ave. at 15th St. • Washington, DC 20004 • Phone: (202) 638-5900 • Fax: (202) 638-1594 • Toll Free: (800) 424-9540

Hunewill Guest Ranch

REGION/HQ: Pacific Northwest/Nevada • **CATEGORY:** Ranch • **POSITION TYPE:** Seasonal • **DURATION:** Spring-Fall • **IDEAL CANDIDATE:** College Students, Career Changers • **APPLICANT POOL:** 30/term • **APPLICANTS ACCEPTED:** 10/term

• •

HUNEWILL RANCH is situated in Bridgeport Valley (California) in the heart of the eastern Sierras, at 6,500 feet. Directly behind the ranch are snow-covered crags which mark the boundary of Yosemite National Park. Staff comes back year after year to work hard and meet vacationers from all over the world while spending free time in the Sierras, breathing fresh, clean air. Positions are available in the kitchen, cleaning cabins, maintenance, as babysitters, and as wranglers. "We are looking for wholesome, robust, and cheerful employees who are willing to pitch in where needed."

Contact Information: Betsy Hunewill Elliott, Personnel Director • Hunewill Guest Ranch • 205 Hunewill Ln. • Wellington, NV 89444 • Phone: (702) 465-2238 • Fax: (702) 465-2056

Kennolyn Camp

REGION/HQ: Pacific Northwest/California
• **CATEGORY:** Camp • **POSITION TYPE:** Seasonal
• **DURATION:** Summer • **IDEAL CANDIDATE:** College Students, Career Changers • **APPLICANT POOL:** Varies
• **APPLICANTS ACCEPTED:** Varies

• •

KENNOLYN CAMP is located in the Santa Cruz Mountains and seeks counselors to lead campers (ages six to fourteen) through extensive ropes courses and other areas. Staff receive $170 to $220 per week salary, plus room and board.

Contact Information: Andrew Townsend, Director • Kennolyn Camp • 8205 Glen Haven Rd. • Soquel, CA 95073 • Phone: (408) 479-6714 • Fax: (408) 479-6718 • E-mail: kennolyn@aol.com • Web Site: www.kennolyn.com

Kiawah Island Resort

REGION/HQ: Southeast/South Carolina • **CATEGORY:** Resort • **POSITION TYPE:** Internship • **DURATION:** Year-Round • **IDEAL CANDIDATE:** College Students, Career Changers • **APPLICANT POOL:** Varies • **APPLICANTS ACCEPTED:** Varies

KIAWAH ISLAND RESORT is located just twenty-one miles south of historic Charleston, South Carolina. Retail, recreation, golf course, lodging, food and beverage, office/clerical, and maintenance positions are available. Kiawah also offers career-growth opportunities, cross-training programs, management development programs, employee relations activities, and discounts on merchandise, golf and tennis, and hotel stays.

Contact Information: Susan Gilinsky, Recruiter/Trainer • Kiawah Island Resort • 12 Kiawah Beach Dr. • Kiawah Island, SC 29455 • Phone: (803) 768-6000 • Fax: (803) 768-6061

Lake of the Woods/ Greenwood Camps

REGION/HQ: Great Lakes/Illinois • **CATEGORY:** Camp • **POSITION TYPE:** Internship/Seasonal • **DURATION:** Summer • **IDEAL CANDIDATE:** College Students, Foreigners • **APPLICANT POOL:** 500/year • **APPLICANTS ACCEPTED:** 60/year

LAKE OF THE WOODS/Greenwood Camps is a traditional, private summer camp, located on a spring-fed lake. Instructors and counselors are needed to assist with over fifty different activities. You will receive a stipend of $1,350 and room and board. Applications must be received by May 31.

Contact Information: Ean Cuthbert, Assistant Director • Lake of the Woods/Greenwood Camps • 1765 Maple St. • Northfield, IL 60093 • Phone: (708) 446-2444

• Fax: (708) 446-2454 • Web Site: www.campchannel.com/lwcgwc

Nelson's Resort

REGION/HQ: Great Lakes/Minnesota • **CATEGORY:** Resort • **POSITION TYPE:** Seasonal • **DURATION:** Spring-Fall • **IDEAL CANDIDATE:** College Students, Career Changers, ForeignerS • **APPLICANT POOL:** 25/term • **APPLICANTS ACCEPTED:** 25/term

IN 1931, THE NELSONS dreamed of a first-class resort on the edge of the wilderness. You can find this dream still alive in the north woods of Minnesota. Still operated by the Nelson family, the tradition of friendly hospitality, impeccable cleanliness, and individual service awaits each and every guest. The resort borders Voyageurs National Park, a wilderness area great for hiking, swimming, fishing, and camping. Summer positions include food service staff, housekeeping, dock attendants, store clerk, office assistant, and maintenance staff. Staff receive $5 per hour, and those who have experience or training can request a higher wage. Also included is free housing and a bonus if your contract is fulfilled. You will have use of boats and the resort facilities and great home-cooked meals for a reasonable cost. "We want employees who are friendly and outgoing, willing to learn, and responsible. Good references are important."

Contact Information: Jacque Eggen, Manager • Nelson's Resort • 7632 Nelson Rd. • Crane Lake, MN 55725-8023 • Phone: (218) 993-2295 • Fax: (218) 993-2242

Ocean Reef Club

REGION/HQ: Southeast/Florida • **CATEGORY:** Resort • **POSITION TYPE:** Internship/Seasonal • **DURATION:** Year-Round • **IDEAL CANDIDATE:** College Students, Career Changers • **APPLICANT POOL:** Varies • **APPLICANTS ACCEPTED:** Varies

OCEAN REEF CLUB is a luxury club on four thousand lush tropical acres on the edge of the Atlantic. Seasonal positions include clubhouse server, palm court expediter, card sound server, front desk, culinary positions, and retail sales. Housing is available in their housing complex.

Contact Information: Larry Wood, Employment Manager • Ocean Reef Club • 31 Ocean Reef Dr. • Key Largo, FL 33037 • Phone: (305) 367-5904 • Fax: (305) 367-

4348 • Job Hotline: (800) 540-1864 • E-mail: reefhr@reefnet.com • Web Site: www.reefnet.com/hrjobs.html

Peaceful Valley Lodge and Ranch

REGION/HQ: Rocky Mountains/Colorado
• **CATEGORY:** Ranch • **POSITION TYPE:** Seasonal
• **DURATION:** Year-Round • **IDEAL CANDIDATE:** College Students, Career Changers, Foreigners
• **APPLICANT POOL:** Varies • **APPLICANTS ACCEPTED:** Varies

PEACEFUL VALLEY LODGE and Ranch is a dude ranch serving 80 to 130 people in weeklong programs. The ranch has a swimming pool, tennis court, fishing pond and stream, playground, and horseback riding in the Rocky Mountains, surrounded by magnificent scenery. Positions include waitstaff, dishwashers, assistant cooks, counselors, wranglers, housekeepers, driver/mechanical personnel, maintenance staff, gardeners/grounds crew, and an office person. All staff will have the opportunity to show off their talents at evening programs, talent show, melodrama, and church choir. In addition, the staff will have the opportunity to work hard while growing on a personal level, meeting unique people among the guests and staff, and learning the art of genuine hospitality. Wages are $600 to $800 per month, including room and board.

Contact Information: Personnel Director • Peaceful Valley Lodge and Ranch • 475 Peaceful Valley Rd. • Lyons, CO 80540-8951 • Phone: (303) 747-2881 • Fax: (303) 747-2167 • Toll Free: (800) 955-6343

Peaks Resort and Spa

REGION/HQ: Rocky Mountains/Colorado
• **CATEGORY:** Resort • **POSITION TYPE:** Seasonal
• **DURATION:** Summer/Winter • **IDEAL CANDIDATE:** College Students, Career Changers, Retired Folks
• **APPLICANT POOL:** Varies • **APPLICANTS ACCEPTED:** Varies

THE PEAKS RESORT AND SPA, in the beautiful San Juan Mountains, offers positions in food and beverage, culinary, front office, spa, massage therapy, retail, and housekeeping. As an employee, you'll have access to the Cybex weight room, the indoor lap pool, racquetball and squash courts, the cardio deck, the climbing wall, and five outdoor tennis courts. After the snow melts and the days of skiing, snowshoeing, and ice climbing are over, the mountains continue to offer a vast array of activities, such as hiking, biking, fishing, horseback riding, white-water rafting, rock climbing, and weekly festivals.

Contact Information: Human Resources • Peaks Resort and Spa • P.O. Box 2702 • Telluride, CO 81435 • Phone: (800) 766-5627 • E-mail: hrpeaks@montrose.net

Redfish Lake Lodge

REGION/HQ: Pacific Northwest/Idaho • **CATEGORY:** Lodge • **POSITION TYPE:** Seasonal • **DURATION:** Summer • **IDEAL CANDIDATE:** College Students, Career Changers, Foreigners • **APPLICANT POOL:** 100/year • **APPLICANTS ACCEPTED:** 55/year

REDFISH LAKE LODGE, established in 1929, is a family-oriented rustic lodge on a lake in the Sawtooth Mountains. Redfish Lodge sits on the border of the beautiful, rugged Sawtooth Wilderness. The area offers incredible backpacking, horseback riding, white-water rafting, rock climbing, mountain bike riding, and fishing. Positions include food service staff, service station, housekeepers, marina staff, store assistants, front-desk clerks, and maintenance people. You will receive $570 per month, plus room and board.

Contact Information: General Manager • Redfish Lake Lodge • Box 9 • Stanley, ID 83278 • Phone: (208) 774-3536 • Fax: (208) 774-3583

Rocky Mountain Village

REGION/HQ: Rocky Mountains/Colorado
• **CATEGORY:** Therapeutic Camp • **POSITION TYPE:** Internship/Seasonal • **DURATION:** Summer • **IDEAL CANDIDATE:** High School Students, College Students, Career Changers, Retired Folks, Foreigners
• **APPLICANT POOL:** 80/year • **APPLICANTS ACCEPTED:** 40/year

ROCKY MOUNTAIN VILLAGE is owned and operated by the Colorado Easter Seal Society and serves as a residential camp serving children and adults with physical and/or cognitive disabilities. Positions include activity director, registered nurse, cabin counselors, kitchen/cooks, maintenance, and specialists in these areas: trips/travel, ropes course, outdoor education, arts and crafts, aquatics, horseback riding/animals, and media. Staff receives a stipend of $1,200 for the summer and those who work the entire season are eligible for a $300 bonus. "We're looking for people who have a desire to work with children and adults with disabilities. Our emphasis is on promoting equality, dignity, and independence in an outdoor recreational environment."

Contact Information: Christine Newell, Director • Rocky Mountain Village • Colorado Easter Seal Society • P.O. Box 115 • Empire, CO 80438 • Phone: (303) 892-6063 • Fax: (303) 825-5004 • Toll Free: (800) 875-4732 • E-mail: campinfo@cess.org

Ski Homewood

REGION/HQ: Pacific Northwest/California • **CATEGORY:** Ski Resort • **POSITION TYPE:** Internship/Seasonal • **DURATION:** Year-Round • **IDEAL CANDIDATE:** High School Students, College Students, Career Changers, Retired Folks, Foreigners • **APPLICANT POOL:** Varies • **APPLICANTS ACCEPTED:** Varies

• •

SKI HOMEWOOD HOLDS a special place in the hearts of skiers and snowboarders who have experienced its extraordinary views. Homewood's great terrain rises dramatically up from the shoreline of beautiful Lake Tahoe, and the result is a skiing experience like no other. Seasonal positions and recreation internships are available, with the biggest perk being a ski pass for the season.

Contact Information: Denise Mix, Human Resources Manager • Ski Homewood • P.O. Box 165 • Homewood, CA 96141 • Phone: (916) 525-2992 • Fax: (916) 525-0417 • E-mail: smile@homewood.com • Web Site: www.skihomewood.com

Snowbird Ski & Summer Resort

REGION/HQ: Rocky Mountains/Utah • **CATEGORY:** Ski Resort • **POSITION TYPE:** Seasonal • **DURATION:** Year-Round • **IDEAL CANDIDATE:** College Students, Career Changers, Retired Folks, Foreigners • **APPLICANT POOL:** Varies • **APPLICANTS ACCEPTED:** 800/year

• •

WITH A MID-MOUNTAIN average annual snowfall of more than 500 inches, Snowbird attracts more fresh powder snow than almost any other resort in the country. Snowbird's mountain trails cover more than 2,000 skiable acres. Seasonal staff positions include food service personnel, front desk clerks, reservation clerks,

sales clerks, security officers, switchboard operators, valets, tram operators, ski hosts/hostesses, housekeeping, parking attendants, warehouse laborers, ski school, and mountain operations. Wages vary. Snowbird's perks feature a generous ski privilege program that includes dependent passes, group health/hospitalization, life insurance, free transportation, and discounts on food, ski lessons, and lodging.

Contact Information: Human Resources Manager • Snowbird Ski & Summer Resort • 7350 S. Wasatch Blvd. • Salt Lake City, UT 84121 • Phone: (801) 943-2243 • Fax: (801) 742-3300

Tamarron Resort

REGION/HQ: Rocky Mountains/Colorado • **CATEGORY:** Ski Resort • **POSITION TYPE:** Seasonal • **DURATION:** Year-Round • **IDEAL CANDIDATE:** College Students, Career Changers, Foreigners • **APPLICANT POOL:** Varies • **APPLICANTS ACCEPTED:** 450/year

• •

TAMARRON RESORT is a 630-acre resort offering elegance and service unmatched in the Rocky Mountains. They actively recruit for food service personnel, golf course greens keepers, ski lift operators, housekeeping, front desk clerks, clerical support, bus drivers, security officers, accounting clerks, banquet staff, purchasing agents, recreation staff, stable wranglers, and a tennis and golf pro. Hourly wages vary. Winter Perks: free lift pass, use of Nordic ski trails, and half-off discounts on alpine/Nordic ski lessons, sleigh rides, and snowmobiling. Summer Perks: one complimentary white-water rafting trip, jeep trips, and discounts on golf and tennis. All employees receive a complimentary health spa membership and numerous social and recreational activities.

Contact Information: Personnel Director • Tamarron Resort • P.O. Box 3131 • Durango, CO 81301 • Phone: (970) 259-2000

Tejas Girl Scout Council

• **REGION/HQ:** South/Midwest/Texas • **CATEGORY:** Camp • **POSITION TYPE:** Seasonal • **DURATION:** Summer • **IDEAL CANDIDATE:** College Students, Career Changers • **APPLICANT POOL:** 120/year • **APPLICANTS ACCEPTED:** 65/year

• •

Thunder is good, thunder is impressive; but it is lightning that does the work.
—MARK TWAIN

"WE NEED STAFF WITH a love of the outdoors, who enjoy working with young women, ages seven to seventeen years, and have the ability to get along with peers."

Contact Information: Carla Weiland, Outdoor Program Manager • Tejas Girl Scout Council • 4411 Skillman • Dallas, TX 75206 • Phone: (214) 823-1342 • Fax: (214) 824-3324 • Toll Free: (800) 442-2260

Teton Valley Ranch Camp

REGION/HQ: Rocky Mountains/Wyoming • **CATEGORY:** Ranch • **POSITION TYPE:** Seasonal • **DURATION:** Summer • **IDEAL CANDIDATE:** College Students, Career Changers, Retired Folks • **APPLICANT POOL:** 150/term • **APPLICANTS ACCEPTED:** 65–70/term

TETON VALLEY RANCH CAMP'S staff provides exceptional five-week experiences for groups of children in the outdoors, around horses and spectacular hiking scenery. All staff goes through a preliminary week of staff training while "on the job." This is definitely not a nine-to-five job, and the ideal candidate has a passion for working with people and is flexible in work hours and situations.

Contact Information: Stuart Palmer, Director • Teton Valley Ranch Camp • P.O. Box 8 • Kelly, WY 83011 • Phone: (307) 733-2958 • Fax: (307) 733-2978

Timberline Ski Area

REGION/HQ: Pacific Northwest/Oregon • **CATEGORY:** Ski Resort • **POSITION TYPE:** Internship/Seasonal • **DURATION:** Year-Round • **IDEAL CANDIDATE:** College Students, Career Changers, Foreigners • **APPLICANT POOL:** Varies • **APPLICANTS ACCEPTED:** Varies

TIMBERLINE LODGE IS A National Historic Landmark, operated by R.L.K., & Co., under a permit with the U.S. Forest Service until the year 2022. You'll recognize a "sense of place" at Timberline. Its qualities are special, it is unique and known to people throughout the world. They are inspired to uphold their duty as stewards of this wonderful place and to provide genuine hospitality to their guests. Positions are available in lift operations, skier services, front desk, rental shop, lodge services, kitchen and banquets, ski school, and the parking lot. Hourly wages range from $4.75 to $14.00, plus tips, depending on position. Interns are unpaid positions, although Timberline supplies housing, skiing privileges, and facility privileges. Employee housing is located nearby, and Timberline offers an employee meal program. Bonuses are given to those who complete their contracts.

Contact Information: Human Resources Director • Timberline Ski Area • Timberline Lodge, OR 97028 • Phone: (503) 272-3716 • Fax: (503) 272-3710

Vail Associates, Inc.

REGION/HQ: Rocky Mountains/Colorado • **CATEGORY:** Ski Resort • **POSITION TYPE:** Seasonal • **DURATION:** Winter/Summer • **IDEAL CANDIDATE:** College Students, Career Changers, Retired Folks, Foreigners • **APPLICANT POOL:** 5,000+ • **APPLICANTS ACCEPTED:** 1,200 Summer; 4,500 Winter

VAIL ASSOCIATES, established in 1962, owns and operates two of America's leading ski resorts—Vail and Beaver Creek. Winter positions include accounting, food service, hospitality, mountain operations, resort operations, retail/rental/vending, ski school, and ticket and lift operations. Summer positions include hospitality, food service, golf course staff, grounds/maintenance, child-care staff, day camp attendants, lift operators, and wranglers. Pay starts at $7.00 per hour. Shared employee housing is available for $310 per month, and spaces will be assigned on a first-come, first-served basis beginning November 1 for the winter. All employees receive a free season ski pass (and discounted passes for dependents), ski-school discounts, retail and ski rental discounts, food-service discounts, employee-assistance program, medical insurance, a daycare program for dependent children at a minimal cost, and lift ticket discounts at other Colorado ski areas. The best way to get in with Vail is to attend their national employment screen held every October.

Contact Information: Human Resources • Vail Associates, Inc. • P.O. Box 7 • Vail, CO 81658 • Phone: (970) 845-2460 • Fax: (970) 845-2465 • Job Hotline: (970) 479-3068 • E-mail: vailpr@vail.net • Web Site: www.vail.net

Wilderness Southeast

REGION/HQ: Southeast/Georgia • **CATEGORY:** Outdoor Education • **POSITION TYPE:** Internship/Seasonal • **DURATION:** Year-Round • **IDEAL CANDIDATE:** College Students, Career Changers • **APPLICANT POOL:** Varies • **APPLICANTS ACCEPTED:** 4–6/year

•••

WILDERNESS SOUTHEAST IS A nonprofit educational organization which promotes the preservation of the natural environment as essential to future well-being and fosters a sense of earth stewardship through immersion trips (natural and cultural history study tours and summer camps for teens). Positions are in Savannah, GA (September-May), and at summer camps in coastal Georgia, North Carolina, and south Florida. For September to May positions, duties include gear and field support, field teaching, and office support. For summer camp positions, primary responsibility is leading and teaching wilderness camps for youth, ages twelve to seventeen. You will receive a stipend of $125 per week, and housing is sometimes provided.

Contact Information: Program Director • Wilderness Southeast • 711 Sandtown Rd. • Savannah, GA 31410 • Phone: (912) 897-5108 • Fax: (912) 897-5116

Wyman Center

REGION/HQ: South/Midwest/Missouri • **CATEGORY:** Experiential Education • **POSITION TYPE:** Internship • **DURATION:** Spring/Fall • **IDEAL CANDIDATE:** College Students, Career Changers, Retired Folks, Foreigners • **APPLICANT POOL:** 75/year • **APPLICANTS ACCEPTED:** 18/year

•••

WYMAN IS AN INNOVATIVE experiential education center serving youth and adults from diverse backgrounds. They are the oldest continuously operating youth camp west of the Mississippi. Programs focus on youth development, environmental awareness, group dynamics, diversity, and enhancing self-esteem. Staff duties include instructing/facilitating groups in educational and life skill programs. Staff is provided training, competitive salary, health/dental insurance, and potential housing. Candidates must have interest in and experience working with children, excellent communication and leadership skills, flexibility, a strong work ethic, and a healthy sense of humor.

Contact Information: Carrie Riker, Program Director • Wyman Center • 600 Kiwanis Dr. • Eureka, MO 63025 • Phone: (314) 938-5245 • Fax: (314) 938-5289

YMCA

REGION/HQ: Nationwide/Illinois • **CATEGORY:** Camp • **POSITION TYPE:** Seasonal • **DURATION:** Year-Round • **IDEAL CANDIDATE:** College Students, Career Changers, Foreigners • **APPLICANT POOL:** Varies • **APPLICANTS ACCEPTED:** Varies

•••

THE YMCA PUTS Christian principles into practice through programs that build a healthy body, mind, and spirit for all. They provide a special issue of the YMCA National Vacancy List directed at college students seeking summer employment in a resident summer camp setting. Wages are $1,000 to $4,000 per month, depending on position, and most include room and board.

Contact Information: Human Resources Director • YMCA • 101 N. Wacker Dr. • Chicago, IL 60606-7386 • Phone: (800) 872-9622 • Fax: (312) 977-9063

YMCA Willson Outdoor Center

REGION/HQ: Great Lakes/Ohio • **CATEGORY:** Outdoor Education • **POSITION TYPE:** Internship/ Seasonal • **DURATION:** Year-Round • **IDEAL CANDIDATE:** College Students, Career Changers • **APPLICANT POOL:** 200/year • **APPLICANTS ACCEPTED:** 8/term

•••

YMCA WILLSON OUTDOOR CENTER is owned and operated by the YMCA of central Ohio. In addition to outdoor education, their programs include summer camp, weekend retreats, and horseback riding. The camp sits on 409 acres of land, with a 40-acre glacial kettlehole lake, a 1860's log cabin, and a 35-foot climbing wall. Interns teach classes about the environment to school children and lead recreational activities. In addition, camp directors, trip leaders, and counselor positions are available. You will receive a stipend of $170 per week plus room and board.

Contact Information: Timothy "Red" Ward, Outdoor Education Director • YMCA Willson Outdoor Center • 2732 County Rd. 11 • Bellefontaine, OH 43311-9382 • Phone: (937) 593-9001 • Fax: (937) 593-6194 •Toll Free: (800) 423-0427 • E-mail: ywillson@bright.net

YWCA Camp Westwind

REGION/HQ: Pacific Northwest/Oregon • **CATEGORY:** Camp • **POSITION TYPE:** Internship/Seasonal • **DURATION:** Spring-Fall • **IDEAL CANDIDATE:** College Students, Career Changers • **APPLICANT POOL:** Varies • **APPLICANTS ACCEPTED:** Varies

CAMP WESTWIND IS A residential camping program, on the Oregon coast, for families and children. Westwind boasts 503 acres of sand dunes, ocean shore, marine tide pools, ranchlands, rainforest, saltwater estuary, and freshwater lakes and streams. Westwind campers are immersed in a positive community where friendships, self-esteem, and confidence develop naturally. Campers participate in nature activities, arts and crafts, camp-fires, overnights, canoeing, and archery. Typical staff positions are available, and you will receive $100 to $230 per week, plus room and board.

Contact Information: Miriam Callaghan, Director • YWCA Camp Westwind • 1111 SW Tenth Ave. • Portland, OR 97205 • Phone: (503) 294-7472 • Fax: (503) 294-7399 • E-mail: miriam.callaghan@ywca.fabrik.com

Addresses

Absaroka Mountain Lodge

REGION/HQ: Rocky Mountains/Wyoming
CATEGORY: Lodge
CONTACT INFORMATION:
David Sweet, Owner
Absaroka Mountain Lodge
1231 E. Yellowstone Highway
Wapiti, WY 82450
Phone: (307) 587-3963

American Hotel & Motel Association

REGION/HQ: Nationwide/Washington, D.C.
CATEGORY: Hotel
CONTACT INFORMATION:
Program Director
American Hotel & Motel Association
1201 New York Ave., NW
Washington, DC 20005
Phone: (202) 289-3100 • Fax: (202) 289-3138

Anderson Ranch Arts Center

REGION/HQ: Rocky Mountains/Colorado
CATEGORY: Ranch
CONTACT INFORMATION:
Shelly Gowen, Public Relations
Anderson Ranch Arts Center
Box 5598
Snowmass, CO 81615
Phone: (970) 923-3181

Attitash Ski Resort

REGION/HQ: Northeast/New Hampshire
CATEGORY: Ski Resort
CONTACT INFORMATION:
Personnel Director
Attitash Ski Resort
P.O. Box 308
Bartlett, NH 03812
Phone: (603) 374-2368

Audubon Camp

REGION/HQ: Rocky Mountains/Wyoming
CATEGORY: Camp
CONTACT INFORMATION:
Program Director
Audubon Camp
Trail Lake Ranch
Dubois, WY 82513
Phone: (307) 455-2457

Bar Lazy J Guest Ranch

REGION/HQ: Rocky Mountains/Colorado
CATEGORY: Ranch
CONTACT INFORMATION:
Jerry & Cheri Helmicki, Owners
Bar Lazy J Guest Ranch
Box ND
Parshall, CO 80468
Phone: (970) 725-3437 • Toll Free: (800) 396-6279

Camp Adventure

REGION/HQ: South/Midwest/Iowa
CATEGORY: Camp
CONTACT INFORMATION:
Program Director
Camp Adventure
University Of Northern Iowa
1223 W. 2nd St.
Cedar Falls, IA 50613-0161
Phone: (319) 273-5960 • Fax: (319) 273-2058

Challenge Wilderness Camp

REGION/HQ: Northeast/Vermont
CATEGORY: Camp
CONTACT INFORMATION:
Program Director
Challenge Wilderness Camp
300 N. Grove St., #4
Rutland, VT 05701
Phone: (800) 832-4295

Deer Valley Resort

REGION/HQ: Rocky Mountains/Utah
CATEGORY: Resort
CONTACT INFORMATION:
Rich Jensen, Recruiting & Training Manager
Deer Valley Resort
P.O. Box 889
Park City, UT 84060
Phone: (801) 645-6663 • Fax: (801) 645-6847
• Toll Free: (800) 475-4562 • Alternate: (801) 649-1000

Don-K Ranch

REGION/HQ: Rocky Mountains/Colorado
CATEGORY: Ranch
CONTACT INFORMATION:
Darlene Smith, Program Coordinator
Don-K Ranch
2677 S. Siloam Rd.
Pueblo, CO 81005
Phone: (303) 784-6600

Dude Rancher's Association

REGION/HQ: Rocky Mountains/Colorado
CATEGORY: Ranch
CONTACT INFORMATION:
Program Director
Dude Rancher's Association
P.O. Box 471
La Porte, CO 80535

Elk Mountain Ranch

REGION/HQ: Rocky Mountains/Colorado
CATEGORY: Ranch
CONTACT INFORMATION:
Owner
Elk Mountain Ranch
P.O. Box 910
Buena Vista, CO 81211
Phone: (719) 539-4430

Elkhorn Ranch

REGION/HQ: Rocky Mountains/Montana
CATEGORY: Ranch
CONTACT INFORMATION:
Personnel Director
Elkhorn Ranch
33133 Gallatin Rd.
Gallatin Gateway, MT 59730
Phone: (406) 995-4291

Flying G Ranch, Tomahawk Ranch

REGION/HQ: Rocky Mountains/Colorado
CATEGORY: Ranch
CONTACT INFORMATION:
Deborah Speicher, Camp Administrator
Flying G Ranch, Tomahawk Ranch
400 South Broadway
Denver, CO 80209
Phone: (303) 778-8774

Guided Discoveries, Inc.

REGION/HQ: Pacific Northwest/California
CATEGORY: Camp
CONTACT INFORMATION:
Ross Turner, Director
Guided Discoveries, Inc.
Catalina Sea Camp
P.O. Box 1360
Claremont, CA 91711
Phone: (909) 625-6194

Gurney's Inn Resort & Spa

REGION/HQ: Northeast/New York
CATEGORY: Resort
CONTACT INFORMATION:
Eleanor Morgan, Human Resources Director
Gurney's Inn Resort & Spa
P.O. Box 5072
Montauk, NY 11954
Phone: (516) 668-2345 • Fax: (516) 668-3576

Heart Six Ranch

REGION/HQ: Rocky Mountains/Wyoming
CATEGORY: Ranch
CONTACT INFORMATION:
Personnel Director
Heart Six Ranch
P.O. Box 70
Moran, WY 83013
Phone: (307) 543-2477

Heavenly Ski Resort

REGION/HQ: Pacific Northwest/Nevada
CATEGORY: SKI Resort
CONTACT INFORMATION:
Personnel Manager
Heavenly Ski Resort
P.O. Box 2180
Stateline, NV 89449
Phone: (702) 586-7000 • E-mail: humres@skiheavenly.com • Web Site: www.skiheavenly.com

Hidden Creek Ranch

REGION/HQ: Pacific Northwest/Idaho
CATEGORY: Ranch
CONTACT INFORMATION:
Iris Behr, Owner
Hidden Creek Ranch
7600 E. Blue Lake Rd.
Harrison, ID 83833
Phone: (208) 689-3209 • Fax: (208) 689-9115

Inn of the Seventh Mountain

REGION/HQ: Pacific Northwest/Oregon
CATEGORY: Ski Resort
CONTACT INFORMATION:
Sharon Thornton, Personnel Department
Inn of the Seventh Mountain
18575 SW Century Dr.
Bend, OR 97702-1950
Phone: (503) 382-8711

International Music Camp

REGION/HQ: Rocky Mountains/North Dakota
CATEGORY: Camp
CONTACT INFORMATION:
Joseph Alme, Camp Director
International Music Camp
1725 11th St., SW
Minot, ND 58701
Phone: (701) 838-8472 • Fax: (701) 838-8472

King Salmon Lodge, Inc.

REGION/HQ: Pacific Northwest/Alaska
CATEGORY: Lodge
CONTACT INFORMATION:
Personnel Director
King Salmon Lodge, Inc.
3340 Providence Dr., Suite 555
Anchorage, AK 99508
Phone: (907) 277-3033

Lazy K Bar Ranch

REGION/HQ: Rocky Mountains/Montana
CATEGORY: Ranch
CONTACT INFORMATION:
Program Director
Lazy K Bar Ranch
P.O. Box 550
Big Timber, MT 59011
Phone: (406) 537-4404

Lone Mountain Ranch

REGION/HQ: Rocky Mountains/Montana
CATEGORY: Ranch
CONTACT INFORMATION:
Personnel Director
Lone Mountain Ranch
P.o. Box 160069
Big Sky, MT 59716
Phone: (406) 995-4644

Loon Mountain Ski Resort

REGION/HQ: Northeast/New Hampshire
CATEGORY: Ski Resort
CONTACT INFORMATION:
Sara Sawyer, Personnel Manager
Loon Mountain Ski Resort
Route 112
Lincoln, NH 03251
Phone: (603) 745-8111

Lost Fork Ranch

REGION/HQ: Rocky Mountains/Montana
CATEGORY: Ranch
CONTACT INFORMATION:
Personnel Director
Lost Fork Ranch
11-12 Highway 287
Cameron, MT 59720
Phone: (406) 682-7690

Mammoth/June Mountain Ski Area

REGION/HQ: Pacific Northwest/California
CATEGORY: Ski Resort
CONTACT INFORMATION:
Personnel Director
Mammoth/June Mountain Ski Area
P.O. Box 24
Mammoth Lakes, CA 93546
Phone: (619) 934-2571

MW Ranch

REGION/HQ: Rocky Mountains/Colorado
CATEGORY: Ranch
CONTACT INFORMATION:
Bill Diekroeger, Owner
MW Ranch
19451 195th Ave.
Hudson, CO 80642
Phone: (303) 536-4206

Nine Quarter Circle Ranch

REGION/HQ: Rocky Mountains/Montana
CATEGORY: Ranch
CONTACT INFORMATION:
Staffing Director
Nine Quarter Circle Ranch
5000 Taylor Fork Rd.
Gallatin Gateway, MT 59730
Phone: (406) 995-4276

Pack Creek Ranch

REGION/HQ: Rocky Mountains/Utah
CATEGORY: Ranch
CONTACT INFORMATION:
Jane Sleight, Program Director
Pack Creek Ranch
P.O. Box 1270
Moab, UT 84532
Phone: (801) 259-5505

Pico Mountain, Inc.

REGION/HQ: Northeast/New Jersey
CATEGORY: Ski Resort
CONTACT INFORMATION:
Paul Denton, Personnel Manager
Pico Mountain, Inc.
184 S. Moetz Dr.
Mill Town, NJ 08850-1321
Phone: (802) 775-4346

Quinnat Landing Hotel

REGION/HQ: Pacific Northwest/Alaska
CATEGORY: Hotel
CONTACT INFORMATION:
Personnel Director
Quinnat Landing Hotel
5520 Lake Otis Parkway, Suite 101
Anchorage, AK 99507
Phone: (907) 561-2310 • Toll Free: (800) 770-3474
• Summer: (907) 246-3000

Royal Gorge Cross Country Ski Resort

REGION/HQ: Pacific Northwest/California
CATEGORY: Ski Resort
CONTACT INFORMATION:
Personnel Director
Royal Gorge Cross Country Ski Resort
P.O. Box 1100
Soda Springs, CA 95728
Phone: (916) 426-3871 • Toll Free: (800) 500-3871
• E-mail: info@RoyalGorge.com • Web Site: www.
royalgorge.com/Jobs.html

Ski Utah

REGION/HQ: Rocky Mountains/Utah
CATEGORY: Ski Resort
CONTACT INFORMATION:
Program Coordinator
Ski Utah
150 W. 500 South
Salt Lake City, UT 84101
Phone: (801) 534-1779

Sky High Ranch

REGION/HQ: Rocky Mountains/Colorado
CATEGORY: Ranch
CONTACT INFORMATION:
Wayne Whyman, Program Director
Sky High Ranch
3535 Parkmoor Village Dr.
Colorado Springs, CO 80917-5298
Phone: (719) 597-8603

Snow Basin

REGION/HQ: Rocky Mountains/Utah
CATEGORY: Ski Resort
CONTACT INFORMATION:
Reeta Young, Office Manager
Snow Basin
P.O. Box 460
Huntsville, UT 84317-0460
Phone: (801) 399-1135

Snow Summit Resort

REGION/HQ: Pacific Northwest/California
CATEGORY: Ski Resort
CONTACT INFORMATION:
Tony Hagmann, Personnel Director
Snow Summit Resort
Box 77
Big Bear Lake, CA 92315
Phone: (714) 866-5766

Don't compete. Create. Find out what everyone else is doing and then don't do it.
—JOEL WELDON

Squaw Valley USA
REGION/HQ: Pacific Northwest/California
CATEGORY: Ski Resort
CONTACT INFORMATION:
Personnel Director
Squaw Valley USA
P.O. Box 2007
Olympic Valley, CA 96146
Phone: (916) 583-6985

Sugarbush Resort
REGION/HQ: Northeast/Vermont
CATEGORY: Ski Resort
CONTACT INFORMATION:
Personnel Director
Sugarbush Resort
RR1, Box 350
Warren, VT 05674
Phone: (802) 583-2385 • Fax: (802) 583-6303

Sugarloaf Mountain Corporation
REGION/HQ: Northeast/Maine
CATEGORY: Ski Resort
CONTACT INFORMATION:
Donna Morey, Personnel Manager
Sugarloaf Mountain Corporation
Box 5000
Kingfield, ME 04947
Phone: (207) 237-2000

Sunny Brook Farm Resort
REGION/HQ: Great Lakes/Michigan
CATEGORY: Ranch
CONTACT INFORMATION:
Mary Ott, Program Director
Sunny Brook Farm Resort
68300 County Rd. 388
South Havens, MI 49090
Phone: (616) 637-4796

Togwotee Mountain Lodge
REGION/HQ: Rocky Mountains/Wyoming
CATEGORY: Lodge
CONTACT INFORMATION:
Peggy Pruitt, General Manager
Togwotee Mountain Lodge
P.O. Box 91
Moran, WY 83013
Phone: (307) 543-2847

Topnotch at Stowe
REGION/HQ: Northeast/Vermont
CATEGORY: Ski Resort
CONTACT INFORMATION:
Personnel Director
Topnotch at Stowe
P.O. Box 1260
Stowe, VT 05672
Phone: (802) 253-8585

Tumbling River Ranch
REGION/HQ: Rocky Mountains/Colorado
CATEGORY: Ranch
CONTACT INFORMATION:
Mary Dale Gordon, Owner
Tumbling River Ranch
P.O. Box 30
Grant, CO 80448
Phone: (303) 838-5981 • Toll Free: (800) 654-8770

Wilderness Trails Ranch
REGION/HQ: Rocky Mountains/Colorado
CATEGORY: Ranch
CONTACT INFORMATION:
Jan Roberts, Owner
Wilderness Trails Ranch
1776 Country Road 302
Durango, CO 81301
Phone: (970) 247-0722 • Fax: (970) 247-1006
• Toll Free: (800) 527-2624

Wind River Wilderness Camp
REGION/HQ: Rocky Mountains/Colorado
CATEGORY: Camp
CONTACT INFORMATION:
Program Director
Wind River Wilderness Camp
6678 S. Arapahoe Dr.
Littleton, CO 80120
Phone: (303) 794-9518

Yakutat Lodge
REGION/HQ: Pacific Northwest/Alaska
CATEGORY: Lodge
CONTACT INFORMATION:
Ken Fanning, Owner/Manager
Yakutat Lodge
Box 287
Yakutat, AK 99689
Phone: (907) 784-3232

Contact the **America Camping Association** for their free brochures: ***Careers in Camping*** and ***The Summer Camp Employment Opportunity Booklet.*** ACA, 5000 State Rd., 67 North, Martinville, IN 46151-7902; (317) 342-8456. You can also call (800) 428-CAMP to order the ACA's *Guide to Accredited Camps* ($12.95), which provides facts on 2,000 ACA-accredited camps coast to coast.

The **Colorado Dude and Guest Ranch Association** publishes a directory of approved ranches in Colorado. Although the directory really acts as a vacationer's guide, it lists thirty-eight ranches (all of whom hire seasonal employees), complete with contact information and phone numbers. To receive your copy, call the association at (970) 887-3128; or write to them at P.O. Box 300, Tabernash, CO 80478.

Directory of Summer Camps for Children with Learning Disabilities. This guide is great for those who want contact information on camps especially geared to working with disabled youth. The guide runs $4. Also inquire about other booklets and pamphlets on different subjects for the learning disabled. Learning Disabilities Association of America, 4156 Library Rd., Pittsburgh, PA 15234

Looking for a job in a summer camp? Visit **Kids Camps** online at www.kidscamps.com

The **Resort and Commercial Recreation Association** puts out a great directory of internships in this field. Call the association at (813) 845-7373; or write to P.O. Box 1208, New Port Richey, FL 34656-1208.

Summer Jobs for Students and ***Summer Opportunities for Kids and Teenagers.*** Great resources providing up-to-date information on summer jobs at camps, resorts, ranches, theatres, amusement parks, and the like. Published by Peterson's, (800) 338-3282, www.petersons.com

6

After spending twenty years working in Corporate America (wholesale, retail, manufacturing, and distribution), I realized that my most rewarding experiences inside work were guiding, educating, and mentoring others. My most rewarding experiences outside work were my artistic pursuits (graphic arts, pottery, creative writing), travel, health and fitness, and environmental projects. Changes in my personal life have made it possible for me to change direction now and integrate my career with the real passions in my life. My resume outlines specific skills, but cannot possibly convey the positive energy, enthusiasm, and creativity I bring to my work. Coming to Yellowstone was just a step in breaking away from the mindset that money and possessions are the measure of a person and their success in life. Being here has shown me that some people value other things and live a totally different way. Now I seek people who are doing what they really love, filled with creative force, shaping their own lives, and having a positive influence on the lives of others.

—SANDRA ALDRICH, A *BACK DOOR* READER
WORKING AT OLD FAITHFUL IN YELLOWSTONE NATIONAL PARK

Photo © Brian Peterson

The Great

A Christian Ministry in the National Parks

REGION/HQ: Nationwide/Massachusetts • **CATEGORY:** Ministry • **POSITION TYPE:** Internship/ Seasonal • **DURATION:** Year-Round • **IDEAL CANDIDATE:** College Students, Career Changers, Retired Folks • **APPLICANT POOL:** Varies • **APPLICANTS ACCEPTED:** Varies

A CHRISTIAN MINISTRY IN THE National Parks is a special Christian movement recognized by over forty Christian denominations. It extends the ministry of Christ to the millions of people who live, work, and vacation in our national park, forest, and resort areas. This ministry serves government personnel and their families who live in these areas, students and professional resort workers who are employed to operate the resort facilities during the summer and winter vacation seasons, and the millions of visitors who come to enjoy the great natural wonders. These people are often isolated from immediate contact with local churches. This ministry cooperates with local committees in each area to provide regular worship services, religious education, and Christian fellowship.

Area and Working Environment: They offer opportunities for service in sixty-five different locations in the United States.

Work/Learn Program Specifics: Worship and work! This theme pervades the whole meaning of the ministry, providing opportunities for witness and service. Each member of the staff has a full-time job with either a park company or the National Park Service. Participants work as desk clerks, housekeepers, bellhops, store clerks, trail crews, rangers, tour guides, waitresses, and such. An important aspect of the program is witnessing on the job. You will function either as a seminary, college, or music leader. All staff leaders are required to attend one of nine regional spring orientation conferences. Applicants must pay for transportation to and from the conference; although the expense of room and board is provided. The twenty-four-hour conferences are held after Easter in California, the Northwest, Texas/Missouri, Minnesota, Chicago, southern Ohio, the Southeast, Northeast, and the Mid-Atlantic areas.

Duration: Most participants arrive at the parks between late May and mid-June and stay through Labor Day. Some parks are open from May 1 through November 1. Year-round and winter placements are available for those who are able to commit themselves for periods of six to fifteen months, depending on the area assigned.

Compensation and Perks: Participants are paid for their work by the park companies. Most earn between $900 and $1,800 in three months after room, board, and taxes. Each participant helps with fund-raising through park offerings and special appeals for administrative support.

The Ideal Candidate: This program seeks trained lay leaders who have a faith in Jesus Christ that is imaginative, dedicated, and open to creative service. The ministry demands maturity of thought and conduct, and applicants must have the ability to understand and live amiably with other people and other faiths. There are positions for singles and married couples, all of whom must be nineteen years of age or older.

Making It Happen: Applications are received year-round. Offers for summer positions are sent to qualified applicants from December through the spring. Early applications are given first preference. Students who wish to qualify for government jobs must apply by January 1 for the following summer.

Contact Information: Richard Camp, Director • A Christian Ministry in the National Parks • 45 School St. • Boston, MA 02108 • Phone: (617) 720-5655 • Fax: (617) 720-7899 • E-mail: acmnp@juno.com • Web Site: www.coolworks.com/showme/acmnp

Outdoors

Adirondack Mountain Club

REGION/HQ: Northeast/New York • **CATEGORY:** Conservation • **POSITION TYPE:** Internship • **DURATION:** Year-Round • **IDEAL CANDIDATE:** High School Students, College Students, Career Changers, Foreigners • **APPLICANT POOL:** Varies • **APPLICANTS ACCEPTED:** Varies

ADIRONDACK MOUNTAIN CLUB (ADK) is dedicated to the protection and responsible recreational use of the New York State Forest Preserve, parks, and other wild lands and waters. The club, founded in 1922, is a member-directed organization committed to public service and stewardship. ADK employs a balanced approach to outdoor recreation, advocacy, environmental education, and natural resource conservation.

Work/Learn Program Specifics: Duties may include assisting with the maintenance and reconstruction of backcountry hiking trails, working in a backcountry information center, interpreting Adirondack natural history, and/or operating two mountain lodges.

Duration: There are a variety of seasonal and full-time positions available, year-round.

Compensation and Perks: Hourly wage based on position, plus room and board.

The Ideal Candidate: Applicants require a strong outdoor orientation and public-service skills. Positions are often filled by outgoing, highly motivated, and independent individuals.

Making It Happen: Call for application form (or check out their web site). Send completed application, cover letter, and resume by February 15 for the summer; other seasons have rolling deadlines.

Contact Information: Bill Brosseau, Trails Director • Adirondack Mountain Club • P.O. Box 367 • Lake Placid, NY 12946 • Phone: (518) 523-3441 • Fax: (518) 523-3518 • E-mail: adkinfo@adk.org • Web Site: www.adk.org

Alaska State Parks

REGION/HQ: Pacific Northwest/Alaska • **CATEGORY:** State Park • **POSITION TYPE:** Seasonal • **DURATION:** Summer/Winter • **IDEAL CANDIDATE:** College Students, Career Changers, Retired Folks, Foreigners • **APPLICANT POOL:** 3,000/year • **APPLICANTS ACCEPTED:** 150/year

CREATED IN 1970, ALASKA STATE PARKS manages more than 130 State Park units with over 6 million visitors each year. These park units range in size and character, from the half-acre Potter Section House State Historic Site to the 1.5-million-acre Wood-Tikchik State Park. In general, state parks are accessible by road and offer a host of visitor facilities including campgrounds, boat launches, hiking trails, and visitor centers.

Area and Working Environment: Statewide, from Kodiak to Fairbanks to Ketchikan.

Work/Learn Program Specifics: Typical positions include archaeological assistant, backcountry ranger assistant, natural history interpreter, park caretaker, ranger assistant, and trail crew. Almost half of the positions offered are campground hosts. Hosts stay in the campground and assist the ranger with campground maintenance and visitor contact.

Duration: Most positions are full-time; however, a few positions are part-time, and approximately ten positions are offered during the winter. Time off is usually given midweek.

Compensation and Perks: Most positions offer an expense allowance ($100 to $300 per month), uniforms, rustic housing, and of course, the state's beauty. Transportation to and from Alaska is the responsibility of the volunteer.

The Ideal Candidate: Applicants must be eighteen years or older and have U.S. citizenship.

Making It Happen: Write or call for the current volunteer program catalog, which includes general information, specific position descriptions, and an application. The catalog becomes available each October, and applications are accepted between November 1 and April 1 (with some exceptions). You may apply for as many positions as you like.

INSIDER TIPS: *If applying for several positions, copy the blank application and fill out an application for each position. Copied, generic applications are not seen in a favorable light.*

Contact Information: Kathryn Reid, Volunteer Coordinator • Alaska State Parks • 3601 C St., Suite 1200 • Anchorage, AK 99503-5921 • Phone: (907) 269-8708 • Fax: (907) 269-8907 • E-mail: volunteer@dnr.state.ak.us • Web Site: www.dnr.state.ak.us/parks

American Hiking Society

REGION/HQ: Nationwide/Maryland • **CATEGORY:** Conservation • **POSITION TYPE:** Work/Learn Adventure • **DURATION:** Year-Round • **IDEAL CANDIDATE:** College Students, Career Changers, Retired Folks, Foreigners • **APPLICANT POOL:** Varies • **APPLICANTS ACCEPTED:** 50/year

AMERICAN HIKING SOCIETY IS A national nonprofit organization dedicated to establishing, protecting, and maintaining foot trails in America. Serving as the voice of the American hiker in our nation's capital, American Hiking works to educate the public about the benefits of hiking and trails, to increase the constituency for trails, and to foster research on trail issues.

Work/Learn Program Specifics: For more than twenty years, AHS's Volunteer Vacations has been sending hundreds of volunteers each year into America's most special places to revitalize trails. Over the years, thousands of vacationers rake, shovel, trim, lop, and chop hundreds of trail miles in America's national parks, forests, and rangelands. Volunteering affords you an opportunity to whip some trail miles—and your mind and body—into shape. You'll spend your days performing rewarding trail work. During afternoon and evening hours you'll explore the countryside, photograph wildlife, relax by a mountain stream, or simply enjoy the fellowship of people who share your passion for the outdoors. AHS Volunteer Vacations also offers an inexpensive way to visit a new part of the United States, work with your hands, and help conserve America's trails. Most projects require a hike into a remote base camp; some offer bunkhouse or cabin accommodations. For each project, American Hiking chooses an experienced volunteer team leader to serve as the liaison between your crew and the host agency. If you are interested in serving as a leader, just indicate that on your registration form.

Duration: On a typical day, you will be on the trail at 9 A.M., after a hearty breakfast, work for six to eight hours, and return to base camp by 4 P.M., just in time to enjoy the long summer afternoons. On two-week vacations, you will get the weekend off.

Compensation and Perks: Host agencies provide tools, safety equipment, workers' compensation, and project leaders. Most agencies also provide food; however, for some projects volunteers may be asked to donate an additional $40 per week. One in three vacationers returns to the program each year. Registration requires a non-refundable $65 registration fee, which includes first-year membership to American Hiking ($10 savings). AHS members pay $50 for the first trip, and each additional trip costs $35. Most expenses, such as travel to and from the site, are tax deductible.

The Ideal Candidate: To participate, you should be in good physical condition, at least eighteen years of age, able to hike five miles or more in a day, supply your own camping equipment (tent, sleeping bag, personal items), and arrange your own transportation to and from the work site (many agencies provide pickups at the major airports nearest to the work sites). Most importantly, an AHS Volunteer Vacations participant should be enthusiastic, able to work well with a diverse group of people, and possess a desire to improve America's trails.

Making It Happen: Call to receive this year's project schedule, which includes a registration form. American Hiking also publishes *Helping Out in the Outdoors*, an annual directory of more than 2,000 volunteer positions and internships on America's public lands. The cost is $7 (add $3 to receive by first-class mail).

INSIDER TIPS: *We'll see you in the backcountry!*

Contact Information: Program Coordinator • American Hiking Society • Volunteer Vacations • 1422 Fenwick Ln. • Silver Spring, MD 20910 • Phone: (301) 565-6704 • Fax: (301) 565-6714 • Toll Free: (800) 972-8608 • E-mail: ahshiking@aol.com • Web Site: www.orca.org/ahs

Bureau of Land Management, Utah

REGION/HQ: Rocky Mountains/Utah • **CATEGORY:** Conservation • **POSITION TYPE:** Seasonal • **DURATION:** Spring-Fall • **IDEAL CANDIDATE:** College Students, Career Changers, Foreigners • **APPLICANT POOL:** 24/year • **APPLICANTS ACCEPTED:** 8/year

THE BUREAU OF LAND MANAGEMENT is responsible for the management, conservation, and development of the resources on more than 270 million acres of public land.

Work/Learn Program Specifics: Recreation/Paleontology: assist in the operation of the Cleveland-Lloyd Dinosaur Quarry. Over 12,000 bones, representing at least 68 individual animals and 11 species, have been recovered from this active, working quarry. In addition to the quarry, there is a visitor center, picnic area interpretive hiking trail. Recreation/Archaeology: assist the outdoor recreation planner with recreation and cultural sites inventory in Nine Mile Canyon (a dedicated backcountry byway). The canyon contains one of the world's highest densities of prehistoric rock art. In addition to the prolific rock art, prehistoric cultures left behind numerous dwellings, villages, and structures. River Ranger/Recreation: assist the outdoor recreation planner with administration of the Desolation and Gray Canyons River Management Program. The eighty-four-mile segment of the Green River through Desolation and Gray Canyons is one of the nation's premier whitewater wilderness adventures. Over 6,000 people engage in multiday float trips on this river segment annually.

Duration: Most positions require at least an eight-week commitment, forty hours per week average. You can either work a five-day workweek or a nine-days-on, five-days-off routine.

Compensation and Perks: All positions include a small stipend, housing, and on-the-job transportation.

The Ideal Candidate: Must be at least eighteen years of age and have an interest in resource management, particularly recreation, paleontology, or wildland recreation management.

Making It Happen: Contact them directly by phone or by letter, expressing your desires and reasons for applying, and some background of your experiences. Enthusiasm is a must! Rolling deadlines.

Contact Information: Outdoor Recreation Planner • Bureau of Land Management, Utah • 125 South, 600 West • Price, UT 84501 • Phone: (801) 636-3600 • Fax: (801) 636-3657

Bureau of Land Management . . . .

The Bureau of Land Management, commonly known as the BLM, is responsible for the management, conservation, and development of the resources on more than 270 million acres of public land. They are responsible for administering rangeland; surveying; carrying out resource management programs; providing recreation areas; issuing leases and overseeing operations for oil, gas, and other mineral development on public land; selling timber from BLM administered lands; and maintaining public land records.

The BLM has volunteer and seasonal programs in a range of fields, including administration, archaeology, botany, information systems, engineering, forestry, geology, hydrology, illustrating, land surveying, natural resources, outdoor recreation programming, personnel management, public affairs, range conservation, soil science, and wildlife biology.

BLM State Offices around the country:

Headquarters
Bureau of Land Management
1849 C St., NW
Washington, DC 20240
(202) 452-5120

Alaska State Office
Bureau of Land Management
222 W. 7th Ave., Suite 13
Anchorage, AK 99513-7599
(907) 271-5043

Arizona State Office
Bureau of Land Management
P.O. Box 16563
Phoenix, AZ 85011
(602) 650-0550

California State Office
Bureau of Land Management
2135 Butano Dr.
Sacramento, CA 95825-0451
(916) 978-4807

Colorado State Office
Bureau of Land Management
2850 Youngfield St.
Lakewood, CO 80215-3900
(303) 236 6681

Eastern State Office
Bureau of Land Management
7450 Boston Blvd.
Springfield, VA 22153
(703) 440-1500

Idaho State Office
Bureau of Land Management
3380 Americana Terrace
Boise, ID 83706
(208) 384-3000

Montana State Office
Bureau of Land Management
P.O. Box 36800
Billings, MT 59107-6800
(406) 255-2913

Nevada State Office
Bureau of Land Management
P.O. Box 12000
Reno, NV 89520-0006
(702) 785-6431

New Mexico State Office
Bureau of Land Management
P.O. Box 27115
Santa Fe, NM 87502-0115
(505) 438-7400

Oregon/Washington State Office
Bureau of Land Management
P.O. Box 2965
Portland, OR 97208-2965
(503) 280-7235

Utah State Office
Bureau of Land Management
P.O. Box 45155
Salt Lake City, UT 84145-0155
(801) 539-4185

Wyoming State Office
Bureau of Land Management
5353 Yellowstone Rd.
P.O. Box 1828
Cheyenne, WY 82003-1828
(307) 775-6034

Carlsbad Caverns National Park

REGION/HQ: South/Midwest/New Mexico
• **CATEGORY:** National Park • **POSITION TYPE:** Seasonal • **DURATION:** Year-Round • **IDEAL CANDIDATE:** College Students, Career Changers, Foreigners • **APPLICANT POOL:** Varies • **APPLICANTS ACCEPTED:** Varies

• •

THIS PARK WAS ESTABLISHED TO PRESERVE Carlsbad Cavern and numerous other caves within a Permian fossil reef. The park contains eighty-three separate caves, including the nation's deepest limestone cave—1,597 feet—and third longest. Carlsbad Cavern, with one of the world's largest underground chambers and countless formations, is also highly accessible, with a variety of tours offered year-round. In addition, the park protects 47,000 acres of the rugged Chihuahuan Desert.

Work/Learn Program Specifics: Special opportunities are available for people interested in caves, natural resources, and working with the public. Positions include park interpretation, visitor services, maintenance, environmental education, history and curatorial, resource management, and cave restoration.

Duration: Duration is flexible. The park asks a minimum of thirty-two hours per week for at least two months in return for housing.

Compensation and Perks: This is a volunteer position for which the park may provide dormitory-style housing or a RV site with full hookups. Volunteers learn new skills, gain valuable work experience, witness the behind-the-scenes activities of a national park, have the opportunity to participate in world-class caving, and meet people from around the world.

The Ideal Candidate: Carlsbad invites motivated, responsible people who would like the opportunity to work with a large, diverse staff in a remote, desert location.

Making It Happen: Call or write for more information and an application. Applications are accepted year-round.

INSIDER TIPS: *Special consideration is given to applicants who are multilingual, flexible in the type of position desired, and/or display a strong conservation ethic. Be prepared to answer these questions: what assets do you feel you will bring to the park? and why do you want to volunteer?*

Contact Information: Paula Bauer, Volunteer Coordinator • Carlsbad Caverns National Park • 3225 National Parks Hwy. • Carlsbad, NM 88220 • Phone: (505) 785-2232 • Fax: (505) 785-2302 • E-mail: caca_interpretation@nps.gov • Web Site: www.nps.gov/cave

Crater Lake Company

REGION/HQ: Pacific Northwest/Oregon
• **CATEGORY:** Concessionaire • **POSITION TYPE:** Seasonal • **DURATION:** Spring-Fall • **IDEAL CANDIDATE:** College Students, Career Changers, Retired Folks, Foreigners • **APPLICANT POOL:** Varies
• **APPLICANTS ACCEPTED:** 200+/year

• •

WHILE THEY HOPE YOU WILL ENJOY exploring Crater Lake National Park, the Oregon Cave, and the southern Oregon coast and mountains on your days off, as the national park's concessionaire, they expect their employees (called "team members") to work hard when they are scheduled to work. All positions, regardless of level, have equal significance in ensuring that their guests have a truly memorable experience.

Area and Working Environment: Crater Lake is located along the crest of the Cascade Mountain Range, approximately seventy-four miles northeast of Medford. With a depth of 1,932 feet, Crater Lake is the deepest lake in the United States and the seventh deepest lake in the world.

Work/Learn Program Specifics: Lodging: lodging manager, room and reservations clerk, front desk clerk/supervisor, campground registration, head housekeeper, laundry worker, night watch/janitor, and night auditor; Food and Beverage: chef, sous chef and assistant, cook, pantry, kitchen utility worker, dining server, lead/coffee shop server, lead server, fast food, host/hostess, bartender, maître d'/banquet manager, team member dining room, lead/stockroom clerk, storeroom clerk, town driver, cashier, and supervisor/assistant supervisor; Retail: assistant manager, lead clerk, gift/convenience store, stock clerk, and store clerk; Maintenance; Administrative: office manager, office clerk, money counter, dormitory coordinators, and activities coordinators; Tour Boats: lead boat pilot, boat pilot, and ticket sales; and Cave Tours: cave guide and registration clerk.

Duration: The season runs from May through October, with two-, four-, and six-month contracts. Most seasonal team members work forty to fifty-six hours per week; however, actual hours worked each week may vary from twenty to forty hours during the early and late seasons.

Compensation and Perks: Most seasonal positions start at $5.50 per hour, plus a season-ending bonus when satisfactorily completing employment agreement. Supervisory and skill positions pay more. Dorm-style housing is provided for $2 per day, with free laundry facilities. RV spaces are also available. Full and partial meal plans are also available for a small cost.

The Ideal Candidate: Team members are needed who are willing to make a commitment to service excellence in their own personal standards and work habits, are able to work at 7,000 feet, and can work from mid-May to mid-October. RVers are encouraged to apply.

Making It Happen: Call or write for application. Also inquire about positions at Oregon Caves, twenty miles east of Cave Junction, Oregon.

INSIDER TIPS: *Be willing to accept any position and be flexible.*

Contact Information: Tammy Roe, Personnel Clerk • Crater Lake Company • 1211 Ave. C • White City, OR 97503 • Phone: (541) 594-2255 • Fax: (541) 594-2622 • Winter: (541) 830-4053

Denali Park Resorts

REGION/HQ: Pacific Northwest/Alaska • **CATEGORY:** Concessionaire • **POSITION TYPE:** Seasonal • **DURATION:** Spring-Fall • **IDEAL CANDIDATE:** College Students, Career Changers, Retired Folks, Foreigners • **APPLICANT POOL:** 1,000+/season • **APPLICANTS ACCEPTED:** 900/season

IN 1917, CONGRESS ESTABLISHED Mt. McKinley National Park in the interior of Alaska. The purpose was to preserve an area of mountain wilderness with a representative population of wildlife found in the western part of North America. In December of 1980 the park was expanded in size, and the name was changed to Denali National Park and Preserve, with the enactment of the Alaska Native Interest Lands Conservation Act. Denali Park Resorts operates four properties. The Denali National Park Hotel is located just inside the park entrance, and the McKinley Chalets, McKinley Village, and Lynx Creek complexes are located just outside the park entrance. In addition to room or campground accommodations, properties have a dining room, bar, gift shop, pizza parlor, convenience store, and gas station facilities. Over 100,000 guests stay overnight at one of the facilities each year. Denali Park Resorts also operates Alaska Raft Adventures and the Tundra Wildlife Tour and Natural History Tour into the park.

Area and Working Environment: Denali National Park has more than six million acres of pristine wilderness, including some of the most awe-inspiring scenery and wildlife in North America, including Mt. McKinley, which rises over 20,000 feet into the Alaskan sky.

Work/Learn Program Specifics: Positions available: Housekeeping (rooms worker, porter, and inspector); Gift Shop and Grocery Store; Food and Beverage Service (snack shop, employee dining room, pizza parlor, kitchen, waitstaff, bus person, bar staff); Front Desk/Tour Activity Desk (clerk/cashier, night audit, reservations, and security); Warehouse; Transportation (tour driver, raft/courtesy driver, buswasher, and river guide); Dinner Theatre Performer; and Maintenance. Employees should expect a busy work environment with extensive guest contact. Those who want to gain experience in the hospitality industry, use professional skills, enjoy the Denali wilderness, and meet a diverse group of people will thrive in this environment.

Duration: The full work season will begin the first week in May and end in mid-September. They give preference to employees who can work the majority of the season.

Compensation and Perks: Jobs pay a variety of wages, commissions, and bonuses, but most first-year employees earn $5.50 to $8.00 per hour and approximately a $300 bonus for the season. Room and board are available for $10 per day and all employees have free use of laundry facilities. A variety of rustic, dormitory-style company housing units exists, with a central bathhouse. Generally you will live with one or two other people. Besides the overall beauty of this region, perks abound in Denali National Park. There are many employee activities, free rafting, and discounted tours, flight-seeing, and retail purchases—not to mention fishing, kayaking, biking, hiking, and more.

The Ideal Candidate: You must be eighteen years or older for housing, and many jobs require at least twenty-one years of age. Almost all jobs have a uniform requirement, and they expect normal standards of grooming to be maintained. Local services are limited in Denali, which is 120 miles from the nearest city, Fairbanks. Therefore, applicants should have a strong desire to enjoy and discover the wilderness. Denali's social emphasis centers on outdoor recreation.

Making It Happen: Call for application. A completed application is all that is required, but you may also submit a resume and/or reference letters. Applications are accepted from December through August.

INSIDER TIPS: *Applicants must be flexible in the work they will do; have the capacity to work May through September*

and experience working in a remote area; and have the ability to work and live with a variety of people in a busy industry and the ability to live dormitory-style.

Contact Information: Human Resources • Denali Park Resorts • 241 W. Ship Creek Ave., Dept. BDP • Anchorage, AK 99501 • Phone: (907) 279-2653 • Fax: (907) 258-3668 • Web Site: www.coolworks.com/showme/denaliak

Florissant Fossil Beds National Monument

REGION/HQ: Rocky Mountains/Colorado • **CATEGORY:** National Monument • **POSITION TYPE:** Internship • **DURATION:** Summer • **IDEAL CANDIDATE:** College Students, Career Changers, Foreigners • **APPLICANT POOL:** 70/year • **APPLICANTS ACCEPTED:** 5/year

FLORISSANT FOSSIL BEDS NATIONAL MONUMENT was established as a unit of the National Park Service in 1969 and offers educational experiences to the public. This national monument preserves fossil remains and geologic evidence of a far different world, from 35 million years ago. The paleontological resources include 35 million-year-old petrified redwood trees and carbon impressions of plants and insects. At 6,000 acres in size, the national monument contains over 12 miles of hiking trails which wander through open grassy meadows, aspens, and ponderosa pine forests.

Area and Working Environment: Florissant Fossil Beds is located forty miles west of Colorado Springs, at an elevation of 8,400 feet. The fossil beds are named after a nearby small town, Florissant, which takes its name from the French word for flowering or blooming.

Work/Learn Program Specifics: Professional field internships are offered in interpretation and paleontology. Interpretative interns provide information on natural and cultural resources, explain area significance, and communicate NPS philosophy and policies to the visiting public. Paleontology interns will be involved with projects relating to the geological or paleontological resources of the park, including resource management; museum collection curation; technical assistance with excavating, inventorying, and monitoring of paleontological sites; and self-directed research. All interns participate in a one-week orientation training session. Topics may include interpretive philosophy, theory, and methods; NPS regulations and agency philosophy; basic geology and paleontology for the area; first aid/CPR; visitor services; and fee-

collection procedures. Training in other park operations, basic wildland firefighting, and natural and paleontological resources monitoring is scheduled throughout the twelve weeks.

Duration: This is a twelve-week program offered during the summer. Interns must be available for training starting in early June and complete the program through mid-late August. Interns usually work a forty hour work week.

Compensation and Perks: Interns receive a $40-per-week stipend, plus housing and full uniforms. Interns also receive insurance, have use of research facilities, and can attend seminars. Paleontology interns may receive a $1,000 to $3,000 stipend in lieu of the daily stipend and housing, depending on project funding and duration of the intern position.

The Ideal Candidate: Interpretive applicants must have effective communication skills, the ability to work comfortably with a variety of people of all ages, ability to work independently and as part of a team, and an interest and ability to work outdoors. A basic knowledge of natural sciences, geology, and paleontology is desirable. Paleontology applicants must have completed basic undergraduate course work for a degree in geology or biology. You are also encouraged to bring your own vehicle.

Making It Happen: Submit cover letter, stating your interest in the position, and a resume with names and telephone numbers of two references by March 15. Selections are made following telephone interviews and reference checks by early April.

Contact Information: Margaret Johnston, Volunteer Coordinator • Florissant Fossil Beds National Monument • P.O. Box 185 • Florissant, CO 80816-0815 • Phone: (719) 748-3253 • Fax: (719) 748-3164

Four Corners School of Outdoor Education

REGION/HQ: Rocky Mountains/Utah • **CATEGORY:** Adventure Travel • **POSITION TYPE:** Internship • **DURATION:** Spring-Fall • **IDEAL CANDIDATE:** High School Students, College Students, Career Changers, Retired Folks, Foreigners • **APPLICANT POOL:** 25–50/year • **APPLICANTS ACCEPTED:** 6/year

FOUR CORNERS SCHOOL OF OUTDOOR EDUCATION has been around since 1984 and offers unique learning vacations, mostly in the Four Corners area of the Un

States. Programs are by foot, van, and raft. They explore areas such as wilderness advocacy, archaeology, and research with the BLM, NPS, USFS, and many others. The school's goal is low-impact adventures with a very healthy dose of education.

Area and Working Environment: Monticello is a small town, with a population of 2,000. The cost of living is very low, the access to beautiful places is very high, and it's a very safe community. The base camp is located approximately twenty miles from town and is even more remote. If you like the outdoors, this is it.

Work/Learn Program Specifics: Each session of internships will vary with the season, program content, special projects, and office load. The school is very conscious about maintaining a balance between office work and field work. Special skills may be put to use, such as public relations, computer programming, painting, and carpentry.

Duration: Internships generally run in three sessions: May to mid-June, mid-June to August, and August to mid-October.

Compensation and Perks: Interns are in the unique position to go on a number of outdoor field programs, which generally last five days. Their programs are so diverse that one week you may be out backpacking, the next on the San Juan River. You'll also have access to their world-class experts.

The Ideal Candidate: All ages are encouraged! No area of interest supersedes another, but some prior knowledge of the outdoors is very helpful.

Making It Happen: Call for application materials. Send in your completed application by December 15. Phone interviews will be conducted.

INSIDER TIPS: *We like applicants who are excited about the outdoors and make good ambassadors for the school. Our participants like friendly, knowledgeable people. We all have to work hard so it helps to have an intern who doesn't mind the work. It doesn't hurt to know about the office environment, as duties will include some office times.*

Contact Information: Joy Stein, Office Manager • Four Corners School of Outdoor Education • P.O. Box 1029 • Monticello, UT 84535 • Phone: (801) 587-2156 • Fax: (801) 587-2193 • Toll Free: (800) 525-4456 • E-mail: fcs@igc.apc.org • Web Site: www.miraclemile.com/fourcorners

Fredericksburg & Spotsylvania National Military Park

REGION/HQ: Southeast/Virginia • **CATEGORY:** History • **POSITION TYPE:** Internship/Seasonal • **DURATION:** Year-Round • **IDEAL CANDIDATE:** College Students, Career Changers, Retired Folks • **APPLICANT POOL:** Varies • **APPLICANTS ACCEPTED:** Varies

THE PARK OFFERS A GREAT DEAL OF VARIETY because it is enormous by the standards of historical parks. The park has a visitor center on the Fredericksburg battlefield, with a library at which much of the research regarding the Union army can be done, and where the staff conducts tours of the Sunken Road fighting. Another visitor center on the Chancellorsville battlefield is also the starting point for conducted tours of the site where Stonewall Jackson was mortally wounded. The park's curatorial collection is also stored at Chancellorsville and the site supervisor also serves as the museum curator and the education coordinator. Tours are conducted of the "Stonewall" Jackson Shrine, the building in which the Confederate general died. Information duty, research on the Confederate Army and other topics, and cultural resource management tasks all occur at the historic structure Chatham, an eighteenth-century manor house.

Area and Working Environment: Fredericksburg was the scene of four major Civil War battles, resulting in more than 100,000 casualties. No other area of similar size witnessed such heavy losses. The boundaries encompass more than 8,000 acres, making the park the largest military preserve in the world.

Work/Learn Program Specifics: Various seasonal, volunteer, and internship positions are available: historical interpreters provide information and conduct walking tours for park visitors; historical researchers complete projects to help the staff access specific information easily; education coordinator assistants develop lesson plans and visuals for the park staff or teachers to use for student programs; curatorial assistants help with cataloging museum artifacts; cultural resource management assistants help to identify and preserve military and civilian landmarks of the Civil War era; restoration assistants properly protect and repair monuments, historic buildings, and other cultural resources; and administrative assistants may learn various federal personnel, budgeting, or purchasing practices.

Duration: Most volunteers must make a commitment of at least 100 hours and internships range from 120 to

480 hours for the term. Schedules vary with each position.

Compensation and Perks: Housing is provided when available. Seasonal wages vary.

The Ideal Candidate: Historical interpreters should be interested in the Civil War and enjoy the prospect of dealing with the public. Historical researchers need a good basic knowledge of the Civil War and military history. Education coordinator assistants must be familiar with the learning characteristics of different ages. Restoration assistants may need special skills in carpentry or masonry. Curatorial and cultural resource management assistants should have exposure to dealing with artifacts or identifying remains of cultural resources.

Making It Happen: Request application materials and specific descriptions of jobs. Telephone or personal interviews will be conducted. It's best to apply at least three months before your desired start date.

Contact Information: Gregory Mertz, Supervisory Historian • Fredericksburg & Spotsylvania National Military Park • 120 Chatham Ln. • Fredericksburg, VA 22405 • Phone: (540) 373-6124 • Fax: (540) 371-1907 • E-mail: Greg_Mertz@nps.gov • Web Site: www.nps.gov/frsp/frspweb.htm

Furnace Creek Inn & Ranch Resort

REGION/HQ: Pacific Northwest/California • **CATEGORY:** Concessionaire • **POSITION TYPE:** Internship/Seasonal • **DURATION:** Year-Round • **IDEAL CANDIDATE:** College Students, Career Changers, Retired Folks, Foreigners • **APPLICANT POOL:** 500/year • **APPLICANTS ACCEPTED:** 400/year

FRED HARVEY COMPANY OPERATES four properties in Death Valley: Furnace Creek Inn, a 68-room historic inn; Furnace Creek Ranch, a 200-room motel resort; Stove Pipe Wells Village, an 82-room motel; and Scotty's Castle. These properties provide lodging, food, retail stores, gas stations, golf, tennis, swimming, horses, and tours to visitors in the area. The summer temperatures can run in the 120°-plus range (great for pool lounging), and the winter temperatures hover around 70° (great for golf).

Area and Working Environment: The resort is located at an oasis within Death Valley National Park, with over 3.3 million acres to explore—including canyons, mountains, sand dunes, and wildlife—only 2 1/2 hours by car from Las Vegas and five hours from Los Angeles.

Work/Learn Program Specifics: This is an opportunity to provide guest services in a unique environment to persons from all parts of the world. The work can be physically demanding and challenging, but also very rewarding. Entry-level positions are also available.

Duration: Schedules can vary and include weekends, holidays, and overtime, as needed.

Compensation and Perks: The hourly wage varies with the position. Perks include low-cost employee meals and housing (including linens, utilities, and cable TV), eight paid holidays (after thirty days), two weeks vacation (after one year), and free golf, tennis, and swimming in a resort environment.

The Ideal Candidate: Must be at least eighteen years old and have an interest in gaining experience in the hospitality industry. A second language is helpful.

Making It Happen: Call for application materials. Rolling deadlines.

Contact Information: David Pizzuti, Human Resources Director • Furnace Creek Inn & Ranch Resort • Death Valley National Park • P.O. Box 187 • Death Valley, CA 92328 • Phone: (619) 786-2311 • Fax: (619) 786-2396

Glacier Park, Inc.

REGION/HQ: Rocky Mountains/Arizona • **CATEGORY:** Concessionaire • **POSITION TYPE:** Seasonal • **DURATION:** Spring-Fall • **IDEAL CANDIDATE:** College Students, Career Changers • **APPLICANT POOL:** 5,000/year • **APPLICANTS ACCEPTED:** 1,000/year

GLACIER PARK OPERATES seven historic hotels, nine restaurants, five retail gift shops, a pro golf shop, four camp stores, and thirty-three famous 1930's red tour buses.

Area and Working Environment: Rising from the plains of northwest Montana and southern Alberta, the jagged peaks of the Rocky Mountains make up the heart of Waterton-Glacier International Peace Park, where you will be working.

Work/Learn Program Specifics: Positions include food and beverage, rooms division, retail, maintenance/engineering, warehouse, property services, and transportation. Students of the performing arts will have the opportunity to be part of a full-scale nightly production. Singers, musicians, dancers, choreographers, stage technicians, and full support personnel are

I only went out for a walk, and finally concluded to stay out until sundown; for going out, I found, was really going in. —JOHN MUIR

all a part of traditional evening performances at both Glacier Park Lodge and the Many Glacier Hotel.

Duration: The season begins in May and runs through September.

Compensation and Perks: Hourly wages range from $4.75 to $6.50 per hour, depending on the position and whether you work in the United States or Canada. Housing in Glacier is extremely rustic. These structures are located in remote Rocky Mountain settings, weathering extreme winter elements and hundreds of new tenants each season. All housing is dormitory-style, with triple or quad accommodations. There is also limited trailer/RV space. Housing is charged at $2.50 per day. The cost of meals is $6 per day.

The Ideal Candidate: The minimum working age is eighteen years old (although waitstaff and bartenders must be at least nineteen and drivers, 21). Applicants will be considered based on their work availability dates, qualifications, and experience in the respective position.

Making It Happen: Call for application materials. Most positions are filled by May 1, although midsummer opportunities are available which can begin as early as June 1 or as late as August 15. May through September you can reach Glacier Park, Inc. at P.O. Box 147, East Glacier, MT 59434; (406) 226-9311.

INSIDER TIPS: *Great emphasis is placed on the applicant's ability to work the entire season.*

Contact Information: Jeff Graybill, HR Recruiting • Glacier Park, Inc. • Viad Tower, Station 0924 • 1850 N. Central Ave. • Phoenix, AZ 85077 • Phone: (602) 207-2612 • Fax: (602) 207-5589 • Web Site: www. coolworks.com/showme/glacier

Grand Canyon, Zion & Bryce Canyon National Park Lodges

REGION/HQ: South/Midwest/Arizona • **CATEGORY:** Concessionaire • **POSITION TYPE:** Seasonal • **DURATION:** Year-Round • **IDEAL CANDIDATE:** College Students, Career Changers, Retired Folks, Foreigners • **APPLICANT POOL:** Varies • **APPLICANTS ACCEPTED:** Varies

GRAND CANYON, ZION & BRYCE CANYON National Park Lodges is the concessionaire providing all lodging, food and beverage, retail, transportation, and support services in Grand Canyon, Zion & Bryce Canyon National Parks.

Area and Working Environment: Located in northern Arizona and southwestern Utah, these parks are the main attraction of the western region of the Colorado plateau. Grand Canyon, Zion & Bryce Canyon National Parks are surrounded by national forest lands, wilderness areas, and other national parks and monuments, including the newly designated Grand Staircase-Escalante National Monument. That means over 2.2 million acres of fun and beauty!

Work/Learn Program Specifics: Positions include guest room attendants, kitchen utility, bussers, F&B servers, cooks, front desk, cashiers, host/hostess, retail sales, transportation/tour guides, camper services, accounting, and maintenance/mechanics.

Duration: Positions are offered on a seasonal basis, starting in March/April/May until mid-October, as well as year-round opportunities. Preference is given to those who can work at least a five-month period.

Compensation and Perks: Wages are $4.75 to $7.00 per hour and higher, depending on position and experience. In-park room and board are provided for a nominal fee, dorm housing, as well as RV/trailer parks are available, and the South Rim at Grand Canyon has upgrade possibilities to apartment-style housing. Medical/dental benefits are available after ninety days. Grand Canyon also sports a new recreation complex/program exclusively for employees.

The Ideal Candidate: Must be at least eighteen years old due to housing regulations.

Making It Happen: Call for application materials. Deadlines are rolling; however it's best to apply in early January.

INSIDER TIPS: *Flexibility in job choice and job offered. Many employees start in entry-level positions and advance during the season, meaning there is much growth potential.*

Contact Information: Employment Office • Grand Canyon, Zion & Bryce Canyon National Park Lodges • AmFac Parks & Resorts • P.O. Box 699 • Grand Canyon, AZ 86023 • Phone: (520) 638-2343 • Fax: (520) 638-0143 • E-mail: gcnpjobs@aol.com • Web Site: www. coolworks.com/showme

Grand Teton Lodge Company

REGION/HQ: Rocky Mountains/Wyoming • **CATEGORY:** Concessionaire • **POSITION TYPE:** Seasonal • **DURATION:** Spring-Fall • **IDEAL**

CANDIDATE: College Students, Career Changers, Retired Folks • **APPLICANT POOL:** Varies • **APPLICANTS ACCEPTED:** 1,000/year

....

GRAND TETON LODGE COMPANY manages three unique resorts—Jackson Lake Lodge, Colter Bay Village, and Jenny Lake Lodge—all located in the heart of Grand Teton National Park. Jackson Lake Lodge is a full-service resort hotel, with 385 guest rooms, situated on a bluff overlooking Jackson Lake and the skyline of the Tetons. Colter Bay Village, on the shores of Jackson Lake, is a family resort offering cabins, tent cabins, and RV park accommodations. Jenny Lake Lodge is a small, elegant resort located in the shadow of the towering Tetons.

Area and Working Environment: You'll discover that exploration of Teton National Park is a soothing and refreshing experience. As you view the rugged mountains, the warm valley, the sparkling lakes, the behavior of wild animals, and the colorful displays of wildflowers, let this special place work its magic on you.

Work/Learn Program Specifics: Whether for a summer or many seasons, employment in Grand Teton National Park provides a unique and gratifying experience in one of the most beautiful and rugged areas in the world. While the work is demanding and the summer cannot be considered a vacation, they offer employees an opportunity to live in an area that annually attracts well over three million visitors. A genuine interest in the park and a positive attitude toward guest service are important in providing a quality experience for their visitors. Available jobs include Hotel Services, Food and Beverage, Kitchen, Accounting, Retail, Guest Activities (wranglers, river guides, and van/bus drivers), Maintenance, and Employee Services (recreation director, dormitory custodians, employee canteen attendants, and personnel clerk).

Duration: Their season runs from May to October. Depending on the position, various starting and ending dates can be accommodated. Preference will be given to applicants who can work until the end of the season. Positions beginning in July and August are also available. Work schedules vary, but in most cases are six days, forty-eight hours per week.

Compensation and Perks: Most positions pay $5.75 to $6.00 per hour. Housing is provided at no charge (RV sites are $4 per day). There is a $40.25 per week charge for employee services, which include cafeteria meals, laundry facilities, and laundered linens. Guest facilities and activities are open to employees on a space-available basis. Employee recreational activities, such as dances and sporting events, are scheduled throughout the summer. You also receive discounts in their gift shops.

The Ideal Candidate: A minimum age of eighteen is required for all employees housed in company-maintained facilities.

Making It Happen: Call for application materials.

Contact Information: Personnel Manager • Grand Teton Lodge Company • P.O. Box 250 • Moran, WY 83013 • Phone: (307) 733-2811 • Toll Free: (800) 350-2068 • Web Site: www.gtlc.com

Hamilton Stores, Inc.

REGION/HQ: Rocky Mountains/Montana • **CATEGORY:** Concessionaire • **POSITION TYPE:** Seasonal • **DURATION:** Spring-Fall • **IDEAL CANDIDATE:** College Students, Career Changers, Retired Folks, Foreigners • **APPLICANT POOL:** Varies • **APPLICANTS ACCEPTED:** Varies

....

SINCE 1915, HAMILTON STORES has owned and run fourteen general stores located throughout Yellowstone National Park.

Work/Learn Program Specifics: Seasonal positions include sales, grocery, food service, employee dining room cooks, servers, and other positions. There are positions also available in their general office and warehouse located in West Yellowstone.

Duration: Positions become available in mid-February in the warehouse and in April in the stores. Most positions are filled from May to September, with the season ending in some stores in late October. You are guaranteed thirty-five- to forty-hour weeks, with two consecutive days off. Most employees work split shifts.

Compensation and Perks: Pay starts at $5.15 per hour (also ask about their contract completion bonus). Room and board are available at all locations in the park except Mammoth Hot Springs. Hamilton Stores is known for dishing out excellent food to its employees, served family-style, and you'll find yourself participating in different events at the store, including crazy hat day or Christmas in Yellowstone—which occurs in August!

The Ideal Candidate: You must be at least nineteen years old upon arrival.

Making It Happen: Call or write for more information and application. There will be a phone interview prior to hiring. Applications are accepted through late August: From November through March, you can reach them at their winter address: 1709 W. College St., Bozeman, MT 59715; (406) 587-2208.

INSIDER TIPS: *Applicants who come early and can stay late have priority.*

Contact Information: Nina Sims, Vice President, Human Resources • Hamilton Stores, Inc. • P.O. Box 250 • West Yellowstone, MT 59758 • Phone: (406) 646-7325 • Fax: (406) 646-7323 • Toll Free: (800) 385-4979 • Web Site: www.coolworks.com/showme/bearsrus

Hopewell Furnace National Historic Site

REGION/HQ: Northeast/Pennsylvania • **CATEGORY:** Historic Site • **POSITION TYPE:** Internship • **DURATION:** Year-Round • **IDEAL CANDIDATE:** College Students, Career Changers, Retired Folks, Foreigners • **APPLICANT POOL:** 30/year • **APPLICANTS ACCEPTED:** 10/year

HOPEWELL FURNACE IS A NATIONAL HISTORIC SITE operated by the National Park Service as one of the finest examples of a restored charcoal-burning iron furnace, which once dominated life in southeastern Pennsylvania and provided the foundations for the industrial development of this country. Hopewell Furnace operated from 1771 until 1883, spanning several generations of our industrial history, from its infancy in the colonial period to the giant steel and railroad industries at the turn of the last century. As an active living history site, Hopewell features first-person interpreta-

tion of moulders, colliers, blacksmiths, farmers, housewives, servants, cooks, and members of the ironmaster's family. The interpretive program also includes an active farm, with horses, sheep, and cows. In addition, Hopewell conducts its own charcoal burn twice a year in an effort to preserve the otherwise lost skill of producing charcoal from cord wood. The charcoal produced in these burns is used as fuel in molding, casting, and blacksmithing demonstrations.

Area and Working Environment: Located in southeast Pennsylvania, just fifteen miles from Reading ("the outlet capital of the world") and forty-five miles west of Philadelphia, but still in a very rural area. It is surrounded on three sides by 7,000-acre French Creek State Park and is close to Amish country.

Work/Learn Program Specifics: Duties are determined by the needs of the site and interest of the intern. Areas include cultural resource preservation and museums, natural resource monitoring and management, historical interpretation, living history, and visitor center operations.

Duration: Internship dates are variable, full- or part-time. In general, positions last three to four months at a minimum of twenty hours per week.

Compensation and Perks: Although no stipend is available, you will receive shared housing and reimbursement for miscellaneous expenses. This is also a great opportunity to learn about the daily operation of a national park while on the job.

The Ideal Candidate: Cultural resources applicants should have a history, public history, archaeology, or museum studies background; natural resources applicants should have a biology, zoology, or natural sciences background; historical interpretation applicants should have a history, theatre, communications, or park management background.

Making It Happen: Call for application. Send completed application, resume, and cover letter. Rolling deadlines. Interviews are conducted over the phone and references will be checked.

INSIDER TIPS: *Must show a willingness to work with and get along with a wide variety of co-workers and visitors. A genuine desire to insure that each visitor has an enjoyable experience at Hopewell Furnace is essential. Must be flexible enough to handle numerous interruptions in work routine by more pressing projects and visitor needs.*

Contact Information: Frank Hebblethwaite, Supervisory Historian • Hopewell Furnace National Historic Site • National Park Service • 2 Mark Bird Ln. • Elverson, PA

19520-9505 • Phone: (610) 582-8773 • Fax: (610) 582-2768 • E-mail: hofu_superintendent@nps.gov

Lassen Volcanic National Park

REGION/HQ: Pacific Northwest/California • **CATEGORY:** National Park • **POSITION TYPE:** Internship • **DURATION:** Winter/Summer • **IDEAL CANDIDATE:** College Students, Career Changers, Foreigners • **APPLICANT POOL:** Varies • **APPLICANTS ACCEPTED:** 1–2/term

THIS 106,000-ACRE NATIONAL PARK, located in the mountains of Northern California, contains outstanding volcanic features, including one of the world's largest plug dome volcanoes—Lassen Peak—reaching an elevation of 10,457 feet.

Work/Learn Program Specifics: The summer intern supports the Junior Ranger, Pioneer, and Field Interpretive programs and assists in the visitor center. The winter intern presents Winter Naturalist programs on snowshoes and assists in the visitor center and with environmental education and interpretive projects. Since there are generally only one or two interns per season, you will receive lots of individual attention. They also have volunteer positions available for campground hosts, maintenance, and interpretation.

Duration: Interns usually work forty hours per week, including weekends.

Compensation and Perks: There may be a small stipend and shared housing. Interns are also eligible to attend summer naturalist training.

The Ideal Candidate: The park is looking for someone with a college background in biological sciences, environmental studies, and/or outdoor education. Candidates should also have public speaking experience and have the ability to learn about park resources and enjoy sharing this knowledge with others. A valid driver's license is required.

Making It Happen: Call for a VIP application. Interviews are often over the telephone, although applicants may need to visit the Park Headquarters for an in-person interview. Deadlines: summer—May 1; winter—November 1.

INSIDER TIPS: *List all of your qualifications on the application. A personal vehicle is useful in this remote location. It helps to talk to the assistant chief park naturalist or education coordinator directly.*

Contact Information: Nancy Bailey, VIP Coordinator • Lassen Volcanic National Park • P.O. Box 100 • Mineral, CA 96063-0100 • Phone: (916) 595-4444 • Fax: (916) 595-3262

Mesa Verde National Park

REGION/HQ: Rocky Mountains/Colorado • **CATEGORY:** Concessionaire • **POSITION TYPE:** Seasonal • **DURATION:** Spring-Fall • **IDEAL CANDIDATE:** College Students, Career Changers, Retired Folks • **APPLICANT POOL:** Varies • **APPLICANTS ACCEPTED:** 250/year

OVER SIX CENTURIES AGO, Mesa Verde was the home to a thriving culture, a creative people who lived in magnificent cliff dwellings of handhewn stone. These ancient ones, the Anasazi, left their beautiful home—for unclear reasons—about A.D. 1300. Their secret legacy remained hidden within the mesa's canyons until cattle ranchers stumbled on the silent ruins in 1888. Today the architectural treasures of the Anasazi are protected by the National Park Service. A visit to the cliff dwellings and mesa-top ruins offers an evocative glimpse into the lives of these resourceful prehistoric people. They made finely decorated pottery, cultivated corn on the mesas, and designed sophisticated architecture in their cliffside homes—all done laboriously by hand. Mesa Verde Company operates the 150-room Far View Lodge, with a dining room, cocktail lounge, and sight-seeing tours. Other services include gift shops, cafeterias, a 425-site campground, service stations, snack bars, and a general office/warehouse in Mancos, Colorado.

Work/Learn Program Specifics: Positions include gift shop sales clerk, cashiers, kitchen staff, waitstaff, buspeople, front desk clerk, night auditor, reservations clerk, bookkeeper, tour driver, maintenance, housekeeper, and campground staff.

Compensation and Perks: Most positions start at or near minimum wage; although some positions have a higher pay rate. Company housing consists of four dormitories, plus cabins and trailers. Single rooms are assigned on a seniority basis. They have a limited number of RV sites for those who have their own travel trailers. The sites have facilities consisting of water, sewer, and electrical hookups. Weekly room charges are $7.50 for double occupancy and $15.00 for singles, trailers, or RV sites. Their employee meal program allows you to eat at cafeterias at reduced prices. Only

One person can make a difference and every person should try.
—JOHN F. KENNEDY

meals that are actually eaten and signed for will be deducted from payroll.

Making It Happen: Call for application materials.

Contact Information: Personnel Director • Mesa Verde National Park • P.O. Box 277 • Mancos, CO 81328 • Phone: (970) 533-7731

Minnesota Conservation Corps

REGION/HQ: Great Lakes/Minnesota • **CATEGORY:** Natural Resources • **POSITION TYPE:** Unique Experience • **DURATION:** Summer • **IDEAL CANDIDATE:** College Students, Career Changers, Retired Folks • **APPLICANT POOL:** 100/year • **APPLICANTS ACCEPTED:** 20/year

THE MINNESOTA CONSERVATION CORPS' summer program employs 70 Minnesota youths, ages fifteen to eighteen, for a period of eight weeks, to work on various natural resource projects. Corps members come from all over Minnesota to live and work at the residential site in St. Croix State Park, which was built by corps members in the 1930's. The projects are often physically demanding, where youths learn basic work skills and help maintain Minnesota's natural resources.

Work/Learn Program Specifics: The MCC is looking for experienced and responsible individuals who are able to supervise and work with high-school aged youth on conservation work projects. Past projects have included erosion control, building and maintaining hiking trails, historical restoration, timber stand improvement, tree planting and pruning, and wildlife projects. Besides the work you'll be doing, you will also teach corps members environmental awareness, life skills, career development, and a wide variety of other subjects. Staff positions include site director, assistant site director, work project coordinator, education/activities coordinator, health coordinator, head cook, assistant cook, crew leaders, and assistant crew leaders. Deaf and hard-of-hearing individuals are especially needed for leadership roles.

Duration: Summer positions are from June through August.

Compensation and Perks: Staff receive $290 to $440 per week and free room, board, and transportation while on the job. This is a chance to challenge yourself and make an impact both on your life and the lives of others.

The Ideal Candidate: Applicants should have positive energy, experience working with high school youth, camping skills, outdoor ethics, and outdoor work experience (landscape, construction, carpentry, trail maintenance, and the like). Those who do best aren't afraid of mosquitoes, rain, heat, and other challenges that the outdoors presents. In addition, individuals who are sign language interpreters and/or skilled in American Sign Language are encouraged to apply.

Making It Happen: Call for application materials. Applications must be received by April 1.

Contact Information: Mark Robbins, Field Specialist • Minnesota Conservation Corps • 1200 Warner Rd. • St. Paul, MN 55106 • Phone: (612) 772-7575 • Fax: (612) 772-7599 • E-mail: mark.robbins@dnr.state.mn.us

Mt. Rainier Guest Services

REGION/HQ: Pacific Northwest/Washington • **CATEGORY:** Concessionaire • **POSITION TYPE:** Seasonal • **DURATION:** Year-Round • **IDEAL CANDIDATE:** College Students, Career Changers, Foreigners • **APPLICANT POOL:** Varies • **APPLICANTS ACCEPTED:** 240/year

MT. RAINIER GUEST SERVICES is the official concessionaire for Mt. Rainier National Park and provides meals and lodging for over two million visitors each year. Employment with Mt. Rainier Guest Services is an excellent opportunity to work in an area of pristine mountain meadows, streams, canyons, lakes, rivers, old-growth forests, and glaciers. It's also an opportunity to meet employees and guests from all over the world. Life in the mountains is physically and mentally invigorating, but work with guest services is hard and serious.

Area and Working Environment: Located in Mt. Rainier National Park, they operate Paradise Inn, Jackson Visitor Center, National Park Inn, and Sunrise Lodge. The centerpiece of the park is 14,410-foot Mt. Rainier.

Work/Learn Program Specifics: Seasonal positions include food and beverage, front desk, gift shop, housekeeping, accounting, security, porter, and supervisory positions. The National Park Service will have an orientation meeting at the beginning of the season to acquaint you with park regulations and how to make the best of your time at the park.

Duration: Positions start as early as mid-April and last as long as mid-October. Most people work between 90 and 120 days during that time period, depending on how long they are available. Those with the longest dates are given the most consideration.

Compensation and Perks: Positions are paid at $5.10 to $10.00 per hour. Room and board are provided at a payroll deduction of $50 per week. Dorm rooms are rustic and within walking distance from work, with two or more persons per room and shared bathrooms (sorry, no housing for children or pets). They offer a bonus to those who complete their work agreement. The possibilities for hiking, climbing, fishing, backpacking, and photography are almost limitless.

The Ideal Candidate: Applicants are considered for all positions based on abilities, skills, and knowledge.

Making It Happen: Call for application materials.

INSIDER TIPS: *Show the exact dates you are available and be realistic about your job choices. Your chances of being selected increase if you are willing to accept an entry-level position. Be sure to give complete information in the area provided for past work references and include an extra sheet or resume to give additional information.*

Contact Information: Sandra Miller, Personnel Manager • Mt. Rainier Guest Services • 55106 Kernahan Rd., East • P.O. Box 108 • Ashford, WA 98304 • Phone: (360) 569-2400 • Fax: (360) 569-2770 • Web Site: www. coolworks.com/showme/rainier

Mt. Rushmore National Memorial

REGION/HQ: Rocky Mountains/South Dakota • **CATEGORY:** Concessionaire • **POSITION TYPE:** Internship/Seasonal • **DURATION:** Summer • **IDEAL CANDIDATE:** High School Students, College Students, Career Changers, Retired Folks, Foreigners • **APPLICANT POOL:** Varies • **APPLICANTS ACCEPTED:** 150/year

MT. RUSHMORE CONCESSIONS IS the concessionaire in charge of operating the public, nongovernment guest services at the memorial. The hospitality services they provide include a cafeteria, ice cream and fudge shops, and a world-class gift shop.

Area and Working Environment: Located in the Black Hills of South Dakota (the nearest airport is in Rapid City).

Work/Learn Program Specifics: As Mt. Rushmore receives millions of visitors each summer, you can imagine the need for many employees, each working with one goal in mind—to make sure visitors enjoy their stay. Not all the jobs are glamorous and, make no mistake about it, they all require work. For some, a summer at Mt. Rushmore is a step on the road to other careers and different places; for others, it is the first step towards a career in the hospitality industry. Positions include Food Department (senior cook, cook, and food attendant), gift shop attendants, maintenance/custodial, accounting/audit clerk, and bus drivers.

Duration: Their busy season begins in May and lasts into September. Some positions start in early April and last until mid-October. Your employment chances improve if you can arrive early and work through September or later. They ask that all applicants work at least ninety days or more during the season. Most employees will average thirty to forty-eight hours per week.

Compensation and Perks: Wages are $4.75 to $7.00 per hour, plus lodging and meals provided at a cost of $56.00 per week. They offer a completely new and handicapped-accessible dormitory and RV sites to those who need them. On your days off box lunches are available and you'll be able to explore places such as Wind Cave National Park, Custer State Park, Badlands National Park, Devil's Tower National Monument, Crazy Horse Monument, and Rapid City. For many, the chance to live and work at Mt. Rushmore is a dream come true. While you are there you'll become closer to the wilderness, closer to different people, and closer to yourself. Applicants who successfully complete their employment agreement will receive free housing.

The Ideal Candidate: Candidates must be willing to work hard, enjoy working with and for others, and take pride in a job well done. You must provide your own transportation to and from Mt. Rushmore.

Making It Happen: Call or write for application materials. Submit completed application. No application will be processed unless reference information is complete (references will be checked). Hiring decisions begin in January and continue throughout the season. It's best not to apply any later than June 30.

Contact Information: Russ Jobman, Human Resources Director • Mt. Rushmore National Memorial • Amfac Parks & Resorts • P.O. Box 178 • Keystone, SD 57751-0178 • Phone: (605) 574-2515 • Fax: (605) 574-2495 • Toll Free: (800) 827-9323 • E-mail: twrs@rapidnet. com

Now I know the secret of making the best persons; It is to grow in the open air and to eat and sleep with the earth. —WALT WHITMAN

169

National Park Concessions, Inc.

REGION/HQ: Nationwide/Kentucky • **CATEGORY:** Concessionaire • **POSITION TYPE: SEASONAL** • **DURATION:** Year-Round • **IDEAL CANDIDATE:** College Students, Career Changers, Foreigners • **APPLICANT POOL:** Varies • **APPLICANTS ACCEPTED:** Varies

NATIONAL PARK CONCESSIONS is authorized by the National Park Service to operate certain facilities in five national parks across our nation, including Big Bend National Park, Texas; Blue Ridge Parkway, Virginia/North Carolina; Isle Royale National Park, Michigan; Mammoth Cave National Park, Kentucky; and Olympic National Park, Washington.

Work/Learn Program Specifics: Many opportunities are available to those seeking employment in the hospitality industry. Combined with the national park setting, the work experiences they offer are both unique and challenging. Positions are available in front office, housekeeping, maintenance, gift shop, kitchen, dining room, camp stores, service stations, and many others.

Duration: Big Bend and Mammoth Cave operations are open year-round, while also offering seasonal employment opportunities. Blue Ridge Parkway, Isle Royale, and Olympic operations offer seasonal work only. Blue Ridge Parkway and Olympic open the first of May and close at the end of October. Isle Royale opens in mid-May and closes after Labor Day.

Compensation and Perks: Pay varies with the park; housing is available at all operations, with the exception of the Blue Ridge Parkway. By living in a national park, you'll have access to all park facilities that are open to the public and some that may only be available to park residents. Also, during the course of the year, there are planned cookouts, tours, and employee get-togethers. Year-round, full-time employees are eligible for paid vacation and insurance benefits.

The Ideal Candidate: All applicants must be eighteen years of age or over. Those seeking seasonal employment must agree to work at least through Labor Day.

Making It Happen: Call for more information and application.

INSIDER TIPS: *Applicants who are available for longer periods of time get careful consideration.*

Contact Information: Garner B. Hanson, President & Chairman • National Park Concessions, Inc. • General

Offices • Mammoth Cave, KY 42259-0027 • Phone: (502) 773-2191 • Fax: (502) 773-5120

Northwest Youth Corps

REGION/HQ: Pacific Northwest/Oregon • **CATEGORY:** Conservation • **POSITION TYPE:** Seasonal • **DURATION:** Spring-Fall • **IDEAL CANDIDATE:** High School Students, College Students, Career Changers, Retired Folks, Foreigners • **APPLICANT POOL:** 200/year • **APPLICANTS ACCEPTED:** 15/year

NORTHWEST YOUTH CORPS (NYC) is a summer education and job training program for high school youth, aged sixteen to nineteen. Youth crews work on projects for government agencies and private landowners in a format stressing environmental education and development of basic job skills. Crews typically live and work in remote locations throughout Oregon and in parts of Washington and Idaho. During the week crews set up primitive camps near their job sites, live in tents, and cook their own meals over a campfire or Coleman stove. On weekends, three to four crews rendezvous for recreational outings and educational activities. NYC is the only fully mobile conservation corps in the country.

Work/Learn Program Specifics: Crew leaders and assistant crew leaders live and work with their crew in a full-time capacity. They put in long days and work shoulder to shoulder with their crew while supervising the successful completion of a wide variety of manual labor projects. They also implement a daily environmental education program, coordinate meal preparation, prepare required paperwork, transport their crew in a fifteen-passenger van, and are required to learn the skills necessary to operate a chainsaw in a safe, efficient manner. Over 400 crew members, aged sixteen to nineteen, are selected each year to participate in the program. You and your crew will work in the woods, building hiking trails with hazel hoes, shovels, and pulaskis. You may pile logging slash, build fences, pull debris from creeks, brush ski trails, restore wildlife habitat, plant trees, enhance fisheries, or work to save endangered species.

Duration: NYC is a residential program requiring long days, high energy, and a love of challenge. Time off is limited.

Compensation and Perks: Crew Leaders average $4,700 to $5,300 per summer, plus meals. Crew members earn $5.00 per hour, and $5.75 per day is deducted for meals.

The Ideal Candidate: Crew Leader applicants should have a youth leadership background, experience in professional positions, a solid environmental ethic, and a diverse set of conservation skills. Current first aid and CPR certifications are required, and lifesaving certification is desirable. Crew members must be between sixteen and nineteen years of age. They also have a special program for fourteen- and fifteen-year-olds.

Making It Happen: Crew leaders: send a cover letter and resume by March 15. Crew members: call Kathleen Colson for current deadlines.

Contact Information: Jeff Parker, Program Director • Northwest Youth Corps • 5120 Franklin Blvd., #7A • Eugene, OR 97403 • Phone: (541) 746-8653 • Fax: (541) 746-5042 • E-mail: nyc@efn.org

Olympic National Park

REGION/HQ: Pacific Northwest/Washington • **CATEGORY:** National Park • **POSITION TYPE:** Internship/Seasonal • **DURATION:** Year-Round • **IDEAL CANDIDATE:** College Students, Career Changers, Retired Folks, Foreigners • **APPLICANT POOL:** Varies • **APPLICANTS ACCEPTED:** Varies

OLYMPIC NATIONAL PARK OCCUPIES over 900,000 acres in Washington State, of which 95 percent is designated wilderness. On October 26, 1976, it was designated a biosphere reserve, and on October 27, 1981, it was designated a world heritage site. The park consists of a rugged and spectacular glacier-capped mountainous core penetrated by deep valleys, some with lush temperate rain forests, a separate 57-mile-long coastal strip, and some 100 offshore islands. The offshore islands are also national wildlife refuges and are contained within the Olympic Coast National Marine Sanctuary. The park was established to preserve primeval forests and the largest natural herd of Roosevelt elk.

Work/Learn Program Specifics: Hurricane Ridge interns will work as entry-level interpretive rangers, preparing and presenting talks and walks in the Hurricane Ridge area during the summer and in the winter will lead interpretive snowshoe walks and short indoor talks.

Sol Duc Valley interns work as entry-level rangers and serve as coordinators for the Sol Duc Ranger Station's wilderness backcountry computerized permit system. The interns will mainly help educate/coordinate other volunteers and the general public about the wilderness permit system.

Wilderness resource/vegetation interns monitor wilderness conditions, which involves extensive backpacking, field mapping, and collection of campsite data in the Olympic Mountains.

Olympic Park visitor center interns will work as interpretive rangers in the Olympic Park Visitor Center in Port Angeles, and may spend one day a week in the Hurricane Ridge area. Interns will assist with the daily operations of the park's main visitor center, which receives over 90,000 visitors annually. Duties include front desk information and sales, radio and phone recording, and some interpretive walks/talks for environmental education.

VIP positions include interpretation, resource management, backcountry ranger, natural sciences, maintenance, and campground host.

Duration: Hurricane Ridge and Sol Duc Valley: June 15 through early September; Wilderness Resources Internship: mid-June through late October; Hurricane Ridge: December 15 through March 31. Visitor center internship positions vary seasonally, and dates can be flexible to coincide with school semesters (plan on two or three months or longer). Jobs one month or less are seldom filled.

Compensation and Perks: Interns receive a $50 to $100 stipend per month, plus free housing in a modern one-bedroom apartment. Apartments are shared with one other park employee. A two-week training program is provided for all positions.

The Ideal Candidate: Hurricane Ridge/Sol Duc applicants should be upper-level undergraduate students or recent graduates of a natural science or park management program. Some knowledge of ecological processes and natural history is desirable. The ability to work independently and with people is required. Visitor center position applicants should be majoring in natural sciences, park management, or interpretation; however, students with interest or experience in visitor information will also be considered.

Making It Happen: Call for application materials. Submit completed application, resume, and list of references. Feel free to call if you have any questions.

INSIDER TIPS: *Many people apply so send in your application one to three months before the season begins.*

Contact Information: Maurie Sprague, VIP Coordinator • Olympic National Park • 600 East Park Ave. • Port Angeles, WA 98362-6798 • Phone: (360) 452-4501 • Fax: (360) 452-0335

Oregon Dunes National Recreation Area

REGION/HQ: Pacific Northwest/Oregon
• **CATEGORY:** Forest Service • **POSITION TYPE:** Unique Experience • **DURATION:** Spring/Summer
• **IDEAL CANDIDATE:** College Students, Career Changers, Retired Folks, Foreigners • **APPLICANT POOL:** Varies • **APPLICANTS ACCEPTED:** Varies

OREGON DUNES NATIONAL RECREATION AREA is 32,000 acres of unbelievable diversity stretching for 40 miles along the central Oregon Coast between Florence and Coos Bay.

Area and Working Environment: This is sand dune country! Ocean winds move sand inland from the beach, building it into great dunes. Year by year, the sand creeps inland, sometimes forming dunes over 400 feet tall. Today's Oregon Dunes began taking form as the Ice Age was ebbing, 10 to 15 thousand years ago.

Work/Learn Program Specifics: Volunteer positions include overlook hosts, headquarters hosts, guided field trips and nature walk interpreters, campground hosts, writers, illustrators, photographers, graphic designers, and office help. If you have a special skill or talent you think is valuable in managing the Oregon Dunes, let them know. Often they need carpenters, data-entry specialists, youth group leaders, Smokey the Bear helpers, or fish tank cleaners. Often projects of this nature can be ideal for a group of friends. Some are one-time deals, others require a significant commitment of time and energy.

Duration: Work one month or six, a few hours a week or full-time! Help is mainly needed from May through September.

Compensation and Perks: A $12 per day stipend and uniforms are provided. Housing is available to volunteers who work at least twenty-four hours per week. Housing is located two miles north of where you will be working, complete with kitchen, bathroom, and laundry facilities. Campground hosts receive a campsite with hookups, along with volunteer jackets and caps. Some host positions include reimbursement for propane.

Making It Happen: Call for details. Rolling deadlines.

Contact Information: Skyanne Housser, Public Affairs Director • Oregon Dunes National Recreation Area • Siuslaw National Forest • 855 Highway Ave. • Reedsport, OR 97467 • Phone: (541) 271-3611 • Fax: (541) 750-7244

Parks Canada Research Adventures

REGION/HQ: Canada/British Columbia
• **CATEGORY:** Conservation • **POSITION TYPE:** Work/Learn Adventure • **DURATION:** Year-Round
• **IDEAL CANDIDATE:** College Students, Career Changers, Retired Folks, Foreigners • **APPLICANT POOL:** Varies • **APPLICANTS ACCEPTED:** Varies

A PARKS CANADA RESEARCH ADVENTURE is a unique opportunity for you to help protect Canada's national parks. It is an exciting chance to work alongside researchers, park wardens, and environmental educators to meet nature face to face. Parks Canada is the government agency entrusted with protecting and preserving Canada's most treasured landscapes and historic sites.

Area and Working Environment: Turquoise mountain lakes, glaciated peaks, tumbling rockfalls, roaring waterfalls, and fabulous hiking trails are images which describe the grandeur of Yoho National Park, where you will be adventuring.

Work/Learn Program Specifics: Broaden your understanding of the Canadian Rockies environment while working with others who share your passion for nature. You may choose from programs that range from tracking wolf packs or checking bluebird nesting success to measuring mountain forest diversity. Research days will be spent outdoors working in the spectacular mountain landscapes of your study area. Projects often involve hiking, flatwater paddling, or in winter, snowshoeing, and skiing.

Duration: Projects last from seven to fourteen days and special educator's weekends are also available.

Compensation and Perks: There is a participation fee that ranges from $80 to $170 (Canadian funds) per day. This covers lodging (in rustic lodges, warden cabins, or field camps), food, local transportation, and some of the project research expenses. Travel to and from Yoho National Park is not included.

The Ideal Candidate: Anyone may participate as long as they are fit, in good health, and are a minimum of eighteen years of age. You need not have scientific training to help—just a sense of adventure, a little outdoor knowhow, and a desire to participate as a team member.

Making It Happen: Apply at least two months prior to project commencement.

Contact Information: Donna Cook, Program Coordinator • Parks Canada Research Adventures • Yoho

National Park • Box 99 • Field, British Columbia V0A 1G0 • Canada • Phone: (250) 343-6324 • Fax: (250) 343-6330 • E-mail: donna_cook@pch.gc.ca • Web Site: www.worldweb.com/ParksCanada-Yoho

Priest Lake State Park

REGION/HQ: Pacific Northwest/Idaho • **CATEGORY:** State Park • **POSITION TYPE:** Internship • **DURATION:** Summer • **IDEAL CANDIDATE:** College Students, Career Changers • **APPLICANT POOL:** Varies • **APPLICANTS ACCEPTED:** Varies

AT AN ELEVATION OF ABOUT 2,400 FEET, Priest Lake State Park offers an abundance of beautiful scenery and recreational opportunities. Visitors enjoy the dense cedar-hemlock forests and have ample opportunity to observe nature's inhabitants such as whitetail deer, black bear, moose, and bald eagles. Noted for its clear water, Priest Lake extends nineteen miles and is connected to the smaller Upper Priest Lake by a placid two-mile-long thoroughfare. Priest Lake offers park visitors a diversity of enjoyment, ranging from boating and fishing to snowmobiling and cross-country skiing.

Work/Learn Program Specifics: Interns will have the opportunity to observe and learn about park-level operational and administrative methods and acquire skills and experience necessary to pursue a career in parks and recreation. Interns will work for the Indian Creek unit as entrance station aides, maintenance aides, or interpretive aides.

Duration: The internship begins one week prior to Memorial Day weekend and lasts through the Labor Day weekend. Various shifts are available depending on the position held. You will be working most weekends and holidays.

Compensation and Perks: There are some paid and some non-paid positions, with housing available at a nominal cost. Maintenance and clerical positions are paid $5.82 per hour, and interpretive positions are paid $6.50 per hour. You will be required to purchase and wear a park-approved uniform.

The Ideal Candidate: CPR and first aid training is required prior to starting employment.

Making It Happen: Write or call for further information and application procedure. Applications are accepted from January 1 through March 15 annually. Normally a personal interview with qualified applicants is required at the park.

Contact Information: Park Manager • Priest Lake State Park • Indian Creek Bay, #423 • Coolin, ID 83821 • Phone: (208) 443-2200

Redwood National Park

REGION/HQ: Pacific Northwest/California • **CATEGORY:** National Park • **POSITION TYPE:** Seasonal • **DURATION:** Year-Round • **IDEAL CANDIDATE:** College Students, Career Changers, Foreigners • **APPLICANT POOL:** 240/year • **APPLICANTS ACCEPTED:** 55/year

EVEN APART FROM THE COAST RANGE and its lofty forests, Redwood's coastline—to which the big tree is intimately related—would justify national park status. Rugged, with stretches of steep, rocky cliffs broken by rolling slopes, it is largely unaltered by humans. Generally rocky, its tidal zone can be difficult to traverse, with exceptions such as Gold Bluff's Beach, a seven-mile stretch of dunes and sandy beach. Redwood National Park was established in 1968 and expanded in 1978 to protect superlative ancient redwood forests growing along the coast. The park is now a world heritage site and international biosphere reserve.

Area and Working Environment: The park is located on the north coast of California and is home to the tallest measured trees in the world—the coast redwood. In addition to the magnificent redwood groves, the park is surrounded by the Pacific Ocean to the west and wilderness mountains to the east. The park is approximately an hour's drive from Humboldt State University.

Work/Learn Program Specifics: Volunteer positions are available in many areas, including trail maintenance, visitor services, campground hosting, interpretation, and resource management. In general, they will try to match your interests and abilities to the variety of positions which they offer. During the school year they offer an environmental education program to elementary school children.

Duration: At least a one month commitment is desired; longer terms are encouraged. Work schedules vary, but are typically twenty-four to forty hours per week and may include weekends and holidays.

Compensation and Perks: No compensation is provided (except a small reimbursement for out-of-pocket expenses); however, you will receive housing, a uniform (if needed), training, recognition, and the opportunity to live and work in a beautiful national park, as well as to help visitors appreciate the park's special resources.

The Ideal Candidate: Applicants must enjoy working with people and have an interest in preserving our nation's national park resources. Having personal transportation (car, bicycle, etc.) is a must, as this is an isolated area with extremely limited public transportation.

Making It Happen: Call for application materials. Type or neatly print on application and attach a resume showing experience working with people and/or working in outdoor environments, along with the names and numbers of three references. Rolling deadlines. Telephone interviews are conducted.

INSIDER TIPS: *Be enthusiastic about people and nature, and make it as easy as possible to get ahold of you.*

Contact Information: Janet Lynch, Budget Clerk • Redwood National Park • 1111 2nd St. • Crescent City, CA 95531 • Phone: (707) 464-6101 • Fax: (707) 464-1812 • Web Site: www.nps.gov/redw

Rocky Mountain National Park

REGION/HQ: Rocky Mountains/Colorado • **CATEGORY:** National Park • **POSITION TYPE:** Internship • **DURATION:** Year-Round • **IDEAL CANDIDATE:** College Students, Career Changers • **APPLICANT POOL:** Varies • **APPLICANTS ACCEPTED:** Varies

••

WORKING FOR THE NATIONAL PARK SERVICE provides interns with an opportunity to work in some of the most spectacular scenery in the nation and to help the public understand and appreciate the natural and cultural resources that the agency is charged with protecting and interpreting.

Work/Learn Program Specifics: The Student Interpretive Internship Program provides a well-rounded experience in environmental interpretation. Duties include developing and presenting walks, talks, and hikes, staffing visitor center information and orientation desks, and conducting roving interpretive assignments. Park staff works closely with each intern to achieve the goals of the student, as well as those of the park. Students will enjoy a challenging season of hard work, companionship, learning, and fun.

Duration: The season generally runs from the beginning of June to early September, but varies from year to year depending on program needs and individual availability rates. Special internships are also available during the academic year in spring, fall, and winter.

Compensation and Perks: Interns receive housing and a stipend of $120 per week.

The Ideal Candidate: They prefer applicants with knowledge of biological or geological sciences or resources management, first aid training, public speaking ability, and foreign language proficiency.

Making It Happen: Submit resume, three references with addresses and phone numbers, transcripts, and a cover letter (outlining reason you are applying, what you hope to achieve from an internship, and dates of availability).

Contact Information: Interpretive Internship Program • Rocky Mountain National Park • Estes Park, CO 80517 • Phone: (970) 586-3565

Rocky Mountain Park Company

REGION/HQ: Rocky Mountains/Colorado • **CATEGORY:** Concessionaire • **POSITION TYPE:** Internship/Seasonal • **DURATION:** Summer/Fall • **IDEAL CANDIDATE:** College Students, Career Changers, Foreigners • **APPLICANT POOL:** 300/year • **APPLICANTS ACCEPTED:** 70/year

••

ROCKY MOUNTAIN PARK COMPANY is a private company which owns and operates the Trail Ridge Store of Rocky Mountain National Park. Trail Ridge Store is located twenty-two miles inside the park and offers high quality fast-food service and a broad selection of gifts, apparel, Native American art/jewelry, and souvenirs to over three million park visitors coming to the park each year.

Area and Working Environment: With 71 peaks over 12,000 feet in elevation and almost 40 miles of the Continental Divide running through it, Rocky Mountain National Park may be described as the top of the Continent. This is truly where the mountains soar above the trees, where only the sturdiest of animals survive, and only the tundra can grow.

Work/Learn Program Specifics: As a seasonal employee, you should enjoy serving people and take pride in a job well done. Positions include retail sales clerk, Native American sales clerk, park/stockroom staff, merchandising clerks, snack bar assistants, and support staff. The privilege of living and working in the spectacular scenery of this mountain region, and the opportunity to form friendships which can last a lifetime are added bonuses.

Duration: Their season is Memorial Day to mid-October. You can expect to receive ten to twenty-two days off (depending on your length of employment) to spend as you choose in the Rocky Mountains.

Compensation and Perks: Most positions are paid at $5.25 per hour. Lodging and meals are provided at the rate of $9.00 per day. Shared employee housing is at the High Country Dorm, with spacious and modern rooms. Travel to and from work (approximately forty-five minutes) is provided by the company. Outdoor recreation will be a big part of your summer experience. Each summer the company organizes a series of weekly activities, including hayrides, canoe races, volleyball, basketball, cookouts, and banquets.

The Ideal Candidate: Though a seasonal job in Rocky Mountain National Park offers many rewards, it may not be for a person whose priority is financial compensation. They are looking for the type of employee whose satisfaction comes not only from a paycheck, but from the knowledge that he or she has made a very special contribution towards the success of a visitor's "once in a lifetime" vacation trip. You must also be able to work at a 12,000-foot level.

Making It Happen: Call for application packet. Send completed application, a resume, and two letters of recommendation from past and present employers. References will be checked. You will be notified by mail on the status of your application within thirty days. It's best to apply early and most hiring is done by April 30.

INSIDER TIPS: *Be available for late summer/autumn work and have a clean and highly regarded set of references.*

Contact Information: Mark Roskam, General Manager • Rocky Mountain Park Company • P.O. Box 2680 • Estes Park, CO 80517 • Phone: (970) 586-3097 • Fax: (970) 586-8590 • Alternate: (970) 586-9308

San Juan/Rio Grande National Forests

REGION/HQ: Rocky Mountains/Colorado • **CATEGORY:** Forest Service • **POSITION TYPE:** Internship • **DURATION:** Summer • **IDEAL CANDIDATE:** College Students, Career Changers, Foreigners • **APPLICANT POOL:** Varies • **APPLICANTS ACCEPTED:** 100+/year

THE RIO GRANDE NATIONAL FOREST and the San Juan National Forest administrations became one in 1993. This move was made in response to President Clinton's "Reinventing Government" efforts and will drastically cut costs by eliminating overhead positions on both forests. The two forests are located in south-central Colorado and contain almost four million acres of publicly-owned lands. They include parts of two spectacular mountain ranges—the San Juan mountains and the Sangre de Cristo mountains—with the Continental Divide separating the two forests. The Rio Grande National Forest surrounds the San Luis Valley and is the headwater for the third longest river in the United States—the Rio Grande. The San Juan National Forest is part of a culturally rich area that contains many artifacts from previous cultures.

Work/Learn Program Specifics: Agencies which have volunteer projects include the U.S. Forest Service (Rio Grande National Forest and San Juan National Forest), San Juan Mountain Association, and the Bureau of Land Management. These agencies are seeking volunteers in these areas: computer and business management, interpretation, photojournalism, campground host, range management, trail/sign maintenance, wildlife biology, archaeology, outdoor recreation, surveys, construction, and computer programming.

Duration: The majority of the positions are during the summer months, although some are available year-round.

Compensation and Perks: A stipend of up to $15 per day may be provided depending on project funding. Housing is usually available.

The Ideal Candidate: Good writing skills and report-preparation experience are highly desirable. Survey and other types of fieldwork entail extensive hiking and possibly backpacking. Interns, therefore, must be in good physical condition, and be willing to endure such discomforts as thunderstorms, steep slopes, wet shoes and pants, tired legs, biting flies, and mosquitoes.

Making It Happen: Call for the application booklet, which is jam-packed with information on their internship/volunteer program. Fill out the application, and a resume is strongly recommended, including one nonacademic and two academic references. No specific deadlines, although most positions are filled by April 1. Applications will be accepted until all openings are filled. Contact the volunteer coordinator directly if you have questions, need further information, or require additional time to respond.

Contact Information: Carolyn Keller, Volunteer Coordinator • San Juan/Rio Grande National Forests • 1803 W. Highway 160 • Monte Vista, CO 81144 • Phone:

(719) 852-5941 • Fax: (719) 852-6250 • Web Site: www.fs.fed.us/srnf/

Sedona Ranger District

REGION/HQ: South/Midwest/Arizona • **CATEGORY:** Forest Service • **POSITION TYPE:** Internship • **DURATION:** Year-Round • **IDEAL CANDIDATE:** College Students, Career Changers, Retired Folks, Foreigners • **APPLICANT POOL:** 30/year • **APPLICANTS ACCEPTED:** 6/year

IF YOU CARE ENOUGH about wilderness to work for no wages, the Sedona Ranger District needs your help. You'll live and work in the beautiful Sedona/Red Rock country, experience the backcountry and urban-interface hiking, go on wilderness overnighters, and learn about public wilderness-use education.

Area and Working Environment: The beautiful Sedona district is located in a semi-arid environment in the Coconino National Forest. There are some major elevation changes that occur on the district, ranging from 3,200 feet along the southern end of the district to 6,600 feet in areas along the northern rims.

Work/Learn Program Specifics: Wilderness Information Specialist: Duties include projecting a positive, good host appearance and attitude and presenting the public with information that is consistent with the USFS; greet, register, and deliver the "leave no trace" message and provide information regarding current wilderness situations to visitors at trailheads and on trails; patrol trails in heaviest use areas, naturalization of campsites, and wilderness trash removal; recruit new volunteers; submit patrol logs, registration data, incident reports, and trail condition reports to the wilderness ranger on a weekly basis; and participate in other related projects and presentations, including group program education, long range patrols, and performing work relating to wilderness implementation schedules. Training and experience will be provided in land ethics, wilderness philosophy, tools, public contact, and environmental education.

Duration: A minimum of a three-month commitment is expected. Although the position is offered year-round, the district has particular interest in the heavy-use period from May to September. The program will require a minimum of forty hours per week.

Compensation and Perks: Interns will be reimbursed for actual costs of food, nonalcoholic beverages, and incidental expenses at the rate of $12 per eight-hour day (reimbursement will be to the extent funding will allow). Housing is provided for full-time volunteers. Single person, barracks-style quarters will be provided. The crew quarter has complete kitchen and bathroom facilities and is located approximately seven miles from the ranger station in the town of Sedona.

The Ideal Candidate: The district desires individuals with experience regarding backcountry/backpacking, trail construction and maintenance, public contact, or any other skills which might pertain to the position. Candidates must be at least eighteen years of age, although no specific age group or education background is necessary.

Making It Happen: Call for their "short" application. Then, send cover letter, resume, references, and completed application. Potential candidates will be interviewed in person or by phone. Rolling deadlines.

INSIDER TIPS: *Enjoy paperwork as well as outdoors work. You should also enjoy (or more than tolerate), extra jobs, errands, post pounding, etc. If possible, visit or call us, we want to get to know you better!*

Contact Information: Terry Adams, Wilderness Ranger • Sedona Ranger District • U.S. Forest Service • P.O. Box 300 • Sedona, AZ 86339-0300 • Phone: (520) 282-4119 • Fax: (520) 282-4119

Sequoia–Kings Canyon Parks Services

REGION/HQ: Pacific Northwest/California • **CATEGORY:** Concessionaire • **POSITION TYPE:** Seasonal • **DURATION:** Spring-Fall • **IDEAL CANDIDATE:** College Students, Career Changers, Retired Folks • **APPLICANT POOL:** Varies • **APPLICANTS ACCEPTED:** 250/year

SEQUOIA–KINGS CANYON PARKS SERVICES operates the visitor services in both parks, including the hotels, restaurants, service stations, markets, gift shops, and a transportation system.

Area and Working Environment: Kings Canyon and Sequoia National Parks are located in the Sierra Nevada Mountains of central California. Here you will find hundreds of square miles of breathtaking scenery: granite mountains, canyons, lush meadows, magnificent forests, lakes, rivers, and waterfalls. The park is also home to the General Sherman Tree, the largest living thing on earth, and Mt. Whitney, the highest mountain in the continental United States.

Work/Learn Program Specifics: If you enjoy mountains and the outdoors, you'll love working here. Seasonal positions include Food and Beverage (cook, prep cook, waitstaff, kitchen help, and busser/dishwasher), Retail (gift shop sales clerk, retail clerk, and warehouse help), Lodging (reservations, front desk, night auditor, room inspector, and housekeeping), Maintenance (general and laborers), and Administrative/General (bus driver, interpretive tour guide, administrative clerk, personnel clerk, account clerk, and recreation/housing coordinator). Seasonal and year-round managerial positions are also available. Interpretive training on park wildlife, native flowers, and ecology of the area, and the opportunity to participate in NPS bear management will be offered throughout the summer.

Duration: The summer season runs May through October. Your dates of availability will directly affect your chances of being hired; and the later you can stay, the better. In addition, you must be willing to work weekends and holidays.

Compensation and Perks: Entry-level position wages range from $5.25 to $8.00 per hour. Employee housing is available for $50 every two weeks, which is deducted from your paycheck. Housing is rustic (one step above camping out), with two to four persons to a cabin, electricity, wood-burning stoves, basic furnishings, and central bath and laundry facilities. A limited number of trailer spaces with full hookups are available. For a fixed priced, employees can also buy one meal per work day in restaurants. Throughout the summer, you'll have the opportunity to participate in sports activities, such as volleyball, as well as barbecues, campfires, jazz get-togethers, trips to the city, and picnics.

The Ideal Candidate: You must be at least eighteen years of age.

Making It Happen: Call for application materials.

Contact Information: Personnel Manager • Sequoia–Kings Canyon Parks Services • P.O. Box 909 • Kings Canyon, CA 93633 • Phone: (209) 335-5501 • Fax: (209) 335-5502

Shenandoah National Park

REGION/HQ: Southeast/Virginia • **CATEGORY:** Concessionaire • **POSITION TYPE:** Seasonal • **DURATION:** Spring-Fall • **IDEAL CANDIDATE:** College Students, Career Changers, Foreigners

• **APPLICANT POOL:** Varies • **APPLICANTS ACCEPTED:** Varies

ARAMARK–VIRGINIA SKYLINE COMPANY is the concessionaire in Shenandoah National Park, operating lodges, dining facilities, craft and gift shops, camp stores, gas stations, and stables throughout the park. Shenandoah is located in northern Virginia, approximately 100 miles southwest of Washington, D.C. The Skyline Drive runs through the middle of the park and connects at its south end to the Blue Ridge Parkway. The northern end of the park begins at Front Royal, Virginia, and runs 105 miles to the southern tip in Waynesboro, Virginia. The park is a mountain area with many scenic overlooks of the Shenandoah Valley and the Blue Ridge Mountains, and offers hiking, backpacking, camping, birding, picnicking, nature walks, and ranger interpretive programs.

Work/Learn Program Specifics: Positions available include desk clerk, bellhop, laundry worker, cook, pantry/salad bar worker, cashier, night auditor, host/hostess, dishwasher, receptionist, housekeeping, server, and linen truck driver.

Duration: The season runs from April through November. Most jobs require forty plus hours per week. Weekends and holidays are the busiest times and all employees must be able to work these days.

Compensation and Perks: Competitive wages are offered based on your experience. A limited amount of dormitory-style housing is available, with shared bath or individual rooms with bath. Costs are $25 per room, per week for single or $15 per room, per week for shared. Trailer pads with electrical hookups are available at $20 per week. Meals are available for $2 per meal.

Making It Happen: Call for application materials.

Contact Information: Human Resources • Shenandoah National Park • Aramark–Virginia Skyline Company • P. O. Box 727 • Luray, VA 22835 • Phone: (540) 743-5108

Signal Mountain Lodge

REGION/HQ: Rocky Mountains/Wyoming • **CATEGORY:** Concessionaire • **POSITION TYPE:** Seasonal • **DURATION:** Spring-Fall • **IDEAL CANDIDATE:** College Students, Career Changers, Foreigners • **APPLICANT POOL:** Varies • **APPLICANTS ACCEPTED:** 140/year

GRAND TETON NATIONAL PARK was first established in 1929 through the joint efforts of Horace Albright, superintendent of Yellowstone National Park, and John D. Rockefeller, Jr., who after forming the Snake River Land Company, purchased most of the private land on the valley floor. Signal Mountain Lodge is a privately-owned company that operates visitor services under a concession agreement with the National Park Service. Their operation includes seventy-nine guest units, two restaurants, two gift shops, a bar, a grocery/gas station, and a marina, along with a second marina and restaurant ten miles north of their location, called Leek's Marina and Restaurant.

Area and Working Environment: Signal Mountain is located directly on Jackson Lake, just thirty miles from the town of Jackson and twenty-five miles from Yellowstone National Park. Grand Teton covers 485 square miles and has over 200 miles of hiking trails and some of the best rock climbing in North America.

Work/Learn Program Specifics: Employment Opportunities: lodging/laundry help, cooks, employee dining room cook, pantry, waiter/waitress, host/hostess, busperson, dishwasher, bartender, gift store sales, service station/grocery store attendant, front desk reservations office, marina attendant, management and staff positions, and day/night auditor.

Duration: Their summer season runs from early May until mid-October. Positions are full-time and a normal work schedule is eight hours per day, five to six days per week, although schedules vary with the season.

Compensation and Perks: Hourly wage varies. All employees eat and live on the property. Meals are $195 per month, and dormitory-style housing is provided at no cost.

The Ideal Candidate: Hiring is based on the applicant's willingness to do the job and give the visitor to Grand Teton National Park the very best in guest services. Applicants with retail/food service, hotel experience, and a genuine, enthusiastic desire to work with the public are most likely to get hired. Those with the longest dates of availability will be given first consideration.

Making It Happen: Call for application. Send completed application and the top section of the two reference forms with any letters of reference. Apply early. Most positions are filled by March.

INSIDER TIPS: *We are looking for good workers who enjoy assisting our visitors and enjoy working in a beautiful National Park with people from all over the world.*

Contact Information: Paulette Philpot, Personnel Manager • Signal Mountain Lodge • Grand Teton National Park • P.O. Box 50 • Moran, WY 83013 • Phone: (307) 543-2831 • Fax: (307) 543-2569 • Toll Free: (800) 672-6012 • E-mail: 102547.1642@compuserve.com • Web Site: www.coolworks.com/showme/signalmt

St. Mary Lodge and Resort

REGION/HQ: Pacific Northwest/Idaho • **CATEGORY:** Concessionaire • **POSITION TYPE:** Seasonal • **DURATION:** Summer • **IDEAL CANDIDATE:** College Students, Career Changers, Retired Folks, Foreigners • **APPLICANT POOL:** Varies • **APPLICANTS ACCEPTED:** 200/year

GLACIER NATIONAL PARK IS A two-million-acre masterpiece of unsurpassed beauty. Hike, bike, or motor through this pristine wilderness. To guests visiting Glacier, St. Mary Lodge and Resort offers the park's most complete guest facilities. Conveniently located at the east entrance of the park, St. Mary Lodge offers distinctive accommodations, the internationally famous Snowgoose Grille, a large supermarket, extensive gift shop, an outdoor store, and one of the most magnificent views in the world.

Area and Working Environment: Imagine hiking over thousands of acres of almost untouched trails, breathing in fresh, crisp, Rocky Mountain air with the lingering scent of pine trees. Imagine crystal clear streams full of colorful rainbow trout just waiting to be caught and rugged mountain goats perched on jagged ledges towering above your head. Conquer the challenge of biking the famous Going-to-the-Sun Highway or completing a fifty-mile hike along the Continental Divide. Glacier has something for everyone!

Work/Learn Program Specifics: Positions include bar staff, cooks (restaurant, pizza parlor, cafe, and prep), kitchen staff (pantry, dishwashing, and baking), housekeeping (room attendants, housemen, and laundry), sales staff (sporting goods, gift shop, and T-shirt shop), cashiers, front desk clerks, dining room staff (host, busser, and server), ice cream servers, pizza and cafe staff, gas station attendants, supermarket staff (shelf stockers, produce people, butcher, and meat processing help), maintenance and grounds personnel, garage mechanics, night security/night steward, warehouse, accounting/general office personnel, resident assistants, and internships in accounting, hospitality, retail management, and recreation. The work required is challenging both mentally and physically; however, the atmosphere of the Rocky Mountains and the companionship of fellow employees make it seem less strenuous than it would elsewhere.

Duration: St. Mary Lodge is open from May 15 to October 1; however, employees are needed from May 1 through October 15. A major emphasis is placed on your ending date.

Compensation and Perks: Most positions pay between $4.25 and $5.50 per hour. Food servers gross about $2,700 for the summer. All employees receive room and board (three meals a day) for $8.75 per day deducted from your biweekly paychecks. Employees are housed in dormitories and one-room cabins, by seniority and age. Be aware that their housing is very rustic and cabins share a central bathroom and shower facilities.

The Ideal Candidate: St. Mary's attracts people who have high energy and are looking for the experience of a lifetime. These employees come from all over the United States and frequently from as far away as Europe and Asia.

Making It Happen: Call for application materials. In the summer you can reach them at the resort: St. Mary Lodge and Resort, St. Mary, Montana 59417.

Contact Information: Personnel Director • St. Mary Lodge and Resort • P.O. Box 1808 • Sun Valley, ID 83353 • Phone: (208) 726-6279 • Summer: (406) 732-4431 • E-mail: glcjobs@magiclink.com • Web Site: www.glcpark.com

Student Conservation Association, Inc.

REGION/HQ: Nationwide/New Hampshire • **CATEGORY:** Conservation • **POSITION TYPE:** Internship/Seasonal • **DURATION:** Year-Round • **IDEAL CANDIDATE:** College Students, Career Changers, Retired Folks, Foreigners • **APPLICANT POOL:** 4,000/year • **APPLICANTS ACCEPTED:** 1,200/year

SINCE 1957, the Student Conservation Association (SCA) has been a nonprofit dedicated to fostering environmental stewardship by providing short-term appointments in many aspects of natural resource management on public lands throughout the United States (with some in Canada) throughout the year. SCA also manages portions of AmeriCorps, part of President Clinton's national service program.

Area and Working Environment: Participating agencies include the National Park Service, Bureau of Land Management, U.S. Forest Service, U.S. Fish and Wildlife Service, National Biological Survey, U.S. Navy and U.S. Army DNR, State Park and Wildlife Agencies, and private conservation organizations throughout the United States.

Work/Learn Program Specifics: Resource Assistant (RA) Program: While most RA positions offer a variety of tasks, generally each position has a main theme or subject matter in which the volunteer participates. Subjects include archaeology, American history, backcountry and wilderness management, environmental education, engineering and survey, forestry, geology and paleontology, hydrology and water resources, interpretation and visitor's assistance, range management and plant taxonomy, recreation management, trail maintenance and construction, and wildlife and fisheries. Each position is listed in one of their semiannually published catalogs. They also just introduced the conservation associates program. Similar to RA's, conservation associates serve in six- to twelve-month positions and receive a $160-per-week stipend amongst other perks.

Duration: Positions are generally twelve weeks in length and offered spring, summer, fall, or early/late winter. Assistants are expected to work forty hours per week.

Compensation and Perks: Each student resource assistant receives round-trip travel, housing, a weekly subsistence allowance of $50 in most cases, accident insurance, a uniform allowance (if required), and the chance to live and work in some of our nation's most beautiful places.

The Ideal Candidate: Anyone eighteen years old or older and out of high school may apply. Students and others, with all backgrounds, are encouraged to apply. Positions are not limited to the natural sciences, and there is no upper age limit.

Making It Happen: Contact SCA to request application form and catalog of positions (do not send your resume). There are no deadlines, although to receive maximum consideration for positions in which you are most interested, and enhance your chances of being selected, you should apply by these dates: spring—January 15; summer—March 1; fall—June 1; early winter—September 15; and late winter—November 15. There is a $10 application fee. SCA begins processing applications on these dates and forwarding them to agency personnel for review and possible selection.

INSIDER TIPS: *Be willing to go anywhere and include positions marked with an asterisk among your choices; these are less requested.*

Contact Information: Mel Tuck, Recruiting Manager • Student Conservation Association, Inc. • Resource Assistant Program • P.O. Box 550 • Charlestown, NH 03603-0550 • Phone: (603) 543-1700 • Fax: (603) 543-1828 • Web Site: www.sca-inc.org

U.S. Fish and Wildlife Service . . . .

Imagine banding birds at a national wildlife refuge, raising fish at a national fish hatchery, conducting wildlife surveys, leading a tour, or assisting in laboratory research. You can do these things by volunteering at national wildlife refuges, fish hatcheries, research stations, and administrative offices. The work may be hard, the conditions harsh, and living quarters primitive, but it is well worth the experience.

The Fish and Wildlife Service administers over 450 wildlife refuges, from the arctic north coast of Alaska to tropical Caribbean islands. These sites cover over ninety million acres and include virtually every kind of habitat necessary for survival of America's wildlife. In addition to the extensive network of refuges, the service operates a host of fish hatcheries, thirteen research centers, and numerous field stations. All these facilities are designed to help continue the agency's mission—"to conserve, protect, and enhance fish and wildlife and their habitat for the continuing benefit of the public."

It's best to contact the Volunteer Coordinator at the various field offices listed below, as all hiring is done through them.

U.S. FISH & WILDLIFE SERVICE FIELD OFFICES:

Region 1
Eastside Federal Complex
911 NE 11th Ave.
Portland, OR 97232-4181
Phone: (503) 231-6136

Region 2
P.O. Box 1306
Albuquerque, NM 87103
Phone: (505) 766-2033

Region 3
Federal Building, Fort Snelling
Twin Cities, MN 55111
Phone: (612) 725-3585

Region 4
Richard B Russell Federal Building
75 Spring St., SW
Atlanta, GA 30303

Region 5
One Gateway Center, Suite 700
Newton Corner, MA 02158
Phone: (413) 253-8251

Region 6
Denver Federal Center
P.O. Box 25486
Denver, CO 80225
Phone: (303) 236-5414

Region 7
1011 E. Tudor Rd.
Anchorage, AK 99503-6199
Phone: (907) 786-3391 • Fax: (907) 786-3635
• Alternate: (907) 786-3301

Headquarters/Research Center
Mail Stop 725 ARLSQ
1849 C St., NW
Washington, DC 20240
Phone: (703) 358-1743

Vega State Park

REGION/HQ: Rocky Mountains/Colorado
• **CATEGORY:** State Park • **POSITION TYPE:** Internship/
Seasonal • **DURATION:** Year-Round • **IDEAL
CANDIDATE:** High School Students, College Students,
Career Changers, Retired Folks, Foreigners
• **APPLICANT POOL:** 100/year • **APPLICANTS
ACCEPTED:** 25/year
••

VEGA STATE PARK IS ONE OF forty state parks in Colorado.
Their mission is to provide a spectrum of safe and high-
quality recreational opportunities to visitors of Colorado.
Vega Reservoir and the meadows that surround it are
rich in history and natural beauty. The area was originally a mountain meadow where cattle ranchers grazed
their herds from the late 1800s until 1962. "Vega" is
actually the Spanish word for "meadow."

Area and Working Environment: Vega State Park is
located at an elevation of 8,000 feet on the eastern edge
of the spectacular Grand Mesa. Scenic aspen and evergreen forests dominate the landscape to the south, and
the remainder of the park is surrounded by a mixture of
public land and private summer homes.

Work/Learn Program Specifics: Seasonal positions
include rangers, maintenance workers, and gate attendants. Internships are offered in collection and management of revenues, interpretation/environmental
education, general maintenance, special projects, administration, and law enforcement. Volunteer campground
hosts are also needed. Training is provided for all positions.

Duration: Full- and part-time positions are available
year-round.

Compensation and Perks: Positions pay $4.75 to
$5.75 per hour, plus low-cost housing. Volunteers
receive free housing or RV site and annual pass to forty
Colorado State Parks after volunteering forty-eight
hours. This is an excellent opportunity to learn about
park management, meet wonderful people, and make
lifelong friendships.

The Ideal Candidate: Applicants must be highly energetic, friendly, outgoing, and motivated, and able to
work independently with little supervision. Good public relations skills are a must.

Making It Happen: Call for application materials.
Deadline: March 31. Top applicants will be interviewed
by phone.

Contact Information: Kevin Tobey, Park Manager • Vega
State Park • P.O. Box 186 • Collbran, CO 81624 • Phone:
(970) 487-3407 • Fax: (970) 487-3404

Wilderness Inquiry

REGION/HQ: Nationwide/Minnesota • **CATEGORY:**
Wilderness • **POSITION TYPE:** Internship
• **DURATION:** Year-Round • **IDEAL CANDIDATE:**
College Students, Career Changers, Retired Folks,
Foreigners • **APPLICANT POOL:** Varies • **APPLICANTS
ACCEPTED:** Varies
••

FOUNDED IN 1978, WILDERNESS INQUIRY (WI) is a
nonprofit organization that conducts wilderness trips
and other outdoor events for youth and adults with and
without disabilities. Goals of the program include providing opportunities for people of diverse backgrounds
and abilities to experience the wilderness, encouraging participant skill development and confidence,
reducing stereotypes about people with disabilities, and
promoting wilderness experience as an avenue for
social and personal growth.

Area and Working Environment: Wilderness Inquiry
is based in Minneapolis, Minnesota, and provides
adventure trips in the United States, Canada, and
abroad.

Work/Learn Program Specifics: Interns are exposed
to various aspects of WI. An intern may work in the
office, help in maintaining outdoor equipment, assist
with marketing and sales, aid in training, or work on
special WI projects. Time is always set aside for interns
to work on academic projects necessary to receive
credit. Field experiences include participating in outdoor recreation events and/or integrated wilderness
adventures. Generally interns will be asked to provide
leadership and technical assistance as deemed appropriate. Trail leaders are responsible for providing
leadership on WI trips throughout the United States,
Canada, and abroad. This would require the ability to
organize, plan, and lead trips, and to maintain gear.
They take pretty rigorous trips, usually traveling five to
twenty miles per day. On each trip, trail leaders sometimes fill the roles of pack horse, teacher, rehabilitation
specialist, folksinger, chef, personal relationship counselor, storyteller, attendant, disciplinarian, dishwasher,
and bush doctor.

Duration: Internships are available year-round, for a
minimum of eight weeks full-time.

Compensation and Perks: Trail leaders receive $25 to $75 per day, amounting to $1,000 to $2,200 per season. Full-time also equals full benefits. The best perk is having the opportunity to participate in outdoor adventures in locations across the country.

The Ideal Candidate: They desire individuals with previous experience in working with people with disabilities and the outdoors. If interns possess Red Cross lifeguard training, advanced first aid, and CPR, they may be given more responsibility during field experiences. Trail leaders must have all certifications and be sensitive, responsible, have good judgment, a sense of humor, and be competent in providing training on all aspects of wilderness travel and living.

Making It Happen: Call for specific job details and application. Submit completed application, cover letter, and resume. Rolling deadlines.

INSIDER TIPS: The number one priority is finding people with good attitudes!

Contact Information: Tom Barrett, Program Director • Wilderness Inquiry • 1313 Fifth St., SE, Box 84 • Minneapolis, MN 55414-1546 • Phone: (612) 379-3858 • Fax: (612) 379-5972 • Toll Free: (800) 728-0719

Yellowstone National Park

REGION/HQ: Rocky Mountains/Wyoming • **CATEGORY:** Concessionaire • **POSITION TYPE:** Internship/Seasonal • **DURATION:** Year-Round • **IDEAL CANDIDATE:** College Students, Career Changers, Foreigners • **APPLICANT POOL:** 10,000/year • **APPLICANTS ACCEPTED:** 3,500/year

AMFAC PARKS & RESORTS OPERATES the major visitor services concession facilities in Yellowstone National Park. The hospitality services provided include lodging, restaurants, shops, boat and horse activities, campgrounds, and transportation services.

Area and Working Environment: You will work at one of seven major locations around the park, including Mammoth Hot Springs, Roosevelt Lodge, Canyon Village, The Lake Area, Grant Village, or Old Faithful, each with its own unique charm and features.

Work/Learn Program Specifics: The work you will be doing will be similar to working at a high-quality resort anywhere in the country. But the privilege of living for a summer in the world's first national park is an experience unmatched anywhere else. Seasonal positions are available in these departments: Accounting, Administrative, Boat, Campground, Employee Recreation, Engineering/Maintenance, Food and Beverage, Gift Shop, Horse, Human Resources, Lodging, Reservations, Support Services, Transportation, Vending, and Warehouse. Internships are available in Hotel/Restaurant Management, Business Administration, Accounting, Food Service, Human Resources, Recreation, Travel/Tourism, and Retail Marketing.

Duration: There are nine locations in Yellowstone, each with varied "seasons," and the park prefers those who can work the entire season. The season runs May 1 to October 15.

Compensation and Perks: Entry-level positions start at $4.75 per hour. Lodging, meals, and laundry facilities are provided at a cost of $57.75 per week. Three meals are served each day, and employee residence facilities vary from very rustic to a typical dorm complex. Seasonal employees will be assigned rooms to share with one or more roommates (you can request to live with a friend or someone that you meet in orientation during your first day in Yellowstone). Perks include an employee recreation program that offers outdoor adventure programs, live bands, sports leagues, a talent show, and many other fun activities. You will be able to enjoy your days off to spend as you choose in this magnificent Rocky Mountain area.

The Ideal Candidate: They are looking for people who are willing to work hard, who enjoy working with and for others, and who take pride in a job well done.

Making It Happen: Call for application. Send resume, two letters of reference, and completed application form. It's best to apply by early February for the summer; positions fill very quickly. However, they do accept applications into the summer and are always looking for applicants who can arrive in August and work through September/October. Call three weeks after you send your application.

Contact Information: Tim Baymiller, Human Resources Director • Yellowstone National Park • Amfac Parks & Resorts • P.O. Box 165 • Yellowstone, WY 82190 • Phone: (307) 344-5324 • Fax: (406) 848-7087 • Alternate: (307) 344-5627 • E-mail: ynpjobs@aol.com • Web Site: www.coolworks.com/showme/ynpjobs

Y ELLOWSTONE NATIONAL PARK remains today just as it has always been—a wilderness area amounting to 3,500 square miles— bigger than the states of Delaware and Rhode Island combined. Yellowstone also contains the world's largest concentration of thermal features, and its rivers, lakes, valleys, forests, and mountains are preserved in natural beauty. Nowhere else are certain forms of wildlife found in such abundance in their natural environments. For many employees, a summer in Yellowstone is an unforgettable and once-in-a-lifetime experience.

Yellowstone must be approached with a "work hard, play hard" mentality. You'll definitely work hard in the position you take on; however, you'll also have the opportunity to play hard in your own "backyard." On days off, many employees find themselves in the backcountry in Yellowstone or nearby Grand Teton National Park, in thousands of miles of maintained trails, taking advantage of the unique opportunity to view rare geological phenomena, wildlife, forests, lakes and rivers, and the many other physical wonders. You'll also find that patiently waiting for a geyser to erupt becomes very addicting, and like many, you may fall victim to becoming an official "geyser gazer." In addition, Yellowstone has long been a favorite for photographers shooting in the wild; not to mention the world-famous fishing in its lakes and streams for fly-fishermen. Meeting employees and visitors from all over the world and making friends from a wide range of backgrounds and ages is what many former employees recall most fondly.

In addition to the park itself, an organized employee recreation program, sponsored and funded by park concessionaires, provides a diverse range of activities: movies; a writing, photography, and T-shirt design contest; various seminars; a club geared exclusively for employees over forty; a hiking club; basketball, softball, and volleyball leagues; white-water rafting; outdoor adventures; talent shows; slide shows; exercise classes; dances; and an outdoor rental program. Could you ask for more?

Yosemite Concession Services Corporation

REGION/HQ: Pacific Northwest/California • **CATEGORY:** Concessionaire • **POSITION TYPE:** Seasonal • **DURATION:** Year-Round • **IDEAL CANDIDATE:** High School Students, College Students, Career Changers, Retired Folks, Foreigners • **APPLICANT POOL:** Varies • **APPLICANTS ACCEPTED:** 1,000+/year

YOSEMITE CONCESSION SERVICES Corporation (YCSC) is the primary concessionaire in Yosemite National Park and provides a variety of guest services to the park's 4 million annual visitors. The Lodging Division operates all guest accommodations, ranging from rustic tent cabins to the impressive National Historic Landmark Ahwahnee Hotel. The Food and Beverage Division hosts a variety of opportunities for their guests' dining needs. Fast food, cafeterias, fine dining, and family-oriented restaurants are available on a year-round basis. Alternate ways to enjoy the splendor of Yosemite are offered through the guest recreation division, with guided tram and horseback tours, rafting along the Merced River, or bicycle rentals. The renowned Yosemite Mountaineering School offers rock climbing lessons, guided climbs, and backpacking trips in both Yosemite Valley and the High Sierra of Tuolumne Meadows. Winter snowfall brings both Nordic and alpine skiers to Badger Pass.

Area and Working Environment: Yosemite National Park is located in the Sierra Nevada mountains of central California about 200 miles east of San Francisco (four hours by car). Within the boundaries of this incredible 1,170-square-mile national park is some of the world's most spectacular scenery, including towering granite cliffs and glaciers, ancient stands of giant sequoias, and thundering waterfalls. So magnificent is this land that it was the first territory ever set aside by Congress "for public use, resort, and recreation...for all time."

Work/Learn Program Specifics: Positions are available in the front office, housekeeping, kitchen, cafeteria, bicycle stands, warehouse, accounting, general offices, gift shops, golf course, pool, refreshment stands, restaurants, service station, transportation, security, maintenance, stables, grocery division, rafting, High Sierra camps, Badger Pass, and ice rink. Available positions are usually entry-level. Employees can also participate in Yosemite's employee recreation program in their time off. This program offers a variety of activities and facilities, including a fitness center and wellness program; numerous organized sports, such as softball, volleyball, and basketball; organized hikes to some of the most spectacular areas in Yosemite; arts and crafts classes; barbecues; rafting trips; dances; movies; and so much more.

Duration: Seasonal and year-round schedules are available; most of which are available during the spring and summer. The average workweek consists of thirty to forty hours of work with two days off, contingent upon business needs. Schedules vary to include day, evening, and night shifts.

Compensation and Perks: Wages begin at $5.49 per hour. Employee housing consists of double- or triple-occupancy, wood-framed canvas tent cabins or dormitory rooms. Rent ranges from $13 to $17 per week, which also includes blankets, pillows, towels, and linen. Employees can also sign up for the employee meals program for $42 per week, which includes three meals, seven days per week. Those not participating in this program can receive half off on the retail price of meals in all cafeterias. All employees receive a 20 percent discount at selected restaurants. In addition, most employee housing areas have a community kitchen where employees may prepare their meals. You will also receive half off on all guest activities, including tours, rafting, ice-skating, ski rentals and lift tickets, and horseback rides. The Village Grocery Store and other retail shops offer a 10 percent discount.

The Ideal Candidate: Successful applicants are enthusiastic individuals who are able to provide the highest level of customer service. If you require employer-provided housing, you must be at least eighteen years of age.

Making It Happen: Call for application materials. Selections are made through application process.

Contact Information: Marty Livingston, Employee Relations Manager • Yosemite Concession Services Corporation • Human Resources Department • P.O. Box 578 • Yosemite National Park, CA 95389 • Phone: (209) 372-1236 • Fax: (209) 372-1050 • E-mail: hr@ycsc.com • Web Site: www.coolworks.com/showme/yosemite

Yosemite National Park

REGION/HQ: Pacific Northwest/California • **CATEGORY:** National Park • **POSITION TYPE:** Internship • **DURATION:** Summer • **IDEAL CANDIDATE:** College Students, Foreigners • **APPLICANT POOL:** Varies • **APPLICANTS ACCEPTED:** 15–30/term

YOSEMITE IS DEDICATED to the preservation and protection of unique geological, natural, and cultural resources of national significance, as well as to providing visitor enjoyment of those resources while leaving them unimpaired for the enjoyment of future generations. The internship program is sponsored by the Yosemite Association, a nonprofit organization that raises money to be used for special projects within Yosemite National Park.

Area and Working Environment: Each intern is assigned to one of Yosemite's three districts: Mather (Tuolumne Meadows, Big Oak Flat, and White Wolf), Valley (Yosemite Valley), and Wawona (Pioneer Yosemite History Center, Mariposa Grove of Giant Sequoias, and Glacier Point).

Work/Learn Program Specifics: Natural resource interpretation interns will spend time working in a visitor center and provide walks, talks, and campfire programs explaining the natural, historical, and cultural significance of the resource. Interns may "rove" a specific area discussing upcoming activities, park policies and regulations, and natural and cultural history with visitors. Wilderness management interns will spend time in a wilderness permit office, issuing backcountry permits and discussing weather conditions, equipment, and trail conditions with day hikers and overnight backpackers. Interns will perform routine campsite maintenance and rehabilitation in the backcountry, including breaking out campfire rings and hauling trash and helping patrol backcountry trails. They also have a volunteer-in-park (VIP) program offered throughout the year. Call for more information.

Duration: The internship is a full-time position lasting twelve weeks during the summer (mid-June through Labor Day). In addition, each year they generally hire one student in the spring and fall.

Compensation and Perks: Interns are technically volunteers; however, the Yosemite Association provides each intern with a $7-per-day stipend to defray the cost of food during the working day. Each intern will also receive a $1,000 tax-free scholarship at the end of the twelve-week commitment. Interns are provided with housing, ranging from canvas-covered tent cabins to large houses. Housing is shared with other employees. Interns must provide their own food, transportation, bedding, and personal items. Interns are also entitled to one Yosemite Association seminar during the summer, a packet of books, maps, and other materials about Yosemite, and a privilege card for discounts with the park concessionaire. Mileage reimbursement may be available for some travel.

The Ideal Candidate: Consideration of candidates for the program is limited to upper-level undergraduates, recent graduates, and graduate students with above-average scholastic records. Applicants should have a strong interest in resource preservation and management and a solid academic base in one or more natural or physical science (typical majors have included parks and recreation, natural resource management, geology, natural history, ecology, environment, and cultural history). Prospective candidates should also have an ability to communicate ideas effectively, a genuine liking for people, and enthusiasm for sharing knowledge with others. Maturity, a sense of responsibility, creativity, and a willingness to work hard are essential attributes.

Making It Happen: Call for details and application. Submit a completed Yosemite application, including essay questions, resume, transcripts, and three references. Your application must be postmarked by February 15 to be considered for their summer program. Selection is based on an evaluation of academic achievements, relevant practical experience, specialized skills, references, personal characteristics, professional goals, and program interest. Interviews are conducted with top-rated applications.

Contact Information: Student Intern Coordinator • Yosemite National Park • Wawona Ranger Station • P.O. Box 2027 • Wawona, CA 95389 • Phone: (209) 372-0563 • Fax: (209) 372-0458

The National Park Service . . . .

Since its inception in 1916, the National Park Service has been dedicated to the preservation and management of this country's priceless natural, historical, and recreational areas. Many Americans have had love affairs with the national parks since Yellowstone—the first national park—was created, in 1872. Today, the National Park Service is entrusted with preserving more than 360 national sites across the United States.

SEASONAL WORK

Each year millions of people from the United States and abroad visit these national park areas. To protect park resources and to serve the public, the National Park Service employs a permanent, seasonal, and volunteer workforce. Seasonals and volunteers are hired every year to help permanent staff at most of these locations, especially during peak visitation seasons. The variety of positions may surprise you: campground rangers, fee collectors, tour guides, naturalists, landscape archi- tects, firefighters, laborers, law enforcement rangers, lifeguards, clerk-typists, carpenters, historians, and many more.

Seasonal jobs are very competitive and are open only to U.S. citizens. Competition is usually less keen at smaller, lesser-known parks and for seasonal jobs in the winter season. Contact any National Park Service regional or park office for a seasonal job application. To apply for a summer seasonal position, submit a completed application postmarked between September 1 and January 15 to Seasonal Employment Unit, National Park Service, P.O. Box 37127, Room 2225, Washington, DC 20013-7127. It is essential that you indicate (1) your earliest reporting date and latest departure date, (2) the types of positions for which application is being made,

Go around asking a lot of damn fool questions and taking chances. Only through curiosity can we discover opportunities, and only by gambling can we take advantage of them. —CLARENCE BIRDSEYE

185

parks where consideration is desired, lowest salary that will be accepted, and particular specialization you might have.

VOLUNTEERS-IN-PARK (VIP) PROGRAM

VIPs work in almost every park in the National Park System and perform varied duties: working at information desks, presenting living history demonstrations in period costume, serving as campground hosts, leading guided nature walks and evening campfire programs, or maintaining and patroling trails, to name just a few. All VIPs are given special training, and some parks reimburse volunteers for some out-of-pocket expenses, such as local travel costs, meals, and uniforms. To apply, call the VIP Coordinator at the national park where you would like to volunteer.

PARK CONCESSIONAIRES

Hotels, lodges, restaurants, stores, transportation services, marinas, and many other visitor facilities in the National Park System areas are operated by private companies who hire their own employees. These jobs are not federal government positions. Contact the National Park Service regional office covering the location in which you'd like to work, or the park itself, for names, addresses, and telephone numbers of the respective concessionaires.

NATIONAL PARK SERVICE RESOURCES

As the official nonprofit partner of the National Park Service, the **National Park Foundation** supports projects in the parks that might otherwise never become reality due to limited federal dollars. They focus on education and outreach, visitor information services and facilities, and support for volunteers and NPS employees. They also publish *The Complete Guide to America's National Parks,* the most comprehensive travel/reference book available on the National Parks. NPF, 1101 17th St., NW, Suite 1102, Washington, DC 20036-4704; (800) 533-6478.

The National Park Service puts out a free directory of service companies and concessionaires operating in our national parks, called *National Parks Visitor Facilities and Services.* It's a little outdated (last revised in 1994), but it's packed with all the contacts you'll need to start your search, and, best of all, it's free. To get your own copy, call any NPS field office; however, I suggest calling the Nebraska NPS office at (402) 221-3611. Their staff does a great job of answering all your questions and will get you the information you need quickly.

The **National Parks and Conservation Association (NPCA)** is a 280,000-member, nonprofit organization dedicated solely to protecting, preserving, and defending America's ecological and cultural resources that are worthy of inclusion in or are already in the U.S. National Park system. NPCA promotes the creation of new parks; monitors the policies and actions of the National Park Service to ensure that parks are adequately and properly managed; defends individual units from development projects that adversely affect park resources; and develops special projects and programs that enhance visitor understanding and appreciation of America's natural and cultural heritage. NPCA, 1776 Massachusetts Ave., NW, Washington, DC 20036; (800) 628-7275.

National Park Field Area Offices:

NPS on the Web: www.nps.gov/personnel/index.htm

Alaska Field Area
National Park Service
2525 Gambell St.
Anchorage, AK 99503-2892
(907) 257-2580

Denali National Park, Gates of the Arctic National Park, Glacier Bay National Park, Katmai National Park, Kenai Fjords National Park, Kobuk Valley National Park, Lake Clark National Park, and Wrangell–St. Elias National Park

Inter-Mountain Field Area

(includes Arizona, Colorado, Montana, New Mexico, Oklahoma, Texas, Utah, and Wyoming)

National Park Service
12795 W. Alameda Parkway
Denver, CO 80225-0287
(303) 969-2506 • Alternate: (303) 969-2630

Arches National Park (UT), Big Bend National Park (TX), Bryce Canyon National Park (UT), Canyonlands National Park (UT), Capitol Reef National Park (UT), Carlsbad Caverns National Park (NM), Glacier National Park (MT), Grand Canyon National Park (AZ), Grand Teton National Park (WY), Guadalupe Mountains National Park (TX), Mesa Verde National Park (CO), Petrified Forest National Park (AZ), Rocky Mountain National Park (CO), Yellowstone National Park (WY), and Zion National Park (UT)

If you are interested in working on trails, roads, and campgrounds for the park or national forest in the Grand Tetons, contact the National Park Service at Grand Teton National Park, Drawer 170, Moose, WY 83012 or Bridger/Teton National Forest, (307) 739-5500 after February.

Midwest Field Area

(includes Arkansas, Illinois, Indiana, Iowa, Kansas, Michigan, Minnesota, Mississippi, Missouri, Nebraska, North Dakota, Ohio, South Dakota, and Wisconsin)

National Park Service
1709 Jackson St.
Omaha, NE 68102-2571
(402) 221-3456

Hot Springs National Park (AR), Isle Royale National Park (MI), Voyageurs National Park (MN), Theodore Roosevelt National Park (ND), Badlands National Park (SD), and Wind Cave National Park (SD)

National Capital Field Area

(includes Washington, D.C., and nearby areas in Maryland, Virginia, and West Virginia)

National Park Service
1100 Ohio Dr., SW
Washington, DC 20242
(202) 619-7224

Northeast Field Area

(includes Connecticut, Delaware, Maine, Massachusetts, New Hampshire, New Jersey, New York, Pennsylvania, Rhode Island, Vermont, and most areas of Maryland, Virginia, and West Virginia)

National Park Service
U.S. Custom House
200 Chestnut St., Room 306
Philadelphia, PA 19106
(215) 597-4056

Shenandoah National Park (VA) and Acadia National Park (ME)

Pacific West Field Area

(includes California, Guam, Hawaii, Idaho, Nevada, Oregon, and Washington)

National Park Service
600 Harrison St., Suite 600
San Francisco, CA 94107-1372
(415) 744-3885

Crater Lake National Park (OR), Mount Rainier National Park (WA), North Cascades National Park (WA), Olympic National Park (WA), Channel Islands National Park (CA), Great Basin National Park (NV), Haleakala National Park (HI), Hawaii Volcanoes National Park (HI), Kings Canyon National Park (CA), Lassen Volcanic National Park (CA), National Park of American Samoa, Redwood National Park (CA), Sequoia National Park (CA), and Yosemite National Park (CA)

Southeast Field Area

(includes Alabama, Florida, Georgia, Kentucky, Louisiana, North Carolina, Puerto Rico, South Carolina, Tennessee, and the Virgin Islands)

National Park Service
Richard B. Russell Federal Building
75 Spring St., SW
Atlanta, GA 30303
(404) 331-3799

Biscayne National Park (FL), Everglades National Park (FL), Great Smoky Mountains National Park (TN), Mammoth Cave National Park (KY), and Virgin Islands National Park

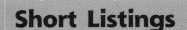

Short Listings

Acadia Corporation

REGION/HQ: Northeast/Maine • **CATEGORY:**
Concessionaire • **POSITION TYPE:** Seasonal
• **DURATION:** Spring-Fall • **IDEAL CANDIDATE:**
College Students, Career Changers, Retired Folks
• **APPLICANT POOL:** Varies • **APPLICANTS ACCEPTED:**
150/year

THE ACADIA CORPORATION is an authorized National
Park Service concessionaire operating in Acadia National
Park on the coast of Maine. They operate gift shops
within the park as well as several in the resort community of Bar Harbor. They also operate the Jordan Pond
House, one of New England's best known restaurants,
serving luncheon, afternoon tea, and dinner. Seasonal
positions are available in the restaurant, gift shops, maintenance, office, warehouse, and dormitory. Room and
board are provided with a weekly payroll deduction. The
season runs from May through October, and the later
you can stay, the better your chances of employment.

Contact Information: Rebecca Ghelli, Personnel
Manager • Acadia Corporation • Acadia National Park
• P.O. Box 24 • Bar Harbor, ME 04609 • Phone: (207)
288-5592 • Fax: (207) 288-2420 • E-mail: acadia@
acadia.net

American Forests

REGION/HQ: Washington, D.C./Washington, D.C.
• **CATEGORY:** Forestry • **POSITION TYPE:** Internship
• **DURATION:** Year-Round • **IDEAL CANDIDATE:**
College Students, Career Changers, Foreigners
• **APPLICANT POOL:** 300/year • **APPLICANTS
ACCEPTED:** Varies

THE MISSION OF AMERICAN FORESTS is to maintain the
countless benefits of trees and forests through the sustainable management of forest ecosystems. Founded in
1875 as the American Forestry Association, American
Forests is the oldest national citizens conservation
group in the United States. Internships are available in
publication, policy, urban forestry, marketing, education, program services, communications, and policy
research. Interns receive a $50-per-week stipend.

Contact Information: Lu Rose, Administration Director
• American Forests • 1516 P St., NW • Washington, DC
20005 • Phone: (202) 667-3300 • Fax: (202) 667-7751
• E-mail: lrose@amfor.org • Web Site: www.amfor.org

Anasazi Heritage Center

REGION/HQ: Rocky Mountains/Colorado
• **CATEGORY:** Museum • **POSITION TYPE:** Internship
• **DURATION:** Summer • **IDEAL CANDIDATE:** College
Students, Career Changers, Foreigners • **APPLICANT
POOL:** 50–75/year • **APPLICANTS ACCEPTED:**
4–6/year

COME SPEND EIGHT WEEKS in beautiful southwestern Colorado working in a state-of-the-art museum committed
to the preservation and interpretation of the northern San
Juan Anasazi. Positions include collections management
and cultural resources management. Interns are expected
to be self-motivated and able to work with a minimum
amount of supervision once the task is understood. The
goal of the position is to provide a realistic and well-
rounded experience of the tasks of cultural resources
management in a federal museum setting. Interns receive
a $50-per-week stipend, plus communal housing.

Contact Information: Curator • Anasazi Heritage Center
• Bureau Of Land Management • 27501 Highway 184
• Dolores, CO 81323 • Phone: (303) 882-4811 • Fax:
(303) 882-7035

Appalachian Trail Conference

REGION/HQ: Southeast/West Virginia • **CATEGORY:**
Conservation • **POSITION TYPE:** Work/Learn
Adventure • **DURATION:** Spring-Fall • **IDEAL
CANDIDATE:** College Students, Career Changers,
Retired Folks, Foreigners • **APPLICANT POOL:** Varies
• **APPLICANTS ACCEPTED:** Varies

HELP BUILD A PIECE OF the Appalachian National Scenic
Trail, one of the most famous footpaths in the world.
Winding along the peaks of the Appalachian chain from
Georgia to Maine, this trail exists thanks to countless
dedicated volunteers who planned, constructed, and
now maintain and manage the trail through this nonprofit organization. Participate in one of these projects
by joining the ATC's Volunteer Trail Crew Program,
which is operated in cooperation with the U.S. Forest
Service, National Park Service, and trail-maintaining

clubs. A professional crewleader directs the crews in designing and building new trail segments, shelters, and bridges, rehabilitating damaged trails, improving wildlife habitat, and preserving open areas. Participants must be at least eighteen years of age. No experience is necessary, as training will be provided. ATC supplies room and board. Crews operate from May through October from base camps in southern Virginia, south-central Pennsylvania, Vermont, and Maine.

Contact Information: Susan Daniels, Crew Program Director • Appalachian Trail Conference • P.O. Box 807 • Harpers Ferry, WV 25425 • Phone: (304) 535-6331 • Fax: (304) 535-2667

Badlands National Park

REGION/HQ: Rocky Mountains/South Dakota • **CATEGORY:** Natural Resources • **POSITION TYPE:** Internship/Seasonal • **DURATION:** Year-Round • **IDEAL CANDIDATE:** College Students, Career Changers, Retired Folks, Foreigners • **APPLICANT POOL:** 50/term • **APPLICANTS ACCEPTED:** 4/term

BADLANDS NATIONAL PARK is the largest national park in South Dakota and consists of 244,000 acres of eroded sedimentary formations and mixed grass prairie. The weather is hot and dry in the summer (up to 110 degrees), cold and icy in the winter (down to -30 degrees), and always windy. It was just voted best sunrises/sunsets in the world by International Nature Photographers (just a hint of its beauty). Positions include staffing visitor center, interpretive walks, children's hikes, slide-show presentations, backcountry patrol, and research and writing programs. You will receive $50-per-week stipend, plus housing. "We are looking for friendly and social people who can work in a high stress environment and/or extremely remote setting."

Contact Information: Marianne Mills, Resource Education Chief • Badlands National Park • P.O. Box 6 • Highway 240 • Interior, SD 57750 • Phone: (605) 433-5361 • Fax: (605) 433-5404 • E-mail: marianne_mills @nps.gov

Canyonlands National Park

REGION/HQ: Rocky Mountains/Utah • **CATEGORY:** National Park • **POSITION TYPE:** Seasonal • **DURATION:** Year-Round • **IDEAL CANDIDATE:** College Students, Career Changers, Retired Folks

• **APPLICANT POOL:** Varies • **APPLICANTS ACCEPTED:** Varies

THIS PARK FEATURES A 337,510-ACRE wilderness in southeastern Utah. Three districts—the Island in the Sky, Needles, and Maze—are located near the confluence of the Green and Colorado Rivers and offer spectacular scenery and trails of hiking, off-road four-by-four exploring, and mountain biking. Positions available include resource management, backcountry, archives, archaeology patrol, interpretation, visitor information services, and maintenance staff. Housing, uniform, and a $5-per-day stipend are provided, dependent on funding. Positions are available both in Canyonlands and Arches National Parks.

Contact Information: Betty White, Volunteer Coordinator • Canyonlands National Park • 2282 S. West Resource Blvd. • Moab, UT 84532-8000 • Phone: (801) 259-3911 • Fax: (801) 259-8628 • E-mail: Betty_ White_at_NP-CANY@ccmail.ltd.NPS.gov

CFAIA

REGION/HQ: Southeast/Kentucky • **CATEGORY:** Forestry • **POSITION TYPE:** Seasonal • **DURATION:** Year-Round • **IDEAL CANDIDATE:** College Students, Career Changers, Retired Folks • **APPLICANT POOL:** Varies • **APPLICANTS ACCEPTED:** Varies

THE CRADLE OF FORESTRY IN AMERICA Interpretive Association, in cooperation with the U.S. Forest Service, manages campgrounds in several national forests in the southeastern United States. Campground host positions are available to perform a variety of duties from North Carolina to Pennsylvania.

Contact Information: Ron Swafford, Program Coordinator • CFAIA • Daniel Boone National Forest • P.O. Box 218 • Salt Lick, KY 40371 • Phone: (606) 768-2722 • Fax: (606) 768-2967 • E-mail: CFAIA@citcom.net • Web Site: www.CradleofForestry.com

Colorado Trail Foundation

REGION/HQ: Rocky Mountains/Colorado • **CATEGORY:** Conservation • **POSITION TYPE:** Unique Experience • **DURATION:** Summer • **IDEAL CANDIDATE:** College Students, Career Changers, Retired Folks • **APPLICANT POOL:** 400/year • **APPLICANTS ACCEPTED:** 350/year

HELP BUILD AND MAINTAIN a 500-mile trail in the beautiful Colorado mountains. Base camps are made up of seventeen individuals and the work is physically demanding. Positions last one week to all summer; you'll work four days a week and have three days off to enjoy the Rockies. The foundation also runs many educational treks and classes on the Colorado Trail all summer long. Write to CTF, P.O. Box 260876, Lakewood, CO 80226-0876 to receive an application. There is a $35 application fee.

Contact Information: Gudy Gaskill, President • Colorado Trail Foundation • 548 Pine Song Trail • Golden, CO 80401 • Phone: (303) 526-0809

Crater Lake National Park

REGION/HQ: Pacific Northwest/Oregon
• **CATEGORY:** National Park • **POSITION TYPE:** Internship • **DURATION:** Year-Round • **IDEAL CANDIDATE:** College Students, Career Changers, Foreigners • **APPLICANT POOL:** Varies • **APPLICANTS ACCEPTED:** Varies

CRATER LAKE IS LOCATED along the crest of the Cascade Mountain Range, approximately seventy-four miles northeast of Medford, Oregon. With a depth of 1,932 feet, Crater Lake is the deepest lake in the United States and the seventh deepest lake in the world. Interpretive interns have a variety of duties, including leading guided walks, giving campfires, and junior ranger programs, providing information at visitor center desks, issuing backcountry permits, and other related assignments. Topics of programs include geology, limnology, winter ecology, and history. Training includes a minimum of eighty hours in visitor center duties, principles and techniques of interpretation, radio and correspondence procedures, and the natural and cultural history of Crater Lake National Park. Interns receive a $10-per-day work stipend, plus housing.

Contact Information: Chief Park Naturalist • Crater Lake National Park • P.O. Box 7 • Crater Lake, OR 97604 • Phone: (503) 594-2211

Denali National Park & Preserve

REGION/HQ: Pacific Northwest/Alaska • **CATEGORY:** National Park • **POSITION TYPE:** Seasonal • **DURATION:** Year-Round • **IDEAL CANDIDATE:**

College Students, Career Changers, Retired Folks
• **APPLICANT POOL:** Varies • **APPLICANTS ACCEPTED:** Varies

VOLUNTEER POSITIONS INCLUDE interpretative naturalists, campground hosts, backcountry patrol, and resource management assistants. Housing is provided; however campground hosts must provide their own RV or trailer. A subsistence stipend of $50 per week may be provided.

Contact Information: VIP Coordinator • Denali National Park & Preserve • Box 9 • Denali Park, AK 99755 • Phone: (907) 683-2294 • Fax: (907) 683-1277

Francis Beidler Forest

REGION/HQ: Southeast/South Carolina
• **CATEGORY:** Wildlife • **POSITION TYPE:** Internship
• **DURATION:** Year-Round • **IDEAL CANDIDATE:** College Students, Career Changers • **APPLICANT POOL:** Varies • **APPLICANTS ACCEPTED:** Varies

FRANCIS BEIDLER FOREST, a 5,800-acre wildlife sanctuary, encompasses the largest stand of virgin cypress-tupelo swamp in the world. A nature center and a 1 3/4-mile boardwalk afford visitors an opportunity to observe and study the swamp. Internship positions are available in interpretation and sanctuary maintenance. Interns receive a stipend of $125 per week and housing.

Contact Information: Norman Brunswig, Internship Coordinator • Francis Beidler Forest • National Audubon Society • 336 Sanctuary Rd. • Harleyville, SC 29448 • Phone: (803) 462-2150 • Fax: (803) 462-2713 • E-mail: nbrunswig@audubon.org • Web Site: www.audubon. org/audubon

Hells Gate State Park

REGION/HQ: Pacific Northwest/Idaho • **CATEGORY:** State Park • **POSITION TYPE:** Internship • **DURATION:** Summer • **IDEAL CANDIDATE:** College Students, Career Changers • **APPLICANT POOL:** Varies • **APPLICANTS ACCEPTED:** Varies

HELLS GATE STATE PARK is part of the Idaho state park system. Intern duties include interpretive programs, community relations, general park maintenance, administrative tasks, and a special work project. You will receive $5.82 per hour. Write or call for an application form and other information. The closing date is March 31.

Contact Information: Program Director • Hells Gate State Park • 3620 Snake River Ave. • Lewiston, ID 83501 • Phone: (208) 799-5015 • E-mail: hel@idpr.state.id.us

Internship Program for Alaska

REGION/HQ: Pacific Northwest/Alaska • **CATEGORY:** Clearinghouse • **POSITION TYPE:** Internship • **DURATION:** Summer • **IDEAL CANDIDATE:** College Students • **APPLICANT POOL:** Varies • **APPLICANTS ACCEPTED:** Varies

THE INTERNSHIP PROGRAM FOR ALASKA is a cooperative effort of Alaskan organizations managed by a small group of volunteers. Its purpose is to offer career-oriented educational experiences to students and recent college graduates by coordinating internships in Alaska. These internships are an opportunity for individuals to gain important job skills in a professional situation. For many participating nonprofit agencies, these internships also expand their ability to achieve their goals. Interns can choose from a broad selection of positions. Internships are offered in the following categories: administration/program planning, environment, law, marketing, recreation/outdoor education, social services, and veterinary medicine. Call or write for their application/directory which describes the organizations and descriptions of each position.

Contact Information: Program Director • Internship Program for Alaska • 519 W. 8th Ave., Suite 201 • Anchorage, AK 99501-3549 • Phone: (907) 276-6593

Isle Royale National Park

REGION/HQ: Great Lakes/Michigan • **CATEGORY:** National Park • **POSITION TYPE:** Internship • **DURATION:** Summer • **IDEAL CANDIDATE:** College Students, Career Changers • **APPLICANT POOL:** 75–100/year • **APPLICANTS ACCEPTED:** 4/year

IN LAKE SUPERIOR'S NORTHWEST CORNER sits a wilderness archipelago, a roadless land of wild creatures, unsoiled forests, refreshing lakes, and rugged, scenic shores accessible only by boat or floatplane. Travel on and around the island is by foot, boat, or floatplane. There are 165 miles of foot trails on Isle Royale, and the island boasts numerous inland lakes. And for more seaworthy craft there is, of course, Lake Superior itself.

Positions are available in park library, photo darkroom, resource management, backcountry campground, interpretation, and assisting in monitoring projects on park wildlife and vegetation. A stipend of $75 per week is provided, as well as comfortable dormitory and living situation on Mott Island, the park's summer headquarters. Food arrives once a week. There are radio and TV hookups.

Contact Information: Park Naturalist • Isle Royale National Park • 808 East Lakeshore Drive • Houghton, MI 49931 • Phone: (906) 482-0986

Lake Tahoe Basin Management Unit

REGION/HQ: Pacific Northwest/California • **CATEGORY:** Natural Resources • **POSITION TYPE:** Internship • **DURATION:** Year-Round • **IDEAL CANDIDATE:** College Students, Career Changers, Foreigners • **APPLICANT POOL:** Varies • **APPLICANTS ACCEPTED:** 2–4/term

THE GOAL OF THE INTERPRETIVE SERVICES program, conducted by the Forest Service at Lake Tahoe, is to provide informational and interpretive material through a visitor center, stream profile chamber, self-guided trails, brochures, displays, and guided activities. Interpretive naturalists will assist with the implementation of these programs and duties include assisting with campfire programs, environmental education activities, living history programs, exhibits for display, natural history information, recreational activities, and various special projects. You will receive a subsistence allowance of $20 per day and free government housing on the shores of Lake Tahoe in a historic estate.

Contact Information: Visitor Center Director • Lake Tahoe Basin Management Unit • U.S. Forest Service • 870 Emerald Bay Rd., Suite #1 • South Lake Tahoe, CA 96150 • Phone: (916) 573-2600 • Fax: (916) 573-2600

Nicolet National Forest

REGION/HQ: Great Lakes/Wisconsin • **CATEGORY:** Conservation • **POSITION TYPE:** Seasonal • **DURATION:** Year-Round • **IDEAL CANDIDATE:** College Students, Career Changers, Foreigners • **APPLICANT POOL:** Varies • **APPLICANTS ACCEPTED:** 10–15/year

THE NICOLET NATIONAL FOREST has internship positions available in these areas: wilderness ranger—

I shall tell you a great secret, my friend. Do not wait for the last judgement.
It takes place every day. —ALBERT CAMUS
191

maintain campsites and trails, construct new trails, and meet wilderness users; naturalist—develop and present informative programs to campers, interpret resources, and conduct walks and tours; campground hosts—greet campers, answer questions, and perform minor maintenance at the campsite; and recreation aid—maintain campgrounds and trails. All interns receive a daily stipend and housing.

Contact Information: Jeff Herrett, Ranger • Nicolet National Forest • Florence Ranger District • P.O. Box 1809 • Eagle River, WI 54521 • Phone: (715) 479-2827 • Fax: (715) 479-6407

Ozette Ranger Station

REGION/HQ: Pacific Northwest/Washington • **CATEGORY:** Natural Resources • **POSITION TYPE:** Internship • **DURATION:** Year-Round • **IDEAL CANDIDATE:** College Students, Career Changers • **APPLICANT POOL:** Varies • **APPLICANTS ACCEPTED:** Varies

INTERNSHIP POSITIONS PROVIDE an opportunity to apply classroom theory in park and recreation area management, environmental and historical interpretation, natural resource studies, wilderness management, outdoor education, and related fields. You will also be provided with exposure to a broad range of park operations. Volunteer positions as well as paid positions through the Student Conservation Association are available. If you receive a salary, there will be a charge for housing. If you are a volunteer, housing is provided free of charge.

Contact Information: Dan Messaros, VIP Coordinator • Ozette Ranger Station • Olympic National Park • 21261 Hoko-Ozette Rd. • Clallam Bay, WA 98326 • Phone: (206) 963-2725 • E-mail: Dan_Messaros@nps.gov

Pacific Crest Trail Association

REGION/HQ: Pacific Northwest/California • **CATEGORY:** Conservation • **POSITION TYPE:** Association • **DURATION:** Spring-Fall • **IDEAL CANDIDATE:** High School Students, College Students, Career Changers, Retired Folks, Foreigners • **APPLICANT POOL:** Varies • **APPLICANTS ACCEPTED:** Varies

THE PACIFIC CREST TRAIL ASSOCIATION conducts volunteer trail maintenance projects in cooperation with U.S. Forest Service, BLM, National Park Service, and private landholders throughout California, Oregon, and Washington. From hot dry deserts to cool windy alpine ridges, one- to ten-day projects offer the opportunity to give something back to the trail.

Contact Information: Program Coordinator • Pacific Crest Trail Association • 5325 Elkhorn Blvd., Box 256 • Sacramento, CA 95842-2526 • Phone: (916) 349-2109 • Toll Free: (888) 728-7245 • E-mail: 71204.1015@compuserve.com • Web Site: www.gorp.com/pcta

Potomac Appalachian Trail Club

REGION/HQ: Southeast/Virginia • **CATEGORY:** Conservation • **POSITION TYPE:** Seasonal • **DURATION:** Summer • **IDEAL CANDIDATE:** College Students, Career Changers, Retired Folks, Foreigners • **APPLICANT POOL:** Varies • **APPLICANTS ACCEPTED:** Varies

INTERNS, CAMP COORDINATORS, cooks, trail crew volunteers, and ridge runners are needed from May through September. Employees receive a $220-per-week stipend, plus $20 per week for mileage or field work.

Contact Information: Heidi Forrest, Trail Management Coordinator • Potomac Appalachian Trail Club • 118 Park St., SE • Vienna, VA 22180-4609 • Phone: (703) 242-0693 • Fax: (703) 242-0968 • E-mail: heidif@erols.com • Web Site: http://patc.simplenet.com

San Francisco Bay National Wildlife Refuge

REGION/HQ: Pacific Northwest/California • **CATEGORY:** Wildlife • **POSITION TYPE:** Internship • **DURATION:** Year-Round • **IDEAL CANDIDATE:** College Students • **APPLICANT POOL:** 40–50/term • **APPLICANTS ACCEPTED:** 4/term

THE SAN FRANCISCO BAY National Wildlife Refuge is located in the south Bay Area and encompasses over 20,000 acres of estuarine habitat, uplands, open water, salt marsh, salt ponds, and tidal mudflats. Interfacing with the fourth largest urban center in the nation, the refuge provides habitat for five endangered species, one threatened species, migratory birds, and other wildlife.

It is also the site of the largest harbor seal pupping area in the San Francisco Bay. They have a Resource Management Biology and Environmental Education Internship Program offered every four months.

Contact Information: Nancy Fries, Interpretive Specialist • San Francisco Bay National Wildlife Refuge • U.S. Fish & Wildlife Service • P.O. Box 524 • Newark, CA 94560 • Phone: (510) 792-0222 • Fax: (510) 792-5828 • E-mail: margaret_kolar@mail.fus.gov

Serve/Maine

REGION/HQ: Northeast/Maine • **CATEGORY:** Conservation • **POSITION TYPE:** Unique Experience • **DURATION:** Year-Round • **IDEAL CANDIDATE:** High School Students, College Students, Career Changers, Retired Folks, Foreigners • **APPLICANT POOL:** Varies • **APPLICANTS ACCEPTED:** Varies

VOLUNTEERS ARE NEEDED throughout the state of Maine in environmental education, water quality monitoring, graphic design, administration, public relations, fundraising, backcountry campsite maintenance, interpretation, trail building, and other areas. Many positions include housing and a stipend. Call to receive their directory of volunteer opportunities.

Contact Information: Lori Dillingham, Program Coordinator • Serve/Maine • Maine Conservation Corps • 124 State House Station • Augusta, ME 04333-0124 • Phone: (207) 287-4931 • Fax: (207) 287-3611

Shoshone National Forest

REGION/HQ: Rocky Mountains/Wyoming • **CATEGORY:** Forest Service • **POSITION TYPE:** Internship/Seasonal • **DURATION:** Summer-Winter • **IDEAL CANDIDATE:** College Students, Retired Folks • **APPLICANT POOL:** Varies • **APPLICANTS ACCEPTED:** Varies

LOCATED ON THE EAST SIDE of Yellowstone National Park, you'll see some of the most beautiful mountains in the country, including both the Beartooth Plateau and the Absorka Range. Seasonal volunteers will work in both the backcountry and front-country, learning the operation of a land management agency. A $10-per-day stipend plus housing is provided.

Contact Information: Phyllis Roseberry, Partnership Coordinator • Shoshone National Forest • Greybull Ranger District • P.O. Box 158 • Meeteetse, WY 82433 • Phone: (307) 868-2536 • Fax: (307) 578-1203

U.S. Forest Service. . . . .

If you've heard of Smokey the Bear or Woodsy Owl, you're familiar with the U.S. Forest Service. With approximately 30,000 permanent employees and a temporary workforce which typically exceeds 15,000 workers in the summer, the Forest Service is one of the government's major conservation organizations. The agency manages 191 million acres of federal lands, assists state and private landowners, conducts research, and works with international organizations and other countries to build a safer, cleaner, and more productive world. Employees are stationed at over 900 separate work locations. Most locations are in the national forests, but many employees work on college campuses, at research laboratories, or in office buildings in cities or towns.

Although the largest number of jobs are in forestry, there's something for everybody. Here's a snapshot of some of the most sought after volunteer positions:

Archaeologists help inventory national forest lands for prehistoric and historic sites (Indian burial grounds, hunting sites, old mining camps, or homesteads). Fieldwork varies but may involve inventory surveys, photography, mapping, and test excavation.

Backcountry rangers are jacks-of-all-trades. They educate the public to practice sound land ethics. They also practice fire prevention, camping ethics, assist in clearing and maintaining trails, maintain fire lookouts, inventory campsites, and record wildlife observations.

Campground hosts serve as picnic ground or campground patrons—greeting visitors, providing information, and maintaining the camp. In return for their services, camp-ground hosts can stay at one campground all summer.

Wilderness rangers meet wilderness visitors and provide information on proper wilder-ness use and ethics. These rangers are usually in the field for one-week to ten-day periods.

Other seasonal and volunteer opportunities include positions in administration, cartog-raphy/graphic arts, education, fire-fighting and management, group volunteer work, guard stations, historical research, hydrol-ogy, interpretation, range management, recreation, research, visitor centers, and wildlife and fish management.

U.S. Forest Service Regional Offices:

Alaska Region
P.O. Box 21628
Juneau, AK 99802
(907) 586-8863

Pacific Northwest Region
P.O. Box 3623
Portland, OR 97208-3623
(503) 326-3816 • Alternate: (503) 326-4091
There are opportunities for volunteer work in the nine-teen national forests in Oregon and Washington.

Pacific Southwest Region
630 Sansome St.
San Francisco, CA 94111
(415) 705-2874
Forests in California and Hawaii

Southwestern Region
Federal Bldg.
517 Gold Ave., SW
Albuquerque, NM 87102
(505) 842-3292
Forests in Arizona and New Mexico.

Intermountain Region
324 25th St.
Ogden, UT 84401
(801) 625-5297 • Alternate: (801) 625-5354
This region covers most of the states of Idaho, Montana, Nevada, Utah, and Wyoming. Research is coordinated and conducted at neighboring universities.

Rocky Mountain Region
P.O. Box 25127
Lakewood, CO 80225
(303) 275-5350
Forests in Colorado, Nebraska, South Dakota, and parts of Wyoming.

Northern Region
Federal Bldg.
P.O. Box 7669
Missoula, MT 59807
(406) 329-3511
Volunteers work on conservation projects, campground hosting, and wildlife management in most of Montana, northern Idaho, western North Dakota, and part of northwestern South Dakota.

Eastern Region
310 W. Wisconsin Ave., Suite 500
Milwaukee, WI 53203
(414) 297-3693

Southern Region
1720 Peachtree Rd., NW
Atlanta, GA 30367
(404) 347-4191

U.S. Forest Service on the Web: www.fs.fed.us

Tips on getting in with the Forest Service:

- **Build your skills through education and/or experi-ence.** If you are a student, participate in many internships and volunteer jobs, which will give you experience in your field of expertise.

- **Contact local Forest Service offices** to learn the types of seasonal positions they fill, how best to find out about them, and what skills and abilities you need to develop. Although the regional offices are the forest hubs, there are over 900 separate work locations across the United States. It is impossible for these hubs to know of all available positions. However, most regional offices publish volunteer opportunity directories.

South Park Ranger District

REGION/HQ: Rocky Mountains/Colorado
• **CATEGORY:** Forest Service • **POSITION TYPE:** Seasonal • **DURATION:** Spring-Fall • **IDEAL CANDIDATE:** College Students, Career Changers
• **APPLICANT POOL:** Varies • **APPLICANTS ACCEPTED:** Varies

THE TOWN OF FAIRPLAY is the site for the South Park Ranger District Office. An Interpretive Center is located on Wilkerson Pass and an information center is at Lake George. Elevations range from 8,000 to 14,000 feet, and the area is excellent for trout fishing and hiking and is located 30 miles from Breckenridge, a world-renowned ski area. Positions available include interpreters, special use permit administrator, visitor information aide, wilderness ranger, non-wilderness dispersed site, trail leader, crew member, fire, work crew, GPS inventory tech, biological aid/tech, and range aid/tech. If you volunteer for more than two weeks at a time, they offer a stipend of $60 per forty-hour week. Limited bunkhouse quarters are available.

Contact Information: Recreation Forester • South Park Ranger District • U.S. Forest Service • P.O. Box 219 • Fairplay, CO 80440 • Phone: (719) 836-2031

Sunset Crater Volcano National Monument

REGION/HQ: South/Midwest/Arizona • **CATEGORY:** National Monument • **POSITION TYPE:** Internship/Seasonal • **DURATION:** Year-Round • **IDEAL CANDIDATE:** High School Students, College Students, Career Changers, Retired Folks, Foreigners
• **APPLICANT POOL:** 100/year • **APPLICANTS ACCEPTED:** 20/year

SUNSET CRATER VOLCANO, surrounded by cliff dwellings and pueblo ruins, is the most recent volcano to erupt in the Flagstaff area. Interns and volunteers help staff visitor centers, develop and conduct interpretive programs, provide educational walks and talks for children, and help with many behind-the-scenes projects. A uniform and shared housing are provided.

Contact Information: SuZan Meiners, Volunteer Coordinator • Sunset Crater Volcano National Monument • Rte. 3, Box 149 • Flagstaff, AZ 86004 • Phone: (520) 526-0502 • Fax: (520) 714-0565 • SuZan_Meiners@ nps.gov

Theodore Roosevelt National Park

REGION/HQ: Rocky Mountains/North Dakota
• **CATEGORY:** National Park • **POSITION TYPE:** Seasonal • **DURATION:** Spring-Fall • **IDEAL CANDIDATE:** College Students, Career Changers, Retired Folks • **APPLICANT POOL:** 50/year
• **APPLICANTS ACCEPTED:** 10/year

THIS PARK, WHICH MEMORIALIZES the twenty-sixth president for his contribution to conservation, preserves the colorful North Dakota badlands along the Little Missouri River, the surrounding prairie, and a variety of wildlife. Interpreters staff information desks at visitor centers, where you will answer questions, sell publications, issue backcountry permits, and act as a radio dispatcher. You will also prepare and present campfire programs, give guided tours of Theodore Roosevelt's cabin, provide demonstrations, and give interpretive talks, guided nature walks, and bus tours. Campground hosts are available in two campgrounds. Resource management volunteers work with the biological control program for the management of the exotic plant leafy spurge; monitor eagle nesting sites; and work with the GIS management system. Depending on length of volunteer work, housing and/or campground space may be provided.

Contact Information: Bruce Kaye, Chief Of Interpretation • Theodore Roosevelt National Park • 315 Second Ave. • Medora, ND 58645 • Phone: (701) 623-4466 • Fax: (701) 623-4840 • E-mail: Bruce_Kaye@nps.gov

Tonto National Forest

REGION/HQ: South/Midwest/Arizona • **CATEGORY:** Wilderness • **POSITION TYPE:** Internship/Seasonal
• **DURATION:** Winter/Summer • **IDEAL CANDIDATE:** College Students, Career Changers • **APPLICANT POOL:** Varies • **APPLICANTS ACCEPTED:** 6–15/season

WORK IN A ENVIRONMENT where the cactus meets the pines. You'll receive hands-on experience in a wide variety of wilderness recreation and environmental education. Interns receive a $19-per-day stipend, plus housing.

Contact Information: Greg Hansen, Recreation Staff • Tonto National Forest • Mesa Ranger District • P.O. Box 5800 • Mesa, AZ 85211-5800 • Phone: (602) 379-6446 • Fax: (602) 379-6448

I have sometimes been wildly, despairingly, acutely miserable, racked with sorrow, but through it all I still know quite certainly that just to be alive is a grand thing. —AGATHA CHRISTIE

U.S. Army Corps of Engineers

REGION/HQ: Nationwide/Tennessee • **CATEGORY:** Conservation • **POSITION TYPE:** Seasonal • **DURATION:** Year-Round • **IDEAL CANDIDATE:** High School Students, College Students, Career Changers, Retired Folks, Foreigners • **APPLICANT POOL:** Varies • **APPLICANTS ACCEPTED:** Varies

THE U.S. ARMY CORPS OF ENGINEERS, which is the steward of almost 12 million acres of land and water, offers many volunteer opportunities in recreation and natural resources management. These include trail building and maintenance, park attendant, campground hosting, wildlife habitat construction, educational interpretation, visitor center staffing, photography, and dozens of other unique and challenging opportunities. Benefits vary with the position and may include reimbursement for out-of-pocket expenses and free camping. To learn of these opportunities, the Corps offers a volunteer clearinghouse, a nationwide, toll-free hotline number for those interested in volunteering their time with the Corps. Before you call, you should be ready to provide information about your interests, talents, and the locations where you may want to volunteer. The clearinghouse, in turn, will provide you with contact information for the area you have requested, as well as written information about volunteer opportunities there.

Contact Information: Volunteer Clearinghouse • U.S. Army Corps of Engineers • P.O. Box 1070 • Nashville, TN 37202-1070 • Phone: (800) 865-8337

U.S. Geological Survey

REGION/HQ: Nationwide/Virginia • **CATEGORY:** Geology • **POSITION TYPE:** Internship • **DURATION:** Year-Round • **IDEAL CANDIDATE:** High School Students, College Students, Career Changers, Retired Folks • **APPLICANT POOL:** Varies • **APPLICANTS ACCEPTED:** Varies

THE MISSION OF THE USGS is to provide geological, topographical, biological, and hydrological information that contributes to the wise management of the nation's natural resources and promotes the health, safety, and welfare of the public. Their commitment to providing accurate and impartial information to all underscores their continued dedication to "Earth Science in the Public Service." Office, laboratory, and field assignments are available nationwide in these divisions:

National Mapping, Water Resources, Geologic, Biological Resources, Information Systems, and administration. Volunteers can work in a laboratory, assist librarians, enter data into a computer, gather water data, provide clerical assistance, help with equipment operation and repairs, monitor geological hazards, provide the public with information about USGS and its products (maps, books, scientific reports, etc.), edit and process manuscripts, design computer graphics and models, or participate in many other activities.

Contact Information: Susan Wells, Volunteer Program Coordinator • U.S. Geological Survey • 601 National Center • Reston, VA 22092 • Phone: (703) 648-7440 • Western Region/HQ: (415) 329-5003 • E-mail: volnteer@usgs.gov • Web Site: www.usgs.gov/volunteer/volunteer.html

Volunteers for Outdoor Colorado

REGION/HQ: Rocky Mountains/Colorado • **CATEGORY:** Conservation • **POSITION TYPE:** Seasonal • **DURATION:** Spring-Fall • **IDEAL CANDIDATE:** High School Students, College Students, Career Changers, Retired Folks, Foreigners • **APPLICANT POOL:** Varies • **APPLICANTS ACCEPTED:** Varies

VOLUNTEERS FOR OUTDOOR COLORADO maintains a listing of more than 400 volunteer opportunities available around Colorado with agencies such as the USFS, BLM, Colorado State Parks, and various other state programs. The projects include trail construction and maintenance, wildlife studies and surveys, field work, botany, backcountry monitoring, urban projects, environmental education, and administrative support. The durations vary and most are conducted April through October. Each spring they publish the *Volunteer Opportunities Catalog.* Call for a copy.

Contact Information: Jennifer Borstein, Programs Associate • Volunteers for Outdoor Colorado • 600 S. Marion Parkway • Denver, CO 80209-2597 • Phone: (303) 715-1010 • Fax: (303) 715-1212 • Toll Free: (800) 925-2220 • E-mail: jenniferb@voc.org • Web Site: aclin.org/code/voc

Wenatchee National Forest

REGION/HQ: Pacific Northwest/Washington • **CATEGORY:** Forestry • **POSITION TYPE:** Seasonal • **DURATION:** Spring-Fall • **IDEAL CANDIDATE:** High

School Students, College Students, Career Changers, Retired Folks, Foreigners • **APPLICANT POOL:** Varies • **APPLICANTS ACCEPTED:** Varies

THE CLE ELUM RANGER DISTRICT is located in central Washington State on the east side of the Cascade Mountains, approximately seventy-five miles from Seattle. The district covers an area from Snoqulamie Pass and the mountainous terrain of the Alpine Lakes Wilderness to drier pine-forested lands north of the town of Ellensburg. Volunteer positions include lookout observers, recreation and backcountry guard, information host, and interpretive naturalist. Candidates must be energetic, responsible, self-starters, who are able to work well with the public and enjoy a rustic lifestyle.

Contact Information: Debbie Kelly, Information Specialist • Wenatchee National Forest • Cle Elum Ranger District • 803 W. Second St. • Cle Elum, WA 98922-1097 • Phone: (509) 674-4411 • Fax: (509) 674-4794

White Sands National Monument

REGION/HQ: South/Midwest/New Mexico • **CATEGORY:** National Monument • **POSITION TYPE:** Internship/Seasonal • **DURATION:** Year-Round • **IDEAL CANDIDATE:** College Students, Career Changers • **APPLICANT POOL:** Varies • **APPLICANTS ACCEPTED:** Varies

ENVIRONMENTAL INTERPRETATION interns work with the interpretive division, staffing the information desk, and giving interpretive talks, slide programs, nature walks, bus tours, and children's programs on the natural and cultural history of White Sands National Monument. You may also provide roving interpretation on foot and bicycle, and assist in exhibit development and various administrative/resource management projects. Benefits include a $12-per-day stipend, housing (with utilities) at the monument, and partial reimbursement for transportation costs to and from the monument.

Contact Information: John Mangimeli, Volunteer Coordinator • White Sands National Monument • P.O. Box 1086 • Holloman AFB, NM 88330 • Phone: (505) 479-6124 • Fax: (505) 479-4333 • E-mail: john_mangimeli @nps.gov

Wind Cave National Park

REGION/HQ: Rocky Mountains/South Dakota • **CATEGORY:** National Park • **POSITION TYPE:** Seasonal • **DURATION:** Year-Round • **IDEAL CANDIDATE:** College Students, Career Changers, Retired Folks • **APPLICANT POOL:** Varies • **APPLICANTS ACCEPTED:** Varies

LOCATED IN THE SOUTHERN BLACK HILLS, this park features some of the most pristine mixed grass prairie found in the United States. Large herds of free-roaming bison, elk, pronghorn, and deer inhabit the grasslands and forest. Wind Cave contains beautiful formations, including rare boxwork, cave popcorn, dogtooth spar, and frostwork. Positions are available in interpretation/visitor services, campground hosts, and resource management. Benefits include training, park housing/campsite, and a stipend.

Contact Information: Kathy Steichen, Assistant Chief Interpreter • Wind Cave National Park • RR1, Box 190 • Hot Springs, SD 57747 • Phone: (605) 745-4600 • Fax: (605) 745-4207 • Alternate: (605) 745-1131

Yellowstone Park Service Stations

REGION/HQ: Rocky Mountains/Montana • **CATEGORY:** Concessionaire • **POSITION TYPE:** Seasonal • **DURATION:** Summer • **IDEAL CANDIDATE:** College Students, Career Changers, Foreigners • **APPLICANT POOL:** Varies • **APPLICANTS ACCEPTED:** 70/season

YELLOWSTONE PARK SERVICE STATIONS operates seven gasoline service stations, four automotive repair shops, and an office and warehouse. Positions include service station attendants, accounting and clerical workers, and automotive technicians. You will make $4.85 per hour, and if you complete your work assignment you will receive a 35¢-per-hour bonus. A payroll deduction of $8.75 per day is made for dormitory-style housing and meals served in employee dining rooms.

Contact Information: Hal Broadhead, General Manager • Yellowstone Park Service Stations • P.O. Box 11 • Gardiner, MT 59030-0011 • Phone: (406) 848-7333 • Fax: (406) 848-7731 • E-mail: ypss@worldnet.att.net • Web Site: www.coolworks.com/showme/ypss

Zion National Park

REGION/HQ: Rocky Mountains/Utah • **CATEGORY:** National Park • **POSITION TYPE:** Seasonal • **DURATION:** Year-Round • **IDEAL CANDIDATE:** College Students, Career Changers • **APPLICANT POOL:** Varies • **APPLICANTS ACCEPTED:** Varies

THIS AREA BOASTS COLORFUL CLIFFS of Navajo sandstone, deep narrow canyons, high forest plateaus, and low rocky deserts. Campground hosts are needed each year for campgrounds adjacent to the Virgin River. You will receive an $8-per-day stipend, five days per week.

Contact Information: Karen Frauson, Volunteer Coordinator • Zion National Park • Springdale, UT 84767 • Phone: (801) 772-3256

Addresses

Black Hills National Forest
REGION/HQ: Rocky Mountains/South Dakota
CATEGORY: Forest Service
CONTACT INFORMATION:
Recreation Forester
Black Hills National Forest
Pactola District
803 Soo San Dr.
Rapid City, SD 57702
Phone: (605) 343-1567 • Fax: (605) 343-7134

Boise National Forest
REGION/HQ: Pacific Northwest/Idaho
CATEGORY: Forest Service
CONTACT INFORMATION:
Range Management
Boise National Forest
Mountain Home Ranger District
5493 Warm Springs Ave.
Boise, ID 83712
Phone: (208) 364-4241

Bridger-Teton National Forest
REGION/HQ: Rocky Mountains/Wyoming
CATEGORY: Forest Service
CONTACT INFORMATION:
Natural Resources Specialist
Bridger-Teton National Forest
Kemmerer Ranger District
P.O. Box 31
Kemmerer, WY 83101
Phone: (307) 877-4415

Caribou National Forest
REGION/HQ: Pacific Northwest/Idaho
CATEGORY: Forest Service
CONTACT INFORMATION:
Supervisory Forester
Caribou National Forest
Soda Springs Ranger District
421 W. 2nd South
Soda Springs, ID 83276
Phone: (208) 547-4356 • Fax: (208) 547-4356

Chattahoochee/Oconee National Forest
REGION/HQ: Southeast/Georgia
CATEGORY: Forest Service
CONTACT INFORMATION:
Staffing Specialist
Chattahoochee/Oconee National Forest
508 Oak St.
Gainesville, GA 30501
Phone: (404) 536-0541 • Fax: (404) 534-4411

Chequamegon National Forest
REGION/HQ: Great Lakes/Wisconsin
CATEGORY: Forest Service
CONTACT INFORMATION:
Resort Naturalist Coordinator
Chequamegon National Forest
U.S. Forest Service
P.O. Box 896
Hayward, WI 54843-0896
Phone: (715) 634-4821

Cibola National Forest
REGION/HQ: South/Midwest/New Mexico
CATEGORY: Forest Service
CONTACT INFORMATION:
Personnel Specialist
Cibola National Forest
2113 Osuna, NE
Albuquerque, NM 87113
Phone: (505) 761-4650 • Fax: (505) 761-4663

Deschutes National Forest

REGION/HQ: Pacific Northwest/Oregon
CATEGORY: Forest Service
CONTACT INFORMATION:
Wilderness Supervisor
Deschutes National Forest
Sisters Ranger District
P.O. Box 249
Sisters, OR 97759
Phone: (503) 549-2111 • Fax: (503) 549-7746

El Malpais National Monument

REGION/HQ: South/Midwest/New Mexico
CATEGORY: National Monument
CONTACT INFORMATION:
Park Ranger
El Malpais National Monument
P.O. Box 846
Grants, NM 87020
Phone: (505) 287-7911

Everglades National Park

REGION/HQ: Southeast/Florida
CATEGORY: Concessionaire
CONTACT INFORMATION:
Personnel Director
Everglades National Park
Amfac
#1 Flamingo Lodge Highway
Flamingo, FL 33034-6798
Phone: (813) 695-3101

Flathead National Forest

REGION/HQ: Rocky Mountains/Montana
CATEGORY: Forestry
CONTACT INFORMATION:
Personnel/Employment
Flathead National Forest
1935 3rd Ave., East
Kalispell, MT 59901
Phone: (406) 758-5273

Glacier National Park Associates

REGION/HQ: Rocky Mountains/Montana
CATEGORY: National Park
CONTACT INFORMATION:
Program Director
Glacier National Park Associates
P.O. Box 91
Kalispell, MT 59904

Lassen National Forest

REGION/HQ: Pacific Northwest/California
CATEGORY: Forestry
CONTACT INFORMATION:
Volunteer Coordinator
Lassen National Forest
55 S. Sacramento St.
Susanville, CA 96130
Phone: (916) 257-2151

Maine Appalachian Trail Club

REGION/HQ: Northeast/Maine
CATEGORY: Outdoor Education
CONTACT INFORMATION:
Program Director
Maine Appalachian Trail Club
15 Westwood Rd.
Bangor, ME 04401

Manti-La Sal National Forest

REGION/HQ: Rocky Mountains/Utah
CATEGORY: Forest Service
CONTACT INFORMATION:
Program Specialist
Manti-La Sal National Forest
Monticello Ranger District
P.O. Box 820
Monticello, UT 84535
Phone: (801) 587-2041

Mt. Hood National Forest

REGION/HQ: Pacific Northwest/Oregon
CATEGORY: Forest Service
CONTACT INFORMATION:
Staffing Coordinator
Mt. Hood National Forest
70220 E. Highway 26
Rhododendron, OR 97049
Phone: (503) 622-3191 • Fax: (503) 622-5622

Pacific Islands National Wildlife Refuge

REGION/HQ: Pacific Northwest/Hawaii
CATEGORY: Wildlife
CONTACT INFORMATION:
Refuge Operations Specialist
Pacific Islands National Wildlife Refuge
P.O. Box 50167
Honolulu, HI 96850
Phone: (808) 541-1201

Pacific Northwest Trail Association
REGION/HQ: Pacific Northwest/Washington
CATEGORY: Wilderness
CONTACT INFORMATION:
Pat Cummins, President
Pacific Northwest Trail Association
22814 135th St., SE
Kent, WA 98031

Salmon & Challis National Forests
REGION/HQ: Pacific Northwest/Idaho
CATEGORY: Forest Service
CONTACT INFORMATION:
Volunteer Program Coordinator
Salmon & Challis National Forests
Highway 93 South
RR 2, Box 600
Salmon, ID 83467-9812
Phone: (208) 756-2215

Society of American Foresters
REGION/HQ: Washington, D.C./Maryland
CATEGORY: Forestry
CONTACT INFORMATION:
Program Director
Society of American Foresters
5400 Grosvenor Ln.
Bethesda, MD 20814
Phone: (301) 897-8720 • Fax: (301) 897-3690

SOLO - Wilderness & Emergency Medicine
REGION/HQ: Nationwide/New Hampshire
CATEGORY: Wilderness
CONTACT INFORMATION:
Program Director
SOLO - Wilderness & Emergency Medicine
P.O. Box 3150
Conway, NH 03818
Phone: (603) 447-6711 • Fax: (603) 447-2310
• E-mail: lfrizzsolo@aol.com • Web Site: www.
stonehearth. com

Timpanogos Cave National Monument
REGION/HQ: Rocky Mountains/Utah
CATEGORY: National Monument
CONTACT INFORMATION:
Chief Ranger
Timpanogos Cave National Monument
RR3, Box 200
American Fork, UT 84003
Phone: (801) 756-5238

Uinta National Forest
REGION/HQ: Rocky Mountains/Utah
CATEGORY: Forest Service
CONTACT INFORMATION:
Chief Ranger
Uinta National Forest
Pleasant Grove Ranger District
390 N. 100 East
Pleasant Grove, UT 84062-2350
Phone: (801) 785-3563 • Fax: (801) 342-5244

Wilderness Medical Associates
REGION/HQ: Nationwide/Maine
CATEGORY: Experiential Education
CONTACT INFORMATION:
Program Director
Wilderness Medical Associates
189 Dudley Rd.
Bryant Pond, ME 04219
Phone: (207) 665-2707

Wilderness Watch
REGION/HQ: Rocky Mountains/Montana
CATEGORY: Wilderness
CONTACT INFORMATION:
Jim Dayton, Executive Director
Wilderness Watch
Box 9175
Missoula, MT 59807
Phone: (406) 542-2048

GORP (gôrp) (1) A concoction of nuts, berries, raisins, chocolate, and more, which fuels travelers in the great outdoors; (2) (abbr) **Great Outdoor Recreation Pages**—a web site packed with valuable information of interest to outdoor recreationists and active travelers. What's in the mix? Attractions—national parks, forests, wilderness, wildlife refuges, historic sites, and more. It describes where to go and what to do on lands throughout the United States. Activities helps the outdoor enthusiast pursue just about anything—hiking, biking, fishing, paddling, skiing, birding, and on and on. Locations lets you throw a dart at a world map and learn about whatever distant corner the point hits. Books, gear, tours, recipes, art—if it has an outdoor and active-travel theme, you'll probably see it in GORP. www.gorp.com

Helping Out in the Outdoors. Each year, the American Hiking Society publishes this directory of more than 2,000 volunteer positions and internships on America's public lands. This great resource is only $7 (add $3 to receive by first-class mail or if you're overseas). Make your checks payable to "AHS Helping Out" and send to AHS, 1422 Fenwick Ln., Silver Spring, MD 20910; (800) 972-8608; ahshiking@aol.com; www.orca.org/ahs

Changing lives through service to nature, **The Student Conservation Association** publishes a couple of great resources to look into. *Earth Work* is a monthly magazine which contains articles on career trends for natural resource and environmental professionals as well as current job classifieds and internships (six-month subscription costs $21.95; one year is $31.95). Another great publication put out by SCA is *Earth Work: Resource Guide to Nationwide Green Jobs* (published by HarperCollins West), which provides you with the tools and information you need for entering the environmental field, whether you're taking the first step or looking for more details about a path you've already chosen ($15, plus $4.75 shipping if you order through SCA). Contact SCA, P.O. Box 550, Charlestown, NH 03603; www.sca-inc.org; (603) 543-1700.

The **Wilderness Education Association** is one of the most comprehensive wilderness education and outdoor leadership training organizations in the country. To get more info, contact Jennifer Tucker, WEA, Colorado State University, Dept. of NRRT, Fort Collins, CO 80521; (970) 223-6252; Fax: (970) 223-2231; wea@lamar.colostate.edu; www.prairienet.org/WEA

7

elp! I'm tired of the day-after-day routine of a job which doesn't inspire me (running a newspaper press). I want to do something to help the planet or something to help people to better appreciate and enjoy it. Anything from building trails to improving wildlife habitat to helping to preserve wilderness. You get the idea. I want to be able to travel around and spend a lot of time in the outdoors, to learn to live simply and truly believe less is more. I don't want to make a lot of money, only enough to live on and a small amount more. I want to meet people who feel and live the same way. I want to experience more in life than the daily grind with weekends off and a short vacation. When I'm old I don't want to regret all the things I didn't do or didn't even attempt. I want to see as much of the world as I can and to better understand it.

—RICKEY SHORTT, *BACK DOOR* READER

The Schuylkill Center for Environmental Education

The Envir

Anita Purves Nature Center

REGION/HQ: Great Lakes/Illinois • **CATEGORY:** Nature Center • **POSITION TYPE:** Internship/Seasonal • **DURATION:** Year-Round • **IDEAL CANDIDATE:** College Students, Career Changers, Foreigners • **APPLICANT POOL:** Varies • **APPLICANTS ACCEPTED:** 1/program

THE ANITA PURVES NATURE CENTER is an environmental education facility operated by the Urbana Park District. Dedicated in 1979, the nature center is named in honor of Anita Parker Purves, a concerned citizen who initiated interest in environmental awareness in Urbana. The mission of the nature center is to serve the community by promoting the wise stewardship of the natural environment, fostering appreciation, understanding, and responsible use of the earth. The center provides environmental recreation programming for all segments of the community.

Work/Learn Program Specifics: Assistantship/Internship Program: These programs are designed to provide graduates an opportunity to develop programming and leadership skills in environmental education activities. Assistants and interns gain practical experience by working with students, park district staff, and cooperating organizations. Duties include developing curricula for environmental programs; providing leadership for programs; recruiting and training volunteers; participating in the planning, implementation, and evaluation of workshops and special events; assisting with development of displays and exhibits; assisting in management of a fifty-nine-acre wood and restoration of a sixty-acre prairie; and preparation and administration of program budgets. You will also complete at least two independent projects that will be of value to the center and your file.

Duration: Both programs run for a minimum of three months and a maximum of twelve months. You will work forty hours per week, some of the time during weekends and evenings.

Compensation and Perks: Assistants receive a stipend of $350 per month; interns receive $150 per month. During the summer you will receive a free pool pass.

The Ideal Candidate: Assistantships: You must have either a bachelor's or master's degree in environmental education, science, education, recreation, or related field. Interns: You must have at least junior status at your university. Courses in biology, zoology, botany, ecology, geology, forestry, wildlife management, and/or education are helpful. All applicants must have a genuine interest in working with people of all ages, have an interest in environmental education, interpretation, and resource management, and intend to pursue a career in environmental education or a related field.

Making It Happen: Call for more information. Rolling deadlines. After reviewing applications, selected applicants are invited for an interview. Phone interviews are conducted for out-of-state candidates. Interviews include a panel interview, tour of the facilities and programs, and a written exercise.

INSIDER TIPS: *Applicants should have a clear idea of what they hope to gain from the program.*

Contact Information: Judy Miller, Environmental Program Manager • Anita Purves Nature Center • Urbana Park District • 1505 N. Broadway Ave. • Urbana, IL 61801 • Phone: (217) 384-4062 • Fax: (217) 384-4052 • Web Site: www.prairienet.org/upd

Archbold Biological Station

REGION/HQ: Southeast/Florida • **CATEGORY:** Research • **POSITION TYPE:** Internship • **DURATION:** Year-Round • **IDEAL CANDIDATE:** College Students, Foreigners • **APPLICANT POOL:** Varies • **APPLICANTS ACCEPTED:** Varies

FOUNDED IN 1941, the Archbold Biological Station is an independent biological research facility that manages

onment

a globally significant nature preserve and is dedicated to the worldwide effort to study, interpret, and preserve the earth's natural biological diversity.

Work/Learn Program Specifics: The Student Intern Program consists of a split work day in which the student works half the day as an assistant to one of the station's scientists and half the day on a project of his or her own. Station staff members research projects that include plant ecology, arthropod ecology and systematics, avian demography, vertebrate population biology, fire ecology, endangered species management, conservation biology, and agro-ecology.

Duration: In general, internships last from three to six months.

Compensation and Perks: Graduate students working on their theses receive $100 per week; undergraduates receive $50 per week. Room and board are also provided.

The Ideal Candidate: Candidates should have a background in biological sciences, ecology, natural resources management, or a related field.

Making It Happen: Please apply in writing, with your cover letter focusing on your special areas of interest and the time frame you will be available. In addition, include your resume and two letters of recommendation from faculty members. The summer deadline is April 1; however, deadlines for other terms are rolling. It is recommended that all materials are submitted at least two months prior to your requested start date.

Contact Information: Hilary Swain, Executive Director • Archbold Biological Station • P.O. Box 2057 • Lake Placid, FL 33862 • Phone: (941) 465-2571 • Fax: (941) 699-1927 • E-mail: hswain@ct.net

Arnold Arboretum

REGION/HQ: Northeast/Massachusetts • **CATEGORY:** Arboretum • **POSITION TYPE:** Internship • **DURATION:** Summer • **IDEAL CANDIDATE:** College Students, Career Changers, Foreigners • **APPLICANT POOL:** Varies • **APPLICANTS ACCEPTED:** 15/year
....

ESTABLISHED IN 1872, the Arnold Arboretum of Harvard University contains one of the world's largest collections of hardy woody ornamental plants, displayed in a historic Olmsted landscape covering over 265 acres.

Work/Learn Program Specifics: Horticultural trainees have opportunities in grounds maintenance, green-

house and nursery operations, mapping and labeling, and library work. As part of the program, trainees are required to attend lectures on intensive horticultural maintenance (seven weeks), woody plant identification (six weeks), and additional lectures and field trips to gardens and historic landscapes.

Duration: Trainees can elect to enter the program between April 1 and June 1, and the program lasts ten to sixteen weeks.

Compensation and Perks: Trainees receive $6.75 per hour.

The Ideal Candidate: Desired qualifications include one or more educational years in horticulture, botany, ecology, forestry, biology, or landscape architecture. Applicants should possess excellent physical health, stamina, maturity, and self-motivation.

Making It Happen: Write for application materials. Applications are due on February 1. Preference is given to applicants who can start on April 1 or shortly thereafter.

Contact Information: Julie Coop, Intern Coordinator • Arnold Arboretum • Horticultural Training Program • 125 Arborway • Jamaica Plain, MA 02130-3519 • Phone: (617) 524-1718 • Fax: (617) 524-1418

Aspen Center for Environmental Studies

REGION/HQ: Rocky Mountains/Colorado • **CATEGORY:** Nature Center • **POSITION TYPE:** Internship • **DURATION:** Summer • **IDEAL CANDIDATE:** College Students, Career Changers • **APPLICANT POOL:** 200/year • **APPLICANTS ACCEPTED:** 12/year
....

SINCE ITS FOUNDING IN 1968 by Aspen resident Elizabeth Paepcke, the private, nonprofit Aspen Center for Environmental Studies has been educating people to be environmentally responsible. Managing the 25-acre Hallam Lake sanctuary and another 175-acre natural area, the center offers hikes and nature classes to children and adults. It also runs the Environmental Learning Center, which houses the Scott Field Laboratory, Pinewood Natural History Library, Gates Visitor Center, and a bookstore informally known as the Den.

Area and Working Environment: The center is positioned at the edge of Hallam Lake, at an elevation of 7,900 feet, in Aspen—one of the best ski resort towns in the United States and a natural paradise.

Work/Learn Program Specifics: Participate in the center's Summer Naturalist Intern Program. The intern's responsibilities include just about everything that has to do with maintaining the center—landscaping, giving talks on the birds of prey program, rehabilitating injured animals and birds, teaching natural-history classes to children and adults, and leading nature walks. Interns teach all the summer programs, from leading a troop of adults on a sunset walk by the lake to teaching children about the rich diversity of insects in the area. After spending a summer leading interpretive walks, learning animal rehabilitation, and teaching children about the environment, interns are sure to leave with a newfound appreciation of nature.

Duration: Twelve to thirteen weeks, full-time, during the summer.

Compensation and Perks: Interns receive a $100-per-week stipend. The center also arranges free accommodations. Interns often cook and eat dinners together, forming friendships that the center's communal atmosphere encourages. Interns are also allowed to take at least one class for free from the center's naturalist field school.

The Ideal Candidate: College juniors, seniors, graduate students, and recent graduates are eligible, although the bulk of interns have received college degrees by the start of the internship. The center strongly prefers students who have studied the natural sciences, environmental studies, or related fields. First-aid certification is required.

Making It Happen: Submit the center's completed application, a resume, and three letters of recommendation (the letters are suggested, but not required). Top candidates are interviewed over the phone. Deadline: March 1.

Contact Information: Education Coordinator • Aspen Center for Environmental Studies • 100 Puppy Smith St. • P.O. Box 8777 • Aspen, CO 81612 • Phone: (303) 925-5756

Audubon Naturalist Society

REGION/HQ: Washington, D.C./Maryland • **CATEGORY:** Environmental Education • **POSITION TYPE:** Internship • **DURATION:** Year-Round • **IDEAL CANDIDATE:** College Students • **APPLICANT POOL:** 100/year • **APPLICANTS ACCEPTED:** 8/year

AS AN INDEPENDENT ENVIRONMENTAL education and conservation organization, the Audubon Naturalist Society

(ANS) seeks to increase environmental awareness and understanding and to encourage action at the local level. Founded in 1897, ANS pioneered linking natural history studies with conservation activities and offers a variety of resources and programs. It is not affiliated with any national group, including the National Audubon Society.

Work/Learn Program Specifics: The internship is a teaching position, and most of the time the intern is co-teaching children's classes (ages four to ten). Other duties include working on an independent project and assisting in general office work. They also offer volunteer positions, including property maintenance, office work, editorial work, and water-quality monitoring.

Duration: Internships last twelve weeks during the summer, full-time; other seasons, part- or full-time.

Compensation and Perks: Interns receive a $100-per-week stipend (for the twelve-week session), plus room and kitchen privileges. Perks include a 20 percent discount at the bookshop and free (or at cost) participation in most programs if you are working over thirty hours per week.

The Ideal Candidate: Applicant should be pursuing a career in environmental education, elementary education, or related field. Experience in natural history and working with children is helpful. First aid and children's CPR certification is required, as is a car or bike.

Making It Happen: Submit a cover letter, resume, and two letters of recommendation three months before starting date. Because of budget constraints, ANS cannot return long-distance intern calls. Either write or leave an address when calling.

Contact Information: Education Program Coordinator • Audubon Naturalist Society • 8940 Jones Mill Rd. • Chevy Chase, MD 20815 • Phone: (301) 652-9188 • Fax: (301) 951-7179

Aullwood Audubon Center & Farm

REGION/HQ: Great Lakes/Ohio • **CATEGORY:** Environmental Education • **POSITION TYPE:** Internship • **DURATION:** Year-Round • **IDEAL CANDIDATE:** College Students, Career Changers, Foreigners • **APPLICANT POOL:** 100/year • **APPLICANTS ACCEPTED:** 12/year

AULLWOOD AUDUBON CENTER and Farm is one of five environmental education centers in the United States owned and operated by the National Audubon Society. The goal is to promote awareness of the relationships within natural and agricultural systems, with humans as an integral element. They also strive to develop environmental ethics. The program is varied in both its media and its audience. With over 75,000 visits per year, they reach far with their messages about natural history, cultural history, and environmental issues.

Area and Working Environment: Aullwood is 350 varied acres of natural area and organic farming along the valley of a state scenic river.

Work/Learn Program Specifics: Environmental Education/Interpretation Program: Participants are involved in an extensive orientation and then gradually assume the same kinds of responsibilities as full-time staff, with a concentration on the activities in the education or farming area. All facets of the operation of an environmental education center and organic farm are explored, meaning "the good, the bad, and the ugly!" Each intern works with the staff to create his or her own individualized program. In addition, the completion of special projects often benefits both the intern and Aullwood.

Duration: The program is designed to last thirteen weeks and interns work forty hours per week, with some weekends and evenings.

Compensation and Perks: A $675 stipend per season is available to each intern. Interns are also provided furnished housing and utilities on the Aullwood property.

The Ideal Candidate: Applicants must have a genuine interest in working with people of all ages and intend to pursue a career in environmental education, natural history, education, or a related field.

Making It Happen: Call for application. Rolling deadlines.

INSIDER TIPS: *Have experience teaching kids or experience with natural history.*

Contact Information: John Wilson, Environmental Education Specialist • Aullwood Audubon Center & Farm • 1000 Aullwood Rd. • Dayton, OH 45414-1129 • Phone: (937) 890-7360

Barrier Island Environmental Education Center

REGION/HQ: Southeast/South Carolina • **CATEGORY:** Environmental Education • **POSITION TYPE:** Seasonal • **DURATION:** Academic year • **IDEAL CANDIDATE:** College Students, Career Changers, Foreigners • **APPLICANT POOL:** 100/year • **APPLICANTS ACCEPTED:** 14/year

CAMP ST. CHRISTOPHER is owned and operated by the Episcopal Diocese of South Carolina and hosts conference groups, Episcopal church groups, summer-camp children, and many public and private school groups. During the school year, the Barrier Island Program teaches over 8,000 elementary and middle school students about the coastal environment.

Area and Working Environment: Located thirty miles from Charleston, the camp is near many historical gardens and plantations. On-site they have one mile of beachfront and 200 acres of undeveloped maritime forest and salt marsh. It is a beautiful area to live, work, teach, and learn.

Work/Learn Program Specifics: Each week you will teach about 260 people about the coastal ecosystems. Most classes are held outdoors for a truly hands-on approach to the ocean, salt marsh, beach, forest, and sand dune habitats. They also take groups seining, dragging nets through the estuary to catch and learn about fish. They have a "touch tank" with touchable salt water creatures and also a "snake den" to teach kids about the local reptiles and amphibians.

Duration: Positions are full-time from August to the following May. Staff training begins at the end of August and the first school group visits the first week of September. Weekends are free (a group of 130 people stays from Monday to Wednesday and another group Wednesday to Friday).

Compensation and Perks: Staff members receive a stipend of $160 per week, plus room and board.

The Ideal Candidate: An undergraduate degree in teaching, biology, environmental studies, or a related field is required. Creativity, independence, and enthusiasm allow for better teaching. You must be able and have a strong desire to learn about plants, animals, insects, and habitats of the local area.

Making It Happen: Send cover letter, resume, and references by July 31.

INSIDER TIPS: *Due to the large number of applicants, personal interviews are desired, but not always possible. A videotape recording of yourself gives you an edge on the competition and lets us get to know you better. Phone calls are always welcome.*

Contact Information: Jim Koenig, Program Director • Barrier Island Environmental Education Center • Camp

St. Christopher • 2810 Seabrook Island Rd. • John's Island, SC 29455-6219 • Phone: (803) 768-1337 • Fax: (803) 768-0918

Berry Botanic Garden

REGION/HQ: Pacific Northwest/Oregon • **CATEGORY:** Botanical Garden • **POSITION TYPE:** Internship • **DURATION:** Summer • **IDEAL CANDIDATE:** College Students, Career Changers, Foreigners • **APPLICANT POOL:** 40/year • **APPLICANTS ACCEPTED:** 2/year

IN ANY SEASON, the Berry Botanic Garden is a wonderful natural place to browse and learn. The garden maintains five major collections: alpine plants and the rock garden, species *lilies*, species *rhododendrons, primulas*, and Northwest natives. The garden is fifty-seven years old and contains mature plantings of rhododendrons from early expeditions and other horticulturally significant collections. They conduct programs in conservation of Northwest native plant species, education, and horticulture.

Area and Working Environment: Located in Portland, the garden's six acres are designed around slopes, natural springs and creeks, open meadows, and towering Douglas firs.

Work/Learn Program Specifics: Horticulture interns will work with garden staff maintaining and developing areas of the garden, work with records and the computer system, propagate, and participate in specific projects.

Duration: Internships generally run for ten weeks, through the summer, full-time. Internships may start any time between April 15 and July 1.

Compensation and Perks: You will receive a stipend of $2,200. Housing may be available for one intern, and the staff is able to provide a place for interns to stay for a few days when they first arrive.

The Ideal Candidate: Applicants should be enthusiastic and excited about plants, horticulture, and working in public gardens. Someone who needs experience for their career is the most likely to get hired.

Making It Happen: Write or call for internship application. Send completed application, resume, and cover letter before March 1.

Contact Information: Will Simonds, Garden Manager • Berry Botanic Garden • 11505 SW Summerville Ave. • Portland, OR 97219-8309 • Phone: (503) 636-4112 • Fax: (503) 636-7496 • E-mail: simonds@agora. rdrop.com

Betsy-Jeff Penn 4-H Educational Center

REGION/HQ: Southeast/North Carolina • **CATEGORY:** Environmental Education • **POSITION TYPE:** Seasonal • **DURATION:** Spring • **IDEAL CANDIDATE:** College Students, Career Changers • **APPLICANT POOL:** 50/year • **APPLICANTS ACCEPTED:** 7/year

THE MISSION OF THE Penn 4-H Educational Center is to provide year-round training and educational programs for youth and those who work with youth. The center's programs are designed to motivate and serve as a laboratory for innovative and effective educational approaches.

Area and Working Environment: The 200-acre site is tucked in the hills and provides a wide variety of examples of typical Piedmont ecosystems. Wetlands, streams, small ponds, and a twenty-five-acre lake provide opportunities for the study of water biology and water quality; while acres of forests demonstrate the effects of various states of succession and provide areas for the study of birds, animals, reptiles, and plants.

Work/Learn Program Specifics: The seasonal staff develops curriculum and teaches classes in environmental sciences, social studies, life skills, communications, and outdoor skills to students in grades three to eight participating in the residential education program. The adventure program instructors facilitate initiatives, group problem solving, trust and group dynamic exercises, and low and high ropes courses for fifth- to twelfth-grade students and adult audiences.

Duration: The spring season runs from the first week in February to the end of May. Exceptional staff will have extended employment opportunities.

Compensation and Perks: You will receive a weekly salary, plus room and board.

The Ideal Candidate: Applicants must have a bachelor's degree in education, community development, counseling, psychology, sociology, human development, biology, wildlife, political science, or a related field.

Making It Happen: Send resume and cover letter requesting application materials and further information.

INSIDER TIPS: *We look for those with a genuine interest in children, a commitment to the environment, and who have enthusiasm, creativity, and are able to work with a team.*

Contact Information: Clare-Marie Hannon, Program Director • Betsy-Jeff Penn 4-H Educational Center • 804 Cedar Ln. • Reidsville, NC 27320 • Phone: (910) 349-9445 • Fax: (910) 634-0110

Bok Tower Gardens

REGION/HQ: Southeast/Florida • **CATEGORY:** Botanical Garden • **POSITION TYPE:** Internship • **DURATION:** Year-Round • **IDEAL CANDIDATE:** College Students • **APPLICANT POOL:** Varies • **APPLICANTS ACCEPTED:** 2/term

BOK TOWER GARDENS was designed by the firm of Frederick Law Olmsted and dedicated as a nonprofit sanctuary and garden in 1929 by former President Calvin Coolidge. Its 157 acres of landscaped gardens and natural area lie atop the highest point in peninsular Florida and surround an internationally known carillon tower. It is a unique experience for visitors to stroll along the quiet wooded paths while listening to the music of the bells.

Work/Learn Program Specifics: Horticulture interns rotate through different departments for on-the-job training in many areas. Work with the horticulture staff will be the major emphasis, learning gardening skills: pruning, weeding, watering, mowing, plant identification, and the use of power equipment. The Round Garden gives an opportunity to work with year-round floral displays. Interns will also help maintain the historic gardens at the Pinewood Estate, a part of Bok Tower Gardens, and explore the natural high pine vegetation of the garden's Pine Ridge Preserve. While working in the endangered plant program, interns learn propagation techniques and the latest in rare plant conservation. In addition, interns will have the opportunity to work with visitors while conducting garden tours for the education department. Interns may work on a special project of particular interest that is approved and overseen by a staff member. A written report is required at the end of the program.

Duration: Internships run for ten weeks, any time of the year, allowing for flexibility with your course schedule. Some work is scheduled on weekends.

Compensation and Perks: Interns receive a stipend of $170 per week, plus room and board. Interns will also have an opportunity to gain practical work experience in one of Florida's finest public gardens.

The Ideal Candidate: The program is primarily open to junior and senior students enrolled in a horticulture or related program. They are looking for individuals with enthusiasm and a commitment to the horticulture profession, who are willing to work hard in all areas of the garden.

Making It Happen: Call for application forms. Send completed application, resume, cover letter stating career goals and reasons for applying, and transcripts. Deadlines: spring—January 15; summer—April 15; fall—July 15; and winter—October 15.

Contact Information: Internship Director • Bok Tower Gardens • 1151 Tower Blvd. • Lake Wales, FL 33853-3412 • Phone: (813) 676-1408 • Fax: (813) 676-6770

Bradford Woods

REGION/HQ: Great Lakes/Indiana • **CATEGORY:** Experiential Education • **POSITION TYPE:** Internship/Seasonal • **DURATION:** Year-Round • **IDEAL CANDIDATE:** College Students, Career Changers, Foreigners • **APPLICANT POOL:** 350/year • **APPLICANTS ACCEPTED:** 100/year

BRADFORD WOODS IS OWNED and operated by Indiana University's Bloomington campus through the Outdoor Education, Recreation, and Camping Center. Programs include residential outdoor education and school camping, residential summer camping, challenge education, group development and managerial training, accessibility training and research programs, and outdoor research laboratory. The campus is also home to Camp Riley, a summer residential camping program serving children and adults with disabilities.

Area and Working Environment: The facility is located on 2,400 wooded acres in south-central Indiana, twenty-five miles north of Indiana University's Bloomington campus.

Work/Learn Program Specifics: Environmental education/recreation interns participate in an intensive three-week training program, teach in the residential environmental education program for elementary students, and facilitate residential and one-day challenge education programs for junior high, high school, and college students. Other responsibilities include assisting with the development of Nature Center displays and programs, participating in professional conferences, completing a season project, and gaining experience in non-program areas of operation which include administration, clerical, food service, and maintenance chores. Seasonal positions include activities coordinator, head counselor, instructors and assistants (creative arts, nature, outdoor living skills, waterfront, adventure challenge, and recreation), cabin head, and cabin counselor. Summer camp internships include recreation administration, therapeutic recreation, and adventure/recreation.

Duration: Spring and fall session—February to May (challenge education and environmental education); summer—May to August (camping programs); winter—November to February (retreat services).

Compensation and Perks: Salary is commensurate with training and experience, ranging from $50 to $200 per week. Room and board, laundry services, and use of facilities and equipment are the biggest perks.

The Ideal Candidate: They prefer applicants who have a background in education, recreation, outdoor recreation, therapeutic recreation, allied health, creative arts, counseling, ecology, natural/earth sciences, natural history, forestry, or environmental studies. CPR and first aid certification is preferred, and all candidates must be at least eighteen years old.

Making It Happen: Call for application materials. Upon receiving application and references, the applicant will be contacted to arrange an interview. Rolling deadlines. Call Jo Burns for summer camp positions.

Contact Information: Margaret Lincoln, Environmental Education Coordinator • Bradford Woods • 5040 State Road 67 North • Martinsville, IN 46151 • Phone: (765) 342-2915 • Fax: (765) 349-1086

Brookfield Zoo

REGION/HQ: Great Lakes/Illinois • **CATEGORY:** Zoo • **POSITION TYPE:** Internship • **DURATION:** Year-Round • **IDEAL CANDIDATE:** College Students • **APPLICANT POOL:** 70–100/year • **APPLICANTS ACCEPTED:** 15–25/term

BROOKFIELD ZOO IS A large zoological park situated on 215 acres and houses over 2,500 animals representing over 400 species of mammals, birds, reptiles, and amphibians. It boasts realistic exhibits designed to promote animal conservation. A world-renowned institution, Brookfield Zoo's mission is "to enhance appreciation of the earth's biological heritage by providing for the recreation and education of the people, the conservation of wildlife and the discovery of biological knowledge."

Work/Learn Program Specifics: For those interested in a zoo career, interns can work in one of these departments: Small Mammal House, the Swamp, Australia House, Animal Hospital, Children's Zoo, Conservation Biology, Birds, Hoofed Stock, Primates, Animal Commissary, or Fragile Kingdom. The program strives to teach the art of maintaining animal well-being and health. Interns interact with the public, directing them to exhibits and answering questions on animals. Programs in non-animal departments include Education, Graphic Arts, Exhibit Design, Marketing, and Public Relations. All interns will keep a journal, and some will work on a special project.

Duration: Interns can work six to twelve weeks. Winter and fall internships are the least competitive.

Compensation and Perks: Interns have access to visiting specialists, who give speeches to the staff. Other perks include an employee pass—which allows interns into the zoo—free parking, use of the zoo library, and discounts on food and gifts.

The Ideal Candidate: Interns must have completed two years of college and convey a career interest in animals.

Making It Happen: Call for an application form. Submit cover letter, resume, completed application form, transcript, and references. Deadlines: winter—December 1; summer—February 1; and fall—August 1.

Contact Information: Jan Rizzo, Intern Program Coordinator • Brookfield Zoo • Chicago Zoological Society • 3300 S. Golf Rd. • Brookfield, IL 60513 • Phone: (708) 485-0263 • Fax: (708) 485-3532 • Alternate: (312) 242-2630

Callaway Gardens

REGION/HQ: Southeast/Georgia • **CATEGORY:** Botanical Garden • **POSITION TYPE:** Internship • **DURATION:** Spring and Summer • **IDEAL CANDIDATE:** College Students, Career Changers, Foreigners • **APPLICANT POOL:** 50+/year • **APPLICANTS ACCEPTED:** 12/year

CALLAWAY GARDENS, a man-made landscape in a unique natural setting, was conceived and created by Cason J. Callaway and his wife, Virginia Hand Callaway, for the benefit of humanity. The purpose is to provide a wholesome family environment where all may find beauty, relaxation, inspiration, and a better understanding of the living world.

Area and Working Environment: Pine Mountain is a rural community of 1,500 located 75 miles southwest of Atlanta. The cities of LaGrange and Columbus can be reached by a thirty-minute drive from Pine Mountain. Many employees find bicycles ideal for commuting to work and for recreation in the gardens.

Work/Learn Program Specifics: Education interns conduct and assist with education programs in home horticulture and natural history. Programs include nature and natural history (on topics such as turtles and snakes) and horticulture interpretation, walks, hikes, demonstrations, and workshops. Horticulture interns are involved in the practical, day-to-day maintenance of the gardens. Work in grounds maintenance, conservatories, greenhouses, trails, and the vegetable garden is assigned on a rotational basis. Interns' daily responsibilities include manual labor and equipment operation, plus exposure to a wealth of native and exotic plants, cultural techniques and technologies, and horticulture professionals. In all programs, interns attend biweekly classes and complete intern projects and journals.

Duration: Spring internships run from March through August; summer positions run late May through August.

Compensation and Perks: Interns will be paid on a biweekly basis. Housing and utilities are provided by the gardens. Benefits available to interns include free gardens and beach admission, access to recreation and sports facilities on a space-available basis, employee discounts in the restaurants and shops on the property, and use of the education department library for research, reading, and work in progress.

The Ideal Candidate: Education candidates must speak and write well, enjoy meeting and teaching a variety of people, and possess enthusiasm, flexibility, and a love of the outdoors. Education applicants come from a variety of backgrounds, including horticulture, natural history, forestry, botany, education, agriculture, entomology, ecology, and landscape design. Horticulture candidates have a background in landscape design, horticulture, entomology, botany, forestry, and related areas.

Making It Happen: Send resume and cover letter describing career goals, professional interests, and reasons for seeking employment with Callaway. You will then receive an application, which should be returned with three letters of recommendation. All application materials must be submitted before the deadline. Deadlines: spring—February 1; summer—March 1. Notification is by April 15.

Contact Information: Gardens Director • Callaway Gardens • P.O. Box 2000 • Pine Mountain, GA 31822-2000 • Phone: (706) 663-5140 • Fax: (706) 663-5004

Center for Coastal Studies

REGION/HQ: Northeast/Massachusetts • **CATEGORY:** Marine Science • **POSITION TYPE:** Internship • **DURATION:** Summer • **IDEAL CANDIDATE:** College Students, Career Changers, Foreigners • **APPLICANT POOL:** 80–100/year • **APPLICANTS ACCEPTED:** 2–4/year

THE CENTER FOR COASTAL STUDIES is a nonprofit organization for research, education, and conservation in the coastal and marine environments. The center supports the idea that wise conservation policy and successful educational outreach must be formulated in conjunction with responsible science. The center is known for its progressive and innovative programs in scientific research, regional conservation initiatives, and its rugged individualism.

Area and Working Environment: The center is located on the tip of Cape Cod, in the midst of a variety of coastal and marine ecosystems.

Work/Learn Program Specifics: Interns in the program may spend about 40 percent of their time engaged in fieldwork on the center's directed research cruises. During these cruises, interns serve as data collectors, learning the basics of field data gathering and system survey techniques. Besides the excitement of fieldwork, the program includes fundamental lab tasks, library research, and report writing. Interns spend as much as 35 percent of their time on various tasks, depending on their projects, in areas such as darkroom production, plankton analysis, and computer data entry. Interns also complete readings of texts and research papers in general ecology and basic marine biology. In addition, all interns at the center are exposed to administrative operations of a nonprofit institution, such as grants management, fund-raising, public relations, and membership management. Most interns work on a project which requires 25 percent of their time. Projects are part of the ongoing research at the center.

Duration: Interns work six days per week engaged in their various assignments. The duration of an internship is generally for a three-month period in the summer.

Compensation and Perks: The center is able to provide communal housing and a modest stipend of $75 per week. Interns also receive discounts on merchandise at their Whale and Dolphin Shop.

The Ideal Candidate: Applicants must have completed at least two years of college, and have backgrounds in biology, zoology, or wildlife ecology.

Making It Happen: Application information and forms should be obtained from the center in the fall of the year preceding the internship. Send completed application, resume, a written statement outlining your interests in the center's program, two recommendations (one from a biology professor), transcripts, and a $10 nonrefundable processing fee payable to the Center for Coastal Studies. Deadline: late January/early February.

INSIDER TIPS: *The applicant needs a strong academic record, must be mature, and be able to get along with others while working and living in close quarters. Recommendations from mentors should be strong and enthusiastic about the applicant's capabilities.*

Contact Information: Internship Coordinator • Center for Coastal Studies • 59 Commercial St. • P.O. Box 1036 • Provincetown, MA 02657 • Phone: (508) 487-3622

Central Wisconsin Environmental Station

REGION/HQ: Great Lakes/Wisconsin • **CATEGORY:** Environmental Education • **POSITION TYPE:** Internship • **DURATION:** Year-Round • **IDEAL CANDIDATE:** College Students, Career Changers, Foreigners • **APPLICANT POOL:** Varies • **APPLICANTS ACCEPTED:** Varies

THE CENTRAL WISCONSIN Environmental Station is a K–12 environmental learning center sponsored by the University of Wisconsin, Stevens Point, through the College of Natural Resources. Programming for groups, on a daily or residential basis, is available throughout the school year. Through hands-on environmental education activities, the station seeks to provide a foundation for the study of ecological principles and concepts as they relate to people and their environment. Over 10,000 children annually participate in school programs at the station.

Area and Working Environment: The station is located on 300 wooded acres on beautiful Sunset Lake, just seventeen miles east of Stevens Point.

Work/Learn Program Specifics: Environmental education/interpretation interns serve as regular staff members and are expected to work with all groups having programs at the station. In this capacity, the intern will provide instruction in environmental studies for groups of K–12 students, direct K–12 programs one day per week, be involved in a variety of administrative responsibilities, and work with weekend groups. Summer staff counselors and specialists are responsible for carrying out overall camp operation, with an emphasis

on environmental education in the residential camp setting. Types of activities conducted vary with the type of camp offered: nature adventure (seven- to thirteen-year-olds), natural resource careers workshop (fifteen- to eighteen-year-olds), or a two-week camp for children with learning disabilities.

Duration: Internships are available for the spring (mid-late January to mid-May) or fall (early September to late December). Summer staff positions run from late May to mid-late August.

Compensation and Perks: Interns will receive a $1,500 stipend, plus an additional $300 living allowance. On-site housing may be available, and some meals are provided. Summer staff pay ranges from $120 to $140 per week, depending on experience and qualifications, plus room and board. All summer staff are expected to live on-site during the employment period.

The Ideal Candidate: Intern applicants must have reached at least their junior year and have completed course work in methods of environmental education or interpretation. Previous practical experience in environmental education, outdoor education, or natural history interpretation is desirable. An understanding of ecological principles and concepts is necessary. Summer staff applicants should have training or experience in one or more of the following areas: recreational activities, environmental education, waterfront supervision, backpacking, canoeing, arts and crafts, first aid, field sports, campfires, or field trips. Preference will be given to applicants with a college background.

Making It Happen: Call for application and further information.

Contact Information: Patty Dreier, Program Director • Central Wisconsin Environmental Station • 7290 County MM • Amherst Junction, WI 54407 • Phone: (715) 824-2428 • Fax: (715) 824-3201

Chicago Botanic Garden

REGION/HQ: Great Lakes/Illinois • **CATEGORY:** Botanical Garden • **POSITION TYPE:** Internship • **DURATION:** Year-Round • **IDEAL CANDIDATE:** College Students, Career Changers, Foreigners • **APPLICANT POOL:** 300/year • **APPLICANTS ACCEPTED:** 25/year

THE CHICAGO BOTANIC GARDEN, recognized for the most diverse botanic garden internship in North

America, is a dynamic horticultural landmark. The garden maintains an extensive collection of herbaceous and woody plants ranging from temperate to tropical. The demonstration, display, and propagation areas hold a reputation for excellence in design, collections, grounds maintenance, integrated pest management, and plant production. The garden's mission is to stimulate and develop an interest in and appreciation for gardening, horticulture, botany, and conservation.

Area and Working Environment: The garden encompasses 385 acres in Glencoe, just 23 miles north of downtown Chicago. Its unique design of islands and water attracts more than a half-million visitors annually and provides a dramatic setting for the interaction of plants and people.

Work/Learn Program Specifics: Horticulture interns work in garden operations, including maintenance, propagation, greenhouse and nursery production, pest control, taxonomy, Japanese garden, fruits and vegetables, aquatics, roses, arboriculture, turf, and bulbs. Horticultural therapy interns assist with horticultural therapy program development, workshop presentation, program evaluation, maintenance of the enabling garden, garden design, and greenhouse maintenance for the only community-based program in the country. Conservation Ecology interns gain practical experience in conservation management of woodlands or prairies and wetlands. Education interns have an opportunity to learn and teach within the framework of one of the largest and most innovative education programs in a public garden. Graphic design interns work with a design team on a variety of projects.

Duration: Internships are three to twelve months long, offered continually throughout the year. Interns will work thirty-seven to forty hours per week, with occasional weekend assignments.

Compensation and Perks: Compensation is $6 per hour for most positions (graphic design and education positions are volunteer positions). Interns have the use of library and research facilities and may attend seminars, classes, and field trips. The garden will help you find affordable housing in the area during your stay with them.

The Ideal Candidate: Applicants should be enthusiastic, energetic, positive-thinking, and willing to "grow" with the gardens. Preference given to those with backgrounds in horticulture, botany, ecology, or conservation.

Making It Happen: Call or write for application form. Applications should be submitted at least three months before starting date for most positions. Applications for summer positions should be received by March 1. Include three letters of reference, a one-page resume, college transcripts, and a short essay describing your long-term career goals and why you are interested in an internship at the garden.

Contact Information: Cynthia Baker, Horticulture Training Manager • Chicago Botanic Garden • P.O. Box 400 • Glencoe, IL 60022-0400 • Phone: (708) 835-8300 • Fax: (708) 835-1635

Christodora-Manice Education Center

REGION/HQ: Northeast/New York • **CATEGORY:** Education • **POSITION TYPE:** Internship • **DURATION:** Spring-Fall • **IDEAL CANDIDATE:** College Students, Career Changers, Retired Folks, Foreigners • **APPLICANT POOL:** Varies • **APPLICANTS ACCEPTED:** Varies

CHRISTODORA WAS FOUNDED as a non-sectarian, youth-oriented settlement house on the Lower East Side of Manhattan in 1897 and has been involved in camping programs, primarily for New York City youth, since 1908. This nonprofit provides challenging and rewarding environmental learning experiences to motivated urban youths, who generally come from economically or experientially disadvantaged families in New York City. The center is a small, high-quality residential center in the Berkshire Mountains, with a strong emphasis on environmental education and adventure programs. The center is unique in that at any time it works with a maximum of thirty-six students taught by a minimum of six staff, giving an excellent six-to-one student-to-staff ratio.

Work/Learn Program Specifics: Field teachers educate and facilitate the growth, understanding, and development of students (aged eleven to eighteen) in program areas such as environmental sciences, wilderness programs, group initiatives, and leadership training. This can also include supervision of overnight trips and wilderness expeditions. Outdoor education interns assist field teachers in program areas while developing skills to teach their own lessons in a supervised setting. Wilderness leadership interns supervise and co-lead six- to nineteen-day courses with field teachers.

Duration: May 1 to October 30.

Compensation and Perks: Field teachers receive a stipend of $250 per week; while interns receive $125

per week. Room, board, and insurance coverage are also provided.

The Ideal Candidate: Field Teachers applicants must have a BS or BA degree. Outdoor education interns must have completed one year of college, and wilderness leadership positions require a minimum of two years of college completed. All positions require a strong interest in the wilderness, interpretation, and experiential education. Current Red Cross safety certificates in first aid, CPR, and lifeguarding are preferred.

Making It Happen: Submit resume, cover letter, and three references.

Contact Information: Director • Christodora-Manice Education Center • 666 Broadway, 9th Floor • New York, NY 10012 • Phone: (212) 529-6868 • Fax: (212) 353-2052

Clearwater

REGION/HQ: Northeast/New York • **CATEGORY:** Sailing • **POSITION TYPE:** Unique Experience • **DURATION:** Year-Round • **IDEAL CANDIDATE:** High School Students, College Students, Career Changers • **APPLICANT POOL:** Varies • **APPLICANTS ACCEPTED:** Varies

CLEARWATER CONDUCTS environmental education, advocacy programs, and celebrations to protect the Hudson River, its tributaries, and related bodies of water and to create awareness of the estuary's complex relationship with the coastal zone. Their flagship, the sloop *Clearwater* (a magnificent 106-foot replica of boats that sailed the Hudson over 100 years ago) is a classroom of waves, carrying unique programs on history, biology, and environmental science to nearly 20,000 adults and children every year.

Work/Learn Program Specifics: Becoming a sailing apprentice involves intense training in the tasks expected of *Clearwater*'s deck crew and in leading groups during education sails. Education Assistants work with professional educators to learn how to conduct the environmental education program. You'll study the ecology of the Hudson, the use of sampling gear, and how to engage and excite students in education activities. Everyone will participate in all crew activities, including education, sailing, and maintenance. You'll also be given the opportunity to contribute your own special talents to the overall effort. Crew positions are available as first, second, and third mate, bosun, engineer, and cook.

Duration: The main sailing season begins mid-April and winds up in November, although positions are available year-round. Crew positions—four months; education assistants—two months; sailing apprentices—one month; and interns/volunteers—flexible time frame. The boat sails seven days per week; you'll only work five days per week.

Compensation and Perks: Apprentices and education assistants receive room and board on the sloop, plus a stipend of $25 per week (in the winter the stipend is $50 per week). Crew position stipends range from $140 to $300 per week. The living quarters are rustic, featuring open bunks, no showers (except, of course, for the ocean), composting, and "unique" sanitary facilities. Meals are cooked over a wood stove, and most are generally vegetarian.

The Ideal Candidate: Candidates must be sixteen years or older and willing and able to work outdoors eight to ten hours per day. Great strength and sailing skill are not as important as coordination, common sense, and an enthusiasm for learning. The ability to deal intelligently with the sloop's hundreds of passengers and casual visitors and to live and work cooperatively in a close and sometimes stressful environment is critical.

Making It Happen: Call for application materials and current deadlines.

INSIDER TIPS: *It's recommended you volunteer for one week to see what it's like before you commit to other positions.*

Contact Information: Cindy Smith, Captain • Clearwater • 112 Market St. • Poughkeepsie, NY 12601-4095 • Phone: (914) 454-7673 • Fax: (914) 454-7953 • Toll Free: (800) 677-5667 • E-mail: clrwtr@clearwater.org • Web Site: www.clearwater.org

The Conservancy of Southwest Florida

REGION/HQ: Southeast/Florida • **CATEGORY:** Conservation • **POSITION TYPE:** Internship • **DURATION:** Year-Round • **IDEAL CANDIDATE:** College Students • **APPLICANT POOL:** 250/year • **APPLICANTS ACCEPTED:** 24/year

"WORKING TO CONSERVE the biodiversity, environmental quality, and natural resources of Southwest Florida's native ecosystems for present and future generations." Since 1965, The Conservancy of Southwest Florida has served as the region's environmental leader, spearheading the conservation of more than 300,000 acres of environmentally sensitive land. In addition to an environmental protection and research division, this progressive organization includes two nature centers, a wildlife rehabilitation center, and an environmental education department.

Area and Working Environment: The climate of Collier County is subtropical, with a strong marine influence from the Gulf of Mexico. The average annual temperature is approximately seventy-five degrees and rainfall averages about fifty-four inches annually, with most precipitation occurring during the summer.

Work/Learn Program Specifics: Internships available at Briggs Nature Center: Naturalists lead interpretive canoe, boat, and beach programs for children and adults. Summer day camp staff develops and implements several week-long specialty day camps for middle school students on canoeing and marine ecology.

Internships at Naples Nature Center: Environmental education programs naturalists teach ecology of south Florida to preschool, elementary, and middle school children. Environmental protection positions include water quality technician, sea turtle monitoring intern, helping coordinate projects with state land acquisition agents, and supervision of volunteers. Nature center museum interns provide interpretation to museum visitors and care for live animal and aquatic collections. Outdoor interpreters educate visitors about south Florida's unique subtropical ecosystem and care for trails. Summer day camp staff teach ecology of south Florida to elementary-aged children. Wildlife rehabilitation center interns assist in care and treatment of injured and orphaned wildlife, along with facility maintenance and participation in education programs.

Compensation and Perks: Interns are paid $823.34 per month and all are required to live in conservancy housing. The value of this housing ($265 per month) will be subtracted from your paycheck. Perks include uniform allotment, some mileage reimbursement, and TC membership.

The Ideal Candidate: Applicants must be college students or graduates with a background in biology, ecology, conservation, wildlife, research, teaching, elementary education, environmental education/science, marine science, or a related field. Applicants who are quick and eager learners and enjoy rustic living conditions are preferred.

Making It Happen: Send cover letter (which describes why you want the internship you are applying to and

what you can contribute), resume, and self-addressed/stamped envelope. Rolling deadlines.

INSIDER TIPS: *Prefer hearty souls who like rustic settings.*

Contact Information: Sharon Truluck, Human Resources Manager • The Conservancy of Southwest Florida • 1450 Merrihue Dr. • Naples, FL 34102 • Phone: (941) 262-0304 • Fax: (941) 262-0672

Conservation & Research Center

REGION/HQ: Southeast/Virginia • **CATEGORY:** Zoo • **POSITION TYPE:** Internship • **DURATION:** Year-Round • **IDEAL CANDIDATE:** College Students, Career Changers, Foreigners • **APPLICANT POOL:** Varies • **APPLICANTS ACCEPTED:** Varies

THE NATIONAL ZOO'S Conservation & Research Center (CRC) is dedicated to the conservation and captive breeding of endangered species. The center maintains breeding populations of over thirty species of endangered birds and mammals, including Przewalski's horse, Eld's deer, black-footed ferret, Guam rail, and several species of Hawaiian birds. In response to increasing requests for practical and intensive experience in conservation biology, the CRC has established a Conservation Biology Internship Program, which focuses on the management of endangered species in captivity and the study of threatened species in their natural habitats. The internship program provides interns with experience in working with zoo, veterinary, and wildlife professionals in a unique institutional setting.

Work/Learn Program Specifics: Captive Management of Endangered Species: Interns work with breeding programs, assist staff in the daily care and husbandry of captive species, assist in record keeping, and assist with animal observations and data analysis. International Conservation Training: Assist the coordinator and instructors for the wildlife management training course and possibly the zoo management course. Interns aid in screening of applicants, researching grants, travel logistics, and preparation for courses. Veterinary and Reproduction Science: Working in the veterinary hospital at CRC, interns assist in endocrine research as it relates to the breeding of endangered species. Animal Behavior: Working with either captive stock or a natural population, interns study reproductive behavior and mating systems. Wildlife Conservation Research: Interns will assist field ecology projects of wild animal populations, including vegetation monitoring, large and small animal capture, and observations of wild animals.

Duration: The internship is a twelve-week, full-time commitment, offered year-round.

Compensation and Perks: All interns are housed at the Conservation Center, and some internships may include communal meals. The cost of the program, including room, partial board (M–F), and research expenses for the twelve-week period, is $1,250. Additional travel costs incurred for the International Conservation Training are the responsibility of the applicant. Partial and full scholarships are available. All interns may attend weekly seminars and special seminars.

The Ideal Candidate: Minimum qualifications for all internships include undergraduate coursework in biology, wildlife management, or animal science.

Making It Happen: Write for application packet. Deadlines: spring—November 15, summer—February 15, fall—June 15, and winter—September 15. Notification of acceptance will be one month after the deadline for each term.

Contact Information: Conservation Intern Program • Conservation & Research Center • National Zoo, Smithsonian Institution • 1500 Remount Rd. • Front Royal, VA 22630 • Phone: (703) 635-6500 • Fax: (703) 635-6551 • E-mail: nzpcrc01@sivm.si.edu

Dahlem Environmental Education Center

REGION/HQ: Great Lakes/Michigan • **CATEGORY:** Nature Center • **POSITION TYPE:** Internship/Seasonal • **DURATION:** Year-Round • **IDEAL CANDIDATE:** College Students, Career Changers, Foreigners • **APPLICANT POOL:** 80/year • **APPLICANTS ACCEPTED:** 9/year

THE DAHLEM ENVIRONMENTAL Education Center is a nonprofit organization that bridges the gap between the human and the natural environment. Operating on Jackson Community College property, the center generates its own revenue via memberships, user fees, gifts, grants, fund-raising projects, and special events. A professional staff, supplemented with seasonal interns and trained community volunteers, provides educational services for more than 26,000 visitors annually, including more than 400 school and youth groups. They have an award-winning elementary education curriculum and host the Bluebird Festival in early March, which attracts over 5,000 visitors.

Area and Working Environment: The center is located less than ninety minutes from Lakes Michigan, Erie, and

Huron; within forty-five minutes of Lansing and Ann Arbor; and sits on a rural setting with plenty of opportunities for outdoor enthusiasts of all persuasions.

Work/Learn Program Specifics: Naturalist interpretive interns are exposed to all aspects of nature-center operations, and primarily will be teaching in the center's award-winning school program. Interns are also afforded the opportunity to experience exhibit design, assist in program development, write for nature-center publications, provide animal care, participate in special events, and work with volunteers. Summer ecology camp counselors develop and implement their own activity plans for ten to twelve elementary school–age campers each week. Staff training is provided, but previous teaching/programming experience is required. Summer wildlife biologist interns coordinate the research and volunteer staff in the center's county-wide bluebird recovery project. Banding and computer experience is helpful, but training will be provided.

Duration: Positions are seasonal, forty hours per week.

Compensation and Perks: Free on-site housing and a weekly stipend of $150 to $200 is provided. You will also gain exposure to and have the opportunity to develop or polish skills through direct experience with resources and interpretive techniques in a cooperative teaching/learning environment.

The Ideal Candidate: Candidates should have college-level training in biology, environmental education, natural history interpretation, field biology, wildlife management, or related fields. Experience working with children in an outdoor educational setting is preferred. Applicants must be responsible, flexible, creative, enthusiastic, and have an innovative personality with a friendly teaching style (i.e., a "do and discover," rather than a "show and tell" teaching style).

Making It Happen: Call or write for application form and job announcement. Written application, resume, and list of three references are required. Telephone interviews are scheduled with best qualified applicants each season. Deadlines: spring—January; summer—April; fall—November; and winter—December.

INSIDER TIPS: *Meet the application deadlines … and be sure to highlight all related experience on your application (this is used for screening).*

Contact Information: Diane Valen, Program Coordinator • Dahlem Environmental Education Center • 7117 S. Jackson Rd. • Jackson, MI 49201 • Phone: (517) 782-3453 • Fax: (517) 796-8633

A pond-frog cannot imagine the ocean, nor can a summer insect conceive of ice. Remember, you are restricted by your own learning. —CHUANG-TSU

Deep Portage Conservation Reserve

REGION/HQ: Great Lakes/Minnesota • **CATEGORY:** Environmental Education • **POSITION TYPE:** Seasonal • **DURATION:** Year-Round • **IDEAL CANDIDATE:** College Students, Career Changers, Foreigners • **APPLICANT POOL:** 30/term • **APPLICANTS ACCEPTED:** 4/term

• •

DEEP PORTAGE CONSERVATION Reserve is a 6,107-acre center for natural resources management, conservation education, outdoor recreation, scientific research, and community service. Each year thousands of students from Midwest schools explore at the reserve in conservation and environmental education activities taught by Deep Portage faculty. In addition, Deep Portage serves area residents and visitors with weekly classes, interpretive programs, wildflower garden displays, land-use demonstrations, and recreational opportunities for birding, hiking, hunting, and skiing.

Area and Working Environment: Hackensack is located in the heart of north-central Minnesota's tourist country with hundreds of lakes, resorts, and miles of recreational trails.

Work/Learn Program Specifics: Duties include preparing and presenting interpretive and environmental education programs for school groups and the general public, hosting visitors in the interpretive center, assisting professional staff in curriculum development and assessment, and special project work. The recreation program teaches every kind of outdoor recreation skill for appreciating lake and forest country. You will learn how to become a forester, wildlife manager, recreation leader, or a K–12 formal-education teacher.

Duration: Positions are offered year-round (beginning in January, June, or September) and last from three to nine months.

Compensation and Perks: Staff members receive a $125 to $200-per-week stipend, plus room and board.

The Ideal Candidate: Along with enthusiasm, applicants should have a variety of skills and, whenever possible, certifications in these skills.

Making It Happen: Submit cover letter, resume, and three letters of reference at least twelve weeks before your requested start date.

Contact Information: Joan Peterson, Program Leader • Deep Portage Conservation Reserve • RR 1, Box 129 • Hackensack, MN 56452-9720 • Phone: (218) 682-2325 • Fax: (218) 682-3121 • E-mail: portage@uslink. net • Web Site: www.uslink.net/~portage

Dodge Nature Center

REGION/HQ: Great Lakes/Minnesota • **CATEGORY:** Nature Center • **POSITION TYPE:** Internship • **DURATION:** Year-Round • **IDEAL CANDIDATE:** College Students, Career Changers, Foreigners • **APPLICANT POOL:** Varies • **APPLICANTS ACCEPTED:** 3/term

• •

THE DODGE NATURE CENTER is a private nature center with a heavy emphasis on environmental education programs for primary schools and the community family audience. The goal is to instill an awareness of and a sense of stewardship for the natural environment. The center, which covers 315 acres, has a very successful model environmental education program involving local schools, organizations, and families. More than 50,000 individual visits are made to the facility annually.

Work/Learn Program Specifics: Environmental education and natural history interpretation interns lead environmental education– and natural history–oriented programs, assist interpretive naturalists, and provide small-animal care, greenhouse/horticultural work, and prairie/woodland management. Interns also assist with programs presented to the public on weekends and special events, such as Earth Day and festivals.

Duration: The internship duration is three to four months or a school-calendar semester/quarter.

Compensation and Perks: You will receive a stipend of $100 per week. Evaluations and letters of recommendations are provided at the end of your term.

The Ideal Candidate: Candidate must have knowledge of natural history, ability to work with or experience teaching children, and a career interest in environmental education. In addition, candidates must have completed at least two years in a related postsecondary program.

Making It Happen: Send letter (with list of relevant/completed college courses) and resume. Rolling deadlines.

Contact Information: Internship Coordinator • Dodge Nature Center • 1795 Charlton St. • West St. Paul, MN 55118 • Phone: (612) 455-4531 • Fax: (612) 455-2575

Eagle's Nest Foundation

REGION/HQ: Southeast/North Carolina • **CATEGORY:** Experiential Education • **POSITION TYPE:** Seasonal • **DURATION:** Year-Round • **IDEAL CANDIDATE:** College Students, Career Changers, Foreigners • **APPLICANT POOL:** 200/term • **APPLICANTS ACCEPTED:** 60/term

EAGLE'S NEST IS AN EXPERIENTIAL outdoor education foundation, with a mission to promote the natural world and the betterment of human character. Eagle's Nest supports Eagle's Nest Camp for boys and girls (celebrating more than seventy years), Birch Tree Fall and Spring Enrichment Programs for school groups, and the Outdoor Academy, a semester program in the southern Appalachians for tenth graders. This school away from school focuses on environmental education, regional studies, and the arts, and centers students and faculty in a close community life. Basically, the Eagle's Nest Foundation is about teaching and nurturing, pure and simple.

Area and Working Environment: Nestled at the base of the Shining Rock escarpment, Eagle's Nest is situated on 180 acres of wooded land that overlooks the Little River Valley. Eagle's Nest is in a mountainous and rustic region of western North Carolina where there are many places to rock-climb, white-water paddle, and soak up the culture of the southern Appalachians. Evenings are cool; summer days are warm.

Work/Learn Program Specifics: There are three facets to Eagle's Nest: (1) Eagle's Nest Camp—staff members teach activities in the arts, music, and drama (batik, West African drum and dance, pottery, musical instrument making, raku—not your everyday arts and crafts class), wilderness (white-water canoeing on a handful of rivers, rock climbing, and backpacking), and athletics (emphasizing skill and teamwork, not competition). You will also double as a trip leader. You will develop/plan/set goals for the courses; then take teenagers on intense wilderness experiences, including hiking 100 miles of the Appalachian Trail, biking the Blue Ridge Parkway, service projects and cultural exchange in Mexico, climbing in Maine, summitting peaks in Colorado, mountain biking in Montana, paddling the chilly waters of northern Ontario, and so much more. (2) Birch Tree runs during the "off season" and staff provides participants with a customized program of natural history, experiential drama, wilderness adventure, and group initiatives. (3) Outdoor Academy teachers emphasize a broad spectrum of knowledge, skills, and attitudes in a college prepara-

tory curriculum of English, history, natural science, fine arts, foreign languages, and mathematics. It combines classroom activities inside and out, with experiential learning as its strength.

Duration: Hours are long but very rewarding, as you are working with kids who are eager to learn and do. Staff have one 24-hour day off per week and at least two hours off per day.

Compensation and Perks: You will receive $145 to $250 per week, plus room and board from their wonderful whole-foods kitchen, which includes meals for vegetarians and vegans. You will also live vivaciously in a community-centered and powered community. Fresh air, mountain music, laughter, and love abound. Other perks include workers' compensation, laundry, and ample time off.

The Ideal Candidate: They look for applicants with experience in outdoor and experiential education who have a strong desire to teach and play in the outdoors. High energy level and creativity are a must.

Making It Happen: Call for a staff application. Applications are reviewed December through January. Summer/Facility address: 43 Hart Rd., Pisgah Forest, NC 28768; (704) 877-4349. If you can't reach Paige, ask for Noni Wiate-Kucera, the Director!

INSIDER TIPS: *The most important aspect of Eagle's Nest is the community itself. Being responsible to the community is at the heart of life at ENF. Consequently, attitude is the most important attribute at Eagle's Nest, that is, a willingness to be a jack-of-all trades, have patience and love of children, a sense of good will and support of others, and a desire to develop one's own potential. It is a place that allows one to reap his or her own rewards.*

Contact Information: Paige Lester-Niles, Assistant Director • Eagle's Nest Foundation • 633 Summit St. • Winston-Salem, NC 27101 • Phone: (910) 761-1040 • Fax: (910) 727-0030 • Summer: (704) 877-4349 • Summer Fax: (704) 884-2788 • E-mail: page@netunlimited.net

Echo Hill Outdoor School

REGION/HQ: Northeast/Maryland • **CATEGORY:** Outdoor Education • **POSITION TYPE:** Internship • **DURATION:** Spring/Fall • **IDEAL CANDIDATE:** College Students • **APPLICANT POOL:** 50+/term • **APPLICANTS ACCEPTED:** 2–6/term

ECHO HILL OUTDOOR SCHOOL, established in 1972, rests on 172 acres of swampland that can be accessed for study by a ³/₄-mile-long wooden walkway. They have an extensive low-challenge course, a "Giant's Ladder" climb up to a zip line and an alpine tower climbing structure. They provide residential learning experiences designed to introduce children to the outdoors and create environmental awareness.

Area and Working Environment: The campus is located directly on the Chesapeake Bay on Maryland's eastern shore. The local culture is rich and focused primarily on life on the Bay.

Work/Learn Program Specifics: Interns will help out with all aspects of the program, from teaching to campus maintenance. Interns, for the most part, will assist teachers with classes and also hold residential responsibilities, like overseeing a tent group throughout a five-day stay.

Duration: Positions last three months, in the spring and fall.

Compensation and Perks: Interns receive a stipend plus room and board.

The Ideal Candidate: Individuals pursuing careers in the areas of education, recreation, and related work with youth are encouraged to apply.

Making It Happen: Send cover letter, resume, and three references.

INSIDER TIPS: *We are looking for creative, energetic, and enthusiastic people who love children of all ages and the outdoors. A strong science or adventure background is helpful because of the nature of our curriculum, which focuses on science, history and the human environment, and adventure.*

Contact Information: Jane Lohmann, Internship Director • Echo Hill Outdoor School • 13655 Bloomingneck Rd. • Worton, MD 21678 • Phone: (410) 348-5880 • Fax: (410) 348-2010

Fernwood Nature Center

REGION/HQ: Great Lakes/Michigan • **CATEGORY:** Nature Center • **POSITION TYPE:** Internship • **DURATION:** Spring/Fall • **IDEAL CANDIDATE:** College Students, Career Changers • **APPLICANT POOL:** 50/year • **APPLICANTS ACCEPTED:** 3/year

FERNWOOD IS A COMBINED 100-acre nature center, botanic garden, and arts and crafts center that provides a sense of environmental awareness, cultural appreciation, and education for the community. They host 30,000 public visitors per year, and 8,000 local school children visit for environmental education programs.

Area and Working Environment: Fernwood is beautifully set on the banks of the St. Joseph River, in scenic Berrien County in southwest Michigan.

Work/Learn Program Specifics: Intern naturalists conduct and lead nature walks and activities for children ranging from preschool to high school age, lead weekend programs for adults and families, develop displays, write articles, work on prairie reconstruction, and maintain nature trails. A project for the center is required, and interns are encouraged to utilize Fernwood's excellent resources to pursue special interests. Seasonal naturalists will develop and conduct natural history programs for school groups and weekend visitors, assist in supervision and training of interns, maintain and design educational displays, supervise care of animals, supervise and assist in the daily operations of the nature center, and provide grounds maintenance.

Duration: Intern positions are available each spring and fall, for a duration of thirteen weeks, forty hours a week. Seasonal naturalist positions run from late March through mid-November.

Compensation and Perks: Pay is $5.15 per hour for intern naturalists, $6.00 per hour for seasonal naturalists. Interns also receive housing, workshops, classroom training, and discounts in gift shops and the cafeteria.

The Ideal Candidate: Applicants should have an interest and training in natural history, ecology, biology, or related subjects, and must enjoy working with children outdoors.

Making It Happen: Submit cover letter, resume, and references. Spring and seasonal positions deadline: January 31; for the fall—July 1.

INSIDER TIPS: *Previous experience (paid or volunteer) in environmental education, or work with children, improves your chances tremendously. Also, a good knowledge of plant and animal identification is very helpful.*

Contact Information: Wendy Jones, Naturalist • Fernwood Nature Center • 13988 Range Line Rd. • Niles, MI 49120-9042 • Phone: (616) 695-6491 • Fax: (616) 695-6688 • Web Site: http://landtrust.org

Five Rivers MetroParks

REGION/HQ: Great Lakes/Ohio • **CATEGORY:** Outdoor Education • **POSITION TYPE:** Internship • **DURATION:** Varies • **IDEAL CANDIDATE:** College Students, Career Changers, Foreigners • **APPLICANT POOL:** 20/term • **APPLICANTS ACCEPTED:** 9/term

FIVE RIVERS METROPARKS offers internships and apprenticeships to further the park and recreation profession and to assist with career decisions. The intern program is designed to provide practical on-the-job experience in outdoor education and park management.

Area and Working Environment: The programs are at Wegerzyn Horticultural Center and Cox Arboretum MetroPark, horticultural facilities; Carriage Hill MetroPark, a living history farm and nature facility; Possum Creek MetroPark Farm, an educational farm; Germantown MetroPark, a large, rural park with an underground nature center; Wesleyan Nature Center, an inner-city nature center; or the North MetroParks.

Work/Learn Program Specifics: Positions are available in the following areas: Possum Creek (lead school tours or youth groups through the barn and on the trails), Carriage Hill (historical farm restoration and agriculture/farm maintenance), Cox Arboretum (horticultural education and grounds maintenance); Germantown MetroPark (natural history), North MetroParks (natural history); Wesleyan Nature Center (natural history); and Wegerzyn Horticultural Center (education). Interns are encouraged to work with their supervisor early in the internships to develop a special project, which is required of your position. In the past, special projects have included slide shows, displays or exhibits, research, production of a brochure, trail design and maintenance, or the planning and execution of a special program or event.

Duration: Internships last three months during the summer or nine months starting in the fall.

Compensation and Perks: The pay is $5 per hour, with free housing available at several work sites.

The Ideal Candidate: Internships are suitable for students majoring in outdoor education, interpretation, natural history, horticulture, living history, or recreation and park management. First priority will be given to students from two- or four-year colleges and graduate programs, who will receive credit for their internship. Apprenticeships are suitable for those seeking work experience and skill development in the above areas.

Making It Happen: Call to receive application. Return completed application along with your resume and references. A personal interview is generally conducted before hiring. Applications are reviewed as received; although, for summer positions, apply early (February or March).

INSIDER TIPS: *It is most difficult to obtain an internship during the summer due to the large number of applicants. I highly recommend considering an apprenticeship with us.*

Contact Information: Lyn Modic, Education Chief • Five Rivers MetroParks • 1375 E. Siebenthaler Ave. • Dayton, OH 45414 • Phone: (937) 275-7275 • Fax: (937) 278-8849 • Web Site: www.dayton.net/MetroParks

Foothill Horizons Outdoor School

REGION/HQ: Pacific Northwest/California • **CATEGORY:** Outdoor Education • **POSITION TYPE:** Internship • **DURATION:** Academic year • **IDEAL CANDIDATE:** College Students, Career Changers • **APPLICANT POOL:** 60/year • **APPLICANTS ACCEPTED:** 6/year

THE STANISLAUS COUNTY Office of Education operates Foothill Horizons Outdoor School for the sixth-grade students of the county. Throughout the year, classes of students, accompanied by their classroom teachers, spend an entire week (five school days) at the center. During this time, the students participate in a variety of activities to increase their knowledge and awareness of and sensitivity to nature. The students take part in nature classes, campfires, square dancing, free play, night hikes, and field trips.

Area and Working Environment: The 143-acre site is located at 2,500 feet (5 miles east of Sonora), primarily within an oak woodland ecosystem, including six species of deciduous and evergreen native oaks, large bull and ponderosa pines, and thick stands of beautiful manzanita. A creek runs through the site.

Work/Learn Program Specifics: The intern will observe a naturalist for the first week and team-teach the second week. From the third week on, the intern will lead a group of sixth graders on hikes, teaching them about ecology, conservation, Native American history and culture, and sensory awareness. The head naturalist will observe and evaluate each intern twice each semester. This is meant to further refine the intern's teaching technique. Interns are encouraged to use any and all resources available to improve their teaching, including Project Learning Tree and Project Wild workshops, regularly scheduled in-services, conferences, curriculum guides in the library and, of course, the knowledge of the naturalists.

Duration: Duration is from mid-August to mid-June, five days a week (M–F).

Compensation and Perks: Interns receive a $40-per-day stipend, plus room, board, health fund, and workers' compensation.

The Ideal Candidate: Applications will be accepted from upper-division college students or graduates concentrating their studies in the areas of natural and environmental sciences, resource management, parks and recreation, child development, education, or related areas.

Making It Happen: Submit cover letter, resume, and two letters of reference. The application process requires either an on-site visit and mini-teaching demo by the applicant or a phone interview and a videotaped lesson presented by the applicant to a group. If you are not willing to commit to the above options, Foothill Horizons will not consider your application. Positions are filled between March and June.

Contact Information: Dan Webster, Head Naturalist • Foothill Horizons Outdoor School • Stanislaus County Office Of Education • 21925 Lyons Bald Mountain Rd. • Sonora, CA 95370 • Phone: (209) 532-6673 • Fax: (209) 533-1390 • E-mail: foothill@sonnet.com • Web Site: http://stan-co.k12.ca.us/scoe/outdoor-ed/foothill

4-H Environmental Education Program

REGION/HQ: Southeast/Georgia • **CATEGORY:** Environmental Education • **POSITION TYPE:** Internship/Seasonal • **DURATION:** Spring/Fall • **IDEAL CANDIDATE:** College Students, Foreigners • **APPLICANT POOL:** Varies • **APPLICANTS ACCEPTED:** 40–45/year

THE 4-H ENVIRONMENTAL Education Program is part of Georgia's 4-H and Youth Program under the Georgia Cooperative Extension Service, and was first implemented at Rock Eagle 4-H Center in 1979. Over 250,000 students from 500 different schools have participated in the program, representing six southeastern states. The program is now established at four 4-H state facilities, including Rock Eagle, Jekyll Island, Wahsega, and Tybee Island.

Area and Working Environment: There are four sites you can work at: Rock Eagle—Central Georgia Piedmont; Jekyll Island—Coastal Barrier Island; Wahsega—North Georgia Mountains; and Tybee Island—Coastal Barrier Island.

Work/Learn Program Specifics: Environmental education and teacher/naturalist specialists teach interdisciplinary morning and afternoon outdoor and environmental education classes, provide leadership to schools participating in the program, conduct evening programs, and maintain teaching laboratories and classes. Extensive training in environmental education is provided.

Duration: Duration varies—some programs are up to nine months long—but generally they are just a semester's length.

Compensation and Perks: Stipend ranges from $160 to $200 per week, depending on location. Interns receive housing and food and have use of educational materials and contacts with school and state officials.

The Ideal Candidate: Applicants should have a genuine interest in children, a dynamic personality, well-developed communication skills, creativity, and leadership abilities. They should be working toward or have completed a bachelor's degree in education, natural science, environmental education, outdoor recreation, or a related field.

Making It Happen: Submit resume, including references and a cover letter. Rock Eagle and Wahsega deadlines: spring—October 15; fall—March 15; Jekyll Island—May 1; and Tybee Island: spring—November 15; fall—June 15. Contacts for each location: Rock Eagle, Cheryl Thompsen, 350 Rock Eagle Rd., NW, Eatonton, GA 31024-9599, (706) 485-2831, Fax: (706) 485-2191, 4henved@uga.cc.uga.edu; Wahsega, Thomas Grudowski, Route 8, Box 1820, Dahlonega, GA 30533, (706) 864-2050, EEEWAH@uga.cc.uga.edu; Jekyll Island, Donna Stewart, 201 S. Beachview Dr., Jekyll Island, GA 31527, (912) 635-4117, Fax: (912) 635-4135, Donnast@uga.cc.uga.edu; Tybee Island, Erik Thompson, P.O. Box 1477, Tybee Island, GA 31328, (912) 786-5534.

Contact Information: Diane Davies, State Coordinator • 4-H Environmental Education Program • 350 Rock Eagle Rd., NW • Eatonton, GA 31024-9599 • Phone: (706) 485-2831 • Fax: (706) 485-2191 • E-mail: ddavies@uga.cc.uga.edu

The Glacier Institute

REGION/HQ: Rocky Mountains/Montana
• **CATEGORY:** Environmental Education • **POSITION TYPE:** Internship/Seasonal • **DURATION:** Spring-Fall • **IDEAL CANDIDATE:** College Students, Career Changers, Retired Folks, Foreigners • **APPLICANT POOL:** Varies • **APPLICANTS ACCEPTED:** 11/year

THE GLACIER INSTITUTE is based at two facilities in and adjacent to Glacier Park in northwest Montana and is governed by a working board of directors who aren't afraid to get dirty. Outdoor enthusiasts will enjoy that most of their work is conducted outside, in beautiful country. The institute courses often bring in local natural resource specialists and employees from Montana Fish, Wildlife, and Parks, Flathead National Forest, Flathead Valley Community College, Glacier National History Association, and Glacier National Park.

Area and Working Environment: Both their facilities are rustic, historic sites in spectacular settings. Opportunities for river floating, hiking, wildlife viewing, and backcountry camping abound. During time off, the towns of Columbia Falls, Kalispell, and Whitefish are close enough for movies, restaurants, and shopping.

Work/Learn Program Specifics: As an intern, you are a full-fledged staff member, acting as a primary teacher of youth programs and an assistant during adult classes. At Big Creek, you will help with all organizational, programmatic, and facility aspects concerning on-site operations of the program. This includes cooking with students, teaching evening programs, creating and implementing curriculum, and helping with facility upkeep. At the field camp, you will fill a similar role. Responsibilities include staffing the office, accompanying instructors on field trips, trail/first aid support, and developing and teaching youth programs. As a teacher/naturalist at Big Creek, your responsibilities increase as you serve as a mentor to interns.

Duration: Programs run from the spring until fall (and interns work two to four months, up to seven months). The work schedule is very irregular and busy. There may be times with no programs and times when programs run nonstop.

Compensation and Perks: Interns—$175 per month; teacher/naturalists—$375 per month. Housing is provided, as well as food or a food stipend. Because they are a small organization, they rely heavily on staff creativity and input, with many opportunities to become involved in program enhancement and development.

The Ideal Candidate: Applicants should be at least nineteen years old and have two years of college or more and some prior experience teaching or working with youth. Interns must have CPR/first aid certification, and teacher/naturalists and the assistant to the director must have at least an advanced first aid certification.

Making It Happen: Call for job descriptions and application. Most interviews are done over the phone, but they prefer personal interviews if at all possible. Deadlines: spring and summer—January 31; fall—February 15.

INSIDER TIPS: *Staff members really enjoy working and living with people of all ages, are enthusiastic and energetic, love learning and being outside, and are creative and flexible. We need people who can be happy working and living in a residential, remote setting with rustic accommodations. Self-directed people who can work without much supervision and are willing to do anything will do very well in our program.*

Contact Information: Jenny Tollefson, Field Camp Director • The Glacier Institute • P.O. Box 7457 • Kalispell, MT 59904 • Phone: (406) 755-1211 • Fax: (406) 755-7154

Glen Helen Outdoor Education Center

REGION/HQ: Great Lakes/Ohio • **CATEGORY:** Environmental Education • **POSITION TYPE:** Internship • **DURATION:** Spring/Fall • **IDEAL CANDIDATE:** College Students, Career Changers, Foreigners • **APPLICANT POOL:** 100/year • **APPLICANTS ACCEPTED:** 10/term

GLEN HELEN OUTDOOR Education Center is a residential environmental education program for sixth grade students. They have six beautiful biotic communities and a raptor center, specializing in education and rehabilitation.

Area and Working Environment: The center is part of a 1,000-acre nature preserve in Yellow Springs.

Work/Learn Program Specifics: Naturalist interns plan and lead small groups of elementary-aged students in residential environmental education programs, care for hawks or owls in their raptor center, and actively participate in a comprehensive training program. After the naturalist internship is fulfilled, there is the possibility of a summer position.

Plan for gradual improvements, not spectacular leaps…a slow & steady stream of water, will, in time, erode the hardest rock.

221

Duration: Internships are offered from early January to early June or from mid-August to mid-December.

Compensation and Perks: Naturalists receive a stipend of $50 per week, plus room and board. Undergraduate or graduate credit is given through Antioch College, and tuition is waived. You will have full-time student status and have use of all college facilities.

The Ideal Candidate: Open to students who have completed two years of college and have an interest in working with children and the outdoors.

Making It Happen: Call for application materials. Send in completed application and you will be contacted for an interview. Rolling deadlines.

INSIDER TIPS: *Send in a well-written application and present yourself as a professional. Let me see that you spent quality time on the essays, and most importantly, ask questions if you have them.*

Contact Information: Gilbert DiSanto, Assistant Director • Glen Helen Outdoor Education Center • 1075 SR 343 • Yellow Springs, OH 45387 • Phone: (937) 767-7648 • Fax: (937) 767-6655 • E-mail: gdisanto@college.antioch.edu

Harbor Branch Oceanographic Institution, Inc.

REGION/HQ: Southeast/Florida • **CATEGORY:** Marine Science • **POSITION TYPE:** Internship • **DURATION:** Summer • **IDEAL CANDIDATE:** College Students, Foreigners • **APPLICANT POOL:** 120/year • **APPLICANTS ACCEPTED:** 10–15/year

HARBOR BRANCH IS A nonprofit institution established in 1971 primarily for research in the marine sciences and for the development of tools and systems for underwater oceanographic investigations. The institution is dedicated to exploring the marine environment, understanding ecological balances, and investigating humanity's impact on the environment. A major portion of the funding for the internship program is provided through the Link Foundation, founded in 1953 by Mr. and Mrs. Edwin A. Link.

Area and Working Environment: The institute is located on 500 acres along the Indian River lagoon portion of the Intracoastal Waterway, between Fort Pierce and Vero Beach, Florida.

Work/Learn Program Specifics: The summer internship program is designed to provide actual work experience in a research environment. The areas of study may include aquaculture, ocean engineering, marine biology, physical oceanography, environmental analysis and monitoring, marine natural products chemistry, cancer biology, microbiology, immunology, sponge physiology and taxonomy, or related research fields. Each intern will be assigned to work with a staff member in the appropriate area of interest. A project of mutual interest will be established, and a plan of action developed. At the completion of the program, each participant will be required to give an oral presentation and submit a comprehensive written report on their individual project.

Duration: The internship is a ten-week program, starting in early June and going through mid-August.

Compensation and Perks: Stipends: $200 per week for undergraduates; $280 per week for graduate students. Interns will be responsible for their own housing and transportation, although the local community college has inexpensive housing for $8 per night. These are single rooms in suites, with kitchens. The biggest perk of the internship is Florida sunshine and beaches!

The Ideal Candidate: Undergraduate and graduate students must be in good academic standing to apply. Applicants must be eighteen years of age, and non-U.S. citizens must have a current visa with authorization to work or be on an educational visa. Graduate interns must be enrolled in a graduate program or accepted to a program. Undergraduate interns must have completed at least two years of college and be seeking a four-year degree.

Making It Happen: Call for application (ask for extension 500). Send completed application, official transcript, three letters of reference from faculty, and a one-page essay outlining experience and career/research interests. Graduate candidates must submit proof of continuing education. Applications must be received by March 15; awards are announced on April 15.

INSIDER TIPS: *Identify potential supervisor and write or call before submitting your application (your application packet will have a list of supervisors). Engineers and chemists have a big edge.*

Contact Information: Susan B. Cook, JSJMECC Director • Harbor Branch Oceanographic Institution, Inc. • 5600 U.S. 1 North • Fort Pierce, FL 34946 • Phone: (407) 465-2400 • Fax: (407) 465-5743 • Home: (407) 595-9575 • E-mail: scook@hboi.edu • Web Site: www.hboi.edu

Hawthorne Valley Farm

REGION/HQ: Northeast/New York • **CATEGORY:** Environmental Education • **POSITION TYPE:** Internship/Seasonal • **DURATION:** Spring-Fall • **IDEAL CANDIDATE:** College Students, Career Changers, Foreigners • **APPLICANT POOL:** 35/year • **APPLICANTS ACCEPTED:** 16/year

• •

HAWTHORNE VALLEY FARM was founded in 1972 by a group of experienced educators and farmers who recognized a growing need to create a place where children and young people might experience life in its wholeness and gain the inner strength and the practical abilities which they would need as adults. At Hawthorne Valley, farmers, artists, and teachers working out the insights of Rudolf Steiner have joined together to create such a place. The bio-dynamic dairy farm, bakery, and cheese-making operation offers apprenticeship training in agriculture; the Hawthorne Valley School provides a Waldorf education for local children; and the visiting students program offers school classes and an experience of farm and country life. A four-acre market garden supplies two Community Support Agricultures, a green market sales in New York City and a retail health food store on the premises.

Area and Working Environment: The farm is located in upstate New York in the Toconic range, surrounded by rolling hills speckled with dairy farms. Hawthorne Valley Farm's 400 acres occupy a wide, sunlit valley that rises to wooded hills and is comprised of croplands, pastures, streams, and ponds.

Work/Learn Program Specifics: Environmental education interns join with the director, assistant director, and permanent staff to plan and lead daily activities. Preparation involves gathering the information, materials, and equipment needed for various activities, including animal feeding, barn cleaning, gardening, bread baking, horseback riding, and seasonal projects, such as maple sugaring or apple-cider pressing. Interns will be in charge of leading activities for small groups of children. Interns also share meals with the children and supervise house and dining hall cleaning tasks. Camp counselors can be group counselors, assistant group counselors, activity counselors, and lifeguard. Experience in horseback riding, craft and nature lore, farm work, camping, hiking, group games, and activities are skills most counselors can draw from.

Duration: Positions are available for an academic year (December/January they are closed) or for their sum-

mer camp. A semester or full year can be done. Scheduling allows for two-day weekends, giving staff members some time away from the program.

Compensation and Perks: Interns receive $200 per month, and camp counselors receive $1,000 per season. All staff receive room and family-style meals.

The Ideal Candidate: Applicants should have experience with children, and an interest in natural history and gardening/farming. They should possess an ability to work well with others, be enthusiastic, and have a love for children, the outdoors, and animals. Homesteading, music, orienteering, or storytelling skills are a plus.

Making It Happen: Call for application materials or send cover letter and resume. Rolling deadlines.

INSIDER TIPS: *Must be open to the philosophy under which we operate.*

Contact Information: Ruth Bruns, Director • Hawthorne Valley Farm • Visiting Students Program • 327 CR 21C • Ghent, NY 12075 • Phone: (518) 672-4790 • Fax: (518) 672-4887

Headlands Institute

REGION/HQ: Pacific Northwest/California • **CATEGORY:** Environmental Education • **POSITION TYPE:** Internship • **DURATION:** Year-Round • **IDEAL CANDIDATE:** College Students, Career Changers, Foreigners • **APPLICANT POOL:** Varies • **APPLICANTS ACCEPTED:** Varies

• •

THE YOSEMITE NATIONAL INSTITUTES (YNI) creates distinctive field science/environmental education programs at three main campuses: Headlands Institute, in the Marin Headlands/Golden Gate National Recreation Area; Yosemite Institute in Yosemite National Park; and Olympic Park Institute in Olympic National Park, in Port Angeles, Washington. YNI is a private, nonprofit organization, founded in 1971, providing outdoor environmental learning experiences to people of all ages.

Work/Learn Program Specifics: Interns will serve as support people for the management team at the institute, which includes administration, computer work, advertising, customer services, development/fundraising, naturalist assistance, and various field-related projects.

Duration: Full-time position offered year-round.

The highest function of the teacher consists not so much in imparting knowledge as in stimulating the pupil in its love and pursuit. To know how is to suggest the art of teaching. —H.H. AMIEL

223

Compensation and Perks: The compensation is negotiable. For example, compensation may include housing and meals, transportation reimbursement, or a stipend. In addition, the institute will provide the opportunity for interns to participate in field science programs.

The Ideal Candidate: They seek individuals who share the values and the mission of the institute, as well as those who can work well with customers and employees of the organization.

Making It Happen: Send cover letter and resume. Rolling deadlines.

Contact Information: Executive Director • Headlands Institute • Yosemite National Institutes • GGNRA, Building 1033 • Sausalito, CA 94965 • Phone: (415) 332-5771 • Fax: (415) 332-5784

Hidden Villa Environmental Education Program

REGION/HQ: Pacific Northwest/California
• **CATEGORY:** Environmental Education • **POSITION TYPE:** Internship • **DURATION:** 6–9 months • **IDEAL CANDIDATE:** College Students, Career Changers, Foreigners • **APPLICANT POOL:** 30+/term
• **APPLICANTS ACCEPTED:** 4/term

HIDDEN VILLA ENGAGES children (preschool to sixth grade) in hands-on, innovative programs promoting environmental awareness, multicultural understanding, and humanitarian values. These programs include the school-year environmental education program that services nearly 15,000 school children each year and multicultural summer camp programs. Hidden Villa's goal is to connect kids to the earth, and by showing these connections, help them develop an appreciation and sense of responsibility for their environment.

Area and Working Environment: The program is located in the Santa Cruz mountains, on a 1,600-acre wilderness preserve and working organic farm.

Work/Learn Program Specifics: Environmental education interns spend one day a week working on the farm and studying agriculture and animal care with the ranch staff. The other four weekdays are divided between the various teaching programs: teaching preschoolers on short tours of the farm, spending all day in the farm and wilderness with elementary school children, or going out to schools in the area and giving presentations about farms, ecology, and Hidden

Villa to classrooms of kids. As an intern you will learn leadership skills and hands-on teaching techniques for environmental education of diverse populations; learn creative techniques for teaching ecological concepts in the classroom through the use of slides, puppets, music, role-playing, and storytelling; experience life on a small farm; become acquainted with organic gardening; and gain practical living skills. They provide training and supervision but encourage interns to take on responsibility and develop their own unique teaching style. Their emphasis is on fun and interactive education.

Duration: Their program runs the academic year, September through June. Interns stay either the full nine months or half a year (September to December or January to June).

Compensation and Perks: Housing is provided, along with partial board (food available from the farm) and a stipend of $500 per month, including medical benefits. Not only that, you will live in a beautiful place, meet inspiring people, and receive lots of experience with children, teaching, and farms.

The Ideal Candidate: They encourage all people with some college-level experience to apply. You should have a demonstrated interest in working with children of extremely diverse backgrounds, a genuine love of people and the outdoors, and a desire to learn about organic farming.

Making It Happen: Call or write for application. Send completed application, resume, and one-page letter explaining why you'd like to participate in the internship and what you would hope to get from it. Deadlines: mid-April for positions starting in September; mid-November for positions starting in January. Applicants will be interviewed by telephone.

INSIDER TIPS: *We look for people who have a long-time interest in farms, the outdoors, and children. Applicants should have lots of experience teaching, counseling, or working with kids in other ways. We want people who can show us how this internship will benefit their future decision or career paths and who are enthusiastic.*

Contact Information: John Fisher, Intern Coordinator • Hidden Villa Environmental Education Program • 26870 Moody Rd. • Los Altos Hills, CA 94022-4209 • Phone: (415) 949-8643 • Fax: (415) 948-1916 • E-mail: hveep@earthlink.net

Holden Arboretum

REGION/HQ: Great Lakes/Ohio • **CATEGORY:** Arboretum • **POSITION TYPE:** Internship • **DURATION:** Summer • **IDEAL CANDIDATE:** College Students, Career Changers • **APPLICANT POOL:** 100/term • **APPLICANTS ACCEPTED:** 11/term

AS A PRIVATE, NONPROFIT MUSEUM with over 3,100 acres of horticultural collections and natural areas, their mission is to promote knowledge and appreciation of plants for personal enjoyment, inspiration and recreation, for scientific research, and for educational and aesthetic improvement purposes. The Holden Arboretum Intern Program is an integral part of their organizational mission.

Area and Working Environment: Located a half-hour from Cleveland, with its museums, professional sports, ethnic areas, and festivals.

Work/Learn Program Specifics: The internship program is designed to give a balance of hands-on experience and educational programming. The educational aspect of the program has four parts: a 1¹/₂-day orientation that combines lectures and tours to help interns understand the Arboretum, its grounds, and its purpose; educational sessions; field trips to eight other horticultural institutions in northeast Ohio and Canada, helping broaden the interns' understanding of public horticulture; and demonstrations which give interns an opportunity to learn additional skills on equipment they might not otherwise use during the summer. Positions are available in horticulture, horticulture maintenance, landscape gardening, conservation, horticulture therapy, and education.

Duration: The internship is a full-time position offered during the summer. Interns spend between five and ten hours each week in educational programs—most of them taking place during work hours.

Compensation and Perks: Interns start at $5.25 per hour and are offered free housing. The intern campus allows the students to bond with each other and develop lasting friendships. The arboretum also has activities for its interns and permanent staff throughout the summer: picnics, ball games, and nights out help the staff get to know one another on a social level.

The Ideal Candidate: Applicants must be studying horticulture, natural history, or related fields. Current students and recent grads receive first consideration.

Making It Happen: Submit cover letter, resume, and names of three references by February 1.

Contact Information: Bruce Cubberley, Intern Coordinator • Holden Arboretum • 9500 Sperry Rd. • Kirtland, OH 44094 • Phone: (216) 256-1110 • Fax: (216) 256-1655 • E-mail: educ@pop.holdenarb.org • Web Site: www.lakeonline.com/holden.html

Joy Outdoor Center

REGION/HQ: Great Lakes/Ohio • **CATEGORY:** Experiential Education • **POSITION TYPE:** Internship/Seasonal • **DURATION:** Year-Round • **IDEAL CANDIDATE:** College Students, Career Changers, Retired Folks, Foreigners • **APPLICANT POOL:** 50 to 100/year • **APPLICANTS ACCEPTED:** Varies

JOY OUTDOOR CENTER is a nonprofit center that provides outdoor school programs, summer camp for children, and team-building and leadership programs for adults. It's known for its excellent food and facilities, and for having an outstanding environmental education program. They offer high and low ropes courses (including an alpine tower, pamper pole, indoor climbing wall, group initiatives, and two 30-foot-tall ropes courses), as well as a cultural history program (including a living history reenactment of the Underground Railroad and the Cherokee Trail of Tears).

Area and Working Environment: This 315-acre, rural community is surrounded by a river, streams, ponds, meadows, and a climax forest. Their nearest community is Wilmington (home of Wilmington College), and they are forty-five minutes from Cincinnati.

Work/Learn Program Specifics: The staff will design and teach daily outdoor education classes, lead evening programs two nights per week, work on a special project, and assist with logistics of a residential program.

Duration: Positions offered August through June (academic schedule).

Compensation and Perks: The base salary for seasonal positions starts at $170 per week, and incentives are given to returning staff and those with advanced degrees. All staff receive housing (separate from students), meals, and health insurance.

The Ideal Candidate: Undergraduate degree preferred in education, science, experiential education, parks and recreation, or a related field.

Making It Happen: Call for application. Rolling deadlines.

The old Lakota was wise. He knew that man's heart, away from nature, becomes hard; he knew that lack of respect for growing, living things soon led to lack of respect for humans too. —LUTHER STANDING BEAR

Contact Information: Mary Pat Bourne-Judd, Outdoor School Programs Director • Joy Outdoor Center • P.O. Box 157 • Clarksville, OH 45113 • Phone: (513) 289-2031 • Fax: (513) 300-7094 • Toll Free: (800) 300-7094

Kalamazoo Nature Center

REGION/HQ: Great Lakes/Michigan • **CATEGORY:** Environmental Education • **POSITION TYPE:** Seasonal • **DURATION:** Summer • **IDEAL CANDIDATE:** College Students, Career Changers, Retired Folks • **APPLICANT POOL:** 100+/year • **APPLICANTS ACCEPTED:** 43/year

THE KALAMAZOO NATURE CENTER is recognized nationally for their outreach, education, and avian research programs. With a unique partnership with Michigan State Parks, they coordinate the Michigan State Parks Adventure Program, which has brought seasonal interpretation back into state parks.

Area and Working Environment: Within the system's 260,000 acres, you'll find 142 miles of Great Lakes frontage; 462 miles of lakes, rivers, and streams; virgin timber stands; waterfalls; and plenty of recreational opportunities.

Work/Learn Program Specifics: Summer staff will develop and implement naturalist programs for adults and youth within one of ninety-six Michigan State Parks, as well as schedule and promote all programs.

Duration: Full-time position with flexible hours.

Compensation and Perks: Staff members receive $220 to $240 per week.

The Ideal Candidate: Candidates must have a degree in environmental education, parks, biology, or a related field. Past experience working for a park, nature center, camp, or outdoor education center is preferred.

Making It Happen: Send resume and cover letter (which includes three references with contact information).

INSIDER TIPS: *We look for high-energy, self-motivated, and organized people.*

Contact Information: Amanda Hathaway, Adventure Program Assistant • Kalamazoo Nature Center • Michigan State Parks • P.O. Box 127 • Kalamazoo, MI 49004-0127 • Phone: (616) 381-1574 • Fax: (616) 381-2557

Keewaydin Environmental Education Center

REGION/HQ: Northeast/Vermont • **CATEGORY:** Environmental Education • **POSITION TYPE:** Internship • **DURATION:** Year-Round • **IDEAL CANDIDATE:** College Students, Career Changers, Foreigners • **APPLICANT POOL:** 50/term • **APPLICANTS ACCEPTED:** 4–12/term

KEEWAYDIN ENVIRONMENTAL Education Center is a non-profit organization which provides public school groups with residential environmental education programs of two to five days. Most of their students are Vermonters between the ages of nine and fourteen years old. They learn about such issues as population dynamics, conservation of resources, habitat destruction, and the need for all to think of the global community. Usually the students and their teachers raise the money to pay for their trip to Keewaydin. This not only allows the whole class to participate, but also gives the kids a sense of ownership; having invested so much energy before they ever arrive at the center, they are determined to get as much as possible out of their stay.

Area and Working Environment: The center has two locations: In the spring and fall, they operate at Keewaydin Camps on Lake Dunmore, which is on the western edge of the Green Mountains, about ten miles south of Middlebury and an hour south of Burlington; their winter location is in eastern Vermont, in Groton State Forest, just an hour north of White River Junction.

Work/Learn Program Specifics: Environmental education instructor: The role of an instructor is challenging, fun, demanding, and rewarding. The primary duty is to lead two-hour study units, called "investigations," with groups of eight or nine kids. There are two of these daily and they revolve around a particular theme. In the spring and fall, they run a "Communities" week for fourth- to sixth-graders, and a week on "The Natural History of Vermont" for seventh- and eighth-grade groups. The students study the natural history and the local history of the area in both five-day programs. The winter programs are shorter; the students and their teachers stay for either an overnight or for two nights. The focus of this program is on adaptations to a winter environment. Everybody works hard, and there isn't a lot of free time. For some people, this is a problem; others seem to thrive on the energy produced by the kids and catch up on their own needs over the weekend. For these people, the demands of the program are more than offset by the rewards of working with young people and helping to foster an environmental awareness in tomorrow's adults.

Duration: Keewaydin has three sessions of environmental education each year. They operate for ten weeks in the winter, eight in the spring, and five to six in the fall, five days per week. Programs start January 1, mid-April, and September 1. Although positions are seasonal, instructors frequently stay on for more than one season. Staff who work in the winter are also expected to stay on for the spring session.

Compensation and Perks: Staff members receive $170 to $190 per week, plus room and board. You will live in wooden cabins close to the lake, and everybody eats together in the large dining hall. Instructors are welcome to stay at the facility on days off to take advantage of the great hiking and canoeing (or skiing and snowshoeing) in the area. Unfortunately they cannot accommodate instructors' dogs; other pets are occasionally permissible.

The Ideal Candidate: Candidates should come with a strong background in ecology or a related field; others should have a wealth of experience working with children. Enthusiasm for learning, living, and working with children and caring deeply for the earth and all its inhabitants are requirements for the position. Smokers, please don't apply!

Making It Happen: Send resume and cover letter to start the application process. Rolling deadlines, but apply at least three to five months ahead of time. An in-person interview is required for the spring positions; telephone interviews are fine for the summer and fall positions.

INSIDER TIPS: *If you possess these qualities and are willing to work hard to achieve sometimes intangible goals, then you are the kind of person Keewaydin needs.*

Contact Information: Intern Director • Keewaydin Environmental Education Center • RD 1, Box 88 • Salisbury, VT 05769-9706 • Phone: (802) 352-9011

Land Between
The Lakes

REGION/HQ: Southeast/Kentucky • **CATEGORY:** Environmental Education • **POSITION TYPE:** Internship • **DURATION:** Year-Round • **IDEAL CANDIDATE:** College Students, Career Changers, Foreigners • **APPLICANT POOL:** 150/year • **APPLICANTS ACCEPTED:** 10/year

LAND BETWEEN THE LAKES (LBL) is a 170,000-acre outdoor recreation, environmental education, and resource management demonstration area administered by the Tennessee Valley Authority. Over 1,500 students have completed internships at LBL since 1964.

Area and Working Environment: You may work in a family campground, a resident center, a living-history farm built in 1850, an educational farm, a nature center, or the main office.

Work/Learn Program Specifics: The internship program is designed to provide cooperating universities a laboratory where the student can apply classroom theories. The goals of the internship program are to provide quality training and practical experience for students in a wide range of disciplines, to introduce students to the operation procedures of a federal agency, and to enhance the quality experiences of the diverse population that visits LBL. You work closely with professionals and receive firsthand knowledge of what it takes to operate and maintain programs related to your major field of interest.

Duration: Internships last from twelve to sixteen weeks, though most last twelve weeks and generally begin mid-May.

Compensation and Perks: Interns receive a stipend of $125 per week and housing at LBL.

The Ideal Candidate: Practical fieldwork experience is not required in all cases, and applicants should have completed at least two years of coursework.

Making It Happen: Call for application. Submit completed application and a written recommendation from your internship advisor. Summer deadline is January 15. Finalists will be interviewed by phone. Apprenticeship positions are filled as vacancies occur.

INSIDER TIPS: *Someone with lots of enthusiasm and commitment has as good a chance as someone with all the experience in the world.*

Contact Information: Jo Travis, Human Resource Assistant • Land Between The Lakes • Tennessee Valley Authority • 100 Van Morgan Dr. • Golden Pond, KY 42211 • Phone: (502) 924-5602 • Fax: (502) 924-1299

Lassen County
Youth Camp

REGION/HQ: Pacific Northwest/California • **CATEGORY:** Outdoor Education • **POSITION TYPE:** Internship • **DURATION:** Fall • **IDEAL CANDIDATE:** College Students, Career Changers, Retired Folks,

Foreigners • **APPLICANT POOL:** Varies • **APPLICANTS ACCEPTED:** 4/year

••

THE LASSEN COUNTY YOUTH CAMP is equipped with dorms, bathrooms, a laboratory, and kitchen facilities. Groups of sixth-grade students from Lassen County schools will attend four-day sessions over a six-week period to study plants, animals, water, and soil of the area.

Area and Working Environment: The camp is located twenty-nine miles northeast of Susanville, on the east shore of Eagle Lake.

Work/Learn Program Specifics: Outdoor education interns assist the outdoor education coordinator. Teacher/naturalists conduct field activities, and teach natural history, physical science, and other environmental-awareness-oriented subjects to sixth-grade students. Additionally, interns and teacher/naturalists will supervise students at all times and help coordinate other aspects of the program.

Compensation and Perks: Interns receive a $25 stipend per day, plus room and board.

The Ideal Candidate: All applicants must have experience working with elementary students, be certified in first aid/CPR, and have the ability to work with others. Prior experience (including volunteer work) in environmental/outdoor education is desirable. The teacher/naturalist also needs a degree in biology or another science, or knowledge of the natural history of Lassen County.

Making It Happen: Call for additional information.

Contact Information: Personnel Director • Lassen County Youth Camp • Lassen County Office Of Education • 472-013 Johnstonville Rd., N • Susanville, CA 96130-9710 • Phone: (916) 257-2196 • Fax: (916) 257-2518

Long Lake Conservation Center

REGION/HQ: Great Lakes/Minnesota • **CATEGORY:** Environmental Education • **POSITION TYPE:** Internship • **DURATION:** Year-Round • **IDEAL CANDIDATE:** College Students, Career Changers, Retired Folks • **APPLICANT POOL:** 30–40/year • **APPLICANTS ACCEPTED:** 4/term

••

LONG LAKE CONSERVATION CENTER is a year-round residential conservation/environmental education facility.

In 1975, LLCC made its facilities and programs available to college students wishing for a site on which to conduct their fieldwork. Since that time, scores of individuals from schools around the country have lived and learned at the center.

Work/Learn Program Specifics: In a spirit of symbiosis, they view each fieldwork experience as an opportunity for the intern and the center to benefit equally. For their part, you'll help keep their teacher-to-student ratios to a more intimate level (of course, the students benefit most!); you'll bring in fresh ideas; you'll provide a helping hand in many areas. For your part, you'll gain teaching experience, leadership and discipline skills, a broadened range of activities, program planning and curriculum development experience, organizational skills, and an introduction to the Midwestern experiential education network. Depending on which season you join, you'll become proficient at teaching a number of topics, including aquatic biology, archery, canoeing, cross-country skiing, deer/wolf relationships, fire building and wilderness ethics, human ecology, initiative games, orienteering, simulation games, snow studies, and snowshoeing.

Duration: Duration can be from one quarter or semester through a nine-month school year.

Compensation and Perks: Interns receive a $75-per-week scholarship, room and board, liability coverage, and limited attendance at professional workshops and meetings.

The Ideal Candidate: They will consider any applicant, eighteen or older, who possesses a strong desire to learn about—and participate in—a vital, ongoing conservation/environmental/outdoor education program in all its phases. A general understanding of the natural world and course work in natural history, though not mandatory, can be quite helpful. Candidates seeking experience in teaching and developing communications skills are ideally suited to this program. Nontraditional students (i.e. older adults seeking a career change or reentry into the workforce) are also welcome to apply.

Making It Happen: Request an application packet. Applications are considered on a first-come, first-served basis and many candidates apply nine to twelve months in advance. If you live in Minnesota, you can call them toll free: (800) 450-5522.

Contact Information: Bob Schwaderer, Executive Director • Long Lake Conservation Center • Route 2, Box 2550 • Palisade, MN 56469 • Phone: (218) 768-4653 • Fax: (218) 768-2309 • E-mail: llcc@informns.k12.mn.us

Mission Springs Christian Conference Center

REGION/HQ: Pacific Northwest/California
• **CATEGORY:** Ministry • **POSITION TYPE:** Internship
• **DURATION:** Year-Round • **IDEAL CANDIDATE:** College Students, Career Changers • **APPLICANT POOL:** 60/year • **APPLICANTS ACCEPTED:** 15+/year

THE MISSION SPRINGS CONFERENCE CENTER holds an outdoor education program for children in grades four to eight from both Christian and public schools. The program is affiliated with the Pacific Southwest Conference of the Evangelical Covenant Church and serves 60 schools with 2,700 students. Activities include natural science classes, recreation, field trips, Bible study, and campfires.

Area and Working Environment: The proximity to Santa Cruz, the beach, and many other natural attractions makes this a great place to work.

Work/Learn Program Specifics: Naturalist/counselors lead outdoor education classes, Bible studies, recreation, and other activities. Naturalists will have the opportunity to gain work experience in outdoor education, Christian camping, and youth ministry; obtain training in educational techniques, natural history interpretation, recreational leadership skills, and camp ministry; and enjoy living in a tight-knit Christian community near the coast.

Duration: The positions are offered year-round. Interns work an average of forty to fifty hours per week.

Compensation and Perks: Interns receive a stipend of $140 per week. Room, board, insurance, and laundry services are provided. This is a superb community, teaching, and ministry experience.

The Ideal Candidate: Desire individuals with backgrounds in biology, environmental science, earth science, theology, education, or Christian education. Other qualifications include excellent physical, emotional, and physical health; enthusiasm; enjoyment of the outdoors; interest and ability to teach Bible classes; concern about environmental issues; and current Red Cross standard first aid certification.

Making It Happen: Submit cover letter, resume, and any applicable letters of recommendation; then follow up with a phone call. Rolling deadlines.

INSIDER TIPS: *I'm looking for solid Christians interested in teaching environmental education. Previous youth ministry, camp, and teaching experience sure helps.*

Contact Information: Mark McReynolds, Outdoor Education Manager • Mission Springs Christian Conference Center • 1050 Lockhart Gulch Rd. • Scotts Valley, CA 95066 • Phone: (408) 335-9133 • E-mail: mike@cruzio.com

Nags Head Woods Preserve

REGION/HQ: Southeast/North Carolina • **CATEGORY:** Conservation • **POSITION TYPE:** Internship
• **DURATION:** Summer • **IDEAL CANDIDATE:** College Students • **APPLICANT POOL:** 50–300/year
• **APPLICANTS ACCEPTED:** 2/summer

THE NATURE CONSERVANCY is an international nonprofit conservation organization committed to preserving rare plants, animals, and natural communities that represent the diversity of life on Earth by protecting the lands and water they need to survive. The North Carolina chapter of The Nature Conservancy, established in 1977, manages forty-seven preserves and natural areas in the state, including Nags Head Woods. Nearly 350,000 acres of natural habitat have been protected in North Carolina thanks to contributors. Nags Head Woods is a mixture of maritime deciduous forest, maritime swamp forest, and several other biological communities.

Area and Working Environment: The Preserve is located on the North Carolina Outer Banks, in the towns of Nags Head and Kill Devil Hills. The preserve is about 90 miles south of Norfolk, Virginia, and 225 miles east of Raleigh, North Carolina.

Work/Learn Program Specifics: The stewardship research internship is designed to link high-priority preserve research needs with the attainment of research requirements for a graduate degree in the natural sciences. Working closely with the preserve steward and the student's advisor, the intern will design and implement a major self-directed research project. The naturalist/environmental education intern will design and lead educational field trips for visitors to the preserve. Under the supervision of the education coordinator, he/she will prepare and conduct interpretive programs for adults and children, including guided canoe trips, hikes, and week-long day camps for children aged nine to twelve.

Duration: Internships run from June 1 through August 31, full-time.

Compensation and Perks: Interns receive a $2,500 to $3,000 stipend, plus housing.

He who is outside his door already has a hard part of his journey behind him.
—DUTCH PROVERB

The Ideal Candidate: Stewardship intern applicants must have been accepted into a graduate program in natural sciences and have experience with related field- and lab-research methodology. Naturalist/environmental education intern applicants must have a minimum of two years of successful academic training in ecology, wildlife biology, or environmental education. All positions require a strong interest in and commitment to conservation, the ability to work well with a variety of people, and the ability to work independently and conscientiously.

Making It Happen: Submit cover letter and resume by mid-February.

Contact Information: Barbara Blonder, Preserve Steward • Nags Head Woods Preserve • The Nature Conservancy • 701 W. Ocean Acres Dr. • Kill Devil Hills, NC 27948 • Phone: (919) 441-2525 • Fax: (919) 441-1271

Nature's Classroom Atop Lookout Mountain

REGION/HQ: Southeast/Alabama • **CATEGORY:** Experiential Education • **POSITION TYPE:** Internship/Seasonal • **DURATION:** Academic year • **IDEAL CANDIDATE:** High School Students, College Students, Career Changers, Retired Folks, Foreigners • **APPLICANT POOL:** 50/year • **APPLICANTS ACCEPTED:** 12/year

NATURE'S CLASSROOM is an experiential education program with an environmental foundation, designed to support traditional classroom learning by teaching creative and practical applications of subjects taught in school. Students enjoy the informal, outdoor atmosphere and open themselves to new growth experiences.

Area and Working Environment: The program is located on the picturesque and rural Lookout Mountain, on the Little River (one of only two rivers that begin and end on a mountain), bordering Tennessee and Georgia.

Work/Learn Program Specifics: Interns/teachers will work with public- and private-school children from the third to seventh grade, teaching hands-on classes in all curriculum areas. You will lead field groups which explore the woods, caves, and river, while focusing on team building, cooperation, and self-esteem. Low elements of ropes course and initiative games will also be used.

Duration: Teaching contracts run one or two semesters. Internship periods vary. You'll be working up to thirteen hours a day.

Compensation and Perks: You'll receive a private room/cabin, all meals, workers' compensation, great staff training, and the chance to work with a wonderfully diverse, top-rate staff. Interns receive $100 per week; teachers, $190 (and up) per week. Teachers also receive health insurance, $150 per year for incidental medical expenses, two paid personal days off per semester, and use of a washer and dryer.

The Ideal Candidate: Teachers must have a four-year degree, be at least twenty-one years old, and pass a criminal background check (which will cost you $25). A sense of humor is very helpful and appreciated, and being able to put the needs of the program and children first is a must. They encourage diversity and offer the opportunity for people to be just who they are.

Making It Happen: Get in touch with Susan for current availability of positions or to schedule a mandatory, on-site interview. You can print out their application form by tapping into their web site. You are welcome to stay for a few days when going on-site for an interview. Rolling deadlines.

INSIDER TIPS: *Although individuality and diversity are celebrated, a professional appearance (woodsy professional, that is) is just as important. Emotional maturity is needed to be a success and have fun.*

Contact Information: Susan Cherones, Director • Nature's Classroom Atop Lookout Mountain • P.O. Box 400 • Mentone, AL 35984 • Phone: (205) 634-4443 • Fax: (205) 634-3601 • Toll Free: (800) 995-4769 • E-mail: TrueSu@aol.com • Web Site: www.naturesclassroom.com

Newfound Harbor Marine Institute

REGION/HQ: Southeast/Florida • **CATEGORY:** Marine Science • **POSITION TYPE:** Internship/Seasonal • **DURATION:** Year-Round • **IDEAL CANDIDATE:** College Students • **APPLICANT POOL:** 50/term • **APPLICANTS ACCEPTED:** 15/term

NEWFOUND HARBOR MARINE INSTITUTE offers programs in marine science and environmental education to groups who want to increase their understanding of the ocean and its ecosystems. Participants snorkel and wade with instructors and experience the wonders of the

Florida Keys. Over 8,000 students participate in the program annually.

Area and Working Environment: The institute is located 120 miles southwest of Miami—an ideal site for exploring the subtropical marine and terrestrial habitats of the Lower Keys—and is within the boundaries of the Florida Keys National Marine Sanctuary. The year-round temperature averages 79 degrees!

Work/Learn Program Specifics: Instructor positions and internships are designed to provide college students and pre-professionals with a variety of experiences, including preparation for teaching tropical marine environmental education to grades four through nine. You will develop the ability to lead interpretive programs and snorkel to coral reefs with visiting school groups. Comprehensive training, including seminars, program observation, teaching field-oriented marine education, program development, boat operation skills, and certifications in first aid, CPR, and ARC lifeguarding, is also provided. Other positions exist in marketing, maintenance, food service, and support staff.

Duration: Interns and instructors work eight to ten hours per day, five or six days per week.

Compensation and Perks: You will receive a monthly stipend, room and board, and a travel bonus. You will also have access to staff boats and a chance to snorkel the coral reef. Other benefits include professional training, skill development, hands-on experience, and future employment opportunities.

The Ideal Candidate: The ideal candidates have interest in marine environment and children, boating and waterfront experience, and a degree (or current study) in biology, environmental science, or a related field.

Newfound Harbor Marine Institute

Making It Happen: Send for application kit.

Contact Information: Keith Jones, Program Director • Newfound Harbor Marine Institute • 1300 Big Pine Ave. • Big Pine Key, FL 33043-3336 • Phone: (305) 872-2331 • Fax: (305) 872-2555

North Woods Resource Center—Widgiwagan

REGION/HQ: Great Lakes/Minnesota • **CATEGORY:** Environmental Education • **POSITION TYPE:** Internship • **DURATION:** Year-Round • **IDEAL CANDIDATE:** College Students, Career Changers, Foreigners • **APPLICANT POOL:** 12/term • **APPLICANTS ACCEPTED:** 4/term

THE NORTH WOODS RESOURCE CENTER is Widgiwagan's wilderness-based environmental education program, which has offered high-quality outdoor experiential education for students since 1973. The program immerses youth in the outdoor classroom in small study groups (eight to twelve students with each instructor) and teaches about the environment, outdoor skills, and teamwork.

Area and Working Environment: The facility is based north of Ely, Minnesota, a half-mile from the Boundary Waters Canoe Area Wilderness. The center has 700,000 acres of wilderness to use as its classroom.

Work/Learn Program Specifics: Their Outdoor Environmental Education Internship is designed to develop the participant's abilities in natural history programming, wilderness skills, and youth leadership. The program includes preseason staff training, seminars on instructing issues, and individual intern projects. Interns co-lead wilderness-based activities and all-day excursions for eight to twelve students, fourth through ninth grade. Two- to three-hour activities develop outdoor skills, encourage teamwork and cooperation, and create curiosity about the natural world. Interns work as part of a staff team (seven naturalists and four interns), and the program is coordinated by a full-time outdoor educator.

Duration: Internships are offered each season except the summer.

Compensation and Perks: Interns receive a $140-per-month stipend, plus room and board.

The Ideal Candidate: Applicant must have a desire to develop youth leadership skills, have confidence working in an outdoor setting, be pursuing (or have) a

The world is moving so fast these days that the man who says it can't be done is generally interrupted by someone doing it. —HARRY EMERSON FOSDICK

231

degree in an environmental field, and have certification in first aid, CPR, and lifeguarding.

Making It Happen: Request application materials. Inquire early as interns are hired on a rolling application basis.

Contact Information: Ann Maxwell, Program Director • North Woods Resource Center–Widgiwagan • 1761 University Ave., W • St. Paul, MN 55104-3599 • Phone: (612) 645-6605 • Fax: (612) 646-5521

NYS Department of Environmental Conservation

REGION/HQ: Northeast/New York • **CATEGORY:** Environmental Education • **POSITION TYPE:** Internship • **DURATION:** Year-Round • **IDEAL CANDIDATE:** College Students, Career Changers • **APPLICANT POOL:** 100/year • **APPLICANTS ACCEPTED:** 6/term

THE NEW YORK STATE Department of Environmental Conservation runs three centers: Five Rivers Environmental Education Center, Rogers Environmental Education Center, and Stony Kill Farm Environmental Center. With programming for teachers, school groups, youth groups, conservation organizations, and the public, the three state-run centers promote an understanding of natural history, ecology, environmental science, and natural resources. Stony Kill uses its working farm to teach agriculture as conservation.

Area and Working Environment: Five Rivers is located in eastern New York, Rogers in central New York, and Stony Kill Farm in southwestern New York.

Work/Learn Program Specifics: Each center offers naturalist training internships to people seeking professional experience in environmental communications and education. Each intern will receive training in a wide variety of education center programs, the operations and activities of a nature center, and in principles of environmental interpretation. Interns plan and lead a wide variety of environmental activities for a broad range of audiences; write newsletter or newspaper articles on natural history; design and construct educational exhibits or off-site displays for the center; prepare slide shows, videos, or other audiovisual materials; prepare written interpretive materials; take care of live animals; and complete a special project.

Duration: Internships are approximately twelve weeks in length, offered year-round.

Compensation and Perks: A stipend of $100 per week is paid to each intern. Each center will provide living space on the grounds, with a fully equipped kitchen, furnished living room, and private bedroom.

The Ideal Candidate: Internship positions are open to adults, eighteen and older, with at least two years of college experience in environmental education, science education, natural resources, or a closely related field. Preference will be given to applicants with a strong background in natural history or education. Enthusiasm, love of the outdoors, and a desire to work with people are required.

Making It Happen: Call for application. Send completed application three months before your desired start date. They also publish *The Conservationist*, a magazine on the environment. Call (800) 678-6399 for more information.

INSIDER TIPS: *Summer is ten times as popular as other seasons, and applicants are less likely to get accepted. Spring (April through June) is actually the most interesting season. Apply early, and type your application.*

Contact Information: Anita Sanchez, Senior Environmental Educator • NYS Department of Environmental Conservation • Game Farm Rd. • Delmar, NY 12054-9776 • Phone: (518) 475-0291 • Fax: (518) 475-0293

Peace Valley Nature Center

REGION/HQ: Northeast/Pennsylvania • **CATEGORY:** Nature Center • **POSITION TYPE:** Internship • **DURATION:** Year-Round • **IDEAL CANDIDATE:** College Students, Career Changers, Foreigners • **APPLICANT POOL:** 20/term • **APPLICANTS ACCEPTED:** 2/term

A BUCKS COUNTY FACILITY, Peace Valley Nature Center began in 1975 with a mission to educate school children and the general public about the natural world. The nature center features nine miles of trail, winding through 300 acres of diverse natural communities, including fields, deciduous forests, thickets, streams, ponds, coniferous forests, and a portion of Lake Galena. The center is home to a solar building which houses displays, a shop, and a clivus multrum composting toilet.

Area and Working Environment: The center is located thirty-five miles north of Philadelphia. The region is full of history from the colonial period, and numerous natural areas are within easy driving distance. The town of Doylestown has colonial charm, a fine library, and many museums.

Work/Learn Program Specifics: Interns are required to observe and teach programs, complete and present a project, write a natural history article, attend a board meeting, participate in bird walks, keep a daily diary, and attend staff meetings. Other responsibilities are assigned at the beginning of the internship and include bird feeding, making phone messages, setting up for programs, and other tasks.

Duration: The spring and fall internships run for twelve weeks. The summer internship is ten weeks. Interns must work every other weekend; Mondays are days off.

Compensation and Perks: Interns receive a $75-per-week stipend, plus room and board. Interns will have the opportunity to gain experience teaching and observe many teaching styles and methods. You will also become familiar with all aspects of nature center operations—an excellent resume builder.

The Ideal Candidate: Preference is given to applicants with two years of college, majoring in environmental education, biology, environmental studies, or a related field. Applicants must be interested in teaching children of all ages about the natural world.

Making It Happen: Send a resume, reference, and cover letter requesting an application. Candidates within a two-hour drive are interviewed on-site; others are interviewed by phone.

INSIDER TIPS: *Applying for the spring or fall internships increases the candidate's chances of employment.*

Contact Information: Craig Olsen, Assistant Naturalist • Peace Valley Nature Center • 170 Chapman Rd. • Doylestown, PA 18901 • Phone: (215) 345-7860 • Fax: (215) 345-4529

Pocono Environmental Education Center

REGION/HQ: Northeast/Pennsylvania • **CATEGORY:** Environmental Education • **POSITION TYPE:** Internship • **DURATION:** Year-Round • **IDEAL CANDIDATE:** College Students, Career Changers, Retired Folks, Foreigners • **APPLICANT POOL:** 1,200/year • **APPLICANTS ACCEPTED:** 40/year

THE MISSION OF Pocono Environmental Education Center (PEEC) is to advance environmental awareness, knowledge, and skills through education so those who inhabit and those who will inherit the planet may better understand the complexities of natural and human-designed environments. Throughout the year, PEEC hosts school groups, religious organizations, universities, professional conferences, and workshops. PEEC also sponsors Elderhostel, Family Nature Study Vacations, and professional development workshops on such topics as ornithology, wildflowers, reptiles and amphibians, photography, and Native American studies.

Area and Working Environment: PEEC is located in the National Park Service's Delaware Water Gap National Recreation Area, twenty miles southwest of where New York, New Jersey, and Pennsylvania meet. The center's outdoor classroom consists of a 38-acre campus with access to over 200,000 acres of public land—fields, forests, ponds, waterfalls, and scenic hemlock gorges.

Work/Learn Program Specifics: Environmental education instructors provide programming, development, and service. The work involved develops personal and professional interactive skills with people from various backgrounds. The instructor's primary duties are teaching and support services. Program planning interns focus on program planning for PEEC guests and visitors by assisting the program coordinator in scheduling, implementing, and coordinating programs for formal and informal education groups. Public relations interns focus on the publications and marketing of PEEC. Interns will assist the PR director in writing, managing, and producing PEEC's publications and promotional materials for events and workshops.

Duration: Employment terms begin in February, June, and September, and range in duration from six to ten months.

Compensation and Perks: Interns receive a $500 to $800-per-month stipend, plus room and board. Lodging is in heated cabins with a private bath, usually shared with one roommate, and meals are served in PEEC's dining hall. There is also a staff lounge with a refrigerator and telephone.

The Ideal Candidate: Enrollment in or completion of a degree program in English, communications, environmental/outdoor education, natural sciences, or related fields is required. The applicant must demonstrate experience working with people and interest in working in a residential setting. Additional consideration is given for applicants with certifications such as lifeguarding, first aid, or CPR, or a commercial driver's license. Since you will live on-site, in a rural area, having a car is helpful, but not required.

Making It Happen: Submit resume, cover letter, and two references. Public relations interns must submit two samples of their writing, editing, photography, or layout design. PEEC will contact you to schedule an on-site interview so that you may observe the typical operation of the center.

Contact Information: Flo Mauro, Director • Pocono Environmental Education Center • R.D. 2, Box 1010 • Dingmans Ferry, PA 18328 • Phone: (717) 828-2319 • Fax: (717) 828-9695 • E-mail: peec@ptd.net

Point Reyes Education Programs

REGION/HQ: Pacific Northwest/California • **CATEGORY:** Environmental Education • **POSITION TYPE:** Internship • **DURATION:** Summer • **IDEAL CANDIDATE:** College Students, Career Changers, Foreigners • **APPLICANT POOL:** 25/year • **APPLICANTS ACCEPTED:** 8/year

POINT REYES EDUCATION PROGRAMS provide educational opportunities for people of all ages. Science Camp is a five-week residential program for kids aged seven to twelve that explores the rich coastal environments and diverse habitats of one of the country's most beautiful national parks. Adventure Camp is six-day program for teens, aged thirteen to sixteen. The highlight of the camp is a four-day backpack trip on the seashore that focuses on self-esteem, teamwork, and backpacking skills.

Area and Working Environment: The education center is close to one of the finest beaches in Point Reyes National Seashore. The seashore boundaries enclose a variety of terrain and vegetation, with a belt of rich marine life along the shores of Tomales Bay and the Pacific Ocean.

Work/Learn Program Specifics: Naturalist intern/counselor: The primary function of this position is to assist with guided natural history and environmental education programs, meal-time supervision, free-time activities, and cabin supervision for children attending the Point Reyes Education Programs' Science Camp. The position allows interns to work with experts in the field of environmental and outdoor education; gain work experience in environmental and science education; be coached by qualified personnel; obtain training in educational techniques, natural history interpretation,

behavior management techniques, and recreational leadership skills; and have a firsthand experience in a rich coastal environment. Other summer staff positions include six naturalists, a director, and three kitchen workers. Come experience the warmth and camaraderie of living and working with other staff members in a residential camp environment.

Duration: Summer positions start in late June (with staff training) and end in mid- to late August.

Compensation and Perks: You will receive a $125-per-week stipend, plus room and board. Staff can remain on-site during weekends and week-long breaks to explore and play in Point Reyes National Seashore.

The Ideal Candidate: Naturalist intern/counselor applicants should enjoy working with children and the outdoors, have a knowledge of ecological concepts/communities, and general knowledge of first aid techniques, with current certification. The ideal student should be creative, enthusiastic, flexible, self-motivated, and have a sense of humor. First aid and CPR certification is required.

Making It Happen: Call for an application. Submit completed application, resume, and any material that can support your qualifications by April 1. On-site interviews preferred, but phone interviews are acceptable.

INSIDER TIPS: *Looking for intern candidates who are college students and are willing to work and live with campers in a rustic setting. Having experience in supervising or teaching students is a bonus.*

Contact Information: Eileen Jones, Intern Director • Point Reyes Education Programs • Point Reyes National Seashore • Point Reyes, CA 94956 • Phone: (415) 663-1200

Pok-O-MacCready Outdoor Education Center

REGION/HQ: Northeast/New York • **CATEGORY:** Outdoor Education • **POSITION TYPE:** Internship • **DURATION:** Year-Round • **IDEAL CANDIDATE:** College Students, Career Changers, Foreigners • **APPLICANT POOL:** 4/year • **APPLICANTS ACCEPTED:** Varies

POK-O-MACCREADY OUTDOOR EDUCATION CENTER provides intensive one- to five-day programs on outdoor skills, environmental studies, Native American studies, and traditional pioneer living principally for students aged twelve to sixteen.

Work/Learn Program Specifics: Interns will participate in program planning, preparation, instruction, and evaluation; design and implementation of evening programs; further development of the center's curriculum; care and maintenance of the facilities; care and feeding of homestead animals; supervision of students; and evaluation sessions with the director. Interns with an emphasis in biology or environmental studies will be responsible for conducting nature walks and pond studies, as well as leading seminars in acid rain or other environmental topics. Interns with an emphasis in social studies or history will assist instructing at the 1812 homestead in a one-room schoolhouse, blacksmithing, shingling, spinning, weaving, dyeing, colonial baking, candle-making, gardening, and other colonial crafts, as well as researching and assisting in the renovation of the homestead.

Duration: Internships are available any time during the academic year, with almost any start date and a minimum duration of two weeks to a maximum duration of six months. No positions are available just for the summer.

Compensation and Perks: Interns receive room and board, plus a stipend of $100 per month.

The Ideal Candidate: Interested candidates should have completed one year of college, with an emphasis in outdoor education, recreation, or environmental studies. Camping, hiking, rock climbing, and waterfront skills are a plus.

Making It Happen: Send resume and cover letter. Rolling deadlines.

Contact Information: Don Watson, Outdoor Education Director • Pok-O-MacCready Outdoor Education Center • 112 N. Reber Rd. • Willsboro, NY 12996 • Phone: (518) 963-7967

Richardson Bay Audubon Center and Sanctuary

REGION/HQ: Pacific Northwest/California • **CATEGORY:** Conservation • **POSITION TYPE:** Internship • **DURATION:** Year-Round • **IDEAL CANDIDATE:** College Students, Career Changers • **APPLICANT POOL:** 10/term • **APPLICANTS ACCEPTED:** 2/term

THE RICHARDSON BAY AUDUBON CENTER and Sanctuary is a wildlife sanctuary and public education center. Thousands of waterbirds winter in the shallow bay, and the center is a focal point of on-site and outreach environmental education activities. Educational programs help the public learn bay and wetland themes and issues.

Area and Working Environment: The center and sanctuary is comprised of 11 acres of land and 900 acres of tidal wetlands on the San Francisco Bay, about nine miles north of San Francisco.

Work/Learn Program Specifics: Environmental education internships provide an opportunity for individuals interested in acquiring work experience in the environmental field to help the center meet its goals of providing public education and preserving wildlife habitat. Interns participate in all aspects of the education center and sanctuary operations. Spring and fall interns participate in teaching natural science classes and programs for children, first as helpers, then as leaders after gaining experience. Interns help with weekend nature walks, slide and film presentations, and lead at least one of these programs. Summer interns will primarily work in the children's program. The program includes three half-day workshops, with a variety of different natural history and environmental science themes, over a four-week period. Participants range in age from three to twelve years. Interns help plan, teach classes, and compile class records. All interns also help with office work, bookstore operations, and sanctuary maintenance projects.

Duration: The internship requires a full-time commitment (minimum of thirty-five hours per week), five days a week for at least three months.

Compensation and Perks: You will receive a $500 food stipend for three months. A historic, 125-year-old Victorian house rests on the edge of the land and houses the interns at no cost. Laundry facilities and utilities are also included.

The Ideal Candidate: Candidates should deal effectively with people, be well-organized, and have an interest in natural history. Experience working with children or teaching is helpful.

Making It Happen: Submit cover letter and resume. Rolling deadlines.

INSIDER TIPS: *Meet the requirements, be a good communicator, and be dependable!*

Contact Information: Meryl Sundove, Education Coordinator • Richardson Bay Audubon Center & Sanc-

Life would be infinitely happier if we could only be born at the age of eighty and gradually approach eighteen. —MARK TWAIN

235

tuary • National Audubon Society • 376 Greenwood Beach Rd. • Tiburon, CA 94920 • Phone: (415) 388-2525 • Fax: (415) 388-0717

River Ridge Environmental Education Program

REGION/HQ: Southeast/Tennessee • **CATEGORY:** Environmental Education • **POSITION TYPE:** Internship/Seasonal • **DURATION:** Spring/Fall • **IDEAL CANDIDATE:** College Students, Career Changers, Retired Folks, Foreigners • **APPLICANT POOL:** 30–50/term • **APPLICANTS ACCEPTED:** 8/term

THE RIVER RIDGE Environmental Education Program is operated by the John Knox Center, a nonprofit Presbyterian Center for Outdoor Ministries. The center sits on 140 acres of natural ecosystems, with a wide variety of plants and animals. Facilities include a large open-air pavilion, low and high ropes courses, a newly remodeled lodge, and three units available for lodging.

Area and Working Environment: The center is located on a three-peninsula bluff overlooking Watts Bar Lake, just one hour west of Knoxville and thirty minutes from Great Smoky Mountains National Park.

Work/Learn Program Specifics: Environmental educators teach environmental education classes and facilitate high and low ropes courses during challenge quest sessions or weekend retreats; provide leadership to ensure students have a fun, safe, and educational experience; and aid in program development by writing new courses, creating displays, and building outdoor classroom stations and ropes course elements. You will learn over thirty environmental education classes and ten evening programs.

Duration: The spring session runs from late February to May, and the fall session runs from September to November.

Compensation and Perks: Those with degrees will make $160 per week; those pursuing a degree will make $80 per week. All staff will receive room, board, and workers' compensation.

The Ideal Candidate: Applicants must have the ability to relate well to others, particularly youth and children; be enthusiastic, creative, and enjoy working outdoors and with people; show care and consideration for other people and the environment; and have a

background in biology, environmental studies, outdoor recreation, education, or a related field.

Making It Happen: Send a cover letter, resume, and contact information for three references.

INSIDER TIPS: *We're looking for people who have a dynamic personality, a love for kids and the outdoors, and teaching experience.*

Contact Information: Kim Bailey, Program Director • River Ridge Environmental Education Program • John Knox Center • 591 W. Rockwood Ferry Rd. • Ten Mile, TN 37880 • Phone: (423) 376-2236 • Fax: (423) 376-1719 • E-mail: Rivridge@aol.com • Web Site: http://users.aol.com/rivridge/homepage/index.html

Ryerson Woods

REGION/HQ: Great Lakes/Illinois • **CATEGORY:** Environmental Education • **POSITION TYPE:** Internship • **DURATION:** Year-Round • **IDEAL CANDIDATE:** College Students, Career Changers • **APPLICANT POOL:** Varies • **APPLICANTS ACCEPTED:** 2/term

THE TAX-SUPPORTED Forest Preserve District is responsible for preserving the flora and fauna of the area in a natural setting while offering recreational opportunities that are harmonious with this setting. The Education Department, stationed at Ryerson, teaches about preservation and wise use of natural resources.

Area and Working Environment: Ryerson Woods is located thirty miles north of Chicago on 550 acres and offers the beauty of a natural area and the cultural benefits of close proximity to a large urban center.

Work/Learn Program Specifics: Environmental Education Internship Program: The purpose of the internship is to develop professional skills in future environmental educators, while strengthening the staff of the Lake County Forest Preserve District's Environmental Education Department. Interns will be exposed to all facets of the Environmental Education Department and as many facets of the Forest Preserve District as is practical. A large portion of time is spent developing, preparing, and presenting programs to youth and adults. The other major priority is the completion of an independent project, which is chosen jointly by the intern and staff. Other responsibilities will vary, depending on the season's needs. They will include special event participation, press release preparation, volunteer coordination, reading assignments, participation in volunteer and teacher training programs, overseeing the preserve on the weekends, enforcement of preserve rules, answering the public's questions about wildlife and the preserve, and other aspects of nature center operation.

Duration: They have an eleven-week summer program beginning in May; a sixteen-week program (mid-August through November and February through early June); and a year-long (fifty-week) program (beginning in August).

Compensation and Perks: Summer stipend—$2,250; sixteen-week stipend—$3,300; year-long stipend—$11,250. Furnished housing can be arranged through the district for a fee of $100 per month, plus phone costs. The housing is located fifteen miles from the primary work site, and thus, interns must have access to a vehicle.

The Ideal Candidate: Applicants must be enrolled in, or have graduated from a college program in biology, education, or a closely related field. Preference is given to those that are pursuing a career in environmental education and have respect and enthusiasm for both people and nature. Some familiarity or experience with nature center programming is preferred.

Making It Happen: Send cover letter (outlining the time frame you wish to work), resume, and transcripts. Deadlines: spring—September 30; summer—March 15; and fall or year-long—March 31.

Contact Information: Intern Coordinator • Ryerson Woods • Lake County Forest Preserve • 21950 Riverwoods Rd. • Deerfield, IL 60015 • Phone: (708) 948-7750

Salish Sea Expeditions

REGION/HQ: Pacific Northwest/Washington • **CATEGORY:** Experiential Education • **POSITION TYPE:** Seasonal • **DURATION:** Spring/Fall • **IDEAL CANDIDATE:** College Students, Career Changers, Retired Folks • **APPLICANT POOL:** 50–75/term • **APPLICANTS ACCEPTED:** 3/term

THE SAILING YAWL CARLYN was completed in late May 1996. She is sixty feet long with a thirteen-foot beam, and displaces twenty tons. The ship is Coast Guard–certified to carry thirty-eight and has the capacity to sleep eighteen. The design and rig support the experiential education interest of Salish Sea and Four Winds Camp (who contracted Salish Sea to build the ship), by allowing maximum student participation in operations.

Student programming operates for five months each spring and fall, with the remainder of the year devoted to development, logistics, and working with teachers to plan programs.

Work/Learn Program Specifics: Science educators teach science topics in the classroom and on the ship. While on the ship, you will also serve as a watch leader, supervising students carrying out communal chores, such as cooking. You will also help the students develop itinerary and research plans. All staff participates in a seven-day training period prior to working with students. Training will familiarize you with Puget Sound ecology, program methodology, safety procedures, and ship operations.

Duration: Five-day workweeks may include weekends or split days off.

Compensation and Perks: Base salary ranges from $30 to $40 per day, depending on prior experience and qualifications. Room and board are provided for the duration of your contract.

The Ideal Candidate: All positions require a college degree and a demonstrated ability to teach and design/implement scientific research projects. Experience with service learning projects is desirable, but not required. Basic first aid and CPR certificates are required; however, advanced certificates and other training, such as EMT or WFR, are highly encouraged.

Making It Happen: Call for more information.

Contact Information: Sophy Johnston, Program Director • Salish Sea Expeditions • P.O. Box 976 • Kingston, WA 98346 • Phone: (360) 297-2512 • E-mail: salish@silverlink.net • Web Site: www.olympic.net/salish

Sarett Nature Center

REGION/HQ: Great Lakes/Michigan • **CATEGORY:** Nature Center • **POSITION TYPE:** Internship • **DURATION:** Year-Round • **IDEAL CANDIDATE:** College Students, Career Changers, Foreigners • **APPLICANT POOL:** Varies • **APPLICANTS ACCEPTED:** 2/term

OVER 25,000 STUDENTS from preschool through college, follow the Sarett Nature Center staff naturalists down the pathway to environmental education each year. The naturalists teach a wide range of environmental topics, including nature awareness, pond study, sand dune ecology, and cross-country skiing.

Area and Working Environment: The center owns 600 acres along the Paw Paw River, manages another 1,200 acres of wooded dunes for the Nature Conservancy, and does nature interpretation at Grand Mere State Park, a wilderness area along Lake Michigan.

Work/Learn Program Specifics: Intern naturalists teach a variety of natural history programs to school groups, primarily preschool through sixth grade. During these programs, interns will lead interpretive nature walks, teach cross-country skiing (winter), lead sixth-grade students on an overnight wilderness camping experience (spring/summer), aid in developing educational programs and weekend activities for the public, build and maintain trails, greet the pubic and answer questions, and care for resident educational animals. Interns are expected to complete a project such as organizing and presenting an interpretive program or display, writing a natural history article for publication, or engaging in field research.

Duration: Positions are available year-round.

Compensation and Perks: Interns receive a $100-per-week stipend, plus room and board.

The Ideal Candidate: Biology or environmental science graduates interested in sharing their knowledge of the natural world with children of all ages are ideal. Useful skills include bird, tree, insect, animal track, and woodland/wetland wildflower identification for the Northeastern United States; cross-country skiing and snowshoeing; canoeing and lifesaving; and low-impact wilderness camping.

Making It Happen: Submit cover letter (including the season you wish to work), resume, and three or four references. Deadlines: winter/spring—October 1; summer—March 1; and fall—June 1.

INSIDER TIPS: *Interns should come eager to learn and willing to take the initiative for projects at hand.*

Contact Information: Dianne Braybrook, Internship Coordinator • Sarett Nature Center • 2300 Benton Center Rd. • Benton Harbor, MI 49022 • Phone: (616) 927-4832 • Fax: (616) 927-2742

Schuylkill Center for Environmental Education

REGION/HQ: Northeast/Pennsylvania • **CATEGORY:** Environmental Education • **POSITION TYPE:** Internship • **DURATION:** Spring/Fall • **IDEAL CANDIDATE:** College Students, Career Changers,

Foreigners • **APPLICANT POOL:** 15–20/term • **APPLICANTS ACCEPTED:** 1–2/term

THE SCHUYLKILL CENTER includes over 500 acres of streams, ponds, old fields, and deciduous forest within the city of Philadelphia. The indoor facilities consist of a 6,000-volume natural history library, 4,000-volume environmental education curriculum and resource library, a computer learning center, hands-on discovery museum, auditorium, bookstore/gift shop, darkroom, classrooms, work areas, and offices—all accessible to wheelchair users. The mission of the Schuylkill Center is to promote, through environmental education, the preservation and improvement of our natural environment by fostering appreciation for and understanding and responsible use of the ecosystem; by disseminating information on current environmental issues; and by encouraging appropriate public response to environmental problems. At the Schuylkill Wildlife Rehabilitation Center, medical treatment and a temporary refuge are provided for birds, mammals, reptiles, and amphibians.

Area and Working Environment: The Schuylkill Center is located near the Schuylkill River in the northwest corner of Philadelphia. The large tract of fields and forests provides visitors with over six miles of hiking trails to experience a variety of wildlife.

Work/Learn Program Specifics: Their environmental education teaching internship is designed to provide an overview of environmental education methods and programs, while allowing maximum opportunities to practice these skills firsthand with the children and adults that visit the center. Interns gradually assume responsibilities during the training period and by the third week are an integral part of the center. Interns are environmental-educators-in-training who work closely with the professional teaching staff to gain expertise in a number of the following areas: teach daily environmental education programs for preschool level through twelfth grade; assist with the center's daily operations; conduct weekend natural history programs for the general public; survey environmental education curriculum materials (including Sharing Nature with Children, Earth Education, Project Learning Tree, and Project Wild); design and construct displays and exhibits for their hands-on discovery museum; and observe and assist with adult workshops, teacher in-services, and college credit courses.

Duration: The internship is for fifteen weeks, held each spring and fall. Interns are required to work forty hours per week, 8:30 A.M. to 5:00 P.M., including some weekend responsibilities.

Compensation and Perks: Interns receive a $1,600 stipend. Periodic teacher workshops in national environmental education curriculum and materials are available.

The Ideal Candidate: Applicants must have a minimum of two years of college in the field of environmental education, biology, natural sciences, elementary education, or a related field, and should have an interest in the environment and desire to work with people.

Making It Happen: Call for application materials. Send a completed application, cover letter, transcripts, and two references by December 1 for the spring and May 1 for the fall. The education staff considers each application and will contact qualified applicants to arrange an in-person interview or a conference call.

INSIDER TIPS: *Those with a combined background of natural sciences and teaching experiences will be given priority.*

Contact Information: Karen Spottiswood, Education Director • Schuylkill Center for Environmental Education • 8480 Hagy's Mill Rd. • Philadelphia, PA 19128-1998 • Phone: (215) 482-7300 • Fax: (215) 482-8158 • E-mail: scee@erols.com

SCICON

REGION/HQ: Pacific Northwest/California • **CATEGORY:** Conservation • **POSITION TYPE:** Internship • **DURATION:** Academic year • **IDEAL CANDIDATE:** College Students, Foreigners • **APPLICANT POOL:** 120/year • **APPLICANTS ACCEPTED:** 10/year

....

SCICON (WHICH STANDS FOR Science and Education) is a resident outdoor education school operated by the Tulare County Office of Education. Over 11,000 students a year attend this outdoor school program to learn and experience nature and science firsthand. SCICON has been developed through thirty-seven years of community involvement. Every acre has been acquired through donations and every building and facility built through volunteers and contributions.

Area and Working Environment: A museum of natural history, planetarium, observatory, raptor rehabilitation center, and over seventeen miles of trails are just some of the highlights of this beautiful 1,200-acre campus.

Work/Learn Program Specifics: Interns gain experience in every facet of outdoor school operation and learn to teach basic concepts of outdoor education in all

areas of natural history. They learn to operate and teach using the various SCICON facilities and gain skills in large-group management, program scheduling, and administration. The internship program starts with an in-depth orientation program at SCICON which includes guest speakers and field trips, as well as intensive training workshops.

Duration: Internships begin in mid-August with three weeks of staff training and continue with program operation through the end of June. Interns can expect long days with irregular hours, Monday through Friday.

Compensation and Perks: You will receive a stipend of $25 to $30 per day, plus room, board, and health insurance.

The Ideal Candidate: Applicants with a bachelor's degree in science, education, or recreation are preferred. Upper-division students will also be considered. Interns must have a high energy level, professional appearance, and a real love for children and the outdoors, and must commit for the entire ten-month program.

Making It Happen: Send your resume and cover letter; an application packet will be sent to you upon receipt. Deadline: February 1 (for a mid-August start date).

Contact Information: Rick Mitchell, Administrator/Director • SCICON • Tulare County Office Of Education • P.O. Box 339 • Visalia, CA 93265 • Phone: (209) 539-2642 • Fax: (209) 539-2643

Science Center of New Hampshire at Squam Lakes

REGION/HQ: Northeast/New Hampshire • **CATEGORY:** Environmental Education • **POSITION TYPE:** Internship • **DURATION:** Year-Round • **IDEAL CANDIDATE:** College Students, Career Changers • **APPLICANT POOL:** 60/term • **APPLICANTS ACCEPTED:** 6/term

....

THE SCIENCE CENTER of New Hampshire is a unique outdoor classroom where people of all ages learn firsthand about native New Hampshire plants and animals. Approximately 25,000 school-age students and 50,000 others visit the center each year.

Area and Working Environment: Located in the beautiful countryside near the shores of Squam Lake in central New Hampshire, the Science Center offers you the opportunity to see and to understand New Hampshire's natural world.

Work/Learn Program Specifics: Teacher-naturalist interns teach and lead programs on natural history and environmental awareness. Programs are done indoors, in classroom format, as well as outdoors using the center's 200-acre site. Interns are also involved in exhibit design and construction, care of the center's native wildlife collection, and the development of pre- and post-trip education materials.

Compensation and Perks: You will receive a $90-per-week stipend. Housing is provided, with a private bedroom, shared bath, and kitchen use.

The Ideal Candidate: College juniors through graduate students majoring in the natural sciences, education, environmental education, or a related field are most desirable. Enthusiasm, motivation, and a desire to work with people and animals are a must. Applicants with personal health insurance get preference in the selection process.

Making It Happen: Submit resume and letter requesting application materials. Candidates should apply three to six months prior to start date.

Contact Information: Dave Chase, Director of Education • Science Center of New Hampshire at Squam Lakes • P.O. Box 173, Route 113 • Holderness, NH 03245-0173 • Phone: (603) 968-7194 • Fax: (603) 968-2229 • E-mail: scnh@lr.net

Sharon Audubon Center

REGION/HQ: Northeast/Connecticut • **CATEGORY:** Nature Center • **POSITION TYPE:** Internship • **DURATION:** Year-Round • **IDEAL CANDIDATE:** College Students, Career Changers, Foreigners • **APPLICANT POOL:** 25/term • **APPLICANTS ACCEPTED:** 2/term

THE SHARON AUDUBON CENTER is one of five environmental education centers in the United States owned and operated by the National Audubon Society. Their purpose is to educate the public about and instill respect for our environment and all living things. This goal is met by providing a protected natural area for self-guided exploration and regularly scheduled programs led by their staff naturalists.

Area and Working Environment: This 754-acre sanctuary provides outstanding learning opportunities in a diverse and beautiful setting in northwestern Connecticut.

Work/Learn Program Specifics: Environmental education interns develop curriculum materials and teach a wide variety of topics (animal adaptation, pond exploration, birds of prey, insect investigation, and maple sugaring) to on-site and outreach audiences of all ages. Interns help care for the turtles and injured birds in the main exhibit room and help admit and care for the injured birds that are brought to the center. Additional duties include creating and maintaining exhibits, answering requests for environmental information, completion of a special project, and helping with many other facets of a nature center's day-to-day operations. The summer naturalist will develop curriculum materials and teach a wide variety of topics (animal adaptation, pond exploration, and insect investigation). Other responsibilities include live animal care and rehabilitation, helping with the annual Sharon Audubon Festival in July, maintaining trails, and all other facets of the nature center's operation.

Duration: Environmental education positions are offered in spring and fall; naturalist positions are for nine weeks during the summer only.

Compensation and Perks: Environmental education interns receive $100 per week; summer naturalists receive $1,800 for the summer. All interns have a furnished suite in the main building, with private bedrooms. They share a kitchen, bath, and living room.

The Ideal Candidate: Some teaching experience or curriculum development is necessary. The most important assets are a strong natural history background, enthusiasm, commitment, a desire to learn, flexibility, and the ability to work well with others (especially children).

Making It Happen: Send cover letter, resume, and contact information for three references. Rolling deadlines.

INSIDER TIPS: *Must have solid outdoor background, not merely experience with environmental issues.*

Contact Information: Scott Heth, Manager • Sharon Audubon Center • 325 Cornwall Bridge Rd. • Sharon, CT 06069 • Phone: (860) 364-0520 • Fax: (860) 364-5792

Shaver's Creek Environmental Center

REGION/HQ: Northeast/Pennsylvania • **CATEGORY:** Environmental Education • **POSITION TYPE:**

Internship • **DURATION:** Year-Round • **IDEAL CANDIDATE:** College Students, Career Changers, Foreigners • **APPLICANT POOL:** 120/year • **APPLICANTS ACCEPTED:** 18/year

SHAVER'S CREEK IS AN environmental education laboratory seeking to enhance the quality of life of the local and global community by providing exemplary outdoor learning opportunities. Administered by Penn State's Division of Continuing and Distance Education, the center functions as a university field campus, providing facilities and programming that meet the education and research needs of several departments. This multifaceted center offers environmental education programs for group visits, natural/cultural history exhibits, live amphibians and reptiles, hiking trails, herb gardens, and more. Their raptor center is one of the few federally and state-licensed raptor facilities in Pennsylvania, providing perpetual care and housing for eagles, falcons, hawks, and owls. Shaver's Creek is a member of the Global Network of Environmental Education Centers and is currently involved in fostering environmental programming in central Europe.

Area and Working Environment: The center is located on 1,000 acres of diverse fields and woodlands in the ridge and valley province of central Pennsylvania, thirteen miles south of State College and the main campus of Penn State.

Work/Learn Program Specifics: Environmental education interns become an integral part of the staff and are encouraged to participate in all aspects of the center's operation. A two-week orientation and training period is followed by seasonal program opportunities in both day and residential settings. Interns work with all ages, preschool to adult, as they lead natural and cultural history programs for school and community groups, families, and the general public. Interns also have the opportunity to contribute articles to their members' newsletter, lead adventure and team-building programs, participate in the care and handling of the live animal collection, and assist in the general operation of the center. Observations, recordings, and videotaping are used in evaluation, and interns are encouraged to keep a journal. The time spent at Shaver's Creek is intense and demanding, but also rewarding.

Duration: Positions are available year-round, for three to six months, and interns have the opportunity to extend their commitment to multiple seasons. The average workweek is forty-five hours.

Compensation and Perks: Interns receive a weekly stipend of $125 and on-site housing (nestled in the woods away from park visitors, with a private sleeping room). Interns are encouraged to participate in professional development workshops and regional conferences, and each season includes a three-day staff trip to another environmental center or a facility of interest. Macintosh computers are used on-site, and access to the Internet is available through Penn State University. They also provide resources on job listings and assistance with resume writing. Former Shaver's Creek interns have taken their skills and moved into the professional world in such places as cultural history centers, natural history institutes, environmental education centers, and many public and private facilities throughout the country.

The Ideal Candidate: Successful candidates have a strong desire to teach and share their knowledge and enthusiasm for the natural world. A background in education or the natural sciences is helpful, but not necessary. International students are encouraged to apply, and the center can assist with the J-1 visa application process.

Making It Happen: Interested candidates can call, fax, or write for an application. Deadlines: winter/spring— November 1; summer—March 1; and fall—July 1. Interviews with top candidates are conducted in person or by phone.

INSIDER TIPS: *Most successful candidates have some experience in working with children. A site visit and meeting with the intern coordinator is beneficial, but not necessary. Many first-time undergraduate candidates who are not accepted, mistakenly fail to reapply for an upcoming season.*

Contact Information: Doug Wentzel, Internship Coordinator • Shaver's Creek Environmental Center • The Pennsylvania State University • 508A Keller Bldg. • University Park, PA 16802-9976 • Phone: (814) 863-2000 • Fax: (814) 865-2706 • Web Site: www.cde.psu.edu/shaverscreek

Slide Ranch

REGION/HQ: Pacific Northwest/California • **CATEGORY:** Environmental Education • **POSITION TYPE:** Internship • **DURATION:** Varies • **IDEAL CANDIDATE:** College Students, Career Changers, Foreigners • **APPLICANT POOL:** 75/year • **APPLICANTS ACCEPTED:** 5/year

SLIDE RANCH IS A nonprofit education center and provides hands-on experiences teaching respect for our human role in the web of life. Through participation in Slide Ranch programs, Bay Area residents can make choices which are ecologically and agriculturally informed, take actions supporting the sustainable use of natural resources, and feel nourished by the natural world. Their programs range from half a day to one week in length and are hands-on and experiential. Their focus is to explore the sources of our food and clothing and to realize and demonstrate our dependence upon natural resources. They offer programs relevant to contemporary life which cultivate an understanding of environmental, agricultural, and human interdependence and effectively galvanize environmentally sound decisions and actions. They strive to create a sense of belonging to the natural world for those who visit the ranch.

Area and Working Environment: Slide Ranch resides on a coastal farm setting.

Work/Learn Program Specifics: The teaching internship program is lead by a head teacher and teaching interns. As a teaching intern, you will gain valuable outdoor education teaching experience leading groups through various on-site activities. You will team-teach, as well as lead-teach, a wide range of programs. The variety of participants that use Slide Ranch will allow you to hone your teaching skills by teaching to groups of all ages. The program is designed to both challenge you and support your growth as a person and professional educator. Under the guidance of the head teacher and program director, you will participate in a two-week intensive training program upon arrival and receive ongoing support, supervision, staff development, and enrichment throughout the internship. Beyond your responsibilities in the teaching programs, you will also be responsible for a chore area, which includes caring for the garden and compost, goats and sheep, chickens and turkeys, or rabbits. You will also be responsible for learning the maintenance of the other chore areas and will work closely with the ranch manager to help in the daily/weekly routines of animal care and site maintenance.

Duration: Positions begin in early September and last 3$^{1}/_{2}$ to 7 months. Living at the Ranch is more than a nine-to-five job; it's a full-time commitment. They are a small community that works, lives, and plays together. All residents are expected to take part in the shared decision-making and domestic responsibilities that go along with being part of a community.

Compensation and Perks: Interns receive a $100-per-month stipend. While each teaching intern is provided with an individual room and full board, cooking and dining space is shared, and all residents help in the preparation of food and the maintenance of the facilities. There is a five-day community trip scheduled, and each intern is given two vacation days to schedule during their tenure. Many former Slide Ranch interns now teach professionally; while others work in the social services, community development organizations, sustainable agriculture, and environmental organizations.

The Ideal Candidate: Candidates must have a keen interest in environmental education and community spirit.

Making It Happen: Send your resume, the names, addresses, and phone numbers of three references, and a self-addressed envelope. Also include a letter telling them more about yourself, including any experience you've had teaching or working with young people, gardening, farming, or working with animals. If you speak other languages or have experience working with low-income or special populations, include this information as well. Also address any experiences you've had working or living in a community.

Contact Information: Marc Lavine, Program Director • Slide Ranch • 2025 Shoreline Highway • Muir Beach, CA 94965 • Phone: (415) 381-6155 • Fax: (415) 381-5762 • E-mail: slideranch@igc.org

Staten Island Zoological Society

REGION/HQ: Northeast/New York • **CATEGORY:** Zoo • **POSITION TYPE:** Internship • **DURATION:** Summer • **IDEAL CANDIDATE:** College Students, Foreigners • **APPLICANT POOL:** Varies • **APPLICANTS ACCEPTED:** 3/year

WHEN THE STATEN ISLAND ZOO opened in 1936, it was a depression-era "modern miracle," with its eight-acre park setting and bylaws creating the first educational zoo in America. For over half a century, millions of people, second and third generations of families, have reaped the recreational and educational benefits of New York City's biggest little zoo.

Area and Working Environment: Positions are located on a small eight-acre zoo in New York City.

Work/Learn Program Specifics: Zoofari day camp instructors are needed for art, science, and recreation to coordinate the development, implementation, and evaluation of Zoofari sessions for preschool through sixth-grade age groups. Art instructors design student activities in which elements of art are explored, plan experiences with various media and methods, and focus on animal subjects. Outdoor recreation instructors plan and conduct noncompetitive activities, organize groups of fifteen to thirty children in both active and quiet activities, develop and reinforce animal characteristics and behavioral concepts through use of games, and coordinate teen volunteers as camp aides. Science instructors engage day campers in participatory learning, plan programs utilizing the zoo's exhibits and collections, and confidently handle and care for a variety of live animals in a group situation.

Duration: Full-time positions are offered from June to late August.

Compensation and Perks: Interns receive a $250-per-week salary.

The Ideal Candidate: They seek individuals experienced in environmental interpretation or elementary education with a concentration in science, art, or recreation, and with preparation for elementary teaching. Instructors should possess appropriate skills for conducting learning activities in an informal setting (often outdoors) and the ability to structure curriculum upon animal themes and examples. A strong background in learning theory, teaching strategies, curriculum/lesson planning, and evaluation is preferred.

Making It Happen: Submit cover letter and resume by April 1.

Contact Information: Education Director • Staten Island Zoological Society • 614 Broadway • Staten Island, NY 10310 • Phone: (718) 442-3174 • Fax: (718) 981-8711

Touch of Nature Environmental Center

REGION/HQ: Great Lakes/Illinois • **CATEGORY:** Experiential Education • **POSITION TYPE:** Internship • **DURATION:** Year-Round • **IDEAL CANDIDATE:** College Students, Career Changers, Foreigners • **APPLICANT POOL:** Varies • **APPLICANTS ACCEPTED:** Varies

SINCE 1969, TOUCH OF NATURE'S wilderness program has provided outdoor education and recreation experiences for a wide variety of groups. Through wilderness settings, initiative courses, and adventure activities, the wilderness program helps participants achieve self-

confidence, self-reliance, cooperation, trust, and appreciation of the outdoors.

Work/Learn Program Specifics: The wilderness program provides a professionally supervised work/learn experience for interns in most aspects of outdoor adventure programming, including backpacking, initiative courses, rock climbing, caving, and canoeing. In addition, you will work at least one, thirty-day wilderness course with youth-at-risk.

Compensation and Perks: Interns receive a $250-per-month stipend, plus basic living quarters and use of the center's equipment and facilities.

The Ideal Candidate: Ideal applicants are college graduates or those nearing completion who have experience working with youth-at-risk and wilderness training, and have certification in first aid and CPR.

Making It Happen: Call for application. Return completed application with resume and letters of reference a minimum of two months prior to desired start date.

INSIDER TIPS: *This program works with a very challenging population in a wilderness setting. A strong desire to work with youth-at-risk is important.*

Contact Information: Tim Humes, Wilderness Program Director • Touch of Nature Environmental Center • Southern Illinois University • Carbondale, IL 62901-6623 • Phone: (618) 453-1121 • Fax: (618) 453-1188 • E-mail: Tonec@siu.edu

Trees For Tomorrow

REGION/HQ: Great Lakes/Wisconsin • **CATEGORY:** Natural Resources • **POSITION TYPE:** Internship • **DURATION:** Year-Round • **IDEAL CANDIDATE:** College Students, Career Changers, Foreigners • **APPLICANT POOL:** 50–100/year • **APPLICANTS ACCEPTED:** 5/year

TREES FOR TOMORROW Natural Resources Education Center is an outdoor school where the teaching is field-based, at woodlots, beaver ponds, lakes, streams, bogs, and forests. Students learn by doing and by first-hand observation of resource management techniques. They specialize in presenting a variety of perspectives on natural resource topics. From water management and forest ecology, to soil science and energy conservation, they provide a balanced, objective education that complements and enhances in-school science and environmental education curricula. After a "Trees" workshop, participants will be prepared to make their own informed decisions about how to manage our renewable resources.

Work/Learn Program Specifics: Interns will teach a variety of educational activities for diverse audiences, both indoors and out; have your teaching style evaluated by professional staff and self; learn about the natural history and resource management techniques of the north woods; design and develop an interpretive project or educational curriculum activity for use in the ongoing programs at the center; write for *Northbound*, a quarterly news magazine on natural resources issues; gain computer skills and the opportunity to develop quality brochures and flyers; keep a daily log of your experiences and development; network with resource professionals for the U.S. Forest Service, Wisconsin Department of Natural Resources, and a variety of forest products industries; and make new friends and lifelong memories while doing a little hard work in the north woods.

Duration: Winter positions run from late December through May; summer/fall positions run June to late November.

Compensation and Perks: Interns receive a stipend of $450 per month, plus room and board. Perks include staff jackets and curriculum guides, the chance to tour other nature centers to get project ideas and network for future employment, and excellent recommendations from your supervisor.

The Ideal Candidate: Candidates should have completed two years of college, with a background in natural resources, biology, outdoor/environmental education, outdoor recreation, or other natural sciences. Recent graduates are preferred. Qualifications they look for include a willingness to learn, high motivation, and good people skills. For winter positions, cross-country ski and snowshoe experience is a plus, but much can be learned at Trees.

Making It Happen: Send cover letter, resume, and a list of three references. Telephone interviews are given to the most promising applicants. Deadlines: winter— November 1; summer/fall—April 4.

INSIDER TIPS: *Again, a willingness to learn and a desire to teach and work with people ranging in age from fourth grade on up to senior citizens is key. We need people who are flexible, always willing to lend a helping hand, and dedicated to the wise use of our environment.*

Contact Information: Sandy Lotto, Internship Coordinator • Trees For Tomorrow • Natural Resources Education Center • P.O. Box 609 • Eagle River, WI 54521-0609 • Phone: (715) 479-6456 • Fax: (715) 479-2318 • Toll Free: (800) 838-9472

Turtle Mountain Environmental Learning Center

REGION/HQ: Rocky Mountains/North Dakota • **CATEGORY:** Environmental Education • **POSITION TYPE:** Internship • **DURATION:** Spring/Summer • **IDEAL CANDIDATE:** College Students, Career Changers, Foreigners • **APPLICANT POOL:** 40/term • **APPLICANTS ACCEPTED:** 2/term

TURTLE MOUNTAIN ENVIRONMENTAL Learning Center (TMELC) was established in 1986, with the goal to provide quality environmental education in a natural setting, for future generations. Over 1,600 acres of forested, rolling hills dotted with many lakes and marshes serve as their outdoor classroom. The TMELC offers a selection of more than twenty hands-on programs available from April to December. The programs can be designed to meet the needs of any group in both content and program length. Groups have the option to come out for just a day or to utilize the center's dorm and kitchen/dining hall facilities for a residential program. The TMELC also offers a Nature in the Classroom program, where TMELC staff brings environmental education to classrooms, community groups, and service organizations wherever they meet. All of their programs strive to develop an awareness, understanding, appreciation, and attitude of change towards the natural environment.

Area and Working Environment: Lake Metigoshe State Park is located in the heart of North Dakota's beautiful Turtle Mountains.

Work/Learn Program Specifics: Outdoor education interns conduct environmental and outdoor recreational education programs for residential camp and day-use student groups (primarily K–10), though adult groups make up a large portion of users. Interns will assist in developing new programs and curricula and are required to complete a project of their own choosing. The position may also include some trail and grounds maintenance and assistance with any special functions sponsored by the TMELC.

Duration: Positions run from April 1 to June 1 (preferable), but the duration is negotiable. If the interns meet state employment standards, there is a possibility of obtaining a three-month summer naturalist position at Lake Metigoshe State Park.

Compensation and Perks: Interns receive a $400 to $500-per-month stipend, plus housing and uniforms. Housing is in a semi-primitive cabin (set in a beautiful area near the lakeshore), which includes a bed, dresser, refrigerator, stove, kitchen table, and running water in the kitchen (bathrooms and showers are away from the cabin).

The Ideal Candidate: Applicants must have completed two semesters of college (or equivalent experience) and have strong organizational skills, the ability to work a flexible schedule, and a basic working knowledge of computers.

Making It Happen: Submit cover letter, resume, transcript, a list of references, and dates available to begin the internship. Applications must be received by February 28, and it's best to apply early. The top candidates will be contacted for a telephone or personal interview.

INSIDER TIPS: *While there are only two positions available, the chance of obtaining one of the positions is quite good if you are available to begin work by April 1. Experience in teaching or working with children is helpful, but not required. Enthusiasm, a willingness to try new and exciting experiences, and a general love of children go just as far in helping you to secure a position. Don't be afraid to try something new, enjoy nature, and be able to laugh and have fun.*

Contact Information: Erica Vollegraaf, TMELC Coordinator • Turtle Mountain Environmental Learning Center • #2 Lake Metigoshe State Park • Bottineau, ND 58318 • Phone: (701) 263-4514 • Fax: (701) 263-4648 • E-mail: tmelc@metigoshe.ndak.net

University of Georgia Marine Extension Service

REGION/HQ: Southeast/Georgia • **CATEGORY:** Marine Science • **POSITION TYPE:** Internship • **DURATION:** Year-Long • **IDEAL CANDIDATE:** College Students, Foreigners • **APPLICANT POOL:** 30 to 50/year • **APPLICANTS ACCEPTED:** 3/year

DEDICATED TO TEACHING students and adults about the coastal environment, the University of Georgia operates the Marine Extension Center. The Center includes a 19,000-square-foot education center with a teaching aquarium, classrooms and exhibit space, a 50-bed dormitory, a cafeteria, and three research vessels. Each year, 13,000 students from Georgia and adjacent states, receive formal education from programs at the Marine Extension Service.

Area and Working Environment: The center is located on scenic Skidaway Island, adjacent to the Skidaway Institute of Oceanography, about fourteen miles from historic Savannah.

Work/Learn Program Specifics: An expert staff of marine environmental educators spend the fall months teaching interns about coastal ecology, oceanography, barrier-island dynamics, ichthyology, archaeology, fisheries biology, the history of the coast, and laboratory and field teaching techniques. These subjects are taught using the living laboratory of the relatively pristine Georgia coast, their well-equipped marine center, boats, and public aquariums. Once training is complete, interns teach a wide variety of students (kindergarten to high school, college students, in-service teachers, and other adults) in formal and informal classes lasting a half-day to several weeks.

Duration: This is a fifty-week program, beginning September 1. In the months of July and August, interns work with a five-week-long day camp program.

Compensation and Perks: You will receive a $200-per-week stipend. Interns live in single occupancy, dorm-style apartments, and have free meals whenever groups are scheduled to eat in the cafeteria. Perks include access to the on-site research library and the opportunity to attend local workshops and educational meetings.

The Ideal Candidate: Open to recent college graduates who are interested in teaching about the marine environment and who enjoy working with children and adults. A degree in science or science education is required.

Making It Happen: Send cover letter expressing career interests and experiences, resume, and official transcript by April 1. Phone interviews will be conducted and references will be contacted.

Contact Information: Associate Director–Education • University of Georgia Marine Extension Service • 30 Ocean Science Circle • Savannah, GA 31411 • Phone: (912) 598-2496 • Fax: (912) 598-2302 • E-mail: eschmidt@uga.cc.uga.edu • Web Site: www.marsci.uga.edu/EXT/MAREX.html

Upham Woods 4-H EE Center

REGION/HQ: Great Lakes/Wisconsin • **CATEGORY:** Environmental Education • **POSITION TYPE:** Internship • **DURATION:** Year-Round • **IDEAL**

CANDIDATE: College Students, Career Changers, Foreigners • **APPLICANT POOL:** 100/year • **APPLICANTS ACCEPTED:** 10/year

UPHAM WOODS 4-H Environmental Education Center has been part of the University of Wisconsin system since 1950 and provides environmental education programs for more than 9,000 adult and youth clients each year. Residential programs focus on animals, plants, water, and their relationship.

Area and Working Environment: Upham Woods is a sandstone, driftless area with unique geologic formations. The center includes a 220-acre island just one mile from the city of Wisconsin Dells.

Work/Learn Program Specifics: Naturalists teach natural science and lead activities primarily for middle-school clientele. Other responsibilities include developing and leading challenge activities on-site and at remote sites by canoe tripping, as well as planning, designing, and developing educational displays, activities, or curriculum.

Duration: Positions are offered year-round, with a five-day, irregular workweek with work between the hours of 7 A.M. and 11 P.M.

Compensation and Perks: Interns receive $150 to $200 per week. Room is provided in "staff-only" housing (on-site), including meals.

The Ideal Candidate: Applicants must have completed introductory courses in either natural resources, recreation, or education (at least junior status). Demonstrated success in working effectively with individuals and groups is preferred. Lifesaving, advanced first aid, and current CPR are required for summer positions and desired for other periods of the year.

Making It Happen: Call for application materials. Rolling deadlines. Personal interviews are preferred, although phone interviews are acceptable.

Contact Information: Bob Nichols, Director • Upham Woods 4-H EE Center • N194, County Highway N • Wisconsin Dells, WI 53965 • Phone: (608) 254-6461 • Fax: (608) 253-7140 • E-mail: bob.nichols@ces.uwex.edu

Vermont Raptor Center

REGION/HQ: Northeast/Vermont • **CATEGORY:** Wildlife • **POSITION TYPE:** Internship • **DURATION:** Year-Round • **IDEAL CANDIDATE:** College Students, Career Changers, Foreigners • **APPLICANT POOL:** 100–150/year • **APPLICANTS ACCEPTED:** Varies

FOUNDED IN 1972, the Vermont Institute of Natural Science (VINS) is a private, nonprofit membership organization reaching 100,000 Vermonters annually, and provides innovative and effective environmental education programs and conducts important natural history research. The Vermont Raptor Center is a living museum which introduces visitors to the owls and hawks of northern New England. The outdoor museum houses twenty-six species of owls, hawks, and eagles in spacious flight habitats.

Work/Learn Program Specifics: Internships with the Vermont Raptor Center offer an experience in bird rehabilitation, with an emphasis on raptors and environmental education (75 percent of your time is spent in rehabilitation work; 25 percent in environmental education). Each intern is trained in basic care, handling, and treatment of injured birds; assists in monitoring the health of approximately eighty nonreleasable raptors (birds of prey) used for public education; works with veterinarian and volunteer networks and supervises volunteers; admits patients and carries out medical treatments; handles nonreleasable hawks and owls in educational presentations; and assists with general operation of the Raptor Center. Summer interns also work extensively with orphaned birds. Additionally, interns are given the opportunity to participate in other VINS research and educational activities.

Duration: The program functions year-round, with internship periods generally beginning in early January, late May, and late August.

Compensation and Perks: You will receive a stipend of $250 per month, plus housing provided at the VINS residence facility nearby.

The Ideal Candidate: Enthusiasm, flexibility, and a strong interest in birds are musts. Experience in ornithology, bird handling, veterinary assistance, or environmental education is preferred. Applicants must be at least eighteen years of age, hold a current driver's license, be physically able to lift fifty pounds and walk/run on the grounds for purposes of patrol and public safety, and be able to carry out routine facility maintenance and property-related duties.

Making It Happen: Send resume, two letters of reference, and a cover letter with dates of availability and a statement of goals and interests relative to the internship at least four months prior to your requested start date.

Contact Information: Michael Cox, Director • Vermont Raptor Center • Vermont Institute Of Natural Science • Church Hill Rd., RR2, Box 532 • Woodstock, VT

05091-9720 • Phone: (802) 457-2779 • Fax: (802) 457-2779 • E-mail: vtraptct@sover.net

Vermont Youth Conservation Corps

REGION/HQ: Northeast/Vermont • **CATEGORY:** Conservation • **POSITION TYPE:** Seasonal • **DURATION:** Spring-Fall • **IDEAL CANDIDATE:** College Students, Career Changers, Retired Folks • **APPLICANT POOL:** Varies • **APPLICANTS ACCEPTED:** Varies

• •

THE YOUTH CORPS IS A private nonprofit organization that hires teams of teenagers who work and study under excellent adult leadership to complete high-priority conservation and park management projects on public lands in Vermont. Youths in the program participate in a daily integrated cycle of reading, discussion, writing, and team building activities. A diverse crew population is a key component of the Youth Corps experience. On each crew there are economically disadvantaged, college-bound, high-school, dropout, and learning-disabled youth. This extraordinary diversity helps break down traditional social and economic barriers and provides a rich and challenging environment for corps members to learn from one another. Crews work on many different types of projects, including trail construction and maintenance, footbridge construction, timber-stand improvement, creek and watershed restoration, park management, and facility improvement.

Area and Working Environment: The Youth Corps operates in Vermont State Parks and National Forest Recreation Areas.

Work/Learn Program Specifics: Crew leaders supervise the work projects; facilitate the daily reading, writing, and discussion program; utilize the local environment to conduct the daily environmental education program; and build teams that communicate well, respect one another, and are fun and productive. The residential camp director manages all aspects of various centers. This person will supervise a staff of four leaders, manage the facility, purchase all food and supplies, and manage the center's budget. Park corps managers are responsible for operating a park with a crew of two to ten youths aged seventeen to twenty-one years and one or two assistant managers (couples are encouraged to apply). Park assistant managers work with the park corps managers in all areas.

Duration: Dates vary and range from April through October.

Compensation and Perks: Crew leader pay ranges from $2,700 to $3,456 per season; camp director— $4,224 to $4,950; park corps assistant—$4,200 to $4,700; and park corps manager—$6,500 to $13,000. All positions include room and board, paid staff training, and reimbursement for travel to Vermont.

The Ideal Candidate: Candidates should have experience with at-risk youth; a background in education, environmental studies, or a related field; excellent organizational and communication skills; cooking skills and enthusiasm for health and tasty food; and standard first aid and CPR certifications.

Making It Happen: Call for application materials.

Contact Information: Dominic Cloud, Trails Coordinator • Vermont Youth Conservation Corps • P.O. Box 482 • Waterbury, VT 05676 • Phone: (802) 241-3903 • Fax: (802) 241-3909 • Toll Free: (800) 639-8922 • E-mail: ycorps@together.net • Web Site: www.state.vt.us/anr/fpr/vycc/index.htm

WildCare

REGION/HQ: Pacific Northwest/California • **CATEGORY:** Nature Center • **POSITION TYPE:** Internship • **DURATION:** Year-Round • **IDEAL CANDIDATE:** College Students, Career Changers, Foreigners • **APPLICANT POOL:** 10/year • **APPLICANTS ACCEPTED:** 1–3/year

• •

WILDCARE: Terwilliger Nature Education and Wildlife Rehabilitation creates a knowledgeable and nurturing relationship with our environment through nature education and wildlife rehabilitation. Environmental education programs reach 60,000 children in nine Bay Area counties. Programs were established over twenty years ago and include habitat discovery trips, nature van outreach programs, classroom nature kits, center tours, family and tot walks, and nature camp. A full-scale, modern wildlife rehabilitation hospital provides specialized diet, shelter, daily care, and veterinary treatment for approximately 4,000 wild animals annually.

Area and Working Environment: The center is located in Marin County, just fifteen minutes from San Francisco. Hiking trails, beaches, museums, restaurants, and other cultural activities abound. A large variety of other nature centers are within an hour's driving distance.

Work/Learn Program Specifics: Interns work under the supervision of the education director on a special project.

Interns are especially needed during the summer to assist the head teacher/naturalist with implementing the summer/nature camp program. Each week has a different nature theme and age group. Internships in the off-season include working on curriculum development, participation in the nature guide training program, or leading field trips for small groups of children.

Duration: Interns may work one or more weeks with varying work schedules. Nature camp interns work from mid-June to late August; other positions are available year-round.

Compensation and Perks: Stipend available. Work with a well-known environmental education group learning interpretive skills; become acquainted with a variety of trail and classroom teaching techniques for children; and practice a multisensory approach, curriculum planning, and group management skills.

The Ideal Candidate: Previous experience working with children in groups is necessary for nature camp interns. A budding knowledge of natural history is helpful, and curiosity, enthusiasm, stamina, and openness to learning are essential.

Making It Happen: Send cover letter, resume, and several letters of recommendation. Rolling deadlines.

INSIDER TIPS: *Someone who is enthusiastic, loves nature, is open to learning, and can be depended upon has the best chance of obtaining a position.*

Contact Information: Education Director • WildCare • P.O. Box 150930 • San Rafael, CA 94915-0930 • Phone: (415) 453-1000 • Fax: (415) 456-0594

Wildlife Prairie Park

REGION/HQ: Great Lakes/Illinois • **CATEGORY:** Wildlife • **POSITION TYPE:** Internship • **DURATION:** Year-Round • **IDEAL CANDIDATE:** College Students, Career Changers • **APPLICANT POOL:** 10–20/year • **APPLICANTS ACCEPTED:** 2/term

WILDLIFE PRAIRIE PARK is a nonprofit park stressing conservation, education, and recreation. The park covers 2,000 acres of grazing land, lakes, and forests, and presents wild animals native to Illinois in their natural habitats. It contrasts the rugged heritage and simple lifestyles of Illinois' past with the complex, energy-demanding society of the future and provides a better understanding of our environment through education, conservation, and recreation.

Work/Learn Program Specifics: Student naturalist interns work under the direction of the park's education department. Duties include those normally associated with the department, including special interpretive projects, trail monitoring and development, plus performance of public educational programs. These varied duties will entail both indoor and outdoor tasks, physical and mental skills, and will provide working experience with park staff, volunteers, and the general public.

Duration: Internships are twelve weeks, offered year-round.

Compensation and Perks: Interns for the summer are provided with a $75-per-week stipend and on-site lodging, or a $125-per-week stipend with no housing. Interns for the remaining semesters are on a voluntary basis. Appropriate park uniforms and all necessary tools will be provided. In addition, each intern will receive the same discounts at the food service and special events as other park employees.

The Ideal Candidate: Qualified applicants are those pursuing a degree in outdoor/environmental education, interpretation, parks and recreation, biology, or other related fields, or recent graduates.

Making It Happen: Submit cover letter and resume. The summer deadline is March 31 and rolling for the remaining terms.

Contact Information: Keelie Lawson, Intern Coordinator • Wildlife Prairie Park • 3826 N. Taylor Rd., RR2, Box 50 • Peoria, IL 61615-9617 • Phone: (309) 676-0998 • Fax: (309) 676-7783 • E-mail: wppark@aol.com

Wolf Ridge Environmental Learning Center

REGION/HQ: Great Lakes/Minnesota • **CATEGORY:** Environmental Education • **POSITION TYPE:** Internship • **DURATION:** Year-Round • **IDEAL CANDIDATE:** College Students, Career Changers, Retired Folks, Foreigners • **APPLICANT POOL:** 200/year • **APPLICANTS ACCEPTED:** 12/year

WOLF RIDGE ENVIRONMENTAL Learning Center is an accredited residential school dedicated to providing all people with opportunities to develop their understanding and appreciation of the environment and their responsibility for stewardship of the earth. Audiences are students of all ages, mostly school-age children.

Area and Working Environment: Wolf Ridge is located on a bluff overlooking Lake Superior, about sixty-five miles northeast of Duluth in northeastern Minnesota.

Work/Learn Program Specifics: Your main responsibility is teaching half-day ecology, cultural history, and recreation classes to students of all ages. You will be guided through the program through initial training, ongoing evaluations, and regular workshops, seminars, and field trips to develop your skills as an educator. Professional interns are simultaneously enrolled in a postbaccalaureate certificate program at a local university. They receive twenty graduate-level credits while participating in this program. This is a one-of-a-kind training program for people thinking of entering the naturalist field or for teachers hoping to enhance their environmental education skills. This carefully designed program leads you through a progression of methodologies and techniques to help you develop your own teaching philosophy. People who spend a year at Wolf Ridge usually say it was a major highlight of their life.

Duration: Positions begin in August and are for nine months, with an option of summer employment.

Compensation and Perks: You will receive a private or shared room, partial board, a scholarship to cover college graduate tuition, and $200 per month if you work during the summer. All program participants share a communal living room, dining room, kitchen, laundry, and bathrooms.

The Ideal Candidate: All candidates are required to have a four-year science degree and should be interested in working with people in the outdoors and teaching and learning about the forests, wetlands, and animals. Basic first aid certification is required, as are a positive attitude and enthusiasm.

Making It Happen: Call for application packet. Submit completed application, resume, college transcript, and names and addresses of three references. Applications are reviewed in March and April, and are accepted continuously with an active waiting list kept. Candidates are interviewed over the phone and offers extended April 31. Note that their toll-free number can only be used from Minnesota or Wisconsin.

INSIDER TIPS: *There are many applicants for this unique training program. Be careful with your application to be clear and communicate well about yourself and your experiences. This position demands a person who truly enjoys being with people, especially children, and is a hard worker with community focus.*

Contact Information: Terry McLaughlin, Naturalist Training Director • Wolf Ridge Environmental Learning Center • 230 Cranberry Road • Finland, MN 55603 • Phone: (218) 353-7414 • Fax: (218) 353-7762 • Toll Free: (800) 523-2733 • E-mail: wrelc@mr.net

Every man has two educations – that which is given to him, and the other, that which he gives to himself. What we are merely taught seldom nourishes the mind like that which we teach ourselves. Indeed, all that is mostly worthy in a man, he must work out and conquer for himself.

—RICKER

Short Listings

AABGA

REGION/HQ: Nationwide/Pennsylvania • **CATEGORY:** Botanical Garden • **POSITION TYPE:** Association • **DURATION:** Year-Round • **IDEAL CANDIDATE:** College Students, Career Changers, Retired Folks, Foreigners • **APPLICANT POOL:** Varies • **APPLICANTS ACCEPTED:** Varies

PARTICIPATION IN THE American Association of Botanical Gardens and Arboreta (AABGA) is one way to further your career goals and to keep in touch with what's happening at other public gardens across the United States and Canada. They publish an annual internship/jobs directory (which you can receive for $10). Internships focus on conservation of rare plants, arid-land horticulture, historic garden restoration, plant inventories, and evaluation of collections, children's programs, integrated pest management, ecology and restoration programs, zoo horticulture, and horticultural therapy.

Contact Information: Nancy Morin, Executive Director • AABGA • 786 Church Road • Wayne, PA 19087 • Phone: (610) 688-1120 • Fax: (610) 293-0149 • E-mail: AABGA@aol.com • Web Site: www. mobot. org/aabga

American Horticultural Society

REGION/HQ: Southeast/Virginia • **CATEGORY:** Agriculture • **POSITION TYPE:** Internship • **DURATION:** Year-Round • **IDEAL CANDIDATE:** College Students, Career Changers, Foreigners • **APPLICANT POOL:** 25–60/year • **APPLICANTS ACCEPTED:** 3/term

THE AMERICAN HORTICULTURAL SOCIETY is located at River Farm, a historic, twenty-six-acre property along the Potomac River. Interns assist with renovation, restoration, and maintenance of gardens and grounds, and help with the children's gardening program and other special projects. Interns also participate in society programs and projects, such as their annual seed program, open-house events, lectures, and seminars. Interns receive $240 per week, and AHS will help arrange housing in a local neighborhood.

Contact Information: Mark Miller, Internship Coordinator • American Horticultural Society • 7931 E. Boulevard Dr. • Alexandria, VA 22308 • Phone: (703) 768-5700 • Fax: (703) 765-8700 • Toll Free: (800) 777-7931 • E-mail: gardenAHS@aol.com

Arboreta & Botanic Gardens

REGION/HQ: Pacific Northwest/California • **CATEGORY:** Botanical Garden • **POSITION TYPE:** Internship • **DURATION:** Summer • **IDEAL CANDIDATE:** College Students, Foreigners • **APPLICANT POOL:** 60/year • **APPLICANTS ACCEPTED:** 6/year

THE ARBORETA & BOTANIC GARDENS cultivates and maintains hundreds of acres of lush greenery and colorful plants at four locations open to the public throughout the year. These gardens offer the casual sightseer and the serious horticulturist a place to see attractive and effective uses of trees, shrubs, and ground covers. Students can participate in their horticulture internship program, where they receive hands-on training sessions in nursery management, equipment maintenance, herbarium operation, labeling, soil preparation, plant propagation, pruning and staking, and irrigation installation. Interns earn $7.52 per hour.

Contact Information: Tim Lindsay, Assistant Superintendent • Arboreta & Botanic Gardens • 301 N. Baldwin Ave. • Arcadia, CA 91007-2697 • Phone: (818) 821-3236 • Fax: (818) 445-1217

Beaver Lake Nature Center

REGION/HQ: Northeast/New York • **CATEGORY:** Nature Center • **POSITION TYPE:** Internship • **DURATION:** Year-Round • **IDEAL CANDIDATE:** College Students, Career Changers, Foreigners • **APPLICANT POOL:** 50/year • **APPLICANTS ACCEPTED:** 4/term

BEAVER LAKE NATURE CENTER sits on 580-acre Onondaga County Park, which includes a 200-acre lake, ten miles of trails, a visitor center with interpretive exhibits, and a wide variety of northeastern communities, including a bog accessible by a floating boardwalk. Interns present a wide range of on-site interpretive programs to school, youth, and family groups, and assist with exhibit production and program development. Opportunities include gaining skills with professional video equipment and use of a Macintosh, as well as assisting on extended trips from the center. Interns receive $100 per week and housing.

Contact Information: Greg Smith, Intern Supervisor • Beaver Lake Nature Center • 8477 E. Mud Lake Rd. • Baldwinsville, NY 13027 • Phone: (315) 638-2519 • Fax: (315) 638-7488

Berkshire Botanical Garden

REGION/HQ: Northeast/Massachusetts • **CATEGORY:** Botanical Garden • **POSITION TYPE:** Internship • **DURATION:** Summer • **IDEAL CANDIDATE:** College Students, Career Changers, Foreigners • **APPLICANT POOL:** Varies • **APPLICANTS ACCEPTED:** 2/year

THIS FIFTEEN-ACRE GARDEN contains a historic terraced herb garden, annual and perennial gardens, a rose garden, pond garden, ornamental vegetables, a woodland trail, a primrose walk, a conservatory of tropical and desert plants, solar greenhouse trees, shrubs, and dwarf conifers. Horticultural interns gain experience while working with staff and volunteers doing general garden maintenance in all areas of the garden. Duties may include weeding, watering, mulching, planting, and cultivation. Housing is provided, and you can participate in the garden's adult education programs.

Contact Information: Dorthe Hviid, Horticulturist • Berkshire Botanical Garden • Rte. 102 & 183 • P.O. Box 826 • Stockbridge, MA 01262 • Phone: (413) 298-3926 • Fax: (413) 298-5355

Bowman's Hill Wildflower Preserve

REGION/HQ: Northeast/Pennsylvania • **CATEGORY:** Botanical Garden • **POSITION TYPE:** Internship • **DURATION:** Summer • **IDEAL CANDIDATE:** College Students, Career Changers • **APPLICANT POOL:** 200/year • **APPLICANTS ACCEPTED:** 2/year

BOWMAN'S HILL WILDFLOWER PRESERVE was established in 1934 to preserve Pennsylvania's native flora and features woods, meadows, ponds, the waters of Pidcock Creek, and special man-made habitats. Native wildflowers, ferns, trees, shrubs, and vines grow in natural settings along the twenty-six trails. The preserve's mission is to lead people to a greater appreciation of the beauty and value of native plants and to inspire in the public an ever-increasing commitment to the conservation of Pennsylvania's natural heritage. Interns will work closely with the preserve staff and receive intense training in native plant propagation, groundskeeping/trail maintenance, and interpretation/education. Field trips to other botanic gardens and natural areas round out the interns' understanding of plants and public gardens. Interns are required to keep a daily journal of their internship and submit it for review upon completion. A stipend is offered for the ten-week program. You must apply by March 1.

Contact Information: Director • Bowman's Hill Wildflower Preserve • Washington Crossing Historic Park • P.O. Box 685 • New Hope, PA 18938-0685 • Phone: (215) 862-2924 • Fax: (215) 862-1846

Brooklyn Botanical Garden

REGION/HQ: Northeast/New York • **CATEGORY:** Botanical Garden • **POSITION TYPE:** Internship • **DURATION:** Summer • **IDEAL CANDIDATE:** College Students, Foreigners • **APPLICANT POOL:** 20–30/year • **APPLICANTS ACCEPTED:** 4–6/year

Brooklyn Botanic Garden is special in as many ways as there are people to enjoy it. And no wonder…the garden maintains a level of excellence in horticulture, education, science, cultural programs, and community service that few institutions can match. The many gardens within the fifty-two-acre grounds are meticulously cared for, and represent an amazingly diverse and extensive collection of plant specimens and garden styles. Garden publications have earned recognition and gained authority nationally and internationally. The Children's Garden is a long-standing, world-renowned program teaching hands-on gardening to urban children. Horticulture education interns are needed to help maintain the Children's Garden and to teach in the program.

Contact Information: Horticulture Education Director • Brooklyn Botanical Garden • 1000 Washington Ave. • Brooklyn, NY 11225 • Phone: (718) 622-4433

Brukner Nature Center

REGION/HQ: Great Lakes/Ohio • **CATEGORY:** Environmental Education • **POSITION TYPE:** Internship • **DURATION:** Year-Round • **IDEAL CANDIDATE:** College Students, Career Changers, Retired Folks, Foreigners • **APPLICANT POOL:** Varies • **APPLICANTS ACCEPTED:** Varies

BRUKNER ENDEAVORS TO provide meaningful experiences that emphasize natural history and the environment. They house over sixty permanently injured native Ohio animals and birds on display and for use in programming.

Contact Information: Debbie Brill, Administrative Director • Brukner Nature Center • 5995 Horseshoe Bend Rd. • Troy, OH 45373 • Phone: (937) 698-6493 • Fax: (937) 698-4619

Cheeseman's Ecology Safaris

REGION/HQ: Worldwide/California • **CATEGORY:** Expedition • **POSITION TYPE:** Unique Experience • **DURATION:** Year-Round • **IDEAL CANDIDATE:** High School Students, College Students, Career Changers, Retired Folks, Foreigners • **APPLICANT POOL:** Varies • **APPLICANTS ACCEPTED:** Varies

CHEESEMAN'S ECOLOGY SAFARIS include natural history trips to Alaska, Antarctica, East Africa, and South America.

Contact Information: Gail Cheeseman, Director • Cheeseman's Ecology Safaris • 20800 Kittredge Rd. • Saratoga, CA 95070 • Phone: (800) 527-5330

Chesapeake Wildlife Sanctuary

REGION/HQ: Northeast/Maryland • **CATEGORY:** Wildlife • **POSITION TYPE:** Internship • **DURATION:** Year-Round • **IDEAL CANDIDATE:** High School Students, College Students, Career Changers, Foreigners • **APPLICANT POOL:** Varies • **APPLICANTS ACCEPTED:** Varies

THE CHESAPEAKE WILDLIFE SANCTUARY is a nonprofit, wildlife rehabilitation center surrounded by eighty-five acres. It is the only organization in the state of Maryland that is open year-round to provide free medical treatment to sick and injured wildlife and hand-rearing care to orphaned wildlife. The main goal of the sanctuary is to provide intensive hands-on training and experience to individuals who wish to pursue a career in wildlife, veterinary medicine, or related fields. Internship positions are available in small mammals, large mammals, avian, wildlife education, and administration categories. Also be prepared to work hard, get dirty, and perform routine and repetitive duties. On-site and off-site housing are provided at a nominal charge. Merit-based scholarships, ranging from $350 to $1,000, are offered after the completion of the internship.

Contact Information: Internship Coordinator • Chesapeake Wildlife Sanctuary • 17308 Queen Anne Bridge Rd. • Bowie, MD 20716-9053 • Phone: (301) 390-7010 • Fax: (301) 871-2699 • E-mail: cheswild@erols.com • Web Site: www.pattersonvideo.com/cws.htm

Cispus Learning Center

REGION/HQ: Pacific Northwest/Washington • **CATEGORY:** Experiential Education • **POSITION TYPE:** Internship • **DURATION:** Year-Round • **IDEAL CANDIDATE:** College Students, Career Changers, Retired Folks, Foreigners • **APPLICANT POOL:** 8/term • **APPLICANTS ACCEPTED:** 2/term

ADMINISTERED BY THE Association of Washington School Principals, the center assists teachers in environmental and outdoor education on the Cispus River, in the Gifford Pinchot National Forest. Outdoor education interns are needed to assist the program coordinator in facilitating ropes courses and developing lessons to present to elementary-age students on environmental education topics. Room and board are provided.

Contact Information: Martin Fortin, Jr., Director • Cispus Learning Center • 2142 Cispus Rd. • Randle, WA 98377-9305 • Phone: (360) 497-7131 • Fax: (360) 497-7132 • E-mail: cispus@igc.apc.org

Club Wilderness

REGION/HQ: Pacific Northwest/California • **CATEGORY:** Outdoor Education • **POSITION TYPE:** Internship • **DURATION:** Spring/Summer • **IDEAL CANDIDATE:** College Students, Career Changers • **APPLICANT POOL:** Varies • **APPLICANTS ACCEPTED:** Varies

THE FOUNDATION OF THE outdoor education program at Club Wilderness is the premise that understanding of the natural world and certain other curricula are best promoted through hands-on encounters with nature. Programs have been designed to strengthen and build each student's character, mind, and ability. Naturalist interns create or adapt existing curricula in the natural science areas and present them to groups of sixteen to twenty students ranging from grades three through seven.

Contact Information: Program Director • Club Wilderness • P.O. Box 751 • Running Springs, CA 92382 • Phone: (909) 867-2155

Clyde E. Buckley Wildlife Sanctuary

REGION/HQ: Southeast/Kentucky • **CATEGORY:** Wildlife • **POSITION TYPE:** Internship • **DURATION:** Year-Round • **IDEAL CANDIDATE:** College Students, Career Changers, Foreigners • **APPLICANT POOL:** 50/year • **APPLICANTS ACCEPTED:** 6/year

THE SANCTUARY'S GOALS are to create, maintain, patrol, and protect the various habitats located on their 275 acres, to protect the native flora and fauna, and to teach the public identification of and the value of these species. Sanctuary operations interns provide nature interpretation, environmental education, wildlife management, research, caretaking, maintenance, administration, exhibits, photography, gift shop operations, and creative writing. They receive a stipend of $55 per week. Housing, utilities, and uniforms are also provided.

Contact Information: Sanctuary Manager • Clyde E. Buckley Wildlife Sanctuary • 1305 Germany Rd. • Frankfort, KY 40601 • Phone: (606) 873-5711

Colorado Wildlife Federation

REGION/HQ: Rocky Mountains/Colorado
• **CATEGORY:** Environmental Education • **POSITION TYPE:** Internship • **DURATION:** Year-Round • **IDEAL CANDIDATE:** College Students • **APPLICANT POOL:** 5–10/year • **APPLICANTS ACCEPTED:** 5–10/year

THE COLORADO WILDLIFE FEDERATION strives to educate, inspire, and assist individuals and organizations to conserve wildlife and other natural resources and to protect the environment. Their environmental education programs teach how to think—not what to think. Interns are needed as classroom educators, teaching about local national wildlife refuges to grades two through eight, and outdoor volunteer educators who teach urban environmental education subjects to school groups on field trips.

Contact Information: Youth Outreach Coordinator • Colorado Wildlife Federation • 445 Union Blvd., Suite 302 • Lakewood, CO 80228-1243 • Phone: (303) 987-0400 • Fax: (303) 987-0200 • E-mail: cwfed@aol.com

Farm & Wilderness Foundation

REGION/HQ: Northeast/Vermont • **CATEGORY:** Outdoor Education • **POSITION TYPE:** Internship • **DURATION:** Year-Round • **IDEAL CANDIDATE:** College Students, Career Changers • **APPLICANT POOL:** Varies • **APPLICANTS ACCEPTED:** Varies

TEACH DAY-LONG IN adventure-based and environmental education programs. Stipends start at $120 per week, plus room and board.

Contact Information: Jeanette Malone, Program Director • Farm & Wilderness Foundation • HCR 70, Box 27 • Plymouth, VT 05056 • Phone: (802) 422-3761

Garden In The Woods

REGION/HQ: Northeast/Massachusetts • **CATEGORY:** Botanical Garden • **POSITION TYPE:** Internship • **DURATION:** Spring-Fall • **IDEAL CANDIDATE:** College Students, Career Changers • **APPLICANT POOL:** 45/year • **APPLICANTS ACCEPTED:** 4/year

THE GARDEN IN THE WOODS, the botanical garden of the New England Wild Flower Society, is one of the loveliest naturalistic gardens in the Northeast. On this forty-five-acre landscape of rolling hills, ponds, and streams grow 1,600 kinds of plants. The botanical collection includes over 200 rare or endangered species.

Contact Information: Cheryl Lowe, Horticulture Director • Garden In The Woods • 180 Hemenway Rd. • Framingham, MA 01701-2699 • Phone: (508) 877-7630 • Fax: (508) 877-3658 • E-mail: lowe@newfs.org

Genessee Valley Outdoor Learning Center

REGION/HQ: Northeast/Maryland • **CATEGORY:** Outdoor Education • **POSITION TYPE:** Internship • **DURATION:** Year-Round • **IDEAL CANDIDATE:** College Students, Career Changers • **APPLICANT POOL:** Varies • **APPLICANTS ACCEPTED:** Varies

GENESSEE VALLEY OUTDOOR LEARNING CENTER is a nonprofit organization operating on 400 acres of fields, woods, and farmland in northern Maryland. The center is primarily adventure-based, working with both public and private schools, youth-at-risk, youth with special needs, scouts, and other organizations.

Contact Information: Program Director • Genessee Valley Outdoor Learning Center • 1700 Rayville Rd. • Parkton, MD 21120 • Phone: (410) 343-0101

Great Smoky Mountains Institute

REGION/HQ: Southeast/Tennessee • **CATEGORY:** Environmental Education • **POSITION TYPE:** Internship/Seasonal • **DURATION:** Year-Long • **IDEAL CANDIDATE:** College Students, Career Changers, Retired Folks • **APPLICANT POOL:** Varies • **APPLICANTS ACCEPTED:** Varies

THE GREAT SMOKY MOUNTAINS INSTITUTE is a residential environmental education center located deep in the heart of the largest mountain wilderness in the east. Their program is dedicated to creating "environmentally literate" students who want to help preserve and protect places like the Smokies for the future. The teaching staff that provides these programs is a small, dedicated team of people who are excited about environmental education and want to gain practical experience in the field. Preference is given to those who are able to commit for one year. Starting teacher/naturalists receive $190 per week, housing, a uniform allowance, and meals when any group is in residence.

Contact Information: Jeanie Hilten, School Program Director • Great Smoky Mountains Institute • 9275 Tremont Rd. • Townsend, TN 37882 • Phone: (423) 448-6709 • Fax: (423) 448-9250 • E-mail: gsmit@ smoky.igc.apc.org

Hawk Mountain Sanctuary

REGION/HQ: Northeast/Pennsylvania • **CATEGORY:** Wildlife • **POSITION TYPE:** Internship • **DURATION:** Year-Round • **IDEAL CANDIDATE:** College Students, Career Changers • **APPLICANT POOL:** Varies • **APPLICANTS ACCEPTED:** Varies

HAWK MOUNTAIN SANCTUARY ASSOCIATION is a private, nonprofit organization with programs in education, research, and conservation policy that are national and international in scope. Hawk Mountain, established in 1934, was the world's first sanctuary for hawks, eagles, and other birds of prey. Environmental education interns help guide field trips and present on-site and off-grounds interpretive programs to school children and the general public. Ecological research interns help the sanctuary study raptors and Appalachian Mountain fauna and flora. Biological survey and monitoring interns assist with censuses of songbirds, raptors, and other flora and fauna and maintain databases. Interns receive a stipend of $375 per month and free housing on sanctuary grounds.

Contact Information: Annette Edwards, Senior Education Specialist • Hawk Mountain Sanctuary • RR 2, Box 191 • Kempton, PA 19529 • Phone: (610) 756-6961 • Fax: (610) 756-4468

Horizons for Youth

REGION/HQ: Northeast/Massachusetts • **CATEGORY:** Environmental Education • **POSITION TYPE:** Seasonal • **DURATION:** Year-Round • **IDEAL CANDIDATE:** College Students, Foreigners • **APPLICANT POOL:** 100/term • **APPLICANTS ACCEPTED:** 14–18/term

HORIZONS FOR YOUTH offers an outdoor environmental education program in the spring and fall, and a summer camp. Field teacher instructors develop and teach lessons and activities in the outdoors, focusing on ecology, environmental science, conservation, and group dynamics. Adventure leaders plan and implement twenty-three-day wilderness trips. Environmental camp leaders plan and implement a five-day environmental camp experience. Most staff receive $175 per week, plus room and board.

Contact Information: Mike Dattilio, School Program Director • Horizons for Youth • 121 Lakeview St. • Sharon, MA 02067 • Phone: (617) 828-7550 • Fax: (617) 784-1287 • E-mail: outdoors@horizons.tiac.net • Web Site: www.hfy.org

Humane Society of the United States

• **REGION/HQ:** Washington, D.C./Washington, D.C. • **CATEGORY:** Wildlife • **POSITION TYPE:** Internship • **DURATION:** Year-Round • **IDEAL CANDIDATE:** College Students, Foreigners • **APPLICANT POOL:** Varies • **APPLICANTS ACCEPTED:** Varies

THEY ARE THE LARGEST animal protection organization in our nation, dedicated to ending animal suffering in all areas. Most of their programs are focused on companion animals, laboratory animals, farm animals, wildlife, habitat protection, and the environment, and they institute changes through investigation, legislation, and public outreach. Duties as an intern include research, writing, monitoring legislative hearings, and limited clerical responsibilities. They prefer college students with coursework in biology, zoology, or ecology; although these are not required.

Contact Information: Program Coordinator • Humane Society of the United States • Wildlife & Habitat Protection Section • 2100 L St., NW • Washington, DC 20037 • Phone: (301) 258-3144 • Fax: (301) 258-3080 • E-mail: hsuswild@ix.netcom.com

International Crane Foundation

REGION/HQ: Great Lakes/Wisconsin • **CATEGORY:** Conservation • **POSITION TYPE:** Internship • **DURATION:** Year-Round • **IDEAL CANDIDATE:** College Students, Career Changers, Foreigners • **APPLICANT POOL:** 100/year • **APPLICANTS ACCEPTED:** 9/year

THE INTERNATIONAL CRANE FOUNDATION is a nonprofit organization dedicated to conservation and preservation of the world's cranes and the natural wetland and grassland communities in which they occur. Aviculture interns receive hands-on training in the care and management of endangered cranes, including husbandry, handling techniques, behavior, stimulating reproduction, incubation, chick rearing, health care, and genetic management. Interns receive a $300-per-month stipend and housing.

Contact Information: Scott Swengel, Curator of Birds • International Crane Foundation • P.O. Box 447 • Baraboo, WI 53913-0447 • Phone: (608) 356-9462 • Fax: (608) 356-9465 • E-mail: cranes@baraboo.com

Longwood Gardens

REGION/HQ: Northeast/Pennsylvania • **CATEGORY:** Botanical Garden • **POSITION TYPE:** Internship • **DURATION:** Year-Round • **IDEAL CANDIDATE:** College Students, Career Changers, Foreigners • **APPLICANT POOL:** 150/year • **APPLICANTS ACCEPTED:** Varies

LONGWOOD GARDENS IS THE world's premier display garden, with nearly four acres of greenhouses and conservatories, flower gardens, fountain gardens, century-old trees, and natural areas within 1,050 acres of property. Nearly 800,000 people visit the garden each year.

Contact Information: David Foresman, Student Programs Coordinator • Longwood Gardens • P.O. Box 501 • Kennett Square, PA 19348-0501 • Phone: (610) 388-1000 • Fax: (610) 388-2908

Marine Sciences Under Sails

REGION/HQ: Southeast/Florida • **CATEGORY:** Sailing • **POSITION TYPE:** Unique Experience • **DURATION:** Year-Round • **IDEAL CANDIDATE:** High School Students, College Students, Career Changers, Retired Folks, Foreigners • **APPLICANT POOL:** Varies • **APPLICANTS ACCEPTED:** Varies

MARINE SCIENCES UNDER SAILS offers short study-cruises for those interested in learning about the sea while sailing and living upon it. Small cruising-size sailboats carry participants to study mangrove islands, barrier islands, shallow seas, coral reefs, open ocean, and the Florida peninsula. Participants learn about the vital role of the sea and coastal zone and the necessity for protecting them as major natural resources.

Contact Information: Ned Webster, Program Director • Marine Sciences Under Sails • P.O. Box 3994 • Hollywood, FL 33023 • Phone: (305) 983-7015

Massachusetts Audubon Society

REGION/HQ: Northeast/Massachusetts • **CATEGORY:** Conservation • **POSITION TYPE:** Internship/Seasonal • **DURATION:** Year-Round • **IDEAL CANDIDATE:** College Students, Career Changers • **APPLICANT POOL:** Varies • **APPLICANTS ACCEPTED:** Varies

THE MASSACHUSETTS AUDUBON SOCIETY produces a directory each year of summer job positions in various environmental organizations throughout the state of Massachusetts (from the Cape to the Berkshires), including wildlife sanctuaries, museums, conservation programs, farms, and camps. Positions include day camp instructors, environmental education interns, naturalists, counselors, teachers, botanists, trip/trek leaders, conservation specialists, sustainable agriculture, and historians.

Contact Information: Claudia Bard Veitch, Human Resources Director • Massachusetts Audubon Society • 208 S. Great Rd. • Lincoln, MA 01773 • Phone: (617) 259-9506 • Fax: (617) 259-8899 • E-mail: cveitch@massaudubon.org

Minnesota Zoo

REGION/HQ: Great Lakes/Minnesota • **CATEGORY:** Zoo • **POSITION TYPE:** Internship • **DURATION:** Year-Round • **IDEAL CANDIDATE:** College Students, Career Changers, Foreigners • **APPLICANT POOL:** Varies • **APPLICANTS ACCEPTED:** Varies

EXPERIENCE THE CHALLENGE and excitement of working side-by-side with professionals at the Minnesota Zoo. Internships are available in animal management, education, marketing, horticulture, conservation biology, animal health, and information technology.

Contact Information: Linda Schmidt, Internship Coordinator • Minnesota Zoo • 13000 Zoo Blvd. • Apple Valley, MN 55124-8199 • Phone: (612) 431-9219 • Fax: (612) 431-9211

Monterey Bay Aquarium

REGION/HQ: Pacific Northwest /California • **CATEGORY:** Aquarium • **POSITION TYPE:** Internship • **DURATION:** Summer • **IDEAL CANDIDATE:** College Students • **APPLICANT POOL:** Varies • **APPLICANTS ACCEPTED:** 15/year

THE MISSION OF THE Monterey Bay Aquarium is to stimulate interest in, increase knowledge of, and promote stewardship of Monterey Bay and the world's ocean environment through innovative exhibits, public education, and scientific research. Interpretive programs college interns assist with interpreting exhibits to the public, develop and deliver educational activities for volunteer guides, and develop interpretive materials. Outreach college interns visit public beaches, schools, and libraries to assist in the delivery of programs about marine life, using live animals and science theater techniques, as well as serving as counselors in a one-week day camp for aquarium members. Deck interpreters deliver presentations to aquarium visitors at the Great Tide Pool. Tide pool divers work outdoors with visitors at the Great Tide Pool exhibit. Divers bring up animals from the tide pool and interpret them to visitors. On-site high school interns assist education staff with the preparation and presentation of field and classroom education programs for preschoolers to adults.

Contact Information: Debbie Keller, Internship Coordinator • Monterey Bay Aquarium • Interpretive Programs Office • 886 Cannery Row • Monterey, CA 93940-1085 • Phone: (408) 648-4866

Moter Marine Laboratory

REGION/HQ: Southeast/Florida • **CATEGORY:** Marine Science • **POSITION TYPE:** Internship • **DURATION:** Year-Round • **IDEAL CANDIDATE:** College Students • **APPLICANT POOL:** 100/year • **APPLICANTS ACCEPTED:** 55/year

MOTER MARINE LABORATORY is an independent, non-profit organization dedicated to excellence in marine and environmental research and education. Interns have the opportunity to participate in scientific literature review, project development, data processing and analysis, and report writing. Internships are available in all research areas of the laboratory, as well as such support areas as the aquarium, communications, and education. Although a volunteer position, interns receive all the benefits of membership, including free aquarium admission, gift shop and Moter Cafe discounts, special event discounts, and lecture and seminar admission.

Contact Information: Andrea Davis, Volunteer/Intern Coordinator • Moter Marine Laboratory • 1600 Ken Thompson Parkway • Sarasota, FL 34236 • Phone: (941) 388-4441 • Fax: (941) 388-4312 • Toll Free: (800) 691-6683 • E-mail: adavis@marinelab.sarasota.fl.us • Web Site: www.marinelab.sarasota.fl.us

National Aquarium in Baltimore

REGION/HQ: Washington, D.C./Maryland • **CATEGORY:** Aquarium • **POSITION TYPE:** Internship • **DURATION:** Year-Round • **IDEAL CANDIDATE:** College Students, Career Changers • **APPLICANT POOL:** 300/year • **APPLICANTS ACCEPTED:** 60/year

THE NATIONAL AQUARIUM IN BALTIMORE is a state-of-the-art aquatic institution dedicated to the conservation and preservation of the environment. The main aquarium and the Marine Mammal Pavilion contain over 2.5 million gallons of fresh- and saltwater, supporting over 5,000 specimens of 500 to 600 different species of mammals, fish, birds, reptiles, amphibians, and invertebrates that make their home at this aquarium. Internships are available in the following departments: Aquaculture, Aquarist, Audiovisual Technology, Aviculture, Development, Gift Shop, Herpetology, Horticulture, Library, Mammalogy, Marine Education, Marketing/Promotions, Membership, Management Information Systems, Publications, Public Relations, and Water Quality/Chemistry.

Contact Information: Education Department—Internships • National Aquarium in Baltimore • 501 E. Pratt Street, Pier 3 • Baltimore, MD 21202-3194 • Phone: (410) 576-8236 • Fax: (410) 659-0116 • Alternate: (410) 576-3800 • Web Site: www.aqua.org

National Marine Fisheries Observer Program

REGION/HQ: Pacific Northwest/Washington • **CATEGORY:** Marine Science • **POSITION TYPE:** Unique Experience • **DURATION:** Year-Round • **IDEAL CANDIDATE:** College Students, Career Changers, Retired Folks • **APPLICANT POOL:** Varies • **APPLICANTS ACCEPTED:** Varies

OBSERVERS ARE PLACED ON foreign and domestic fishing vessels operating off the Alaskan and the northwestern coast of the United States, or are stationed at shoreside processing plants in Alaska, to collect data required for fisheries management and enforcement purposes. Salary, expenses, benefits, and insurance are provided.

Contact Information: Program Director • National Marine Fisheries Observer Program • BIN C15700, Bldg. 4 • 7600 Sand Point Way, NE • Seattle, WA 98115-0070 • Phone: (206) 526-4191

New Canaan Nature Center

REGION/HQ: Northeast/Connecticut • **CATEGORY:** Environmental Education • **POSITION TYPE:** Internship • **DURATION:** Academic Year • **IDEAL CANDIDATE:** College Students, Career Changers, Foreigners • **APPLICANT POOL:** 150–200/year • **APPLICANTS ACCEPTED:** 10–15/term

ESTABLISHED IN 1936, New Canaan County School (NCCS) is a leading independent coeducational day school with approximately 500 students in grades K–9 and 100 staff members. The fundamental goal of the school is to stimulate and guide each student toward the realization of his or her intellectual, creative, physical, and moral potential. NCCS is committed to the nurturing of human relationships and to the experience of service in the larger community. Positions include teacher/naturalist and Adventurers Program assistant. Interns receive a $230- to $260-per-week stipend, plus room and board.

Contact Information: Camp Director • New Canaan Nature Center • 144 Oenoke Ridge • New Canaan, CT 06840 • Phone: (203) 966-9577 • Fax: (203) 966-6536

New England Aquarium

REGION/HQ: Northeast/Massachusetts • **CATEGORY:** Aquarium • **POSITION TYPE:** Internship • **DURATION:** Year-Round • **IDEAL CANDIDATE:** High School Students, College Students, Career Changers, Retired Folks, Foreigners • **APPLICANT POOL:** 700–900/year • **APPLICANTS ACCEPTED:** 200–270/year

THE MISSION OF THE New England Aquarium is to increase understanding of aquatic life and environments, to enable people to act to conserve the world of water, and to provide leadership for preservation and sustainable use of aquatic resources. This mission is fulfilled through exhibits, education, conservation, and research programs. Exhibits showcase the diversity, importance, and beauty of aquatic life and habitats. Internships are available in these departments: Curatorial, Administrative, Conservation, Veterinary Services, Media, Information Systems, Marine Mammal, Education, and Research.

Contact Information: Marueen Crawford, Volunteer Programs Supervisor • New England Aquarium • Central Wharf • Boston, MA 02110-3399 • Phone: (617) 973-5235 • Fax: (617) 720-5098 • E-mail: vols@neaq.org • Web Site: www.neaq.org

North Carolina Aquarium on Roanoke Island

REGION/HQ: Southeast/North Carolina • **CATEGORY:** Aquarium • **POSITION TYPE:** Internship • **DURATION:** Year-Round • **IDEAL CANDIDATE:** College Students, Foreigners • **APPLICANT POOL:** 40/year • **APPLICANTS ACCEPTED:** Varies

NORTH CAROLINA AQUARIUM on Roanoke Island is a state-operated public aquarium. The aquarium promotes an awareness, understanding, and appreciation of the diverse natural and cultural resources associated with North Carolina's ocean, estuaries, rivers, streams, and other aquatic environments. Marvel at the sharks, eels, sea turtles, and countless other fascinating forms of marine life on display. Seasonal positions and internships are available in the education department, working with children and the general public. Duties include developing and conducting programs that include beach and marsh field trips, live-animal presentations, lectures, and slide programs. A ten-week intern will speak to over 10,000 people on a variety of marine and aquatic topics. An internship is also available in aquarium husbandry, which includes fish feeding, water chemistry, and collecting and maintaining fresh- and saltwater fishes and marine life. Interns receive $5 per hour, but the best perk is living and working on North Carolina's Outer Banks, with miles of ocean beaches, water recreation, and hang gliding sites.

Contact Information: Rhett White, Director • North Carolina Aquarium on Roanoke Island • P.O. Box 967, Airport Rd. • Manteo, NC 27954-0967 • Phone: (919) 473-3494 • Fax: (919) 473-1980

North Cascades Institute

REGION/HQ: Pacific Northwest/Washington • **CATEGORY:** Experiential Education • **POSITION TYPE:** Work/Learn Adventure • **DURATION:** Year-Round • **IDEAL CANDIDATE:** College Students, Career Changers, Retired Folks, Foreigners • **APPLICANT POOL:** 80/year • **APPLICANTS ACCEPTED:** 40/year

NORTH CASCADES INSTITUTE is a nonprofit organization dedicated to increasing understanding and appreciation of the natural, historical, and cultural landscapes of the Pacific Northwest. Their primary focus is on field-based, experiential, environmental education for children and adults. Internship positions are offered in these areas: Mountain School (room and board provided), watershed education, Mountain Camp, field seminar, and administrative. Although these positions are not paid, you will be able to participate in field seminars, go through extensive training, and get a free T-shirt.

Contact Information: Wendy Scherrer, Youth Program Coordinator • North Cascades Institute • 2105 Highway 20 • Sedro Woolley, WA 98284-9394 • Phone: (360) 856-5700 • Fax: (360) 856-1934 • E-mail: nci@ncascades.org • Web Site: http://ncascades.org/nci

Olympic Park Institute

REGION/HQ: Pacific Northwest/Washington • **CATEGORY:** Environmental Education • **POSITION TYPE:** Internship • **DURATION:** Year-Round • **IDEAL CANDIDATE:** College Students, Career Changers, Retired Folks, Foreigners • **APPLICANT POOL:** Varies • **APPLICANTS ACCEPTED:** Varies

OLYMPIC PARK INSTITUTE is a nonprofit organization founded in 1971, providing outdoor environmental learning to people of all ages. The intern will serve as a support person for the management team at the institute, with duties including administration, computer work, advertising, customer services, naturalist assistance, and various field-related projects. There is a limited stipend, which may include housing and meals or transportation reimbursement. In addition, the institute will provide the opportunity for interns to participate in field science programs.

Contact Information: Maitland Peet, Executive Director • Olympic Park Institute • 111 Barnes Point Rd. • Port Angeles, WA 98363 • Phone: (360) 928-3720 • Fax: (360) 928-3046 • E-mail: opi@olympus.net • Web Site: www.olympus.net/opi

Philadelphia Zoo

REGION/HQ: Northeast/Pennsylvania • **CATEGORY:** Zoo • **POSITION TYPE:** Internship • **DURATION:** Year-Round • **IDEAL CANDIDATE:** College Students • **APPLICANT POOL:** Varies • **APPLICANTS ACCEPTED:** Varies

THE PHILADELPHIA ZOO is run by the Zoological Society of Philadelphia, a nonprofit corporation chartered in 1859. Today more than 1,500 animals, a picturesque Victorian setting, outstanding art and architecture, and a wealth of botanical splendor set the scene at America's first zoo, visited by more than one million people each year. Internships are offered in AFZ Camera Club, administrative office, Backyard Bugs, children's zoo, docent council, hospitality team, zoo gardening group, and zoo shop.

Contact Information: Connie Poole, Recruiter • Philadelphia Zoo • 3400 W. Girard Ave. • Philadelphia, PA 19104-1196 • Phone: (215) 243-5326 • Fax: (215) 243-5385 • Web Site: www.phillyzoo.org

Riverbend Environmental Education Center

REGION/HQ: Northeast/Pennsylvania • **CATEGORY:** Environmental Education • **POSITION TYPE:** Internship/Seasonal • **DURATION:** Summer • **IDEAL CANDIDATE:** College Students, Career Changers, Foreigners • **APPLICANT POOL:** Varies • **APPLICANTS ACCEPTED:** 10/year

RIVERBEND IS A PRIVATE, nonprofit organization which stimulates awareness, appreciation, and understanding of our environment and works to preserve a natural wildlife habitat. They are situated in a 1923 Sears catalog barn on twenty-eight acres of forest, fields, and streams. They offer positions for environmental education interns and environmental educators. Interns receive $100 per week, and environmental educators receive $250 to $300 per week. Housing is provided if needed.

Contact Information: Kathleen Geist, Senior Educator • Riverbend Environmental Education Center • Spring Mill Rd. • P.O. Box 2 • Gladwyne, PA 19035-0002 • Phone: (610) 527-5234 • Fax: (610) 527-5234 • E-mail: rvrbend@aol.com • Web Site: http://members. aol.com/rvrbend

Rodale Institute Research Center

REGION/HQ: Northeast/Pennsylvania • **CATEGORY:** Agriculture • **POSITION TYPE:** Internship • **DURATION:** Year-Round • **IDEAL CANDIDATE:** College Students, Career Changers, Foreigners

• **APPLICANT POOL:** Varies • **APPLICANTS ACCEPTED:** Varies

THE RODALE INSTITUTE RESEARCH CENTER is a nonprofit dedicated to promoting healthful, low-input regenerative agriculture systems. Its purpose is to produce scientific information on regenerative agriculture.

Contact Information: Internship Coordinator • Rodale Institute Research Center • 611 Siegfriedale Rd. • Kutztown, PA 19530 • Phone: (215) 683-1400 • Fax: (215) 683-8548

Sail Caribbean

REGION/HQ: Caribbean/New York • **CATEGORY:** Sailing • **POSITION TYPE:** Internship/Seasonal • **DURATION:** Summer • **IDEAL CANDIDATE:** College Students, Career Changers • **APPLICANT POOL:** Varies • **APPLICANTS ACCEPTED:** Varies

SAILING, MARINE BIOLOGY, and oceanography are combined to take advantage of the living laboratory of the Caribbean. Marine biology/oceanography instructors plan and conduct classes which explore oceanography (geography and wonders of water), marine biology (marine life—adaptations and interactions), and environmental considerations (human hazards and possible solutions to these problems). Location dictates what activities will take place, some of which include day and night snorkels, plankton tows, or island hikes. Instructors also serve as assistant skippers each day. You will receive a salary, plus room and board.

Contact Information: Michael Liese, Director • Sail Caribbean • 79 Church St. • Northport, NY 11768 • Phone: (800) 321-0994

The Scott Arboretum of Swarthmore College

REGION/HQ: Northeast/Pennsylvania • **CATEGORY:** Arboretum • **POSITION TYPE:** Internship • **DURATION:** Summer/One Year • **IDEAL CANDIDATE:** College Students, Career Changers, Foreigners • **APPLICANT POOL:** Varies • **APPLICANTS ACCEPTED:** 3–5/year

THE SCOTT ARBORETUM was established in 1929 for the purpose of cultivating and displaying the better kinds of trees, shrubs, and herbaceous plants suited to the climate of eastern Pennsylvania and which are suitable for planting by home gardeners. The arboretum covers more than 300 acres and grows over 2,000 woody taxa.

Contact Information: Claire Sawyers, Director • The Scott Arboretum of Swarthmore College • 500 College Ave. • Swarthmore, PA 19081-1397 • Phone: (610) 328-8025 • Fax: (610) 328-8673 • E-mail: csawyer1@cc.swarthmore.edu

Teton Science School

REGION/HQ: Rocky Mountains/Wyoming • **CATEGORY:** Natural Resources • **POSITION TYPE:** Training Program • **DURATION:** Academic year • **IDEAL CANDIDATE:** College Students, Career Changers • **APPLICANT POOL:** Varies • **APPLICANTS ACCEPTED:** 16/year

THE TETON SCIENCE SCHOOL provides and encourages experiential education in natural science and ecology while fostering an appreciation for conservation ethics and practices. The Greater Yellowstone region serves as your outdoor classroom and model for year-round programs that offer academic, professional, and personal benefits to students of all ages. Students participate in field studies involving a hands-on approach to natural science learning. The permanent staff is composed of professional natural science teachers with many years of experience. The $11,000-per-year fee includes TSS tuition, academic credit at Utah State University, wilderness first responder certification or local internship, room and board, and a $100-per-month stipend.

Contact Information: Nancy Shea, Education Director • Teton Science School • P.O. Box 68-BD • Kelly, WY 83011 • Phone: (307) 733-4765 • Fax: (307) 739-9388 • E-mail: tss@wyoming.com • Web Site: www.jacksonwy.com/tss/tssovr.htm

Westwood Hills Nature Center

REGION/HQ: Great Lakes/Minnesota • **CATEGORY:** Nature Center • **POSITION TYPE:** Internship • **DURATION:** Year-Round • **IDEAL CANDIDATE:** College Students, Career Changers • **APPLICANT POOL:** Varies • **APPLICANTS ACCEPTED:** Varies

DURING THE SUMMER, Westwood runs a nature camp, which is made up of eight, one-week classes for preschoolers through sixth grade; during the other seasons a school curriculum program for elementary students is offered. Westwood's naturalist internship program revolves around environmental, natural history, and outdoor education. Training includes content for each program topic, teaching techniques, and natural history information. As groups begin, interns first observe experienced naturalists leading the groups. On-site, free lodging is available, and each season one applicant is selected and will receive a $1,200 stipend for the eleven-week period.

Contact Information: Mark Oestreich, Naturalist • Westwood Hills Nature Center • 8300 W. Franklin Ave. • St. Louis Park, MN 55426 • Phone: (612) 924-2543 • Fax: (612) 924-2663

Wetlands Institute

REGION/HQ: Northeast/New Jersey • **CATEGORY:** Conservation • **POSITION TYPE:** Internship • **DURATION:** Year-Round • **IDEAL CANDIDATE:** College Students, Career Changers • **APPLICANT POOL:** 15–30/year • **APPLICANTS ACCEPTED:** 10/term

THE WETLANDS INSTITUTE is a nonprofit involved in research and educational programs dealing with the coastal environment. Located on coastal wetlands in south Jersey, the Wetlands Institute features an attractive cedar-shake building and includes an aquarium and exhibit building, classroom offices, research laboratories, a book and gift shop, dorm rooms, and a full

Wetlands Institute

kitchen. Outdoor facilities include a salt-marsh trail, sixty-foot pier, boat slip, classroom, and an elevated boardwalk. Volunteer positions include aquarist/guide, birding guide, environmental education, exhibits, public relations, and research. You will also assist with special events and in any capacity required for the good of the Wetlands Institute. Free housing at the institute is available.

Contact Information: Cindy O'Connor, Executive Director • Wetlands Institute • 1075 Stone Harbor Blvd. • Stone Harbor, NJ 08247-1424 • Phone: (609) 368-1211 • Fax: (609) 368-3871 • Web Site: www.netteck.com/wetlands

The Wildlife Society

REGION/HQ: Washington, D.C./Maryland • **CATEGORY:** Wildlife • **POSITION TYPE:** Internship • **DURATION:** Six months • **IDEAL CANDIDATE:** College Students • **APPLICANT POOL:** Varies • **APPLICANTS ACCEPTED:** Varies

Interns at the Wildlife Society research conservation issues, prepare background information for use in testimony or comments, attend briefings/hearings, and write for and assist with Society publications. Actual activities will depend upon the ability and interest of each intern and the needs of the Society. A $500 stipend is paid every two weeks for this six-month-long position beginning in either January or July.

Contact Information: Thomas Franklin, Wildlife Policy Director • The Wildlife Society • 5410 Grosvenor Ln. • Bethesda, MD 20814-2197 • Phone: (301) 897-9770 • Fax: (301) 530-2471 • E-mail: tws@wildlife.org

Willowbrook Wildlife Center

REGION/HQ: Great Lakes/Illinois • **CATEGORY:** Wildlife • **POSITION TYPE:** Internship • **DURATION:** Year-Round • **IDEAL CANDIDATE:** College Students, Career Changers • **APPLICANT POOL:** Varies • **APPLICANTS ACCEPTED:** Varies

WILLOWBROOK WILDLIFE CENTER offers internships to students in the areas of wildlife rehabilitation, veterinary work, wildlife technicians, and environmental education. All interns will receive training and gain experience in public service, organizational philosophies, education strategies, and rehabilitation techniques utilized at Willowbrook. Positions run twelve weeks, and interns will receive a stipend of $240 per week.

Contact Information: Curator • Willowbrook Wildlife Center • 525 S. Park Blvd. • Glen Ellyn, IL 60137 • Fax: (708) 469-0034

Wing Haven Gardens & Bird Sanctuary

REGION/HQ: Southeast/North Carolina • **CATEGORY:** Botanical Garden • **POSITION TYPE:** Internship • **DURATION:** Summer • **IDEAL CANDIDATE:** College Students, Career Changers, Foreigners • **APPLICANT POOL:** Varies • **APPLICANTS ACCEPTED:** Varies

WING HAVEN IS A four-acre public garden and bird sanctuary that combines formal gardens with wild woodlands and has been a unique part of Charlotte since 1927. The formal gardens are designed so that visitors may stroll along brick paths and enjoy the many lovely vistas and beautiful trees, flowers, and shrubs. Beyond the formal gardens are wooded areas filled with ferns and wildflowers. Throughout the gardens, emphasis is on plantings for bird attraction—providing cover, nesting sites, and food. Many pools, recirculating fountains, and dripping bird baths delight visitors and birds alike. Integrated into the garden walls and paths are plaques and statues which provide interest and reflect the gentle spirit and beauty of Wing Haven and its creators. Horticulture interns assist the gardening staff with the basic maintenance of the garden and will be responsible for all bird feeding and the care of specific garden areas, including watering, weeding, pruning, and sweeping.

Contact Information: Gardens/Grounds Director • Wing Haven Gardens & Bird Sanctuary • 248 Ridgewood Ave. • Charlotte, NC 28209 • Phone: (704) 331-4726

Wolf Creek Outdoor School

REGION/HQ: Pacific Northwest/California • **CATEGORY:** Environmental Education • **POSITION TYPE:** Internship • **DURATION:** Spring/Fall • **IDEAL CANDIDATE:** College Students, Career Changers, Retired Folks • **APPLICANT POOL:** Varies • **APPLICANTS ACCEPTED:** 2/term

THE WOLF CREEK OUTDOOR SCHOOL is a residential environmental education facility which includes six cab-ins, a small dining hall, new staff cabins, and a new lodge. Nearby old-growth redwood forests and freshwater streams serve as outdoor classrooms. The curriculum for environmental education interns includes old growth studies, stream studies, awareness activities, values clarification activities, and campfire programs. Housing, a uniform, and a food stipend are provided.

Contact Information: Jay Moeller, Internship Coordinator • Wolf Creek Outdoor School • Redwood National Park • P.O. Box 7 • Orick, CA 95555 • Phone: (707) 822-7611 • Web Site: www.nps.gov/redw

Wolverine Outdoor Education Center

REGION/HQ: Great Lakes/Michigan • **CATEGORY:** Outdoor Education • **POSITION TYPE:** Internship/ Seasonal • **DURATION:** Academic Year • **IDEAL CANDIDATE:** College Students, Foreigners • **APPLICANT POOL:** Varies • **APPLICANTS ACCEPTED:** 4/year

THE WOLVERINE OUTDOOR EDUCATION CENTER offers residential outdoor education programs for fifth to eighth graders. Outdoor education interns teach natural history classes, pioneer living, group initiatives course, ropes course, outdoor survival skills, orienteering, the history of Native Americans, and an evening program series (astronomy, night hikes, wildlife, logging history, and American history). Interns receive $85 per week, plus room and board.

Contact Information: Outdoor Education Director • Wolverine Outdoor Education Center • N. Old 27 • Wolverine, MI 49799 • Phone: (616) 525-8211

I come now, at the late juncture of my life, to this sudden realization: I have no destination, no real destination in the literal sense. The destination, the place toward which my life is tending, is the journey itself and not the final stopping place. How I get there is more important than whether I arrive, although I know I will arrive.

—RICHARD BODE

The secret of success is to do the common duty uncommonly well.
—JOHN D. ROCKEFELLER, JR.

Addresses

African Wildlife Foundation
REGION/HQ: Washington, D.C./Washington, D.C.
CATEGORY: Wildlife
CONTACT INFORMATION:
Program Director
African Wildlife Foundation
1717 Massachusetts Ave., NW
Washington, DC 20036
Phone: (202) 265-8393

American Federation of Teachers
REGION/HQ: Washington, D.C./Washington, D.C.
CATEGORY: Teaching
CONTACT INFORMATION:
Charmayne March, Assistant Director
American Federation of Teachers
555 New Jersey Ave., NW
Washington, DC 20001
Fax: (202) 879-4556

AYF—Merrowvista Education Center
REGION/HQ: Northeast/New Hampshire
CATEGORY: Experiential Education
CONTACT INFORMATION:
Anna Kay Vorstag, Program Director
AYF—Merrowvista Education Center
147 Canaan Rd
Ossipee, NH 03864-9604
Phone: (603) 539-6607 • Fax: (603) 539-7504

Blackwater National Wildlife Refuge
REGION/HQ: Washington, D.C./Maryland
CATEGORY: Wildlife
CONTACT INFORMATION:
Outdoor Recreation Planner
Blackwater National Wildlife Refuge
2145 Key Wallace Dr.
Cambridge, MD 21613
Phone: (410) 228-2677 • Fax: (410) 228-3261

Caribbean Conservation Corporation
REGION/HQ: Southeast/Florida
CATEGORY: Conservation
CONTACT INFORMATION:
Caroline Reiners, Volunteer Coordinator
Caribbean Conservation Corporation
P.O. Box 2866
Gainesville, FL 32601-2866
Phone: (904) 373-6441 • Fax: (904) 375-2449

Catalina Island Marine Institute
REGION/HQ: Pacific Northwest/California
CATEGORY: Marine Science
CONTACT INFORMATION:
Program Director
Catalina Island Marine Institute
P.O. Box 796
Avalon, CA 90704

Chincoteague National Wildlife Refuge
REGION/HQ: Southeast/Virginia
CATEGORY: Wildlife
CONTACT INFORMATION:
Refuge Manager
Chincoteague National Wildlife Refuge
P.O. Box 62
Chincoteague, VA 23336
Phone: (804) 336-6122

Earth Conservation Corps
REGION/HQ: Washington, D.C./Washington, D.C.
CATEGORY: Conservation
CONTACT INFORMATION:
Leib Kaminsky, Program Director
Earth Conservation Corps
1st & Potomac Ave., SE
Washington, DC 20003
Phone: (202) 554-1960

Environmental Resource Center
REGION/HQ: Rocky Mountains/Idaho
CATEGORY: Environment
CONTACT INFORMATION:
Anita Smith, Program Director
Environmental Resource Center
411 E. Sixth
P.O. Box 819
Ketchum, ID 83340
Phone: (208) 726-4333 • Fax: (208) 726-1531 • E-mail:
ERC@sunvalley.net

Erie National Wildlife Refuge

REGION/HQ: Northeast/Pennsylvania

CATEGORY: Wildlife

CONTACT INFORMATION:
Volunteer Coordinator
Erie National Wildlife Refuge
RD 1, Wood Duck Ln.
Guys Mills , PA 16327
Phone: (814) 789-3585 • Fax: (814) 789-2909

4-H Outdoor Education Centers

REGION/HQ: Northeast/New Jersey

CATEGORY: Outdoor Education

CONTACT INFORMATION:
Kevin Mitchell, Program Director
4-H Outdoor Education Centers
New Jersey 4-H Camps
50 Nielson Rd.
Sussex, NJ 07461
Phone: (201) 875-4715 • Fax: (201) 875-1289

Hotchkiss Ecology & Great Whales Programs

REGION/HQ: Northeast/Connecticut

CATEGORY: Marine Science

CONTACT INFORMATION:
Richard Hughes, Program Director
Hotchkiss Ecology & Great Whales Programs
The Hotchkiss School
Lakeville, CT 06039
Phone: (203) 435-0410

Marine Environmental Sciences Consortium

REGION/HQ: Southeast/Alabama

CATEGORY: Marine Science

CONTACT INFORMATION:
Jenny Cook, Program Director
Marine Environmental Sciences Consortium
Dauphin Island Sea Lab
P.O. Box 369-370
Dauphin Island, AL 36528
Phone: (205) 861-2141

National Tropical Botanical Gardens

REGION/HQ: Pacific Northwest/Hawaii

CATEGORY: Botanical Garden

CONTACT INFORMATION:
Supervisor of Education
National Tropical Botanical Gardens
College Intern Program
P.O. Box 340
Lawai, HI 96765
Phone: (808) 332-7324

Natural Habitat Adventures

REGION/HQ: Pacific Northwest/California

CATEGORY: Natural Resources

CONTACT INFORMATION:
Program Coordinator
Natural Habitat Adventures
1696 Ocean Dr.
McKinleyville, CA 95521
Phone: (800) 548-7555

The Road Less Travelled

REGION/HQ: Great Lakes/Illinois

CATEGORY: Outdoor Education

CONTACT INFORMATION:
Jessica Larson, Program Coordinator
The Road Less Travelled
2053 N. Magnolia Ave.
Chicago, IL 60614
Phone: (773) 348-4100 • Fax: (773) 348-4399

Sea Life Park Hawaii

REGION/HQ: Pacific Northwest/Hawaii

CATEGORY: Marine Science

CONTACT INFORMATION:
Marilyn Lee, Director
Sea Life Park Hawaii
Volunteer Student Programs
Makapu'u Point
Waimanalo, HI 96815
Phone: (808) 259-6476

Thayer Academy Summer Programs

REGION/HQ: Northeast/Massachusetts

CATEGORY: Outdoor Education

CONTACT INFORMATION:
Steve Savage, Program Director
Thayer Academy Summer Programs
745 Washington St.
Braintree, MA 02184
Phone: (617) 843-3580

Wildlife Habitat Enhancement Council

REGION/HQ: Washington, D.C./Maryland

CATEGORY: Wildlife

CONTACT INFORMATION:
Field Programs Director
Wildlife Habitat Enhancement Council
1010 Wayne Ave.
Silver Springs, MD 20910
Phone: (301) 588-8994

Do you have a green thumb? **The American Association of Botanical Gardens and Arboreta** (AABGA) is a great network for professional contacts. Membership in AABGA has a number of benefits, including: a directory of internships and summer jobs at public gardens, a quarterly magazine, a newsletter, a resource center, a membership directory, and professional education. Participation in AABGA is one way to further your career goals and to keep in touch with what's happening at other public gardens across the United States and Canada. AABGA, 786 Church Rd., Wayne, PA 19087; (215) 688-1120 (E-mail and Web site: see page 249)

The **American Birding Association** publishes an outstanding directory of volunteer opportunities for birding enthusiasts, listing hundreds of projects in the United States and abroad. By becoming a volunteer, you'll have the chance to give something back to the birds that give you so much pleasure. In addition, studying birds as a project volunteer will bring you much closer to the birds than you'd likely get out on a hike or out birding, and some of the projects even offer a small stipend. The association also sponsors youth birding camps and conventions. To receive the ***Directory of Volunteer Opportunities for Birders*** (updated each year), contact Dr. Paul Green, Conservation/Education Director, American Birding Association, P.O. Box 6599, Colorado Springs, CO 80934-6599; (800) 850-2473; paulgrn@aba.org; www.mobot.org/aabga

An excellent Web resource for aquatic sciences is **Aquanet,** which gives worldwide information, including job listings, business opportunities, and research information. www.aquanet.com

The American Fisheries Society puts out a free brochure, ***Careers in Fisheries,*** which acquaints interested students with the educational background needed for employment and fishery career opportunities. 5410 Grosvenor Ln., Suite 110, Bethesda, MD 20814-2199; (301) 897-8616; main@fisheries.org

The American Institute of Biological Sciences publishes ***Careers in Biology***, which you can receive for free by writing AIBS, 730 11th St., NW, Washington, DC 20001-4584; (202) 628-1500.

The free brochure ***Careers in Ecology*** shares experiences and opinions of ecologists on education, training, and job information in this field. It's published by the Ecological Society of America, Center for Environmental Studies, Arizona State University, Tempe, AZ 85287-3211; (602) 965-3000.

Environmental Opportunities, a monthly newsletter, lists environmental work opportunities throughout the United States. A free sample copy will be sent upon request, or you can subscribe for six months ($26) or a year ($47). Get in touch with Sanford Berry for more information: P.O. Box 4379, Arcata, CA 95518; (707) 826-1909; msandsl@tidepool.com

The Job Seeker is a bimonthly newsletter which lists environmental- and natural resource–related seasonal, part-time jobs, and internships nationwide. You can receive it either through the mail or E-mail. Subscriptions are available for three months ($19.50), six months ($36), or one year ($60), or you may want to invest in their ***Summer Jobs Special*** which costs $10 for 9 issues during the months of December through April. Contact *The Job Seeker,* 28672 Cty EW, Warrens, WI 54666; (608) 378-4290; jobseeker@tomah.com; www./tomah.com/jobseeker

The New Complete Guide to Environmental Careers by the Environmental Careers Organization. Environmental Careers are big news today. This book is filled with detailed information about the environmental career opportunities available to you and also provides you with a broad overview of career search strategies and information on education, volunteering, and internships. Contact the Environmental Careers Organization at (617) 426-4375; khibbard@ eco.org; www.eco.org

Are you interested in internship or volunteer opportunities with a nonprofit in the Pacific Northwest? ***Sound Opportunities,*** a biweekly newsletter, can help you find work in social service and environmental change in Washington and Oregon, with a particular emphasis on the Seattle metropolitan area. For a complimentary copy of their newsletter contact: Sound Opportunities, P.O. Box 16722, Seattle, WA 98116; (206) 933-6556; Fax: (206) 933-6566; soundop@halcyon.com; www.halcyon.com/soundop

Authors Joy Herriott and Betty Herrin have included over 250 jobs, internships, study and travel programs, and camps, all related to the natural science field in their handbook, ***Summer Opportunities in Marine and Environmental Science.*** Although the guide is geared mainly to students, it provides a comprehensive list of resources and opportunities that are great information for anyone. To pick up a copy, send $14.95 plus $2 shipping to Summer Opportunities Guide, 38 Litchfield Rd., Londonderry, NH, 03053 or call (603) 432-5588.

The **Traveler's Earth Repair Network** (TERN) is a networking service for travelers wanting to make a positive contribution to the environment in the course of their travels. For a $50 fee, TERN links travelers with contacts and hosts involved in reforestation, forest preservation, sustainable agriculture, permaculture, and other areas of work related to trees and earth repair. Visits range from weekends to seasonal apprenticeships. Most hosts offer room and board in exchange for help, but sometimes there is a nominal charge to cover living expenses. The director, Michael Pilarski, also writes and publishes a handful of super resource guides related to the field. Friends of the Trees Society, P.O. Box 4469, Bellingham, WA 98855; (360) 738-4972 (Phone/Fax).

The aim of education is to impel people into value forming experiences…to ensure the survival of these qualities: an enterprising curiosity, an undefeatable spirit, tenacity in pursuit, readiness for sensible self-denial, and above all compassion.

—Kurt Hahn

Academy of Television Arts & Sciences

REGION/HQ: Pacific Northwest/California
• **CATEGORY:** Media • **POSITION TYPE:** Internship
• **DURATION:** Summer • **IDEAL CANDIDATE:** College Students, Foreigners • **APPLICANT POOL:** 1,000/year
• **APPLICANTS ACCEPTED:** 30/year

THE ACADEMY OF TELEVISION ARTS and Sciences (ATAS) is a nonprofit awards organization with a professional membership of nearly 7,000, which represents the largest in the U.S. television industry. In addition to sponsoring the Emmy Awards, ATAS holds filmmaking contests, publishes *Emmy* magazine, sponsors industry-wide meetings, and maintains the ATAS/UCLA Television Archives.

Work/Learn Program Specifics: Opportunities in all areas of professional television production, including agency, animation (traditional and computer-generated), art direction, broadcast advertising and promotion, business affairs, casting, commercials, children's programming/development, cinematography, commercials, costume design, development, editing, entertainment news, episodic series, movies for TV, music, network programming management, production management, public relations and publicity, sound, syndication/distribution, TV directing and scriptwriting, and videotape postproduction. Each internship is hosted by an organization—children's shows, prime-time sitcoms, talent agencies, studios, and production companies. Interns receive in-depth exposure to facilities, techniques, and practices and are paired with past interns through the academy's mentor program.

Duration: Internships last eight weeks, full-time (forty- to sixty-hour experience) in the summer.

Compensation and Perks: Interns are paid $1,000 halfway through the program and an additional $1,000 upon successful completion. Those residing outside L.A. County receive $400 to offset travel expenses. Interns also receive free passes to first-run movie screenings and are honored at a large mid-season party attended by over 300 people.

The Ideal Candidate: Any full-time college student can apply, although junior, senior, or graduate students are preferred. Successful candidates are typically pursuing degrees in art, theatre arts, business (advertising, marketing, or journalism), cinema, music, TV, film, law, or English.

Making It Happen: Call for detailed instructions and an application. Submit completed application, cover letter, written statement of approximately 250 words (outlining professional and personal goals), resume, three letters of recommendation, and transcripts. The entry period is from January through March 15. Finalists will be notified by April 15. All finalists will then have to submit a videotaped interview on half-inch VHS (not BETA) in response to questions posed in the notice of final candidacy.

Contact Information: Price Hicks, Director of Education • Academy of Television Arts & Sciences • Internship Program • 5220 Lankershim Blvd. • North Hollywood, CA 91601-3109 • Phone: (818) 754-2830 • Fax: (818) 761-2827 • Web Site: www.emmys.org

Alabama Sports Festival

REGION/HQ: Southeast/Alabama • **CATEGORY:** Festival
• **POSITION TYPE:** Internship • **DURATION:** Six/Nine Months • **IDEAL CANDIDATE:** College Students, Career Changers, Foreigners • **APPLICANT POOL:** 2–3/term
• **APPLICANTS ACCEPTED:** 2–3/term

THE ALABAMA SPORTS FESTIVAL is a statewide Olympic-style competition for amateur athletes of all ages and abilities, including the physically challenged and seniors.

Artistic A

The festival offers forty-two sporting events and has an annual participation of over 7,000 athletes in regional and state games competition. Alabama Sports Festival is recognized as a United States Olympic Committee State Games Program Participant and is a part of the nationwide network of state games programs which introduce young athletes to the Olympic traditions.

Work/Learn Program Specifics: The internship will provide individuals with experience in planning, management, marketing, fund-raising, recruiting, desktop publishing/graphics, sport development/management/implementation, and development of computer skills. The intern will participate in all staff meetings along with regular staff members and has the opportunity to function on an executive level.

Duration: Internships are offered for six- to nine-month periods: January through July 15 and May/June through November/December.

Compensation and Perks: Interns are provided housing, food, and a $100-per-month stipend for personal items. Expenses are reimbursed for transportation and other items that are required for carrying out job responsibilities.

The Ideal Candidate: Undergraduate and graduate students are encouraged to apply. Computer experience is essential.

Making It Happen: Submit cover letter and resume. Rolling deadlines.

INSIDER TIPS: *Students with Macintosh computer experience should highlight this on their resume, as well as outline software/hardware that they have a thorough knowledge of.*

Contact Information: Ron Creel, Chief Executive Officer • Alabama Sports Festival • 801 Adams Ave. • P.O. Box 1110 • Montgomery, AL 36101-1110 • Phone: (205) 263-3411 • Fax: (334) 263-3717 • Toll Free: (800) 467-0422 • E-mail: alagames@aol.com • Web Site: http://members.aol.com/alagames

American Conservatory Theatre

REGION/HQ: Pacific Northwest/California • **CATEGORY:** Theatre • **POSITION TYPE:** Internship • **DURATION:** Academic Year • **IDEAL CANDIDATE:** College Students, Career Changers • **APPLICANT POOL:** 100/year • **APPLICANTS ACCEPTED:** 15/year

SAN FRANCISCO'S TONY Award–winning American Conservatory Theatre is one of the largest and most active of the nation's resident professional theaters. ACT houses a prestigious actor training program and employs more than 475 persons annually. Each year ACT presents a season that is approximately 35 weeks in length and offers about 250 performances to an audience numbering more than 450,000. ACT draws its repertoire from the classics of dramatic literature and outstanding works of modern theater. ACT's historic Geary Theater was badly damaged during the Loma Prieta earthquake, in October 1989. In January 1996, ACT returned home. The magnificent Geary has been seismically stabilized and lovingly restored and features new state-of-the-art stage technology.

Work/Learn Program Specifics: Since 1976, ACT has provided excellent training for individuals seeking a career in theatre arts by offering internships in theater production. In 1993, ACT expanded the program to include intern positions in theater administration. These programs provide students and other interested persons the opportunity to work closely with top professionals in each field. The Production Department offers stage management, production, properties, technical design, sound design, lighting design, costume rentals, and wig construction/makeup. The Artistic and Administrative Department offers assistant directors/observers, general artistic staff, marketing/public relations and publications, and graphic design.

Duration: Internships are during the theatre season—August/September to May, forty to sixty hours per week. Summer-only positions are not available. Due to the variable hours of the program and the intense

dventures

nature of the work, it is impossible to hold an outside job during the internship period.

Compensation and Perks: Production interns are provided with a $165-per-week stipend. Artistic/administrative internships are nonpaid. ACT will provide housing assistance, but securing housing is the responsibility of each intern. Perks include free parking at the costume shop (a blessing for those of you that know how scarce and expensive parking can be in San Francisco), two tickets to any ACT production, and tickets to Berkeley and San Jose Repertory Theatre productions. Students needing financial aid should inquire.

The Ideal Candidate: Undergraduates or graduates of any age are eligible. Most departments require previous experience in their area of production, but a sincere and enthusiastic personality may compensate for a lack of experience in some cases. Due to the high costs of living in the Bay Area, all applicants must have additional independent funding for living expenses while in residence.

Making It Happen: Call for details on the program and to obtain an application. Submit completed application form, a personal statement, a resume, a photograph, three letters of recommendation, and a $10 nonrefundable application fee (the fee is waived for nonpaid interns). The deadline is April 15 and applicants are interviewed in person or over the phone. Notification of acceptance will be made by June 1.

Contact Information: Susan West, Intern Coordinator • American Conservatory Theatre • 30 Grant Ave. • San Francisco, CA 94108-5800 • Phone: (415) 834-3200 • Fax: (415) 834-3326

American Dance Festival

REGION/HQ: Southeast/North Carolina • **CATEGORY:** Festival • **POSITION TYPE:** Internship • **DURATION:** Summer • **IDEAL CANDIDATE:** College Students, Career Changers, Foreigners • **APPLICANT POOL:** Varies • **APPLICANTS ACCEPTED:** 300/year

SINCE ITS FOUNDING IN 1934, the American Dance Festival has remained committed to serving the needs of dance, dancers, and choreographers.

Area and Working Environment: The ADF is held for six weeks each summer at Duke University in Durham, North Carolina. ADF students use Duke facilities, including swimming pools, tennis courts, bookstores, and libraries. The grounds of the university include the formal Sarah P. Duke Gardens and an 8,000-acre forest. Durham is easily accessible by car, bus, and plane (Raleigh/Durham Airport is located approximately 18 miles away). It is a 3 $1/2$-hour drive from both the seashore and the mountains; either is accessible to festival participants for a weekend excursion.

Work/Learn Program Specifics: Don't miss this chance to become a part of this exciting community of dancers, students, choreographers, teachers, performers, critics, body therapists, dance medical specialists, scholars, and arts managers from all over the United States and around the world. Internships are available in ADF on Tour, box office, central services, community development, development/hospitality, finance, merchandising, performances, press, school, and production.

Duration: The intern program begins late in May and ends late in July.

Compensation and Perks: In addition to the $950 to $1,100 stipend, interns will receive one complimentary ticket to one night of all performances in the ADF's exciting 6 $1/2$-week modern dance season. Interns may also take one dance class per day and can observe panel discussions, seminars, and lectures by distinguished visitors as the work schedule permits. Apartments and shared housing are conveniently located near the festival site. Those needing housing assistance are encouraged to seek the festival's assistance.

Making It Happen: Call for application. Send completed application, cover letter (dealing with your interest in working with the festival, your particular skills, and what you hope to accomplish with the internship), resume, and two letters of recommendation. All applications must be received by February 1.

Contact Information: Art Waber, Intern Program Coordinator • American Dance Festival • Box 90772 • Durham, NC 27708-0772 • Phone: (919) 684-6402 • Fax: (919) 684-5459 • E-mail: adfnc@acpub.duke.edu • Web Site: www.duke.edu/~srn/adf.html

Aperture Foundation

REGION/HQ: Northeast/New York • **CATEGORY:** Visual Arts • **POSITION TYPE:** Internship • **DURATION:** Year-Round • **IDEAL CANDIDATE:** College Students, Career Changers, Foreigners • **APPLICANT POOL:** 250/year • **APPLICANTS ACCEPTED:** 26/year

APERTURE FOUNDATION is a nonprofit organization devoted to photography and the visual arts. Their mission is to promote the development of photography as one of the most powerful forms of human expression and to use photography's unique capabilities to illuminate important social, environmental, and cultural issues. To realize these objectives, Aperture has established an effective combination of programs, including publications, exhibitions, education, archival maintenance, and research.

Area and Working Environment: Aperture Publications and the Burden Gallery are located in New York City, and the Paul Strand Archive is located in Millerton, New York.

Work/Learn Program Specifics: Work-Scholar Program: The purpose of the program is to offer individuals of special promise an opportunity to become involved with the writing, editing, design, production, distribution, and marketing of publications and magazines; exhibition planning and the packaging of traveling shows; archival work; and nonprofit business practices. Positions are available in the following departments: Circulation, Development, Director's Office, Editorial, Foreign Rights, Marketing, Production, Publicity, Traveling Exhibition, the Burden Gallery, and the Paul Strand Archive. The program offers the opportunity to become involved in a nonprofit organization while learning and working for a senior member of the staff. Aperture's small size also allows interns to become familiar with the many aspects of publishing.

Duration: A commitment of at least six months is preferred, but concessions can be made. Positions are full-time and offered year-round. Part-time positions are available as projects arise.

Compensation and Perks: A monthly stipend of $250 is available. Living arrangements must be made by applicant. Upon completion of the internship, work-scholars are provided with letters of recommendation and referrals. While at Aperture, work-scholars receive a discount on books, magazines, and prints. After the internship is completed, interns receive a limited edition print.

The Ideal Candidate: Work-scholars will be selected on the basis of interest and experience in photography, publishing, and the visual arts; experience in their respective field; the ability to contribute significantly; and openness to gaining meaningful experience from the program. Skills such as typing, computer knowledge, copyediting, design, printing, business management, sales and marketing, and print preparation will enhance a candidate's application.

Making It Happen: Send a resume, two writing samples, and cover letter describing background, special skills, and personal objectives in becoming involved with the program. Rolling deadlines.

INSIDER TIPS: *Be concise in your letter; please let us know what positions you are most interested in and exactly when you can start. Enthusiasm and interest are the most important tips on getting accepted into the program. Staff members want to know that you are interested and that you will work hard once you arrive.*

Contact Information: Maria Décsey, Work-Scholar Coordinator • Aperture Foundation • 20 E. 23rd St. • New York, NY 10010-4463 • Phone: (212) 505-5555 • Fax: (212) 979-7759

Appel Farm Arts & Music Center

REGION/HQ: Northeast/New Jersey • **CATEGORY:** Performing Arts • **POSITION TYPE:** Internship • **DURATION:** Year-Round • **IDEAL CANDIDATE:** College Students, Career Changers • **APPLICANT POOL:** Varies • **APPLICANTS ACCEPTED:** Varies

APPEL FARM IS A NONPROFIT organization that provides people of all ages, cultures, and backgrounds a supportive environment to study, appreciate, and present work in creative and performing arts. There is a year-round conference center, arts outreach program, and performing arts series. During the summer months, Appel Farm operates a residential summer camp program for children ages nine to seventeen.

Area and Working Environment: Appel Farm is located in rural South Jersey, about thirty miles from Philadelphia and Wilmington.

Work/Learn Program Specifics: As an intern you will work with the Appel Farm staff in one or more of the following areas: festival management, arts administration, arts programming, marketing, development, conference center. They also have summer teaching/counselor staff positions, where you will work in the fields of theatre, music, fine arts, media, dance, or swimming/sports. Along with specific projects, interns will be expected, as is everyone at Appel Farm, to pitch in where help is needed. Everyone will do their share of envelope stuffing, data entry, filing, and other office work.

Duration: Applicants should plan to make at least a three-month commitment, although internships may

No one can whistle a symphony. It takes an orchestra to play it.
—HALFORD LUCCOCK

269

be extended up to twelve months. Openings available year-round.

Compensation and Perks: Interns—$150-per-month stipend; summer teaching/counselors—$1,000- to $1,300-per-month stipend. All staff are offered free room and board and live on-site in the Appel's original farmhouse. Life in the country can be very relaxing and quiet. Their senior residential staff member is more than willing to point out local and regional attractions, restaurants, and transportation. You may wish to bring a car with you, as Appel Farm is located in a country setting, away from the city. Additional benefits include use of Appel Farm arts and sports facilities, participation in conferences and training sessions, and encouragement of artistic freedom.

The Ideal Candidate: If you want to gain administrative experience in the arts while being in a supportive atmosphere, contribute to a growing arts center, thrive on being given responsibility and hard work, and if you genuinely like people, then this is the place for you. Teaching/counselor staff must be at least twenty-one years of age, available for entire camp duration during the summer (generally mid-June to mid-August), and nonsmokers.

Making It Happen: Call for application form. Send completed application, resume, and the names and telephone numbers of three references. Rolling deadlines.

Contact Information: Kathleen Bagby, Office Manager • Appel Farm Arts & Music Center • P.O. Box 888 • Elmer, NJ 08318-0888 • Phone: (609) 358-2472 • Fax: (609) 358-6513 • Toll Free: (800) 394-8478 • E-mail: appelarts@aol.com • Web Site: www.rowan.edu/appel

Arcosanti

REGION/HQ: South/Midwest/Arizona • **CATEGORY:** Conservation • **POSITION TYPE:** Unique Experience • **DURATION:** Year-Round • **IDEAL CANDIDATE:** High School Students, College Students, Career Changers, Retired Folks, Foreigners • **APPLICANT POOL:** 10–30/month • **APPLICANTS ACCEPTED:** 10–30/month

ARCOSANTI IS A NONPROFIT educational institution advancing the concept of arcology: the synthesis of architecture and ecology. Arcosanti is a prototype for an energy-efficient town, begun in 1970. It is intended to house approximately five thousand people in its final phase, providing an urban infrastructure with workplaces, cultural centers, and facilities for a diverse

population while simultaneously allowing accessibility to and interactions with the surrounding natural environment.

Area and Working Environment: The construction site is located on a mesa in the high desert of Arizona, within a 4,000-acre desert preserve and 70 miles north of metropolitan Phoenix.

Work/Learn Program Specifics: Learn about arcology (architecture and ecology) as an alternative to current urban dilemmas of expanding populations within limited spaces. Workshops generally involve a one-week seminar and four weeks of hands-on work. They've also introduced a Silt, Clay, Bronze Workshop, which goes into Paolo's methods in these materials, where you will produce your own siltcast clay bell, plaster tile, or sculpture. Call for the most current workshop listings.

Duration: Workshops are offered February through November, for five weeks.

Compensation and Perks: For five-week construction workshops there is a fee of $700; the Silt, Clay, Bronze Workshop runs $385. Housing and meals are provided as part of the cost of attending workshops. You also have co-use of the woodshop and other facilities.

The Ideal Candidate: Previous construction or architectural experience is not a prerequisite for participation in their programs; however, they are in need of people who have skills in mechanics, carpentry, welding, concrete, electrical, landscaping, cooking, accounting, baking, programming, drafting, tour guiding, model making, ceramics, and foundry work.

Making It Happen: Call for application form. Send application, a short statement about your interest in Arcosanti, a resume, three references with phone listings, and a $50 nonrefundable registration fee. Apply at least two weeks prior to workshop date.

INSIDER TIPS: *You can apply and receive more information about our workshops from our web site.*

Contact Information: Beth Greene, Workshops Registrar • Arcosanti • HC 74, Box 4136 • Mayer, AZ 86333 • Phone: (520) 632-7135 • Fax: (520) 632-6229 • E-mail: bgreene@getnet.com • Web Site: www. Arcosanti.org

Arena Stage

REGION/HQ: Washington, D.C./Washington, D.C. • **CATEGORY:** Theatre • **POSITION TYPE:** Internship • **DURATION:** Year-Round • **IDEAL CANDIDATE:**

College Students, Career Changers, Foreigners
• **APPLICANT POOL:** Varies • **APPLICANTS ACCEPTED:** Varies

• •

CO-FOUNDED IN 1950 by Zelda Fichandler, Thomas C. Fichandler, and Edward Mangum, Arena Stage was an early pioneer in the resident theatre movement, which sought to establish living theatre in communities outside of New York. Over the next forty years, under the visionary leadership of Zelda Fichandler, Arena Stage set the pace for the growth of the resident theater movement in this country and evolved in the process from a fledgling theatre into an internationally renowned institution. The three-theatre complex houses the 800-seat Fichandler Stage, the 500-seat Kreeger Theatre, and the 150-seat intimate Old Vat Theatre, as well as shops and offices necessary to support the art.

Area and Working Environment: Arena Stage provides the Washington metropolitan area and the nation with theatre of the highest artistic quality.

Work/Learn Program Specifics: The internship program is committed to providing the highest standard of training to future generations of theater professionals. Interns are treated as members of the Arena staff and are expected to perform a wide variety of tasks. Administrative: accessibility, arts in education, business management/personnel, casting, production office, communication/PR, development/fundraising, executive director's office, computer/information systems, literary management/dramaturgy, living stage administration (with Arena's social outreach company), and ticket operations. Artistic/Production: costume design, directing, electrics/lighting design, living stage production (with Arena's social outreach company), properties, scenic construction, paints, sound design, and stage management. Also inquire about their fellows program!

Duration: Internships are available throughout the calendar year for administrative interns. Directing, stage management, and technical production internships are available during the season (August through June) only. The duration of internships may vary from eight weeks (a production schedule) to forty weeks (a full season).

Compensation and Perks: A $100-per-week stipend is provided. Interns will also receive complimentary tickets to Arena performances and regular informational seminars with Arena's staff of professionals and guest artists.

The Ideal Candidate: The program is designed for people interested in pursuing a career in the professional theater. Applicants should be serious-minded, highly motivated individuals who have basic training and experience in theater and are willing to engage in the creative process and to test the limits of their own ingenuity.

Making It Happen: Send a cover letter (indicating which internship you are applying for and the dates you are available), resume, your most current transcript, two letters of recommendation, and responses to the following questions: 1) What is your eventual career goal in theatre? 2) Why are you applying to the internship program? 3) What do you hope to gain from your internship experience? Deadlines: winter/spring—October 1; summer—March 1; and fall—May 1. An interview is mandatory and can be handled in person or by telephone.

INSIDER TIPS: *Don't wait until the last minute to apply. Keep the coordinator abreast of the progress of your application if you are having trouble getting all of the materials in on time.*

Contact Information: Fellows & Interns Program Coordinator • Arena Stage • 6th & Maine Ave., SW • Washington, DC 20024 • Phone: (202) 554-9066 • Fax: (202) 488-4056 • Web Site: www.arena-stage.org

Arkansas Repertory Theater

REGION/HQ: South/Midwest/Arkansas • **CATEGORY:** Theatre • **POSITION TYPE:** Internship • **DURATION:** Year-Round • **IDEAL CANDIDATE:** College Students • **APPLICANT POOL:** 700/year • **APPLICANTS ACCEPTED:** 12/year

• •

THE ARKANSAS REPERTORY THEATER has provided Arkansas and the region with many opportunities and services. Its programs include an 8-play Main Stage series, a three-play Second Stage series, an annual regional or national Main Stage tour, and seven educational programs. The latter serves over 30,000 junior and senior high school students, teachers, and college students, in over 35 communities. Their mission is to be a professional theatre of excellence which entertains and challenges local, regional, and national audiences. Through its educational outreach and as a creative forum for artists, the Rep strives to provide valuable services to the community and make significant contributions to the national theatre agenda.

Work/Learn Program Specifics: Technical/production: costuming, set construction, lighting, sound and properties/set decoration. Stage Management: interns work directly with the resident equity stage manager and production manager on Main Stage, Second Stage, in-state and regional touring productions, and the Playreading series. Administration: development/fundraising, box office, house management, business management, and marketing/public relations. Acting: interns audition for and understudy selected Main Stage, Second Stage, and touring productions, as well as the Playreading series. Interns assist in all production and administrative areas and gain valuable experience as actors and teachers throughout the Arts in Education tour.

Duration: Positions are nine months, beginning in September and running through March, although they have done shorter internships, including just the summer.

Compensation and Perks: Interns receive $150 per week and casting opportunities. The Rep will also assist in locating housing for you.

Making It Happen: Submit cover letter and resume. Student must audition/interview in person and provide three letters of recommendation at that time. The nine-month program deadline is mid-March; call for other time periods.

INSIDER TIPS: *Actors—choosing material suited to you which demonstrates your emotional range, sense of humor, and honesty; technicians—a well put together portfolio; management—a detailed statement of your year's goals.*

Contact Information: Artistic Associate • Arkansas Repertory Theater • P.O. Box 110 • Little Rock, AR 72203-0110 • Phone: (501) 378-0445 • Fax: (501) 378-0012

Art Institute of Chicago

REGION/HQ: Great Lakes/Illinois • **CATEGORY:** Museum • **POSITION TYPE:** Internship • **DURATION:** Year-Round • **IDEAL CANDIDATE:** College Students, Career Changers • **APPLICANT POOL:** Varies • **APPLICANTS ACCEPTED:** Varies

IT IS THE OBJECTIVE OF the Art Institute of Chicago to collect, preserve, exhibit, and interpret for the public one of the finest collections of the visual arts in the nation. The museum was founded in 1879, and today the permanent collection has grown to include 250,000 objects held in 10 curatorial departments. As they move forward, the institute is committed to bringing more and more diverse people face to face with original works of art. Last year, over 145,000 students toured the collection and almost 1.5 million people visited the museum.

Work/Learn Program Specifics: Internships are offered in the Art Institute's many departments throughout the year and enable students to gain firsthand experience in their areas of interest or study. Interns work under the guidance of curators or department heads, and they assist in routine departmental work that ranges from special projects and research to clerical support. The following departments offer internships: Accounting, Africa, Oceania and the Americas, American Art, Architecture, Archives, Asian Art, Conservation, Design and Construction, Development, Energy and Facilities Planning, End-User Computing, European Decorative Arts, European Painting, Imaging and Technical Services, Information Support, Installation and Packing, Museum Education, Museum Registration, Operations, Photo Collections, Personnel, Prints and Drawings, Public Affairs, Purchasing, Ryerson/Burnham Library, and Twentieth Century Art.

Duration: Hours vary and are flexible; however, a minimum of four hours per week is generally expected.

Compensation and Perks: Many positions are paid, while others are offered for work-study. During the internship duration, the Art Institute will offer employee discounts at the museum shop and cafeteria, as well as admission to the museum and most Chicago cultural institutes.

The Ideal Candidate: Interns are usually junior- or senior-level college students or graduate students; however, in some cases, those individuals with related work will be considered. A major in art history or fine arts is not essential.

Making It Happen: Call for application materials. Applications should include a resume and cover letter indicating specific areas of interest and availability, including the number of hours per week, and the goals to be achieved if selected for an internship. Applicants will be considered for those internships that most closely match their study, background, and interest.

Contact Information: Kim Kruskop, Coordinator of Internship Programs • Art Institute of Chicago • 111 S. Michigan Ave. • Chicago, IL 60603-6110 • Phone: (312) 443-3555 • Fax: (312) 443-0111

Astors' Beechwood Mansion

REGION/HQ: Northeast/Rhode Island • **CATEGORY:** Living History • **POSITION TYPE:** Internship • **DURATION:** Varies • **IDEAL CANDIDATE:** College Students, Foreigners • **APPLICANT POOL:** Varies • **APPLICANTS ACCEPTED:** Varies

THE BEECHWOOD THEATRE COMPANY is a resident company housed in the Astors' Beechwood Victorian mansion. The company of actors play Astor family members, their guests, and servants, as they re-create the Victorian era. Beechwood's grounds are also the site of tea dances (a re-creation of a Victorian ball) and murder mysteries.

Area and Working Environment: Newport is a very cosmopolitan area and tourist resort town.

Work/Learn Program Specifics: Intern actors work with the professional staff on living history tours and are required to take part in tea dances and murder mysteries. Interns also have weekly classes for improvisation, audition technique, and acting.

Duration: The summer season is usually from the beginning of May to mid-August; the fall season is from mid-August to late December.

Compensation and Perks: A $90-per-week stipend is provided, plus room and board.

The Ideal Candidate: The company desires students who are working to make theatre and acting a career. Improvisational skills are very important.

Making It Happen: Submit cover letter, resume, and photo. Auditions usually include two contrasting monologues and a song. Beechwood Theatre Company attends three conference auditions: NETC, ITA, and the Midwest Theatre Conference. There is also an in-house audition which is by appointment only. Rolling deadlines.

INSIDER TIPS: *Beechwood is an opportunity for the young actor to gain confidence in self and skills. Living in a mansion is also a lifetime highlight for many.*

Contact Information: Sheli Beck, Artistic Director • Astors' Beechwood Mansion • 580 Bellevue Ave. • Newport, RI 02840 • Phone: (401) 846-3772 • Fax: (401) 849-6998

Berkeley Repertory Theatre

REGION/HQ: Pacific Northwest/California • **CATEGORY:** Theatre • **POSITION TYPE:** Internship • **DURATION:** Ten months • **IDEAL CANDIDATE:** College Students, Career Changers, Retired Folks, Foreigners • **APPLICANT POOL:** 100–200/year • **APPLICANTS ACCEPTED:** 7–12/year

BERKELEY REPERTORY ATTRACTS over 20,000 subscribers each season to its multimillion-dollar facility and reaches out into the entire Bay Area with its popular school touring program. It's one of the most successful theatre companies in the Bay Area and has earned an impressive national reputation for the production of classic and new plays, attracting some of the finest theatre professionals working today. Five challenging productions are mounted each season in the 401-seat mainstage, along with the innovative Parallel Season productions and one fully produced school touring production. Since its founding in 1968, Berkeley Rep has focused on the development of a resident company of theatre artists, including actors, playwrights, directors, designers, and theatre artisans. The sense of community and shared growth and knowledge that now exists within the Rep is one of its real strengths.

Area and Working Environment: Berkeley is one of many cities in the culturally rich and diverse San Francisco Bay Area.

Work/Learn Program Specifics: The internship program provides an opportunity to work under Berkeley Rep's professional staff, helping to support the high-quality production standards for which the Rep continues to win numerous awards. Interns will work closely with an accomplished company of artists, administrators, guest directors, and designers. The program includes regularly scheduled informal seminars every month throughout the season as the production schedule allows. The partnership between the Theatre and the intern is intended to fulfill as many career-building goals and objectives as possible and to provide the intern with a variety of professional contacts and craft-building experiences. Areas of specialization include development, marketing/public relations, theatre administration, properties, costumes, sound, lighting/electrics, scenic construction, scenic painting, stage management, literary/dramaturgy, and education.

Duration: Positions are for ten months, usually beginning in August or September. A full-time commitment, forty hours per week, is required.

No one can tell you how to live your life. You are the artist...and must shape your experiences with your own hand.

Compensation and Perks: A $300 stipend per month is provided, plus local housing for most positions.

The Ideal Candidate: Applicants should be serious-minded, highly motivated individuals who have already acquired basic training and experience in the theatre and are ready for the next step toward a career in professional theatre. They should be willing to engage in the creative process and to test the limits of their own ingenuity. Work outside of school is a great benefit.

Making It Happen: Submit a resume, three letters of recommendation, and a cover letter addressing why you think an internship will further your career, why you should be chosen as an intern, and how you heard about Berkeley Rep's internship program. Literary applicants must include two samples of critical writing. The deadline for all programs is April 15, except for the Stage Management Program which is March 15.

INSIDER TIPS: *If you have some solid experience, even if it's only in college, and you proofread your application, then you'll get an interview. In the interview make sure you think about what you are going to say before you say it. Don't be afraid to take your time in an interview.*

Contact Information: Intern Coordinator • Berkeley Repertory Theatre • 2025 Addison St. • Berkeley, CA 94704 • Phone: (510) 204-8901 • Fax: (510) 841-7711 • Web Site: www.berkeleyrep.org

Berkshire Public Theatre

REGION/HQ: Northeast/Massachusetts • **CATEGORY:** Theatre • **POSITION TYPE:** Internship • **DURATION:** Year-Round • **IDEAL CANDIDATE:** College Students, Career Changers, Foreigners • **APPLICANT POOL:** 100/year • **APPLICANTS ACCEPTED:** 18/year

THE BERKSHIRE PUBLIC THEATRE is the only year-round repertory theatre in Berkshire County. Since 1976, this ensemble company has performed an eclectic repertoire encompassing drama, comedy, musicals, original works, and children's theatre. The Public Theatre is in residence in a partially restored 1912 Vaudeville House in downtown Pittsfield.

Area and Working Environment: Pittsfield is a small industrial city in the center of the Berkshires, an area renowned for its rural beauty and cultural attractions, including Tanglewood, The Williamstown Theatre Festival, The Berkshire Theatre Festival, Jacob's Pillow Dance Festival, and the Norman Rockwell Museum.

Work/Learn Program Specifics: Theatre Administration: management, public relations, development, marketing, and box office. Theatre Technology: set construction, lighting and sound, costume construction and maintenance, stage management, and production management. Education: in-school/after-school programs, summer camp, and children's theatre. Directing and Acting: Interns attend their staff meetings once a week and participate in set change, strikes, and the maintenance of the theatre, regardless of their specific area of interest.

Duration: Three month minimum.

Compensation and Perks: Interns can be housed in the Berkshire Public Theatre's Annex, known as the Octagon. This house sits across the street from the theatre and contains administrative offices, costume shop, and a communal kitchen on the first floor. The sixth floor is where you will live, where there are six dormitory rooms. Rooms could be singles, doubles, or triples, depending on the number of interns. The fee is $25 per week. Since this is an unpaid position, many interns seek part-time employment in the area.

The Ideal Candidate: Interns must be at least eighteen years of age.

Making It Happen: Call for application. Send completed application, cover letter, resume, headshot (actors), and two letters of recommendation. Rolling deadlines. Interviews are required for all prospective interns. Phone interviews can be conducted in certain cases. If you are interested in acting, please be prepared to audition at the time of your interview, with two pieces of contrasting material, either classical or contemporary.

Contact Information: Company Manager • Berkshire Public Theatre • 30 Union St. • P.O. Box 860 • Pittsfield, MA 01202-0860 • Phone: (413) 445-4631 • Fax: (413) 445-4640

California Institute for Peruvian Studies

REGION/HQ: Peru/Colorado • **CATEGORY:** Expedition • **POSITION TYPE:** Unique Experience • **DURATION:** Spring/Summer • **IDEAL CANDIDATE:** High School Students, College Students, Career Changers, Retired Folks, Foreigners • **APPLICANT POOL:** 100/term • **APPLICANTS ACCEPTED:** 10/term

ARE YOU SEARCHING FOR KNOWLEDGE, yearning for adventure, wishing for an unparalleled cultural exchange?

If you are, this unique experience could change your life. The California Institute for Peruvian Studies (CIPS) invites you to become a part of history by joining its archaeological expedition team. Through hands-on research, you will learn how to locate lost ruins, identify early civilizations, seek out cultural artifacts, and document your findings—all in the magical setting of Peru's southern coast.

Area and Working Environment: The CIPS "home" is located in a small pueblo called Bella Union (pronounced *Bay-you-yawn*), situated near the sea, eight hours south of Lima, Peru. It is considered one of the longest towns in Peru, reaching eight kilometers, and is one block wide.

Work/Learn Program Specifics: Digging in the sun-baked ground, you may uncover an infant mummy bundle or the head of an Incan war club. You can't help but wonder what happened to these people. More questions are uncovered with each shovel full of loosened earth. An overwhelming intellectual curiosity develops in the quest to know "the ancient ones." Delving into the culture, textiles, ceramics, and human remains of long ago, many have experienced a new beginning, of sorts, while participating in this work. Field-school topics include culture history, physical anthropology, excavation, museology, archaeotourism, archaeological illustration, survey, and more. The center is staffed with a resident archaeologist coordinator, maid, and cook, providing ideal conditions for the workshops.

Duration: CIPS offers several three-week-long field schools each year.

Compensation and Perks: In a large, eight-room house, complete with cobblestone courtyard, lab, outdoor patio, and cactus garden, CIPS participants carry out their research and educational programs. The gourmet cuisine is said by some to be the highlight of the trip. Discounted group airfare is offered in conjunction with each field school.

The Ideal Candidate: The ability to speak Spanish is helpful, but not required, as the bilingual staff provides all necessary interpretation. Each field school, while it may be used for college credit, is equally enjoyed by the avocational student and the adventure seeker.

Making It Happen: Call for application and current schedule. At time of press, Bella Union was recovering from a massive earthquake. Most of the trips will be geared to rebuilding what has been destroyed through hard work, evaluation, humanitarian efforts, and rustic living.

Contact Information: Sandy Asmussen, Operations Administrator • California Institute for Peruvian Studies • 45 Quakie Way • Bailey, CO 80421 • Phone: (303) 838-1215 • Fax: (303) 838-5526 • E-mail: cips@juno.com

Center for Investigative Reporting

REGION/HQ: California/D.C./California
• **CATEGORY:** Media • **POSITION TYPE:** Internship
• **DURATION:** Six months • **IDEAL CANDIDATE:** College Students, Career Changers, Foreigners
• **APPLICANT POOL:** 80–100/term • **APPLICANTS ACCEPTED:** 5–10/term

THE CENTER FOR INVESTIGATIVE REPORTING (CIR) serves as a base for journalists in pursuit of hidden stories about the individuals and institutions that shape our lives. Since the center's founding in 1977, CIR staff and associates have completed hundreds of major investigations and have become an important source of information for media outlets, community and public-interest groups, and other journalists, as well as government officials and the concerned public. Their stories have spurred interest and action in Congress, the courts, and the United Nations, and have forced changes in multinational corporations, government agencies, and other organizations. Media outlets such as *60 Minutes*, *20/20*, CNN, and the *Washington Post* have relied on CIR to produce similar types of stories for them.

Area and Working Environment: Most positions are offered in San Francisco; however some are available in Washington, D.C.

Work/Learn Program Specifics: Investigative Reporting Intern: One of the center's most important functions is to teach investigative reporting skills to novice reporters. After a half-day orientation in CIR procedures and administration, interns are paired with senior reporters. Under the guidance of these senior journalists, interns follow the full cycle of a major project from concept to publication or broadcast. CIR interns will conduct interviews, gather information and search through public records, and often contribute to final stories with sidebars or other reporting. Research projects generally include investigations into environmental, public health, constitutional government, economic, social justice, and public-trust issues. In addition, interns participate in a series of seminars on investigative techniques, media law, ethics, and other

You've got to dance like there's nobody watching; you've go to love like you've never been hurt; you've got to sing like there's nobody listening; you've got to live like it's heaven on earth.

275

issues. They also have access to files of staff members and holdings of the center's library. For most participants, the internship launches a promising career in reporting.

Duration: Duration is approximately six months, with a minimum commitment of fifteen hours per week. Regular starting dates for internships are approximately January 15 for winter/spring and June 15 for summer/fall.

Compensation and Perks: The stipend is $100/month. Interns who write stories under the watchful eye of CIR's editors will take home 85 percent of what an outside news organization pays for the piece. Interns also interact with prominent local and national producers, reporters, and journalism instructors, as well as journalists visiting from foreign countries.

The Ideal Candidate: Desire students and career-changers with good writing and research skills, as well as an interest in investigative reporting and a self-directed work style.

Making It Happen: Submit resume, cover letter (describing interests and background), and a few clippings or writing samples (if you haven't been published, make sure you send in vivid writing samples that avoid academic/stuffy tones). After a phone or on-site interview, you will need to provide them with two or three personal references. Deadlines: winter/spring—December 1; summer/fall—May 1. Please call before applicable deadline for written material.

Contact Information: James Curtiss, Communications Director • Center for Investigative Reporting • 530 Howard St., 5th Floor • San Francisco, CA 94105-3008 • Phone: (415) 543-1200 • Fax: (415) 543-8311 • E-mail: cir@igc.apc.org

Center for Photography at Woodstock

REGION/HQ: Northeast/New York • **CATEGORY:** Photography • **POSITION TYPE:** Unique Experience • **DURATION:** Summer • **IDEAL CANDIDATE:** College Students, Career Changers, Foreigners • **APPLICANT POOL:** 40–50/year • **APPLICANTS ACCEPTED:** 4/year

SINCE 1979, THE CENTER has presented the Woodstock Photography Workshops, an education series where national/international photographers serve as teachers. Workshop students come from all over the United States, as well as from other countries, to study with working photographers who have the skills and desire to share their experiences with a peer group.

Work/Learn Program Specifics: Interns participate in the workshops and the photography lecture series (which is valued at over $3,000). The intern experience is unlike traditional classroom education. In a matter of months, interns have the opportunity to meet an average of fifteen different guest teachers and hundreds of students. An entire range of topics is presented in a relatively short span. Interns learn strategies in teaching, arts administration, and professional image making. A fully-equipped professional darkroom and use of library are also available free of charge.

Duration: June through September.

The Ideal Candidate: CPW seeks individuals who are curious, highly motivated, technically skilled, and can handle a diverse audience and a fast-paced work environment. Interns should plan to live or relocate to the Woodstock, New York area and have transportation.

Making It Happen: Each spring, interns may schedule a personal interview on Fridays at 2 P.M., during the last two weeks of March and the month of April. A personal portfolio (ten prints), resume, and personal references (with phone numbers) are required for an appointment.

Contact Information: Kathleen Kenyon, Associate Director • Center for Photography at Woodstock • 59 Tinker St. • Woodstock, NY 12498 • Phone: (914) 679-9957 • Fax: (914) 679-6337 • E-mail: CPWphoto@aol.com

Center Stage

REGION/HQ: Washington, D.C./ Maryland • **CATEGORY:** Theatre • **POSITION TYPE:** Internship • **DURATION:** Academic year • **IDEAL CANDIDATE:** College Students, Career Changers • **APPLICANT POOL:** 100/year • **APPLICANTS ACCEPTED:** 13/year

FOUNDED IN BALTIMORE IN 1963, Center Stage has grown to prominence locally, regionally, and nationally as a leader in the resident theatre community. Honored as the state theatre of Maryland, Center Stage performs to more than 110,000 theatre-goers annually. In February of 1991, following extensive alterations and additions to its 135-year-old building, Center Stage opened the Head Theatre, a flexible space seating between 250 and 350 people. The Pearlstone Theatre, featuring a modified thrust, seats 541 people. Center

Stage strives to explore a wide range of dramatic literature and production approaches, from fresh visions of the classics to active support of contemporary writing. In addition to six main-stage productions, there are three in the Off-Center series, which features cutting-edge performance artists.

Area and Working Environment: Located in the historic Mount Vernon area of Baltimore.

Work/Learn Program Specifics: Production internships are available in stage management, scenic artist, properties, costumes, electrics, and sound. Administrative internships are available in development/ fund-raising, public relations, marketing, dramaturgy, education, and company management. Center Stage provides biweekly seminars to increase interns' knowledge and understanding of the organization as a whole.

Duration: Internships are from August/September through May/June, full-time.

Compensation and Perks: Interns receive a stipend of $75 per week, plus housing. Center Stage recently acquired three row houses close to the theatre, where each intern has a furnished efficiency apartment. The only charge to the intern is for long-distance phone calls. Perks include tickets to all productions at Center Stage and often to other local theatres and concerts.

The Ideal Candidate: Applicants should have proven ability in area of specialization. They expect a willingness of interns to work hard and have high standards of performance.

Making It Happen: Call for application. Send completed application, resume, a brief personal statement (your long-range goals and what you expect to gain from an internship), and two letters of recommendation (which can be sent under separate letter). It's best to apply by March/April for the following season.

Contact Information: Katharyn Davies, Internship Coordinator • Center Stage • 700 N. Calvert St. • Baltimore, MD 21202 • Phone: (410) 685-3200 • Fax: (410) 539-3912 • E-mail: info@centerstage.org

Central City Opera House Association

REGION/HQ: Rocky Mountains/Colorado • **CATEGORY:** Festival • **POSITION TYPE:** Internship/ Seasonal • **DURATION:** Summer • **IDEAL CANDIDATE:** College Students • **APPLICANT POOL:** 85/year • **APPLICANTS ACCEPTED:** 16/year

CENTRAL CITY OPERA WAS BUILT IN 1878 by Cornish and Welsh miners and is one of the oldest opera festivals in the United States. The 750-seat theatre, a historic landmark in Central City, affords an intimate experience with grand opera and operetta. It is one of the very few opera companies in America to own its own opera house.

Area and Working Environment: Central City Opera is at the hub of this historic mining town, located forty-five minutes from Denver.

Work/Learn Program Specifics: Festival season staff positions include music librarian, public relations assistant, house management, switchboard, costume shop/wardrobe, gardening, gift shop, facility maintenance, production assistance, and general office positions.

Duration: The festival runs from the beginning of June to the middle of August. The workweek is six days, Tuesday through Sunday.

Compensation and Perks: Stipends start at $175 per week, plus housing with a kitchen and laundry facilities. A travel reimbursement is also paid to those residing outside of Colorado.

The Ideal Candidate: Applicants must be at least eighteen years of age and have lots of energy and a positive attitude. Some positions require a driver's license.

Making It Happen: It's best to request an application by January with all materials due by April 1. Personal interviews are preferred, although phone interviews can be arranged.

INSIDER TIPS: *It helps to have an interest in opera or a desire to become more familiar with the art form, but it's not necessary.*

Contact Information: Curt Hancock, Artistic Administrator • Central City Opera House Association • 621 17th St., Suite 1601 • Denver, CO 80293-1601 • Phone: (303) 292-6500 • Fax: (303) 292-4958 • Web Site: www.artstozoo.org/ccopera

Chesterwood Estate & Museum

REGION/HQ: Northeast/Massachusetts • **CATEGORY:** Museum • **POSITION TYPE:** Internship • **DURATION:** Year-Round • **IDEAL CANDIDATE:** College Students, Career Changers, Retired Folks, Foreigners • **APPLICANT POOL:** Varies • **APPLICANTS ACCEPTED:** Varies

THE CHESTERWOOD MUSEUM is the former summer estate of sculptor Daniel Chester French (1850-1931), who is best known for creating two great national symbols—the seated *Abraham Lincoln* (at the Lincoln Memorial in Washington, D.C.) and the *Minute Man* (in Concord, Massachusetts). The site includes French's studio and residence (operated as historic house museums), a barn (circa 1820) adapted for use as an exhibition gallery and a collections storage facility, the Country Place garden, woodland walks, a visitor reception area, and several outbuildings. Chesterwood also houses the largest collection of works by a single major American sculptor and a 100,000-piece archive.

Area and Working Environment: This unique historic site sits on over 130 acres in the Berkshire mountains.

Work/Learn Program Specifics: The student intern/adult volunteer program offers the opportunity for work experience in a variety of museum operations, including administration, curatorial, education, historic horticulture research, interpretation, special events, the museum shop, and historic site maintenance. In addition to completing assigned projects, volunteers are required to perform such regular activities as presenting guided tours, greeting and directing group tours, operating special events, and assisting with museum maintenance. During the off-season (November through April), volunteers undertake specific projects, such as research, exhibit preparation, and serving as guest editor of the museum's newsletter.

Duration: Positions vary from three to twelve months, depending on the availability of the volunteers and projects. It is suggested that volunteers should plan at least a three-month program to include time for training, preparation, and implementation of projects.

Compensation and Perks: Although an unpaid position, volunteers receive a membership to the Friends of Chesterwood and participate in special events and parties, including the volunteer reception held in the fall. Volunteers also receive complimentary tickets to many local programs and performances in the Berkshire region.

The Ideal Candidate: Open to those wishing to contribute their time and abilities to the preservation and interpretation of the site.

Making It Happen: Call for application materials. Deadlines: spring—October 15; summer—April 1; and fall—July 15. Applicants will be notified within six weeks of the application deadline.

Contact Information: Susan Frisch Lehrer, Education & Visitor Services Manager • Chesterwood Estate & Museum • P.O. Box 827 • Stockbridge, MA 01262-0827 • Phone: (413) 298-3579 • Fax: (413) 298-3973

The Children's Museum

REGION/HQ: Northeast/Massachusetts • **CATEGORY:** Museum • **POSITION TYPE:** Internship • **DURATION:** Varies • **IDEAL CANDIDATE:** College Students, Career Changers, Foreigners • **APPLICANT POOL:** 175/term • **APPLICANTS ACCEPTED:** 15/term

THE CHILDREN'S MUSEUM, characterized as a laboratory museum and national research and development center, exists to help children understand and enjoy the world in which they live. Central to their philosophy is the belief that real objects, direct experiences, and enjoyment support learning. They want children to grow up feeling secure and self-confident, with respect for others and the natural world.

Work/Learn Program Specifics: Exhibit instructors will open and clean the exhibits each morning, staff a different exhibit each hour according to assignment, do drop-in activities with visitors, be available to answer visitors' questions and help them with special requests, and, finally, close the exhibits every evening. School program interpreters open the exhibits, escort school groups through the museum, and perform school programs in the exhibits as needed. Public program interpreters staff a different exhibit every hour according to assignment, run drop-in activities for children, answer questions, and close the exhibits at the end of the day.

Duration: Positions are available for the summer beginning mid-June, and for the academic year beginning mid-August (fall and spring semesters combined).

Compensation and Perks: Interns receive $6.30 per hour. You will also receive free admission to Boston area museums.

The Ideal Candidate: Someone who has experience with children, a strong interest in education, is comfortable with the public, flexible, and energetic.

Making It Happen: Send a resume, three letters of recommendation, and a one-page statement of interest. Deadlines: summer—March 30; academic year—May 30. Selected applicants will be interviewed and a formal application will be filled out at time of interview.

INSIDER TIPS: *We like high-energy individuals. A second language is a plus.*

Contact Information: Human Resource Director • The Children's Museum • 300 Congress St. • Boston, MA 02210-1034 • Phone: (617) 426-6500 • Fax: (617) 426-1944

Children's Museum of Indianapolis

REGION/HQ: Great Lakes/Indiana • **CATEGORY:** Museum • **POSITION TYPE:** Internship • **DURATION:** Year-Round • **IDEAL CANDIDATE:** College Students, Career Changers • **APPLICANT POOL:** 200/year • **APPLICANTS ACCEPTED:** 65+/year

THE CHILDREN'S MUSEUM OF INDIANAPOLIS is the largest and fourth oldest children's museum in the world. This five-story brick museum (325,000 square feet) houses ten major galleries exploring the sciences, history, foreign cultures, and the arts. In addition, it regularly hosts thousands of nontraditional programs for children and their adults, hosting over 1.3 million visitors each year. The museum itself includes a sweeping atrium entrance, complete with a unique water clock, an education center, a world-class planetarium, and the IWERKS CineDome Theater. The museum also operates Ritchey Woods, a 180-acre environmental learning center for children and their families.

Area and Working Environment: Indianapolis is home to a strong arts community, the Indianapolis 500, the Circle Centre Mall, and booming growth.

Work/Learn Program Specifics: The museum offers enthusiastic professionals as mentors and a customized experience for each intern. Interns are placed primarily in the Education, Programs, Collections, Exhibit Production, Marketing, Communications, and Development departments. You will have the opportunity to work with the public, design and implement activities, develop future job skills, discover the inner workings of a major museum, experience the day-to-day business of meetings and brainstorming, and have fun. During the internship, interns attend field trips to area and regional arts institutions to learn more about career options and to add perspective to their experience.

Duration: Internships are available year-round for a minimum of eight weeks; however, the best experiences usually come from a full-time internship for a three- to four-month period. The longer you stay, the more you learn and the more substantive assignments you receive.

Compensation and Perks: Although the positions are on a volunteer basis, they offer behind-the-scenes field trips to area and regional arts institutions, staff training, and networking possibilities. Subsidized housing is also in the works.

The Ideal Candidate: The internship program is highly selective. They look for people who are interested in working with and for children, have good interpersonal skills, and a high energy level.

Making It Happen: Call for more information and application materials. At least six to eight weeks prior to your anticipated start date, send your resume, a cover letter describing your interests, and completed application. After an interview with a staff member, they will provide a more specific job description proposal and try to accommodate any other needs.

INSIDER TIPS: *Museums are an increasingly tough field to break into, so previous experience is more important than ever. We are dedicated to providing professional, positive experiences for interns interested in working with children. We are looking for people who are enthusiastic, motivated, and thoughtful.*

Contact Information: Derek Drockelman, Intern/Youth Coordinator • Children's Museum of Indianapolis • P.O. Box 3000 • Indianapolis, IN 46206-3000 • Phone: (317) 924-5431 • Fax: (317) 921-4019 • Toll Free: (800) 826-5431 • E-mail: interns@childrensmuseum.org • Web Site: www.childrensmuseum.org

Children's Studio School

REGION/HQ: Washington, D.C./Washington, D.C. • **CATEGORY:** Arts Administration • **POSITION TYPE:** Internship • **DURATION:** Year-Round • **IDEAL CANDIDATE:** College Students, Career Changers • **APPLICANT POOL:** Varies • **APPLICANTS ACCEPTED:** 100/year

CHILDREN'S STUDIO SCHOOL is a twenty-year-old community-based institution with national recognition for its transcultural "Arts-As-Education" approach to developing multidimensional thinking in children. Believing that the younger the child, the more developed the student's teacher should be, the Studio School employs mature visual and performing artists, architects, and writers of diverse cultural backgrounds, all respected professionals in their disciplines, to teach three-to nine-year-olds throughout the day. As the children work through the intense process of investigating concepts and ideas in the arts, they naturally draw upon

It is the function of art to renew our perception. What we are familiar with we cease to see. The writer shakes up the familiar scene, and as if by magic, we see new meaning in it. —ANAïS NIN

their cultural histories and, incidentally, develop superior capabilities in all academic areas. The school stimulates divergent ways of thinking and solving problems in participants of all ages through workshops, conferences, and performances for families, teachers, and others in the community.

Work/Learn Program Specifics: Artist/teacher interns will assist artists and children in the "Arts-As-Education" process. Duties include working directly with children, participating in meetings and workshops, documenting children's working process and progress, and self-evaluation. Interns work closely with the school's artists to develop their own teaching capabilities. Interns are expected to help challenge the children to actively investigate, imagine, design, create, contemplate, and analyze their ideas and productions as a means of developing divergent ways of thinking, knowing, and acting. Administrative interns will work directly with the president on many aspects of running the organization. This may include researching and drafting grant proposals, recruiting and working with volunteers, financial and resource development, and communicating the purpose and philosophy of the school to the wider community. Designer/graphic artist interns organize and install exhibits, mat and frame, prepare graphic presentation portfolios, and catalog slides and photographs of student work and working processes.

Compensation and Perks: This is a volunteer position; however, they will provide assistance in finding housing.

The Ideal Candidate: Artist/teacher intern applicants should have a background in the arts or education and a serious commitment to developing an experiential understanding of the Studio School philosophy and approach. Administrative intern applicants should be interested in developing an in-depth understanding of, and ability to communicate, the underlying concepts of Children's Studio School. Designer/graphic artist intern applicants should have experience in visual art/design and preferably the ability to write well.

Making It Happen: Send resume and a statement of philosophy/approach to the arts as a process of education. Rolling deadlines.

Contact Information: Marcia McDonell, President • Children's Studio School • 1824 Biltmore St., NW • Washington, DC 20009-1904 • Phone: (202) 387-5880 • Fax: (202) 986-1202

The Cloisters

REGION/HQ: Northeast/New York • **CATEGORY:** Museum • **POSITION TYPE:** Internship • **DURATION:** Summer • **IDEAL CANDIDATE:** College Students, Foreigners • **APPLICANT POOL:** 250/year • **APPLICANTS ACCEPTED:** 8/year

THE CLOISTERS, OPENED IN 1938, is a branch of The Metropolitan Museum of Art devoted to the art of medieval Europe. It resembles a twelfth-century monastery and got its name from the sections of four medieval cloisters (covered walkways enclosing courtyards and leading to monastic buildings) that are part of the modern architecture of the museum. The four cloisters provide an inviting place for rest and contemplation.

Work/Learn Program Specifics: The program begins with three weeks of intensive training to prepare the interns to become medievalists. This knowledge prepares the interns to conduct gallery workshops for groups of New York City day campers (ages four to twelve) and for developing a public gallery talk which they will deliver in the last week. Interns will learn all facets of curatorship: handling art objects, setting up exhibits, meeting art dealers, and interacting with the public.

Duration: Summer positions are from mid-June to mid-August, full-time.

Compensation and Perks: Each intern will receive an honorarium of $2,250 for the summer. A list of summer housing opportunities is mailed to all finalists. Besides all the intensive training you will receive on medieval art history and museum teaching techniques, you will also participate in field trips to New York City art institutions and meetings with museum curators and conservators.

The Ideal Candidate: Applicants must be undergraduate students (with special consideration given to first- and second-year students) who are interested in art and museum careers and who enjoy working with young people. In addition, applicants are expected to be responsible and mature individuals who are able to work well both independently and in a group.

Making It Happen: Contact the Education Department in the fall for an application flyer. A typed application must be received by the first Friday in February. Interviews will be conducted in March and all applicants will be notified by April 15.

INSIDER TIPS: *Applicants should have an enthusiasm for teaching children and for medieval art.*

Contact Information: Michael Norris, Assistant Museum Educator • The Cloisters • Education Department • Fort Tryon Park • New York, NY 10040 • Phone: (212) 650-2280 • Fax: (212) 795-3640

Creede Repertory Theatre

REGION/HQ: Rocky Mountains/Colorado • **CATEGORY:** Theatre • **POSITION TYPE:** Internship • **DURATION:** Year-Round • **IDEAL CANDIDATE:** High School Students, College Students, Career Changers, Retired Folks • **APPLICANT POOL:** 1,000/year • **APPLICANTS ACCEPTED:** 10/term

THE CREEDE REPERTORY THEATRE strives to raise the standards of practice, to make the performing arts more accessible to the public, and to promote greater understanding of the performing arts.

Area and Working Environment: At 9,000 feet and near the headwaters of the Rio Grande, you'll be immersed in some spectacular scenery while working here.

Work/Learn Program Specifics: Business interns work with bookkeeping, advertising, payroll, fund-raising, box office, and front-of-house. Shop set interns build, paint, and assemble sets; conduct set changeovers and backstage scene changes; and run shows by performing crew work. Stage management interns assist the stage manager, schedule, type, and work backstage, as well as function as a stage manager for one show. Costume interns sew costumes, dress actors, and maintain costumes. Light/sound interns assist the technical director in hanging and changing light plans/design, and assist lighting designer during shows and set changeovers.

Duration: Positions are offered year-round for four months.

Compensation and Perks: You'll receive $115 per week, plus housing.

Making It Happen: Call for application. Rolling deadlines.

Contact Information: Richard Baxter, Chief Executive Officer • Creede Repertory Theatre • P.O. Box 269 • Creede, CO 81130 • Phone: (719) 658-2541 • Fax: (719) 658-2343 • E-mail: crt@creederep.com • Web Site: www.creederep.com

Crow Canyon Archaeological Center

REGION/HQ: Rocky Mountains/Colorado • **CATEGORY:** Archaeology • **POSITION TYPE:** Internship • **DURATION:** Year-Round • **IDEAL CANDIDATE:** College Students, Career Changers, Foreigners • **APPLICANT POOL:** 90–120/year • **APPLICANTS ACCEPTED:** 14–18/year

CROW CANYON ARCHAEOLOGICAL CENTER was formed in 1984 as a nonprofit organization dedicated to archaeological research and education. The Center has developed a high standard of exacting research and scholarship, and offers an established program that enables lay people to participate with professional archaeologists in scientific research. Crow Canyon archaeologists have been carefully piecing together information that will help them understand the prehistoric people who once flourished in this majestic land of mesas, mountains, and canyons. The center's goal is to reconstruct the prehistoric cultural and natural environment in order to understand how the relationship between the two brought about a change in ancestral Pueblo life. With that knowledge, they may also recognize those dynamics in modern cultures and environments, including our own.

Area and Working Environment: 400 miles southwest of Denver and ten miles from the entrance to Mesa Verde National Park, Crow Canyon is situated in one of the most pristine natural areas in America. On the Crow Canyon campus, adobe architecture is everywhere and hiking trails snake through the juniper-covered terrain. Sunny weather is the norm.

Work/Learn Program Specifics: Research Internship: Field, laboratory, and environmental archaeology interns work closely with experienced professionals to assist them in excavating and recording archaeological contexts, in site surveying and mapping, in laboratory processing and analysis, or in studies of present and past environments. In addition, interns will be responsible for helping supervise small groups of program participants who are engaged in field or lab work. Interns may also be asked to give lectures or demonstrations to help participants prepare for fieldwork. Interns will attend research staff meetings where they may participate in discussions of research strategies, organization, and scheduling of work. Interns are welcome to attend evening educational programs and have the option of giving an evening lecture.

** _ation Internship:** Interns will work closely with **__perienced educators to assist them in preparation and teaching. In addition, interns will be responsible for developing a content lesson and a research project which assesses how and what students are learning. Interns will attend education staff meetings at which programs and logistics are discussed.

Duration: Positions are offered year-round; call for specific time frames. Interns will work a five-day week, normally Monday through Friday. Modification of the program terms to meet individual needs may be possible.

Compensation and Perks: There is a modest stipend of $50 to $100 per week, depending on whether meals and a $350 travel allowance are provided. All internships include meals at the center's dining hall and lodging in rustic cabins. Interns scheduled in the cold season will be provided with indoor housing. Everyone eats well at Crow Canyon; the resident chef serves up three delicious meals every day, including homemade salsas, luscious guacamole, gourmet tacos, and blue-corn chicken enchiladas!

The Ideal Candidate: Advanced undergraduate or graduate coursework in archaeology, anthropology, ethnobotany, botany, museum studies, or related fields; ability to work as an effective member of a small research team; ability to perform technical work, make careful observations, and record data legibly and accurately; ability to work well with lay participants ranging from secondary-school students to adults who often have no previous archaeological experience; good health and the ability to perform moderate levels of outdoor physical activity under high daytime temperatures; and a strong interest in improving field, lab, and teaching skills. Experience either in archaeological field or lab/museum work is a must to be accepted for a research internship.

Making It Happen: Call for application form (and it's preferable to call in December for internships the following year). The application is a three-page questionnaire that asks about academic coursework, related work experience, reasons for wanting the job, and three references. Deadlines vary and interviews are not conducted.

INSIDER TIPS: _We do call references, so it's advisable to list people who have actually worked with you and are accessible by phone. Research internships are highly competitive; list any and all experiences that are applicable. Education internships are not as competitive, but a demonstrated interest in teaching is necessary._

Contact Information: Melita Romasco, Laboratory Director • Crow Canyon Archaeological Center • 23390 County Rd. K • Cortez, CO 81321 • Phone: (303) 565-8975 • Fax: (303) 565-4859 • Toll Free: (800) 422-8975 • E-mail: interns@crowcanyon.org • Web Site: www.crowcanyon.org

David R. Godine, Publisher, Inc.

REGION/HQ: Northeast/Massachusetts • **CATEGORY:** Publishing • **POSITION TYPE:** Internship • **DURATION:** Year-Round • **IDEAL CANDIDATE:** College Students, Career Changers, Foreigners • **APPLICANT POOL:** 100/year • **APPLICANTS ACCEPTED:** 10/year

DAVID R. GODINE, PUBLISHER is a small, independent publisher of fine trade books. They publish books on all subjects, including typography, poetry, children's books, biography, essays, art, fiction, nonfiction, and collections of high quality photographs and illustrations.

Work/Learn Program Specifics: Editorial/publicity interns will write letters to reviewers, enter books in award competitions, and wade through the "slush" (their name for the piles of unsolicited manuscripts they receive). Production interns will copyedit books, catalogues, and press releases, and if qualified, will design them using Quark. Both types of internships involve some staff-support tasks, such as xeroxing, mailing, filing, and faxing, but they try to keep those to a minimum. On occasion, an intern might be asked to help out their customer service staff by taking phone orders from customers or providing them with availability information.

Compensation and Perks: None.

The Ideal Candidate: Editorial/publicity applicants should have a strong college background in writing; production applicants should have a strong college background in graphic design. All candidates should have a commitment to a career in publishing, excellent communication and organizational skills, and the ability to meet deadlines and work on several different projects at a time.

Making It Happen: Send cover letter and resume. Deadlines: spring—November 1; summer—April 1; and fall—July 1.

INSIDER TIPS: _If you want a career in the competitive publishing field, an internship is the best, if not the only, way to break in._

Contact Information: Lissa Warren, Editorial Director • David R. Godine, Publisher, Inc. • P.O. Box 9103 • Lincoln, MA 01773-9103 • Phone: (617) 259-0700 • Fax: (617) 259-9198 • Web Site: www.godine.com

Directors Guild— Producer Training Plan

REGION/HQ: Pacific Northwest/California • **CATEGORY:** Film • **POSITION TYPE:** Training Program • **DURATION:** Year-Round • **IDEAL CANDIDATE:** College Students, Career Changers, Foreigners • **APPLICANT POOL:** 1,000+/year • **APPLICANTS ACCEPTED:** 8–20/year

THE ASSISTANT DIRECTORS TRAINING PROGRAM was established in 1965. Sponsored by the Directors Guild of America and the Alliance of Motion Picture and Television Producers, the program's purpose is to train second assistant directors for the motion picture and television industry. Since its inception, over 400 participants of diverse backgrounds have graduated from the program and gone on to successful careers in the business.

Work/Learn Program Specifics: As a trainee, you will be assigned to work on episodic television, television movies, pilots, miniseries, and feature films with various studios and production companies. The program is designed to give you a basic knowledge of the organization and logistics of motion picture and television production, including set operations, paperwork, and the working conditions and collective bargaining agreements of more than twenty guilds and unions. You will learn to deal with all types of cast and crew members while you're solving problems in highly varied and sometimes difficult situations. The trainee work is physically demanding and is characterized by long hours.

Duration: This is a 400-day trainee program, five to six days per week, twelve- to eighteen-hour days. Because of the freelance nature of production work, you may experience periods of layoff, and you may be eligible for unemployment benefits during these periods.

Compensation and Perks: Trainees receive $439 to $539 per week, plus medical benefits. Upon satisfactory completion of the program, your name will be placed on the Southern California Area Qualification List, making you eligible for employment as a second assistant director.

The Ideal Candidate: Applicant must have either an associate or baccalaureate degree from an accredited institution or two years of paid work in film or television

production, and must be at least twenty-one years old. If you are accepted into the program, you are expected to make a commitment to complete it in its entirety.

Making It Happen: Applicants who meet the basic eligibility requirements must first take a written test ($50 fee). The test assesses job-related skills, including verbal, reasoning, and mathematical abilities, as well as organizational and interpersonal skills. The test is given once per year, usually between January and March, and is administered in Los Angeles and Chicago. The final selection of trainees is based on test scores and group and individual interviews. Deadline: mid-November for the following year.

Contact Information: Elizabeth Stanley, Administrator • Directors Guild—Producer Training Plan • 15503 Ventura Blvd. • Encino, CA 91436 • Phone: (818) 386-2545 • Fax: (818) 382-1794 • Web Site: www.leonardo.net/trainingprogram

Festivals, Inc.

REGION/HQ: Pacific Northwest/Washington • **CATEGORY:** Festival • **POSITION TYPE:** Internship • **DURATION:** Year-Round • **IDEAL CANDIDATE:** College Students, Career Changers, Foreigners • **APPLICANT POOL:** Varies • **APPLICANTS ACCEPTED:** Varies

FESTIVALS, INC. IS A SPECIAL EVENTS production company. Founded by Alan Silverman in 1982 with the creation of the Bite of Seattle, Festivals is known in the Northwest for high-quality events and trade shows, specializing in promoting the food and beverage industry. With attendance growing from 75,000 to over 500,000, the Bite of Seattle is now one of the largest events held in the entire Northwest. Not only has Festivals developed and expanded the concepts behind a successful food event, it has created and produced festivals that cover a variety of themes. Events on tap this year include a Taste of Tacoma, Great Northwest Microbrewery Invitational, Brewstock, and Coffee Fest. Festivals has been hired as a professional consultant on such events as the World's Fair in Vancouver, Canada and the Tulip Festival in Washington State.

Area and Working Environment: The business office is conveniently located on Mercer Island and is only fifteen minutes from Seattle's downtown and the Eastside suburbs by car. Beautiful parks that overlook Lake Washington are also close by and offer paths for walking, jogging, cycling, and in-line skating.

Work/Learn Program Specifics: Special Events Intern: Responsibilities include event marketing, coordination in all advertising campaigns (local and national), writing of news releases, media exposure, event management, and all operational procedures, in addition to many administrative projects. Most importantly, interns are viewed as important members of the Festivals team, and are respected as executives of the company. The success of the internship program is largely due to the amount of responsibility that students are given. Each will be involved in projects that they can call their own (great portfolio material). With supervision and guidance from a creative and highly professional staff, students will experience firsthand all facets of the special events industry.

Duration: Summer internships are full-time, starting mid-May through mid-August. Schedules are more flexible during other parts of the year. Students must be available on the event weekends.

Compensation and Perks: This is a paid internship; however, students are not paid until the end of the program. Each student will be paid according to individual performance. Financial compensation has ranged from $700 to $1,400 in the past. The business office has a small gym with workout equipment and a shower. Festivals also covers basic business expenses. Parking at the office is free.

The Ideal Candidate: Most students who participate are communications, recreation and leisure studies, business/marketing, or hotel/restaurant management majors; however, it is not mandatory to fall into one of these categories. If you have high energy, are creative, work well with people, like parties and huge crowds, and most importantly, are a team player, you will be a good candidate for an internship at Festivals.

Making It Happen: Submit cover letter and resume, then follow up with a phone call. The summer deadline is mid-February; all others are rolling.

INSIDER TIPS: *If you just want to taste the events business without taking on a full-time internship, they also offer hourly wage jobs at the individual events. Hiring for those events does not take place until June.*

Contact Information: General Manager • Festivals, Inc. • 7525 Southeast 24th St., Suite #480 • P.O. Box 1158 • Mercer Island, WA 98040 • Phone: (206) 232-2982 • Fax: (206) 236-5241

Flat Rock Playhouse

REGION/HQ: Southeast/North Carolina • **CATEGORY:** Theatre • **POSITION TYPE:** Internship • **DURATION:** Summer • **IDEAL CANDIDATE:** College Students, Career Changers, Foreigners • **APPLICANT POOL:** Varies • **APPLICANTS ACCEPTED:** Varies

FLAT ROCK PLAYHOUSE (FRP) is considered one of the top summer theatres in the United States. Producing nine shows annually, the season runs from late May through mid-October. Broadway and London hits are carefully selected for their audience appeal and entertainment value.

Area and Working Environment: Flat Rock is located in the mountains of western North Carolina.

Work/Learn Program Specifics: From building and running shows, to attending classes, assisting patrons, or performing at the Sandburg Home and on the Mainstage, apprentices are constantly on the move. FRP believes that hands-on professional training is essential to any drama student's education. They are dedicated to providing a program that fosters a respect and understanding of all elements of the theatrical process. They feel the best way to accomplish this goal is through exposure to as many facets of theatre as possible. Daily "Master Classes" range from acting and improvisation to scene/lighting/costume design, and professional preparation. You'll also have the opportunity to perform in as many as five venues and weekly technical crew assignments.

Duration: Internships are for ten weeks, from early June to mid-August.

Compensation and Perks: The room and board fee is $850, which includes three meals a day and dormitory-style housing on-site. Some scholarship and work-study money is available and is based on talent and financial need.

The Ideal Candidate: Apprentices must be high school graduates with prior theatrical experience and be committed to the development of the art form.

Making It Happen: Write requesting an application and an audition/interview time (appointments can be scheduled at spring SETC). Return completed application by April 15 (you will be notified by May 1). If you cannot audition in person videotapes are welcome.

Contact Information: Dale Bartlett, Apprentice Director • Flat Rock Playhouse • 2661 Greenville Highway

• P.O. Box 310 • Flat Rock, NC 28731-0310 • Phone: (704) 693-0731 • Fax: (704) 693-6795 • E-mail: flatrock@ioa.com • Web Site: www.ioa.com/home/flatrock

Franklin D. Roosevelt Library

REGION/HQ: Northeast/New York • **CATEGORY:** Library • **POSITION TYPE:** Internship • **DURATION:** Summer • **IDEAL CANDIDATE:** College Students • **APPLICANT POOL:** 5–10/year • **APPLICANTS ACCEPTED:** 5/year

THE FRANKLIN D. ROOSEVELT LIBRARY was the nation's first presidential library and the only one to be used by a sitting president. Its educational programs reach out to students of all ages and the museum displays are seen by over 200,000 visitors yearly. Both the museum and library reflect President Roosevelt's service to the American people and his great contributions to humanity.

Work/Learn Program Specifics: William R. Emerson Archival Internship: Interns will assist the library staff in current processing, reference, and museum projects. Opportunities include working on *Creating FDR—Day by Day*, a computerized chronology of President Roosevelt's life to be made accessible to scholars through the Internet; the development of educational programs and materials for teachers and students of all grade levels; computer projects that help streamline the research process; development of exhibits; public relations; archival research; and a wide variety of other activities. Your experience at the library will broaden your historical perspective and give you an opportunity to work in the creative process of history, while encouraging you to learn more about the era of Franklin and Eleanor Roosevelt.

Duration: A minimum commitment of twenty hours per week is required, but beyond that, scheduling is flexible.

Compensation and Perks: Interns receive a $7-per-hour stipend.

The Ideal Candidate: Students come from varied educational backgrounds.

Making It Happen: Call for application materials. The Emerson Internship is very competitive. The deadline for the following summer is March 10 each year (so plan ahead). Decisions are made by mid-April.

Contact Information: Raymond Teichman, Supervisory Archivist • Franklin D. Roosevelt Library • 511 Albany Post Rd. • Hyde Park, NY 12538 • Phone: (914) 229-8114 • Fax: (914) 229-0872 • E-mail: Library@Roosevelt.nara.gov

Georgia Agrirama

REGION/HQ: Southeast/Georgia • **CATEGORY:** Living History • **POSITION TYPE:** Internship • **DURATION:** Summer • **IDEAL CANDIDATE:** College Students • **APPLICANT POOL:** Varies • **APPLICANTS ACCEPTED:** Varies

GEORGIA AGRIRAMA IS THE STATE'S living history museum, located on a ninety-five-acre site in the wiregrass region of southern Georgia. The site has an 1870s home/farm site, an 1890s home/farm site, a grist mill, saw mill, cotton gin, blacksmith shop, cooper shed and turpentine still, a train, print shop, commissary, feed and seed store, and a village area which includes a drugstore, lawyer's office, dentist's office, Masonic lodge, Victorian house, gardens, orchards, livestock, a lake, and numerous staff buildings. Georgia Agrirama has about forty-five interpreters, who all help with special events throughout the year, long- and short-term special exhibits, special tours, and international programs.

Work/Learn Program Specifics: Curatorial interns start off with a one-week orientation, covering the collection at Georgia Agrirama and instructions on accessing, researching, inventorying, and preservation and conservation methods. The remainder of the internship will be applied to updating the collection inventory, assisting the curator, and participating in special events on the site.

Duration: Internships are for 400 hours during the months of June through August. An exact time schedule will be worked out.

Compensation and Perks: Interns receive $1,700 for the summer. The compensation may or may not include housing. The community college has dorm rooms available for $380 to $430 for interns.

The Ideal Candidate: A historic preservation or history major (with a strong background in American history) in the junior or senior year makes the best applicant. The student must be able to research in both primary and secondary sources in libraries, archives, and government facilities, and to conduct oral interviews. Some computer knowledge in data processing/word processing (WordPerfect, Professor Write, Pagemaker, Lotus 123) is very helpful.

Making It Happen: Send a completed application form (call for one), two letters of reference from professors, and an example of your writing abilities (such as a research paper) by May 15.

Contact Information: Personnel Curator • Georgia Agrirama • P.O. Box Q • Tifton, GA 31793 • Phone: (912) 386-3344 • Fax: (912) 386-3386

The Hermitage

REGION/HQ: Southeast/Tennessee • **CATEGORY:** Historic Site • **POSITION TYPE:** Internship • **DURATION:** Summer • **IDEAL CANDIDATE:** College Students, Career Changers, Foreigners • **APPLICANT POOL:** 60/term • **APPLICANTS ACCEPTED:** 10/term

SINCE 1987 ARCHAEOLOGICAL fieldwork has been performed on the grounds of the Hermitage. By exploring the foundations and other subsurface artifacts adjacent to President Andrew Jackson's family mansion, archaeologists and interns reconstruct what plantation life was like at the Hermitage of Jackson's time.

Area and Working Environment: The Hermitage is about a fifteen-minute drive from downtown Nashville.

Work/Learn Program Specifics: Historical Archaeology Internship: After a brief orientation meeting and a welcoming barbecue, interns begin their adventure in historical archaeology. Trowel in hand and sweat on brow, interns are fully immersed in archaeological excavation. The internship program provides a full range of experiences, from testing and model building through excavation, lab work, initial coding, and model testing. Interns unearth all sorts of artifacts, including pieces of pottery and glass, animal bones, rusty nails, glass beads, and coins from the 1850s. An integral part of life as a Hermitage intern is interaction with the public. Hundreds of tourists visit the grounds every day, and inevitably they encounter interns hard at work excavating. Although a sign explains the basics of the project, it's up to interns to answer any questions visitors have about the excavation. The Hermitage's current fieldwork focus is on investigations of slave dwelling sites in two different areas of Hermitage property.

Duration: They offer two types of work terms: one is for five weeks (two sessions), the other for two (three sessions). All fall during the humid summer months.

Compensation and Perks: The five-week session stipend is $1,000 and the two-week session provides a $400 stipend, with room and board included for both.

Interns live in one of two 1930s-era farm houses located on the Hermitage property, about a half-mile from the mansion. Each has a bathroom, a few pieces of furniture, and a fully equipped kitchen. Six people live in each house, with two or three to a bedroom.

The Ideal Candidate: The five-week session is intended for advanced undergraduates and early-phase graduate students who have had some field training in archaeology and who are looking for more experience in a research-oriented setting. The two-week session is intended primarily for advanced undergraduates and graduate students in such fields as history, African-American studies, American studies, folklore, and geography who are interested in gaining exposure to the archaeological study of the recent past. No archaeological experience is necessary.

Making It Happen: Submit a cover letter summarizing your education and research experience and a statement detailing your specific interest in the program. Be sure to indicate if you are applying for the two- or five-week internship, and include a first- and second-session preference. Applicants must have a letter of recommendation sent under separate cover. The application deadline is April 10. All applicants will be notified of selection decisions by no later than May 1.

INSIDER TIPS: *The letter of recommendation is by far the most critical element in the decision process.*

Contact Information: Internship Coordinator • The Hermitage • 4580 Rachel's Ln. • Hermitage, TN 37076-1331 • Phone: (615) 889-2941 • Fax: (615) 889-9289

Hi Desert Nature Museum

REGION/HQ: Pacific Northwest/California • **CATEGORY:** Museum • **POSITION TYPE:** Internship • **DURATION:** Year-Round • **IDEAL CANDIDATE:** College Students, Career Changers • **APPLICANT POOL:** Varies • **APPLICANTS ACCEPTED:** Varies

THE HI DESERT NATURE MUSEUM is a small family-oriented museum with collections and exhibitions related to the high desert's unique natural and historical elements. The museum has a full range of educational activities for visitors of all ages. It's a place where you don't need to be quiet and listen, and that encourages active participation so that all members of the family will have a fun and educational time.

Area and Working Environment: Nestled in the mountains of Southern California lies a series of high valleys known as the Morongo Basin. These valleys are situated between the Colorado and the Mojave Deserts and take the best from both worlds. Small streams allow flora and fauna not found in other areas of the desert to flourish. This unique area is called the high desert.

Work/Learn Program Specifics: Interns will assist the museum staff with a variety of duties related to the operation of a small natural history/general museum, including, but not limited to, collections management, exhibition design and installation, educational programs, and day-to-day management. Because of the small size of the museum and staff, participants will get a hands-on experience in the operations of museums.

Duration: The internship will generally last one semester. The student will be expected to work a thirty- to forty-hour week, which may include some weekends.

Compensation and Perks: Although the internship is unpaid, they may be able to offer housing with enough notice.

The Ideal Candidate: Open to all interested candidates, particularly appropriate for those majoring in museum studies, history, natural history, anthropology, or biology.

Making It Happen: Send cover letter (with dates of availability), resume, and three letters of recommendation (one must be from advisor). Rolling deadlines.

INSIDER TIPS: *We are looking for those interested in gaining an well-rounded museum experience in a museum that is representative of the vast majority of museums in this country—small, understaffed, and underfunded.*

Contact Information: Jim DeMersman, Director • Hi Desert Nature Museum • 57116 29 Palms Hwy. • Yucca Valley, CA 92284 • Phone: (619) 369-7212 • Fax: (619) 369-1605

The History Factory

REGION/HQ: Washington, D.C./Virginia • **CATEGORY:** History • **POSITION TYPE:** Internship • **DURATION:** Year-Round • **IDEAL CANDIDATE:** College Students, Foreigners • **APPLICANT POOL:** Varies • **APPLICANTS ACCEPTED:** Varies

THE HISTORY FACTORY PROVIDES creative management of historical resources and records and advises businesses on how to preserve and use their history for a variety of communications needs. They process, catalog, and store corporate archives in their Washington facility and answer their clients' research requests and inquiries.

Their approach is very user-oriented, meaning that they make history accessible via exhibits, videos, publications, and anniversary programs.

Work/Learn Program Specifics: An internship at The History Factory will provide students with an overview of the many facets of their services. Interns can expect to do research both at The History Factory and at Washington repositories such as the Library of Congress and the Smithsonian. Often interns learn about the history of a company by processing or labeling in-house archives. When special research or writing projects come up, the intern can be given the responsibility to see the project through. Internships in the past have included researching brand histories, compiling company chronologies, answering daily research requests, processing and cataloging archives, labeling and moving collections, creating image binders for exhibit purposes, historical research, writing articles for company newsletters, contacting local media, and researching upcoming anniversaries.

Duration: Internships are offered year-round, depending on the individual's preference and/or availability.

Compensation and Perks: Internships are offered for pay or school credit. The dress is casual and you'll have the opportunity to work with rare and interesting historical materials and do research in Washington, D.C. repositories.

The Ideal Candidate: Students with the following skills and characteristics will be given greater consideration: highly motivated, flexible, ability to work with others and meet deadlines, historical research and excellent writing skills, an appreciation for rare and valuable archival documents, and work experience in museums, special collections, or archives.

Making It Happen: Submit resume and cover letter (addressing your expectations of an internship and hours of availability). A personal interview will be required. You should apply about three months prior to expected start date.

INSIDER TIPS: *We work for several Fortune 500 companies. Ongoing client service is very important to our business.*

Contact Information: Debbie Waller, Archival Services Director • The History Factory • 14140 Parke Long Ct. • Chantilly, VA 20151 • Phone: (703) 631-0500 • Fax: (703) 631-1124 • Toll Free: (800) 937-4001 • E-mail: information@historyfact.com • Web Site: www.historyfact.com

Independent Curators, Inc.

REGION/HQ: Northeast/New York • **CATEGORY:** Arts Administration • **POSITION TYPE:** Internship • **DURATION:** Year-Round • **IDEAL CANDIDATE:** College Students, Career Changers, Foreigners • **APPLICANT POOL:** 30–50/year • **APPLICANTS ACCEPTED:** Varies

INDEPENDENT CURATORS INCORPORATED (ICI) is a national, nonprofit traveling exhibition service specializing in contemporary art. Founded in 1975, ICI organizes and circulates exhibitions which are presented in museums, university galleries, art centers, and alternative spaces throughout the United States, Canada, Mexico, and abroad.

Work/Learn Program Specifics: Exhibition interns provide assistance in all phases of the development of traveling exhibitions, including maintenance of files and records related to exhibitions, preparation and execution of checklists, target mailings, loan forms, press packets, and other exhibition-related projects, and with the collection and maintenance of visual materials. Development department interns assist with all development activities, including planning and preparation of the biannual benefit dinner and annual benefit series of studio visits with prominent artists. Interns will also assist with individual, foundation, and corporate prospect research and with the preparation of grant applications and other proposals. Registrarial interns assist in maintaining the files and records related to exhibitions, and preparation of registrarial forms.

Duration: The internships are of flexible duration, with a minimum of fifteen hours per week to fall within their regular office hours.

Compensation and Perks: Local transportation expenses are reimbursed and interns may receive a small stipend.

The Ideal Candidate: Applicants must have a background in art history, business, or studio art and a demonstrated interest in contemporary art.

Making It Happen: Call for application materials. Rolling deadlines.

Contact Information: Director • Independent Curators, Inc. • 799 Broadway, Suite 205 • New York, NY 10003 • Phone: (212) 254-8200 • Fax: (212) 477-4781

Jacob's Pillow Dance Festival

REGION/HQ: Northeast/Massachusetts • **CATEGORY:** Festival • **POSITION TYPE:** Internship • **DURATION:** Summer • **IDEAL CANDIDATE:** College Students, Career Changers, Foreigners • **APPLICANT POOL:** Varies • **APPLICANTS ACCEPTED:** 22/summer

JACOB'S PILLOW DANCE FESTIVAL is America's oldest dance festival, presenting ten weeks of dance performances and conducting a professional dance school each summer. Companies, students, and administrators from across the United States and around the world come together to create a unique and exciting environment. "How fitting that many in the dance world refer to Jacob's Pillow as the Dance Farm, for it is indeed a place that nurtures."

Area and Working Environment: Located in the Berkshire Hills of western Massachusetts, the campus includes 150 acres of woodlands, two theatres, four studios, and an outdoor stage.

Work/Learn Program Specifics: Working closely with staff members in all aspects of festival operation, interns receive on-the-job training and experience. Visiting artists and professionals offer additional insights and the opportunity to make valuable contacts. Positions are available in development, marketing/press, technical theatre/production, education/resources, operations, business office, programming/special projects, video, and archives/preservation assistant.

Duration: All positions are for the summer season, beginning in late May and finishing in the end of August.

Compensation and Perks: Interns receive a stipend of $100 per month, with housing provided at the Pillow's cottages and meals served in the Pillow's resident cafeteria.

The Ideal Candidate: Applicants should have general office skills and technical theatre interns should have a demonstrated interest in dance-related production work.

Making It Happen: Send a resume and cover letter indicating your primary area of interest. In your letter include a brief statement describing your goals and expectations for this internship, the names and phone numbers of two work-related references, and a daytime telephone number for yourself. Applicants for marketing/press and development positions should also include writing samples. Applications are due at the beginning of March.

Contact Information: Debbie Markowitz, Company Manager • Jacob's Pillow Dance Festival • P.O. Box 287 • Lee, MA 01238 • Phone: (413) 637-1322 • Fax: (413) 243-4744

Juilliard School

REGION/HQ: Northeast/New York • **CATEGORY:** Theatre • **POSITION TYPE:** Internship • **DURATION:** Academic year • **IDEAL CANDIDATE:** College Students, Career Changers • **APPLICANT POOL:** Varies • **APPLICANTS ACCEPTED:** Varies
....

THE JUILLIARD SCHOOL HAS VARIOUS facilities which serve different performances. The Juilliard Theatre, seating 933 with a 60-foot proscenium stage, houses Juilliard's opera and dance productions, concerts, recitals, and special events. The Drama Theatre, which seats 206, contains a large thrust stage which supports drama productions ranging from classical Greek to modern avant-garde plays, as well as lectures, workshops, and spring repertory. They also have black box studios for performance, drama, and opera.

Work/Learn Program Specifics: Technical theatre interns positions include costumes, wigs and makeup, props, electrics, stage management, scene painting, stage carpentry, and sound. The arts administration internship covers a variety of areas and departments which include public relations, orchestra library, drama division, performance activities, facilities management, pre-college, intern program, production administration, vocal arts, and dance division.

Duration: Internships begin in September and end in May. Expect to work forty hours per week. Although reasonable working hours are generally maintained, the interns' weekly schedules will vary with their duties and the requirements of the overall production schedule. Interns are closely monitored and evaluated in November, before the December holiday break, by the intern director and by the interns' appropriate supervisors.

Compensation and Perks: Each intern receives a stipend of $205 each week (keep in mind that will you be living in New York and may need more income in order to cover living expenses). Housing in New York City is expensive and requires careful consideration.

Making It Happen: To apply, each candidate must submit the following: a completed application form; a

$15 nonrefundable application fee; a current resume, and snapshot or photo; three letters of reference which discuss the candidate's personal working style, an evaluation of skills, and if applicable, an evaluation of design abilities; and a personal statement of at least 250 words describing the candidate's expectations of the internship program and how it relates to their individual career goals. All this must be submitted by June 1.

INSIDER TIPS: *Calls are always welcome.*

Contact Information: Helen Taynton, Professional Intern Program Director • Juilliard School • 60 Lincoln Center Plaza • New York, NY 10023-6588 • Phone: (212) 799-5000 • Fax: (212) 724-0263

The Kennedy Center

REGION/HQ: Washington, D.C./Washington, D.C. • **CATEGORY:** Performing Arts • **POSITION TYPE:** Internship • **DURATION:** Year-Round • **IDEAL CANDIDATE:** College Students, Career Changers, Retired Folks • **APPLICANT POOL:** 70–200/term • **APPLICANTS ACCEPTED:** 20/term
....

THE KENNEDY CENTER IS ONE OF the country's foremost performing arts institutions. Founded in 1971 as a memorial to JFK, the center not only was a sorely needed addition to Washington's cultural scene, but also quickly became an arts center of national and international importance. Today the center has the drawing power to attract the country's finest music, dance, and theatre companies, while also providing a home to the National Symphony Orchestra, the American Film Institute, and the Washington Opera. It also runs an admirable array of educational programs and competitions for students of all ages. The center's grand marble exterior is matched by a foyer, regal red carpet, and an eighteen-foot bust of JFK.

Work/Learn Program Specifics: Internships are available in these program areas: advertising, Alliance for Arts Education, American College Theater Festival, National Symphony Orchestra education programs/administration, marketing, development, events for teachers, government liaison, Performance Plus, press office, member services, special events, programming, youth and family program, production, and education. Intern duties may include assistance with the technical, administrative, presentational, and/or promotional aspects of the Center. Internships are designed to increase each participant's understanding and appreciation of the performing arts in Washington, D.C. and throughout the nation.

Duration: Internship assignments are full-time, last for three to four months, and are offered year-round.

Compensation and Perks: A stipend of $650 per month is provided. Interns also have dibs on two seats to any event and are welcome at special events, such as cast parties and the annual open house (a free festival in the fall featuring performances by local artists).

The Ideal Candidate: Upper-level undergraduate college students, graduate students, and teachers of the arts are eligible to apply. Specific requirements vary, depending on program assignment.

Making It Happen: Write or call for information. Then submit a cover letter (stating career goals), resume, two current letters of recommendation, transcripts, and writing samples. Phone interviews may be conducted. Deadlines: spring—November 1; summer—March 1; and fall—June 1.

INSIDER TIPS: *Your odds of being selected into the program are much better if you apply for the fall or winter/spring sessions. We receive 70 to 100 applications at this time and over 400 for the summer.*

Contact Information: Darrell Ayers, Internship Program Manager • The Kennedy Center • Education Department • 2700 F St., NW • Washington, DC 20566 • Phone: (202) 416-8807 • Fax: (202) 416-8802 • E-mail: DMAyers@mail.kennedy-center.org • Web Site: www. kennedy-center.org

The Kitchen

REGION/HQ: Northeast/New York • **CATEGORY:** Theatre • **POSITION TYPE:** Internship • **DURATION:** Year-Round • **IDEAL CANDIDATE:** College Students, Career Changers, Foreigners • **APPLICANT POOL:** Varies • **APPLICANTS ACCEPTED:** Varies

THE KITCHEN IS A SMALL, nonprofit organization dedicated to the presentation and promotion of emerging artists and experimental art forms. Its performance season annually features over 150 evenings of dance, music, performance, literature, and media, from September through the end of May. In the past year, The Kitchen has become the New York site of Electronic Cafe International, a worldwide link, with sites in Santa Monica, Paris, Tokyo, and other cities around the world. For the artists of The Kitchen, this opens a new era of artistic and technical challenges, combined with the possibility of simultaneously international exposure.

Area and Working Environment: All positions are at their permanent home in the Chelsea neighborhood of New York City, which houses two of the largest uncolumned black box theatres in the United States.

Work/Learn Program Specifics: Curatorial interns assist one of the curators (performance, dance, music) with artist contacts, preproduction planning, and review and response to submissions. Technical interns assist the production manager and technical director with installation and strike of productions, preproduction planning, and maintenance of the theaters and equipment. Technical interns may also be asked to function as running crew for selected performances. Publicity interns assist the director of communications in all aspects of publicity and public relations. Fund-raising interns assist the director of development in grant writing and fund-raising. Administrative interns assist the executive director and administrative staff on special projects as well as assisting in the day-to-day office management. Media services interns are responsible for the organization and upkeep of The Kitchen's video archives, database entry, and day-to-day administrative organization in the Media Services Office. Media services interns also assist the director of media services with international video distribution and setup of rotating video installations. Electronic Cafe interns assist the Electronic Cafe coordinators in a variety of tasks including administration, publicity, and technical.

Duration: Internship lengths and hours are flexible with the intern's schedule. Most positions require at least a two- to three-month commitment.

Compensation and Perks: No compensation is provided; however, they do offer interns contact with world-class artists, invaluable work experience within a major international arts organization, and free access to all Kitchen performances during the internship period.

The Ideal Candidate: Students from all disciplines are welcome to apply, especially those with an interest in the arts. A background in the area of interest and computer skills are also very useful.

Making It Happen: No phone calls, please! Send resume and cover letter which covers what internship you are applying to, what you would like to learn from your internship, the dates of availability, and approximately how many hours per week you are willing to devote to your internship. There is no deadline for application. Upon receipt of your information, it will be forwarded to the appropriate department and an interview will be set up. After your interview you will receive a letter or phone call within six to eight weeks to let you know if you have been accepted.

INSIDER TIPS: *Specific letters and well-written, detailed resumes get more attention than vague inquiries. Knowing specifically what you want to learn is also a bonus.*

Contact Information: Internship Coordinator • The Kitchen • 512 W. 19th St. • New York, NY 10011 • Phone: (212) 255-5793 • Fax: (212) 645-4258 • E-mail: kitchen@panix.com

Kohl Children's Museum

REGION/HQ: Great Lakes/Illinois • **CATEGORY:** Museum • **POSITION TYPE:** Internship • **DURATION:** Year-Round • **IDEAL CANDIDATE:** College Students, Career Changers, Foreigners • **APPLICANT POOL:** 10/term • **APPLICANTS ACCEPTED:** 6/term

THE KOHL CHILDREN'S MUSEUM is a nonprofit education institution. Each year the museum serves over 260,000 children, their families, school groups, and teachers from Chicago and its suburbs. Children from diverse backgrounds delight in learning through unique interactive exhibits and participatory educational programs.

Area and Working Environment: Wilmette is located just twenty-five miles north of Chicago, near Lake Michigan on the border of Evanston, Illinois.

Work/Learn Program Specifics: Education/programming interns assist in the planning, facilitation, and evaluation of various theme-based, interdisciplinary educational programs. Communications interns assist the PR director in researching media outlets, writing press releases, filing, and updating media lists. Marketing/development interns handle tasks in development research, grant writing, membership recruitment and retention, admissions, promotion, and information gathering for individual solicitations. Exhibit facilitator interns interact with museum visitors, organizing crafts activities, storytelling, puppeteering, music, dance, or role-playing to insure a positive experience. Events departments interns assist in all areas of event planning. These areas include library and phone research, talent information files, brainstorming, calendars, fairs, and festivals.

Duration: The duration consists of a minimum time commitment of twenty hours per week over a six-week period.

Compensation and Perks: No compensation is provided; however, you will work with an outstanding team of early childhood educators, attend recognition events, and receive gifts of appreciation.

The Ideal Candidate: Education: outgoing, patient, responsible, timely student who is accepting of other cultures. Communications: word-processing skills, organizational abilities, and experience in public speaking (for phone) and writing. Marketing: strong interpersonal skills, the ability to work with the public, professionalism, strong writing skills, computer literacy, and an understanding of math/statistics. Exhibit: ability to deal with people in a positive upbeat manner, warm, friendly, outgoing, and courteous. Events: organized, good with detail, an excellent communicator, resourceful, and creative.

Making It Happen: Call for Internship brochure/application. Once your application is received, they will call you for an interview. Rolling deadlines.

INSIDER TIPS: *Have enthusiasm and a love for young children.*

Contact Information: Charlene Podolsky, Volunteer/Intern Services Director • Kohl Children's Museum • 165 Green Bay Rd • Wilmette, IL 60091 • Phone: (708) 256-6056 • Fax: (708) 256-2921

The Library of Congress

REGION/HQ: Washington, D.C./Washington, D.C. • **CATEGORY:** Library • **POSITION TYPE:** Internship • **DURATION:** Summer • **IDEAL CANDIDATE:** College Students, Foreigners • **APPLICANT POOL:** 500+/year • **APPLICANTS ACCEPTED:** 18–24/year

THE LIBRARY OF CONGRESS (LC) is not exclusively for members of Congress, as it once was back in the 1800s. Today anyone over the age of eighteen can peruse through its 90 million books, manuscripts, maps, photographs, and films. Originally housed in the U.S. Capitol, the Library of Congress now comprises three buildings on the corner of Independence Avenue and Second Street SE. The buildings are named after John Adams, James Madison, and Thomas Jefferson. Underneath the library are extensive catacombs leading to the subway and congressional buildings. Only those with passes may burrow through them—a perk given to interns!

Work/Learn Program Specifics: Interns are scattered among the following divisions: Africa and Middle East;

Asia; Europe; Geography and Maps; Hispanic; Manuscript; Motion Pictures, Broadcasting, and Recording; Music; National Preservation Program; Prints and Photographs; Rare Books and Special Collections; and Serial and Government Publications. Within these divisions they work toward "arrearage" (piles of uncataloged work) reduction goals by doing bibliographical research, producing finding aids and bibliographical records, organizing and documenting archival collections, and working closely with primary source materials. The objective is to increase knowledge and use of the library's collections throughout the nation, help the library inventory, chronicle, and make available hitherto unexplored materials, give selected fellows an opportunity to explore the library's unique collections, and expose the fellows to the challenging career opportunities available at the Library of Congress.

Duration: Fellowships are available in the summer and last two to three months, according to the needs and schedules of the library and the fellow. Full-time positions.

Compensation and Perks: Fellows will be paid a taxable stipend of $300 per week and housing assistance is provided. Perks include tours and orientations of extensive LC collections, borrowing privileges, and possible stack access privileges.

The Ideal Candidate: College juniors and seniors, graduate students, and recent graduates are eligible for the program. Although it is open to all majors, the majority of interns study American studies, history, languages, geography, or cartography.

Making It Happen: Call for application materials. Submit cover letter indicating the subject area/division in which you are interested, a completed SF-171 or resume (including social security number, telephone number, date of birth, and citizenship), a letter of recommendation from a professor attesting to your reliability and proficiency, as well as an official transcript. Deadline: March 1. Final selections are determined after phone interviews, with final decisions coming in April.

INSIDER TIPS: *Highly selective application process; follow all instructions accurately and thoroughly; a lucid cover letter is valuable to applicant's application.*

Contact Information: Junior Fellows Program Coordinator • The Library of Congress • Collections Services, LM-642 • Washington, DC 20540-4700 • Phone: (202) 707-8253 • E-mail: coll@loc.gov

Lincoln Center for the Performing Arts

REGION/HQ: Northeast/New York • **CATEGORY:** Arts Administration • **POSITION TYPE:** Internship • **DURATION:** Summer • **IDEAL CANDIDATE:** College Students, Foreigners • **APPLICANT POOL:** 100/year • **APPLICANTS ACCEPTED:** 2/year

LINCOLN CENTER FOR THE PERFORMING ARTS is the organization that created and built Lincoln Center, one of the world's largest and most prominent arts centers. Some of their programs include Mostly Mozart, Great Performers, Lincoln Center Festival, and Lincoln Center Out-of-Doors. They also provide services to nine independent resident companies.

Work/Learn Program Specifics: Interns are often surprised to learn that no prearranged project awaits their arrival at Lincoln Center. Instead, they spend their first few days interviewing with key staff members, with whom they develop a project meeting the needs of the organization and interests of the intern. The emphasis is placed on creating a project that will give interns broad exposure to a range of departments, including Planning and Development, Programming, Finance, Marketing, Operations, and Fundraising. At the end of the summer, interns submit a project report to management…and management listens. More often than not, the interns' work has a meaningful impact on Lincoln Center's operations.

Duration: Internships are for twelve weeks, beginning in June.

Compensation and Perks: Interns receive a $450-per-week stipend. Interns also receive concert tickets.

The Ideal Candidate: The program is open only to students who have had at least one year of graduate coursework. Students should also demonstrate interest in and commitment to a career in arts management; strong verbal and analytic skills; and arts experience (helpful, but not required).

Making It Happen: Submit cover letter describing qualifications and career goals and a resume by early February.

Contact Information: Jay Spivack, Human Resources Director • Lincoln Center for the Performing Arts • 70 Lincoln Center Plaza • New York, NY 10023-6583 • Phone: (212) 875-5184 • Fax: (212) 875-5185

The Metropolitan Museum of Art

REGION/HQ: Northeast/New York • **CATEGORY:** Art Museum • **POSITION TYPE:** Internship • **DURATION:** Summer • **IDEAL CANDIDATE:** College Students • **APPLICANT POOL:** 700/year • **APPLICANTS ACCEPTED:** 24/year

⋯⋯⋯⋯⋯⋯⋯⋯⋯⋯⋯⋯⋯⋯⋯⋯

THE METROPOLITAN MUSEUM OF ART (The Met) is the largest and most diverse museum in the Western Hemisphere, containing two million pieces that cover nearly 5,000 years of history. Unlike the majority of the world's museums, which tend to limit their scope to particular styles and periods, the Met satisfies the tastes of everyone.

Work/Learn Program Specifics: Summer interns are placed in Conservation, Library, Education, Administration, or one of their nineteen curatorial departments. The program begins with a two-week whirlwind orientation, and each intern visits each curatorial department. This prepares interns to give gallery talks and work at the visitor information center. Most interns also spend two full days each week in their respective departments. The Met also sponsors other programs, including a six- or nine-month internship program, the Graduate Lecturing Internship, and an internship program at The Cloisters. Call The Met for details on these programs.

Duration: Ten weeks during the summer, full-time.

Compensation and Perks: Honorariums of $2,500 for undergraduates; $2,750 for graduate students. On Mondays, when The Met is closed to the public, interns visit other museums and attend lectures.

The Ideal Candidate: Applicants must be juniors, seniors, recent graduates, or graduate students. A strong background in art history is preferred.

Making It Happen: Submit a resume, a separate list of foreign language ability and art history courses completed, two academic recommendations, official transcripts, and an essay of not more than 500 words indicating career goals, interest in museum work, and reasons for applying to the internship program. Deadlines: undergraduates—the third Friday in January; graduate students—the fourth Friday in January.

Contact Information: Esther Morales Cacchione, Assistant Museum Educator • The Metropolitan Museum of Art • 1000 Fifth Ave. • New York, NY 10028-0198 • Phone: (212) 879-5500 • Fax: (212) 570-3879

Montshire Museum of Science

REGION/HQ: Northeast/Vermont • **CATEGORY:** Museum • **POSITION TYPE:** Internship • **DURATION:** Year-Round • **IDEAL CANDIDATE:** College Students, Career Changers, Retired Folks • **APPLICANT POOL:** Varies • **APPLICANTS ACCEPTED:** 10/year

⋯⋯⋯⋯⋯⋯⋯⋯⋯⋯⋯⋯⋯⋯⋯⋯

MONTSHIRE MUSEUM OF SCIENCE is a hands-on education center serving northern New England. The museum's innovative programming and management have earned national and regional recognition for excellence. Montshire creates its own changing natural history, physical science, and technology exhibits and sponsors exhibits from other science centers. The museum conducts a variety of programs, trips, and other activities for preschool children and families, as well as courses, workshops, and forums for business leaders and community groups.

Area and Working Environment: Located in Norwich, one mile from Dartmouth College, the museum's site features 100 acres of woodland and nature trails along the Connecticut River.

Work/Learn Program Specifics: Science education interns will have the opportunity to teach a variety of science concepts to preschoolers and school children, to develop curricula and design demonstrations for kids and families, to interpret exhibits, to work in day camps and other environmental education activities, and to assist with special events. Exhibit interns will be involved in the research, design, and construction of exhibits. Internet and education interns work with Valley Net, a nonprofit internet access provider for schools and community organizations in this area. Membership and development interns work with varied membership programs and a strong development effort. Public relations interns work in the various avenues of communication, including radio, TV, articles, ads, video, desktop publishing, and graphic design.

Duration: The fifteen-week, full-time internship program is held during all seasons of the year. Other schedules may be available to meet the needs of an individual intern, including part-time work.

Compensation and Perks: Housing and a small stipend are provided. Local families welcome interns into their homes. The stipend of $600 is intended to help offset food and gas expenses.

The Ideal Candidate: Prerequisites include an interest in science and a desire to work with people. Priority will be given to those interested in working in the field after the program. Familiarity with natural and physical science, communications, and education is useful.

Making It Happen: Call for an application. Send resume and completed application. Upon receiving your application, they will call or send you a letter to arrange an interview. They hold in-person interviews with applicants who live nearby and telephone interviews with most distant applications.

Contact Information: Ginger Wallis, Intern Coordinator • Montshire Museum of Science • P.O. Box 770 • Norwich, VT 05055 • Phone: (802) 649-2200 • Fax: (802) 649-3637 • E-mail: montshire@valley.net • Web Site: www.valley.net/~mms

National Museum of Women in the Arts

REGION/HQ: Washington, D.C./Washington, D.C.
• **CATEGORY:** Art Museum • **POSITION TYPE:** Internship • **DURATION:** Year-Round • **IDEAL CANDIDATE:** College Students, Career Changers, Foreigners • **APPLICANT POOL:** 100/year • **APPLICANTS ACCEPTED:** 10/term

DESIGNED BY ARCHITECT Waddy Butler Wood in 1907, the elegant Renaissance-revival structure once served as the Masonic Grand Lodge of the national capital. The National Museum of Women in the Arts recognizes the achievements of women artists of all periods and nationalities by exhibiting, collecting, preserving, and researching art by women and by educating the public as to their accomplishments. To fulfill this mission, the museum holds and displays a permanent collection, presents special exhibitions, conducts education programs, maintains a library and research center, and supports a network of national and international chapters. It also serves as a center for the performing arts and other creative disciplines in which women have excelled.

Work/Learn Program Specifics: The internship program (sponsored by Coca-Cola) is available in the following departments: Accounting, Administration, Corporate Relations, Curatorial, Education, Exhibition Design and Production, Library and Research Center, Membership, National Programs, Publications, Public Relations, Registrar, Retail Operations, and Special Events. All internships are project-oriented, and each intern will complete a project. Also inquire about The Lebovitz Internship, which was established by the family of Mrs. Lebovitz in honor of her lifetime interest in promoting the careers of young artists.

Duration: Coca-Cola internship positions are available year-round, full-time, for ten to twelve weeks. The Lebovitz Internship is during the fall semester only, full-time.

Compensation and Perks: Coca-Cola interns receive a $2,000 stipend and the Lebovitz Internship Program carries a $1,500 stipend. Perks include college-level art history training with the docent class, an opportunity to work with museum professionals on a one-to-one basis, tours to other arts institutions in the Washington, D.C. area, free or reduced admissions to public education and performing arts events at NMWA, and discounts in the museum shop and mezzanine cafe.

The Ideal Candidate: Coca-Cola applicants must have a minimum 3.25 or higher GPA and have completed their sophomore year. Some departments want interns who have experience in their specific areas, although candidates who indicate more than one department have a better chance at being chosen than those who do not. Qualities they seek are excellent writing skills, flexibility, and a team-player attitude. Lebovitz applicants must have a 3.25 or higher GPA and have not yet entered graduate school.

Making It Happen: All interns should send a cover letter stating the preferred department and how a NMWA internship will further their personal and professional goals, a resume, transcript, a brief writing sample, and two letters of recommendation (one academic/one personal). Coca-Cola deadlines: spring—October 30; summer—March 15; and fall—May 31; the Lebovitz deadline is May 31. All materials must be postmarked by these dates.

Contact Information: Jill Wexler Greenstein, Volunteer/Visitor Services Manager • National Museum of Women in the Arts • 1250 New York Ave., NW • Washington, DC 20005-3920 • Phone: (202) 783-7996 • Fax: (202) 393-3235 • Alternate: (202) 783-5000 • Web Site: www.nmwa.org

Naval Historical Center

REGION/HQ: Washington, D.C./Washington, D.C.
• **CATEGORY:** Museum • **POSITION TYPE:** Internship • **DURATION:** Year-Round • **IDEAL CANDIDATE:** College Students, Career Changers, Foreigners • **APPLICANT POOL:** Varies • **APPLICANTS ACCEPTED:** Varies

TIRED OF CONDESCENDING INTERNSHIPS, the Naval Historical Center treats its interns well (admittedly, they must perform herculean amounts of work, but isn't that the nature of the position?). Internships here excite people about history. With a staff of less than 100, the center produces books, exhibits, and brochures. The museum and art gallery has less than a tenth of the National Air and Space Museum's annual visitors, but they provide their interns with greater insight into museum operations. The center serves a large branch of the federal government—the only organization dedicated to the history of all aspects of the U.S. Navy. Internships here consistently garner good reviews, and many former interns return as volunteers. It is no platitude to say that an internship at the center enhances one's academic and employment prospects.

Area and Working Environment: The museum is located just east of the Capitol Hill area of Washington, D.C.

Work/Learn Program Specifics: Each intern works on a personal project, with possibilities in archives, editing, design, historical research and writing, collections management, curation, education, publicity, documentary editing, and library science. Archival and collections management interns catalogue new material and assist with accounting for items already in the collection. Editing interns help with their publication program. In design, interns work on invitation and exhibit layouts and silkscreening. Research and writing forms the backbone of work in the branches dealing with post-1945 history, ships, and naval aviation, but interns also learn about museum curation. Library interns work in one of the oldest federal libraries. Everyone, just like the paid staff, turns to the more mundane pursuits: answering inquiries, addressing mass mailings, short bursts of office work, assisting with public programs, and organizing education tour materials.

Duration: Have your weekends free. Interning hours are Monday through Friday, excluding federal holidays. You won't make a fortune at the Naval Historical Center, but you will be able to arrange a schedule convenient for your academic or employment needs.

Compensation and Perks: A small stipend is offered, and you will receive sound information on housing options. When intern numbers warrant (generally in the summer), the coordinator arranges field trips; and on the same note, intern T-shirts are designed and produced in-house. Interns have the social cachet of inviting their friends to public programs and private exhibit openings. In addition, each branch sends off its interns with a farewell lunch, and each intern will receive the services of excellent reference writers.

The Ideal Candidate: They want everybody to have the opportunity to work in naval history. Past interns have included history majors (naturally), but also those in museum studies, studio art, anthropology, English, French, political science, computer science, international relations, and geography.

Making It Happen: Call for application materials (or download them from their Web site). Send completed application along with a writing sample, unofficial transcripts, and an academic letter of reference. Design interns must submit a portfolio, even just slides in the mail. Interviews by telephone or in person form part of the application process.

INSIDER TIPS: *Being enthusiastic and open to new experiences. It's hard sometimes, but try to submit a complete application packet. We love organizational skills. Try The Navy Museum and you'll find yourself heading down the museum career path.*

Contact Information: Edward Furgol, Curator • Naval Historical Center • The Navy Museum • 901 M. St., SE • Washington, DC 20374-5060 • Phone: (202) 433-6901 • Fax: (202) 433-8200 • Web Site: www.history.navy.mil

New Stage Theatre

REGION/HQ: Southeast/Mississippi • **CATEGORY:** Theatre • **POSITION TYPE:** Internship • **DURATION:** Academic year • **IDEAL CANDIDATE:** College Students, Career Changers, Foreigners • **APPLICANT POOL:** 200/year • **APPLICANTS ACCEPTED:** 8/year

FOUNDED IN 1965, New Stage Theatre is the only fully professional theatre in the state of Mississippi. Under the leadership of its staff, the theatre operates year-round, offering an ambitious season which includes six mainstage productions, two second-stage shows, the premiere of a new play, and a mainstage production for young audiences.

Area and Working Environment: Jackson, the state capital, has a good variety of arts events/organizations and great local restaurants.

Work/Learn Program Specifics: Acting Intern Company Members: Interns tour the state of Mississippi with three Arts-in-Education productions. These productions include one Shakespeare tour, one Southern writers show, and one fairy tale theatre production.

Interns also teach creative dramatics for children, conduct theatre workshops in area schools, assist with teacher workshops, participate in the New Play Series, and help coordinate equity auditions. When not performing or rehearsing, acting interns assist in the daily operation of the theater, including technical and administrative duties as well as the strike of all productions. Technical Intern Program: Interns participate in the building of all New Stage productions by assisting in the areas of design, carpentry, scenic painting, props, lighting, sound, and costuming. Program participants are assigned running crew and strike duties on all New Stage productions. Interns are given the opportunity to spend an entire season continuing their education with New Stage Theatre's professional staff while earning professional theatre experience in a caring and nurturing environment.

Duration: An internship is a nine-month position, starting in mid-August. Interns usually work an average of fifty hours per week with one day off. The internship is a full-time commitment; outside employment is rarely possible.

Compensation and Perks: Stipends range from $5,000 to $6,000. Housing is available within walking distance of the theatre. Acting interns are given an opportunity to earn equity points toward their Actor's Equity Association card by being cast in understudy roles in equity production. Interns also gain valuable experience in conducting dramatic classes and workshops for children.

The Ideal Candidate: New Stage prefers recent college graduates with theatre experience, although others may apply.

Making It Happen: Call for application materials. Send completed application, resume, two letters of recommendation, and a brief personal statement explaining your expectations and reasons for applying for an internship. Acting intern company applicants also send a current photo (8x10 b/w preferred) and a VHS tape with two contrasting monologues. Technical intern applicants also send six photography samples of recent work in a mini-portfolio format. An interview/audition is required of all applicants. Deadline: mid-March.

INSIDER TIPS: *Have a good attitude, dedication to the theatre, ability to adapt, and get along with others.*

Contact Information: Education Director • New Stage Theatre • P.O. Box 4792 • Jackson, MS 39296-4792 • Phone: (601) 948-0142 • Fax: (601) 948-3538 • Alternate: (601) 948-3533

The Pearl Theatre Company, Inc.

REGION/HQ: Northeast/New York • **CATEGORY:** Theatre • **POSITION TYPE:** Internship • **DURATION:** Academic year • **IDEAL CANDIDATE:** College Students, Career Changers, Foreigners • **APPLICANT POOL:** Varies • **APPLICANTS ACCEPTED:** Varies

THE PEARL IS NEW YORK'S SMALLEST off-Broadway theatre, performing a full range of the classics from the ancient Greeks to the beginning of the twentieth century. Their emphasis is on craft, so that they transport their audience to the world of the play rather than adapt the play in order to make it accessible.

Work/Learn Program Specifics: Administration: assist the managing director in fiscal management, office management, front of house, and box office management. Stage management: assist equity stage managers in rehearsal and performance, the casting director in the audition process, all running crew positions, and the designers and tech director at strike and put-in. Acting: play supporting roles in three of five plays; understudy in all five; participate in warm-ups and classes in voice, speech, approach to text, and other crafts; assist casting director at auditions; and assist artistic associate/director. Costumes: assist designer of each of five plays, research and concept all aspects of construction, alteration, shopping, fittings, and dress rehearsals. Assistant to the Artistic Director: duties include all administrative aspects of artistic direction. Development: duties include acknowledging and recording individual donations, updating donor and prospect databases, and identifying potential corporate/foundation sponsors. Marketing: assist in subscription campaign, program, mailer and ticket ads, group sales, lobby and window displays, preparing playbills and mailers, and some box office and house management work.

Duration: Candidates who accept internships are asked to commit to eight months (August through May) and work a minimum of fifty to sixty hours per week. This period begins with the first rehearsal of the first of their five-classical-play season and ends with the final performance of the fifth. Shorter commitments are possible, especially in the case of school-sponsored programs and administrative interns.

Compensation and Perks: Interns receive a $75-per-week stipend. EMC points are available for acting and stage management interns.

The Ideal Candidate: Must show evidence of skills that pertain to each position (computer literacy, writing, good telephone presentation, organization, acting, basic sewing skills, etc.).

Making It Happen: Send cover letter and resume. All candidates are chosen on the basis of seriousness of their intent (as indicated in their letters of application), their training and educational background, and through a personal or telephone interview. In the case of acting interns, an audition with the artistic director and the artistic associate is also required. The best time to apply is January through March.

Contact Information: Mary Perez, Associate Director Of Marketing • The Pearl Theatre Company, Inc. • 80 St. Mark's Pl. • New York, NY 10003 • Phone: (212) 505-3401 • Fax: (212) 505-3404

Pentangle Council on the Arts

REGION/HQ: Northeast/Vermont • **CATEGORY:** Arts Council • **POSITION TYPE:** Internship • **DURATION:** Year-Round • **IDEAL CANDIDATE:** College Students, Career Changers, Foreigners • **APPLICANT POOL:** 8–10/term • **APPLICANTS ACCEPTED:** 1–2/term

THE PENTANGLE COUNCIL ON THE ARTS is a nonprofit, performing arts presenting organization with the goal to enrich the greater Woodstock area with the finest possible creative entertainment and education in the arts. Pentangle shows are presented regularly in two local theatres, as well as many nontraditional spaces, such as the lawn in front of the library. In addition, they are very committed to the presentation of arts in area schools and sponsor arts residencies each school year.

Area and Working Environment: All positions are located in Woodstock, a beautiful New England town whose population is about 5,000. It's a wonderful place to hike, bike, ski, and have fun.

Work/Learn Program Specifics: A Pentangle intern is expected to be involved in all areas of arts presentation. Duties will include the writing of press releases for upcoming events, reviewing contracts, layout and design of posters, postering, ticket sales, dealing with artists, stage managing, grant application writing, mailing lists management, setting up for performances, assisting both the director and the Arts-in-Education director, and coordinating fund-raising. As one of the employees in a small company, interns will have a great deal of auton-

omy but will also be expected to provide assistance whenever and wherever needed.

Duration: Positions are available year-round.

Compensation and Perks: A $50-per-week stipend and housing are provided.

The Ideal Candidate: Applicants must have a strong interest in the arts, arts management, education, teaching, or children.

Making It Happen: Submit resume, two writing samples, and a cover letter indicating what aspects of the internship program appeal to you, what skills you might bring to the program, and your level of expertise with computers, office equipment, or theatre equipment. Deadlines: winter/spring—November 15; summer—April 15; and fall—July 15.

Contact Information: C. P. Boswell, Assistant Director • Pentangle Council on the Arts • P. O. Box 172 • Woodstock, VT 05091 • Phone: (802) 457-3981 • Fax: (802) 457-4972

Playhouse on the Square

REGION/HQ: Southeast/Tennessee • **CATEGORY:** Theatre • **POSITION TYPE:** Internship • **DURATION:** Year-Round • **IDEAL CANDIDATE:** College Students, Career Changers, Foreigners • **APPLICANT POOL:** Varies • **APPLICANTS ACCEPTED:** Varies

PLAYHOUSE ON THE SQUARE, founded in 1969, is a member of the Theatre Communications Group, the national organization for nonprofit professional theatre.

Work/Learn Program Specifics: Each season, Playhouse on the Square offers several acting and technical internships. Interns at Playhouse are regarded as professional staff members and work in both the 260-seat Playhouse on the Square and the 136-seat Circuit Playhouse. Assignments will be consistent with the needs of the theatre and, as much as possible, with the interests of the intern. Acting interns will generally be in four to five productions if they are at the theatre for a year.

Duration: Participation in the Playhouse intern program is a full-time commitment.

Compensation and Perks: All positions receive a weekly stipend, plus housing. Playhouse helps interns who want to work on off-hours conduct workshops with the Memphis Arts Council's Artist-in-the-Schools

If all the year were playing holidays, to sport would be as tedious as to work.
—WILLIAM SHAKESPEARE

program. This provides extra income to interns having interests in this area.

The Ideal Candidate: Individuals in school or professional training programs, or those out of school seeking to further their professional careers.

Making It Happen: Call for application. Send resume, cover letter, and completed application. Rolling deadlines.

Contact Information: Jackie Nichols, Executive Producer • Playhouse on the Square • 51 S. Cooper • Memphis, TN 38104 • Phone: (901) 725-0776 • Fax: (901) 272-7530

Seattle Repertory Theatre

REGION/HQ: Pacific Northwest/Washington
• **CATEGORY:** Theatre • **POSITION TYPE:** Internship
• **DURATION:** Year-Round • **IDEAL CANDIDATE:** College Students, Career Changers • **APPLICANT POOL:** Varies • **APPLICANTS ACCEPTED:** Varies

THE SEATTLE REPERTORY THEATRE is a major resident theatre which enjoys a subscriber base of 21,000 and plays to an audience of nearly a quarter million a year. Productions range from classic to contemporary and from the well-known to world premieres.

Work/Learn Program Specifics: The Professional Arts Training Program functions on several levels. It not only gives participants comprehensive work in their areas of interest, but exposes them to the workings of the entire organization, and beyond that, to the arts community in which the Seattle Repertory Theatre operates. Internships are offered in arts management, communications, development, directing, finance, literary/dramaturgy, production management, properties, scenic art, scenic design, stage management, technical production, and wardrobe. Intern seminars are held twice a month and are designed to make contact between interns and the full range of the Rep's professions, including staff, guest artists, and members of the acting company. Seminars also include off-site field trips to other arts organizations in the area, with guest speakers from their staff or company.

Duration: Every intern is expected to commit to a full-time workweek for the agreed-upon term of his or her internship.

Compensation and Perks: Interns receive a limited stipend. Because of your time commitment, additional employment is not recommended.

Making It Happen: Applications are accepted no earlier than January 1 and the deadline is April 15 for the following September through May season. Send a resume, two letters of recommendation, and a brief personal statement about your goals and areas of interest. On April 15, your application will be forwarded to the department supervisor of the area to which you are applying. You will be notified no sooner than May 15 as to the status of your application.

Contact Information: Christy Bain, Company Manager • Seattle Repertory Theatre • 155 Mercer St. • Seattle, WA 98109 • Phone: (206) 443-2210

Smithsonian Institution

REGION/HQ: Washington, D.C./Washington, D.C.
• **CATEGORY:** Museum • **POSITION TYPE:** Internship
• **DURATION:** Year-Round • **IDEAL CANDIDATE:** College Students, Career Changers • **APPLICANT POOL:** 1,000/year • **APPLICANTS ACCEPTED:** 700/year

THE CENTER FOR MUSEUM STUDIES (CMS) coordinates a central referral service for all internship programs at the Smithsonian Institution. Incorporating sixteen museums and galleries plus the National Zoo, the Smithsonian is the world's largest museum complex and offers, quite possibly, the world's largest museum internship program.

Area and Working Environment: Washington, D.C.; Edgewater, Maryland; New York City; Fort Royal, Virginia; and the Republic of Panama.

Work/Learn Program Specifics: Interns at the Smithsonian develop job skills, expand expertise in academic disciplines, learn about museum careers, and see the workings of a major institution from the inside-out. Smithsonian interns "learn by doing," working closely with an internship supervisor in a tutorial setting. Interns are placed in one of forty museums, administrative offices, and research programs—there is truly something for everyone. Remember that the Smithsonian Institution is more than just the science, art, and history museums. The great size of this cultural institution means that there are many interns here doing a wide variety of work, from exhibit design to research to conservation to public programs and education. There are also internships in areas not normally associated with a museum, such as photography, computer science, public affairs, administration, product development, and library science. Most museums also have enrichment programs for interns, which include career seminars, behind-the-scenes tours, and such.

Duration: Most interns work at the Smithsonian for a period of two months to one year, for a minimum of twenty hours per week.

Compensation and Perks: Unless otherwise noted, internships at the Smithsonian do not carry a stipend. CMS provides a resource guide to area housing opportunities. Other perks include a 20 percent discount at museum gift shops and an available gym facility.

Making It Happen: Contact CMS for *Internships and Fellowships*, a free booklet containing program descriptions, contact information, and an application. Submit one set of application materials for each museum/office where you wish to be considered for an internship. This includes a completed application form, a two to three page essay and two letters of reference and transcripts. If you are not certain which program may be appropriate for you, submit five sets of application materials to CMS. Deadlines: spring—October 15; summer—February 15; and fall—June 15. No interviews are conducted.

INSIDER TIPS: *The internships and fellowships brochure is very useful in answering initial questions and providing you with the names and numbers of intern coordinators for each specific program. Make sure you find out about the program you are applying for. A good way to get information is to contact the intern coordinator for each specific program because it is better to ask any questions you might have about the process before you apply. Don't ever think a question is stupid or irrelevant. Some of us were interns before and probably had the very same question. The most important thing to remember when applying is being yourself and letting you and your interests be apparent in your application. This way the project you may be selected for will truly match your interests and help you to fulfill your goals. The application essay gives you the opportunity to do this.*

Contact Information: Elena Piquer Mayberry, Intern Services Coordinator • Smithsonian Institution • Center For Museum Studies • 900 Jefferson Dr., Suite 2235/MRC 427 • Washington, DC 20560 • Phone: (202) 357-3102 • Fax: (202) 357-3346 • E-mail: siintern@sivm.si.edu • Web Site: www.si.edu

Solomon R. Guggenheim Museum

REGION/HQ: Northeast/New York • **CATEGORY:** Museum • **POSITION TYPE:** Internship/Volunteer • **DURATION:** Year-Round • **IDEAL CANDIDATE:** College Students, Career Changers, Retired Folks, Foreigners • **APPLICANT POOL:** 100/term • **APPLICANTS ACCEPTED:** 20/term

THE INTERNSHIP PROGRAM at The Solomon R. Guggenheim Museum is a twenty-five-year-old tradition that is still going strong! With the museum's renovation and expansion project nearing completion, the museum is fast becoming an international center for modern and contemporary art. There is no better time than the present to be a part of the Guggenheim Museum's internship program and participate in the museum's development into the twenty-first century.

Area and Working Environment: The uptown Solomon R. Guggenheim Museum is a landmark Frank Lloyd Wright building located in the Upper East Side of Manhattan, while the downtown Guggenheim Museum is located in Soho.

Work/Learn Program Specifics: The Guggenheim designs its programs to give students an overall glimpse into the world of modern and contemporary art. Their summer internship is a formal program in which interns are taken on trips once a week to out-of-the-way places to hear guest speakers or be given tours of other museums. Interns may work in education, curatorial, conservation, legal, information technology, membership, special events, photography, design, development, archives/library, finance, public affairs, director's office, registrar, publications, personnel, or visitor services. Interns should be willing to do a lot of administrative work and gain exposure in the process.

The Ideal Candidate: Interns from all over the United States, Europe, and Asia participate in the Guggenheim Internship Program each year. College students are preferred, but it is not limited to this group.

Making It Happen: Call for application. Send completed application, cover letter, resume, two essays, and letters of recommendation. Volunteers should contact Diane Maas at (212) 423-3648.

Contact Information: Beth Rosenberg, Education Program Manager • Solomon R. Guggenheim Museum • 1071 Fifth Ave. • New York, NY 10128-0173 • Phone: (212) 423-3557 • Fax: (212) 423-3560 • E-mail: brosenberg@guggenheim.org • Web Site: www.guggenheim.org

Spoleto Festival USA

REGION/HQ: Southeast/South Carolina • **CATEGORY:** Festival • **POSITION TYPE:** Unique Experience • **DURATION:** Spring • **IDEAL CANDIDATE:** College Students, Career Changers, Retired Folks, Foreigners • **APPLICANT POOL:** 300/year • **APPLICANTS ACCEPTED:** 75/year

THE SPOLETO FESTIVAL PRODUCES and presents world-class opera, dance, theatre, chamber music, symphonic and choral music, jazz, and the literary and visual arts. The festival produces over 120 events in 17 days, playing to an international audience of more than 75,000 in a variety of theaters and other performance sites throughout historic Charleston. The festival was founded by world-renowned composer and director Gian Carlo Menotti. The *Washington Post* calls the Spoleto Festival "the most varied arts festival given on this continent."

Work/Learn Program Specifics: A short-term, intensive, and exciting opportunity to learn about the world of the performing arts through apprenticeships in a variety of disciplines. Apprentices work with arts professionals to produce and operate an international arts festival. Administrative apprenticeships are available in media relations, development, finance, box office, housing, general administration, merchandising, orchestra management, chamber music assistant, and rehearsal assistant. Production apprenticeships include stage carpenters, stage electricians, sound, properties, wardrobe, wigs and makeup, and production administration.

Duration: Employment period is from mid-May to mid-June, full-time.

Compensation and Perks: A $200-per-week stipend is provided, plus housing at the College of Charleston. Out-of-town apprentices also receive $50 toward travel expenses. Other perks include a welcoming cruise around Charleston's harbor, a participant badge (open access to all events), and excellent career training in the arts.

The Ideal Candidate: Applicant should have excellent organization, communication, and administrative skills. Familiarity with the arts is also a plus.

Making It Happen: Call for application. Submit completed application, resume, and two letters of recommendation by mid-February. Secondary material or interview may be required.

Contact Information: Nunally Kersh, Operations Director • Spoleto Festival USA • P.O. Box 157 • Charleston, SC 29402-0157 • Phone: (803) 722-2764 • Fax: (803) 723-6383

Stagedoor Manor Performing Arts Center

REGION/HQ: Northeast/Tennessee • **CATEGORY:** Performing Arts • **POSITION TYPE:** Seasonal • **DURATION:** Summer • **IDEAL CANDIDATE:** College Students, Career Changers, Foreigners • **APPLICANT POOL:** 300/year • **APPLICANTS ACCEPTED:** 60/year

STAGEDOOR IS A PERFORMING ARTS center for boys and girls, ages eight to eighteen. Every summer over 240 talented kids and 117 staff members from all over the world travel to Stagedoor to produce 33 full-scale productions in the 5 on-site theatres. In addition to performance, Stagedoor offers a full program of classes in dance, TV, video production, directing, vocal training, acting technique, stage combat, technical skills—every facet of theatre and performance is covered. Staff and campers alike come to Stagedoor for experience and to fulfill professional and personal goals. They also come for fun, laughter, and friendships that last a lifetime. Their classrooms, video labs, dance studios, and costume and scenic shops are alive with the energy and enthusiasm of theatre.

Area and Working Environment: Stagedoor is located in the Catskill Mountains of New York State, only 2½ hours from New York City and close to Woodstock and Monticello. The camp is located in an old resort hotel with indoor/outdoor pools and tennis courts.

Work/Learn Program Specifics: Positions at Stagedoor require great flexibility. The staff must have a commitment to teamwork and a true enjoyment of the energy and honesty of children. The days are long and the daily schedule of each staff member includes a variety of responsibilities and functions. Counselors double as stage managers, production assistants, dance captains, or sports personnel. Directors, musical directors, and choreographers teach classes in their craft and must hold professional credits. They also hire office, housekeeping, and kitchen personnel, registered nurses, American Red Cross lifeguards, and swim and tennis instructors.

Duration: The program lasts ten weeks, from mid-June to late August.

Compensation and Perks: Salaries vary according to age and experience and range from $900 to $2,500 for the season. Full room and board (dormitory-style housing) and transportation from New York City are provided. Perks include working for an internationally famous training center with staff and children from all over the world. You'll have the chance to go to Broadway shows and meet visiting celebrities. This is a fast-paced summer stock environment.

The Ideal Candidate: Staff members must be twenty-one or older, with previous experience working with children and the theatre. Average staff age is twenty-three to thirty.

Making It Happen: Send resume and cover letter, including references and also requesting an application and brochure. Deadline: May 15.

Contact Information: Konnie Kittrell, Production Director • Stagedoor Manor Performing Arts Center • 269 Moneymaker Cr. • Gatlinburg, TN 37738 • Phone: (423) 436-3030

Strong Museum

REGION/HQ: Northeast/New York • **CATEGORY:** Museum • **POSITION TYPE:** Internship • **DURATION:** Summer • **IDEAL CANDIDATE:** College Students • **APPLICANT POOL:** Varies • **APPLICANTS ACCEPTED:** 2/year

STRONG MUSEUM'S WORLD-RENOWNED collections and award-winning exhibitions tell the extraordinary story of everyday life in America since 1820. The museum also offers entertaining and engaging activities and programs for all ages year-round: festivals, performances, family and children's events, talks, school programs, and more.

Work/Learn Program Specifics: Interns will work with staff in area of interest, which includes collections, conservation, administration and finance, public affairs, research, interpretation, education, publications, and exhibitions design. Interns will be expected to complete a specific project by the end of the internship period.

Duration: Internship positions are approximately twelve weeks in length, from June through August, full-time.

Compensation and Perks: You will receive a $4,000 stipend.

The Ideal Candidate: Graduate students in museum studies or conservation of historic artifacts and works of art are given special consideration.

Making It Happen: Send a cover letter stating your area of specialty and interest in program, a resume, and

three references (one from an individual not affiliated with your graduate program) by December 15.

Contact Information: Education/Internship Director • Strong Museum • 1 Manhattan Square • Rochester, NY 14607 • Phone: (716) 263-2700 • Fax: (716) 263-2493 • Web Site: www.strongmuseum.org

Swetcharnik Studio

REGION/HQ: Northeast/Maryland • **CATEGORY:** Arts Administration • **POSITION TYPE:** Internship • **DURATION:** Year-Round • **IDEAL CANDIDATE:** College Students, Career Changers, Foreigners • **APPLICANT POOL:** Varies • **APPLICANTS ACCEPTED:** Varies

WILLIAM AND SARA SWETCHARNIK have been working professionally as artists for over twenty years, William primarily as a painter of complex, installation-oriented still-life/figure/interior compositions, and Sara as a sculptor of animals and the human figure. Their work has been the subject of numerous museum and gallery exhibitions both in the U.S. and abroad. Between them they count many professional distinctions, including a series of Fulbright grants to Spain and Central America, additional fellowships from the Cintas and Stacey Foundations, and multiple fellowships to Yaddo and other residency programs. William is also the founder of the Latin American Art Resource Project (LAARP), a program that enables underprivileged artists and artisans to create work with low-cost, local resources. Internships are available both for LAARP (see additional listing under that name) and studio work, either in their Maryland or Central American studio, depending on time frame.

Area and Working Environment: William and Sara Swetcharnik normally live in a converted barn/studio in the Maryland countryside about an hour north of Washington, D.C. While working on the art resource project, they maintain a home and studio in the mountains outside of Tegucigalpa, Honduras, at the foot of a cloud forest. Interns usually like to do a bit of exploring/vacationing, so it should be mentioned that the studio in Maryland is an excellent jumping-off point for day-tripping to museums in Washington, Baltimore, Philadelphia, and even New York. The home base in Honduras is a great point of departure for Mayan ruins, tropical rainforests, and coral reef islands. When the team takes off for workshop tours in remote areas of the isthmus, there are usually weekend opportunities, as well, to explore. It should also be mentioned that there is a slight language difference between Maryland and Honduras, but depending on the kinds of activities contemplated, this is not necessarily a limiting factor.

Work/Learn Program Specifics: The studio internship is modeled on the traditional apprenticeship approach, in which the apprentice helps with work around the studio in exchange for a practical educational experience, learning firsthand the artistic and business skills necessary to maintain an art studio. Depending on your skills, tasks may include preparation of art materials, secretarial and accounting duties, photographic documentation and cataloguing of artwork, public relations, and various carpentry and other construction/maintenance tasks. Interns have the choice of working with either William or Sara, or a combination of both. Sara is presently working on sculptures of indigenous animals at a nearby Honduran zoo, in conjunction with an environmental education program, and needs an assistant to help demonstrate and talk with the school children. Since much of the art produced by William is oriented around a development project that teaches the use of traditional art methods with low-cost local resources, his interns have a special opportunity to learn how to work with raw materials, making works of art in egg tempera, fresco, and other exotic media, on supports including carved wood, stone, ceramic, and local fibers. In some cases, studio internships can be combined with work for the Latin American Art Resource Project (see internship listings under that name).

Duration: Internships are normally arranged for a minimum of three months, full-time.

Compensation and Perks: Interns do not receive salaries or any other employment benefits. Structured weekly art classes are provided at no cost. Nearby room and board are available for $400 per month in Honduras and $700 per month in Maryland.

The Ideal Candidate: Prerequisites are emotional maturity and eagerness to learn, attested through good school records, work history, and letters of reference.

Making It Happen: Send a cover letter and resume.

Contact Information: William and Sara Swetcharnik, Artists • Swetcharnik Studio • 7044 Woodville Rd. • Mt. Airy, MD 21771 • Phone: (301) 831-7286 • Fax: (301) 694-7653 • E-mail: wswetcharnik@nimue.hood.edu • Web Site: www.hood.edu/academic/art/laarp

The Theater at Monmouth

REGION/HQ: Northeast/Maine • **CATEGORY:** Theatre • **POSITION TYPE:** Internship • **DURATION:** Summer • **IDEAL CANDIDATE:** College Students, Career Changers, Foreigners • **APPLICANT POOL:** 1,500/year • **APPLICANTS ACCEPTED:** 20/year

THE THEATER AT MONMOUTH is a classical summer theatre which performs in the time-honored tradition of rotating repertory in an intimate Victorian opera house, Cumston Hall. A large and loyal audience of 12,000 travels each summer to their rural location to enjoy the only professional classical theater in the state. Recognized by the state legislature as "The Shakespearean Theatre of Maine" and awarded with a Citation for Excellence from the New England Theater Conference, The Theater at Monmouth has enjoyed critical success and achieves consistently high artistic quality.

Work/Learn Program Specifics: The internship program provides the unique opportunity for interns to work side-by-side with the professional company on the mainstage productions as staff members, rather than being relegated to a second stage or the classroom. Interns are the backbone of their summer staff and enjoy appropriate departmental responsibility while honing their skills under the supervision of seasoned professionals. The Theater offers internships in acting (performing on the mainstage and in children's shows and assisting in technical and administrative ways), costuming (stitchers and craftspersons), technical theatre production (involved in all aspects of physical production, including scenery construction, props, electrics, and run crew), stage management (assist in stage managing the mainstage productions and stage manage the children's shows), and theatre administration (staff the box office, manage concessions and volunteers, and assist with PR, marketing, fund-raising, and bookkeeping).

Duration: Internships run about June 1 through Labor Day.

Compensation and Perks: Interns are paid a modest stipend of $40 to $60 per week and provided with free room and board.

Making It Happen: Send cover letter, resume, and the names and phone numbers of at least three references by April 15. Actors must audition at New England Theater Conference or travel to Maine for an audition.

Contact Information: Managing Director • The Theater at Monmouth • P.O. Box 385 • Monmouth, ME 04259-

0385 • Phone: (207) 933-2952 • Fax: (207) 933-2952 • Box Office: (207) 933-9999 • Web Site: www.biddeford.com/tam

TheatreVirginia

REGION/HQ: Southeast/Virginia • **CATEGORY:** Theatre • **POSITION TYPE:** Internship/Seasonal • **DURATION:** Varies • **IDEAL CANDIDATE:** College Students, Career Changers, Foreigners • **APPLICANT POOL:** 250/year • **APPLICANTS ACCEPTED:** 10–15/year

••

THEATREVIRGINIA, LOCATED IN the Virginia Museum of Fine Arts, is one of America's oldest regional theatres. Classic and contemporary dramas, musicals, and comedies have been part of their repertoire for over forty years. In addition, the theatre provides technical support for the Virginia Museum's performance art and lecture series.

Area and Working Environment: Richmond is an incredibly beautiful city, with a little bit of everything you could want in a city—museums, symphony, ballet, opera, and, of course, the theatre. It's also a great place for the history buff.

Work/Learn Program Specifics: TheatreVirginia offers a training/internship program for young theatre artists, artisans, and administrators. The program is designed to give the participant concentrated experience in specific aspects of theatre. While these young professionals gain the training and credentials needed to pursue a career in the professional theatre, TheatreVirginia derives invaluable assistance from them. Although advancement into a staff position is not guaranteed, many current staff started as apprentices with TheatreVirginia. Seasonally, over fifty persons staff the theatre. Administrative Specialization: development, ticket operations, marketing/ public relations, education/outreach, and house management. Production Specialization: production assistant, scenic carpentry/properties, electrics/sound, scenic artistry, and costume production.

Duration: The theatre's season runs from September through April. Apprentice positions last the full season; internships normally last one semester. Participation in the program requires a full-time commitment. Although the workweek exceeds forty hours, depending on the level of responsibility and the theatre's production schedule, the week may exceed sixty hours. The theatre has a comp-time policy in an effort to keep the average to forty hours or less.

Compensation and Perks: Interns receive a stipend of $175 per week, plus limited benefits. This experience is supplemented by minimal workshops, seminars, and other activities, but is essentially nonacademic.

The Ideal Candidate: Apprentices usually have completed college and have some theatre experience outside of academia. Apprentices are expected to have chosen a specific area of interest and to be relatively certain about a career in theatre. No theatre experience is necessary for internships.

Making It Happen: Send your resume and a letter stating your area of interest and the names of references with phone numbers. Applications are accepted throughout the year. Recruitment begins in March for the following season.

Contact Information: Donna Coghill, Education & Outreach Director • TheatreVirginia • 2800 Grove Ave. • Richmond, VA 23221 • Phone: (804) 353-6100 • Fax: (804) 353-8799

U.S. Olympic Committee

REGION/HQ: Nationwide/Colorado • **CATEGORY:** Sports Management • **POSITION TYPE:** Internship • **DURATION:** Year-Round • **IDEAL CANDIDATE:** College Students • **APPLICANT POOL:** 100–500/term • **APPLICANTS ACCEPTED:** 20–25/term

••

THE U.S. OLYMPIC COMMITTEE is a nonprofit organization dedicated to providing opportunities for American athletes and to preparing and training those athletes for challenges that range from domestic competitions to the Olympic Games.

Area and Working Environment: The majority of internships are at their headquarters in Colorado Springs; however, you may work at Lake Placid, New York or Chula Vista, California.

Work/Learn Program Specifics: The internship program seeks to provide a quality work experience to students and a unique opportunity for exposure to the Olympic movement and spirit in the United States. Colorado Springs positions include accounting (one or two students), broadcasting (one), computer science (one or two), journalism (four to six), marketing (two), sports administration (four to six), and sport science/weightroom (one or two). Lake Placid positions include sport science/weightroom (one or two), sports administration (one), and journalism (one or two). Chula Vista positions include sports administration (one) and sports science (two).

Duration: Winter/spring—twenty-one weeks; summer—thirteen weeks; and fall—fifteen weeks.

Compensation and Perks: Interns will receive $45 per week, plus room and board. The center houses athletes and interns in dormitories on a double occupancy basis and meals are provided at the athletes' dining hall. The complex in Colorado Springs is an athlete's paradise—gyms, weight room, pool, and recreational facilities.

The Ideal Candidate: Most of the positions are for students studying journalism, public relations, marketing, and sports administration. Applicants must be enrolled in an undergraduate or graduate program and have completed at least two years of college before the start of their internship. Applicants must have basic computer skills, and most who get accepted have a GPA of 3.0 or higher and have good writing skills. Work experience, volunteer experience, and college extracurricular activities are seriously considered in the selection process.

Making It Happen: Call for a student program application. Submit completed application (which requires three faculty references), cover letter, official transcript, and resume. Applications must be received by these dates: spring—October 1; summer—February 15; and fall—June 1. You will be notified four to eight weeks after submitting your application.

INSIDER TIPS: *Get your application mailed in a timely manner. Make sure it is complete and accurate and that you have followed directions carefully.*

Contact Information: Intern Program Manager • U.S. Olympic Committee • One Olympic Plaza • Colorado Springs, CO 80909-5760 • Phone: (719) 632-5551 • Fax: (719) 578-4817

Washington Performing Arts Society

REGION/HQ: Washington, D.C./Washington, D.C. • **CATEGORY:** Performing Arts • **POSITION TYPE:** Internship • **DURATION:** Year-Round • **IDEAL CANDIDATE:** College Students, Career Changers • **APPLICANT POOL:** Varies • **APPLICANTS ACCEPTED:** Varies

WASHINGTON PERFORMING ARTS SOCIETY is the second largest user of the Kennedy Center, annually presenting over 100 performances on major stages in Washington, D.C. Performances include major orchestras, solo recitalists, chamber ensembles, jazz, gospel, American modern-dance troupes, and specialty shows. They also present over 1,000 free concerts each year in metropolitan schools, using local performers.

Work/Learn Program Specifics: Internships are offered in public relations/marketing, development, or programming. Volunteer summer positions are available and consist of research and office work, as there are no performances during this time.

Duration: Positions are available year-round.

Compensation and Perks: A $100-per-week stipend is provided.

The Ideal Candidate: Applicants must have an interest or background in music, dance, or performance; computer literacy (WordPerfect preferred); good speaking skills; good writing skills (it is assumed that the applicant knows how to write a press release, for example); and the ability to learn quickly and take initiative.

Making It Happen: Send cover letter and resume. Rolling deadlines.

Contact Information: Linda Soma, PR/Marketing Director • Washington Performing Arts Society • 2000 L St., NW, Suite 810 • Washington, DC 20036-4907 • Phone: (202) 833-9800 • Fax: (202) 331-7678 • E-mail: wpas@wpas.org • Web Site: www.wpas.org

Westport Country Playhouse

REGION/HQ: Northeast/Connecticut • **CATEGORY:** Theatre • **POSITION TYPE:** Internship/Seasonal • **DURATION:** Summer • **IDEAL CANDIDATE:** College Students, Career Changers, Foreigners • **APPLICANT POOL:** 100/year • **APPLICANTS ACCEPTED:** 10/year

EACH SUMMER, SINCE 1931, a series of plays and musicals has been presented in the Westport County Playhouse, mostly contemporary plays or new works. Each production is separately cast, often with well-known stars from Broadway, film, and television. Actors, directors, designers, technicians, and managers are all union professionals with strong credits. As an intern, you will learn about the history of this theatre, through oral tradition or just a glimpse at the theatre lobby walls, which are covered with posters advertising shows dating from the beginning of the theatre's history.

Area and Working Environment: Westport, Connecticut is a charming suburban town, about an hour away from New York City by train. The Playhouse itself is a converted barn, just five minutes from the center of Westport.

Work/Learn Program Specifics: Each intern will work directly under a department head, switching departments throughout the season, acquiring a full range of experience by the season's end. Areas of concentration include stage management, scenery, lighting, props, costumes, and sound. Assignments are based on the needs of each show as well as the individual intern's aptitude for specialized work. Some projects, such as strike and setup, involve everyone, while other projects call for individual responsibilities. Periodic seminars are conducted, each led by a director, designer, stage manager, actor, producer, or union representative. Each season they produce six plays, including one or two musicals. Internships are also available in administration and public relations.

Duration: Internships begin in early June and continue through mid-September. Shorter schedules can be arranged if necessary, but must be in place before the season begins. A typical schedule for interns: shop duty from nine to five, with a lunch break; dinner break between 5:00 and 7:30; and back at the theatre from 8:00 to 11:00 to run the current show.

Compensation and Perks: Interns receive an $80-per-week stipend, or a $40-per-week stipend plus housing. The Actor's Equity Association accepts the Westport Playhouse in its Membership Candidate Program. Upon application, an intern's work at the theatre may be credited toward membership in that union.

The Ideal Candidate: The internship is best suited for those who are ready to begin a career in the theatre and need hands-on experience in a professional setting. Some experience in technical theatre is preferred, but not required.

Making It Happen: Call for application form. A personal interview is preferred, although a telephone interview may be substituted, if necessary. Deadline: May 1.

INSIDER TIPS: *Interns must be excited and enthusiastic about learning all about the world of backstage theatre, and be willing to work long hours with only an occasional day off. In exchange, they will receive a wealth of experience in every area of theatre ranging from carpentry to wardrobe. Little, if any, acting or other performance experience is offered, yet acting students are welcome so that they may learn the total universe of the theatre before specializing.*

Contact Information: Julie Monahan, General Manager • Westport Country Playhouse • P.O. Box 629

• Westport, CT 06881 • Phone: (203) 227-5137 • Fax: (203) 221-7482

Williamstown Theatre Festival

REGION/HQ: Northeast/Massachusetts • **CATEGORY:** Festival • **POSITION TYPE:** Internship • **DURATION:** Summer • **IDEAL CANDIDATE:** High School Students, College Students, Career Changers, Retired Folks, Foreigners • **APPLICANT POOL:** 500/year • **APPLICANTS ACCEPTED:** 50/year

BEGINNING AS A SMALL SUMMER company, the Williamstown Theatre Festival (WTF) has grown into a major theatrical event and has acquired a national reputation for the artists it attracts and the gifted young actors, designers, and directors it sends out into the world. The theatre performs on five stages. The Main Stage presents productions of modern classics in Williams College's 521-seat Adams Memorial Theatre, one of the finest small proscenium houses in America. New plays are presented on the Other Stage, a ninety-six-seat open thrust house. The Cabaret presents four musical revues, and Sunday Special Events, a highly eclectic series of one-time events, are presented at the Clark Art Institute. The Children's Theatre and Greylock Theatre Project involves the community and provides entertainment for all ages.

Area and Working Environment: Located in the scenic Berkshire region of Massachusetts, WTF is one of many fine artistic institutions in the area. The festival is three hours from New York City and Boston.

Work/Learn Program Specifics: Interning at WTF offers a chance to bridge the gap between academic and professional theatre by concentrating in one of the following areas of the festival: design, tech production, stage management, publicity, production management, directing, box office, general/company management, artistic, publications management, photography, and literary management. They also offer an acting apprentice program.

Duration: The theatre's season lasts from mid-June through the end of August.

Compensation and Perks: Interns are responsible for their own daily living expenses and pay $425 for Williams College housing. A few fellowships and paid staff positions are also available.

The Ideal Candidate: Anyone may apply.

There comes a time in every rightly constructed boy's life when he has a raging desire to go somewhere and dig for hidden treasure. —MARK TWAIN

Making It Happen: Call for more information and application materials. Send cover letter, resume, two letters of recommendation, and completed application. You are chosen on the basis of experience, recommendations, and an interview.

Contact Information: Anne Lowfie, Company Manager • Williamstown Theatre Festival • P.O. Box 517 • Williamstown, MA 01267-0517 • Phone: (212) 228-2286 • Fax: (212) 228-9091 • E-mail: wtfcm@aol.com

Wolf Trap Foundation for the Performing Arts

REGION/HQ: Southeast/Virginia • **CATEGORY:** Performing Arts • **POSITION TYPE:** Internship • **DURATION:** Year-Round • **IDEAL CANDIDATE:** College Students, Career Changers • **APPLICANT POOL:** 400/year • **APPLICANTS ACCEPTED:** 30/year

AS AMERICA'S ONLY NATIONAL PARK for the performing arts, Wolf Trap's mission since its inception in 1971 has been to enrich, educate, and provide enjoyment to the widest possible audiences through a broad range of accessible, high-quality activities in the performing arts. To reach the community, the country, and the world, Wolf Trap not only presents outstanding performances, including world premieres, national radio and television broadcasts, and events that preserve culturally diverse art forms, but provides educational opportunities in the arts to people of all ages and backgrounds.

Area and Working Environment: Wolf Trap is situated on an expanse of Virginia farmland a half-hour from Washington, D.C., and has an open-air amphitheater with thousands of lawn seats.

Work/Learn Program Specifics: Wolf Trap provides meaningful hands-on training and experience in the areas of arts administration and technical theatre. These internships offer the practical opportunity to become an integral member of the staff and work side-by-side with professionals producing, promoting, and administering the full spectrum of the performing arts. They have positions available in these offices: accounting, development, education, food and beverage, graphic design (advertising), group sales/box office, human resources, media relations, opera administration, photography, publications, special events, special programs, and technical and production. Interns also attend "brown bag lunch" presentations by department heads and attend educational seminars on the topic of arts management careers.

Duration: Internships are approximately twelve weeks long, part-time (twenty-four hours per week) in the spring and fall, and full-time in the summer; however, the duration and hours required of an intern can vary.

Compensation and Perks: Stipends depend on length of the internship and whether it is full- or part-time. Generally it's about $150 per week. Other perks include the opportunity to attend a variety of performances and events (two complimentary tickets for each); observe pre- and post-performance discussions; and attend dress rehearsals of the Wolf Trap Opera Company.

The Ideal Candidate: All administrative interns should possess enthusiasm and self-motivation, strong writing and organizational skills, the ability to work under pressure and meet deadlines, knowledge of word processing, and an articulate and professional phone manner. Production and technical interns are required to have prior experience in technical theater (minimum of one year of undergraduate work or equivalent) and the willingness to work long hours. Additional qualifications pertaining to each of the various internships are listed with the individual descriptions in Wolf Trap's brochure.

Making It Happen: Submit cover letter, with brief personal statement and outline of career goals; a resume listing relevant courses, previous experience, and special skills; two academic or professional references; and two contrasting samples of writing (except technical and accounting applicants). The majority of interviews take place over the phone, but in-person meetings can be arranged. Deadlines: spring—November 1; summer—March 1; and fall—July 1. An early application is advised.

Contact Information: Internship Coordinator • Wolf Trap Foundation for the Performing Arts • 1624 Trap Rd. • Vienna, VA 22182 • Phone: (703) 255-1933 • Fax: (703) 255-1924 • Web Site: www.wolf-trap.org/

Women's Sports Foundation

REGION/HQ: Northeast/New York • **CATEGORY:** Sports Management • **POSITION TYPE:** Internship • **DURATION:** Year-Round • **IDEAL CANDIDATE:** College Students, Career Changers, Foreigners • **APPLICANT POOL:** 30/term • **APPLICANTS ACCEPTED:** 10–12/term

In 1974, a small group of elite women athletes came together (including Billie Jean King, the founder) out of a belief that all girls and women deserve the opportunities and benefits of sports and that the inequalities existing between men's and women's sports are simply not right. The Women's Sports Foundation (WSF) was formed and dedicated to providing comprehensive programs of recognition, information, education, and the means for all girls and women to have the opportunity for sports experience, and to realize their full sports potential. Their programs of advocacy are aimed at enhancing and influencing public policy and general awareness.

Work/Learn Program Specifics: The Women's Sports Foundation internship program consists of four areas of activity and responsibility: 1) Direct Information Response—assist in answering the thousands of requests for information on their toll free line; 2) In-House Assignments—These may include assisting an event coordinator with scheduling airline reservations for athletes, distributing educational or promotional materials at an event, or writing articles for the WSF newsletter. Each intern will also have an individual project which meets their specific interests; 3) Ongoing WSF Projects—depending on the time of year, interns may be involved in scholarship guide research, awards balloting, National Girls and Women in Sports Day, the WSF Annual Conference, or the New York Dinner; and 4) Supplemental Opportunities—these vary widely and may include awards dinners, press conferences, attendance at workshops, seminars, and conferences, and visits to related organizations.

Duration: Ideal start dates are January 1, May 15, and September 1, although positions are available at any time during the year.

Compensation and Perks: Stipends for full-time interns range from $350 to $1,000 per month. Part-time interns receive a transportation reimbursement of up to $5 per day. Although housing is not provided, they will assist you in housing needs.

The Ideal Candidate: Excellent organizational and communication skills are required.

Making It Happen: Call for application. Submit completed application and two letters of reference. You should apply at least ninety days in advance of your proposed start date. Interviews may be in person or over the phone.

Contact Information: Marjorie Snyder, Associate Executive Director • Women's Sports Foundation • Eisenhower Park • East Meadow, NY 11554 • Phone: (516) 542-4700 • Fax: (516) 542-4716 • Toll Free: (800) 227-3988

Women's Studio Workshop

REGION/HQ: Northeast/New York • **CATEGORY:** Visual Arts • **POSITION TYPE:** Internship • **DURATION:** Year-Round • **IDEAL CANDIDATE:** College Students, Foreigners • **APPLICANT POOL:** Varies • **APPLICANTS ACCEPTED:** Varies

Women's Studio Workshop (WSW), since 1974, is a nonprofit artist's space founded and run by women to serve as a supportive working environment for all people interested in the visual arts. WSW staff artists coordinate grants, fellowships, internships, exhibition opportunities, and the Summer Arts Institute—WSW's primary education program for visual artists. Membership currently totals over 800 and is drawn from across the country and abroad.

Area and Working Environment: Located in the beautiful Hudson Valley, in the foothills of the Shawangunk and Catskill Mountains, WSW is surrounded by acres of marsh and woodlands. It is housed in the Binnewater Arts Center, a 100-year-old mercantile building that has been completely renovated to accommodate specialized studios in printmaking, papermaking, photography, and book arts. The 5,000 square feet of studio space have been carefully designed, localizing work and printing areas, all with plenty of natural light and direct access to the outdoors.

Work/Learn Program Specifics: Interns work alongside the artists/staff, learning about papermaking, print media, book arts, and arts administration. Interns assist in day-to-day running of the organization, including general maintenance and housekeeping. During the summer session, interns spend half their time taking classes at no charge, during the intensive summer workshop series they run each year. In the spring and fall, WSW's studios are used by visiting artists who are working on their own projects or are working with WSW to produce a limited edition artist's book. One month each spring and fall is devoted to art-in-education projects with students from the local public schools.

Duration: They offer three sessions of four- to five-month duration, with start dates of January, early June, and September. Internships require a full-time commitment to the organization.

Compensation and Perks: A $75-per-month stipend, plus housing, is provided. Interns are allowed unlimited access to studios after hours and may seek advice and/or instruction from staff concerning their own work.

The Ideal Candidate: Applicants must be interested in printing, studio arts, or marketing, and be able to relocate temporarily to New York. A car is recommended, and all serious candidates will be considered.

Making It Happen: Applicants should send a cover letter, resume, ten to twenty slides of your work, and three letters of reference. Postmark deadlines: spring—November 1; summer—March 15; and fall—July 15.

INSIDER TIPS: *Do not send old recommendation letters. We would rather hear from a friend who knows you well than a professor who does not. In your letter, address why you want to come here, specifically how we will benefit from having you here, as well as how a WSW internship can help further your professional ambitions. A strong body of work is essential, as shown through good-quality slides. Applicants must show that they understand that this is not an artists' residency.*

Contact Information: Laura Moriarty, Program Director • Women's Studio Workshop • P.O. Box 489 • Rosendale, NY 12472 • Phone: (914) 658-9133 • Fax: (914) 658-9031 • E-mail: wsw@mhv.net • Web Site: www.webmark.com/wsw/wswhome.htm

Short Listings

Agora, Inc.

REGION/HQ: Southeast/Florida • **CATEGORY:** Publishing • **POSITION TYPE:** Internship • **DURATION:** Year-Round • **IDEAL CANDIDATE:** College Students, Career Changers, Foreigners • **APPLICANT POOL:** 25/year • **APPLICANTS ACCEPTED:** Varies

AGORA IS AN INTERNATIONAL NEWSLETTER publisher with over twenty-five titles and one million paid subscribers worldwide. The bulk of their publications are financial investment newsletters, though they also have other very successful newsletters that cover areas ranging from home-based business opportunities to retirement to personal health. Editorial interns primarily provide editorial research, but will also be in contact with their contributing writers, or "stringers," from around the world. Additional duties will range from proofreading to administrative work. Marketing assistant interns help to conceive, design, and implement a direct mail campaign, as well as provide supportive marketing, such as follow-up phone calls. The intern is also involved in marketing arrangements with major business groups, from international chambers of commerce to sponsors of international seminars and trade shows.

Contact Information: Internship Coordinator • Agora, Inc. • 1050 SE 5th Ave., Suite #100 • Delray Beach, FL 33483 • Phone: (561) 279-0157

Alliance Theatre Company

REGION/HQ: Southeast/Georgia • **CATEGORY:** Theatre • **POSITION TYPE:** Internship • **DURATION:** Varies • **IDEAL CANDIDATE:** College Students • **APPLICANT POOL:** Varies • **APPLICANTS ACCEPTED:** Varies

THE ALLIANCE THEATRE COMPANY offers a diverse 7-play season of contemporary plays, musical theatre, world and regional premieres, and classics (as well as two plays for children) in its 784-seat mainstage and 200-seat studio theatres. Acting interns perform Lunchtime Theatre roles, understudy mainstage, studio, and children's theatre roles, and work-study in the office or as teaching assistant. Technical apprentices work in specific departments on all ATC productions, including Properties, Scenery, Stage Management, Stage Operations, or Sound. Acting interns receive no pay and make a commitment of two years, part-time; technical apprentices receive minimum wage and make a commitment for nine months, full-time. For acting internships, contact Al Hamcher at (404) 733-4706; for technical theatre internships, contact Steve Lindsley at (404) 733-4776.

Contact Information: Rixon Hammond, Production Manager • Alliance Theatre Company • Robert W. Woodruff Arts Center • 1280 Peachtree St., NE • Atlanta, GA 30309 • Phone: (404) 733-4777 • Fax: (404) 733-4773

American Repertory Theatre

REGION/HQ: Northeast/Massachusetts • **CATEGORY:** Theatre • **POSITION TYPE:** Internship • **DURATION:** Year-Round • **IDEAL CANDIDATE:** College Students, Career Changers • **APPLICANT POOL:** Varies • **APPLICANTS ACCEPTED:** Varies

THE AMERICAN REPERTORY THEATRE (ART) is a fully professional resident theatre company which makes its home at Harvard University's Loeb Drama Center. ART produces a variety of works throughout the year, including a five-play Mainstage season, a New Stages series, and a number of special events. The ART also engages in national and international touring and has established its own professional theatre training program, the Institute for Advanced Theatre Training at Harvard. Artistic, Management, and Technical internships are available.

Contact Information: Internship Program Coordinator • American Repertory Theatre • 64 Brattle St. • Cambridge, MA 02138 • Phone: (617) 495-2668 • Fax: (617) 495-1705

American Stage Festival

REGION/HQ: Northeast/New Hampshire • **CATEGORY:** Festival • **POSITION TYPE:** Internship • **DURATION:** Summer • **IDEAL CANDIDATE:** College Students, Career Changers, Retired Folks, Foreigners • **APPLICANT POOL:** 300/year • **APPLICANTS ACCEPTED:** 30/year

SINCE 1974, THE AMERICAN STAGE FESTIVAL has been providing New England with exhilarating, quality performances of classic and contemporary plays and musicals, educational children's theatre pieces, and new American works. Act in "The Young Company" touring ensemble, collaborating with playwrights and directors to mount five creative theatre pieces for young audiences. Audition for available non-equity mainstage roles and benefit from workshops with professional actors and directors. Production internships are available in stage management, production management, stage direction, technical direction, music direction, properties, administrative (marketing/publicity, development, company and house management, and box office), lighting and sound design, scenic design, and costume design. They will also customize an internship for the right individual. Performance interns receive $650

tuition, and housing is provided; production interns may receive a stipend, and housing is negotiable.

Contact Information: Troy Siebels, Managing Director • American Stage Festival • P.O. Box 225 • Milford, NH 03055-0225 • Phone: (603) 889-2330 • Fax: (603) 889-2336 • E-mail: Trsiebels@aol.com

American Theatre Works, Inc.

REGION/HQ: Northeast/Vermont • **CATEGORY:** Theatre • **POSITION TYPE:** Internship • **DURATION:** Summer • **IDEAL CANDIDATE:** College Students, Career Changers • **APPLICANT POOL:** 50/year • **APPLICANTS ACCEPTED:** 10–15/year

THE AMERICAN THEATRE WORKS, built from two pre-revolutionary barns, is a professional nonprofit equity theatre company producing summer seasons of five mainstage plays, plus two children's plays. Dorset is a beautiful historical village located in the Green Mountains in southwestern Vermont. Internships are available in arts management, technical theatre, and the acting apprentice company. Interns receive $85 to $100 per week, plus housing. Also note that they publish the *Summer Theatre Directory* (listing more than 400 opportunities) and the *Directory of Theatre Training* (listing 350 programs for grads and undergrads).

Contact Information: Jill Charles, Artistic Director • American Theatre Works, Inc. • P.O. Box 519 • Dorset, VT 05251 • Phone: (802) 867-2223 • Fax: (802) 867-0144 • E-mail: theatre@sover.net • Web Site: www.genghis.com/theatre.htm

Archive Films, Inc.

REGION/HQ: Northeast/New York • **CATEGORY:** Film • **POSITION TYPE:** Internship • **DURATION:** Year-Round • **IDEAL CANDIDATE:** College Students, Career Changers, Foreigners • **APPLICANT POOL:** 75/year • **APPLICANTS ACCEPTED:** 12–15/term

ARCHIVE FILMS IS A LIBRARY OF ALL types of pre-1970 film footage. This footage, from old newsreels and features to rock and roll performances, is made available to filmmakers who are producing everything from national television commercials to feature films. The library uses state-of-the-art on-line computers to help researchers gain immediate access to information regarding entire films and clips within films. They have

I owe my success to having listened respectfully to the very best advice, and then going away and doing the exact opposite. —G.K. CHESTERTON

309

developed a unique method for handling the voluminous material they process each day. They are constantly evolving new and more effective methods as demand increases.

Contact Information: Internship Coordinator • Archive Films, Inc. • 530 W. 25th St. • New York, NY 10001 • Phone: (212) 620-3955 • Fax: (212) 645-2137

ARChive of Contemporary Music

REGION/HQ: Northeast/New York • **CATEGORY:** Library • **POSITION TYPE:** Internship • **DURATION:** Year-Round • **IDEAL CANDIDATE:** College Students, Career Changers, Foreigners • **APPLICANT POOL:** Varies • **APPLICANTS ACCEPTED:** Varies

THE ARCHIVE OF CONTEMPORARY MUSIC is a nonprofit music library and research center that collects and preserves all forms of popular music from around the world since 1950. In addition to over 250,000 sound recordings, the ARChive also maintains music books, periodicals, photos, and clipping files.

Contact Information: Program Director • ARChive of Contemporary Music • 54 White St. • New York, NY 10013-3508 • Phone: (212) 226-6967 • Fax: (212) 226-6540

Atlanta Ballet

REGION/HQ: Southeast/Georgia • **CATEGORY:** Performing Arts • **POSITION TYPE:** Internship • **DURATION:** Year-Round • **IDEAL CANDIDATE:** College Students, Career Changers, Foreigners • **APPLICANT POOL:** Varies • **APPLICANTS ACCEPTED:** Varies

THE ATLANTA BALLET COMPANY is a professional ballet company with forty-one dancers and a technical and administrative staff of twenty-three people. They provide educational programs and some touring. Internship participants will be exposed to development (fundraising, grant writing, and special events coordination), marketing (ticket sales and advertising), and public relations (working with the dancers to promote their careers and the Atlanta Ballet).

Contact Information: Christine Mentzer, Marketing & Development Assistant • Atlanta Ballet • 1400 W. Peachtree St., NW • Atlanta, GA 30309 • Phone: (404) 873-5811 • Fax: (404) 874-7905

BalletMet

REGION/HQ: Great Lakes/Ohio • **CATEGORY:** Performing Arts • **POSITION TYPE:** Internship • **DURATION:** Year-Round • **IDEAL CANDIDATE:** College Students, Career Changers, Foreigners • **APPLICANT POOL:** 20/year • **APPLICANTS ACCEPTED:** 3–4/term

ONE OF THE TOP FIFTEEN professional dance companies in the United States, BalletMet is a dynamic arts organization. Marketing and public relations interns assist with promotions, special events, public relations, media relations, and graphics. The Marketing Department is responsible for audience development, increasing the number of students enrolled in the dance academy, as well as promoting the professional dance company when touring nationally and internationally. Development interns help with fund-raising, special events, donor prospect research, and database management. The internship would involve daily support to a four-member department and exposure to the working committees of the board of trustees. The position also would include a specific project for which the intern would have primary responsibility (possibilities include research, proposal/grant writing, statistical analysis, documentation of a special event, or a campaign component). A small stipend, free parking, and complimentary tickets to performances are provided.

Contact Information: Marketing Director • BalletMet • 322 Mt. Vernon Ave. • Columbus, OH 43215 • Phone: (614) 229-4860 • Fax: (614) 229-4858

Bathhouse Theatre

REGION/HQ: Pacific Northwest/Washington • **CATEGORY:** Theatre • **POSITION TYPE:** Internship • **DURATION:** Year-Round • **IDEAL CANDIDATE:** College Students, Career Changers • **APPLICANT POOL:** 150/year • **APPLICANTS ACCEPTED:** 2–10/year

THE BATHHOUSE THEATRE is a nonprofit professional theatre that produces and presents year-round theatre. Internships are available in development, costuming, audio, outreach, managing, marketing, production, and the scene shop. Interns receive a $75-per-week stipend and free tickets to Bathhouse and other area theatres.

Contact Information: Intern Program Coordinator • Bathhouse Theatre • 7312 W. Greenlake Dr., North

• Seattle, WA 98103 • Fax: (207) 783-0053 • Web Site: www.seattlesquare.com/bathhouse

Biltmore House

REGION/HQ: Southeast/North Carolina • **CATEGORY:** Historic Site • **POSITION TYPE:** Internship • **DURATION:** Year Long • **IDEAL CANDIDATE:** College Students, Career Changers, Foreigners • **APPLICANT POOL:** 50–100/year • **APPLICANTS ACCEPTED:** 3–6/year

THE BILTMORE HOUSE IS THE largest privately owned home in the United States. It was built by George Washington Vanderbilt, grandson of Cornelius Vanderbilt, in 1895. Opened to the public in 1930, the 255-room Biltmore House is a self-supporting historic house museum. Each internship focuses on a particular aspect of the 50,000-object Biltmore collection and also acquaints the intern with the overall operation of a historic house museum. Interns work in one of three areas: object cataloging, archives management, or collections management.

Contact Information: Internship Coordinator • Biltmore House • One North Pack Square • Asheville, NC 28801 • Phone: (704) 274-6270 • Fax: (704) 274-6269

Boarshead: Michigan's Public Theater

REGION/HQ: Great Lakes/Michigan • **CATEGORY:** Theatre • **POSITION TYPE:** Internship • **DURATION:** Academic Year • **IDEAL CANDIDATE:** College Students, Career Changers, Foreigners • **APPLICANT POOL:** Varies • **APPLICANTS ACCEPTED:** 6/year

BOARSHEAD: MICHIGAN'S PUBLIC THEATER produces six mainstage productions during their season using professional actors, and produces two mainstage children's theatre productions and one touring production that tours statewide. Performance interns work and perform in all children's productions and usually perform in at least one mainstage production. Not only is performance part of the program, but all interns work on technical aspects of all shows, from building scenery to running light and sound boards. Stage management and design internships are also available. You will receive a $75-per-week stipend and housing.

Contact Information: Education Director • Boarshead: Michigan's Public Theater • 425 S. Cesar Chavez Ave.

• Lansing, MI 48933 • Phone: (517) 484-7800 • Fax: (517) 484-2564

California Council for the Humanities

REGION/HQ: Pacific Northwest/California • **CATEGORY:** Arts Council • **POSITION TYPE:** Internship • **DURATION:** Year-Round • **IDEAL CANDIDATE:** College Students, Career Changers, Foreigners • **APPLICANT POOL:** Varies • **APPLICANTS ACCEPTED:** Varies

THE HUMANITIES EXPLORE human histories, cultures, and values. The purpose of the California Council for the Humanities is to make this exploration of the state's diverse cultural heritage available to all Californians. The council accomplishes this by creating and supporting such public humanities projects as museum exhibits, documentary film and radio programs, public lecture series, and reading/discussion groups. Interns will participate in all phases of publication production, from planning and design meetings to blue lines and press checks. Interns will also gain valuable knowledge about the day-to-day functioning of a non-profit organization.

Contact Information: Alden Mudge, Communications Director • California Council for the Humanities • 312 Sutter St., Suite 601 • San Francisco, CA 94108 • Phone: (415) 391-1474 • Fax: (415) 391-1312 • Web Site: www.calhum.org

Cape Cod Life Magazine

REGION/HQ: Northeast/Massachusetts • **CATEGORY:** Media • **POSITION TYPE:** Internship • **DURATION:** Year-Round • **IDEAL CANDIDATE:** College Students, Career Changers • **APPLICANT POOL:** 20/year • **APPLICANTS ACCEPTED:** 2/term

CAPE COD LIFE IS A BIMONTHLY, regional magazine covering Cape Cod, Nantucket, and Martha's Vineyard. The staff is small, friendly, and they share a love for the area. In each issue they try to relate what is unique about their region in a way that informs and entertains. They have a paid circulation of roughly 35,000, with newsstand sales throughout the Cape and Islands, Massachusetts, and New England. Positions are available as photographers and editorial and advertising interns. This internship is a great way to gain valuable experience in magazine publishing. Interns have the opportunity to see how an award-winning publication is put together from start to finish and to be an important part of that process. They don't believe their interns should spend their summers chained to the Xerox machine or glued to a computer screen. "Because we require a personal interview, applicants with a Cape connection, either residents or summer visitors with housing, are much more likely to be chosen than applicants from afar who have no plans finalized for spending the summer on the Cape. Applicants who are familiar with or have a particular interest in the area, and our publication, are also a more likely choice for us."

Contact Information: Publishing/Editorial Director • Cape Cod Life Magazine • P.O. Box 1385 • Pocasset, MA 02559-1385 • Phone: (508) 564-4466 • Fax: (508) 564-4470

Capital Children's Museum

REGION/HQ: Washington, D.C./Washington, D.C. • **CATEGORY:** Museum • **POSITION TYPE:** Internship • **DURATION:** Year-Round • **IDEAL CANDIDATE:** College Students, Career Changers, Retired Folks • **APPLICANT POOL:** Varies • **APPLICANTS ACCEPTED:** Varies

THE CAPITAL CHILDREN'S MUSEUM is a multifaceted organization that researches and develops innovative educational programs. Its primary mission is the development of new educational structures, methods, and materials. The museum receives over 300,000 visitors annually from throughout the world, as well as 100,000 children visiting in organized school tours. Internships are available in public relations, special exhibits, volunteer department, administration, exhibit construction, museum tour guides, special events, guest artist/performer, U-TV Studio, animation lab, media arts, development and fund-raising, options school, and Model Early Learning Center

Contact Information: Susan Albers, Intern Director • Capital Children's Museum • 800 3rd St., NE • Washington, DC 20002 • Phone: (202) 675-4124 • Fax: (202) 675-4140

CEC International Partners

REGION/HQ: Northeast/New York • **CATEGORY:** Arts Administration • **POSITION TYPE:** Internship • **DURATION:** Year-Round • **IDEAL CANDIDATE:** College Students, Foreigners • **APPLICANT POOL:** Varies • **APPLICANTS ACCEPTED:** Varies

CEC (CITIZENS EXCHANGE COUNCIL) International Partners is an international environmental education and professional exchange organization. Its activities—transformed in response to the needs of the newly independent states of the former Soviet Union and the countries of Eastern Europe—now focus on the arts and the environment. ArtsLink interns assist the director, program manager, and program coordinator in administering programs linking the United States and the countries of Central/Eastern Europe and the former Soviet Union. Duties will include grants management and arts administration.

Contact Information: Cecilia Eguia, ArtsLink Coordinator • CEC International Partners • 12 W. 31st St., 4th Floor • New York, NY 10001-4415 • Phone: (212) 643-1985 • Fax: (212) 643-1996 • E-mail: cecny@igc.apc.org

Center for Folklife Programs/Cultural Studies

REGION/HQ: Washington, D.C./Washington, D.C. • **CATEGORY:** Cultural Resources • **POSITION TYPE:** Internship • **DURATION:** Year-Round • **IDEAL CANDIDATE:** College Students, Career Changers, Foreigners • **APPLICANT POOL:** 25–50/year • **APPLICANTS ACCEPTED:** Varies

THROUGH SCHOLARLY RESEARCH and public programming, the Center for Folklife Programs/Cultural Studies seeks to promote continuity, integrity, and equity for traditional ethnic, tribal, regional, minority, and working-class cultures in the United States and abroad. Staff folklorists, anthropologists, and ethnomusicologists conduct research on American and worldwide grassroots cultural traditions and make research findings available to scholarly and general audiences through the Festival of American Folklife, the Folklife Monograph/Film Series, Smithsonian/Folkways Recordings, and the Folklife archives. Internships are offered year-round in the fields of folklore, cultural anthropology, and ethnomusicology of the United States and other countries. Intern projects often center around research, design, and production for the Festival of American Folklife, the Smithsonian/Folkways Collection, or the Folklife Archives.

Contact Information: Arlene Reiniger, Intern Coordinator • Center for Folklife Programs/Cultural Studies

• Smithsonian Institution • 955 L'Enfant Plaza, Suite 2600, MRC 914 • Washington, DC 20560 • Phone: (202) 287-3259 • Fax: (202) 287-3699 • E-mail: siwp08.cfpcs.arlene@ic.si.edu

Chicago Children's Museum

REGION/HQ: Great Lakes/Illinois • **CATEGORY:** Museum • **POSITION TYPE:** Internship • **DURATION:** Year-Round • **IDEAL CANDIDATE:** College Students, Career Changers, Foreigners • **APPLICANT POOL:** Varies • **APPLICANTS ACCEPTED:** Varies

THE CHICAGO CHILDREN'S MUSEUM is an interactive children's museum that inspires creative and interactive learning and leads children to the discovery and love of learning. Positions are available in education, development, marketing, exhibits, recycle arts, video/TV education, outreach, and human resources.

Contact Information: Volunteer/Intern Services Director • Chicago Children's Museum • North Pier Chicago • 435 E. Illinois, Suite 370 • Chicago, IL 60611 • Phone: (312) 527-1000 • Fax: (312) 527-9082

City of Los Angeles Marathon

REGION/HQ: Pacific Northwest/California • **CATEGORY:** Sports Management • **POSITION TYPE:** Internship • **DURATION: SPRING** • **IDEAL CANDIDATE:** College Students, Career Changers, Retired Folks, Foreigners • **APPLICANT POOL:** Varies • **APPLICANTS ACCEPTED:** Varies

THE CITY OF LOS ANGELES MARATHON (held in March) is the third largest marathon in the world and the biggest single-day sporting event in L.A., with more than 20,000 participants, 15,000 volunteers, and one million spectators. On the same day there is also a 13,000-person bike ride, a 2,500-person 5K race, and a 10K inline-skate tour. The day before is a free senior walk (1K and 5K) and a 5,000-person pasta party. After the marathon there is a three-day health and fitness expo at the L.A. Convention Center, with over 400 booths and 100,000 attendees. People with a desire to be an integral part of the inner workings of this event have the opportunity to assist in the following areas: community relations, operations, human resources/ personnel, promotions, press, computer systems, and marketing.

Contact Information: Nick Curl, Vice President • City of Los Angeles Marathon • 11110 W. Ohio Ave., Suite 100

• Los Angeles, CA 90025 • Phone: (310) 444-5544 • Fax: (310) 473-8105 • E-mail: LAMarathon@aol.com • Web Site: www.lamarathon.com

Colonial Williamsburg Foundation

REGION/HQ: Southeast/Virginia • **CATEGORY:** Living History • **POSITION TYPE:** Internship • **DURATION:** Year-Round • **IDEAL CANDIDATE:** College Students, Career Changers, Foreigners • **APPLICANT POOL:** 100–150/year • **APPLICANTS ACCEPTED:** 30/year

THE COLONIAL WILLIAMSBURG FOUNDATION has an active program of internships administered by the Department of Museum Studies. They seek an understanding of the history and people of eighteenth-century Williamsburg and Virginia. Some areas where interns have served include architecture, architectural research, archives and records, crafts programs, decorative arts administration, historic research, interpretive education, marketing, program development, personnel, and public affairs. Tasks vary from one department to another, but often include some research.

Contact Information: Peggy McDonald-Howells, Museum Professional Services Manager • Colonial Williamsburg Foundation • P.O. Box 1776 • Williamsburg, VA 23187-1776 • Phone: (757) 220-7211 • Fax: (757) 220-7398 • Web Site: www.history.org

Colorado Historical Society

REGION/HQ: Rocky Mountains/Colorado • **CATEGORY:** Museum • **POSITION TYPE:** Internship • **DURATION:** Year-Round • **IDEAL CANDIDATE:** College Students, Career Changers • **APPLICANT POOL:** 40/year • **APPLICANTS ACCEPTED:** 5–10/term

THE PURPOSE OF THE Colorado Historical Society is to educate through collecting, preserving, and interpreting the material culture, documentary resources, and buildings and sites of the past and the present of Colorado in particular and the West in general. Areas of study include archaeology and ethnology. The society also encourages and fosters preservation, conservation, restoration, and appreciation of such resources through exhibitions, research, publications, programs, and related activities. The society operates fourteen museums and historic sites throughout Colorado, operates an extensive research library for Western history, has active publications and education programs, and has extensive collections of documents, photographs, and material culture. Internship positions are available in material culture, office of history, and roadside interpretation program, decorative and fine arts, photography and film, public relations, newspaper, education, and museum collections. Applicants should be enrolled in a degree program with a major in history, anthropology, education, or museum studies.

Contact Information: Andrew Masich, Vice President • Colorado Historical Society • 1300 Broadway • Denver, CO 80203-2137 • Phone: (303) 866-3917 • Fax: (303) 866-5739

Concord Pavilion

REGION/HQ: Pacific Northwest/California • **CATEGORY:** Performing Arts • **POSITION TYPE:** Internship • **DURATION:** Spring-Fall • **IDEAL CANDIDATE:** College Students, Career Changers, Foreigners • **APPLICANT POOL:** Varies • **APPLICANTS ACCEPTED:** Varies

THE 12,500-SEAT CONCORD PAVILION is the San Francisco Bay Area's premier outdoor amphitheatre. A variety of popular, cultural, and community performing arts events, featuring internationally renowned performers as well as local performance groups, are presented. Marketing assistant interns will work in the areas of entertainment publicity and promotion during the outdoor amphitheatre's April through October summer concert season.

Contact Information: Linda Worley, Internship Coordinator • Concord Pavilion • 2000 Kirker Pass Rd. • P.O. Box 6166 • Concord, CA 94524-1166 • Phone: (510) 798-3318 • Fax: (510) 676-7262 • Web Site: www.ci.concord.ca.us:80

Dance Theater Workshop

REGION/HQ: Northeast/New York • **CATEGORY:** Performing Arts • **POSITION TYPE:** Internship • **DURATION:** Year-Round • **IDEAL CANDIDATE:** College Students, Career Changers, Foreigners • **APPLICANT POOL:** Varies • **APPLICANTS ACCEPTED:** Varies

THE DANCE THEATER WORKSHOP is celebrating over thirty years as an organization devoted to the imaginative and innovative support of independent dance and performing artists and of the local, national, and international communities where these artists live, work, and interact. Internships are available in marketing/public relations, membership services, technical direction, finance, development, community affairs/public imaginations, and presenting/NPN and Suitcase Fund. Internship tasks are decided on a case-by-case basis, depending on the needs of the department and of the student.

Contact Information: Internship Coordinator • Dance Theater Workshop • 219 W. 19th St. • New York, NY 10011-4079 • Phone: (212) 691-6500 • Fax: (212) 633-1974

DanceAspen

REGION/HQ: Rocky Mountains/Colorado • **CATEGORY:** Festival • **POSITION TYPE:** Internship • **DURATION:** Summer • **IDEAL CANDIDATE:** College Students, Career Changers, Retired Folks, Foreigners • **APPLICANT POOL:** Varies • **APPLICANTS ACCEPTED:** 1–4/summer

THE DANCEASPEN FESTIVAL AND SCHOOL has been a significant force in American dance for over two decades. It is considered, along with Jacob's Pillow and the American Dance Festival, to be one of the three major summer festivals committed to dance in the nation. Walk in the footsteps of the world's great artists and thinkers by participating in their internship program. DanceAspen offers internships in development/fund-raising, marketing/public relations, box office management, and administration. All areas overlap each other so that the intern receives a well-rounded knowledge of the theatre/business field. Interns receive a stipend of $75 per week and housing for the summer.

Contact Information: Henry Young, Program Director • DanceAspen • P.O. Box 8745 • Aspen, CO 81612 • Phone: (970) 925-7718 • Fax: (970) 925-3041 • Web Site: www.aspenonline.com/danceaspen

Denver Art Museum

REGION/HQ: Rocky Mountains/Colorado • **CATEGORY:** Art Museum • **POSITION TYPE:** Internship • **DURATION:** Year-Round • **IDEAL CANDIDATE:** College Students • **APPLICANT POOL:** 30/year • **APPLICANTS ACCEPTED:** 15/year

INTERNS WILL ASSIST IN THE Education Department (adult programs, family and youth, school, outreach, and visitor evaluation) and a particular collection area (i.e., American/European, Asian, Pre-Columbian, American-Indian). Although a volunteer position, you will receive free membership to the museum and any programs sponsored by the Education Department.

Contact Information: Rogene Cuerden, Education Administrator • Denver Art Museum • 100 W. 14th Ave. Parkway • Denver, CO 80204 • Phone: (303) 640-2953 • Fax: (303) 640-7711

Denver Center Theatre Company

REGION/HQ: Rocky Mountains/Colorado
• **CATEGORY:** Theatre • **POSITION TYPE:** Internship
• **DURATION:** Year-Round • **IDEAL CANDIDATE:** College Students, Career Changers, Foreigners
• **APPLICANT POOL:** Varies • **APPLICANTS ACCEPTED:** Varies

THE DENVER CENTER THEATRE COMPANY is a nonprofit regional theatre which produces twelve productions in four theatres and tours productions locally, nationally, and internationally. Internships are available in lighting design, scene painting, technical production, properties, sound, costume/wigs/wardrobe, scene design, stage management/production, literary, and administration/marketing. A limited scholarship stipend may be available, pending qualifications and availability. Perks include complimentary or discount tickets to DCTC productions. "These internships are not glamorous. They will involve hard work, long hours, and a willingness to contribute to the entire process in the most professional and positive manner possible. Only the most dedicated people should apply."

Contact Information: Brad Russell, Assistant to the Producing Director • Denver Center Theatre Company • 1050 13th St. • Denver, CO 80204 • Phone: (303) 893-4000 • Fax: (303) 825-2117 • Web Site: www. artstozoo.org/denvercenter

Florida Studio Theatre

REGION/HQ: Southeast/Florida • **CATEGORY:** Theatre • **POSITION TYPE:** Internship • **DURATION:** Year-Round • **IDEAL CANDIDATE:** College Students, Career Changers, Foreigners • **APPLICANT POOL:** 300/year • **APPLICANTS ACCEPTED:** 20–25/year

THE FLORIDA STUDIO THEATRE (FST) has been in operation in Sarasota since 1973. FST presents mainly contemporary works which have been produced on or off-Broadway within the last five years. By focusing on the works of contemporary authors, they are able to offer plays to their audiences that are not normally produced by other area theatres. The FST intern program offers intensive, practical experience in a variety of areas of the professional theatre. Each intern receives hands-on experience while working closely with one or more professionals in his or her discipline. Internships are available in acting, stage management/ directing, administrative, technical/ design, playwriting/dramaturgy, and pianist/music director. Interns can expect to work primarily in their areas of interest, but should also be willing to work in other areas as the need arises. Stipends are $40 per week, plus housing.

Contact Information: James Ashford, Assistant To The Artistic Director • Florida Studio Theatre • 1241 N. Palm Ave. • Sarasota, FL 34236-5602 • Phone: (941) 366-9017 • Fax: (941) 955-4137

GeVa Theatre

REGION/HQ: Northeast/New York • **CATEGORY:** Theatre • **POSITION TYPE:** Internship • **DURATION:** Year-Long • **IDEAL CANDIDATE:** College Students, Career Changers • **APPLICANT POOL:** Varies • **APPLICANTS ACCEPTED:** Varies

GEVA THEATRE WAS FOUNDED in 1973 and occupies a building that is on the National Registry of Historic Places. The theatre offers a distinctive season that includes a wide variety of classics, revivals, musicals, and contemporary drama representing the whole body of American and international dramatic literature. Year-long apprenticeships are available in administration, costumes, electrics, production, stage management, and the scene shop. A stipend of $170 per week is provided. Submit resume, cover letter, and two letters of recommendation by May 15.

Contact Information: Skip Greer, Education Director • GeVa Theatre • 75 Woodbury Blvd. • Rochester, NY 14607 • Phone: (716) 232-1366 • Fax: (716) 232-4031

Greek Dances Theater–Dora Stratou

REGION/HQ: Greece/Greece • **CATEGORY:** Performing Arts • **POSITION TYPE:** Unique Experience • **DURATION:** Year-Round • **IDEAL CANDIDATE:** High School Students, College Students, Career Changers, Retired Folks, Foreigners • **APPLICANT POOL:** Varies • **APPLICANTS ACCEPTED:** Varies

THIS SOCIETY WAS FOUNDED in 1953 by Dora Stratou, who remained its president until 1983. She believed in the preservation of dances as a proof of the continuity of the Greek race since antiquity. It's an institution unique in the world, with varied activities, all centered around Greek dance. As a theatre it differs from all other theatres and as a dance company it differs from other dance companies. The society has positions in dance, theatre management, ethnographic field research, and costume maintenance. Interns receive a small stipend (most have morning jobs) and are able to use the facilities and attend seminars.

Contact Information: Alkis Raftis, President • Greek Dances Theater–Dora Stratou • 8 Sholiou Str., Plaka • Athens, 105 58 • Greece • Phone: (331) 324-4395 • Fax: (331) 324-6921 • Alternate: (331) 324-6188

Headlands Center for the Arts

REGION/HQ: Pacific Northwest/California • **CATEGORY:** Arts Administration • **POSITION TYPE:** Internship • **DURATION:** Year-Round • **IDEAL CANDIDATE:** High School Students, College Students, Career Changers, Retired Folks, Foreigners • **APPLICANT POOL:** Varies • **APPLICANTS ACCEPTED:** Varies

HEADLANDS CENTER FOR THE ARTS is located in a 13,000-acre section of the Golden Gate National Recreation Area just north and west of the Golden Gate Bridge in San Francisco, and is housed in a former military fort in eleven turn-of-the-century buildings. The center is dedicated to the exploration and interpretation of the relationship between place and the creative process. It functions as a laboratory where the focus is on the artist's process of investigation and creation, rather than on presentation of work. The center offers residencies to artists of all media from the Bay Area, around the country, and the world. Arts administration and facilities technician intern positions are available.

Contact Information: Residency Coordinator • Headlands Center for the Arts • 944 Fort Barry • Sausalito, CA 94965 • Phone: (415) 331-2787 • Fax: (415) 331-3857

International Documentary Association

REGION/HQ: Pacific Northwest/California • **CATEGORY:** Film • **POSITION TYPE:** Internship • **DURATION:** Year-Round • **IDEAL CANDIDATE:** College Students, Foreigners • **APPLICANT POOL:** 50–75/year • **APPLICANTS ACCEPTED:** 1–3/term

THE INTERNATIONAL DOCUMENTARY Association is a nonprofit association founded in 1982 to promote non-fiction film and video, to support the efforts of documentary film and video makers around the world, and to increase public appreciation and demand for documentary films for television programs. IDA and its cultural/educational arm, the International Documentary Foundation, work to raise public consciousness of the documentary's importance to a free society and to encourage international understanding and cooperation through the medium of documentary film. Interning is a great way of finding out what is going on in the microcosm of nonfiction filmmakers—the first step towards getting a foot in the door (and a job).

Contact Information: Thomas Gianakopoulos, Administrative Coordinator • International Documentary Association • 1551 S. Robertson Blvd., Suite 201 • Los Angeles, CA 90035-4257 • Phone: (310) 284-8422 • Fax: (310) 785-9334 • E-mail: idf@netcom.com

Judah L. Magnes Museum

REGION/HQ: Pacific Northwest/California • **CATEGORY:** Museum • **POSITION TYPE:** Internship • **DURATION:** Year-Round • **IDEAL CANDIDATE:** College Students, Career Changers, Foreigners • **APPLICANT POOL:** 10/year • **APPLICANTS ACCEPTED:** 3/year

THE MAGNES MUSEUM has a permanent collection of approximately 10,000 art and historical objects that reflect the culture of Jewish communities from many different countries and periods. The Magnes has a collecting emphasis on rescuing and preserving objects from vanishing Oriental and Sephardic Jewish communities, such as those from India, Yemen, Turkey, Morocco, and Greece. The museum also houses the Western Jewish History

Center—which collects and preserves over 20,000 pieces of archival material on Western American pioneer Jewish organizations, businesses, and families—and the Harry and Dorathy Blumenthal Rare Book and Manuscript Library. Because the Magnes is a small museum, interns have the opportunity to work closely with upper-level staff and make a uniquely significant contribution to a variety of museum activities, such as research and care of the art, history, archive, and library collections; publicity and coordination of exhibitions; fund-raising and administration; and daily operations. All internship projects are planned to provide the highest level of training possible, and projects are individually tailored to the skills and experience of each intern.

Contact Information: Marni Welch, Registrar • Judah L. Magnes Museum • The Jewish Museum of the West • 2911 Russell St. • Berkeley, CA 94705 • Phone: (510) 549-6955 • Fax: (510) 849-3650

Kidsnet

REGION/HQ: Washington, D.C./Washington, D.C. • **CATEGORY:** Media • **POSITION TYPE:** Internship • **DURATION:** Year-Round • **IDEAL CANDIDATE:** College Students • **APPLICANT POOL:** Varies • **APPLICANTS ACCEPTED:** Varies

KIDSNET, THE COMPUTERIZED clearinghouse for children's electronic media, is seeking enthusiastic, imaginative individuals to serve as interns in its Washington, D.C. office. Interns will work in research/special projects, on-line/computerized services, or general operations/public affairs. Most interns are studying communications, media studies, English, journalism, or K–12 education.

Contact Information: Beth Myhre, Research Manager • Kidsnet • 6856 Eastern Ave., NW, Suite 208 • Washington, DC 20012 • Phone: (202) 291-1400 • Fax: (202) 882-7315 • E-mail: kidsnet@aol.com

Loggins Promotion/ Backstage Management

REGION/HQ: Pacific Northwest/California • **CATEGORY:** Entertainment • **POSITION TYPE:** Internship 8 **DURATION:** Year-Round • **IDEAL CANDIDATE:** College Students, Career Changers, Retired Folks, Foreigners • **APPLICANT POOL:** Varies • **APPLICANTS ACCEPTED:** Varies

LOGGINS PROMOTION/BACKSTAGE MANAGEMENT is an entertainment management and promotions company. Internship positions include entertainment management/radio promotion (book live performances, oversee contracts, bookkeeping, marketing/public relations, and work with merchants, manufacturers, and the general public); talent scout (search for new talent/potential clients); and producer (oversee recordings for tonal and sonic quality and book studio times).

Contact Information: Paul Loggins, Internship Coordinator • Loggins Promotion/Backstage Management • 26239 Senater Ave. • Harbor City, CA 90710 • Phone: (310) 325-2500 • Fax: (310) 325-2560 • E-mail: LogProd@aol.com

Maine State Music Theatre

REGION/HQ: Northeast/Maine • **CATEGORY:** Theatre • **POSITION TYPE:** Internship • **DURATION:** Summer • **IDEAL CANDIDATE:** College Students • **APPLICANT POOL:** Varies • **APPLICANTS ACCEPTED:** Varies

MAINE STATE MUSIC THEATRE, located on the Bowdoin College campus, is Maine's only professional resident music theatre. Their internship program is hands-on and puts you in the midst of some of the best professionals from around the country. All interns attend classes given by various members of the professional company and are overseen by an academic supervisor. Internships are available in both performance and production. Production includes administration, box office, carpentry, costumes, house management, lighting, marketing, music direction, painting, props, stage management, and sound. Because team playing is essential for the summer, each intern will be required to work outside his or her particular concentration. Everyone should be prepared to work running crews for shows and log many hours during hectic changeovers. Interns receive a weekly stipend of $30 to $50 plus room and board.

Contact Information: Julie Ray, Company Manager • Maine State Music Theatre • 14 Maine St., Suite 109 • Brunswick, ME 04011 • Phone: (207) 725-8769 • Fax: (207) 725-1199 • E-mail: msmtstev@biddeford. com • Web Site: www.msmt.org

McCarter Theatre

REGION/HQ: Northeast/New Jersey • **CATEGORY:** Theatre • **POSITION TYPE:** Internship • **DURATION:** Academic year • **IDEAL CANDIDATE:** College Students, Career Changers • **APPLICANT POOL:** 100/year • **APPLICANTS ACCEPTED:** 12/year

THE McCARTER THEATRE CENTER for the Performing Arts is a nationally recognized, nonprofit performing arts organization which presents an annual series of theatre, music, dance, and special events. Over 200 events are produced annually at McCarter, which resides on the campus of Princeton University. Internships are available in front-of-house/special events, company/production management, directing, development, library management, marketing, properties, stage management, costumes/wardrobe, and technical direction/scene shop. Interns can also expect to perform basic, everyday tasks for the benefit of the theatre, such as answering phones, staffing student matinees, stuffing envelopes, and running errands. All interns will be directly involved with the production of McCarter's annual new-play festival. McCarter provides housing and a $50-per-week stipend. It's also possible for some interns to obtain employment within the theatre for additional compensation.

Contact Information: Kathleen Kund Nolan, General Manager • McCarter Theatre • 91 University Pl. • Princeton, NJ 08540 • Phone: (609) 683-9100 • Fax: (609) 497-0369

Museum of Contemporary Art

REGION/HQ: Great Lakes/Illinois • **CATEGORY:** Art Museum • **POSITION TYPE:** Internship • **DURATION:** Year-Round • **IDEAL CANDIDATE:** College Students, Career Changers, Foreigners • **APPLICANT POOL:** 100–300/year • **APPLICANTS ACCEPTED:** Varies

THE MUSEUM OF CONTEMPORARY ART, established in 1967, focuses on international, multimedia work from 1945 to the present and maintains a permanent collection of over 2,000 works and over 3,000 artist's books. Positions are available in administration, curatorial, collections and exhibitions, development, corporate and foundation relations, editorial, education, graphic design, information systems, library, marketing, membership, photo archives, public relations, registrar, retail/wholesale, and special events/hospitality. Interns are exposed to a diversity of events within the program and the museum, as well as the day-to-day practical operations of the internal departments in the museum.

Contact Information: Intern Coordinator • Museum of Contemporary Art • 220 E. Chicago Ave. • Chicago, IL 60611 • Phone: (312) 280-2660 • Fax: (312) 280-2687

National Building Museum

REGION/HQ: Washington, D.C./Washington, D.C. • **CATEGORY:** Museum • **POSITION TYPE:** Internship • **DURATION:** Year-Round • **IDEAL CANDIDATE:** College Students, Career Changers, Foreigners • **APPLICANT POOL:** 15/term • **APPLICANTS ACCEPTED:** 8/term

THE NATIONAL BUILDING MUSEUM was mandated by an act of Congress in 1980 to explore American achievements in building and to foster awareness and concern for the built environment. The museum's exhibitions and educational programs interpret the world of engineering and architectural design, environmental and urban planning, building crafts and materials, and historic preservation. As an intern, you may work in the following departments: Exhibitions, Collections, Education, Public Affairs, Development, and Administration. All interns participate in an initial training program that includes background information about the organization and history of the museum and its programs, information specific to their assignment, and sessions on communication techniques and learning styles.

Contact Information: Marcia Gregory, Volunteer/Visitor Services Coordinator • National Building Museum • 401 F St., NW • Washington, DC 20001 • Phone: (202) 272-2448 • Fax: (202) 272-2564 • E-mail: mgregory@nbm.org • Web Site: www.nbm.org

National Museum of American Art

REGION/HQ: Washington, D.C./Washington, D.C. • **CATEGORY:** Art Museum • **POSITION TYPE:** Internship • **DURATION:** Year-Round • **IDEAL CANDIDATE:** College Students • **APPLICANT POOL:** Varies • **APPLICANTS ACCEPTED:** Varies

THE SMITHSONIAN INSTITUTION'S National Museum of American Art, the nation's oldest federal art collection, is dedicated to the preservation, exhibition, and study of the visual arts of the United States. Interns work in any of the museum's nine offices including Curatorial Division, Design and Production, Publications, Registration and Collections Management, Educational Programs, The Renwick Gallery, Research and Scholars Center, External Affairs, and Administration.

Contact Information: Intern Program Officer • National Museum of American Art • Research & Scholars Center • Smithsonian Institution • Washington, DC 20560 • Phone: (202) 357-2714 • Fax: (202) 786-2607

New Tuners Theatre

REGION/HQ: Great Lakes/Illinois • **CATEGORY:** Theatre • **POSITION TYPE:** Internship • **DURATION:** Year-Round • **IDEAL CANDIDATE:** College Students, Career Changers, Foreigners • **APPLICANT POOL:** 50/year • **APPLICANTS ACCEPTED:** 3/year

THIS GREAT OPPORTUNITY to meet and work with a variety of theatre personnel. New Tuners offers a workshop for composers, bookwriters, and lyricists of the musical theatre, which interns may also participate in as part of their remuneration. New Tuners gives hands-on opportunities to work on new musical projects while the projects are developing. With a small staff, interns are given a chance to work intensely in different areas of interest. You will receive a $500-per-month stipend.

Contact Information: General Manager • New Tuners Theatre • 1225 W. Belmont Ave. • Chicago, IL 60657-3205 • Phone: (312) 929-7367 • Fax: (312) 327-1404

New York Foundation for the Arts

REGION/HQ: Northeast/New York • **CATEGORY:** Arts Council • **POSITION TYPE:** Internship • **DURATION:** Year-Round • **IDEAL CANDIDATE:** College Students, Career Changers, Foreigners • **APPLICANT POOL:** 30–40/year • **APPLICANTS ACCEPTED:** Varies

THE NEW YORK FOUNDATION FOR THE ARTS is one of the largest providers of grants and services to individual artists of all artistic disciplines in the United States. Through fellowships, artist residencies, project support, loans, and information services, the foundation works with artists and organizations throughout New York State to bring the work of contemporary artists to the public. Interns are needed in nearly all of the foundation's pro-

grams, as well as in general administrative areas such as planning/special projects, development, and finance. Specific responsibilities will vary according to the experience and interests of the intern.

Contact Information: Internship Program Director • New York Foundation for the Arts • 155 Avenue of the Americas • New York, NY 10013-1507 • Phone: (212) 366-6900 • Fax: (212) 366-1778

Norlands Living History Center

REGION/HQ: Northeast/Maine • **CATEGORY:** Living History • **POSITION TYPE:** Internship • **DURATION:** Year-Round • **IDEAL CANDIDATE:** College Students, Career Changers, Foreigners • **APPLICANT POOL:** Varies • **APPLICANTS ACCEPTED:** Varies

NORLANDS IS AN OUTDOOR museum and living history farm located on a windswept hillside in southwestern Maine. The site is designated a national historic district consisting of 445 acres of rolling farmland and woodland, and five buildings, the remnants of a nineteenth-century crossroads community. The buildings include the Norlands mansion, home of the Washburns, a nationally prominent nineteenth-century family. Interns will become familiar with the local history and everyday lifestyles of the area, including economics, social values, and recreation. They will then choose a nineteenth-century local character whose life they will portray while doing first-person interpretation. As part of their training, interns will participate in an adult live-in, a three-day, in-depth experience of nineteenth-century rural New England life. A $200-per-month stipend, plus housing, is provided.

Contact Information: Director • Norlands Living History Center • RFD 2, Box 1740 • Livermore Falls, ME 04254 • Phone: (207) 897-4366

North Carolina Amateur Sports

REGION/HQ: Southeast/North Carolina • **CATEGORY:** Sports Management • **POSITION TYPE:** Internship • **DURATION:** Spring/Summer • **IDEAL CANDIDATE:** College Students, Career Changers, Foreigners • **APPLICANT POOL:** Varies • **APPLICANTS ACCEPTED:** 7–11/year

THE MISSION OF North Carolina Amateur Sports is to promote the Olympic movement through amateur sports in North Carolina. The goals of the organization are to produce the State Games of North Carolina, sponsor state conferences on the Olympic movement and amateur sports, attract national and international events and conferences to North Carolina, assist other amateur sports events in the state, and increase public awareness of the ideals and benefits of the Olympic movement and amateur sports. Internship opportunities are varied and allow interns to gain hands-on experience in sports promotions and event management. Interns may work in these program areas: operations, media/promotions, data services/finance, volunteer services, and special projects. Interns have tremendous responsibility placed on them, which is believed will prepare interns for any job that they pursue in the future.

Contact Information: Chuck Hobgood, Associate Executive Director • North Carolina Amateur Sports • P.O. Box 12727 • Research Triangle Park, NC 27709 • Phone: (919) 361-1133 • Fax: (919) 361-2559 • E-mail: ncamateur@aol.com

North Carolina Arts Council

REGION/HQ: Southeast/North Carolina • **CATEGORY:** Arts Council • **POSITION TYPE:** Internship • **DURATION:** Year-Round • **IDEAL CANDIDATE:** College Students, Career Changers • **APPLICANT POOL:** Varies • **APPLICANTS ACCEPTED:** Varies

THE NORTH CAROLINA ARTS COUNCIL strives to enrich the cultural life of the state by nurturing and supporting excellence in the arts and by providing opportunities for every North Carolinian to experience the arts. They offer Community Arts Administration internships, with a $3,000 stipend for three months.

Contact Information: Viola Bullock, Arts in Communities Assistant • North Carolina Arts Council • Department Of Cultural Resources • Raleigh, NC 27601-2807 • Phone: (919) 733-7897 • Fax: (919) 715-5406 • E-mail: vbullock@ncacmail.dcr.state.nc.us

Northwest Folklife

REGION/HQ: Pacific Northwest/Washington • **CATEGORY:** Cultural Resources • **POSITION TYPE:** Internship • **DURATION:** Year-Round • **IDEAL**

CANDIDATE: College Students, Career Changers, Retired Folks, Foreigners • **APPLICANT POOL:** Varies • **APPLICANTS ACCEPTED:** Varies

NORTHWEST FOLKLIFE is a comprehensive multicultural arts organization dedicated to serving the ethnic, traditional, and folk arts communities of the Northwest. Northwest Folklife creates opportunities for individuals and communities to celebrate, share, and sustain the vitality of ethnic and traditional arts for present and future generations. Programs include the annual Northwest Folklife Festival, the Folklife Museum, Traditional World Cultures in Contemporary Education (teacher training seminars), Families Together (professional artists working with low-income families' children on arts projects), and more. Interns are needed in marketing, development, program, volunteers, exhibits, production, and various special projects. They also have a number of volunteer and paid production positions available for the annual Festival. Most positions receive a $200-per-month stipend.

Contact Information: Sheila Daniels, Customer Service • Northwest Folklife • 305 Harrison St. • Seattle, WA 98109-4695 • Phone: (206) 684-7300 • Fax: (206) 684-7190 • E-mail: folklife@nwfolklife.org • Web Site: www.nwfolklife.org/folklife

Southern Exposure

REGION/HQ: Pacific Northwest/California • **CATEGORY:** Arts Administration • **POSITION TYPE:** Internship • **DURATION:** Year-Round • **IDEAL CANDIDATE:** College Students, Career Changers, Retired Folks, Foreigners • **APPLICANT POOL:** 20–40/year • **APPLICANTS ACCEPTED:** 6–10/term

ANYONE INTERESTED IN live/work co-op spaces will be happy with this gallery. Called "Southern Exposure" because of its south of Market Street location, the gallery is a nonprofit that showcases emerging artists. Although many of the featured pieces are by local talent, the gallery's art exchange program salutes pieces from around the globe. The offerings run the gamut in terms of both media and quality, all the way from obscure, backwater Czech pieces to mainstream, commercial art. A range of exhibitions, lectures, panel discussions, workshops, and performances are available to the public.

Interns are vital elements of Southern Exposure's staffing picture. They provide thorough orientation, training, evaluation, and recognition of their interns and volunteers. They view their internship program as an extension of their educational outreach service that helps to expand and diversify community interaction. Internships are offered in the following areas: arts administration, artists in education, live events, installation/exhibition coordination, curatorial, and membership coordination.

Contact Information: Susan López, Intern Coordinator • Southern Exposure • 401 Alabama at 17th St. • San Francisco, CA 94110 • Phone: (415) 863-2141 • Fax: (415) 863-1841 • E-mail: soex@artswire.org • Web Site: www.soex.org

Stage One

REGION/HQ: Southeast/Kentucky • **CATEGORY:** Theatre • **POSITION TYPE:** Internship • **DURATION:** Academic year • **IDEAL CANDIDATE:** College Students, Career Changers, Foreigners • **APPLICANT POOL:** Varies • **APPLICANTS ACCEPTED:** Varies

STAGE ONE IS AN equity theatre for young audiences, with a staff of professional actors, directors, administrators, designers, and educators dedicated to bringing the finest quality live theatre to children and young people. Acting, public relations/marketing, and production/company management positions are available to students who are intelligent, skilled, enthusiastic, and dependable in their field of expertise. A $150-per-week stipend is provided.

Contact Information: J. Daniel Herring, Associate Director • Stage One • Professional Theatre for Young Audiences • 5 Riverfront Plaza • Louisville, KY 40202-2957 • Phone: (502) 589-5946 • Fax: (502) 588-5910 • E-mail: kystageone@aol.com

TADA!

REGION/HQ: Northeast/New York • **CATEGORY:** Theatre • **POSITION TYPE:** Internship • **DURATION:** Year-Round • **IDEAL CANDIDATE:** College Students, Career Changers, Foreigners • **APPLICANT POOL:** Varies • **APPLICANTS ACCEPTED:** Varies

TADA! IS NEW YORK'S only children's theatre ensemble company producing professional productions performed by children for family audiences. All interns work directly with professional, New York–based designers and directors and receive a practical education through experience. The following are paid positions

(which require experience): stage manager, ass stage manager, theater electrician/board op wardrobe mistress/seamstress, house manager, a office. The following positions are unpaid: assistant to set, costume or lighting designers, assistant to technical director, props coordinator, production assistant, assistant to the producer, administrative assistant, and literary intern.

Contact Information: Tobe Sevush, Managing Director • TADA! • 120 West 28th St. • New York, NY 10001 • Phone: (212) 627-1732 • Fax: (212) 243-6736 • E-mail: TADA@ziplink.net • Web Site: www.tadatheater.com

Wadsworth Atheneum

REGION/HQ: Northeast/Connecticut • **CATEGORY:** Art Museum • **POSITION TYPE:** Internship • **DURATION:** Spring-Fall • **IDEAL CANDIDATE:** College Students • **APPLICANT POOL:** 12–15/term • **APPLICANTS ACCEPTED:** 10–12/term

THE WADSWORTH ATHENEUM is the oldest public art museum in the country. It houses a fine arts collection with particular strengths in nineteenth-century American painting, Renaissance and Baroque European painting, European and American decorative arts, the Amistad Foundation Collection of African-American art and artifacts, contemporary art, and the Nutting collection of Colonial American furniture. Students are assigned to work in specific departments, according to their interests and skills. Internships are available in the following departments: Curatorial, Development, Design and Installation, Photographic Services, Business Office, the Museum Shop, Education, Library, Registrar, Membership, and Public Information. In addition, interns will participate in weekly museum-studies seminars. The seminars provide the intern with an overview of the various departments and the ways in which these departments interact within the museum.

Contact Information: Linda Friedlaender, Associate Curator of Education • Wadsworth Atheneum • 600 Main St. • Hartford, CT 06103-2990 • Phone: (860) 278-2670 • Fax: (860) 527-0803

Writers Corps

REGION/HQ: Washington, D.C./Washington, D.C. • **CATEGORY:** Community Service • **POSITION TYPE:** Internship/Seasonal • **DURATION:** Year-Round

• **IDEAL CANDIDATE:** College Students • **APPLICANT POOL:** 250/year • **APPLICANTS ACCEPTED:** 30/year

TEACH WRITING IN COMMUNITY settings to groups of people, from elementary age to seniors. You might work in schools, hospitals, jails, homeless shelters, community centers, and service organizations. The best candidates are writers with teaching experience in a community setting and those who are committed to community service. An education award is provided.

Contact Information: Ed Taylor, National Coordinator • Writers Corps • National Endowment For The Arts • 1100 Pennsylvania Ave., NW • Washington, DC 20506 • Phone: (202) 682-5796 • Fax: (202) 682-5660

Holistic Learning Centers . . . .

Esalen Institute

Big Sur, California

Founded in the sixties, the world's first holistic center has flourished, continually pushing the envelope of human potential. Its activities consist of public seminars, residential work-study programs, invitational conferences, research, and semiautonomous projects. This unique "experiment" has become more of a success than anyone, even its co-founders, could have dreamed. Esalen Institute, Highway 1, Big Sur, CA 93920-9616; Fax: (408) 667-2724; friends@esalen.org; www.esalen.org/ns1.1

Hollyhock

Cortes Island, British Columbia, Canada

Located on an island 150 kilometers north of Vancouver, Hollyhock offers over seventy workshops from March through October and on holidays: naturalist programs, massage, kayaking, sailing, etc. Hollyhock— Holistic Learning Center, Box 127, Manson's Landing, Cortes Island, BC V0P 1K0, Canada; (800) 933-6339, (250) 935-6576; hollyhock@oberon.ark.com; www. hollyhock.bc.ca

New York Open Center

New York City

In the past decade the New York Open Center has become the largest urban holistic learning center in the United States, serving some 20,000 participants each year. The center presents nearly 1,000 courses annually on topics of alternative health and bodywork disciplines, in-depth psychologies, sociocultural issues, spiritual and meditative teachings, and multicultural arts. The New York Open Center, 83 Spring St., New York, NY 10012; (212) 219-2527; box@opencenter.org; www.opencenter.org

Omega Institute for Holistic Studies

Rhinebeck, New York

The Omega Institute has a work exchange program for the summer. For details, write to: Omega Institute, 260 Lake Dr., Rhinebeck, NY 12572-3212

Addresses

American Association of Museums
REGION/HQ: Washington, D.C./Washington, D.C.
CATEGORY: Museum
CONTACT INFORMATION:
Program Director
American Association of Museums
1225 I St., NW
Washington, DC 20005
Phone: (202) 289-1818

American Council for the Arts
REGION/HQ: Northeast/New York
CATEGORY: Arts Council
CONTACT INFORMATION:
Program Director
American Council for the Arts
One E. 53rd St.
New York, NY 10022
Phone: (212) 223-2787

The Archaeological Conservancy
REGION/HQ: South/Midwest/New Mexico
CATEGORY: Archaeology
CONTACT INFORMATION:
Program Director
The Archaeological Conservancy
5301 Central Ave., NE, Suite 1218
Albuquerque, NM 87108
Phone: (505) 266-1540

Aspen Music Festival & School
REGION/HQ: Rocky Mountains/Colorado
CATEGORY: Festival
CONTACT INFORMATION:
Program Director
Aspen Music Festival & School
2 Music School Rd.
Aspen, CO 81611-8500
Phone: (303) 925-3254

Association of Independent Video & Filmmakers
REGION/HQ: Northeast/New York
CATEGORY: Film
CONTACT INFORMATION:
Administrative Director
Association of Independent Video & Filmmakers
625 Broadway, 9th Floor
New York, NY 10012
Phone: (212) 473-3400 • Fax: (212) 677-8732

Banff Festival of the Arts
REGION/HQ: Canada/Alberta
CATEGORY: Festival
CONTACT INFORMATION:
Program Director
Banff Festival of the Arts
Banff Center For The Arts
Box 1020
Banff, Alberta T0L 0C0
Canada
Phone: (403) 762-6100

Bar Harbor Music Festival
REGION/HQ: Northeast/Maine
CATEGORY: Festival
CONTACT INFORMATION:
Staffing Director
Bar Harbor Music Festival
59 Cottage St.
Bar Harbor, ME 04609
Phone: (212) 222-1026

Center for American Archaeology
REGION/HQ: Great Lakes/Illinois
CATEGORY: Archaeology
CONTACT INFORMATION:
Education Director
Center for American Archaeology
P.O. Box 366
Kampsville, IL 62053
Phone: (618) 653-4316 • Fax: (618) 653-4232

Corporation for Public Broadcasting
REGION/HQ: Washington, D.C./Washington, D.C.
CATEGORY: Broadcasting
CONTACT INFORMATION:
Internship Coordinator
Corporation for Public Broadcasting
901 E St., NW
Washington, DC 20004
Phone: (202) 879-9600 • Fax: (202) 783-1019

Detroit Free Press
REGION/HQ: Great Lakes/Michigan
CATEGORY: Media
CONTACT INFORMATION:
Joe Grimm, Recruiter
Detroit Free Press
321 W. Lafayette Blvd.
Detroit, MI 48226
Phone: (313) 222-6490 • Fax: (313) 222-5981
• Toll Free: (800) 678-6400

Dow Jones Newspaper Fund, Inc.
REGION/HQ: Northeast/New Jersey
CATEGORY: Media
CONTACT INFORMATION:
Editing Intern Program Coordinator
Dow Jones Newspaper Fund, Inc.
P.O. Box 300
Princeton, NJ 08543-0300
Phone: (609) 452-2820 • Fax: (609) 520-5804
• Toll Free: (800) 369-3863

Howell Living History Farm
REGION/HQ: Northeast/New Jersey
CATEGORY: Living History
CONTACT INFORMATION:
Robert Flory, Intern Program Coordinator
Howell Living History Farm
101 Hunter Rd.
Titusville, NJ 08560

Institute for Wellness and Sports Medicine
REGION/HQ: Southeast/Mississippi
CATEGORY: Sports Management
CONTACT INFORMATION:
Program Director
Institute for Wellness and Sports Medicine
P.O. Box 16796
Hattiesburg, MS 39402
Phone: (601) 268-5010 • Fax: (601) 268-8007

League of American Theatres & Producers
REGION/HQ: Northeast/New York
CATEGORY: Theatre
CONTACT INFORMATION:
Program Administrator
League of American Theatres & Producers
226 W. 47th St.
New York, NY 10036
Phone: (212) 764-1122

Maya Research Program
REGION/HQ: South/Midwest/Texas
CATEGORY: Research
CONTACT INFORMATION:
Program Director
Maya Research Program
P.O. Box 15376
San Antonio, TX 78212

National Association of College Broadcasters
REGION/HQ: Nationwide/Rhode Island
CATEGORY: Broadcasting
CONTACT INFORMATION:
Program Director
National Association of College Broadcasters
71 George St.
Providence, RI 02912-1824
Phone: (401) 863-2225 • Fax: (401) 863-2221

National Endowment for the Humanities
REGION/HQ: Washington, D.C./Washington, D.C.
CATEGORY: Arts Council
CONTACT INFORMATION:
Deputy Chairman
National Endowment for the Humanities
1100 Pennsylvania Ave., NW
Washington, DC 20506
Phone: (202) 606-8623

National News Bureau
REGION/HQ: Northeast/Pennsylvania
CATEGORY: Media
CONTACT INFORMATION:
Publisher
National News Bureau
P.O. Box 43039
Philadelphia, PA 19129

National Public Radio
REGION/HQ: Washington, D.C./Washington, D.C.
CATEGORY: Broadcasting
CONTACT INFORMATION:
Internship Coordinator
National Public Radio
635 Massachusetts Ave.
Washington, DC 20001-3753
Phone: (202) 414-2000

Ogunquit Playhouse

REGION/HQ: Northeast/Maine

CATEGORY: Theatre

CONTACT INFORMATION:
John Lane, Producer
Ogunquit Playhouse
P.O. Box 915
Ogunquit, ME 03907
Phone: (207) 646-2402

Olympic Music Festival

REGION/HQ: Pacific Northwest/Washington

CATEGORY: Festival

CONTACT INFORMATION:
Program Director
Olympic Music Festival
P.O. Box 45776
Seattle, WA 98145
Phone: (206) 527-8839

Tanglewood Music Festival

REGION/HQ: Northeast/Massachusetts

CATEGORY: Festival

CONTACT INFORMATION:
Staffing Director
Tanglewood Music Festival
Lenox, MA 01240
Phone: (413) 637-1600

Utah Arts Council

REGION/HQ: Rocky Mountains/Utah

CATEGORY: Arts Council

CONTACT INFORMATION:
Program Director
Utah Arts Council
617 E. South Temple
Salt Lake City, UT 84102
Phone: (801) 533-5895

Women's Sports & Fitness Magazine

REGION/HQ: Rocky Mountains/Colorado

CATEGORY: Sports Management

CONTACT INFORMATION:
Associate Editor
Women's Sports & Fitness Magazine
2025 Pearl St.
Boulder, CO 80302
Phone: (303) 440-5111 • Fax: (303) 440-3313

Wyoming Arts Council

REGION/HQ: Rocky Mountains/Wyoming

CATEGORY: Arts Council

CONTACT INFORMATION:
Internship Program Manager
Wyoming Arts Council
2320 Capitol Ave.
Cheyenne, WY 82002
Phone: (307) 777-7742

Youth Volunteer Corps of America

REGION/HQ: South/Midwest/Kansas

CATEGORY: Youth Service

CONTACT INFORMATION:
Program Director
Youth Volunteer Corps of America
6310 Lamar Ave., Suite 145
Overland Park, KS 66202-4247
Phone: (913) 432-9822 • Fax: (913) 432-3313

Knowledge and experience do not necessarily speak the same language. But isn't the knowledge that comes from experience more valuable than the knowledge that doesn't?

325

The 100 Best Small Art Towns in America by John Villani. You won't find any jobs listed in this unique guide; however, it will provide you with insider information on communities that are loaded with the arts, including festivals, galleries, museums, arts agencies, and the like. (John Muir Publications, $15.95)

Each January the Archaeological Institute of America publishes the *Archaeological Fieldwork Opportunities Bulletin,* listing digs, projects, field schools, and programs open to volunteers, students, and staff all over the world. The bulletin costs $12.50, from Kendall Hunt Publishing;(800) 228-0810.

American Theatre Works publishes the annual *Summer Theatre Directory,* listing more than 400 opportunities (many of which are internships), and the *Directory of Theatre Training,* listing 350 programs for college students and recent graduates. ATW, P.O. Box 519, Dorset, VT 05251; (802) 867-2223; theatre@sover.net; www.genghis. com/theatre.htm

The **Directory of National and Regional Cultural Services Organizations**—this site lists about every credible performing arts association in the United States (with an emphasis on East Coast organizations): www.hartnet.org/~artsinct/NatRegOrg.html

Passport in Time Clearinghouse, also know as PIT, is a volunteer program that invites you to share in the thrill of discovery through archaeological and historical research. Forest Service archaeologists and historians guide volunteers in activities ranging from excavation sites to historic building restoration. Many projects involve backcountry camping in which volunteers supply their own gear and food. Some projects offer meals for a small fee; others might provide hookups for your RV. Project length generally ranges from a weekend up to a month. There is no registration fee or cost for participating. The *PIT Traveler,* a free newsletter/directory, announces current projects and is published every March and September. Contact Passport in Time Clearinghouse, Carol Ellick, Project Manager, P.O. Box 31315, Tucson, AZ 85751-1315; (800) 281-9176; sriarc@aol.com

Call for your free brochure, *What It Takes to Teach,* published by Recruiting New Teachers, 385 Concord Avenue, Suite 100, Belmont, MA 02178; (800) 45-TEACH. You can also order their book, *Careers in Teaching Handbook.*

The **U.S. Institute for Theatre Technology** publishes a directory for internships in design, management, and technical production. USITT, 10 W. 19th St., Suite 5A, New York, NY 10011

*Individuality is the salt of common life.
You may have to live in a crowd, but
you do not have to like it, nor subsist
on its food. You may have your own
orchard. You may drink at a hidden
spring. Be yourself if you would serve
others.*

—HENRY VAN DYKE

*Be not the slave of your own past.
Plunge into the sublime seas, dive deep,
and swim far, so you shall come back
with self-respect, with new power, with
an advanced experience, that shall
explain and overlook the old.*

—RALPH WALDO EMERSON

9

It is not by accident that the happiest people are those who make a conscious effort to live useful lives. Their happiness, of course, is not a shallow exhilaration where life is one continuous intoxicating party. Rather, their happiness is a deep sense of inner peace that comes when they believe their lives have meaning and that they are making a difference of good in the world.

—ERNEST FITZGERALD

Emandal—A Farm on a River

Socially R

Academy for Advanced & Strategic Studies

REGION/HQ: Washington, D.C./Washington, D.C.
• **CATEGORY:** Social Service • **POSITION TYPE:** Unique Experience • **DURATION:** Year-Round • **IDEAL CANDIDATE:** College Students, Career Changers, Foreigners • **APPLICANT POOL:** Varies • **APPLICANTS ACCEPTED:** 3–5/term

THE ACADEMY FOR ADVANCED & STRATEGIC STUDIES is a small, future-oriented think tank fostering exploration of issues that are strategic to social and personal progress. Their projects cut across current concerns, for example, the productive use of knowledge and computer operating systems; small community and economic development; arts and multimedia relations and corporate cultures; global culture wars and defense industry right-sizing; policy analysis and researchable libraries; new patterns for organizing education, health care, and transportation; appropriate tech and the smart house; and the governance of cities and the built environment. They work out of an older, four-story, 86-room building with shops, studios, theatre space, a 250,000-item library, an advanced multiserver computer network, and living space for a dozen visiting fellows, interns, or associates.

Area and Working Environment: You'll be working two miles north of the White House, at the edge of an ethnically diverse neighborhood with rows of embassies, parks, restaurants, mansions, and a skid row.

Work/Learn Program Specifics: Interns are expected to participate fully in the research and education projects of the academy, and to take responsibility for the maintenance and development of administrative functions and facilities. Your program will be created with an assigned counselor, to link your interests and abilities with their current projects and changing research priorities, and you will receive detailed and constructive criticism. This is neither a job nor exploratory employment, but a full-time learning and developmental experience that you should approach with the intensity of graduate training. Moreover, you should function as a creative professional cultivating diverse projects, as an independent consultant juggling divergent priorities, and as an adroit colleague whose first priority is providing valued products.

Duration: A minimum of fifteen weeks is required of the interns (but thirteen is well justified). Internships are available throughout the year, with three to five positions available each semester.

Compensation and Perks: Lodging and meals are available on site. A bonus of $500 ($1,000 for advanced students or excellence) is given upon successful completion of a 15-week internship.

The Ideal Candidate: Come if you want to thoroughly engage yourself in research and design; to write extensively for exploration, analysis, and exposition; and to develop a broad range of skills via hands-on projects with significant intellectual flexibility, self-initiative, and responsibility to a team effort. Especially for short terms, they look for skills that help interns begin a substantial project without lengthy preparation: a command of formal English, a practical technology or computer savvy, and a developed craft or a portfolio of finished initiatives.

Making It Happen: Send a cover letter and resume, and they'll send you details. There are no fixed application dates or particular prerequisites; still, competition for summer-only terms is brisk. They receive a heavy load of inquiries and ask that you defer phone calls or visits until you have sent your materials and have read theirs. However, if you haven't heard from them in three weeks, do call.

Contact Information: Intern Coordinator • Academy for Advanced & Strategic Studies • 1647 Lamont St., NW • Washington, DC 20010-2796 • Phone: (202) 234-6646 • Fax: (202) 667-4042

esponsible

Advocacy Institute

REGION/HQ: Washington, D.C./Washington, D.C.
• **CATEGORY:** Public Interest • **POSITION TYPE:** Internship • **DURATION:** Year-Round • **IDEAL CANDIDATE:** College Students, Career Changers • **APPLICANT POOL:** Varies • **APPLICANTS ACCEPTED:** Varies

THE ADVOCACY INSTITUTE, created in 1985, pursues a vision of the just society. Its core mission is to share the skills, guidance, and inspiration that we gain from working together with those who are advocates for social and economic justice. In a "just" society, all people must be able to participate fully in public debate, public decision-making, and the shaping of public values and policies. Such values and policies should include justice for those denied justice, economic equity for the poor and disadvantaged, public health and security for those at risk, and access to equal political power for those who have been denied a voice in the policy-making process.

Work/Learn Program Specifics: Interns generally concentrate on one of the institute's program areas, working closely with professional staff. Training interns work on a broad range of issues, across the public-interest spectrum. Development interns explore the world of philanthropy, seeking ways to increase support for advocacy and social change. Smoking control, gun violence, and transportation interns focus more specifically on these distinct issue areas. Electronic advocacy interns work with their networking team to support and develop computer networks that link advocates for social change. Administrative and management internships are also available. Also inquire about their nationwide Gas Guzzler Campaign internships! Intern tasks have included preparing curricula and materials to train public-interest advocates, interviewing issue leaders and developing case studies of advocacy campaigns, monitoring congressional hearings and tracking legislation, conducting surveys and analyzing findings, developing media and communications strategies, compiling information for publication, organizing seminars and workshops, and researching and writing action alerts and newsletter articles.

Duration: Interns are expected to work a minimum of forty hours per week, and internships generally run three to four months in length.

Compensation and Perks: The pay is $6.25 per hour.

The Ideal Candidate: Candidates should have a devotion to public-interest issues and superior writing, research, and communication skills. Word-processing skills are a must.

Making It Happen: Call or write for application materials.

Contact Information: Internship Coordinator • Advocacy Institute • 1707 L St., NW, Suite 400 • Washington, DC 20036 • Phone: (202) 659-8475 • Fax: (202) 659-8484 • E-mail: intern_info@advocacy.org

American Geographical Society

REGION/HQ: Northeast/New York • **CATEGORY:** Geography • **POSITION TYPE:** Internship • **DURATION:** Year-Round • **IDEAL CANDIDATE:** College Students, Career Changers, Foreigners • **APPLICANT POOL:** 20/year • **APPLICANTS ACCEPTED:** 3 at a time

THE AMERICAN GEOGRAPHICAL SOCIETY is the oldest geographical organization in North America. They work to expand knowledge in the field of geography through scholarly and semi-popular publications; educational travel programs; business geography teaching programs in cooperation with Junior Achievement of America; involvement with the business community (providing speakers and consulting); and promotion of better K–12 geographic education.

Work/Learn Program Specifics: Responsibilities vary according to the interns' abilities, experience, and education. Interns generally handle correspondence, organize programs in geographic education, assist with seminars and other events, conduct library research, assemble mailings, write press releases, index publications, and proof documents.

Duration: Full- or part-time positions are available, any day. They do not accept interns for less than ten weeks and never have more than three interns at once.

Compensation and Perks: No pay is provided, although they write job and graduate school recommendations for interns.

The Ideal Candidate: They prefer geography majors, although they accept those studying international affairs, economics, history, environmental affairs, or English. Foreign languages ability and computer knowledge are helpful. International students must be fluent in English.

Making It Happen: Send cover letter and resume.

INSIDER TIPS: *Know what you want from the program and be ready to describe your strongest personal assets and talents.*

Contact Information: Mary Lynne Bird, Executive Director • American Geographical Society • 120 Wall St., Suite 100 • New York, NY 10005-3904 • Phone: (212) 422-5456 • Fax: (212) 422-5480 • E-mail: amgeosoc@ earthlink.net

AmeriCorps

REGION/HQ: Nationwide/Washington, D.C.
• **CATEGORY:** Service Learning • **POSITION TYPE:** Unique Experience • **DURATION:** Year-Round • **IDEAL CANDIDATE:** College Students, Career Changers, Retired Folks • **APPLICANT POOL:** 4,000+
• **APPLICANTS ACCEPTED:** Varies

AMERICORPS IS A national service movement that engages thousands of Americans of all ages and backgrounds in a domestic Peace Corps—that is, getting things done across America by meeting our education, public safety, environmental, and human needs. Also ask about the National Senior Service Corps, which helps people aged fifty-five and older find service opportunities related to their interests and close to home. This program includes three components: foster grandparents provide support to children with special needs; senior companions offer assistance to help elderly individuals live independently; retired and senior volunteers tend to a variety of local services that range from leading local museum tours to teaching adult education computer classes. Together, these programs involve over a half-million seniors serving in tens of thousands of sites across the country. For more information call (800) 424-8867.

Area and Working Environment: More than 25,000 AmeriCorps members serve in over 430 programs across the country.

Work/Learn Program Specifics: AmeriCorps is a network of hundreds of national service programs, as diverse as America's people and its problems. The work will be tough, and AmeriCorps members won't solve all of America's problems. But if you join, you'll make a difference. AmeriCorps members get things done in the areas of education, public safety, human needs, and the environment. You might mentor teens or teach elementary school children; counsel victims of domestic violence or walk the beat with community police officers; renovate low-income housing or help the home-bound and disabled achieve self-sufficiency; test for lead paint in city apartments or restore national parks and coastlines; or tackle others of the thousands of projects AmeriCorps members are conducting right now to help their communities. First, you'll attend AmeriCorps pre-service training of up to five days. Then, you can look forward to on-the-job training by your sponsoring organization, usually a public agency or nonprofit organization. There's also in-service training like workshops and conferences to help you hone your skills.

Duration: Depending on the program, you could serve for nine months or up to three years, full- or part-time; and before, during, or after college or job training.

Compensation and Perks: AmeriCorps members receive a modest living allowance, health coverage, and a post-service education award of $4,725 ($2,362 for part-time service). Alternatively, members may elect to receive a cash award of $100 per month, payable at the end of service. Travel to your pre-service training, to your project, and back to your home after service is provided. You'll also receive noncompetitive eligibility for federal employment upon completion of one year. Beyond these benefits, AmeriCorps members learn job skills, take on new responsibilities, and become part of a national network of people committed to service, community, and country.

The Ideal Candidate: Any citizen or permanent resident age eighteen or over, with a deep desire to make a difference is eligible to join.

Making It Happen: Call for information and an application form. Joining AmeriCorps is a highly competitive process. Members are selected through a review process involving an initial screening of the application, an interview, and a review of references. Once an applicant qualifies for service, a placement officer attempts to locate a suitable assignment, taking skills and preferences into account. This process may take a few months, so an early application is advised.

Contact Information: Patricia Booker, Recruitment Administrator • AmeriCorps • Corporation For National Service • 1201 New York Ave., NW • Washington, DC 20525 • Phone: (202) 606-5000 • Fax: (202) 565-2789 • Toll Free: (800) 942-2677 • Web Site: www.cns. gov/americorps.html

Amnesty International USA—Chicago

REGION/HQ: Great Lakes/Illinois • **CATEGORY:** Human Rights • **POSITION TYPE:** Internship • **DURATION:** Year-Round • **IDEAL CANDIDATE:** High School Students, College Students, Career Changers, Retired Folks, Foreigners • **APPLICANT POOL:** Varies • **APPLICANTS ACCEPTED:** Varies

FOUNDED IN 1961, Amnesty International is a worldwide human rights movement which works impartially for the release of prisoners of conscience, for fair trials for political prisoners, and for an end to torture and executions.

Area and Working Environment: You'll work in a small and casual, yet productive and fast-paced, office.

Work/Learn Program Specifics: Community and Student Network Program coordinators will coordinate the Midwest's student program and assist with community group servicing. Internships are available in media, student/membership servicing, project, human rights literary library development, and those which are self-designed.

Duration: Program coordinator is a full-time, ten-month position, August through June; internships are available year-round, part- or full-time.

Compensation and Perks: Program coordinators receive a stipend to cover living expenses; internships are volunteer positions.

The Ideal Candidate: Interns must be able to work well, both as part of a team and independently, and have good written and verbal communication skills. In addition, a familiarity with Amnesty International, a general knowledge of international human rights issues, organizing skills, and computer experience are desired.

Making It Happen: Call/write for application. Submit completed application, resume, cover letter, and a list of two references (either academic or work-related). The program coordinator deadline is April 15; internship deadlines are rolling.

Contact Information: Intern Coordinator • Amnesty International USA—Chicago • 53 W. Jackson Blvd., Suite 1162 • Chicago, IL 60604-3606 • Phone: (312) 427-2060 • Fax: (312) 427-2589 • E-mail: aiusamwro@igc.apc.org

Amnesty International USA—D.C.

REGION/HQ: Washington, D.C./Washington, D.C. • **CATEGORY:** Human Rights • **POSITION TYPE:** Internship • **DURATION:** Year-Round • **IDEAL CANDIDATE:** College Students, Foreigners • **APPLICANT POOL:** 100/year • **APPLICANTS ACCEPTED:** Varies

THE WASHINGTON OFFICE monitors U.S. legislation concerning refugee policy, the death penalty, and international human rights treaties. Its goal is to bring about improvements in the lives of men, women, and children around the world whose human rights are being violated.

Work/Learn Program Specifics: Interns will work with staff that monitors human rights developments in one of four world regions: Africa, Asia, Latin America, and Europe/Middle East. These staff and interns ask government officials to press for improvements in specific areas of concern to Amnesty International. Usually, in the course of an internship, these interns will attend Congressional hearings; compile materials from Amnesty reports for briefing government officials, congressional aides, and others; and answer requests for human rights information from government officials and others. The office also offers legislation, media/public relations, co-groups, and campaign/country action internships.

Duration: The Washington office offers internships year-round. Most internships require a minimum commitment of thirty hours per week for ten weeks (shorter internships are possible in January; contact the office for details).

The Ideal Candidate: Applicants should possess strong written and verbal communications skills, be capable of taking on significant responsibility, be familiar with Amnesty and human rights issues, and work well as part of a team and independently.

Making It Happen: Mail or fax your resume, a cover letter expressing your interest (and please include the dates you would be available for an internship, the number of days per week you could work, and what specific internship[s] interests you), two letters of recommendation, and a brief writing sample. Deadlines: winter—November 15; spring—February 1; summer—April 1; fall—No deadline.

Contact Information: Intern Coordinator • Amnesty International USA—D.C. • 304 Pennsylvania Ave., SE

• Washington, DC 20003 • Phone: (202) 675-8573
• Fax: (202) 546-7142

Aprovecho Research Center

REGION/HQ: Pacific Northwest/Oregon
• **CATEGORY:** Sustainable Living • **POSITION TYPE:** Internship • **DURATION:** Spring-Fall • **IDEAL CANDIDATE:** College Students, Career Changers, Retired Folks, Foreigners • **APPLICANT POOL:** 20/term • **APPLICANTS ACCEPTED:** 14/term

··

APROVECHO, WHICH MEANS "make best use of" in Spanish, is the central theme of the Center—to learn how to live together sustainably and ecologically and to help others to do the same, around the world.

Area and Working Environment: The center is located in the abundant ecosystem of Oregon's Willamette Valley. Culturally-rich Eugene is just thirty minutes away.

Work/Learn Program Specifics: Daily classes teach interns basic principles of sustainable forestry, organic gardening, indigenous skills, and appropriate technology. Classes combine a holistic approach of lecture and discussion formats with practical, hands-on activities. Readings, independent projects, and field trips supplement other coursework. You'll cook with food from the garden, heat and build with wood from the forest, and utilize native plant species for food, medicine, and crafts.

Duration: Internships are ten weeks, beginning on March 1, June 1, and September 1. Classes typically run from eight to five, Monday through Friday. Weekends are open so interns can take advantage of Oregon's beautiful coastline, mountain ranges, and lakes and rivers.

Compensation and Perks: The $1,500 tuition covers room, board, and instruction for the team. One full scholarship is offered each session, usually to a student from overseas. Interns generally need only a small amount of spending money, as most necessities are provided on-site. All interns live in an eco-friendly, straw-bale dormitory.

The Ideal Candidate: The main criteria for acceptance into the program are enthusiasm, a sincere interest in the subjects of study, and a willingness to join in a cooperative learning experience. There are no specific educational or work-related prerequisites.

Making It Happen: Call for a brochure and application. Rolling admission.

INSIDER TIPS: *Interns want to learn how to live in ways that are more ecologically and socially sustainable and to acquire specific practical and intellectual skills that will aid them on this path.*

Contact Information: Interns Coordinator • Aprovecho Research Center • 80574 Hazelton Rd. • Cottage Grove, OR 97424 • Phone: (541) 942-8198 • Fax: (541) 942-0302 • E-mail: apro@efn.org • Web Site: www.efn.org/~apro

Bay Area Action

REGION/HQ: Pacific Northwest/California
• **CATEGORY:** Grassroots • **POSITION TYPE:** Internship
• **DURATION:** Year-Round • **IDEAL CANDIDATE:** College Students, Career Changers, Foreigners
• **APPLICANT POOL:** Varies • **APPLICANTS ACCEPTED:** Varies

··

BAY AREA ACTION IS A citizen education organization working in the San Francisco Bay Area to preserve and restore the environment. They are dedicated to the creation of an ecologically sound society grounded in justice, equity, and peace.

Work/Learn Program Specifics: Current projects include restoring different natural habitats around the Bay Area, educating people in organic gardening in the city, educational outreach program for grade school children, converting regular cars to electricity, developing leadership skills for high schoolers around environmental issues, educating people on the connection between food and the environment through dinners and special events, and continuing work in forest education and protection.

Duration: Opportunities are designed to fit the availability of the person.

Compensation and Perks: No compensation, although you will enjoy great social interaction, meet new friends, and have interesting conversations.

The Ideal Candidate: Basic office and computer skills are nice, but the best tool they can use is a positive, energetic attitude.

Making It Happen: Call for details. Rolling deadlines.

INSIDER TIPS: *Be interested more in getting things done than just talking about them. Keep positive, as environmental work can get negative very quickly; we try to keep it light.*

Far away there in the sunshine are my highest aspirations. I may not reach them, but I can look up and see their beauty. Believe in them and try to follow where they lead. —LOUISA MAY ALCOTT

333

Contact Information: Laura Stec, Special Projects Coordinator • Bay Area Action • 715 Colorado Ave., Suite #1 • Palo Alto, CA 94303-3913 • Phone: (415) 321-1994 • Fax: (415) 321-1995 • E-mail: baaction@igc.apc.org

Bike-Aid

REGION/HQ: Nationwide/California • **CATEGORY:** Cycling • **POSITION TYPE:** Unique Experience • **DURATION:** Year-Round • **IDEAL CANDIDATE:** College Students, Career Changers, Retired Folks, Foreigners • **APPLICANT POOL:** 250/year • **APPLICANTS ACCEPTED:** 85/year

BIKE-AID IS A VIBRANT, innovative program that coordinates an annual cross-country cycling adventure. Eighty-five individuals from around the world will cycle along three different routes, meeting, sharing with, and learning from local community groups and environmental organizations. The staff at their headquarters is young, energetic, and committed to creating positive social change through providing hands-on learning experiences relating to international development, environmental education, and activism.

Area and Working Environment: Cyclists ride from Seattle, Portland, San Francisco, or Los Angeles to Washington, D.C. Shorter routes may also be available.

Work/Learn Program Specifics: Have you ever wanted to: bicycle across the U.S.? learn about global development issues? do something for yourself and make the world a more humane place? get experience working with a nonprofit organization? If you said yes to any of the above, get involved with Bike-Aid as a participant or office intern, helping organize the rides. Bike-Aid combines physical challenge, community interaction, education, leadership, fund-raising, and community service in the empowering experience of a lifetime. Bike-Aid is an unprecedented success and a unique way to experience the United States, where you'll meet people from all walks of life, from huge cities to small hamlets.

Duration: The ride begins in mid-June and ends the third week of August in Washington, D.C. Internships and volunteer positions are available year-round.

Compensation and Perks: As a cyclist, you will raise $1 for every mile ridden, totaling $3,600. Overnight lodging is donated by schools, community organizations, and individuals, and will include some camping. Some food is donated by hosts; riders pay for the remaining food, personal expenses, equipment, occa-

sional campsites, and transportation to and from the starting and finishing points. Intern/volunteer positions are unpaid, but you will work in an upbeat, casual office atmosphere, with regularly scheduled social and educational events with other Bay Area nonprofits.

The Ideal Candidate: Beginners to prize-winning racers have participated in Bike-Aid, and riders from the ages of sixteen to sixty have met the challenge. It is not a race, and it encourages the participation of people from all backgrounds, ages, and abilities. Cyclists must be willing to live in a community throughout the summer, and intern/volunteers must be resourceful and able to work in a team environment.

Making It Happen: Call for an intern or cyclist application packet. Intern applications are accepted throughout the year; cyclists are encouraged to register by mid-March to ensure your first choice of routes.

INSIDER TIPS: *For cyclists: apply by March 31 to save on your registration fee and don't let fund-raising stop you—we have an endless source of creative ideas; after college is an excellent time to join Bike-Aid, allowing you to explore the United States in a unique way, see some towns where you may want to live or go to graduate school, and meet organizations working to build better communities across the country. For interns: apply early for summer internships which include an exciting schedule of guest speakers, field trips, social events, and participation in the Summer Leadership Conference, bringing together campus activists from around the country.*

Contact Information: Rachel Glickman, Outreach Coordinator • Bike-Aid • Overseas Development Network • 333 Valencia St., Suite 330 • San Francisco, CA 94103-3547 • Phone: (415) 431-4480 • Fax: (415) 431-5953 • Toll Free: (800) 743-3808 • E-mail: odn@igc.org • Web Site: www.igc.apc.org/odn

Boston Mobilization for Survival

REGION/HQ: Northeast/Massachusetts • **CATEGORY:** Grassroots • **POSITION TYPE:** Internship • **DURATION:** Year-Round • **IDEAL CANDIDATE:** College Students, Career Changers, Foreigners • **APPLICANT POOL:** Varies • **APPLICANTS ACCEPTED:** Varies

BOSTON MOBILIZATION FOR SURVIVAL is a leading grassroots peace and justice organization that has been organizing in Massachusetts since 1978. Current projects include organizing for single-payer health care, for cuts in military spending, and funding human needs.

Their tactics include demonstrations, direct action, lobbying, petition drives, and public education through workshops and forums.

Work/Learn Program Specifics: Interns will help end military and economic policies of the United States which maintain U.S. dominance over other nations and plunder society's resources for militarism and corporate profit; affirm self-determination, human rights, and access to a life of dignity for all people; bring about deep cuts in military spending and oppose unjust U.S. military intervention; and pass single-payer health care legislation at the state and/or national level. Internship positions include grassroots organizing, fund-raising, and development. Possible activities include outreach to religious, labor, campus, and community groups; writing campaign brochures and letters; speaking at public gatherings; promoting media coverage of issues; organizing meetings to plan and support campaigns; organizing public events, discussion groups, and demonstrations; planning and holding fund-raising events; designing an individual project; and helping with general office work.

Duration: Internships are available for any time period, for ten to twenty hours per week, or even more in the summer. Convenient schedules for both parties are easily arranged.

Compensation and Perks: They cannot pay interns at this time; however, they will help applicants find free/low-cost housing and/or part-time jobs.

The Ideal Candidate: Successful interns are organized, committed to social justice, have good people skills, and are willing to work independently. Organizing experience and computer skills are very helpful.

Making It Happen: Send a cover letter (including how many hours a week you would like to intern and what dates you plan to start and finish) and a resume or a summary of relevant experience.

Contact Information: Wells Wilkinson, Internship Coordinator • Boston Mobilization for Survival • 11 Garden St. • Cambridge, MA 02138 • Phone: (617) 354-0008 • Fax: (617) 354-2146 • E-mail: bostonmobe @igc.apc.org

Bread for the World

REGION/HQ: Washington, D.C./Maryland • **CATEGORY: HUMAN RIGHTS** • **POSITION TYPE: INTERNSHIP** • **DURATION:** Year-Round • **IDEAL CANDIDATE:** College Students, Career Changers, Retired Folks, Foreigners • **APPLICANT POOL:** Varies • **APPLICANTS ACCEPTED:** Varies

BREAD FOR THE WORLD, a Christian citizen's movement, is a national "citizen's lobby" focusing solely on hunger. The organization attempts to shape government policies that address the causes of hunger in this country and in other parts of the world. Over 42,000 members across the country write letters, make phone calls, and visit their members of Congress about legislation that addresses the immediate and root causes of hunger.

Work/Learn Program Specifics: The Bread for the World intern program allows students and others to work in departments such as media, organizing, domestic hunger issues, international hunger, annual hunger report, development, church relations, communications, administration, accounting, personnel, and library. Interns may research hunger issues, organize citizens for grassroots political action, promote BFW to churches across the denominational spectrum, produce educational materials, assist in fund-raising, develop educational services, gain managerial experience, organize seminars and workshops, and work on media projects such as videos, PSAs, and talk show tours.

Duration: Internships vary from three months to two years in the summer and spring/fall semesters with part-time and full-time positions available.

Compensation and Perks: A stipend of $13,300, plus medical benefits, is provided. Transportation expenses to and from work are reimbursed; however, interns must cover their transportation costs to and from Washington, D.C. and their own housing and living expenses. BFW will assist in finding inexpensive, or occasionally, free housing.

The Ideal Candidate: All interested students are encouraged to apply. A Christian-faith perspective; good writing, speaking, typing, and filing skills; and a background in political science, international relations, communications, economics, or grassroots organizing are preferred.

Making It Happen: Call for application form. Send completed application, cover letter with GPA stated and course listing, resume, three letters of reference, and a writing sample. An interview in person or by phone may be required. Deadlines: spring—October 1; summer—March 1; and fall—June 1.

Contact Information: Human Resources Director • Bread for the World • 1100 Wayne Ave., Suite 100

• Silver Spring, MD 20910-5603 • Phone: (301) 608-2400 • Fax: (301) 608-2401

Carrying Capacity Network

REGION/HQ: Washington, D.C./Washington, D.C.
• **CATEGORY:** Advocacy • **POSITION TYPE:** Internship
• **DURATION:** Year-Round • **IDEAL CANDIDATE:**
College Students, Career Changers, Foreigners
• **APPLICANT POOL:** Varies • **APPLICANTS ACCEPTED:**
Varies

• •

CARRYING CAPACITY NETWORK conducts an advocacy-oriented program focusing on solutions such as economic sustainability, U.S. population stabilization, immigration limitation, and resource conservation, all to preserve our quality of life. "Carrying Capacity" refers to the number of individuals who can be supported without degrading the natural, cultural, and social environment, without reducing the ability of the environment to sustain the desired quality of life over the long term.

Area and Working Environment: They are located in the Dupont Circle area of northwest Washington, D.C., within walking distance of a number of other non-profits, night spots, and embassies.

Work/Learn Program Specifics: Administrative interns assist in managing the database; answer phones; contact the media, environmental groups, and activists; and, dependent upon the applicant's skills and the organization's needs, research and write for educational and outreach purposes.

Duration: Interns should be available for a minimum commitment of three months.

Compensation and Perks: Interns receive $8 per hour, depending on experience.

The Ideal Candidate: Positions are open to college students with an interest in Carrying Capacity issues. Applicants must demonstrate enthusiasm, initiative, and responsibility, and possess strong writing, verbal, and computer skills. Previous volunteer or work experience is helpful.

Making It Happen: Send resume, cover letter, and references. Rolling deadlines.

INSIDER TIPS: *We like applicants with a genuine commitment to the environment and sustainability, but we prefer those who acknowledge the need for tough choices now and in our nation's future, rather than starry-eyed, fuzzy-thinking idealists.*

Contact Information: Leon Kolankiewicz, Network Coordinator • Carrying Capacity Network • 2000 P St., NW, Suite 240 • Washington, DC 20036-5915 • Phone: (202) 296-4548 • Fax: (202) 296-4609 • E-mail: CCN@igc.apc.org

Center for Science in the Public Interest

REGION/HQ: Washington, D.C./Washington, D.C.
• **CATEGORY:** Public Interest • **POSITION TYPE:**
Internship • **DURATION:** Year-Round • **IDEAL
CANDIDATE:** College Students, Career Changers
• **APPLICANT POOL:** Varies • **APPLICANTS ACCEPTED:**
Varies

• •

THE CENTER FOR SCIENCE in the Public Interest (CSPI) was started in 1971 by three scientists who saw the need for an organization to evaluate the effects of science and technology on society and to promote national policies responsive to consumers' interest. CSPI focuses primarily on health and nutrition issues, disclosing deceptive marketing practices, dangerous food additives or contaminants, and flawed science propagated by desire for profits. Findings are communicated in press interviews and a variety of educational materials, which include reports, books, posters, software, videos, and the center's *Nutrition Action Healthletter*.

Work/Learn Program Specifics: Nutrition and Public Policy: This project covers a broad array of topics related to nutrition and health policies, including the *Nutrition Action Healthletter*, where you will assist the editor with many aspects of the publication, including research for future articles. Legal Affairs Office: help prepare legal documents and research issues involving food and drug law and consumer protection. Alcohol and Public Policy: The project campaigns to reduce the health and social consequences of alcohol use and abuse and to counter the industry view that alcohol is a necessary part of the good life. Food Safety: This project covers animal drugs and seafood, meat and poultry inspection, sustainable agriculture, and food inspection. Marketing: review and analyze demographic data and coordinate and track the placement of acquisition packages in newspapers and advertisements. Technology: assist with software training and support, hardware troubleshooting, and basic programming.

Duration: Generally an internship is for ten weeks. The specific dates are flexible and depend on the Center's needs and the applicant's schedule.

Compensation and Perks: Undergraduate interns are paid an hourly wage of $5.25 graduate students receive $6.25 per hour.

The Ideal Candidate: Applicants should have a background in public policy, law, science, children's health, consumer law, biology, public health, marketing, or management. Experience with advocacy groups is not required, but would be advantageous.

Making It Happen: Send a cover letter indicating issues of interest, future plans, and the dates that you are available; a resume; writing sample (an informal written piece is preferred over a technical report); two letters of recommendation from instructors or employers that address your academic/work ability and character; and an official transcript. Applications are taken on a rolling basis until all positions are filled.

INSIDER TIPS: *Awards for internships are very competitive. Applicants are advised to follow the application guidelines and apply as early as possible.*

Contact Information: Human Resources Manager • Center for Science in the Public Interest • 1875 Connecticut Ave., NW, Suite 300 • Washington, DC 20009-5728 • Phone: (202) 332-9110 • Fax: (202) 265-4954 • Web Site: www.cspinet.com

Children's Defense Fund

REGION/HQ: Washington, D.C./Washington, D.C.
• **CATEGORY:** Advocacy • **POSITION TYPE:** Internship
• **DURATION:** Year-Round • **IDEAL CANDIDATE:**
College Students, Career Changers, Foreigners
• **APPLICANT POOL:** 450/year • **APPLICANTS ACCEPTED:** 50/year

"DEAR LORD. Be good to me. The sea is so wide, and my boat is so small." The Children's Defense Fund (CDF) is a nonprofit, child advocacy organization that exists to provide a strong and effective voice for American children, who cannot speak, vote, or lobby for themselves. They pay particular attention to the needs of poor, minority, and handicapped children. CDF's goal is to educate the nation about the needs of children and encourage preventative investment in children before they get sick, drop out of school, or get into trouble. They believe that preventative investment in children— through carefully planned, long-term programs and policies—is a crucial investment in the nation's future well-being.

Work/Learn Program Specifics: CDF engages in research, policy analysis, public education, training, and grassroots mobilization. Interns provide important support to staff members who carry out these activities. Interns will work on at least one major project that requires critical thinking and problem-solving and perform research, surveys, or office duties as deemed necessary by the department head. Departments that need interns include Development, the Violence Prevention Project, Child Care and Development, Office of Government Affairs, Juvenile and Family Court Judges Leadership Council, Field Division, Family Income Division, and Office of Interns and Volunteers. Although assigned to a particular project or division within CDF, interns also learn about the organization as a whole by attending weekly brown-bag discussions on substantive issues, engaging in hands-on advocacy skills training, participating in national grass roots and mobilization efforts, and having (with some limits) free access to publications, reports, materials, and staff expertise.

Duration: Preference is given to those who can commit to at least twenty-eight hours per week for three months.

Compensation and Perks: Travel reimbursement of up to $6 per day is provided.

The Ideal Candidate: They are seeking interns who have a passion for progressive social change; are interested in working on children's issues; have a track record of activism or community involvement; have realistic expectations of their role and involvement as CDF interns; and can work interdependently, as well as independently, as needs dictate. Preference is given to college juniors, seniors, and graduate students.

Making It Happen: Call for application materials. Rolling deadlines.

Contact Information: Kathie Villa, Internship Coordinator • Children's Defense Fund • 25 E St., NW • Washington, DC 20001 • Phone: (202) 628-8787 • Fax: (202) 662-3510 • Job Hotline: (202) 662-3680 • E-mail: kvilla@childrensdefense.org • Web Site: www.childrensdefense.org

Citizens Clearinghouse for Hazardous Waste

REGION/HQ: Southeast/Virginia • **CATEGORY:** Grassroots • **POSITION TYPE:** Internship • **DURATION:** Year-Round • **IDEAL CANDIDATE:**

College Students, Career Changers, Foreigners
• **APPLICANT POOL:** Varies • **APPLICANTS ACCEPTED:** 50/year

THE CITIZENS CLEARINGHOUSE for Hazardous Waste (CCHW) has been assisting disenfranchised communities struggling for environmental justice since 1981. Through their organizing, leadership development, research, and technical assistance, they empower individuals with skills and sound information to start local environmental groups, strengthen existing groups, and develop networks that reach beyond the limits of class and race to protect public health and the environment.

Work/Learn Program Specifics: Interns work on such topics as environmental racism, pesticide misuse, hazardous- and solid-waste incineration, sham recycling technologies, solid waste landfills, and corporate greenwashing. Specific positions include science, journalism, writing, grassroots organizing, nonprofit management, research, and development. Interns are given tasks to match their interests, skills, and background with CCHW's need. Because their national office is small and utilizes team-based work techniques, CCHW interns are likely to have a more diverse experience than interns at organizations with larger staff and rigid departmental structures.

Duration: Flexible duration and schedule.

Compensation and Perks: CCHW does not generally compensate interns, but this is a general rule that has often been overruled when presented with an outstanding intern.

The Ideal Candidate: People of all backgrounds, who are committed in making a difference and rebuilding democracy, are welcome.

Making It Happen: Send resume and cover letter outlining what type of internship you want, what you hope to gain from the experience, and what time frame you are available.

Contact Information: Barbara Sullivan, Intern Coordinator • Citizens Clearinghouse for Hazardous Waste • P.O. Box 6806 • Falls Church, VA 22040-6806 • Phone: (703) 237-2249 • Fax: (703) 237-8389 • E-mail: cchw@essential.org

City Year

REGION/HQ: Nationwide/Massachusetts • **CATEGORY:** Service Learning • **POSITION TYPE:** Unique Experience • **DURATION:** One Year • **IDEAL**

CANDIDATE: High School Students, College Students
• **APPLICANT POOL:** Varies • **APPLICANTS ACCEPTED:** Varies

CITY YEAR, AN AMERICORPS PROGRAM, is an innovative service organization which seeks to address unmet community needs, break down barriers of class and race, inspire citizens to civic action, and strengthen the bonds of community. By tapping the energy and commitment of young people, City Year is "putting idealism to work."

Area and Working Environment: Corps members will work in Boston (MA), Chicago (IL), Cleveland (OH), Columbia (SC), Columbus (OH), San Jose (CA), Providence (RI), and San Antonio (TX).

Work/Learn Program Specifics: Corps members begin each weekday morning with a regimen of high-spirited calisthenics to prepare themselves for a day of excellent service. After their "community huddle," corps members—in distinctive red, tan, and black uniforms—fan out in teams of ten to twelve to serve their community. Corps members serve as teachers' aides in public schools, renovate housing for the homeless, turn vacant lots into community gardens, operate recreational programs for senior citizens, teach health and public safety curriculums, and run after-school programs. Through their service work and coordinated Leadership Training Days, City Year corps members learn the value of community, realize their potential to improve the lives of others, and develop the skills necessary to excel in educational and professional endeavors.

Compensation and Perks: Corps members receive a weekly stipend of $125 and upon graduation are eligible for up to $4,725 in post-service awards for college tuition, job training, or other life-changing opportunities.

The Ideal Candidate: Applicants must be aged seventeen to twenty-three.

Making It Happen: Call for application materials. Rolling deadlines.

Contact Information: Program Director • City Year • 285 Columbus Ave. • Boston, MA 02116 • Phone: (617) 927-2500 • Fax: (617) 927-2510

Co-op America

REGION/HQ: Washington, D.C./Washington, D.C.
• **CATEGORY:** Grassroots • **POSITION TYPE:** Internship
• **DURATION:** Year-Round • **IDEAL CANDIDATE:**

College Students, Career Changers, Foreigners • **APPLICANT POOL:** 150/year • **APPLICANTS ACCEPTED:** 20/year

• •

CO-OP AMERICA IS A nonprofit membership association of individuals and organizations working to build a more cooperative and socially responsible economy. They strive to educate their members to use their buying power more effectively to create change. Co-op America serves as a link between socially conscious consumers and responsible businesses by providing a variety of benefits, including a quarterly publication and the *National Green Page* to their members.

Work/Learn Program Specifics: All positions involve the intern in developing programs, researching and writing, and general organizational strategy. Each offers excellent exposure to the world of marketing and development in the nonprofit, social change sector. Internships are available in accounting and finance, membership marketing, development, executive department, magazine reporting/writing, public education and public relations, general research, internet technical assistant, and more. They have a progressive office, treat their interns as part of their team, and encourage interns to participate in all staff activities.

Duration: They offer internships year-round and prefer the interns work a minimum of two months. Schedules and length of internships vary depending on the project and intern's availability. They are fairly flexible about scheduling.

Compensation and Perks: Interns receive a $50-per-month stipend. In addition, each intern receives a free two-year membership to Co-op America.

The Ideal Candidate: They look for applicants who are interested in the environmental and social-change movement, hardworking, able to work independently and as part of a team, and willing to work in a cooperative environment.

Making It Happen: Send cover letter and resume at least one month prior to your requested start date. You may also want to purchase their publication, *Action Guide: How to Find a Socially Responsible Job*, which provides resources and job listings in the environmental, nonprofit, and public affairs sectors, with references and directories of socially responsible organizations. Just send $2, along with your name and address.

INSIDER TIPS: *Let us know which internship you would like. Don't make us guess. Make sure there are no typos in your letter and resume. Be clear and concise about what you*

are looking for and what your skills are. Know something about the organization you are writing to.

Contact Information: Debby Leopold, Internship Coordinator • Co-op America • 1612 K Street, NW, Suite 600 • Washington, DC 20006 • Phone: (202) 872-5307 • Fax: (202) 331-8166 • Web Site: www. coopamerica.org

Cystic Fibrosis Foundation

REGION/HQ: Pacific Northwest/California • **CATEGORY:** Human Service • **POSITION TYPE:** Internship • **DURATION:** Year-Round • **IDEAL CANDIDATE:** High School Students, College Students, Career Changers, Foreigners • **APPLICANT POOL:** 50/year • **APPLICANTS ACCEPTED:** 16/year

• •

THE CYSTIC FIBROSIS FOUNDATION (CFF) is a nonprofit organization and one of seventy field and branch offices across the country. CFF was established in 1955 to raise money to fund research to find a cure for cystic fibrosis and improve the quality of life for the 30,000 children and young adults with this fatal genetic disease. The disease causes grossly abnormal amounts of thick, sticky mucus that clogs the lungs, causing irreparable damage to the respiratory and digestive systems. The Northern California chapter produces over twenty high-profile events each year, ranging from sporting events to black-tie galas. The foundation operates at less than 10 percent overhead cost, which means that nearly every cent of each dollar raised goes to medical research.

Work/Learn Program Specifics: Sports and special events marketing has grown into a $10 billion industry. If you are considering entering this field and being successful, you need to understand the marketing techniques and practices used in the industry and to develop the skills specific to this business. The internship program at CFF is designed to teach you how to implement an integrated marketing program in order to raise substantial dollars for medical research. Their office produces sporting events such as walk-a-thons, golf tournaments, a sports challenge, and a tennis/volleyball tournament. They also produce several black-tie affairs which have major auctions.

As an intern, you will work closely with an event director on all aspects of planning, production, and follow-up of an event. You will learn to formulate effective sponsorship proposals, recruit corporate teams and participants, and organize the specifics of the event-day production. You will also develop a strong understanding of sales techniques by working as an event promoter.

Duration: Internships are for three months; they prefer you work three days a week for a total of 15 hours per week.

The Ideal Candidate: Applicant should be interested in learning the event-planning business in its entirety.

Making It Happen: You must go to their office for an interview, and at that time, you will fill out an application. Rolling deadlines.

INSIDER TIPS: *Must be extremely outgoing, willing to make cold calls, and able to make a serious commitment.*

Contact Information: Julie Westhead, Special Events Coordinator • Cystic Fibrosis Foundation • 417 Montgomery St., Suite 404 • San Francisco, CA 94104 • Phone: (415) 677-0155 • Fax: (415) 677-0156

Emandal— A Farm on a River

REGION/HQ: Pacific Northwest/California • **CATEGORY:** Sustainable Living • **POSITION TYPE:** Seasonal • **DURATION:** Year-Round • **IDEAL CANDIDATE:** College Students, Career Changers, Retired Folks • **APPLICANT POOL:** Varies • **APPLICANTS ACCEPTED:** Varies

EMANDAL—A FARM ON A RIVER is the Adams's family home, as well as an environmental education facility for school groups, a small children's camp for five weeks (during June and July), a family vacation farm during August, a weekend getaway for families in the fall, a varietal wine-grape vineyard, a working cattle and pig ranch, and producer of fine jams, jellies, pickles and salsas. The philosophy is one of self-sufficiency, both mental and physical, as an individual and as part of a community, to ensure viability in our changing world.

Area and Working Environment: Emandal is located in the heart of Mendocino County, on the main fork of the Eel River. This is a land where biomes of the arid Southwest and rainy Northwest overlap and interact, creating an incredible diversity of plants and wildlife. Set into this wilderness is the farm, with acres of organic fruits, vegetables, and vineyards that help feed all who experience life on the farm.

Work/Learn Program Specifics: Emandal provides a learning environment and a chance to do something constructive while pondering life's choices. Explore the cycle of employment opportunities: January—gardener and farm workers; March—environmental education coordinator; April—naturalists, cook, and assistant gardeners; June—children's camp counselors, camp cooks, backpack counselor, program director, and teen programs director; July—family camp workers, pickle packers, and scrapbook editor; September through November—farm workers; November through December—mail-order workers. Typical job assignments include trail building, firewood gathering, painting cabins, fixing fences, planting seeds, washing clothes, making jam, labeling brochures, feeding animals, butchering chickens, building compost, teaching soap-making, building rock walls, gardening, making meals, and the list goes on and on.

Duration: Positions are full- or part-time or any other times that can be negotiated. The days in summer are long—working up to twelve hours per day. A farmworker follows the sun. Days off and time off change dramatically with the seasons.

Compensation and Perks: Most stipends range from $180 to $250 per week, plus room and board. Emandal is known for its incredible, family-style meals. The living space is either in bunkhouses, cabins, the schoolhouse, or the carriage house, depending on the season.

The Ideal Candidate: The farm is ideal for transitioning from one experience to another—whether the end of school, between jobs, prior to graduate education, before a trip around the world, or while making a decision about a career change.

Making It Happen: Call for application materials. Rolling deadlines.

INSIDER TIPS: *We're always looking for good people, eager to learn and work, who are interested in others. We especially need grandparents for the Summer Camp!*

Contact Information: Clive and Tamara Adams, Owners • Emandal—A Farm on a River • 16500 Hearst Post Office Rd. • Willits, CA 95490 • Phone: (707) 459-5439 • Fax: (707) 459-1808 • E-mail: emandal@pacific.net

Environmental Careers Organization

REGION/HQ: Nationwide/Massachusetts • **CATEGORY:** Environment • **POSITION TYPE:** Internship • **DURATION:** Year-Round • **IDEAL CANDIDATE:** College Students, Career Changers

• APPLICANT POOL: 2,500/year • **APPLICANTS ACCEPTED:** 600/year

••

THE ENVIRONMENTAL CAREERS ORGANIZATION (ECO) is a national nonprofit organization that protects and enhances the environment through the development of professionals, the promotion of careers, and the inspiration of individual action. Founded in 1972, ECO has five regional offices located in Boston, Cleveland, Seattle, San Francisco, and Tampa and an alumni network of over 5,000. The organization sponsors an annual environmental career conference (late October), publishes books on environmental careers, maintains environmental career libraries, and places students into environmental internships.

Area and Working Environment: Positions are available throughout the entire United States.

Work/Learn Program Specifics: Environmental Placement Services Program: Approximately 175 organizations sponsor ECO interns and almost every type of environmental career is covered, including government agencies, corporations, consulting firms, and nonprofit organizations. Positions are entry-level and are designed to utilize your education, interests, and skills. The program prepares students to become the next generation of environmental scientists and engineers, chemists and biologists, teachers, recycling coordinators, and environmental lawyers.

Duration: Positions vary from as short as three months to as long as two years. The average project length is six months, and it is not uncommon for projects to be extended.

Compensation and Perks: Typical stipends range from $300 to $600 per week (with the average being $425 per week).

The Ideal Candidate: Candidates from all backgrounds have been placed in ECO's program; approximately two-thirds of interns have science and technology backgrounds, and the other third concentrate in liberal arts.

Making It Happen: Call for an application (or fill it out on their web page). Once they receive your application (which is kept active for twelve months), they attempt to match your skills to organizations which have openings in your field. ECO recommends six to eight candidates for each internship; the sponsor then selects how many they would actually like to interview. Apply at least three months prior to your ideal start date.

Contact Information: Kim Hibbard, Career Services Coordinator • Environmental Careers Organization • 179 South St. • Boston, MA 02211 • Phone: (617) 426-4375 • Fax: (617) 423-0998 • E-mail: khibbard@eco.org • Web Site: www.eco.org

Farm Sanctuary

REGION/HQ: Northeast/New York • **CATEGORY:** Wildlife • **POSITION TYPE:** Internship • **DURATION:** Year-Round • **IDEAL CANDIDATE:** High School Students, College Students, Career Changers, Retired Folks, Foreigners • **APPLICANT POOL:** Varies • **APPLICANTS ACCEPTED:** Varies

••

FARM SANCTUARY IS THE LARGEST nonprofit farm animal advocacy and shelter organization in the world dedicated to saving farm animals from systematic cruelty and abuse. They provide rescue, rehabilitation, and permanent shelter for abused or neglected farm animals, educate the public and encourage individuals to adopt lifestyles that foster the protection of farm animals, and initiate investigations and campaigns to prevent cruelty to farm animals at livestock and poultry facilities.

Area and Working Environment: Interns can work at either Watkins Glen, New York or Orland, California (or perhaps both!).

Work/Learn Program Specifics: Sanctuary volunteer/interns are assigned to a specific department involved in shelter and education center operations. Duties may include animal care and feeding, office work, farm maintenance, or educational tours. This is a unique opportunity to make a vital contribution to the saving of animal lives.

Duration: Positions are available year-round, so you can join them any time. Interns work a full-time, forty-hour-a-week schedule. The minimum commitment for the program is one month, although two- or three-month internships are preferred.

Compensation and Perks: Housing is free of charge for all interns. Interns share a bedroom and have twenty-four-hour access to kitchen facilities. Food is bought and prepared individually; a weekly grocery shopping trip is provided for interns without transportation.

The Ideal Candidate: Everybody is welcome! The primary qualification is a strong commitment to animals and the joy of doing outdoor work.

Making It Happen: Call for application. Send completed application at least several months in advance.

Contact Information: Gene Bauston, Education Coordinator • Farm Sanctuary • P.O. Box 150 • Watkins Glen, NY 14891-0150 • Phone: (607) 583-2225 • Fax: (607) 583-2041 • Web Site: www.farmsanctuary.org

Feminist Majority

REGION/HQ: Washington, D.C./Virginia • **CATEGORY:** Feminism • **POSITION TYPE:** Internship • **DURATION:** Year-Round • **IDEAL CANDIDATE:** College Students, Career Changers, Foreigners • **APPLICANT POOL:** 120/year • **APPLICANTS ACCEPTED:** 20/year

SPEARHEADED BY ELEANOR SMEAL, former president of the National Organization for Women (NOW), the Feminist Majority and the Feminist Majority Foundation are nonprofit research and advocacy organizations dedicated to promoting equality for women. The Feminist Majority leads action campaigns to inspire women to take power in all sectors of society. Feminist Majority organizers also track legislative issues of concern to women and speak out to the government on behalf of women's rights. The Feminist Majority Foundation, a feminist think tank, develops creative long-term strategies and permanent solutions for the pervasive social, political, and economic obstacles facing women. Through educational and research projects, the foundation seeks to transform the public debate on issues of importance to women's lives.

Work/Learn Program Specifics: Internships provide the students with a behind-the-scenes look at the women's movement. Each internship is tailored to meet the needs of the individual student and includes a wide variety of responsibilities, such as monitoring press conferences and congressional hearings, researching, writing, policy analysis, organizing demonstrations, and clinic defense. Interns will choose projects that best match their interests. Current projects/positions include violence and sexual harassment against women; empowering women internationally; press assistant; working for the passage of abortion-rights laws and women's rights laws; Rock for Choice—helping to organize fund-raising concerts; women in police; empowering women to seek leadership in all areas of society, such as business, medicine, and law; the Task Force on Women and Girls in Sports to end discrimination against women and girls in sports; and the Feminization of Power campaign to inspire women to seek leadership positions in politics and on college campuses.

Duration: Internships are flexible in duration, thirty-five to forty hours per week for at least two months.

Compensation and Perks: From September through May they offer a stipend of $70 per week (in exchange, interns are expected to do up to ten hours per week of clerical work). There is no stipend offered during the summer, but there is some opportunity to earn pocket money by doing clerical work as needed. They do provide reimbursement of local transportation costs.

The Ideal Candidate: Feminist women and men in all majors are encouraged to apply—especially political science and women's studies majors. They prefer applicants who have experience working on women's issues on campus, in their communities, or through a previous internship.

Making It Happen: Send cover letter, resume, and writing sample. Rolling deadlines.

INSIDER TIPS: *We are interested in applicants from diverse ethnic backgrounds. Men are welcome to apply.*

Contact Information: Christine Onyango, Intern Coordinator • Feminist Majority • 1600 Wilson Blvd., Suite 801 • Arlington, VA 22209 • Phone: (703) 522-2214 • Fax: (703) 522-2219

Friends of the National Zoo

REGION/HQ: Washington, D.C./Washington, D.C. • **CATEGORY:** Zoo • **POSITION TYPE:** Internship • **DURATION:** Summer • **IDEAL CANDIDATE:** College Students, Career Changers, Foreigners • **APPLICANT POOL:** 300–350/year • **APPLICANTS ACCEPTED:** Varies

THE NATIONAL ZOOLOGICAL PARK occupies 163 acres in Washington's Rock Creek Park. It is a place of public education and recreation, a center for research in zoology, and it preserves many rare and endangered species. The zoo's collection of reptiles, birds, insects, amphibians, and mammals also includes many endangered species, some of which are being studied as a part of long-term captive-breeding efforts.

Work/Learn Program Specifics: Each trainee will be responsible to an advisor while participating in ongoing or special projects, and each will receive guidance in research methodology. Responsibilities may include animal observation and handling, data recording, laboratory analyses, data processing, and report writing. Research traineeships include: animal behavior, animal medicine, veterinary pathology, reproductive physiology, nutrition, genetics, and husbandry. Other traineeships include exhibit interpretation, photography, public affairs, education, horticulture, landscaping, video production, and design.

Duration: Internships are twelve weeks, during the summer.

Compensation and Perks: Interns receive a $2,400 stipend. Optional dormitory space is available at Front Royal, although you are responsible for your own housing.

The Ideal Candidate: Selection criteria focus on applicant's statement of interest, scholastic achievement, relevant experience, and letters of reference. Preference is given to advanced undergraduates and recent graduates, except in certain positions which are only open to veterinary college students.

Making It Happen: Call for announcement. Submit essay, transcript, and two letters of recommendation.

Contact Information: Human Resources • Friends of the National Zoo • National Zoological Park • 3001 Connecticut Ave., NW • Washington, DC 20008 • Phone: (202) 673-4640 • Fax: (202) 673-4890 • E-mail: fonzhr@aol.com

Frontier Nursing Service

REGION/HQ: Southeast/Kentucky • **CATEGORY:** Social Service • **POSITION TYPE:** Unique Experience • **DURATION:** Year-Round • **IDEAL CANDIDATE:** College Students, Career Changers, Retired Folks, Foreigner • **APPLICANT POOL:** 60/year • **APPLICANTS ACCEPTED:** 4/term

THE WORK OF FRONTIER NURSING SERVICE was begun by Mary Breckinridge in Leslie County, Kentucky in 1925. Mrs. Breckinridge introduced the use of professionally trained nurses/midwives into the United States, established district nursing centers to provide a decentralized system of health care to serve families in rural areas, and made the teaching of nurses/midwives as much a part of the program as providing care. Today, the Frontier Nursing Service operates the forty-bed Mary Breckinridge Hospital, three outpost clinics, a women's health clinic, and a distance-learning nursing/midwifery program. FNS also has a long history of volunteers who are known as couriers.

Area and Working Environment: FNS is the only building located in Wendover, a ten-minute drive from the city of Hayden, a community of about 500 residents.

It's also located in the heart of the Appalachian mountains, with a rich historical and cultural tradition.

Work/Learn Program Specifics: Couriers deliver supplies to the outpost clinics, host dinners at Wendover (the historical headquarters of FNS), help out around the offices, watch over Wendover, and participate in various local community events. Couriers also participate in community education, which includes acting as teaching aides in local schools and assisting adults in the adult learning center. Through assisting in educational initiatives, couriers can experience the local Appalachian community on many different levels and attain a greater understanding of the big picture, in which health care plays a vital component.

Duration: Positions last eight to twelve weeks, although there is a possibility for extended stays. Couriers are on call at times in the evening to host dinners and deliver supplies.

Compensation and Perks: All couriers are provided room and board and will live at the historical Wendover. You will have your own room, each with a bed, desk, closet, and linens. Lunch and dinner are served "family-style" in Mrs. Breckinridge's two-story log home. There is also a common room located on the second floor, with both cable TV and a VCR.

The Ideal Candidate: Because of the program's nature, a great deal of maturity and self-motivation is required of all volunteers. All successful applicants must be over eighteen years of age and have graduated from high school. Couriers must hold a valid driver's license and are asked to provide their own vehicles (all work-related mileage will be reimbursed).

Making It Happen: Call for application materials. Even though acceptance is on a rolling basis, admissions tend to correspond with the months of March, June, September, and December. A $250 registration fee is required upon acceptance into the program to help offset the cost of room and board.

INSIDER TIPS: *We are looking for couriers who are independent, self-initiators, flexible, patient, and enjoy working with people.*

Contact Information: Karen Thomisee, Courier Coordinator • Frontier Nursing Service • P.O. Box 4 • Wendover, KY 41775 • Phone: (606) 672-2317 • Fax: (606) 672-3022 • Web Site: www.barefoot.com/fns

The future must be seen in terms of what a person can do to contribute something, to make something better, to make it go where he believes with all his being it ought to go. —FREDERICK KAPPEL

343

Global Exchange

REGION/HQ: Pacific Northwest/California • **CATEGORY:** Global Development • **POSITION TYPE:** Internship • **DURATION:** Year-Round • **IDEAL CANDIDATE:** College Students, Career Changers, Foreigners • **APPLICANT POOL:** 50/year • **APPLICANTS ACCEPTED:** 15/year

GLOBAL EXCHANGE IS A NONPROFIT research, education, and action center that works to build people-to-people ties between First- and Third-World countries and promotes social justice and sustainable development. Their programs include study tours to developing countries, retail stores that promote alternative trade, and development of educational resources, including writing articles, publishing books, and coordinating speaking tours and forums on current political issues.

Area and Working Environment: Positions are in Berkeley and San Francisco, California.

Work/Learn Program Specifics: Activism? Education? Travel? Other Cultures? Justice? Human Rights? Social Responsibility? Yes? Yes? Then this may be the internship for you. They have a great program for interns who are interested in gaining real-life experience and working for a more equitable world. Positions include: Realty Tours—a wonderful learning experience for interns who are interested in Third World traveling and research. Long-term interns become part of their work team. Fund-raising—opportunity for interns to learn the ins and outs of fund-raising on a variety of levels, including proposal writing, foundation research, event planning, and membership development. Fair Trade—Interns will participate in bridging the gap between North American consumers and Third World producers. Their dual mission is selling crafts and educating consumers about fair trade. Possible ways of participating include producing educational material, expanding community links, coordinating special events, and becoming a communications liaison. Campaign Program—help promote peace and justice in Cuba or Mexico. Public Education—possibilities include publications, research, media outreach, and speakers bureau. Human Rights—research and write reports on human rights issues and provide outreach to other human rights organizations.

Duration: One- to six-month positions are available, part- or full-time.

The Ideal Candidate: Candidates should be self-motivated, creative, and willing to make a set time commitment, depending on the project.

Making It Happen: Call for application. Send completed application, cover letter, resume, and two letters of recommendation. Rolling deadlines, but apply one month before your requested start date.

Contact Information: Kirsten Moller, Internship Coordinator • Global Exchange • 2017 Mission St., Room 303 • San Francisco, CA 94110 • Phone: (415) 255-7296 • Fax: (415) 255-7498 • E-mail: gx-info@globalexchange.org • Web Site: www.globalexchange.org

Green Chimneys Children's Services

REGION/HQ: Northeast/New York • **CATEGORY:** Therapeutic Recreation • **POSITION TYPE:** Internship • **DURATION:** Year-Round • **IDEAL CANDIDATE:** College Students, Career Changers, Foreigners • **APPLICANT POOL:** Varies • **APPLICANTS ACCEPTED:** Varies

GREEN CHIMNEYS IS DEDICATED to the development of basic education and daily living skills for children and adults to restore and strengthen their emotional health and well-being. Their programs are designed to help all recipients of services achieve optimal functioning and a high degree of independence. They strive to provide an atmosphere that is as normal and home-like as possible.

Area and Working Environment: The main campus is situated on a 150-acre farm, a quiet rural setting that provides an environment conducive to learning and emotional rehabilitation. You'll also enjoy a smoke-free campus!

Work/Learn Program Specifics: Interns assist with farm science, riding and greenhouse classes, daily chores, and public programs, and participate with public tours and other outdoor activities, such as nature walks and cross-country skiing. Interns also assist with public tours, teacher workshops, and weekend events. All responsibilities are carried out with residents of their treatment center.

Duration: Start dates are in January, May, and September, and you must make at least a four-month commitment.

Compensation and Perks: Room and board are provided, and you'll live in a brick Cape Cod residence located across the street from the campus. Rooms may be private or shared with one other person, as available.

The Ideal Candidate: Applicants must have keen interest in children, animals, farms, and outdoor education; be at least twenty years of age, a junior in college, or equivalent; and have a background in farming, social service, special education, environmental education, or outdoor education recreation.

Making It Happen: Call for application. Submit cover letter, completed application, and resume.

Contact Information: Joan O'Connell, Internship Coordinator • Green Chimneys Children's Services • Caller Box 719, Putnam Lake Road • Brewster, NY 10509 • Phone: (914) 279-2996 • Fax: (914) 279-2714

Habitat for Humanity International

REGION/HQ: Southeast/Georgia • **CATEGORY:** Service Learning • **POSITION TYPE:** Work/Learn Adventure • **DURATION:** Year-Round • **IDEAL CANDIDATE:** High School Students, College Students, Career Changers, Retired Folks, Foreigners • **APPLICANT POOL:** Varies • **APPLICANTS ACCEPTED:** Varies

HABITAT IS A MOVEMENT OF individuals and groups working in partnership to build houses with those who otherwise would be unable to afford decent shelter. Habitat volunteers provide their construction and administrative skills for the vision of eliminating poverty housing from the face of the earth.

Area and Working Environment: Besides the projects offered in North America, Habitat serves in over forty nations around the world.

Work/Learn Program Specifics: Short-term and long-term volunteers are needed to fill positions at the international headquarters in Georgia, or you may choose to become involved with Habitat on a grassroots level by working with a local affiliate or support projects overseas. Projects may include construction, administration, childcare, photography, fund-raising, graphic arts, information systems, language translation, and public relations. Internships are available in the summer for college students.

Duration: Terms of service vary—from one week up to three years. A summer internship is available.

Compensation and Perks: Furnished housing, a food stipend, and insurance are available at their headquar-

ters. Benefits also include paid utilities, laundry facilities, cleaning supplies, and childcare. Transportation is the responsibility of volunteers assigned to North American affiliates. However, transportation is provided for volunteers assigned to overseas affiliates.

The Ideal Candidate: Habitat welcomes people of all ages and backgrounds. For North American projects you must be at least sixteen years of age and for international projects you must be at least twenty-one.

Making It Happen: Call for an application. Rolling deadlines.

Contact Information: Kathyie Doyle, Volunteer Support Services • Habitat for Humanity International • 121 Habitat St. • Americus, GA 31709-3498 • Phone: (912) 924-6935 • Fax: (912) 924-0641 • Toll Free: (800) 422-4828 • E-mail: DVR@habitat.org • Web Site: www.habitat.org

IAAY Summer Programs

REGION/HQ: Washington, D.C./Maryland • **CATEGORY:** Education • **POSITION TYPE:** Unique Experience • **DURATION:** Summer • **IDEAL CANDIDATE:** College Students • **APPLICANT POOL:** 1,500/year • **APPLICANTS ACCEPTED:** 850/year

THE INSTITUTE FOR THE Academic Advancement of Youth (IAAY) is a comprehensive, university-based initiative that promotes the academic ability of children and youth throughout the world. The institute, which includes the Center for Talented Youth (CTY) and Center for Academic Advancement (CAA), holds summer residential and commuter programs which provide the opportunity for their participants to take rigorous courses in mathematics, science, computer science, humanities, and writing.

Area and Working Environment: Residential programs are offered at fourteen sites around the country and held on beautiful college campuses in California, Connecticut, Maryland/Washington, D.C., New York, and Pennsylvania.

Work/Learn Program Specifics: Positions available include general assistants, instructors, office managers, resident assistants (similar to a college RA), program assistants, teaching assistants/laboratory assistants, academic counselors, academic deans, dean of residential life, dean of students, and site directors. You will have the opportunity to work with unique and exciting highly able youngsters in dynamic settings.

Duration: There are two, three-week sessions, beginning in late June and ending in early August. All positions are full-time, from 9 A.M. to 9 P.M., and weekend work is required.

Compensation and Perks: A salary is provided for all employees and at residential sites. You will also receive room and board. All employees, residential and commuter, are responsible for the costs of their travel to and from the sites.

The Ideal Candidate: Candidates should be motivated and energetic and have experience with young people.

Making It Happen: E-mail users can request an application packet by sending a message to academic@ jhunix.hcf.jhu.edu. Applications must be accompanied by a cover letter, resume, transcripts, and three letters of recommendation. Deadline: January 31. Applications received later will be considered only if needed.

INSIDER TIPS: *We are looking for creative, dynamic individuals who are interested in working with children in an academic setting. Candidates must be energetic and able to handle multiple tasks.*

Contact Information: Kimberley Theobald, Assistant Coordinator • IAAY Summer Programs • The Johns Hopkins University • 3400 N. Charles St. • Baltimore, MD 21218 • Phone: (410) 516-0240 • Fax: (410) 516-0804 • E-mail: kat@jhu.edu • Web Site: www.jhu.edu/~gifted/acadprog/jobs.html

Jackson Hole Land Trust

REGION/HQ: Rocky Mountains/Wyoming • **CATEGORY:** Conservation • **POSITION TYPE:** Internship • **DURATION:** Year-Round • **IDEAL CANDIDATE:** College Students • **APPLICANT POOL:** 20/year • **APPLICANTS ACCEPTED:** 1–2/term

THE JACKSON HOLE LAND TRUST, founded in 1980, is one of the oldest and best established trusts in the West. It currently protects over 7,000 acres and holds over 50 easements. The Land Trust aims at preserving the scenic, natural, and agricultural values of Jackson Hole, so the valley may retain its unique Western flavor and abundant wildlife. With the help of such tools as the conservation easement and the Conservation Buyer Project, as well as through direct purchases, the Land Trust has been able to preserve nearly 10 percent of the private lands in Teton County.

Area and Working Environment: Jackson Hole has excellent access to national parks and forests and hiking, skiing, climbing, biking, birding, and water sports.

Work/Learn Program Specifics: An internship at the Jackson Hole Land Trust is a great opportunity to become involved in the day-to-day work of a successful land conservation organization. Interns have the opportunity to gain a detailed understanding of private land protection as well as a better understanding of how the growing community of land trusts fits into the conservation movement as a whole. Areas of possible involvement include local wildlife biology, community planning, special events coordination, grant writing, biomonitoring, easement formation and/or summation, landowner and property research, mapping/aerials, and fund-raising. Interns are also expected to be available for office support in addition to their project work.

Duration: The internship is for three months, starting any time of year. A minimum of twenty hours per week is required.

Compensation and Perks: A $200-per-month stipend is provided. You will be working with an energetic and friendly staff. Because the staff is small, its members rely on their interns a great deal. For this reason, interns will find it easy to become involved in the constant list of projects.

The Ideal Candidate: Applicants must have experience or demonstrated interest in natural resources, field studies, private land protection, ranching, conservation, real estate transactions, or legal work. Macintosh experience is also very important. College students and graduates are encouraged to apply.

Making It Happen: Send resume, list of references, and a cover letter addressing: (1) why you want to work at the Land Trust; (2) any skills or interests that would make you a particularly strong candidate; and (3) dates of availability. Rolling deadlines.

Contact Information: Intern Coordinator • Jackson Hole Land Trust • P.O. Box 2897 • Jackson, WY 83001 • Phone: (307) 733-4707 • Fax: (307) 733-4144

The Land Institute

REGION/HQ: South/Midwest/Kansas • **CATEGORY:** Agriculture • **POSITION TYPE:** Internship • **DURATION:** Ten months • **IDEAL CANDIDATE:** College Students, Career Changers, Foreigners • **APPLICANT POOL:** 50/year • **APPLICANTS ACCEPTED:** 8–10/year

THE LAND INSTITUTE, established in 1976, is a nonprofit research and education organization devoted to sustainable agriculture and good stewardship of the earth. They serve as a center for the study of environmental and agricultural issues and conduct pioneering research in the development of sustainable agriculture and communities based on the model of the prairie.

Area and Working Environment: Located along the Smoky Hill River, southeast of Salina, a thriving small city, the Institute occupies about 277 acres, including 100 acres of native tallgrass prairie, 60 acres of restored prairie, 75 acres of arable bottomland, and 30 acres of woodlands, gardens, and facilities.

Work/Learn Program Specifics: Interns are a vital part of the Land Institute's sustainable-agriculture research program. Each intern chooses an experiment that has been designed by staff as part of the ongoing perennial polyculture and Sunshine Farm research; for example, cultivating or caring for a particular species or measuring yields and analyzing the resulting data. At the end of the term, the intern presents the results in a formal paper at Kansas State University or the University of Kansas. The schedule follows the growing season. During the spring and fall, interns discuss assigned readings three or four mornings per week and do research and maintenance work the rest of the time. The summer is primarily devoted to fieldwork. Staff and interns meet twice a week throughout the year to plan work and have informal discussions. Interns also contribute articles and illustrations to the Land Report, published three times per term. They help host public programs, such as the annual spring Prairie Festival and fall Visitors' Day, give tours to their many visitors, and occasionally represent the Land Institute at area events, festivals, and conferences.

Duration: Internship duration is forty-three weeks, beginning mid-February and ending mid-December. Internships are offered once a year.

Compensation and Perks: The stipend is $139 per week for forty-three weeks. Interns find their own housing in Salina and provide their own meals. Produce is available seasonally from the garden and orchard. Special seminars, guests, and field trips vary the routine of your experience.

The Ideal Candidate: College graduates and upper-level graduate students are encouraged to apply. Good health, stamina, and a love of working outside in sometimes extreme conditions are essential. Training in the biological sciences is not required, but they do prefer candidates with agricultural or biological field experience.

Making It Happen: Call for application details. You will need to answer essay questions and provide transcripts, a resume, and two letters of recommendation. Applications must be postmarked by October 1.

Contact Information: Brian Donahue, Education Director • The Land Institute • 2440 E. Water Well Rd. • Salina, KS 67401 • Phone: (913) 823-5376 • Fax: (913) 823-8728 • E-mail: theland@igc.apc.org

Little Brothers– Friends of the Elderly

REGION/HQ: Great Lakes/Illinois • **CATEGORY:** Human Service • **POSITION TYPE:** Internship • **DURATION:** Summer/Year-long • **IDEAL CANDIDATE:** College Students, Career Changers, Foreigners • **APPLICANT POOL:** Varies • **APPLICANTS ACCEPTED:** Varies

LITTLE BROTHERS—FRIENDS OF THE ELDERLY serves lonely and isolated elderly over the age of seventy who live within the city of Chicago. These people most often lack a social network of family and friends, or have few social skills to build friendships, and identify themselves as lonely.

Area and Working Environment: Little Brothers are found in France, Canada, Germany, Ireland, Mexico, Morocco, Spain, and in six United States cities. Chicago is the original home of Little Brothers in the United States.

Work/Learn Program Specifics: Summer interns will be part of a team of helpers who, together with the elderly, organize and go to their vacation home, a fifteen-room house set on seven acres just two hours outside of Chicago. You will have constant interaction with the elderly, prepare and assist with various group activities, help with personal hygiene, assist with meal preparation, drive passenger vans, and help with house-/groundskeeping. Year-long positions include human resources/volunteer management, nonprofit management, public relations assistant, and program site assistant. They also offer part-time volunteer positions.

Duration: They offer summer and year-long positions, full-time, with a flexible schedule, including some evenings and weekends.

Compensation and Perks: Summer interns receive $150 per week; year-long interns receive $450 per month, and all receive room and board. You will also receive excellent training and experience in the field of aging, working under the guidance of experienced volunteers and staff.

The Ideal Candidate: Applicants must have a sensitivity to the needs of elderly people who are growing old alone, a personal value system that emphasizes respect for the individual and a belief that friendship is essential in the lives of elderly people, and strong communication/interpersonal skills. Bilingual English/Spanish skills are welcomed.

Making It Happen: Call for application materials.

Contact Information: Christine Bertrand, Internship Coordinator • Little Brothers–Friends of the Elderly • 355 N. Ashland Ave. • Chicago, IL 60607 • Phone: (312) 455-1000 • Fax: (312) 455-9674

Lost Valley Educational Center

REGION/HQ: Pacific Northwest/Oregon • **CATEGORY:** Sustainable Living • **POSITION TYPE:** Unique Experience • **DURATION:** Summer • **IDEAL CANDIDATE:** High School Students, College Students, Career Changers • **APPLICANT POOL:** 50/year • **APPLICANTS ACCEPTED:** 12–15/year

LOST VALLEY EDUCATIONAL CENTER is a nonprofit educational organization that consists of an educational center, a hostel, and an international community. The center hosts and organizes conferences, workshops, and retreats that focus on personal growth and sustainable living. Fifteen adults and ten children live on the grounds year-round, and all are committed to the pursuit of a more sustainable lifestyle.

Area and Working Environment: The center is located on eighty-seven acres in the foothills of the Cascades, eighteen miles southeast of Eugene, complete with a growing young forest, perennial stream, meadow, oak savanna, and three food and herb gardens.

Work/Learn Program Specifics: The apprentice program combines practical hands-on experience in the center's gardens with lectures, seminars, field trips, and exercises in personal growth. Apprentices will learn organic gardening by helping center gardeners produce vegetables for the conference center and community. You will learn how to make your own herbal medicines and how to identify and harvest medicinal herbs, as well as learn counseling skills to enhance your own personal growth.

Duration: This is a full-time three-month program, and it involves strenuous physical work and scheduled classes, eight hours a day, five days a week. Most weekends are geared toward rest, play, and work on personal projects on or off the property.

Compensation and Perks: Tuition for the three-month program is $1,830, or $610 per month. This includes organic vegetarian food, use of facilities, class materials, and instruction. Limited work trade/scholarship opportunities are available. Apprentices will camp in the meadow in their own tents and have access to an outdoor kitchen and solar showers, as well as an indoor study space and bathrooms, showers, and laundry facilities. In addition, a swimming hole, sauna, and a sweat lodge are available to use and enjoy.

The Ideal Candidate: All who are excited about the program and learning and living in an intentional community!

Making It Happen: Call for application materials.

Contact Information: Julianne Ruben, Owner • Lost Valley Educational Center • 81868 Lost Valley Ln. • Dexter, OR 97431 • Phone: (541) 937-3351

Mono Lake Committee

REGION/HQ: Pacific Northwest/California • **CATEGORY:** Grassroots • **POSITION TYPE:** Internship • **DURATION:** Year-Round • **IDEAL CANDIDATE:** College Students, Career Changers, Retired Folks, Foreigners • **APPLICANT POOL:** Varies • **APPLICANTS ACCEPTED:** Varies

THE MONO LAKE COMMITTEE is a nonprofit grassroots environmental organization dedicated to the protection of Mono Lake. Their internship program is an excellent introduction to a grassroots organization.

Area and Working Environment: Lee Vining is located on the eastern edge of Yosemite National Park, near Mono Lake, California.

Work/Learn Program Specifics: Mono Lake Committee Intern Program: Interns assist the information center manager in providing general support for the Mono Lake Committee (a 20,000-member citizen's group dedicated to the permanent protection and restoration of the Mono Basin ecosystem). Responsibilities include staffing the information center desk, providing information and answering questions for visitors, and gaining support for the Mono Lake Committee; handling sales and general office duties; providing public education and outreach programs, including interpretative and canoe tours; and assisting the public education coordinator with providing educational programs to groups from Los Angeles. Interns will also attend seminars and meetings, as offered, to gain a greater knowledge of the natural history of the Mono Basin and to keep abreast of the current political news. Special assignments are given based on skills and abilities.

Duration: Positions are available for three to six months, offered year-round. Interns work forty hours per week, with two consecutive days off.

Compensation and Perks: Interns are paid $4.75 per hour, and housing is available at $75 per month. A car is required for work-related travel (mileage reimbursed) and for personal use. Sorry, no pets.

The Ideal Candidate: The ability to work independently and work well in a close-knit office setting is necessary. Candidates must have an enthusiastic and outgoing personality, be dedicated to the protection of the environment, and have the ability to quickly understand complicated natural history and legal/political information.

Making It Happen: Send cover letter and resume. The summer deadline is February 28; all others—rolling.

Contact Information: Shannon Nelson, Internship Coordinator • Mono Lake Committee • P.O. Box 29 • Lee Vining, CA 93541 • Phone: (619) 647-6595 • Fax: (619) 647-6377

National Geographic Society

REGION/HQ: Washington, D.C./Washington, D.C. • **CATEGORY:** Geography • **POSITION TYPE:** Internship • **DURATION:** Year-Round • **IDEAL CANDIDATE:** College Students, Foreigners • **APPLICANT POOL:** 165/year • **APPLICANTS ACCEPTED:** 20–25/year

THE NATIONAL GEOGRAPHIC SOCIETY internship program is designed to furnish qualified students a professional learning experience through participation in various projects aimed at the diffusion of geographic knowledge. Interns are given the opportunity to apply knowledge and classroom techniques to practical publication procedures or other geographic outreach programs at the National Geographic Society.

Work/Learn Program Specifics: Interns may be assigned to an editorial project team to carry out editorial research, cartographic design, or cartographic production for one of their magazines, books, or maps,

depending upon departmental needs. There is a heavy emphasis on research skills. Assignments may include work on an increasing number of geographic projects or initiatives.

Duration: Fourteen- to sixteen-week positions are offered each season. If you are available for more than one work period, please indicate that on your application. Greater availability increases your chances.

Compensation and Perks: Interns are paid $425 per week, plus a stipend to cover travel expenses between your home and Washington, D.C. Interns are responsible for living arrangements in the D.C. area.

The Ideal Candidate: Candidates must be in their junior or senior year or be graduate students and must be majoring in geography or cartography.

Making It Happen: Call for application. Send completed application, a short essay, resume, official transcript, and three letters of recommendation. All application materials must be received by early October for each program the following year. You will be notified by early December if you will be accepted into the program. This is a very competitive internship program, and generally the spring and fall semesters are less competitive than the summer.

Contact Information: Internship Coordinator • National Geographic Society • Geography Intern Program • 1145 17th M St., NW • Washington, DC 20036-4688 • Phone: (202) 857-7161 • Fax: (202) 429-5729

National Organization for Women, Inc.

REGION/HQ: Washington, D.C./Washington, D.C. • **CATEGORY:** Feminism • **POSITION TYPE:** Internship • **DURATION:** Year-Round • **IDEAL CANDIDATE:** High School Students, College Students, Career Changers, Retired Folks, Foreigners • **APPLICANT POOL:** 180/year • **APPLICANTS ACCEPTED:** 30/year

THE NATIONAL ORGANIZATION OF WOMEN (NOW), with over 250,000 members, is the largest feminist organization in the nation. NOW was founded in 1966 and has struggled to end the injustice and inequality women face daily. NOW strives to eliminate discrimination and harassment in the workplace; secure abortion and birth control rights for all women; stop all forms of violence against women; eradicate racism, sexism, and heterosexism; and promote equality and justice through mass actions, intensive lobbying, nonviolent civil disobedience, direct action, and litigation.

Work/Learn Program Specifics: Interns will work with one of the following teams: Government Relations/Public Policy; Field Organizing; Direct Mail, Fund-raising, Membership, and Internet; Communications; or Political Action Committee. Activities include: Intern Lobby Day, which includes a workshop and a tour of Capitol Hill; weekly intern discussion group meetings and workshops on a wide range of feminist issues, which are led by national NOW staff and officers; experience with their successful, grassroots organizing techniques, including the components and application of nonviolent civil disobedience; exploring different career opportunities (journalism, marketing, lobbying, and organizing) and developing connections in the nonprofit world; and firsthand observation of how a sexist, classist, and racist political and judicial system impacts women in this country.

Duration: Positions are offered year-round and are generally one semester in length. Internships may be full- or part-time, but a minimum commitment of twenty hours per week is necessary for the spring and fall. Summer internships have a minimum of twenty-four hours per week.

Compensation and Perks: These are all volunteer positions. They will assist in helping find affordable housing.

The Ideal Candidate: Anyone over the age of fifteen is eligible to apply. Candidates should be hardworking, enthusiastic, flexible, and possess/seek a working knowledge of women's issues and feminist organizing.

Making It Happen: Call for application. Send completed application, a cover letter detailing your ability to work in a fast-paced feminist environment, resume, and two letters of recommendation. Deadlines: spring—November 20; summer—March 15; and fall—July 30.

Contact Information: Dee Dee Anderson, Intern/Volunteer Coordinator • National Organization for Women, Inc. • 1000 16th St., NW, Suite 700 • Washington, DC 20036-5705 • Phone: (202) 331-0066 • Fax: (202) 785-8576 • E-mail: volunteer@now.org • Web Site: www.now.org/intern

National Wildlife Federation

REGION/HQ: Washington, D.C./Washington, D.C.
• **CATEGORY:** Conservation • **POSITION TYPE:** Internship • **DURATION:** Spring/Fall • **IDEAL CANDIDATE:** College Students, Career Changers, Foreigners • **APPLICANT POOL:** 300–400/term
• **APPLICANTS ACCEPTED:** 7/term

THE NATIONAL WILDLIFE FEDERATION (NWF), founded in 1936, is the world's largest private, nonprofit conservation education organization, whose mission is to educate, inspire, and assist individuals and organizations of diverse cultures to conserve wildlife and other natural resources and to protect the earth's environment in order to achieve a peaceful, equitable, and sustainable future. They are also well-known for innovative publications, including *National Wildlife, International Wildlife, Ranger Rick, Your Big Backyard, National Wildlife Week* curriculum kits, the *Conservation Directory,* and *EnviroAction,* their monthly newsletter.

Area and Working Environment: The federation is located in the heart of Washington, D.C., in the Dupont Circle neighborhood, convenient to Metro (subway) and bus lines.

Work/Learn Program Specifics: An opportunity to influence environmental policy-making! All interns will work in the Resources Conservation and International Affairs Departments. These departments work on a wide range of issues, seeking agency compliance with environmental laws and regulations, identifying and filling legislative gaps in protection of critical natural resources, and litigating issues which cannot be resolved by other means. The approach is a multidisciplinary one—with a scientist, lawyer, and lobbyist working together as a team in each program area. Each intern is assigned to a program area, is given a responsible role, and becomes an essential part of a team's efforts. Internships are available in the following areas: endangered species/biodiversity; water quality; international, public and private lands; wetlands; grassroots communication; and Corporate Conservation Council. Much of an intern's time is spent researching environmental-policy issues and covering congressional activity. Responsibilities may include attending congressional hearings, briefings, and seminars; drafting testimony to be presented by the federation to congressional and executive panels; lobbying on environmental legislation; commenting on environmental impact statements and resource management plans; writing for some NWF publications; and assisting generally in the activities of the program and the department.

Duration: Internships are offered in two 24-week sessions starting in January or July.

Compensation and Perks: A stipend of $275 per week is offered, plus health insurance. Perks also include a nonsmoking office and casual dress. You will definitely make vital contacts with influential nature lovers.

The Ideal Candidate: Applicants must be college graduates with academic background and experience in areas of wildlife biology or management, wetlands ecology, fisheries science, natural resource management, land management, forestry, environmental science/policy, biology, chemistry, toxicology, energy, international environmental/development issues, political science, grassroots organizing, and/or journalism. The applicant pool is very competitive. Interns must be able to conduct independent research on difficult environmental policy issues and must be prepared to advocate the positions of NWF.

Making It Happen: No application form is required. Send cover letter indicating areas of interest; a resume; names and telephone numbers of three to five academic or professional references (not letters of reference); and a two- to four-page sample of nontechnical academic or professional writing (such as an excerpt from a research paper, not a personal essay). Personal interviews are generally not conducted, due to the large number of applications they receive. Deadlines: January start date, September 15; and July start date, March 15.

INSIDER TIPS: *Previous environmental policy experience, legislative ("Hill") experience, and work experience (paid or volunteer) with similar organizations, such as the Sierra Club or the Audubon Society, are a plus.*

Contact Information: Leevannah Washington, Volunteer/Internship Coordinator • National Wildlife Federation • Resources Conservation Internship Program • 1400 16th St., NW, Suite 501 • Washington, DC 20036-2266 • Phone: (202) 797-6819 • Fax: (202) 797-6646 • Alternate: (202) 790-6800 • E-mail: washington_l@nwf.org • Web Site: www.nwf.org/nwf

The Nation Institute

REGION/HQ: Northeast/New York • **CATEGORY:** Media • **POSITION TYPE:** Internship • **DURATION:** Year-Round • **IDEAL CANDIDATE:** College Students, Career Changers, Foreigners • **APPLICANT POOL:** Varies • **APPLICANTS ACCEPTED:** 8/term

THE NATION INSTITUTE is a private nonprofit foundation that supports research, conferences, seminars, educational programs, and other projects with an emphasis on social justice, civil liberties, and peace and disarmament. The Nation, America's oldest weekly magazine, is a journal of politics and the arts that focuses primarily on foreign and domestic policy, civil liberties, and literature.

Work/Learn Program Specifics: To gain editorial experience, interns check facts, do research, read and evaluate manuscripts, and are encouraged to write editorials, articles, or reviews for the magazine. On the publishing side, interns assist the advertising, circulation, and promotions staffs with day-to-day business and in creating and carrying out developmental and research projects for the magazine and the Institute. Intern duties also include filing, photocopying, running errands, and other routine office work. An additional position is available in the Washington, D.C. office, where this intern works closely with the magazine's Washington editor, attending press conferences and congressional hearings, as well as doing research and some clerical work.

Duration: Positions are offered year-round, full-time (10:00 to 6:00), five days a week.

Compensation and Perks: The internship carries a $100-per-week stipend. Weekly seminars are an important part of the program in New York.

Making It Happen: Send a resume, a cover letter (stating interest in The Nation and describing your prospective career goals), two letters of recommendation, and two writing samples. Published clips are preferred, though academic papers and creative writing samples are acceptable. Call for current deadlines and program duration before you submit your materials.

Contact Information: Peter Meyer, Director • The Nation Institute • 72 Fifth Ave. • New York, NY 10011 • Phone: (212) 242-8400 • Fax: (212) 463-9712 • E-mail: institute@thenation.com • Web Site: www.thenation.com

Nature Conservancy— Virginia

REGION/HQ: Washington, D.C./Virginia • **CATEGORY:** Conservation • **POSITION TYPE:** Internship • **DURATION:** Summer • **IDEAL CANDIDATE:** College Students, Career Changers, Retired Folks

• **APPLICANT POOL:** Varies • **APPLICANTS ACCEPTED:** Varies

••

THE NATURE CONSERVANCY, founded in 1951, is an international conservation organization committed to preserving natural diversity by finding and protecting lands and waters supporting the best examples of all elements of the natural world. The Conservancy's single, overriding goal is the preservation of biological diversity.

Work/Learn Program Specifics: Administrative and specialist/technical positions are offered in varied departments, including Conservation Operations, Government Relations, Board of Governors, Conservation Science (Botany), and Records Management. Hands-on conservation internships at nationwide field offices and preserves include preserve, stewardship, naturalist, and administrative positions.

Duration: Unless specifically noted, the positions are for the summer.

Compensation and Perks: Most positions are unpaid; however, botany internships pay $5 to $7 per hour.

The Ideal Candidate: Most positions require computer proficiency and excellent writing, communications, and organizational skills.

Making It Happen: Call for application materials and latest line on available positions. Rolling deadlines. There are Nature Conservancy state offices all over the United States, with each conducting its own recruiting; so it's best to apply to the state office which interests you.

Contact Information: Employment Specialist • Nature Conservancy—Virginia • 1815 N. Lynn St. • Arlington, VA 22209 • Phone: (703) 841-5379 • Fax: (703) 841-7292 • Job Hotline: (703) 247-3721 • Toll Free: (800) 628-6860 • Web Site: www.tnc.org

NETWORK

REGION/HQ: Washington, D.C./Washington, D.C.
• **CATEGORY:** Ministry • **POSITION TYPE:** Internship
• **DURATION:** Year-Round • **IDEAL CANDIDATE:** College Students, Career Changers, Retired Folks, Foreigners • **APPLICANT POOL:** 10/year
• **APPLICANTS ACCEPTED:** 3/year

••

NETWORK IS A national Catholic social-justice lobby founded in 1971 by forty-seven religious women. It operates as a nonprofit, membership organization of lay and religious women and men who put their faith into action by lobbying to influence public policy in Washington. NETWORK's political lobbying goals are securing just access to economic resources (housing, health care, employment, and income support), reordering federal budget priorities (military spending cuts, economic conversion, human needs increases, deficit reduction, and progressive taxation), and transforming global relationships (the Philippines, Central America, and South Africa).

Work/Learn Program Specifics: As a NETWORK associate or intern you will be involved in a variety of projects and in many facets of the organization. During an orientation process, you will be briefed on NETWORK's history, their alternative management processes (informed by feminist thinking and practice), current legislative issues, and will be given several issues to follow during the course of your program. For your selected issues, you will assist their lobbyists with phone calls and deliveries to congressional offices, and participate in occasional lobbying of Congressional staff. You will also attend a variety of coalition groups on the issues and may attend hearings and briefings on legislation as it moves through Congress.

Duration: Associate Program: September through July; internships are offered year-round.

Compensation and Perks: Associates are compensated with an in-depth learning experience and a stipend of $550 per month (a total of $6,000 for the eleven-month program) and a partial health-care program. There is no stipend available for interns. Information on local housing opportunities is also provided.

The Ideal Candidate: Looking for excellent written and oral communication skills, being comfortable with a progressive, faith-based approach to public policy (however, you do not need to be Catholic), and willingness to do everything from analyzing legislation to stuffing envelopes.

Making It Happen: Call for application. The deadline for the associate and the summer intern program is February 15; other terms are accepted on a rolling basis.

Contact Information: Linda Rich, Intern Coordinator • NETWORK • 801 Pennsylvania Ave., SE, Suite 460 • Washington, DC 20003-2167 • Phone: (202) 547-5556 • Fax: (202) 547-5510 • E-mail: network@ igc.apc.org

Planet Drum Foundation

REGION/HQ: Pacific Northwest/California
• **CATEGORY:** Grassroots • **POSITION TYPE:**
Internship/Seasonal • **DURATION:** Year-Round
• **IDEAL CANDIDATE:** High School Students, College
Students, Career Changers, Retired Folks, Foreigners
• **APPLICANT POOL:** 100/year • **APPLICANTS**
ACCEPTED: 4 at one time

PLANET DRUM FOUNDATION has been working for over twenty-one years to research, communicate, and disseminate information about bioregionalism. Bioregionalism promotes an understanding of and concern for the unique natural systems of each region. It provides an effective grassroots approach to ecology that emphasizes sustainability, community self-determination, and regional self-reliance. It holds that people who know and care about their life-places will work to maintain and restore them. Responding to the need for urban sustainability in a bioregional context, Planet Drum initiated the Green City Project in 1990. They also publish the *Green City Calendar* on a bimonthly basis. Call for your own copy.

Work/Learn Program Specifics: Planet Drum has a need for people in these positions: Green City assistant (help develop, plan, and implement workshop/workdays with groups in the volunteer network); environmental education assistant (develop curricula and teach classes, empowering students to make other positive changes in their immediate surroundings); editorial assistants; art layout and design; fund-raising assistant; public relations manager; Green City resource researcher; and administrative assistant.

Duration: A three-month, twenty-hours-per-week commitment is needed.

Compensation and Perks: The positions are unpaid, although a local transportation stipend is provided. They're a small office, so an internship at Planet Drum is a great way to gain new job skills, make contacts, and immerse yourself in the bioregional, ecological, and urban sustainability scenes.

The Ideal Candidate: Candidates should have education or experience in ecological issues, writing ability, and a willingness to accept responsibilities.

Making It Happen: Call to receive an internship/volunteer packet and ask about their current openings. Submit completed application, cover letter, and resume. Rolling deadlines.

INSIDER TIPS: *We are looking for candidates with enthusiasm and an ability to work well independently, as well as with a group.*

Contact Information: Maggie Weadick, Volunteer Network Coordinator • Planet Drum Foundation • P.O. Box 31251 • San Francisco, CA 94131 • Phone: (415) 285-6556 • Fax: (415) 285-6563 • E-mail: planetdrum@ igc.apc.org • Web Site: Coming soon!

Population Institute

REGION/HQ: Washington, D.C./Washington, D.C.
• **CATEGORY:** Public Interest • **POSITION TYPE:**
Internship • **DURATION:** Spring/Fall • **IDEAL**
CANDIDATE: College Students, Career Changers,
Foreigners • **APPLICANT POOL:** Varies • **APPLICANTS**
ACCEPTED: 4–6/term

THE POPULATION INSTITUTE is a small nonprofit organization working to increase public awareness of the world's constantly increasing population and to foster leadership that works on solutions to the overpopulation problem. Its headquarters are on Capitol Hill, with affiliates in Brussels, Belgium; Colombo, Sri Lanka; and Bogota, Columbia.

Work/Learn Program Specifics: Staff assistants participate fully in all organizational activities, working with experienced professionals in seeking practical solutions to population-related problems. One to three staff assistants work with public policy, assisting on legislative alerts, providing information to legislators and key staff, and following up on community leaders recruited during field trips across the nation. Duties include the maintenance of a press list, liaison with media, writing, reporting, proofreading, and editing.

Duration: They have two, six-month work periods, one starting in January and the other in July.

Compensation and Perks: The stipend provided to participants in this program is $1,000 per month, plus medical insurance. The internship also includes one day of sick leave and three days of personal-need time.

The Ideal Candidate: Applicants must be able to demonstrate leadership qualities through prior experience, have a high academic record, and possess strong writing and oral skills. Candidates must have a mature sense of purpose and commitment and must be interested in a career in public or nonprofit service. Applicants must have completed at least two years of college and be over twenty-one years of age.

Making It Happen: Send resume, cover letter, transcript, and three letters of recommendation (two must be from academic instructors). A personal interview is required. Rolling deadlines.

Contact Information: Devinka Abeysinghe, Education Coordinator • Population Institute • 107 2nd St., NE • Washington, DC 20002 • Phone: (202) 544-3300 • Fax: (202) 544-0068 • E-mail: popline@primanet. com • Web Site: www.populationinstitute.org

Rainforest Action Network

REGION/HQ: Pacific Northwest/California
• **CATEGORY:** Grassroots • **POSITION TYPE:** Internship
• **DURATION:** Year-Round • **IDEAL CANDIDATE:**
College Students, Career Changers, Foreigners
• **APPLICANT POOL:** Varies • **APPLICANTS ACCEPTED:** 30/year

RAINFOREST ACTION NETWORK is a nonprofit activist organization working to protect the earth's rainforests and support the rights of their inhabitants through education, grassroots organizing, and nonviolent direct action. Major education and advocacy programs include Amazon Program, Boycott-Mitsubishi Campaign, Wood-Use Reduction Campaign, Rainforest Action Groups, International Information Clearinghouse, Protect-An-Acre Program, and World Rainforest Week.

Work/Learn Program Specifics: Intern opportunities include media operations, database coordination, campaign administration and coordination, library assistance, on-line information, executive administration, information assistance, and development assistance.

Duration: Internships require a time commitment of twelve hours per week for three months.

Compensation and Perks: Internships are unpaid, although commuting costs are reimbursed. Interns also receive a one-year complimentary membership and a T-shirt.

The Ideal Candidate: Applicants should have basic Macintosh computer skills, knowledge of environmental issues, and a passion to help save the environment.

Making It Happen: Call for application or fill it out on their Web page.

Contact Information: Adrienne Blum, Volunteer & Intern Coordinator • Rainforest Action Network • 221 Pine St., Suite 500 • San Francisco, CA 94104 • Phone:

(415) 398-4404 • Fax: (415) 398-2732 • E-mail: helpran@ran.org • Web Site: www.ran.org/ran

Renew America

REGION/HQ: Washington, D.C./Washington, D.C.
• **CATEGORY:** Grassroots • **POSITION TYPE:** Internship
• **DURATION:** Year-Round • **IDEAL CANDIDATE:**
College Students, Career Changers, Retired Folks, Foreigners • **APPLICANT POOL:** 250/year
• **APPLICANTS ACCEPTED:** Up to 4/year

RENEW AMERICA'S GOAL is to encourage the rapid expansion of programs that effectively protect, restore, or enhance the environment at all levels—national, state, regional, and local. They recognize and promote successful projects that can serve as models for others seeking to implement similar initiatives elsewhere. More than 1,600 success stories have already been verified nationwide and are included in the Environmental Success Index. This clearinghouse of information includes environmental programs initiated by individuals; volunteer groups; religious, consumer, and environmental organizations; schools; business and industry; and government agencies at every level.

Area and Working Environment: Located in downtown Washington, D.C., Renew America has a small office with a staff of about seven people.

Work/Learn Program Specifics: Interns work on identifying successful environmental programs nationwide, in twenty-six policy areas, under such broad categories as natural resource conservation, economic progress, and human development. Much of the intern's time is spent working with local grassroots environmental organizations (state contact groups) nationwide to identify and verify projects for inclusion in the Index. As part of this effort, interns will have the opportunity to work with staff members of national environmental organizations in Washington, D.C. to search for programs that deal effectively with those issues. Interns will also respond to individual requests for information on programs included on the Index in the twenty-six environmental policy areas. All interns will assist with general activities of the program and routine office work, including use of computers.

Duration: This is a six-month program; however, short-term and part-time arrangements are possible.

Compensation and Perks: Six-month interns will receive a $7,500 stipend; other assignments vary in compensation.

The Ideal Candidate: The program is definitely aimed at recent college grads, but is open to all who have an interest in the environment.

Making It Happen: Send a resume and cover letter, expanding on your interest in the program. Rolling deadlines.

Contact Information: Internship Coordinator • Renew America • 1400 16th St., NW, Suite 710 • Washington, DC 20036 • Phone: (202) 232-2252 • Fax: (202) 232-2617 • Toll Free: (800) 922-7363 • E-mail: renewamerica@igc.org • Web Site: www.crest.org/ renew_america

Reporters Committee for Freedom of the Press

REGION/HQ: Washington, D.C./Virginia• **CATEGORY:** Public Interest • **POSITION TYPE:** Internship • **DURATION:** Year-Round • **IDEAL CANDIDATE:** College Students • **APPLICANT POOL:** 75/year • **APPLICANTS ACCEPTED:** 2/term

THE REPORTERS COMMITTEE for Freedom of the Press is a voluntary, unincorporated association of reporters and editors dedicated to protecting the First Amendment interests of the news media. It provides cost-free legal defense and research services to journalists throughout the United States, and also operates the FOI Service Center to assist the news media with federal and state open records and open meetings issues.

Work/Learn Program Specifics: Journalism interns have the opportunity to report, write, and edit the committee's publications. These stories cover a broad range of issues, from the arrests of journalists to military press pool restrictions and access to executions. Editorial interns will prepare their annual legislative update, an analysis of bills in Congress that could affect the news media. Interns also attend weekly seminars by prominent media and legal experts in freedom of the press, members of the Steering Committee, and in-house attorneys, and attend congressional hearings, U.S. Court of Appeals and Supreme Court arguments, and media conferences relevant to the committee's work.

Duration: Internships are offered three times a year, each term lasting twelve to fourteen weeks. Full-time interns work forty or more hours a week; part-time interns, twenty to thirty hours.

Compensation and Perks: Full-time interns receive a stipend of $650 to $1,000 per semester; part-time interns receive proportional shares, based on hours worked.

The Ideal Candidate: Juniors, seniors, or graduate students are encouraged to apply. A strong background in journalism or political science is required.

Making It Happen: Submit resume, short writing sample (clips and/or a short research paper), and a cover letter describing interest. Rolling deadlines.

INSIDER TIPS: *Our interns go immediately to work here. They are very much a part of the committee's work in this small-staffed office. We generally consider the best writers, and the candidates who are clearly professional in attitude and demeanor.*

Contact Information: Internship Coordinator • Reporters Committee for Freedom of the Press • 1101 Wilson Blvd., Suite 1910 • Arlington, VA 22209 • Phone: (703) 807-2100 • Fax: (703) 807-2109

River Network

REGION/HQ: Nationwide/Oregon • **CATEGORY:** Conservation • **POSITION TYPE:** Internship • **DURATION:** Year-Round • **IDEAL CANDIDATE:** College Students, Career Changers • **APPLICANT POOL:** Varies • **APPLICANTS ACCEPTED:** 4/year

RIVER NETWORK IS A national river conservation organization dedicated to helping people save rivers. They support river conservationists in America at the grassroots, state, and regional levels, help them build effective organizations, and link them together in a national movement to protect and restore America's rivers and watersheds. They also work with river conservationists to acquire and conserve riverlands that are critical for wildlife, fisheries, and recreation.

Area and Working Environment: The Riverlands Conservancy Program is in Portland, Oregon; the Watershed Program is in Washington, D.C.

Work/Learn Program Specifics: The Riverlands Conservancy internship duties include researching land ownership along specific rivers, assisting in closing land projects, researching new markets with municipal watershed agencies and Corps of Engineers mitigation programs, producing publications and organizing photos of rivers that they work on, and providing any related administrative tasks. The Watershed internship duties include knowledge and experience with on-line services, researching and writing about technical issues related to river protection, identifying and recruiting river experts, responding to requests for assistance from activists, assisting in administrative tasks, and compiling fund-raising information for river activists.

Duration: River Network prefers interns to stay for one year, working forty hours per week, with a flexible schedule.

Compensation and Perks: A $1,000-per-month stipend, plus vacation and sick days are provided. Perks include attending work-related river-rafting trips, conferences and trainings, and meetings with people in the environmental/river protection fields.

The Ideal Candidate: Applicants must have an interest in river protection or environmental issues. The ideal candidate is someone who has just graduated or will be graduating with a bachelor's or master's in environmental studies or a related field. Applicants must be well-organized, work well both as team members and individuals, and be computer literate.

Making It Happen: Send a cover letter describing why and when you are interested in an internship and your major areas of interest, a resume, a nontechnical writing sample about an environmental issue you've researched, and a list of three personal references. Rolling deadlines.

INSIDER TIPS: *Send complete application, including cover letter; let your personality show in your writing; have a good understanding of River Network's programs and convey that in your cover letter; be persistent without being a pest; and are you working on local river or environmental issues?*

Contact Information: Jean Hamilla, Office Manager • River Network • P.O. Box 8787 • Portland, OR 97207-8787 • Phone: (503) 241-3506 • Fax: (503) 241-9256 • Toll Free: (800) 423-6747 • E-mail: rivernet@igc.apc.org • Web Site: www.rivernetwork. org/~rivernet

Save The Bay

REGION/HQ: Northeast/Rhode Island • **CATEGORY:** Grassroots • **POSITION TYPE:** Internship • **DURATION:** Year-Round • **IDEAL CANDIDATE:** College Students, Career Changers, Foreigners • **APPLICANT POOL:** 80/year • **APPLICANTS ACCEPTED:** Varies

SAVE THE BAY IS A privately-funded nonprofit organization dedicated to protecting and maximizing the assets of Rhode Island's greatest natural resource—

Narrangansett Bay. Recent accomplishments include production of a video on storm-drain-painting, development of an elementary school curriculum manual, production of a *Tips for Better Boating* and a *Septic System Manual*, and tracking the legislative agenda.

Work/Learn Program Specifics: Internships include educational, development and marketing, and policy. Responsibilities may include assisting with development of educational publications and displays, assisting with the development and teaching of Explore the Bay (on-the-water program for children), assisting the communications director with all aspects of Save The Bay's public and media relations requirements, and prospecting major gifts from foundations, corporations, and individuals.

Duration: Duration is approximately twelve to thirteen weeks, offered year-round.

Compensation and Perks: Stipend is $125 per week, plus participation in professional development activities. Another bonus is a smoke-free office and free parking.

The Ideal Candidate: Applicants must have a background in education, natural science, natural history, environmental study, or one of the life sciences. Experience in working with children and knowledge of marine science are desirable, but not necessary. You must have your own transportation.

Making It Happen: Send cover letter and resume. Rolling deadlines.

Contact Information: Volunteer Coordinator • Save The Bay • 434 Smith St. • Providence, RI 02908-3770 • Phone: (401) 272-3540 • Fax: (401) 273-7153

Southface Energy Institute

REGION/HQ: Southeast/Georgia • **CATEGORY:** Conservation • **POSITION TYPE:** Internship • **DURATION:** Year-Round • **IDEAL CANDIDATE:** College Students, Career Changers, Foreigners • **APPLICANT POOL:** 150/year • **APPLICANTS ACCEPTED:** 8/year

SOUTHFACE ENERGY INSTITUTE is a nonprofit public interest group that conducts research and educational activities on energy conservation and renewable energy technologies. Since its inception in 1978, the Southface staff has taught thousands of building and energy professionals and consumers how to save energy and money through a variety of projects, workshops, seminars, free publications, and services. One of the institute's most exciting projects is the Southface Energy and Environmental Resource Center, a new, state-of-the-art demonstration facility. New technologies and materials are combined to demonstrate to the public what can be done in the context of residential construction.

Work/Learn Program Specifics: Approximately half of the workweek for interns will be spent in general staff assistance. This may include monitoring of the in-house recycling program, maintaining membership databases, and participating in weekly staff meetings. Another quarter of the workweek will be spent in project work. This might consist of assisting the staff in leading hands-on workshops at high schools, setting up and staffing exhibits at home shows and festivals, or conducting research for the institute's quarterly periodical. The final quarter of time is left open for an independent project chosen in conjunction with the internship coordinator. Past projects have included designing and updating a building products file, researching and planting an organic herb garden for the southern climate, and creating an exhibit relating sun angle to thermal gain in a passive solar house.

Duration: Internships are from three to six months in length.

Compensation and Perks: Interns receive a $335-per-month stipend; and unless free housing is available, interns will also receive $200 to $250 per month for housing. Interns may attend free courses taught by Southface and receive free publications.

The Ideal Candidate: Southface has a need for interns who have knowledge of or an interest in and willingness to learn about organic gardening and landscaping, building construction and design, or environmental issues in relation to the use of energy. Interns must be willing to do physical work, mostly related to light construction, carpentry, and building maintenance. Foreign students must have excellent English skills.

Making It Happen: Write for application form. Rolling deadlines.

INSIDER TIPS: *Be flexible and enthusiastic!*

Contact Information: Steve Byers, Internship Coordinator • Southface Energy Institute • 241 Pine St. • Atlanta, GA 30308 • Phone: (404) 872-3549 • Fax: (404) 872-5009 • E-mail: interns@southface.org • Web Site: www.southface.org

Spring Lake Ranch, Inc.

REGION/HQ: Northeast/Vermont • **CATEGORY:** Therapeutic Camp • **POSITION TYPE:** Internship • **DURATION:** Year-Round • **IDEAL CANDIDATE:** College Students, Career Changers, Foreigners • **APPLICANT POOL:** 40/year • **APPLICANTS ACCEPTED:** 10/year

SPRING LAKE RANCH IS A SMALL, therapeutic-work community founded in 1932. Residents decide to come to the ranch because stress, breakdown, or illness has interrupted the normal progress of their lives. All share a need for time to identify and work on problems and to assess and develop abilities that can be a foundation for future life. It is much easier to make friends and focus on what one can do rather than what one can't when working together on a common task.

Area and Working Environment: The ranch is situated in a small, rural New England town located in the Green Mountains of Vermont. The ranch covers 500 acres, most of which is either farmland or forested, with the Appalachian Trail crossing the property.

Work/Learn Program Specifics: House advisor/work crew leaders are both responsible for the residents with whom they share living space. They also lead or participate in a wide variety of manual tasks appropriate to the rural environment and dramatically changing seasons. These include cutting wood, caring for animals, growing vegetables in their gardens for sale at the Farmer's Market in town, shoveling snow, maple sugaring, haying in meadows, and helping with ongoing chores of cooking, cleaning, sewing, and construction. The majority of people who have worked in the ranch community have found the experience both physically and emotionally demanding, but intensely rewarding as well. Unlike many institutions for the chronically ill, the ranch program has little structure or job description and demands flexibility and emotional spontaneity from its staff. It is an extremely demanding life experience, requiring balance, stability, and an ability to set limits on one's involvement and the use of one's energy to achieve a positive end.

Duration: There is a minimum six-month commitment.

Compensation and Perks: Interns receive a $100-per-week stipend, plus room and board. You will live in one of nine cottages as a house advisor, supervising from two to nine residents. Other perks include two weeks'

vacation, comprehensive health insurance, and personal use of their auto shop, woodworking shop, computers, and laundry facilities. You will also have the opportunity to attend seminars/workshops and other benefits that only come from working and living in a small community.

The Ideal Candidate: Applicants must be twenty years of age or older. Applicants must show a willingness to share life with a community of diverse people, the ability to interact and relate to others and motivate self and others, and flexibility. A basic knowledge of and experience in farming, gardening, carpentry, cooking, sewing, auto mechanics, landscaping, and recreational skills are not necessary, but can be very helpful.

Making It Happen: Send resume and cover letter. A twenty-four-hour visit is strongly recommended as part of the interview process.

Contact Information: Lynn McDermott, Personnel Director • Spring Lake Ranch, Inc. • Spring Lake Rd. • Box 310 • Cuttingsville, VT 05738 • Phone: (802) 492-3322 • Fax: (802) 492-3331

Surfrider Foundation

REGION/HQ: Nationwide/California • **CATEGORY:** Marine Science • **POSITION TYPE:** Internship • **DURATION:** Year-Round • **IDEAL CANDIDATE:** High School Students, College Students, Career Changers, Retired Folks, Foreigners • **APPLICANT POOL: Varies** • **APPLICANTS ACCEPTED:** Varies

FED UP WITH SOUTHERN CALIFORNIA'S increasingly polluted waters, a circle of surfers banded together in 1984 to create a group dedicated to the preservation of coastal waters and beaches. Today, Surfrider is an international organization with over 25,000 members. Its track record as a coastal watchdog is impressive—it stopped the California Coastal Commission from building a $200-million beach-destroying breakwater at Bolsa Chica State Beach and helped to divert storm-drain water from Santa Monica Bay to the city's sewage treatment system. Surfrider staff also spends time educating local students and lifeguard associations.

Area and Working Environment: The foundation is based in San Clemente, California, a beach community known for its health food stores, trinket shops, and great surf. Positions are available in one of their thirty-five local chapters across the United States (including seventeen California coastal communities, Delaware, Florida, Hawaii, North Carolina, New Jersey, Maine,

New York, Oregon, Puerto Rico, Rhode Island, Texas, Virginia, Washington, and Washington, D.C.).

Work/Learn Program Specifics: They are a small, dedicated group of individuals sincerely trying to make a difference and have to perform a wide range of tasks to get the job done. Their program is informal, and it's what you make of it. Current projects interns will participate in include Blue Water Task Force (interns assist in gathering water samples along seashores in an effort to demonstrate the severity and extent of near shore pollution); Respect the Beach (a coastal educational program that includes videos and booklets designed to teach the basics about beach safety, marine ecology, and ocean stewardship); and Wave Watch (an environmental advocacy program that is conceived to empower Surfrider Foundation members to take individual action that will make a difference in their own ocean backyards).

Duration: Positions are available year-round.

Compensation and Perks: Although this is an unpaid position, you will receive industry exposure and contacts and an opportunity to interface with top-notch professionals.

The Ideal Candidate: Surfrider looks for candidates who are outgoing and environmentally aware. Knowledge of the surf industry and computer proficiency are very helpful. Foreign student applicants must speak English.

Making It Happen: Call for application. Rolling deadlines.

INSIDER TIPS: *Flexibility and a strong desire and commitment will be valued assets. Candidates must be willing to perform other needs/functions apart from their chosen area of interest, when necessary.*

Contact Information: Angi Guiton, Internship/Volunteer Director • Surfrider Foundation • 122 S. El Camino Real, #67 • San Clemente, CA 92672 • Phone: (714) 492-8170 • Fax: (714) 492-8142 • Toll Free: (800) 743-7873 • E-mail: surfrider0@aol.com • Web Site: www.surfrider.org

UCSF AIDS Health Project

REGION/HQ: Pacific Northwest/California • **CATEGORY:** Education • **POSITION TYPE:** Internship • **DURATION:** Year-Round • **IDEAL CANDIDATE:** College Students, Career Changers, Foreigners • **APPLICANT POOL:** Varies • **APPLICANTS ACCEPTED:** 10/year

THE AIDS HEALTH PROJECT (AHP) was founded in 1984 by a group of mental health professionals from the University of California, San Francisco and the private practice community in San Francisco. Since that time, it has provided direct service to more than 20,000 individuals and more than 1,000 providers annually. AHP seeks to help people reduce the risk of HIV transmission, cope with the emotional challenges of HIV infection, and support friends, lovers, family members, and co-workers who face the challenges of the epidemic.

Work/Learn Program Specifics: Whenever possible, internships will be tailored to capitalize on those unique skills and personal interests that each intern brings to the position. The intern will be an integral part of the UCSF AIDS Health Project, and interns are expected to take on many of the professional responsibilities of permanent staff. The intern will attend monthly staff meetings, unit cluster meetings, and other meetings as needed. Encouragement and assistance whenever possible will be given for the individual intern's pursuit of academic and professional goals. Positions include publications, marketing and public relations, computer support, client support services, development, research, and HIV counseling/testing services.

Duration: Internship assignments are twelve months and you will work thirty-two hours per week.

Compensation and Perks: Although the positions are unpaid, they can provide guest house accommodations (either provided at approved sites or as a $500 monthly payment to a landlord for rent) and a wealth of learning experience. You will also receive student/staff privileges at UCSF, including reduced rate membership in the Milberry Union health and fitness program (including gym and pool), use of the UCSF library, and other programs. Since you won't work a full week, you may try getting part-time paid work to supplement your internship experience.

The Ideal Candidate: Applicants should have a strong knowledge of Macintosh or PC computers and Microsoft Word; excellent interpersonal skills, including the ability and sensitivity to work with clinical and nonclinical staff; sensitivity to HIV-related needs and concerns; and ability and sensitivity to work in a culturally diverse work setting that includes gays, lesbians, people of various ethnicities, persons with substance abuse problems, and people with HIV.

Making It Happen: Call for application. Submit completed application and resume (with two writing samples for publications, marketing, or development positions) by March 31. You will be notified no later than May 31.

INSIDER TIPS: *Bilingual Spanish/English ability is very desirable; previous HIV/AIDS experience is a plus.*

Contact Information: Staffing Coordinator • UCSF AIDS Health Project • P.O. Box 0884 • San Francisco, CA 94143-0884 • Phone: (415) 476-3890 • Fax: (415) 476-3613 • E-mail: susan_sunshine.ahp_mcb @quickmail.ucsf.edu

United Nations Association of the USA

REGION/HQ: Northeast/New York • **CATEGORY:** Global Development • **POSITION TYPE:** Internship • **DURATION:** Year-Round • **IDEAL CANDIDATE:** College Students, Foreigners • **APPLICANT POOL:** 200-300/year • **APPLICANTS ACCEPTED:** 10–15/term

THE UNITED NATIONS ASSOCIATION (UNA) is the nation's leading center for research and information on the work and structure of the UN system. Through a unique combination of grassroots activism and high-level policy studies, UNA, through its 26,000 members nationwide, pioneers efforts to involve the American public, government, and business leaders in the discussion of foreign policy priorities.

Work/Learn Program Specifics: Internships are available in these departments: Communications, Model UN and Education, Policy Studies, Media Relations/Public Affairs, and Corporate Affairs. Interns leave UNA with a broad understanding of how the UN works and the issues it faces. Besides important research and writing assignments, UNA Interns are given coveted UN grounds passes with which they may observe UN meetings and briefings.

Duration: Both part-time and full-time positions are available year-round, for ten to twelve weeks.

Compensation and Perks: Interns have use of research facilities and can attend various UN meetings, functions, and seminars.

The Ideal Candidate: Candidates should have an interest in and some knowledge of the UN and international affairs.

Making It Happen: Write for an application package. The application package calls for a resume, a completed application, and short responses to three questions. Interviewing is generally not required. Selections may begin before the deadline, so submit early. Deadlines: spring—January 15; summer—April 1; and fall—August 15.

INSIDER TIPS: *All writing samples should be extremely short—not more than five pages. Considering such length, applicants should not try to submit writing samples on topics on which the staff members are experts. Errors in facts and attribution tend to stick out. Writing samples are required only because internship duties most often include writing and editing, research, and correspondence with high-level officials; therefore, clear, concise, and consistent writing is preferred. Topics for these samples should be meaningful to the author.*

Contact Information: Melanie Andrich, Internship Program Coordinator • United Nations Association of the USA • 801 Second Ave. • New York, NY 10017 • Phone: (212) 907-1326 • Fax: (212) 682-9185 • Alternate: (212) 697-3232 • E-mail: unany@igc.apc.org • Web Site: www.unausa.org

The White House

REGION/HQ: Washington, D.C./Washington, D.C. • **CATEGORY:** Government • **POSITION TYPE:** Internship • **DURATION:** Year-Round • **IDEAL CANDIDATE:** College Students, Career Changers • **APPLICANT POOL:** 600/year • **APPLICANTS ACCEPTED:** 200/year

THE WHITE HOUSE internship program is a rare chance for students to experience life on the doorstep of a world power center.

Work/Learn Program Specifics: The duties of an intern often entail assisting in the operations of press conferences, briefings, and public events—some of which are of national importance! This is an unparalleled experience for a student who wishes to see the workings of the executive branch, and interns will have the opportunity to work in various departments of the White House. These departments include Cabinet Affairs, Chief of Staff, Correspondence, Office of Counsel to the President, Domestic Policy, First Lady's Office, Intergovernmental Affairs, Legislative Affairs, Management/Administration/Operations, National AIDS Policy Office, National Economic Council, Photo Office, Political Affairs, Presidential Personnel, Office of the Press Secretary, Scheduling and Advance, Strategic Planning and Communications, and the Office of

the Vice President (which includes Visitors Office and Women's Initiative and Outreach).

Duration: There are four intern sessions each year: twelve-week sessions in the spring and fall, and two six-week summer sessions (early June to early July or mid-July to late August). Spring and fall interns must be able to work at least twenty-five hours per week.

Compensation and Perks: The White House is prohibited by law from seeking private funds to underwrite its internship program. They can, however, provide you with guidelines and suggestions for obtaining funds for your internship. Although unpaid, the program includes a weekly speaker series, job-skill workshops, and evening issue lectures. Speakers include White House staff, cabinet secretaries, and congressional leaders. Seminars are on a wide range of job-related issues ranging from time management to career planning.

The Ideal Candidate: Applicants must be at least eighteen years of age and the program is ideal for undergraduates, graduate students, and recent graduates who have demonstrated academic excellence and display a commitment to public service. Only U.S. citizens are eligible to apply.

Making It Happen: Call for application and details of the program. Along with your completed application, you'll need to include your resume, two letters of recommendation, a 500-word writing sample, unofficial transcripts, and a brief description of any significant information regarding family, upbringing, or heritage. Deadlines: spring—November 1; summer—March 1; and fall—July 1. Applicants should hear a decision at least one month prior to the start date of the internship. No interviews are given.

Contact Information: Madge Henning, Intern Program Director • The White House • Room 98 • Washington, DC 20500 • Phone: (202) 456-2742 • Fax: (202) 456-5123

Make your voice heard by dropping a note to President Clinton—on-line. President@ whitehouse.gov

Short Listings

Amerind Foundation, Inc.

REGION/HQ: South/Midwest/Arizona • **CATEGORY:** Anthropology • **POSITION TYPE:** Internship • **DURATION:** Year-Round • **IDEAL CANDIDATE:** College Students, Career Changers, Foreigners • **APPLICANT POOL:** 200/year • **APPLICANTS ACCEPTED:** Varies

THE AMERIND FOUNDATION is an anthropological research facility and museum. The name "Amerind," a contraction of American Indian, illustrates the purpose of the foundation, which is devoted to the study of Native American culture and history. Internships vary depending on current projects. Interns will be appointed in anthropological research, museum studies, and the library. The stipend depends on the intern's project and previous experience. Housing is provided. Apply at least sixteen weeks before desired start date.

Contact Information: Anne Woosley, Director • Amerind Foundation, Inc. • P.O. Box 400 • Dragoon, AZ 85609 • Phone: (520) 586-3666 • Fax: (520) 586-3667 • E-mail: amerindinc@aol.com

Amnesty International USA—New York

REGION/HQ: Northeast/New York • **CATEGORY:** Human Rights • **POSITION TYPE:** Internship • **DURATION:** Year-Round • **IDEAL CANDIDATE:** College Students, Foreigners • **APPLICANT POOL:** 200–300/year • **APPLICANTS ACCEPTED:** Varies

THE NEW YORK OFFICE has internship positions available in casework/country actions, death penalty, refugee, religious affiliation, information services/computer systems, finance and administration, women's program, advertising and marketing, membership communications, press, special projects, video, comment mailer, legal/policy advisor/board liaison, development, and national programs.

Contact Information: Program/Internship Director • Amnesty International USA—New York • 322 Eighth Ave. • New York, NY 10001 • Phone: (212) 807-8400 • Fax: (212) 627-1451

Amnesty International USA— San Francisco

REGION/HQ: Pacific Northwest/California • **CATEGORY:** Human Rights • **POSITION TYPE:** Internship • **DURATION:** Year-Round • **IDEAL CANDIDATE:** College Students, Career Changers, Retired Folks, Foreigners • **APPLICANT POOL:** 20/term • **APPLICANTS ACCEPTED:** 5/term

WHEN THE TELEPHONE is answered at Amnesty International's Refuge Program in San Francisco, interns can hear the pleas of people who have fled to the United States because they've been kidnapped or tortured or because they've witnessed the brutal murders of relatives and friends. More often than not these crimes occurred at the hands of their own governments. Interns provide the research and documentation to be used as evidence in political asylum hearings. Because of the contact with refugees and asylum seekers, Amnesty prefers interns with fluency in more than one language. Although a volunteer position, interns are provided with a travel stipend to help cover transportation costs.

Contact Information: Coleen Liebmann, Program Assistant • Amnesty International USA—San Francisco • National Refugee Office • 500 Sansome St., Suite 615 • San Francisco, CA 94111-3222 • Phone: (415) 291-0601 • Fax: (415) 291-8722 • E-mail: cliebman@ aiusa.usa.com

Bikes Not Bombs

REGION/HQ: Worldwide/Massachusetts • **CATEGORY:** Conservation • **POSITION TYPE:** Unique Experience • **DURATION:** Year-Round • **IDEAL CANDIDATE:** High School Students, College Students, Career Changers, Retired Folks, Foreigners • **APPLICANT POOL:** Varies • **APPLICANTS ACCEPTED:** Varies

BIKES NOT BOMBS (BNB) is a nonprofit development and solidarity organization that helps local groups form ecologically viable bicycle workshops and related projects in Central America, Haiti, and in the United States. These projects have involved the collecting of over 12,000 donated bicycles and tons of parts from across the United States, recycling them to Nicaragua, Haiti, and recently, to U.S. inner-city youth programs. BNB provides technical assistance, training, tools, and financing for these projects and funds a bicycle-purchaser-revolving-loan fund for campesinos in Nicaragua. Experienced, bilingual mechanics and personnel are placed to carry out fieldwork.

Contact Information: Program Director • Bikes Not Bombs • 59 Amory, #103A • Roxbury, MA 02119 • Phone: (617) 442-0004 • E-mail: bnbrox@igc.apc.org

Campaign to Save the Environment

REGION/HQ: Nationwide/Massachusetts • **CATEGORY:** Advocacy • **POSITION TYPE:** Internship/Seasonal • **DURATION:** Summer • **IDEAL CANDIDATE:** College Students, Career Changers, Retired Folks, Foreigners • **APPLICANT POOL:** Thousands • **APPLICANTS ACCEPTED:** Thousands

WORK WITH STATE PIRGs, the Sierra Club, Southern Utah Wilderness Alliance, or American Oceans Campaign helping preserve our environment and protect public health. Positions are available in over thirty states throughout the United States, where you'll gain experience working on an exciting campaign to save the environment and put political power where it belongs—with the people, not the special interests. In addition, you'll learn powerful skills, like fund-raising, media relations, public education, and community organizing. You can also expect to earn $2,500 to $4,000 during the summer.

Contact Information: Program Coordinator • Campaign to Save the Environment • 29 Temple Place, 5th Floor • Boston, MA 02111 • Phone: (800) 753-2784 • E-mail: greenjobs@juno.com

The Carter Center

REGION/HQ: Southeast/Georgia • **CATEGORY:** Public Interest • **POSITION TYPE:** Internship • **DURATION:** Year-Round • **IDEAL CANDIDATE:** College Students • **APPLICANT POOL:** 60/year • **APPLICANTS ACCEPTED:** 25/year

IN 1982 JIMMY CARTER founded the Carter Center, a think tank to improve the quality of life for people around the world. Guided by Carter and staffed with distinguished professors, the Carter Center works with world leaders and dignitaries to promote democracy, resolve conflicts, protect human rights, eradicate disease, improve agriculture in developing countries, and tackle social problems in urban areas.

Contact Information: Internship Coordinator • The Carter Center • 453 Freedom Parkway • One Copenhill • Atlanta, GA 30307 • Phone: (404) 420-5151 • Fax: (404) 420-5196 • Web Site: www.emory.edu/CARTER_CENTER/homepage.htm

Center for Marine Conservation

REGION/HQ: Washington, D.C./Washington, D.C. • **CATEGORY:** Marine Science • **POSITION TYPE:** Internship • **DURATION:** Year-Round • **IDEAL CANDIDATE:** College Students, Foreigners • **APPLICANT POOL:** 500/year • **APPLICANTS ACCEPTED:** Varies

THE CENTER FOR MARINE CONSERVATION is a nonprofit, environmental organization with headquarters in Washington, D.C. and regional offices in Virginia, Florida, Texas, and California. The center is dedicated to protection of the marine environment and its wildlife through public awareness and education, political lobbying, grassroots activities, and collaborative efforts with others. Internships are available in such areas as marine debris and entanglement, sea turtle conservation, marine mammal conservation, marine habitat protection, fisheries conservation, marine biological diversity, press relations and art/publications, and administration.

Contact Information: Denise Thomas, Internship Coordinator • Center for Marine Conservation • 1725 DeSales St., NW, Suite 500 • Washington, DC 20036 • Phone: (202) 429-5609 • Fax: (202) 872-0619

Citizen Action

REGION/HQ: Washington, D.C./Washington, D.C. • **CATEGORY:** Advocacy • **POSITION TYPE:** Internship • **DURATION:** Year-Round • **IDEAL CANDIDATE:** High School Students, College Students, Career Changers, Retired Folks, Foreigners • **APPLICANT POOL:** Varies • **PPLICANTS ACCEPTED:** Varies

CITIZEN ACTION WORKS on a variety of issues that affect people in their daily lives. These include affordable and accessible national health care, reduction of toxic wastes, promotion of energy efficiency, fair energy prices and utility rates, campaign finance reform, and consumer reforms of the insurance industry. Interns engage in a wide variety of substantive work, including research, congressional advocacy, and grassroots organizing.

Contact Information: Internship Coordinator • Citizen Action • 1730 Rhode Island Ave., NW, Suite 403 • Washington, DC 20036 • Phone: (202) 775-1580 • Fax: (202) 296-4054

Colorado Association of Nonprofit Organizations

REGION/HQ: Rocky Mountains/Colorado • **CATEGORY:** Clearinghouse • **POSITION TYPE:** Association • **DURATION:** Year-Round • **IDEAL CANDIDATE:** High School Students, College Students, Career Changers, Retired Folks • **APPLICANT POOL:** Varies • **APPLICANTS ACCEPTED:** Varies

THE COLORADO ASSOCIATION of Nonprofit Organizations promotes and strengthens the nonprofit sector through advocacy, information, networking, and group purchasing programs for over 950 members. They have various volunteer internships available. This a great resource for those needing more information on the nonprofit industry.

Contact Information: Associate Director • Colorado Association of Nonprofit Organizations • 225 E. 16th Ave., Suite 1060 • Denver, CO 80203-1614 • Phone: (303) 832-5710 • Fax: (303) 894-0161 • E-mail: canpo@canpo.org • Web Site: www.aclin.org/code/canpo

Concern, Inc.

REGION/HQ: Washington, D.C./Washington, D.C. • **CATEGORY:** Environment • **POSITION TYPE:** Internship • **DURATION:** Year-Round • **IDEAL CANDIDATE:** College Students, Career Changers, Foreigners • **APPLICANT POOL:** Varies • **APPLICANTS ACCEPTED:** Varies

FOUNDED IN 1970, CONCERN is a nonprofit organization that provides environmental information to individuals, community groups, educational institutions, public officials, and others involved with the environment, public education, and policy development. Interns assist with research and writing of Concern's Community Action Guide Series. Each Community Action Guide provides a comprehensive overview of an environmental issue and includes pertinent legislation

and guidelines for specific actions individuals may take at home and in their communities. Interns may also take part in community outreach programs, contribute to the design and layout of Concern information sheets, and assist with management of data entry and distribution of materials. Interns receive a $75-per-week stipend.

Contact Information: Outreach Coordinator • Concern, Inc. • 1794 Columbia Rd., NW • Washington, DC 20009 • Phone: (202) 328-8160 • Fax: (202) 387-3378

Congressional Youth Leadership Council

REGION/HQ: Washington, D.C./Washington, D.C. • **CATEGORY:** Education • **POSITION TYPE:** Association • **DURATION:** Year-Round • **IDEAL CANDIDATE:** College Students, Career Changers, Foreigners • **APPLICANT POOL:** Varies • **APPLICANTS ACCEPTED:** Varies

THE COUNCIL IS A NONPROFIT, educational organization committed to providing a hands-on learning experience for over 7,000 outstanding high school students nationwide annually. In addition to sponsoring leadership training for high school students, the council provides internships for college students. They produce a nice internship directory for positions in the Washington, D.C. area. Call for details. Council internships are available in admissions, alumni affairs, conference, curriculum, information systems, finance, and public affairs (just to name a few).

Contact Information: Marguerite Regan, Executive Director • Congressional Youth Leadership Council • 1511 K Street, NW, Suite 842 • Washington, DC 20005 • Phone: (202) 638-0008 • Fax: (202) 638-4257 • E-mail: mregan@cylc.org • Web Site: www.cylc.org

Delaware Nature Society

REGION/HQ: Northeast/Delaware • **CATEGORY:** Environmental Education • **POSITION TYPE:** Internship • **DURATION:** Year-Round • **IDEAL CANDIDATE:** High School Students, College Students, Career Changers, Retired Folks, Foreigners • **APPLICANT POOL:** 15/year • **APPLICANTS ACCEPTED:** Varies

THE DELAWARE NATURE SOCIETY fosters understanding, appreciation, and enjoyment of the natural world through education, preservation of ecologically significant areas, and advocation of stewardship of natural resources. Created by a handful of concerned people in 1964, the organization has grown to include over 5,000 members. Internships are available in environmental education, conservation advocacy, communications, photography, or illustration. Interns will have opportunities to work with people of all ages and interests, design curriculum, attend environmental workshops and training programs, work with live farm and wild animals, and develop their own special skills and interests, which help to enrich the society's programs. Interns receive a stipend to cover the costs of housing, food, and transportation.

Contact Information: Education Manager • Delaware Nature Society • P.O. Box 700 • Hockessin, DE 19707 • Phone: (302) 239-2334 • Fax: (302) 239-2473

EarthAction

REGION/HQ: Worldwide/Massachusetts • **CATEGORY:** Global Development • **POSITION TYPE:** Internship • **DURATION:** Year-Round • **IDEAL CANDIDATE:** High School Students, College Students, Career Changers, Retired Folks, Foreigners • **APPLICANT POOL:** 10/year • **APPLICANTS ACCEPTED:** 2/term

EARTHACTION IS A global network of over 1,500 organizations in more than 140 countries that work together on environment, development, peace, and human rights issues. They focus on a different issue every month and prepare an information and action kit that they send to all the organizations in their network. Internships are available in their offices in Massachusetts, London, and Santiago, Chile. Interns help with the day-to-day activities of carrying out their work as well as work on special projects. Interns stay anywhere from two months to a year and usually spend twenty to thirty hours a week at their office. They are looking for people who are bright, eager to learn, detail oriented, and have good communication and computer skills.

Contact Information: Lois Barber, International Coordinator • EarthAction • 30 Cottage St. • Amherst, MA 01002 • Phone: (413) 549-8118 • Fax: (413) 549-0544 • E-mail: amherst@earthaction.com • Web Site: www.oneworld.org/earthaction

Elderhostel

REGION/HQ: Worldwide/Massachusetts • **CATEGORY:** Service Learning • **POSITION TYPE:** Unique Experience • **DURATION:** Year-Round • **IDEAL CANDIDATE:** Retired Folks • **APPLICANT POOL:** Varies • **APPLICANTS ACCEPTED:** Varies

ELDERHOSTEL HAS volunteer and learning programs in the United States and abroad lasting two to four weeks. Participants assist in a variety of tasks, from teaching English and computer skills, to building low-cost housing in needy communities, to ecological/scientific research. Applicants must be age fifty-five or older (although a younger spouse may accompany). During free times, participants engage in cultural interaction and educational service. The fee is from $315 to $4,000 depending on program.

Contact Information: Program Director • Elderhostel • 75 Federal St. • Boston, MA 02110-1941 • Phone: (617) 426-7788 • Fax: (617) 426-8351

Friends of the Earth

REGION/HQ: Washington, D.C./Washington, D.C. • **CATEGORY:** Advocacy • **POSITION TYPE:** Internship • **DURATION:** Year-Round • **IDEAL CANDIDATE:** College Students, Career Changers • **APPLICANT POOL:** Varies • **APPLICANTS ACCEPTED:** Varies

FRIENDS OF THE EARTH is an independent, global, environmental advocacy organization which will work—at local, national, and international levels—to protect the planet from environmental disaster, preserve biological, cultural, and ethnic diversity, and involve citizens in decisions affecting their environment and their lives.

Contact Information: Fellowship Coordinator • Friends of the Earth • 1025 Vermont Ave., NW • Washington, DC 20005 • Phone: (202) 544-2600

Frontiers Foundation/ Operation Beaver

REGION/HQ: Canada/Ontario • **CATEGORY:** Community Service • **POSITION TYPE:** Unique Experience • **DURATION:** Year-Round • **IDEAL CANDIDATE:** College Students, Career Changers, Retired Folks, Foreigners • **APPLICANT POOL:** Varies • **APPLICANTS ACCEPTED:** Varies

FRONTIERS FOUNDATION IS A community-development service organization which works in partnership with communities in low-income, rural areas across northern Canada. These locally initiated projects build and improve housing, conduct training programs, and organize recreational activities in developing regions. Projects run year-round, but new volunteers begin in April and November. Placements up to eighteen months are possible. Volunteers must be eighteen or older and be available for a minimum of twelve weeks. Accommodations, food, and travel inside Canada are provided.

Contact Information: Program Director • Frontiers Foundation/Operation Beaver • 2615 Danforth Ave., Suite 203 • Toronto, Ontario M4C 1L6 • Canada • Phone: (416) 690-3930 • Fax: (416) 690-3934

Greenpeace USA

REGION/HQ: Washington, D.C./Washington, D.C.
• **CATEGORY:** Grassroots • **POSITION TYPE:** Internship
• **DURATION:** Year-Round • **IDEAL CANDIDATE:**
College Students, Career Changers, Retired Folks, Foreigners • **APPLICANT POOL:** Varies • **APPLICANTS ACCEPTED:** Varies

GREENPEACE IS A NONPROFIT environmental organization dedicated to preserving the earth. Positions are available in ocean ecology, toxics, or nuclear disarmament campaigns. Duties include research, administrative duties, and information gathering.

Contact Information: Program Coordinator • Greenpeace USA • 1436 U St., NW • Washington, DC 20009 • Phone: (202) 462-1177

Hartford Food System

REGION/HQ: Northeast/Connecticut • **CATEGORY:** Public Interest • **POSITION TYPE:** Internship
• **DURATION:** Summer • **IDEAL CANDIDATE:** College Students, Career Changers, Foreigners • **APPLICANT POOL:** 25/year • **APPLICANTS ACCEPTED:** 4/year

THE HARTFORD FOOD SYSTEM is a private nonprofit organization founded in 1978 that increases the access of lower-income and elderly Hartford residents to high-quality, affordable food. In addition to its development and management of community food programs, such as farmer's markets, a community-supported agriculture farm, and grocery delivery service, the Food System develops policy options designed to influence the

response of the local, state, and federal governments to the food system. Food policy and community-supported agriculture interns are needed and receive stipends of $200 to 250 per week. "We look for people with a strong commitment to social justice and hunger issues, as well as an interest in sustainable agriculture."

Contact Information: Elizabeth Wheeler, Farm to Family Director • Hartford Food System • 509 Wethersfield Ave. • Hartford, CT 06114 • Phone: (203) 296-9325 • Fax: (203) 296-8326

International Expeditions, Inc.

REGION/HQ: Southeast/Alabama • **CATEGORY:** Adventure Travel • **POSITION TYPE:** Seasonal
• **DURATION:** Year-Round • **IDEAL CANDIDATE:** College Students, Career Changers, Retired Folks
• **APPLICANT POOL:** Varies • **APPLICANTS ACCEPTED:** Varies

SINCE 1980, INTERNATIONAL EXPEDITIONS has offered the highest quality natural history expeditions worldwide. The purpose of IE is "to stimulate an interest in, develop an understanding of, and create an appreciation for the great natural wonders of our earth." Today, IE is among the largest and most respected nature travel organizations in America. It has long been recognized as the pioneer in ecologically responsible travel and is an ally to many conservation organizations.

Contact Information: Veronica Rhoads, Program Director • International Expeditions, Inc. • One Environs Park • Helena, AL 35080 • Phone: (800) 633-4734 • E-mail: intlexp@aol.com • Web Site: www.ietravel.com/intexp

International Rivers Network

REGION/HQ: Pacific Northwest/California
• **CATEGORY:** Conservation • **POSITION TYPE:** Internship • **DURATION:** Year-Round • **IDEAL CANDIDATE:** College Students, Career Changers, Foreigners • **APPLICANT POOL:** Varies • **APPLICANTS ACCEPTED:** Varies

INTERNATIONAL RIVERS NETWORK is the world's principal organization dedicated to defending the world's rivers. Their successes have been possible only because they work as part of a global network of environmental, human rights, and social organizations and have a demonstrated commitment to grassroots, bottom-up decision making and coalition development. Internships are available in research, campaigns, and media.

Contact Information: Petra Yee, Operations Director • International Rivers Network • 1847 Berkeley Way • Berkeley, CA 94703 • Phone: (510) 848-1155 • Fax: (510) 848-1008 • E-mail: irn@igc.apc.org • Web Site: www.irn.org/irn/

Jackson Hole Alliance for Responsible Planning

REGION/HQ: Rocky Mountains/Wyoming • **CATEGORY:** Conservation • **POSITION TYPE:** Internship • **DURATION:** Summer • **IDEAL CANDIDATE:** College Students, Career Changers • **APPLICANT POOL:** Varies • **APPLICANTS ACCEPTED:** 2–3/season

THE JACKSON HOLE ALLIANCE has approximately 1,300 members united by a strong concern for Jackson Hole and its future. The company is a local organization dedicated to protecting Jackson Hole's wildlife, scenic, and natural resources. The internship program is loosely structured in terms of supervision and project selection. An intern will typically spend 60 percent of their time on an independent project which will be of mutual interest both to the student and to the alliance. The remainder of their time will be involved in helping with the day-to-day office administration of a nonprofit and grassroots organization, which includes assisting at meetings and special events, coordinating volunteers, maintaining community contacts, and completing general clerical tasks. There is a stipend of $300 per month.

Contact Information: Heather Thomas, Outreach Coordinator • Jackson Hole Alliance for Responsible Planning • Box 2728 • Jackson, WY 83001 • Phone: (307) 733-9417 • Fax: (307) 733-9008 • E-mail: jharp@wyoming.com

Kellogg Child Development Center

REGION/HQ: Rocky Mountains/Colorado • **CATEGORY:** Child Development • **POSITION TYPE:** Internship • **DURATION:** Year-Round • **IDEAL CANDIDATE:** College Students, Career Changers • **APPLICANT POOL:** Varies • **APPLICANTS ACCEPTED:** Varies

THE KELLOGG CHILD DEVELOPMENT CENTER, one of the most innovative programs in the country, supports children (ages three months to six years) and educators in growing together, family-style. The program is designed to nurture each individual child in a deep and holistic way. Each child is provided with one primary caregiver with whom a meaningful, in-depth relationship is developed. Internship positions include Teacher Assistants, Fund Development Assistants, or Marketing/Public Relations Assistant. A stipend of $300 per month, plus a $350 housing stipend, is provided.

Contact Information: Program Director • Kellogg Child Development Center • 2580 Iris Ave. • Boulder, CO 80304 • Phone: (303) 938-8233

Lutheran Volunteer Corps

REGION/HQ: Nationwide/Washington, D.C. • **CATEGORY:** Service Learning • **POSITION TYPE:** Unique Experience • **DURATION:** Year-Round • **IDEAL CANDIDATE:** High School Students, College Students, Career Changers, Retired Folks, Foreigners • **APPLICANT POOL:** Varies • **APPLICANTS ACCEPTED:** Varies

LUTHERAN VOLUNTEER CORPS volunteers work through agencies in a number of areas, including direct service, public policy, advocacy, community organizing, and education. Volunteers live communally with three to seven other volunteers in various places across the United States, including Maryland, Delaware, Washington, D.C., Illinois, Wisconsin, Minnesota, and Washington. Travel, room and board, medical coverage, and daily work-related transportation expenses are covered. The program is open to people of all faiths.

Contact Information: Program Director • Lutheran Volunteer Corps • 1226 Vermont Ave., NW • Washington, DC 20005 • Phone: (202) 387-3222

Make-A-Wish Foundation

REGION/HQ: Great Lakes/Illinois • **CATEGORY:** Social Service • **POSITION TYPE:** Internship • **DURATION:** Year-Round • **IDEAL CANDIDATE:** College Students, Career Changers • **APPLICANT POOL:** Varies • **APPLICANTS ACCEPTED:** Varies

MAKE-A-WISH FOUNDATION fulfills wishes of children between the ages of $2\frac{1}{2}$ and 11 who have life-threatening illnesses. Internships are available in communications/ special events, programming, administration, historian/archivist, development, volunteer administration, and MIS/development.

Contact Information: Internship Coordinator • Make-A-Wish Foundation • 640 N. La Salle St., Suite 289 • Chicago, IL 60610 • Phone: (312) 943-8956 • Fax: (312) 943-8913

Merck Forest & Farmland Center

REGION/HQ: Northeast/Vermont • **CATEGORY:** Sustainable Living • **POSITION TYPE:** Internship • **DURATION:** Year-Round • **IDEAL CANDIDATE:** College Students, Career Changers, Retired Folks • **APPLICANT POOL:** 20–30/term • **APPLICANTS ACCEPTED:** 4/term

MERCK FOREST & FARMLAND CENTER, a 2,800-acre preserve located in the Taconic Mountains of southwestern Vermont, is an independent nonprofit conservation and education organization. Facilities include a small diversified farm, a working forest, maple sugar operation, rustic cabins and shelters, group camping area, a solar-powered visitor center, and twenty-eight miles of trails for hiking and skiing. Depending on seasonal needs and your interests, responsibilities include forest and back-country management, sugaring, livestock care, lambing and wool products, gardening and food preservation, pasture management, sustainable farming, environmental education, public and school programs, and visitor center administration. Interns receive a stipend of $65 per week, housing, and free farm produce, maple sugar, and meats.

Contact Information: Angela Cannon, Program Director • Merck Forest & Farmland Center • Route 315 Rupert Mountain Rd. • P.O. Box 86 • Rupert, VT 05768 • Phone: (802) 394-7836

Minnesota International Center

REGION/HQ: Great Lakes/Minnesota • **CATEGORY:** Global Development • **POSITION TYPE:** Internship • **DURATION:** Year-Round • **IDEAL CANDIDATE:** College Students, Career Changers, Foreigners • **APPLICANT POOL:** 60/year • **APPLICANTS ACCEPTED:** 5–6/term

THE MINNESOTA INTERNATIONAL CENTER (MIC) is a nonprofit community organization promoting international exchange and understanding between Minnesotans and the world. Interns work directly in one of six areas at MIC and assist in the other areas as time and circumstance permit. The internships are designed to give you an in-depth understanding of one program area and a general overview of MIC. Departments include World Affairs Program, Professional Exchange Program, Intercultural Programs, Membership/Development, Volunteer Coordination/Administration, and International Classroom Connection. Knowledge of a second language is not necessary.

Contact Information: Kathleen Oscarson, Administrative Manager • Minnesota International Center • 711 E. River Rd. • Minneapolis, MN 55455 • Phone: (612) 625-4421 • Fax: (612) 624-1984 • E-mail: koscarso@ globe.mic.umn.edu

My Sister's Place

REGION/HQ: Washington, D.C./Washington, D.C. • **CATEGORY:** Human Service • **POSITION TYPE:** Internship • **DURATION:** Year-Round • **IDEAL CANDIDATE:** College Students, Career Changers, Retired Folks, Foreigners • **APPLICANT POOL:** 300/year • **APPLICANTS ACCEPTED:** 150/year

MY SISTER'S PLACE IS A shelter for battered women and their children. They offer counseling, advocacy, and other kinds of help that women need to re-establish themselves in society. They also have a twenty-four-hour crisis hotline for women in trouble, and they refer women to legal services, counseling, parenting classes, job training, schools, and prospective employers. Positions are available in Children's Program, Community Education/Speaker's Bureau, Development/Fund-raising, Hotline, House Management, Latino Outreach/Sister-to-Sister, Legal Committee, Office Work/Statistics, Sister-to-Sister, Transitional Housing, Transportation, Women's Advocacy, and Volunteer Program. Applicants must be at least eighteen years old and attend their training program. "It's not hard to get into a My Sister's Place program. It helps if you can send a cover letter being specific about the needs of your internship, times available to work, and supervision needed. This helps us to better determine how we can work together to get our mutual needs met."

Contact Information: Aléna Biagas, Volunteer Coordinator • My Sister's Place • P.O. Box 29596 • Washington, DC 20017 • Phone: (202) 529-5991 • Fax: (202) 529-5984

National 4-H Council

REGION/HQ: Washington, D.C./Maryland • **CATEGORY:** Youth Service • **POSITION TYPE:** Internship • **DURATION:** Year-Round • **IDEAL CANDIDATE:** College Students, Career Changers • **APPLICANT POOL:** 150/year • **APPLICANTS ACCEPTED:** 4–17/term

THE NATIONAL 4-H COUNCIL builds partnerships valuing and involving youth in issues critical to their lives and society. Interns lead groups on educational field trips to historic sites such as Arlington Cemetery, Kennedy Center, U.S. Capitol, and the Vietnam Veterans Memorial. Interns also serve as role models for 4-H members and other youth visiting the National 4-H Center. Responsibilities include conducting workshops on life skills, government in action, citizenship, our national heritage, and current events. You'll share on-campus, dormitory-style living quarters (for $8 per night). Ten meals a week are also provided.

Contact Information: Kimberlee Morgan, Internship Coordinator • National 4-H Council • 7100 Connecticut Ave. • Chevy Chase, MD 20815-4999 • Phone: (301) 961-2994 • Fax: (301) 961-2894 • Web Site: www.fourhcouncil.edu

National Audubon Society, Washington

REGION/HQ: Washington, D.C./Washington, D.C. • **CATEGORY:** Grassroots • **POSITION TYPE:** Internship • **DURATION:** Year-Round • **IDEAL CANDIDATE:** College Students, Foreigners • **APPLICANT POOL:** 100–200/year • **APPLICANTS ACCEPTED:** 20/year

FOUNDED IN 1886 AS AN organization to protect the lives of birds, the National Audubon Society now also defends wetlands, water sources, and ancient forests. Managing more than 100 sanctuaries nationwide, the society works to restore natural ecosystems for the benefit of humanity and the earth's biological diversity. With 516 chapters and over 600,000 members, they have made a significant impact, helping to establish parks, halt the building of environmentally damaging infrastructures, and create various refuges and preserves. The Government Affairs internship program exposes students to environmental policy-making, grassroots organizing, and lobbying in one of the following departments: Wildlife, Wetlands,

Population, International, Public Lands, and Water Resources.

Contact Information: Internship Coordinator • National Audubon Society, Washington • 1901 Pennsylvania Ave., Suite 1100 • Washington, DC 20006-3405 • Phone: (202) 547-9009 • Fax: (202) 547-9022

WWOOFing Around the Globe

Established in the UK in the seventies, WWOOF (Willing Workers on Organic Farms) was initially designed to allow people from the city to experience rural areas of the UK. Today its purpose is to promote the organic agricultural movement in the "global village" in which we live. As a volunteer, you help with organic farming, gardening, or other environmentally-conscious activities, in exchange for room and board. The length of stay can vary from a few days to several months. This way of life affords the opportunity to exchange knowledge and skills, live and work harmoniously with others, and learn about the land. It also allows one to explore areas of a country that may have otherwise been virtually impossible to reach, since workers are often included in family excursions.

• United States

New England Small Farm Institute, NEWOOF, P.O. Box 608, Belchertown, MA 01007-0608; (413) 323-4531. The New England Small Farm Institute promotes the increased and sustainable use of New England's agricultural resources. Founded in 1978, it manages over 400 acres of public forest and farmland, working to refine viable small-farm management systems and to provide information and training in ecologically responsible, commercial production of fuel and food. The North East Workers on Organic Farms (NEWOOF) is a regional farm apprenticeship placement service. Sponsored by the New England Small Farm Institute, NEWOOF publishes an annual list of organic farms seeking apprentices. You can receive this publication for $8, and subscribers receive bimonthly updates throughout the year. Preferably, applicants should have farm experience and share the goal of promoting organic/alternative farming.

• Canada

In exchange for help on one of over 200 farms or homesteads (animal care, weeding, harvesting, and construction projects), volunteers receive accommodations, three meals daily, and a wonderful learning experience. Most opportunites are spring through fall; however, volunteers are needed year-round. Send $25 (single) or $35 (couple) plus 2 IRCs. WWOOF—Canada; RR2, S. 18, C. 9, Nelson, BC VIL 5P5, Canada; (604) 354-4417.

• Australia/New Zealand

Australia: Lionel Pollard, Mt. Murrindal Cooperative Reserve, Buchan, Victoria 3885, Australia; (011) 61-51-550218. Issues a list of 400 member farms in Australia for US$25 and publishes a worldwide list of farms and volunteer work opportunities for US$15.

New Zealand: P.O. Box 1172, Nelson, New Zealand; (011) 64-25-345711. Provides a list of over 300 organic growers for $12.

• Europe and the UK

Europe: The European Centre for Ecological Agriculture and Tourism, P.O. Box 10899, 1001 EW Amsterdam, The Netherlands. The centre provides WWOOF-type listings in Holland, the Baltic States, Czech Republic, Hungary, Poland, Portugal, and Slovakia.

Britain: WWOOF-England, 19 Bradford Rd., Lewes, Sussex BN7 1RB, England, UK. Annual membership is £8. They also have a coordinator based in France who provides additional European farm and homestead contacts. For this info, get in touch with Dominic Goddard, Le Broqua, Semezies-Cachon, 32450, Soramon, France.

Denmark: V.H.H. Alternative Travelclub, Bent and Inga Nielsen, Asenvej 35, 9881 Bindslev, Denmark

Germany: Stettiner, Str. 3, D-35415 Pohlheim, Germany. Volunteer openings on organic farms. Membership costs DM30.

Hungary: Biokultura Association, Gödöllö ATE, 2130 Práter Karoly u. 1, Budapest, Hungary; (011) 36-28-310-200. Refers applicants to organic farms in Hungary looking for volunteers. WWOOF, H-2105 Godollo, Gate Kollegium, Ungarn, Hungary

Ireland: c/o Annie Sampson, Tulla P.O., Tulla, Clare, Ireland. Membership is IR£5.

Norway: APOG, Torbjorbn Dahl, Lokkegt 23, 2600 Lillehammer, Norway

Spain: Integral, Agricultural Ecologica, Apdo 2580, E-08080, Barcelona, Spain

Switzerland: Postfach b15, 9001 St. Gallen, Switzerland; tel/fax (011) 41-71-232415. For details on working for your keep on an organic farm send 1 IRC.

• Africa

GHANA: WWOOF, Ebenezer Nortey-Mensah, P.O. Box 154, Trade Fair Site, La Accra, Ghana

NFIE

REGION/HQ: Washington, D.C./Washington, D.C.
• **CATEGORY:** Education • **POSITION TYPE:** Internship
• **DURATION:** Year-Round • **IDEAL CANDIDATE:** College Students, Career Changers, Foreigners
• **APPLICANT POOL:** 10–20/year • **APPLICANTS ACCEPTED:** 1–2/year

CREATED IN 1969 BY THE National Education Association, the National Foundation for the Improvement of Education (NFIE) seeks to improve the quality of public education in the United States through the empowerment of teachers and through policy recommendation. The Foundation's grant programs—focusing on dropout prevention, teacher leadership, classroom technology, global education, and teacher professionalism—have assisted hundreds of teachers who have directed NFIE-funded projects, and thousands of students and educators who have been touched by these teachers.

Research/development assistant interns assist staff by gathering and analyzing information relevant to the foundation's program areas, typically working on one substantial research project which lasts the duration of the intern's term. Interns are encouraged to become involved in program planning sessions and staff meetings and to contribute professionally, ultimately leaving NFIE with the feeling of having made significant accomplishments which will serve them well in their future endeavors. This is a wonderful opportunity for networking with other units within the NEA and other agencies in Washington.

Contact Information: Rosilyn Alter, Program Assistant • NFIE • 1201 16th St., NW • Washington, DC 20036-3207 • Phone: (202) 822-7708 • Fax: (202) 822-7779 • Alternate: (202) 822-7840 • E-mail: ralter@nfie.org • Web Site: www.nfie.org

Rails-to-Trails Conservancy

REGION/HQ: Washington, D.C./Washington, D.C. • **CATEGORY:** Conservation • **POSITION TYPE:** Internship • **DURATION:** Year-Round • **IDEAL CANDIDATE:** College Students, Career Changers • **APPLICANT POOL:** Varies • **APPLICANTS ACCEPTED:** Varies

THE RAILS-TO-TRAILS CONSERVANCY is a national non-profit conservation organization which promotes the conversion of suitable abandoned railroad rights-of-way to trails for bicycling, running, wildlife conservation, nature interpretation, and other uses. Program interns research issues and provide telephone/written outreach work. Development/communications interns will prepare and distribute news releases, research and develop publishing, special events, and fund-raisers. Benefits include $225 per week, five days paid leave, health insurance (employer pays 75 percent), and a non-smoking office.

Contact Information: Program Coordinator • Rails-to-Trails Conservancy • 1400 16th St., NW, Suite 300 • Washington, DC 20036 • Phone: (202) 797-5400 • Fax: (202) 797-5411

Reachout Expeditions

REGION/HQ: Pacific Northwest/Washington • **CATEGORY:** Ministry • **POSITION TYPE:** Internship/Seasonal • **DURATION:** Year-Round • **IDEAL CANDIDATE:** College Students, Career Changers, Retired Folks • **APPLICANT POOL:** 30/year • **APPLICANTS ACCEPTED:** 12/year

ARE YOU INTERESTED IN and committed to helping lead youth and adults closer to Christ? Do you enjoy spending time adventuring in the outdoors? Do you have a heart for service? Are you willing to work long hours and go the extra mile for others? If so, Reachout may have a job for you—from outdoor to adminis-

trative positions! Staff raise their own salaries (also known as pledge support) via monthly donations from family, friends, churches, and others, who believe in and support the vision of Reachout. Housing and food are provided through families and individuals in the community.

Contact Information: Robert Bavis, Director • Reachout Expeditions • A Ministry of Youth Dynamics • P.O. Box 464 • Anacortes, WA 98221 • Phone: (360) 293-3788 • Toll Free: (800) 697-3847 • E-mail: rew@cnw.com

St. Elizabeth Shelter

REGION/HQ: South/Midwest/New Mexico • **CATEGORY:** Social Service • **POSITION TYPE:** Internship • **DURATION:** Year-Round • **IDEAL CANDIDATE:** College Students, Career Changers, Retired Folks, Foreigners • **APPLICANT POOL:** 20/year • **APPLICANTS ACCEPTED:** 5/year

THE ST. ELIZABETH SHELTER is a homeless shelter providing services to homeless individuals and families. Interns assist homeless guests, organize meals, process donations, maintain facilities, and assist with writing the newsletter. Interns receive a $40 to $80-per-week stipend, plus room and board.

Contact Information: Hank Hughes, Executive Director • St. Elizabeth Shelter • 804 Alarid St. • Santa Fe, NM 87501 • Phone: (505) 982-6611 • Fax: (505) 982-5347

Student Pugwash USA

REGION/HQ: Washington, D.C./Washington, D.C. • **CATEGORY:** Education • **POSITION TYPE:** Internship • **DURATION:** Year-Round • **IDEAL CANDIDATE:** College Students, Career Changers • **APPLICANT POOL:** Varies • **APPLICANTS ACCEPTED:** Varies

STUDENT PUGWASH USA, a nonprofit, education organization run by a staff of young professionals, provides university students with a range of programs to prepare them, as future leaders and concerned citizens, to make thoughtful decisions about the use of technology. They organize international conferences, coordinate a network of chapters on campuses nationwide, compile and publish an employment directory, and sponsor a number of national and regional events each year. Interns work as staff members, taking part in office discussions and decisions. Interns are encouraged to take individual initiative and responsibility and will be expected to work well as part of a team. All positions require energetic and creative individuals committed to sensitizing young people and the wider public to social issues posed by technology. They also publish *The Mentorship Guide: A Directory of Resource People and Advisors in Social Change*. It profiles nearly 200 socially committed professionals who are interested in providing career guidance to students and recent graduates.

Contact Information: Susan Higman, Assistant Director • Student Pugwash USA • 815 15th St., NW, Suite 814 • Washington, DC 20005 • Phone: (202) 328-6555 • Fax: (202) 797-4664 • Toll Free: (800) 969-2784

Teach for America

REGION/HQ: Nationwide/New York • **CATEGORY:** Teaching • **POSITION TYPE:** Unique Experience • **DURATION:** Two Years • **IDEAL CANDIDATE:** College Students, Career Changers • **APPLICANT POOL:** 3,000/year • **APPLICANTS ACCEPTED:** 500/year

TEACH FOR AMERICA PLACES corps members in K–12 positions in public school districts that traditionally have difficulty filling all of their teaching positions. These districts hire corps members at first-year teacher salaries ($17,000 to $30,000) for a two-year contract. Corps members can assume teaching positions in these shortage areas without meeting conventional licensure requirements, although they are usually required to work toward certification by enrolling in local university programs or in programs run by their school districts or states. They place corps members in urban sites in Baltimore, the Bay Area (CA), Houston, Los Angeles, New Jersey, New York City, Phoenix, and Washington, D.C.; in urban areas of the Mississippi Delta (MS and AR), North Carolina, and the Rio Grande Valley (TX); and in both urban and rural sites in northern and southern Louisiana.

Contact Information: Bridget Hogan, Assistant Admissions Director • Teach for America • 20 Exchange Pl., 8th Floor • New York, NY 10005 • Phone: (212) 425-9039 • Fax: (212) 425-9347 • Toll Free: (800) 832-1230 • E-mail: TFAadm@aol.com • Web Site: www. teachforamerica.org

TreePeople

REGION/HQ: Pacific Northwest/California • **CATEGORY:** Environment • **POSITION TYPE:** Internship • **DURATION:** Year-Round • **IDEAL**

CANDIDATE: College Students, Career Changers, Foreigners • **APPLICANT POOL:** Varies • **APPLICANTS ACCEPTED:** Open

TREEPEOPLE'S MISSION IS TO inspire people to take personal responsibility for improving their immediate environment. TreePeople supports the planting and care of trees, provides educational tools for environmental stewardship, serves as a catalyst for cooperative action among the diverse communities of Los Angeles, and communicates the importance of the urban forest. TreePeople's environmental leadership program gives park tours and presentations at school assemblies for more than 100,000 children each year. TreePeople is also playing a key role in helping to restore and beautify areas ravaged by recent fires and floods. Internships are available in Urban, Mountain, and Campus Forestry; School Education Program; Park Program; and special projects related to fund-raising, volunteer management, and community outreach/ government relations.

Contact Information: Jack Carone, Volunteer Coordinator • TreePeople • 12601 Mulholland Dr. • Beverly Hills, CA 90210 • Phone: (818) 753-4600 • Fax: (818) 753-4625

U.S. Information Agency

REGION/HQ: Washington, D.C./Washington, D.C. • **CATEGORY:** Global Development • **POSITION TYPE:** Internship • **DURATION:** Summer • **IDEAL CANDIDATE:** College Students, Career Changers • **APPLICANT POOL:** Varies • **APPLICANTS ACCEPTED:** 50/year

THE UNITED STATES INFORMATION AGENCY (USIA) is an independent foreign affairs agency within the executive branch of the U.S. government. USIA explains and supports American foreign policy and promotes U.S. national interests through a wide range of overseas information programs. The agency promotes mutual understanding between the United States and other nations by conducting educational and cultural activities. USIA maintains more than 211 posts in over 147 countries, where it is known as USIS, the U.S. Information Service. Volunteers will be assigned to positions throughout the agency, depending on the relevancy of their educational major, previous work experience, and personal interests. Volunteers will support their overseas operations divisions, including: Bureau of Educational and Cultural Affairs, the Bureau of Information, the Bureau of Management, the Office of Research, the Office of Public Liaison, and the Office of the General Counsel.

Contact Information: Intern Coordinator • U.S. Information Agency • Domestic Personnel Division, Room 518 • 301 4th St., SW • Washington, DC 20547 • Phone: (202) 619-4355 • Fax: (202) 619-6988

United Cerebral Palsy of New York

REGION/HQ: Northeast/New York • **CATEGORY:** Human Service • **POSITION TYPE:** Internship • **DURATION:** Year-Round • **IDEAL CANDIDATE:** College Students, Career Changers • **APPLICANT POOL:** Varies • **APPLICANTS ACCEPTED:** Varies

UNITED CEREBRAL PALSY (UCP) is the sole voluntary health agency devoted entirely to the problems and needs of children and adults of our community with cerebral palsy and related disabilities. UCP offers people with disabilities and their families supportive programs designed to meet five basic needs: education and learning; vocational training and work; appropriate health services; recreation and social services; and housing and living arrangements. In addition, UCP, through its state and national affiliations, publishes educational material for both lay and professional use. Its aim is to help people with disabilities achieve independent lives to the fullest extent possible. Its ultimate goal is prevention. The Fund-raising Department seeks an intern to work with their eight-person staff. The Fund-raising Department raises money from special events, foundations, corporations, government, and individuals. The intern will gain knowledge of fundraising, including special events, grant writing, corporate and foundation research, and database management.

Contact Information: Public Relations Director • United Cerebral Palsy of New York • 105 Madison Ave. • New York, NY 10016-7450 • Phone: (212) 683-6700 • Fax: (212) 685-8394

United Nations

REGION/HQ: Northeast/New York • **CATEGORY:** Global Development • **POSITION TYPE:** Internship • **DURATION:** Year-Round • **IDEAL CANDIDATE:** College Students • **APPLICANT POOL:** 2,000–3,000/year • **APPLICANTS ACCEPTED:** Varies

THE UNITED NATIONS, established in 1945, promotes understanding of major problems confronting the world and how to find solutions. The UN Headquarters Internship Programme aims to promote a better understanding of issues and problems facing the international community and how the UN responds to them. Applicants should be enrolled in a graduate program in a field related to the UN and should apply six months prior to the start date. In addition to the New York program, the UN Information Service in Geneva, Switzerland offers a similar program. For more information, contact Graduate Study Program, UN Information Service, Palais des Nations, 1211 Geneva 10, Switzerland; Phone: (41 22) 734 60 11; Fax: (41 22) 733 32 46.

Contact Information: Patricia Perret, Internship Coordinator • United Nations • Human Resources Management • Room S-2570 • New York, NY 10017 • Phone: (212) 963-4437 • Fax: (212) 963-3683

Woodrow Wilson Center

REGION/HQ: Washington, D.C./Washington, D.C. • **CATEGORY:** Global Development • **POSITION TYPE:** Internship • **DURATION:** Year-Round • **IDEAL CANDIDATE:** College Students, Foreigners • **APPLICANT POOL:** Varies • **APPLICANTS ACCEPTED:** Varies

THE WOODROW WILSON International Center for Scholars was established in 1968 by Congress as an international institute for advanced study and as the nation's official "living memorial" to the twenty-eighth president, "symbolizing and strengthening the fruitful relation between the world of learning and the world of public affairs." Open competitions have brought more than 1,200 fellows and guest scholars to the center since 1970. Fellows carry out advanced research, write books, and join in dialogues with other scholars, public officials, reporters, and business leaders. The center matches the needs and interests of the interns with those of the fellows (whenever possible). The duties of an intern at the center include, but are not bound by, the searching for source materials at area institutions, the analysis and summarization of research materials, the compilation of bibliographies, the proofreading and editing of written work, the clarification of quotations in response to references, and the locating and transporting of interlibrary loan materials.

Contact Information: Bahman Amini, Internship Coordinator • Woodrow Wilson Center • 1000 Jefferson Dr.,

SW • Washington, DC 20560 • Phone: (202) 357-2429 • Fax: (202) 357-4439

Youth Enrichment Services

REGION/HQ: Northeast/Massachusetts • **CATEGORY:** Youth Service • **POSITION TYPE:** Internship • **DURATION:** Year-Round • **IDEAL CANDIDATE:** High School Students, College Students, Career Changers, Retired Folks • **APPLICANT POOL:** Varies • **APPLICANTS ACCEPTED:** Varies

YOUTH ENRICHMENT SERVICES (YES) is a nonprofit youth services agency with the mission to provide outdoor activity programs for low- to moderate-income youth in the greater Boston area. Through YES programs, young people gain a sense of accomplishment and self-confidence. These positive experiences carry over to their education, family, community, and employment. While youth services is the mainstay of their agency, they also conduct Elderhostel programs during the summer at their lodge in the western part of Massachusetts—the Berkshire region. Interns' duties include agency marketing and community outreach, equipment maintenance, database information management, assistance with youth/Elderhostel groups, and acting as a youth activity chaperone. Housing is offered during the summer.

Contact Information: Eric Pinckney, Executive Director • Youth Enrichment Services • 412 Massachusetts Ave. • Boston, MA 02118 • Phone: (617) 267-5877 • Fax: (617) 266-6168

Youth With A Mission

REGION/HQ: Pacific Northwest/California • **CATEGORY:** Ministry • **POSITION TYPE:** Unique Experience • **DURATION:** Year-Round • **IDEAL CANDIDATE:** College Students, Career Changers, Retired Folks • **APPLICANT POOL:** Varies • **APPLICANTS ACCEPTED:** Varies

YOUTH WITH A MISSION sends high school– and college-aged youth on Christian missions around the world. Programs emphasize hands-on service projects as well as spreading the Gospel. Call for a copy of their *Steppin Out* publication, which is about going on a mission, and their *Go Manual*, which lists missions all over the world.

Contact Information: Prudence Elliott, Personnel Coordinator • Youth With A Mission • Springs Of Living Water • 15850 Richardson Springs Rd. • Chico, CA 95973 • Phone: (916) 893-6750 • Fax: (916) 893-6759 • Alternate: (503) 364-3837 • E-mail: 76752.3427@compuserve.com

• • • • • • • • • • • • • • • • •

Addresses

Alliance for the Wild Rockies
REGION/HQ: Rocky Mountains/Montana
CATEGORY: Environment
CONTACT INFORMATION:
Program Director
Alliance for the Wild Rockies
P.O. Box 8731
Missoula, MT 59807
Phone: (406) 721-5420

American Rivers
REGION/HQ: Washington, D.C./Washington, D.C.
CATEGORY: Marine Science
CONTACT INFORMATION:
Director
American Rivers
1025 Vermont Ave., NW, Suite 720
Washington, DC 20005-3516
Phone: (202) 547-6900 • Fax: (202) 543-6142

Amnesty International USA—Atlanta
REGION/HQ: Southeast/Georgia
CATEGORY: Human Rights
CONTACT INFORMATION:
Southern Regional Administrator
Amnesty International USA—Atlanta
131 Ponce De Leon Ave., NE, Suite 220
Atlanta, GA 30308-1979
Phone: (404) 876-5661

Anorexia Nervosa & Associated Disorders

REGION/HQ: Great Lakes/Illinois
CATEGORY: Health
CONTACT INFORMATION:
Internship Director
Anorexia Nervosa & Associated Disorders
National Association
Box 7
Highland Park, IL 60035
Phone: (847) 831-3438 • Fax: (847) 433-4632

Asia Watch

REGION/HQ: Northeast/New York
CATEGORY: Human Rights
CONTACT INFORMATION:
Paul Lall, Internship Coordinator
Asia Watch
485 Fifth Ave., 3rd Floor
New York, NY 10017
Phone: (212) 972-8400 • Fax: (212) 687-9786

Green Corps

REGION/HQ: Washington, D.C./Washington, D.C.
CATEGORY: Conservation
CONTACT INFORMATION:
Kelly Wark, Program Director
Green Corps
218 D St., NE
Washington, DC 20003
Phone: (202) 547-9178 • Fax: (202) 546-2461

Idaho Rivers United

REGION/HQ: Pacific Northwest/Idaho
CATEGORY: Conservation
CONTACT INFORMATION:
Wendy Wilson, Executive Director
Idaho Rivers United
P.O. Box 633
Boise, ID 83701
Phone: (208) 343-7481 • Fax: (208) 343-8184

National Audubon Society, New York

REGION/HQ: Northeast/New York
CATEGORY: Conservation
CONTACT INFORMATION:
Staffing Coordinator
National Audubon Society, New York
700 Broadway
New York, NY 10003
Phone: (212) 979-3000 • Fax: (212) 353-0508

Nature Conservancy—California

REGION/HQ: Pacific Northwest/California
CATEGORY: Conservation
CONTACT INFORMATION:
Human Resources
Nature Conservancy—California
201 Mission St., 4th Floor
San Francisco, CA 94105
Phone: (415) 777-0487 • Fax: (415) 777-0244

Nature Conservancy—North Carolina

REGION/HQ: Southeast/North Carolina
CATEGORY: Conservation
CONTACT INFORMATION:
Stewardship Director
Nature Conservancy—North Carolina
North Carolina Field Office
4011 University Dr., Suite 201
Durham, NC 27707-2519
Phone: (919) 967-7007 • Fax: (919) 929-7710

Old Mill Farm School of Country Living

REGION/HQ: Pacific Northwest/California
CATEGORY: Sustainable Living
CONTACT INFORMATION:
Charles Hinsch, Director
Old Mill Farm School of Country Living
P.O. Box 463
Mendocino, CA 95460
Phone: (707) 937-0244

Pacific Environment & Resources Center

REGION/HQ: Pacific Northwest/California
CATEGORY: Environment
CONTACT INFORMATION:
Octavja Morgan, Intern Coordinator
Pacific Environment & Resources Center
1055 Fort Cronkhite
Sausalito, CA 94965
Phone: (415) 332-8200 • Fax: (415) 332-8167

Sierra Club—California

REGION/HQ: Pacific Northwest/California
CATEGORY: Conservation
CONTACT INFORMATION:
Program Director
Sierra Club—California
85 2nd St., 2nd Floor
San Francisco, CA 94105-3441
Phone: (415) 776-2211 • Fax: (415) 776-0350

Sierra Club—Washington

REGION/HQ: Washington, D.C./Washington, D.C.
CATEGORY: Conservation
CONTACT INFORMATION:
Annette Henkin, Program Director
Sierra Club—Washington
408 C Street, NE
Washington, DC 20002
Phone: (202) 547-1141

World Wildlife Fund

REGION/HQ: Washington, D.C./Washington, D.C.
CATEGORY: Wildlife
CONTACT INFORMATION:
Staffing Director
World Wildlife Fund
1225 24th St., NW
Washington, DC 20037
Phone: (202) 293-4800 • Fax: (202) 293-2911

Wyoming Wildlife Federation

REGION/HQ: Rocky Mountains/Wyoming
CATEGORY: Wildlife
CONTACT INFORMATION:
Office Manager
Wyoming Wildlife Federation
P.O. Box 106
Cheyenne, WY 82003
Phone: (307) 637-5433 • Fax: (307) 637-6629

Action Guide: How to Find a Socially Responsible Job, published by Co-op America, provides resources and job listings in the environmental, nonprofit, and public affairs sectors, with references and directories of socially responsible organizations. Just send $2, along with your name and address, to Co-op America, 1612 K St., NW, Suite 600, Washington, DC 20006; (202) 872-5307; www.coopamerica.org

The **Directory of Internships in Youth Development** Web site is continually updated and describes over 2,000 internship and career opportunities in youth development agencies across the United States. www.nassembly.org/nonprofit

The **Ecotourism Society** is dedicated to finding the resources and building the expertise to make tourism a viable tool for conservation and sustainable development. To get the info you need, contact Kathy Murphy, Membership Director, P.O. Box 755, North Bennington, VT 05257; (802) 447-2121; Fax: (802) 447-2122; ecotsocy@igc.apc.org; www. ecotourism.org

The **EcoSource** Web site (helping to conserve and protect our fragile ecosystems, endangered species, and indigenous peoples) continues to work on creating the world's most comprehensive, informative, fun, and useful site on ecotourism. Highlights include destinations (visit exotic-sounding places like Vanuatu), ecotours and tour operators (participate in off-the-wall activities like bamboo rafting), ecolodges (bungle in the jungle), and ecotourism career information (get answers to your ecotourism industry job and career questions). www.podi.com/ecosource

The pay is modest. The work is important. The satisfaction is incredible. **Good Works** is the largest and most authoritative national directory of social change organizations. It lists more than 1,000 career opportunities for people who want to be pioneers of a more just society. www.tripod.com/work/goodworks

Good Works: A Guide to Careers in Social Change, presents alternatives to traditional corporate employment and is packed with information on public interest occupations. It costs $24, plus $2.50 for postage and handling for the first copy and $.50 for each additional copy. Make checks payable to Essential Information. Good Works, P.O. Box 19405, Washington, DC 20036

Community jobs: the *National Employment Newspaper for the Nonprofit Sector* is a monthly newspaper including features, resource lists, book reviews, profiles of nonprofit organizations and leaders, and nonprofit job listings at all experience levels in all types of nonprofit organizations nationwide. Contact ACCESS: Networking in the Public Interest, 1001 Connecticut Ave., NW, Suite 838, Washington, D.C. 20036; (202) 785-4233; Fax: (202) 785-4212; www.essential.org/access

The New Social Worker is the only national magazine devoted to social-work students and recent graduates. Sections include: social-work practice specialties, social-work ethics, people in the profession, job search/career guidance, student field-placement issues, book reviews, and news from campuses. www.xmission.com/~gastown/newsocwk/index.html

Are you about to go on your adventure with a disability? With adequate preparation and precautions, much of the world is accessible to a disabled traveler—especially with help from Mobility International. They publish a quarterly newsletter, **Over the Rainbow,** which costs $15 for the year, and the book *A World of Options: A Guide to International Exchange, Community Service, and Travel for Persons with Disabilities* ($30, plus $5 postage). This super guide is jam-packed with over 650 pages of great information. From spending a study abroad year in Spain to working in Australia, the book explores everything conceivable for the disabled (and the non-disabled), with personal experience stories scattered throughout. MIUSA, P.O. Box 10767, Eugene, OR 97440; (541) 343-1284; miusa@ igc.apc.org

Volunteer Vacations by Bill McMillon is a detailed guide for travelers who want to combine adventure and personal growth with service to others. Over 500 short-term opportunities are listed. (Chicago Review Press, $13.95)

Confidence comes from knowing that you have the talent to do a job. Confidence also comes from a good education, work and life experiences, and from a general belief in yourself and your abilities.

For many, living and working abroad for extended periods of time becomes the adventure of a lifetime. Many trek off to unknown lands to fill a gap of time in their lives, improve their fluency in a foreign language, meet new and interesting people, and/or build self-reliance. Whatever your case, by traveling to a new land, you'll have the chance to immerse yourself in the culture and meet people on their own terms, rather than experiencing a culture as a tourist would.

Do be prepared, though: landing a job overseas often takes months of preparation. But the hard work you put into preparing for your journey will give you the confidence to find and land a job on any soil.

Where to begin? First, broadcast your intentions to the world. Do you have friends, family, or pen pals who are scattered throughout the world? How about coworkers or colleagues who have worked or lived on foreign soil? The more widely publicized your plans, the better chance you'll pick up a lead or two and learn about what to expect and plan for.

Perhaps you don't have an aunt in Italy or a pen pal in Fiji. So then what? For the person who needs the security of having a job before departure, you'll find that there are plenty of organizations who will provide you with packaged work arrangements. These programs provide you with a job, set up living arrangements, and take care of all the red tape (work permits, visas, health insurance). However, these programs also charge participation fees, which does not fit into some people's adventure budgets.

An alternative to this "packaged" deal is to do as much initial legwork as you can at home prior to departure, then begin exploring local job possibilities upon arrival. Besides the leads provided in this guidebook, there are plenty of other great travel guides that provide leads specific to the foreign land you've decided to travel to. You'll also find that the fellow travelers you meet undoubtedly become a gold mine of leads and other great information. Job boards at youth hostels, universities, or cafes, or listings in local newspapers also serve as potential starting points for your search.

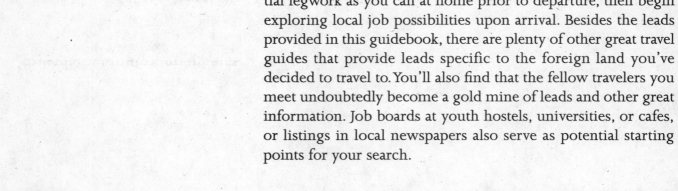

Goin' Wo

Just like job-hunting on your home turf, landing a job becomes easier when you meet your prospective employer face-to-face. You'll find that walking in to a place where you really want to work and asking for a job is by far the most effective method of landing a job overseas. The fact is, most employers don't want to deal with someone who is ten thousand miles away: when you physically make your presence and your passion known, you begin to seem like a real possibility. If there are no openings at the time (and it's financially feasible), ask if you can volunteer. You'll prove your abilities and you'll have an excellent chance of filling a vacancy when one opens.

No matter what your reasons are for working and living abroad (or how you do it), you are bound to meet many interesting characters, collect a wealth of tales to bring back home, and learn a lot more about yourself. Bon voyage!

Alliances Abroad

REGION/HQ: Worldwide/California • **CATEGORY:** Service Learning • **POSITION TYPE:** Unique Experience • **DURATION:** Year-Round • **IDEAL CANDIDATE:** High School Students, College Students, Foreigners • **APPLICANT POOL:** 4,000/year • **APPLICANTS ACCEPTED:** 65%/year

ALLIANCES ABROAD OFFERS language study, service projects and internships, work au pair, homestays, and language tutor and high school programs. They strive to give you firsthand experience of different lifestyles, cultures, and traditions in the safest, most organized way. Their representatives are experienced travelers who use the knowledge they have gained living in the exchange country to make your trip as exciting and educational as you can imagine.

Area and Working Environment: Programs are available in Africa, Australia, Ecuador, England, France, Germany, Italy, Mexico, and Spain.

Work/Learn Program Specifics: Service projects give you a unique opportunity to get to know a Third World country that would otherwise be out of range. The cultural component is the most important aspect of the program, and you will be given the opportunity to immerse yourself in the culture. In order for you to achieve this they personally design programs to fit your interests. You will live with a host family and take part in a service project, which may focus on health care, education, social projects, and the environment. Internship program opportunities are endless. They offer several programs designed to integrate experiential learning and cross-cultural international education. All of their programs involve immersion in the culture and language. An internship allows you the opportunity to improve your language skills while immersing yourself in the culture and establishing contacts for the future. Placements are usually in or near large cities.

Duration: Typical service projects consist of thirty hours per week. Internships generally last one to three months.

rldwide

Compensation and Perks: Each participant will receive predeparture information on staying abroad, living and working in a developing country, cultural aspects, communication, project information, and local lifestyle. Tuition includes predeparture materials, room and board with a carefully selected host family, transportation from airport to host family, orientation, support from local staff, basic health and accident insurance, placement in the service project, and a certificate of completion. Tuition does not include airfare or personal expenses.

The Ideal Candidate: Programs are open to those who are independent, flexible, and who are willing to show initiative in their learning. Previous language experience is not necessary.

Making It Happen: Program fees vary; call for current application materials and a brochure.

Contact Information: Program Director • Alliances Abroad • 2830 Alameda • San Francisco, CA 94103 • Phone: (415) 487-0691 • Fax: (415) 621-1609 • Toll Free: (800) 266-8047 • E-mail: AlliancesA@aol.com • Web Site: www.studyabroad.com/alliances

American Friends Service Committee

REGION/HQ: Mexico/Pennsylvania • **CATEGORY:** Workcamp • **POSITION TYPE:** Unique Experience • **DURATION:** Summer • **IDEAL CANDIDATE:** College Students, Career Changers, Foreigners • **APPLICANT POOL:** Varies • **APPLICANTS ACCEPTED:** 50/year

THE AMERICAN FRIENDS SERVICE COMMITTEE (AFSC) is a Quaker organization supported by individuals who care about peace, social justice, and humanitarian service. Its work is based on the profound Quaker belief in the dignity and worth of every person and faith in the power of love and nonviolence to bring about change. Many divisions separate the people of North America, Latin America, and the Caribbean—divisions of history, economics, culture, and language. The understanding that enables people to overcome these divisions is best established by personal encounter, reflection, and action. To help in this process, the AFSC has supported short-term community service projects in Latin America since 1939. More than 4,000 volunteers have participated and many say their lives have been profoundly affected by their work-camp experience.

Work/Learn Program Specifics: Small groups of participants (ten to twelve people from different back-

grounds) are assigned to a particular community, where they work side-by-side with residents. Some of the communities are located in indigenous regions. This is not a program of adventure and travel; it is an opportunity to experience a single community in some depth. The daily experience of participants follows the patterns of rural life, and volunteers must fit into and respect local social customs. Recent work projects have included construction and repair of schools, clinics, roads, small stores, irrigation, and water supply systems. Participants also help organize activities related to recreation, education, agriculture, women's issues, health, and local culture and history. The nature of the projects depends on the needs and interests of the local people.

Duration: The program is approximately seven weeks, beginning in July.

Compensation and Perks: The participant's contribution of $900 ($150 of that amount is a nonrefundable registration fee) covers orientation, food, lodging, transportation during the project, and health and accident insurance. Volunteers are responsible for their own transportation to Mexico, a required health examination and inoculations, and personal spending money.

The Ideal Candidate: Please note that Spanish is the only language used in the program. Every participant must be able to communicate effectively in Spanish. All applicants should be eighteen to twenty-six years old, healthy, hardworking, flexible, willing to adapt to group living, and familiar with issues in the developing world. Construction, gardening, crafts, and recreation skills are needed as well.

Making It Happen: Call or write for application. Applications must be received by April 1.

Contact Information: Helene Pollock, Recruitment Coordinator • American Friends Service Committee • Latin America Summer Projects • 1501 Cherry St. • Philadelphia, PA 19102-1479 • Phone: (215) 241-7295 • Fax: (215) 241-7247 • E-mail: hpollock@afsc.org • Web Site: www.afsc.org

Amigos de las Americas

REGION/HQ: Latin America/Texas • **CATEGORY:** Service Learning • **POSITION TYPE:** Unique Experience • **DURATION:** Summer • **IDEAL CANDIDATE:** High School Students, College Students, Career Changers, Retired Folks, Foreigners • **APPLICANT POOL:** Varies • **APPLICANTS ACCEPTED:** Varies

AMIGOS DE LAS AMERICAS is an international, voluntary nonprofit, which, through service, provides leadership development opportunities for young people, promotes community health for the people of Latin America, and facilitates cross-cultural understanding for the people of the Americas. Since Amigos's birth in 1965, more than 18,000 volunteers have provided approximately 11 million health services in 15 Latin American countries.

Area and Working Environment: Countries served include Brazil, Costa Rica, Dominican Republic, Ecuador, Honduras, Mexico, and Paraguay.

Work/Learn Program Specifics: Each summer, hundreds of high school and college students (Amigos volunteers and their supervisors) travel to Latin America during the summer for four to eight weeks of service. They live in rural, semi-urban, or urban communities. They work together in teams of two or three in schools, health clinics, and house-to-house. Amigos become members of a community, and usually of a family. Services include community health education, latrine education, human immunizations, school renovations, construction, reforestation, and environmental education. Amigos also has field supervisor, assistant project director, and project director positions. The training you will receive before you go includes cross-cultural sensitivity; first aid; interpersonal relations; Latin American language, history, geography, politics, and economy; leadership skills; medical self-care; problem solving; project management; and records management.

Duration: Program lasts four to eight weeks during the summer.

Compensation and Perks: There is a fee of $3,000 to $3,400, which includes round-trip international airfare, training materials, orientation, weekly training sessions, field-project supplies, chapter support, host-country room, board, and transportation, and professional staff support. Participation fee scholarships and college tuition scholarships up to $1,400 are available to applicants with proven financial need.

The Ideal Candidate: Volunteers must be at least sixteen years of age, have one year of Spanish/Portuguese completed before training, six months of Amigos training, successful completion of several screenings or proficiency tests, active participation in fund-raising, and proof of health insurance.

Making It Happen: Call for application materials.

INSIDER TIPS: *Amigos are flexible, motivated, able to work independently and as team members, energetic,* *adventuresome, enthusiastic, and interested in public health, quality of life, and community service.*

Contact Information: Joe Crownover, Field Program Director • Amigos de las Americas • 5618 Star Ln. • Houston, TX 77057 • Phone: (713) 782-5290 • Fax: (713) 782-9267 • Toll Free: (800) 231-7796 • E-mail: info@amigoslink.org • Web Site: www.amigoslink.org

Association of Episcopal Colleges

REGION/HQ: Worldwide/New York • **CATEGORY:** Service Learning • **POSITION TYPE:** Unique Experience • **DURATION:** Year-Round • **IDEAL CANDIDATE:** College Students, Career Changers, Retired Folks, Foreigners • **APPLICANT POOL:** Varies • **APPLICANTS ACCEPTED:** Varies

THE ASSOCIATION OF EPISCOPAL COLLEGES is an international consortium of colleges that have historic and present ties to the Episcopal Church, and is also the sponsor of thirty-five independent and church-related service agencies.

Area and Working Environment: Choose from thirty-five rural, urban, and wilderness sites in the U.S. and around the world, from a South American port city to the Appalachian mountains.

Work/Learn Program Specifics: Volunteer opportunities combine learning and travel with service to people in need. You may teach reading to the illiterate, recreation to young people, or useful skills to the jobless; care for the young, the sick, the troubled, the handicapped, or the elderly; or help organize community projects—all of which are under the supervision of professional caregivers.

Duration: Programs last from one month up to one year.

Compensation and Perks: Some programs with academic credit have tuition fees; others may provide room and board or a modest stipend. Financial aid may cover some programs with academic study.

The Ideal Candidate: Open to people of any faith who want to use their talents to help make a difference in the lives of others while learning more about the world.

Making It Happen: Call or write for information. Rolling deadlines.

Contact Information: Program Director • Association of Episcopal Colleges • Learning Through Service • 815

Though we travel the world over to find the beautiful, we must carry it with us or we will find it not. —RALPH WALDO EMERSON

381

Second Ave., Suite 315 • New York, NY 10017 • Phone: (212) 986-0989 • Fax: (212) 986-5039 • Toll Free: (800) 334-7626 • E-mail: pmerchant@worldnet.att.net

Atlantis Youth Exchange

REGION/HQ: Norway/Norway • **CATEGORY:** International Exchange • **POSITION TYPE:** Seasonal • **DURATION:** Year-Round • **IDEAL CANDIDATE:** High School Students, College Students, Career Changers, Foreigners • **APPLICANT POOL:** 700/year • **APPLICANTS ACCEPTED:** 350/year

ATLANTIS YOUTH EXCHANGE is a nonprofit foundation established by the Norwegian Youth Council in 1987. The objective of Atlantis is to promote intercultural understanding. This goal is pursued by exposing young people to foreign cultures through various kinds of exchange programs. Also, information and counseling on international youth exchange and international youth organizations make up part of the work in the area of furthering international communication and respect.

Area and Working Environment: Enjoy a few months living with a Norwegian host family on a farm, living somewhere in this beautiful country of only 4.2 million inhabitants, of Vikings and trolls, of high mountains and long fjords, of the midnight sun and pure nature.

Work/Learn Program Specifics: Get involved in their Working Guest Program. A working guest is a young person who is invited to stay for some months with a Norwegian family running a farm. Living and working in Norway for a period of time, you get to know the Norwegian people, culture, customs, and lifestyle from the inside, more deeply than as an ordinary tourist. As a working guest you take part in the daily life on the farm, both in work and in leisure, as a member of the host family and the local community where you are staying. During working hours you are expected to help in the agricultural work on the farm. Tasks can include haymaking, weeding, milking, picking berries and vegetables, painting, and light housework.

Duration: Homestays are two to three months long and are continuously offered year-round. You will work up to thirty-five hours per week and are entitled to have one-and-a-half days off per week. Note: It's much easier to get a position in seasons other than the summer.

Compensation and Perks: You will receive a minimum payment of 600 Norwegian kroner per week. In addition, you will have free board and lodging, like a member of the family, and you will most likely have your own bedroom in the main building. Prepare for a different stay abroad—contact your nearest Norwegian embassy for booklets and brochures about their exciting country.

The Ideal Candidate: The program is open to anyone eighteen to thirty years old, preferably with some agricultural experience. You are not expected to have any knowledge of Norwegian, but must be able to communicate in English. To have a successful stay, you have to be open-minded and tolerant and able to adapt to your host family's way of life. Things will often be quite different from what you are used to at home.

Making It Happen: Write for an application packet. Send completed application, a personal letter from you to your prospective host family, a medical certificate not older than three months, a reference of conduct from a teacher/employer, copy of payment of the registration fee, and two recent photos of yourself. Applicants pay a fee of 1,000 Norwegian kroner to cover application expenses; 750 NOK refunded if no placements are being made (see application for details!). Please submit your application at least three months ahead of preferred arrival date.

INSIDER TIPS: *Try to give a positive, honest, and smiling impression in your application. This is a very popular program.*

Contact Information: Inbound Manager • Atlantis Youth Exchange • Rolf Hofmos Gate 18 • Oslo, N-0655 • Norway • Phone: 47 22 67 00 43 • Fax: 47 22 68 68 08

Brethren Volunteer Service

REGION/HQ: Worldwide/Illinois • **CATEGORY:** Service Learning • **POSITION TYPE:** Unique Experience • **DURATION:** Year-Round • **IDEAL CANDIDATE:** College Students, Career Changers, Retired Folks, Foreigners • **APPLICANT POOL:** 175/year • **APPLICANTS ACCEPTED:** 95%

BRETHREN VOLUNTEER SERVICE (BVS) is a Christian service program sponsored by the Church of the Brethren. As sponsor of the program, the Church of the Brethren exemplifies its heritage in peacemaking and service through the goals of BVS: working for peace, advocating justice, serving basic human needs, and maintaining the integrity of creation. Volunteers come from varied backgrounds with different motivations. BVSers are young adults and retirees. They are persons with little formal training and others with advanced degrees, others still exploring possible options. They are citizens from the United States and those from other nations. They are individuals wanting to live out their religious convictions and persons seeking to reach out beyond themselves. "I slept and dreamt that life was pleasure, I woke and saw that life was service, I served and discovered that service was pleasure!"

Area and Working Environment: Over 150 positions are available in 24 states in the United States and in 17 nations abroad.

Work/Learn Program Specifics: BVS people give their time and skills to help a world in need. It is a way for people to work at issues greater than themselves, recognizing that their efforts may not immediately solve deep-rooted problems but can be a part of ongoing work for justice, peace, and the integrity of creation. Volunteers choose from a variety of projects including programs involving children, youth/young adults, senior citizens, general community services, farmworkers, disabled persons, agriculture, hunger/homelessness, prisoners and the prison systems, refugees, peace, domestic violence, housing, health care, camping ministries, community organizing/development/advocacy, education/teaching, and the environment. A booklet describes the specifics of each position. Volunteers begin their term of service with twelve to thirty other volunteers in a BVS three-week orientation (scheduled four times per year), which examines a wide range of topics, including peace and justice issues, hunger, stress management, Third World concerns, cross-cultural understanding, and poverty.

Duration: Positions in the United States require a one-year commitment; overseas positions require two years.

Compensation and Perks: Volunteers receive room, board, medical insurance, transportation to the project, and a monthly allowance of $45 to $55. Volunteers may live in a group situation or an apartment, or with a family. The financial costs to an individual include a $15 application fee, transportation to orientation, an overseas travel fee ($400) covering a portion of the transportation costs and costs for medical, dental, and optical exams before orientation.

The Ideal Candidate: BVS seeks those who are willing to act on their commitment and values. They challenge individuals to offer themselves, their time, and their talents to work that is both difficult and demanding, rewarding and joyful. The minimum requirements include: twenty years of age, sound physical and mental health, high school education (or equivalent), willingness to examine and study the Christian faith, and commitment to the goals of BVS. A college degree or equivalent life experience is required for overseas assignment.

Making It Happen: Submit letter or call and request application. Applications are accepted year-round. Applicants are encouraged to apply six months prior to their availability.

INSIDER TIPS: *It is essential that each volunteer bring a willingness to grow and a desire to serve. Important work towards peace, justice, meeting the needs of humanity and the environment calls out for persons willing to serve.*

Contact Information: Dan McFadden, Director • Brethren Volunteer Service • 1451 Dundee Ave. • Elgin, IL 60120-1694 • Phone: (847) 742-5100 • Fax: (847) 742-6103 • Toll Free: (800) 323-8039 • E-mail: cob.bvs.parti@ ecunet.org • Web Site: www.tgx.com/cob/bvs.htm

Catholic Network of Volunteer Service

REGION/HQ: Worldwide/Washington, D.C. • **CATEGORY:** Ministry • **POSITION TYPE:** Unique Experience • **DURATION:** Year-Round • **IDEAL CANDIDATE:** College Students, Career Changers, Retired Folks, Foreigners • **APPLICANT POOL:** Varies • **APPLICANTS ACCEPTED:** Varies

THE CATHOLIC NETWORK OF Volunteer Service is the official U.S. Catholic return to lay mission programs. Currently 5,500 men and women are serving in member programs, offering their gifts and abilities in full-time service to people in need. Their member programs recruit, screen, place, train, and support volunteers during their time of service.

Work/Learn Program Specifics: Volunteers work in a variety of positions, which may include working in soup kitchens or family shelters, directing programs for at-risk youth, teaching in schools, ministering to the abused, providing health care, building houses, offering service to refugees, and so much more. All these opportunities can be found in their annual volunteer directory, *Response*, which includes close to 200 programs operating all over the United States and in 90 countries worldwide.

Duration: Programs vary in length from a few weeks to a few years. The average length of a domestic placement is one year and an international program, two years. All are full-time, forty-hour-per-week positions.

Compensation and Perks: Each program has their own combination of benefits and compensation; most include a stipend, room and board, health insurance, and workmen's compensation. All provide orientation and training, and some may offer retreats or language training.

The Ideal Candidate: The best applicants are those who are committed to social justice, spirituality, a simple lifestyle, and in some instances, community living. They are single, married, recent graduates, early retirees—just about anybody can become involved.

Making It Happen: Call for your free copy of their volunteer directory, *Response*. Application involves applying directly to the programs listed in this directory. Rolling deadlines.

Contact Information: Mary Ellen Moore, Recruitment Coordinator • Catholic Network of Volunteer Service • 4121 Harewood Rd., NE • Washington, DC 20017 • Phone: (202) 529-1100 • Fax: (202) 526-1094 • Toll Free: (800) 543-5046 • E-mail: cnvs@ari.net • Web Site: www2.ari.net/home3/cnvs/cnvshome.html

CDS International, Inc.

REGION/HQ: Germany/New York • **CATEGORY:** International Education • **POSITION TYPE:** Unique Experience • **DURATION:** Year-Round • **IDEAL CANDIDATE:** College Students, Career Changers • **APPLICANT POOL:** Varies • **APPLICANTS ACCEPTED:** Varies

CDS INTERNATIONAL IS A nonprofit organization dedicated to promoting international awareness in business and education through various exchange programs, professional work internships, study tours, and seminars. They offer individuals the chance to learn new skills and technologies, build relationships with their foreign counterparts, learn and perfect a foreign language in its native setting, and gain the special confidence that comes from taking risks. Their programs give participants a chance to broaden their professional and life experience so that, no matter the work, they will do a better job because of their broader experience.

Work/Learn Program Specifics: Career Training: an eighteen-month exchange program for Americans/Europeans between the ages of twenty-two and thirty

with a college degree in a business, hotel management, or a technical field and one or two years of practical work experience. Congress-Bundestag Youth Exchange Program for Young Professionals: a twelve-month exchange program for Americans/Germans between the ages of eighteen and twenty-four with a high school diploma and practical work experience in a business, vocational, or technical field. They also have the same program for Americans/Germans between the ages of twenty and twenty-four with experience in agriculture. Internships: a six-month exchange program for American/German college seniors/recent graduates with majors in business/technical/agriculture fields and one year of work experience. Robert Bosch Foundation Fellowship: a nine-month fellowship in Germany for Americans with a graduate degree in business, economics, public policy, law, journalism, or mass communications and relevant work experience. Study Tours: a program which offers business and educational groups in the United States the opportunity to participate in customized two- or three-week study tours and seminars in European countries.

Duration: Programs are anywhere from three to eighteen months, offered at various times throughout the year.

Compensation and Perks: A limited number of scholarships are available. Salaries vary depending on previous experience and training, but average 1,500 deutsche marks (DM) per month, which is generally enough to cover basic living expenses. Fellowship: Stipend is DM3,500 per month and DM800 for accompanying spouse. Round-trip transportation between U.S. residence and Germany, related travel to seminars in Europe, and health insurance are provided.

The Ideal Candidate: All programs require German language proficiency.

Making It Happen: Request an application from CDS. Applications are requested five months before planned departure date, which include application, resume, German Lebenslauf, official transcripts, letters of recommendation, essay, language test, and a $325 administration fee (which is returned in full should you not be eligible for participation in the program).

INSIDER TIPS: *You need a high level of interest for working in and acclimating yourself to Germany and its culture.*

Contact Information: Program Director • CDS International, Inc. • 330 7th Ave., 19th Floor • New York, NY 10001-5010 • Phone: (212) 760-1400 • Fax: (212) 268-1288

Center for Global Education

REGION/HQ: Worldwide/Minnesota • **CATEGORY:** Educational Travel • **POSITION TYPE:** Unique Experience • **DURATION:** Year-Round • **IDEAL CANDIDATE:** High School Students, College Students, Career Changers, Retired Folks, Foreigners • **APPLICANT POOL:** 250/year • **APPLICANTS ACCEPTED:** 250/year

THE CENTER FOR GLOBAL EDUCATION at Augsburg College is nationally recognized for its work on experiential education in the Two-Thirds World. The center was founded in 1982 to help North Americans think more critically about global issues so that they might work toward a more just and sustainable world.

Work/Learn Program Specifics: Short Term International Travel Seminars: The center takes learning adults around the world on short-term travel seminars, bringing them into encounters with the peoples and situations of Mexico, Central America, the Caribbean, southern Africa, the Middle East, and the Asia/Pacific region. These one- to three-week educational trips bring North Americans face to face with people of other cultures—people struggling for justice and human dignity. Each day consists of two to four meetings with community representatives, ranging from grassroots organizers to business leaders and representatives of the ruling and opposition political parties, as well as visits to key historical or archaeological sites. Programs enable you to learn about the current political, economic, and social realities of the host community through meeting with people who represent varying perspectives. Group sessions will help you reflect on what you have learned.

Duration: Seminars are one to three weeks and take place year-round.

Compensation and Perks: Seminar fees range from $1,295 to $3,795. Costs include meetings with community representatives, lodging, all meals, translation, local travel, and usually round-trip airfare.

The Ideal Candidate: Participants must be at least sixteen years of age, unless accompanied by an adult. No language skills are necessary.

Making It Happen: Call for application materials. Apply at least one month prior to departure.

INSIDER TIPS: *Programs attract a broad range of participants, from ages sixteen to eighty, from all ethnic backgrounds and from all professional areas. All have an interest in listening to and learning from people in the community.*

Contact Information: Regina McGoff, Travel Counselor • Center for Global Education • Augsburg College • 2211 Riverside Ave., Box 307 • Minneapolis, MN 55454 • Phone: (612) 330-1159 • Fax: (612) 330-1695 • Toll Free: (800) 299-8889 • E-mail: globaled @augsburg.edu • Web Site: www.augsburg.edu/global

College Year in Athens

REGION/HQ: Greece/Massachusetts • **CATEGORY:** History • **POSITION TYPE:** Learning Adventure • **DURATION:** Spring-Fall • **IDEAL CANDIDATE:** College Students, Career Changers, Retired Folks, Foreigners • **APPLICANT POOL:** Varies • **APPLICANTS ACCEPTED:** 80/term

COLLEGE YEAR IN ATHENS is an independent study-abroad program in Greece offering university-level programs on ancient and modern Greece. Participants have the chance to study and travel to many historically important sites in Attica, Crete, the Peloponnese, central Greece, and Macedonia. The summer program is held on the island of Paros.

Area and Working Environment: Athens is a vibrant capital city, with charming neighborhood shops and squares and all of the amenities of a modern European city. The beauty of Greece's mountains, plains, and islands is readily accessible by public transportation, and Athens is an unrivaled base from which to explore the sites and monuments of ancient Greece, as well as modern Greek culture.

Work/Learn Program Specifics: During the academic year, students choose from courses in two tracks: Ancient Greek Civilization and Mediterranean Studies. Summer programs are offered in study and travel to the sites and monuments of Athens and the surrounding countryside, and intensive modern Greek. Many fields of study are offered, including classics, art history, Greek language and literature in translation, history, archaeology, and Mediterranean studies.

Duration: Semester or year-long programs are available. Summer, six-week study/travel, or three-week modules are offered.

Compensation and Perks: The per-semester fees are $9,900 (tuition—$7,200; housing—$1,950; board—$650; and damage deposit—$100). Students who

The traveler's-eye view of men and women is not satisfying. A man might spend his life in trains and restaurants and know nothing of humanity at the end. To know, one must be an actor as well as a spectator. —ALDOUS HUXLEY

385

attend College Year in Athens for two consecutive semesters receive a 13-percent discount on tuition and housing for the second semester. Students are often able to transfer some or all of their financial aid package toward the College Year in Athens fees. For its semester programs, College Year in Athens has a few supplemental scholarships, based on need and academic merit. These are awarded as credit, ranging from $500 to $3,000 against the semester fees. Program and extracurricular activities include theatrical performances, Greek cooking and dancing, hiking/climbing trips, dinners with Greek families, and sports.

The Ideal Candidate: Semester/year programs are normally open to those in their junior year of undergraduate study, although sophomores are considered. Summer programs are open to those that are at least eighteen years old. Students who are academically motivated, inquisitive, self-reliant, self-disciplined, and flexible are most likely to be accepted into the program.

Making It Happen: Call for details and application/registration materials. Deadlines: fall—May 15; spring—October 15; and summer study/travel—May 1. Other summer program applications are accepted until the course is full.

Contact Information: Jana Van Der Veer, Coordinator • College Year in Athens • North American Office • P.O. Box 390890 • Cambridge, MA 02139 • Phone: (617) 494-1008 • Fax: (617) 494-1662 • E-mail: cyathens@aol.com • Web Site: www.cyathens.org

Concern America

REGION/HQ: Worldwide/California • **CATEGORY:** Global Development • **POSITION TYPE:** Unique Experience • **DURATION:** Year-Round • **IDEAL CANDIDATE:** College Students, Career Changers, Retired Folks • **APPLICANT POOL:** Varies • **APPLICANTS ACCEPTED:** Varies

CONCERN AMERICA IS AN international development and refugee aid organization incorporated as an independent nonprofit in California in 1972. Funding for Concern America programs comes primarily from individual donors.

Area and Working Environment: Volunteers currently serve in development projects in El Salvador, Guatemala, Honduras, Mexico, and Mozambique.

Work/Learn Program Specifics: Through the work of volunteers, who are professionals in the fields of health, public health, nutrition, health education, adult literacy, sanitation, agroforestry, appropriate technology, and community organizing, Concern America assists impoverished communities and refugees in developing countries in their efforts to improve their living conditions. The programs emphasize training of community members in order to impart skills and knowledge that remain with the community long after the volunteer is gone.

Duration: A minimum commitment of one year is required. There are no short-term internships or assignments.

Compensation and Perks: Concern America provides room and board, round-trip transportation, health insurance, a small monthly stipend of $250 per month, support services from the home office, a repatriation allowance (first year—$50 per month, second year—$100 per month, third year—$150 per month) and support services from the home office.

The Ideal Candidate: Applicants must have a degree/experience in public health, medicine, nutrition, nursing, agriculture, community development, education, or appropriate technology. Fluency in Spanish (except for the project in Mozambique, where Portuguese is required) or ability to learn Spanish at one's own expense is also required. All candidates must be at least twenty-one years of age.

Making It Happen: Send cover letter and resume. Rolling deadlines.

Contact Information: Janine Mills, Recruitment Coordinator • Concern America • 2024 N. Broadway, Suite 104 • P.O. Box 1790 • Santa Ana, CA 92702 • Phone: (714) 953-8575 • Fax: (714) 953-1242

Council on Hemispheric Affairs

REGION/HQ: Washington, D.C./Washington, D.C. • **CATEGORY:** Research • **POSITION TYPE:** Internship • **DURATION: YEAR-ROUND** • **IDEAL CANDIDATE:** College Students, Career Changers, Foreigners • **APPLICANT POOL:** 300/term • **APPLICANTS ACCEPTED:** 20/term

THE COUNCIL ON HEMISPHERIC AFFAIRS (COHA) is a hard-hitting and highly regarded research group that specializes in monitoring the full spectrum of U.S.–Latin American political, economic, diplomatic, trade, social, and cultural relations. The organization also closely follows Canadian relations with the rest of the hemisphere.

COHA has been described on the floor of the Senate, by Senator Edward Kennedy, as "one of our nation's most respected bodies of scholars and policymakers." COHA publishes the biweekly *Washington Report on the Hemisphere* as well as frequent memoranda on breaking regional issues to major national media.

Area and Working Environment: Located in an office building in the heart of downtown Washington, D.C., close to Chinatown and the Martin Luther King Public Library (the city's largest), the National Press Building, and an abundance of restaurants and stores, COHA's office is extremely convenient to bus and metro stations.

Work/Learn Program Specifics: COHA's interns, called research associates, are renowned for their extraordinary output and have the opportunity to work closely with senior regional specialists and also pursue research topics of their own interest. In general, research associates can expect to have two-thirds of their time devoted to research/writing activities and less than one-third to administrative functions. The heavy demands placed on research associates and the strong writing style which they develop as the result of relentless deadlines and rounds of editing, are reflected in the noticeable achievements of its alumni. They quickly come to see themselves as autonomous investigators whose mission is to validate a thesis by generating a critical mass of information that will illuminate an emerging issue in which important elements of basic policy are involved.

Duration: Schedules for the sixteen-week internships (thirteen weeks in the summer) can be arranged to meet the individual's needs, although full-time and full-term applicants are usually given preference in the selection process.

Compensation and Perks: None, but the intern will attend meetings, congressional hearings, legislative seminars, and substantive discussions on topics relevant to COHA's work. COHA is generally considered to be one of the most congenial offices in Washington for enterprising, entry-level, young professionals to become adept at the policy-making process. The high attainment of alumni in various fields gives testimony to the vigorous training and substantive responsibilities given to interns.

The Ideal Candidate: Intern candidates should have some knowledge of or interest in U.S.–Latin American affairs or international relations and should display impressive research and writing skills. Language ability in Spanish or Portuguese is desired, although an interest/major in journalism, English, or one of the social sciences may be substituted for the normal background requirements.

Making It Happen: Send cover letter, resume, and two strong writing samples. An application form will be sent to you, which you must then complete and return. Vacancies are competitively filled on a rolling basis.

INSIDER TIPS: *Convince us that you have the right background mix to thrive in a large, busy, very informal, very hardworking, and productive setting. Within a quintessentially messy setting, you will be expected to turn out press releases, write articles, draft bylines which will appear in the national press, and prepare for radio and TV appearances. Show us that you have the flexibility, talent, and brightness to blossom here.*

Contact Information: Larry Birns, Director • Council on Hemispheric Affairs • 724 9th St., NW, Suite 401 • Washington, DC 20001 • Phone: (202) 393-3322 • Fax: (202) 393-3423 • E-mail: www@coha.org • Web Site: www.coha.org

Council on International Educational Exchange

REGION/HQ: Worldwide/New York • **CATEGORY:** International Education • **POSITION TYPE:** Unique Experience • **DURATION:** Year-Round • **IDEAL CANDIDATE:** College Students, Career Changers, Foreigners • **APPLICANT POOL:** 5,000+/year • **APPLICANTS ACCEPTED:** 5,000+/year

SINCE ITS FOUNDING IN 1947, the Council on International Education Exchange (commonly known as Council) has been active in the development and administration of study, work, travel, and volunteer programs worldwide. Today Council assumes important educational responsibilities and develops, facilitates, and administers programs throughout the world on behalf of its North American and international constituencies.

Area and Working Environment: Programs are available in Britain, Ireland, France, Germany, Canada, New Zealand, Jamaica, and Costa Rica, but call for more opportunities, as new programs are developed each year.

Work/Learn Program Specifics: Over 5,000 students from over 1,000 United States colleges take advantage of this program each year and find work shortly after arrival. Council provides a handbook and general program information prior to departure and then an orientation, employment information, counseling services, and the use of a Council or cooperating organization office from which to job-hunt after arrival.

What makes working abroad unique is not so much the job you find but the opportunity to get an insider's perspective on another culture. Working in another country also means participating in its daily life. The sky's the limit for jobs! Most participants find short-term or seasonal service-industry positions, such as waiting tables, bartending, office temping, and retail sales. Others find jobs or paid internships in finance, law, and other professional fields. Students who are seeking professional/ degree-related positions have the most success by working towards landing a job prior to actually going overseas; while others interested in spending a summer working in a cafe or as a secretary typically find work within the first week after their arrival.

Duration: Britain (any time of the year, up to six months), Ireland (any time of the year, up to four months), France (any time of the year, up to three months), Germany (summer option—May 15 to October 15, three to six months; internship option—any time of the year, up to six months), New Zealand (April 1 to October 31, up to six months), Costa Rica and Jamaica (June 1 to October 1, up to three months) and Canada (any time of the year, up to five months).

Compensation and Perks: The current program fee is $225, and while working and living, most participants earn enough money to cover day-to-day expenses. Also inquire about Council's travel agency (which offers discount tickets to full-time students), how to purchase an International Student Identity Card ($19), and how to receive other discounts.

The Ideal Candidate: You must be at least eighteen years old and a full-time student or within one semester of your last period of full-time study. There is no language requirement for most countries; however, for programs in France, Germany, and Costa Rica, you must have completed intermediate-level study in the appropriate language.

Making It Happen: Contact Council for their work-abroad brochure and application materials. Council also publishes a free magazine for international travel, study, and work, called *Student Travels*. Look for all of this great information on their Web site.

Contact Information: Information Center • Council on International Educational Exchange • 205 East 42nd St. • New York, NY 10017-5706 • Phone: (888) 268-6245 • Fax: (212) 822-2699 • E-mail: info@ciee.org • Web Site: www.ciee.org

Educational Programs Abroad

REGION/HQ: Europe/New York • **CATEGORY:** International Exchange • **POSITION TYPE:** Internship • **DURATION:** Year-Round • **IDEAL CANDIDATE:** College Students • **APPLICANT POOL:** Varies • **APPLICANTS ACCEPTED:** Varies

EDUCATIONAL PROGRAMS ABROAD (EPA) was formed in 1971 to organize study programs for American universities and colleges unable to set up their own organizations in the host country. An internship with EPA gives you the opportunity of getting valuable work experience in an area related to your course of study or intended career field in an overseas location. Those internships lasting a semester or longer also involve academic credit. All commence with an orientation, and in non-English-speaking countries, include intensive language orientation as well.

Area and Working Environment: London, Brussels, Bonn/Cologne, Paris, and Madrid.

Work/Learn Program Specifics: Internships in Europe: There are a wide range of placements available, including advertising and public relations, arts administration, architecture, banking, business, education, environment, graphic design, health care, law firms, medical research, museums/art galleries, politics/pressure groups, publishing, social services, theatre, and town/urban planning. EPA has a professional staff in each host country. Applicants may request a particular institution or department, but EPA cannot guarantee placement there. With sufficient notice, it is often possible to make special arrangements for placements.

Duration: Most programs run for the summer or a semester.

Compensation and Perks: Application fees start at $3,550 and run up to $7,600. Housing is either with families, in apartments, or in hostels. A substantial part of the program fee is used to help students cover board and lodging expenses. The application has a schedule of fees. Academic credit, airfare, daily commuting, some meals, and personal expenses are not included in program fees.

The Ideal Candidate: In French-, German-, or Spanish-speaking countries, you should be able to understand the language. You will be working in a non-English-speaking environment.

Making It Happen: Call for details on program. EPA requires receipt of applications no later then ten weeks before the program begins.

Contact Information: Maura Staker, U.S. Administrator • Educational Programs Abroad • 2815 Sarles Dr. • Yorktown Heights, NY 10598 • Phone: (914) 245-6882 • Fax: (914) 245-6811 • E-mail: edproab@aol.com

Global Routes

REGION/HQ: Worldwide/California • **CATEGORY:** Global Development • **POSITION TYPE:** Seasonal • **DURATION:** Year-Round • **IDEAL CANDIDATE:** College Students, Career Changers, Retired Folks, Foreigners • **APPLICANT POOL:** 150/year • **APPLICANTS ACCEPTED:** 15/year

GLOBAL ROUTES IS A nonprofit organization committed to offering experiences that allow people with different world views to engage each other in creating a global community. The future of that community is dependent upon understanding, open communication, mutual respect, and interdependence between diverse peoples. It also depends on the preservation of the cultural and natural environments in which we all live. To further this end, Global Routes designs educational service projects and internships that allow people of all ages to extend themselves by living and working with people in communities throughout our world. Learning, achieved primarily through experiential methods, covers such areas as international development, language, government and politics, history, geology, ecology, art, and culture.

Area and Working Environment: "Our locale is the world!" More specifically, programs exist in Belize, Costa Rica, Ecuador, Kenya, Navajo Nation, Nepal/Thailand/Vietnam, and Zimbabwe.

Work/Learn Program Specifics: Adventure Leaders: Two leaders (one man, one woman) will lead a group of up to eighteen high school students. Staff will coordinate and support the students, who live either singly or in pairs in villages, as they teach at local primary and secondary schools. The leader is also responsible for organizing the group's in-country orientation and managing the debriefing process prior to their return. These programs require that leaders have a deep commitment to fostering their own growth and that of the group participants. The purpose of the programs is to place students in an environment radically different from their own, where they can reflect on their own lives and cultures. Leaders must facilitate this process in a fun and creative way, in addition to meeting the logistical demands of managing a group in a developing country. Typical projects are the building of classrooms for village schools, starting a business in conjunction with a women's cooperative, running daycare centers, teaching ESL, or preserving and extending natural environments through reforestation and other work.

Duration: Positions are offered year-round and roughly correspond to summer vacation and academic terms.

Compensation and Perks: Global Routes pays new leaders $225 per week for four-to-seven week programs and $2,000 for 2 1/2-month-long programs. They also cover all living expenses incurred by a leader during a program and round-trip travel to/from the program site. The biggest perk is the opportunity to see amazing places and meet interesting people.

The Ideal Candidate: Leaders must have graduated from college and have travel experience and the ability to work with groups of young people. Costa Rica and Ecuador leaders must be fluent in Spanish.

Making It Happen: Call for application form. In-person interviews will be arranged and the sooner you get your application in, the better. Rolling deadlines.

INSIDER TIPS: *We look for people with a passion for adventure, learning, and working with young people.*

Contact Information: Lara Mendel, Program Director • Global Routes • 1814 7th St., Suite A • Berkeley, CA 94710 • Phone: (510) 848-4800 • Fax: (510) 848-4801 • E-mail: globalrts@aol.com • Web Site: www.lanka.net/globalrts

Global Service Corps

REGION/HQ: Worldwide/California • **CATEGORY:** Conservation • **POSITION TYPE:** Unique Experience • **DURATION:** Year-Round • **IDEAL CANDIDATE:** College Students, Career Changers, Retired Folks, Foreigners • **APPLICANT POOL:** 10/project • **APPLICANTS ACCEPTED:** All

GLOBAL SERVICE CORPS (GSC) creates opportunities for adult volunteers to live in developing nations and work on projects that serve Earth's people and her environment. These projects emphasize grassroots collaboration on the local level, promote mutual transfer of skills, and foster cross-cultural understanding. GSC hopes to provide developing communities with the means to function sustainably and to widen the perspectives of volunteers as responsible global citizens by revealing the challenges of life in developing nations.

Area and Working Environment: Each town in each country is unique. Volunteers may wake up to the sounds of Buddhist prayers in Pasang, Thailand, or go to sleep watching the dim red glow of the Arenal Volcano in Monteverde, Costa Rica.

Work/Learn Program Specifics: GSC offers a unique opportunity to live in a small village in Kenya, Costa Rica, Thailand, or Guatemala. While living with your host family, you will be working on a community project that will be of real benefit to your host and community. You'll work with villagers teaching, learning, and doing real work to help each other. Projects include building trails, providing health education, teaching English, or training in biointensive agriculture. Also inquire about interning at their headquarters in San Francisco.

Duration: Most projects average three weeks; however, they offer projects which last two months or more.

Compensation and Perks: The most rewarding aspect of this experience is spending time with the people of the host communities, sharing ideas, and breaking down cultural stereotypes. In your spare time, you may visit nearby temples, rain forests, hot springs, or volcanic lakes, depending on the country.

The Ideal Candidate: Volunteers must be flexible, adaptable to the customs and culture of their host country, and willing to perform a valuable service to a community in need.

Making It Happen: Call for application materials. Apply at least sixty days prior to departure date. There is a fee of $1,500 to $1,700.

Contact Information: Tom Parker, Coordinator • Global Service Corps • 300 Broadway, Suite 28 • San Francisco, CA 94133-3312 • Phone: (415) 788-3666 • Fax: (415) 788-7324 • E-mail: gsc@igc.apc.org • Web Site: www.earthisland.org/ei/gsc/gschome.html

Global Volunteers

REGION/HQ: Worldwide/Minnesota • **CATEGORY:** Service Learning • **POSITION TYPE:** Unique Experience • **DURATION:** Year-Round • **IDEAL CANDIDATE:** High School Students, College Students, Career Changers, Retired Folks, Foreigners • **APPLICANT POOL:** Varies • **APPLICANTS ACCEPTED:** 90%

GLOBAL VOLUNTEERS WAS founded in 1984 with the goal of helping to establish a foundation for peace through mutual international understanding. At the request of local leaders and indigenous host organizations, Global Volunteers sends teams of volunteers to live and work with local people on human and economic development projects identified by the community as important to their long-term development. In this way, the volunteers' energy, creativity, and labor are put to use as they gain a genuine, firsthand understanding of how other people live day-to-day.

Area and Working Environment: Developing Countries Program (Costa Rica, Indonesia, Jamaica, Mexico, Tanzania, and Vietnam), European Program (Greece, Italy, Poland, Russia, and Spain) and USA Program (Ozark Mountains, Mississippi Delta, and Rio Grande Valley).

Work/Learn Program Specifics: Each volunteer selects a service program that best employs their experience and interests and can feel engaged in a community project of lasting benefit. Volunteers in developing countries live in communities under conditions similar to that of local people and thereby learn firsthand about how the vast majority of the world's people live day-to-day. You'll lend a hand with construction, education, health care, and environmental projects. European volunteers help build bridges of understanding in classrooms, in business and government offices, and in small groups in rural and urban communities. USA volunteers work with local citizens on broad-based community development projects, such as building playgrounds, repairing housing, and assisting with public works and general beautification efforts.

Duration: Program trips generally last one to three weeks, depending on the destination. Over 100 departure dates are offered throughout the year.

Compensation and Perks: There is a tax-deductible fee for this program ranging from $350 to $2,090. Your fee provides food, accommodations, ground transportation, an experienced team leader, project materials and consultants, program coordination, and administration. Airfare is not included in this fee.

The Ideal Candidate: Global Volunteers has no language or professional requirements for participation. Volunteers typically share common characteristics, such as flexibility, compassion, a sense of adventure, and most important, the desire to work with and learn from local people in the host community. Volunteers are drawn from all occupations and backgrounds, and from throughout the United States and Canada. Approximately

60 percent are women. While many of their team members are students, most are between the ages of thirty and seventy-five.

Making It Happen: Call for complete program description, along with departure dates. Applicants must complete the Global Volunteers application and submit it two to three months prior to departure date.

Contact Information: Volunteer Coordinator • Global Volunteers • 375 E. Little Canada Rd. • St. Paul, MN 55117 • Phone: (612) 482-1074 • Fax: (612) 482-0915 • Toll Free: (800) 487-1074 • E-mail: e-mail@ globalvlntrs.org • Web Site: www.globalvlntrs.org

Institute for International Cooperation & Development

REGION/HQ: Worldwide/Massachusetts • **CATEGORY:** Global Development • **POSITION TYPE:** Work/Learn Adventure • **DURATION:** 6–18 months • **IDEAL CANDIDATE:** College Students, Career Changers, Retired Folks, Foreigners • **APPLICANT POOL:** Varies • **APPLICANTS ACCEPTED:** Varies

THE INSTITUTE FOR International Cooperation and Development (IICD) is a nonprofit organization inspired by the Scandinavian folk education idea—"education for common people independent of their skills or schooling." The learning takes place for the sole purpose of gaining knowledge and experience, not for fame or credit. IICD organizes travel, study, and solidarity courses in Africa and Latin America.

Area and Working Environment: Mozambique, Zimbabwe, Angola, southern Africa, Nicaragua, and Brazil.

Work/Learn Program Specifics: You will participate in three components of the program: (1) the preparation period, which includes regional studies, language studies (Portuguese or Spanish), practical training, and fund-raising; (2) the international period, which includes travel to Africa or Latin America and work in community projects involving tree planting, health care, teaching, and construction work; and (3) the follow-up period in the United States, which includes the creation of educational materials such as a slide presentation, videos, films, exhibitions, booklets, or articles. Becoming a part of IICD means expecting the unexpected and learning new things with others and by yourself. You definitely won't be the same person when you finish their program.

Duration: The duration varies depending on the assignment and programs start throughout the year. Programs last anywhere from six to eighteen months, with preparation and follow-up periods in the United States.

Compensation and Perks: IICD receives no funding from the government or any other organization. The costs of running the programs are covered through the fee that each participant pays and through fund-raising. The students participate in extensive fund-raising efforts in support of the institute. The institute covers the expenses for training, room and board, international health insurance, and airfare. Fees range from $3,400 to $4,600. Limited financial aid is available.

The Ideal Candidate: The programs are open to anyone who is eighteen or older. There are no specific academic or skill requirements. They welcome applications from all people who are ready to accept the challenge of undertaking new and demanding tasks, working in a group, and opening themselves to new understandings of the world—and of their own potential.

Making It Happen: Call for application materials. Applications are evaluated on a rolling basis, so the sooner they receive your application, the sooner you will know if you are able to go. After sending your application, your next step is a personal orientation where you will learn more about the program to which you are applying and discuss your needs and ideas. When sending your completed application, please also include a $10 processing fee.

Contact Information: Josefin Jonsson, Promotion Director • Institute for International Cooperation & Development • P.O. Box 103 • Williamstown, MA 01267 • Phone: (413) 458-9828 • Fax: (413) 458-3323 • E-mail: iicd1@berkshire.net • Web Site: www.berkshire. net/~iicd1

Institute of International Education

REGION/HQ: Washington, D.C./Washington, D.C. • **CATEGORY:** International Education • **POSITION TYPE:** Internship • **DURATION:** Year-Round • **IDEAL CANDIDATE:** College Students, Career Changers, Foreigners • **APPLICANT POOL:** 6–20/term • **APPLICANTS ACCEPTED:** 3–5/term

THE INSTITUTE OF International Education (IIE), founded in 1919, is a nonprofit educational exchange organization dedicated to fostering international collaboration and economic development through pro-fessional and academic exchanges, training, publications, and other services. The IIE Professional Exchange Program Division (PEP) designs and implements programs that broaden the expertise of leaders and specialists from abroad. PEP tailors these professional development and policy analysis programs to meet the specific interests of the participants. Briefings, panel discussions, site visits, and hands-on learning are integrated into each group or individual project. PEP develops programs for a variety of public and private sponsors, including the U.S. Information Agency (USIA), the Japanese government, and the German Marshall Fund. Through its contractual relationship with USIA, and in conjunction with the National Council of International Visitors (NCIV) affiliates, PEP has organized three-to-six week programs for more than 600 international visitors annually since 1972.

Area and Working Environment: Interns will be in their Washington, D.C. office; however, the organization itself is headquartered in New York, with regional offices in Washington, D.C., Denver, Chicago, Houston, and San Francisco, and overseas offices in Budapest, Hong Kong, Bangkok, Jakarta, and Mexico City.

Work/Learn Program Specifics: Interns assist with the development and implementation of programs for international visitors participating in group and individual programs, with assignments being quite diverse. Often interns are asked to research resources nationwide that match the professional and cultural interests of international visitors; identify and contact appropriate organizations in Washington to request appointments for international visitors; research specific but diverse topics such as small business development, free trade zones, women's programs, nontraditional higher education programs, agricultural research centers, or museums of traditional American folk culture; write short biographic statements for speakers and presenters; assist in the preparation of program booklets and welcome packets; and escort visitors to occasional Washington appointments. Interns are requested to submit a written evaluation at the conclusion of their internship.

Duration: Internships are a semester in duration, with a flexible work schedule (full- or part-time).

Compensation and Perks: There is a $500 stipend for full-time interns. As part of the program, interns also are able to meet international visitors almost every week. In addition to working with the International Visitor Program, all IIE interns have the opportunity to

become familiar with many organizations in Washington and with the professional operation of a large and dynamic office. Interns are highly valued for their contribution to their fast-paced and "something different everyday" work.

The Ideal Candidate: Interested applicants should have a background and interest in international relations, American studies, cross-cultural communications, government and politics, or language/regional studies. You must also have the ability to work under minimum supervision, meet deadlines, communicate effectively with individuals from other cultures, and possess maturity, flexibility, and strong writing skills.

Making It Happen: Send resume, writing sample, unofficial transcript, and two letters of recommendation. Deadlines: spring—December 10; summer—April 15; and fall—August 20.

INSIDER TIPS: *Call to follow up your application. Know the organization. Reek enthusiasm!*

Contact Information: Jeanne Thum, Internship Coordinator • Institute of International Education • 1400 K Street, NW, Suite 650 • Washington, DC 20005-2403 • Phone: (202) 326-7679 • Fax: (202) 326-7696 • Toll Free: (800) 424-8030 • E-mail: jthum@iie.org • Web Site: www.iie.org

Institute of International Education, Latin America

REGION/HQ: Mexico/Texas • **CATEGORY:** Education • **POSITION TYPE:** Internship • **DURATION:** Year-Round • **IDEAL CANDIDATE:** College Students, Career Changers, Foreigners • **APPLICANT POOL:** 30/year • **APPLICANTS ACCEPTED:** 3–4/term

THE INSTITUTE OF International Education (IIE), Regional Offices for Latin America, functions as an integral part of the U.S. Information Service in Mexico, providing information about U.S. education to more than 40,000 people per year. IIE maintains close ties with the American Embassy, Mexican government offices, and universities and schools both in Mexico and the United States.

Work/Learn Program Specifics: Interns working at the IIE office in Mexico will have the opportunity to work as student advisors, giving out information about U.S. educational opportunities. Interns will also have the chance to observe and familiarize themselves with operations of a large U.S. Embassy. Interns will be able to take advantage of the vast cultural opportunities found in Mexico City and other parts of the republic while they are there. Those who wish to undertake an independent study or research project during their internship may do so.

Duration: Internships are generally two to three months in the summer, although internships are available during the fall and spring as well.

Compensation and Perks: Interns will receive a $400 stipend to defray expenses for the two to three months that are expected. Interns can arrange to stay longer but with no additional pay. Perks include a great cultural experience and contacts with U.S. Embassy and Mexican institutions. You must cover travel, lodging, meals, and personal expenses while on assignment.

The Ideal Candidate: Applicants must have an interest in Latin America, the ability to communicate well in Spanish and English, and have a general knowledge of Mexican history and culture. Interns are expected to keep abreast of current political, economic, educational, and social events in Mexico.

Making It Happen: Call for application. Submit application form, university transcripts, and two letters of recommendation (one from someone who can attest to your ability in Spanish). There is no formal deadline, but you should apply at least three months before desired starting date.

Contact Information: Josephine Griffin, Assistant Director • Institute of International Education, Latin America • AmEmbassy Educational Center • P.O. Box 3087 • Laredo, TX 78044-3087 • Phone: (525) 703-0167 • Fax: (525) 535-5597 • E-mail: jgriffin@usia.gov

InterExchange, Inc.

REGION/HQ: Europe/New York • **CATEGORY:** International Exchange • **POSITION TYPE:** Unique Experience • **DURATION:** Year-Round • **IDEAL CANDIDATE:** College Students, Career Changers, Retired Folks, Foreigners • **APPLICANT POOL:** Varies • **APPLICANTS ACCEPTED:** Varies

INTEREXCHANGE IS A private, nonprofit cultural exchange organization which operates a variety of work-abroad programs for both Americans and foreigners. They are strongly committed to promoting the benefits of an international experience for personal growth, and working abroad is a great way to actually experience life in another country, not just observe it as a tourist. Students are able to improve their foreign language skills and gain greater insight into another way of life while earning money to help offset travel costs. During the past twenty years, InterExchange has enabled thousands of students to experience and appreciate another way of life.

Area and Working Environment: Austria, Czech Republic, Finland, France, Germany, Holland, Hungary, Italy, Norway, Poland, Spain, and Switzerland.

Work/Learn Program Specifics: Have you ever: enjoyed a real Finnish sauna? dreamed about ordering a croissant and café au lait in Paris? or wanted to become a part of a real Italian family? If so, InterExchange is the program for you. They have dozens of positions in dozens of countries. Typical jobs include picking rhubarb and blackberries, tending livestock, teaching English, being a camp counselor, looking after children (au pair), working in a resort, internships for hotel management graduates, and in the fields of trade, environmental protection, agriculture, and forestry (and this list keeps growing).

Duration: Placements can be from one month to one year, dependent on the program. Teaching and au pair positions are generally from six months to a year; farm programs, two to four months; and internships range from summer positions to year-long ventures.

Compensation and Perks: There is a program fee for placement of $125 to $300. Pay and housing vary according to the program you chose, although your salary will be merely sufficient to sustain you during your time abroad.

The Ideal Candidate: Starting from the age of eighteen, the programs are open to a variety of different age groups, some are even open to all ages (although some are, by the nature of the work, more suited to the younger generation—no offense intended). Additionally, all participants must be covered by health and accident insurance for the length of involvement in the program. Participants on any of the farm programs must also be covered for accidents occurring while performing manual labor. Some programs have language and degree requirements.

Making It Happen: Call for program information. You are required to purchase a country kit for $2, which explains the details of that particular program. After the proper paperwork is completed, most participants receive word of placement anywhere from four to eight weeks before their requested departure date.

INSIDER TIPS: *Have a neat application, proofread, and provide solid references. For teaching positions, get some experience tutoring, volunteering, or take a TEFL class.*

We must not cease from exploration. And the end of all our exploring will be to arrive where we began and to know the place for the first time. —T.S. ELIOT

393

Contact Information: Casey Slamin, Program Coordinator • InterExchange, Inc. • 161 Sixth Ave. • New York, NY 10013 • Phone: (212) 924-0446 • Fax: (212) 924-0575 • E-mail: interex@earthlink.net

International Agricultural Exchange Association

REGION/HQ: Worldwide/Montana • **CATEGORY:** Agriculture • **POSITION TYPE:** Unique Experience • **DURATION:** Year-Round • **IDEAL CANDIDATE:** College Students, Career Changers, Foreigners • **APPLICANT POOL:** Varies • **APPLICANTS ACCEPTED:** Varies

THE INTERNATIONAL AGRICULTURAL Exchange Association (IAEA) was founded in 1963, with a strong international network of past trainees and host families. Worldwide, IAEA has over 1,000 participants every year. In many member countries, IAEA works closely with rural youth organizations and agricultural colleges.

Area and Working Environment: Australia, New Zealand, Japan, and Europe (Denmark, Netherlands, Sweden, Norway, and Germany).

Work/Learn Program Specifics: Do you have an agricultural or horticultural background and have always dreamed of working abroad? If so, get in touch with IAEA. Experience the thrill of herding cattle in the outback of Australia, milking 200 cows in less than two hours in New Zealand, or working in the flower market in Amsterdam—not to mention the adventures you can experience on your days off and during your holiday time. IAEA is a great way to meet young people from all over the world, just by your traveling to one country. In addition, it is a great way to experience a different culture, living with and being accepted as a member of your host family. There is more to life than what you can see out your back door.

Duration: Departure dates are in March, April, July, August, September, October, and November, and range from four to thirteen months in length.

Compensation and Perks: The up-front fee for this program covers a "training allowance" paid to the student which is approximately equal to the program cost. Host families generally pay allowances per month, plus room and board. Perks include a work visa and medical insurance, as well as two day-long stopovers in Hawaii for various programs, and seminars in the host country.

The Ideal Candidate: Candidates must be citizens of one of the member countries; have the desire to work overseas; be eighteen to thirty years old; have practical experience in agriculture, horticulture, or home management; have a valid driver's license; have no criminal record; have no children; be in good mental and physical health; and have a basic understanding of the English language.

Making It Happen: Call or write for information, application, and current program fees. Rolling deadlines.

Contact Information: Monica Heisler, Office Manager • International Agricultural Exchange Association • 1000 1st Ave. South • Great Falls, MT 59401 • Phone: (406) 727-1999 • Fax: (406) 727-1997 • Toll Free: (800) 272-4996

International Christian Youth Exchange

REGION/HQ: Worldwide/New York • **CATEGORY:** International Exchange • **POSITION TYPE:** Unique Experience • **DURATION:** Year-Round • **IDEAL CANDIDATE:** College Students, Career Changers, Retired Folks • **APPLICANT POOL:** Varies • **APPLICANTS ACCEPTED:** Varies

ICYE IS PEOPLE AROUND the world, participants and volunteers alike, striving to make the world a better place to live. In 1949, with the world still recovering from the horrors of war, fifty courageous German teenagers ventured across the Atlantic and were welcomed into American host families as ICYE exchangees—and ICYE was born. Building bridges of peace, justice, and understanding through personal encounters has been their goal throughout the past forty years, with the program now reaching over thirty countries around the globe.

Work/Learn Program Specifics: There are several programs available for individuals that are interested in making a difference in the world. You can become an ICYE exchangee, host a young person from another country, or volunteer for ICYE projects at home.

Duration: Depending on the program in which you decide to participate, your stay can last from four weeks for summer workcamps to a year.

Compensation and Perks: Program fees range from $500 to $5,000. ICYE provides room and board and a monthly stipend for exchangees.

The Ideal Candidate: Anyone and everyone with an interest in helping build bridges of peace between countries is encouraged to apply. For six-month and year-long programs, participants must be sixteen to thirty years old. Summer workcamps are open to those sixteen and older.

Making It Happen: The application procedure is tailored for each program—call for details. Complete the application and return it to ICYE by May 15. If you are considering being a host family or agency, call for information.

Contact Information: Outbound Program Director • International Christian Youth Exchange • 134 W. 26th St. • New York, NY 10001-6803 • Phone: (212) 206-7307 • Fax: (212) 633-9085

International Cooperative Education Program

REGION/HQ: Europe/California • **CATEGORY:** International Education • **POSITION TYPE:** Internship/SeasonaL • **DURATION:** Summer • **IDEAL CANDIDATE:** College Students, Career Changers • **APPLICANT POOL:** Varies • **APPLICANTS ACCEPTED:** 200–250

EACH SUMMER, OVER 200 Americans from 65 colleges go to work overseas through the sponsorship of the International Cooperative Education Program. Günter Seefeldt, the director, is also the director of the International Education Program—Work Abroad, which is sponsored by Foothill College. The only difference in this program is that it is for California residents only, and it places about 400 Californians overseas each year. For more information, call Günter at (415) 949-7066/E-mail: iepnorcal@aol.com.

Area and Working Environment: Germany, Belgium, Switzerland, Finland, and Japan.

Work/Learn Program Specifics: Linguistic/Cultural Immersion Program: Employment positions are matched, when possible, with each participant's work experience and educational preparation. Work experience is available in many fields, including banking, hotels and restaurants, retail sales, teaching and recreation, health care, clerical work, tourism, agriculture, engineering, computer science, and chemistry. Housing is in host homes or in student housing. At the conclusion of the summer, each student writes an analysis report describing his or her employment and cultural observations as compared to business and customs in America.

Duration: Programs run from June through early September. Work periods last from one to three months.

Compensation and Perks: Participants receive a modest salary and gain international work experience. Housing is arranged by employers or IEP coordinators in Europe. Program costs include insurance, round-trip airfare, placement fees, and financial reserves.

The Ideal Candidate: For this program you must attend school or live outside California (ask Günter about the International Education Program—Work Abroad if you're from California), have U.S./Canadian citizenship, and be eighteen to thirty. You must also be currently enrolled in a German, French, Dutch, Italian, or Japanese language class (or have proficiency in one of these languages).

Making It Happen: Request an application and informational brochure. Mail your typed application to IEP as early as possible (no later than February). Attach four passport photos (signed on the back). Personal interviews are conducted with a coordinator at local orientation meetings in the fall/winter to determine the student's language ability, experience, and job preferences. Telephone interviews can also be arranged.

Contact Information: Günter Seefeldt, Director • International Cooperative Education Program • 15 Spiros Way • Menlo Park, CA 94025 • Phone: (415) 323-4944 • Fax: (415) 323-1104 • E-mail: icemenlo@aol.com

International Law Institute

REGION/HQ: Washington, D.C./Washington, D.C. • **CATEGORY:** Education • **POSITION TYPE:** Internship • **DURATION:** Year-Round • **IDEAL CANDIDATE:** College Students, Career Changers, Foreigners • **APPLICANT POOL:** Varies • **APPLICANTS ACCEPTED:** 2–3/term

THE INTERNATIONAL LAW INSTITUTE is a nonprofit educational institute that hosts conferences and runs training seminars for officials from developing countries on the substance and practice of negotiation, policy execution, and management in different fields. The institute was founded at Georgetown University in 1955. Since that time, over 4,000 bankers, lawyers, and government officials from 140 countries have attended courses at the institute.

Area and Working Environment: Washington is a great place to be as an intern! It's a large city, but very visitor-friendly and accessible to all sorts of activities and festivals.

Work/Learn Program Specifics: Interns act as program assistants to seminar administrators. They are involved in all aspects of the seminar, including the marketing, planning, and administration of the seminars. There is some research involved, however. This is really a hands-on internship. Seminar participants and staff interact frequently, providing a unique opportunity for students to meet and network with people from all over the world. Interns will also be able to network with a great many of the faculty members, who are lawyers, engineers, bankers, and officials from government and international organizations. Interns are welcome to sit in on any of the lectures and may accompany groups to on-site meetings, with some seminars conducted in New York.

Duration: The institute offers year-round positions, full- or part-time.

Compensation and Perks: All internships are unpaid. Housing is not provided; however, they could offer some suggestions. The ILI is a small organization and has an easygoing staff. Interns are considered part of the staff and are included in everything. Along with the academic part of the seminars, lots of social events are planned for the participants, faculty, and staff. This is a big part of the seminar, a chance for the participants to socialize with faculty and staff outside of the classroom and office—and a big part of the internship, too! It's their hope that interns will want to participate in these activities—welcome receptions and luncheons, dinners, tours of Washington, and shopping trips. The ILI incorporates all of these activities into each seminar, so there are always events to attend.

The Ideal Candidate: Applicants should have an interest in international legal and economic issues and a desire to work with people from developing countries. Computer and research skills are helpful. Working knowledge of a second language is preferred, but not required. Any Russian skills are helpful, as the ILI plans a number of seminars taking place in Washington and in the former Soviet Republics.

Making It Happen: Send a cover letter and resume. In the letter, applicants should explain why they want to intern, what their interests are, and include dates/hours of availability. There are no deadlines, but it is best to send information a few months before desired start date.

INSIDER TIPS: *As a former ILI intern, I think this is a fantastic internship. There are lots of different activities to get involved in and lots of interesting people to meet (lots of social events to attend, too). Interns don't sit at desks for* eight hours a day researching, instead we encourage them to get involved and stay active. It makes for a much more interesting internship experience.

Contact Information: Brenda Smith, Assistant to the Executive Director • International Law Institute • 1615 New Hampshire Ave., NW • Washington, DC 20009 • Phone: (202) 483-3036 • Fax: (202) 483-3029 • E-mail: training@ili.org • Web Site: www.ili.org

International Volunteer Projects

REGION/HQ: Worldwide/New York • **CATEGORY:** Workcamp • **POSITION TYPE:** Seasonal • **DURATION:** Summer • **COMPENSATION:** Volunteer • **IDEAL CANDIDATE:** College Students, Career Changers, Foreigners • **APPLICANT POOL:** Varies • **APPLICANTS ACCEPTED:** 600/year

INTERNATIONAL VOLUNTEER PROJECTS, coordinated by CIEE, has established extensive international links with voluntary service organizations in thirty countries, which offer volunteers access to over 600 projects on four continents. Workcamps are about adapting, sharing, cooperating, letting go of prejudices, and appreciating the cultural diversity of our world. The first workcamp was organized in France after World War I by a Swiss pacifist and a British Quaker. They brought youth from all over Europe together to help rebuild farmhouses destroyed during the war. By creating an atmosphere of cooperation, they also hoped to rebuild understanding between the young people of Europe and to promote peace. Today, the same spirit remains.

Area and Working Environment: Projects take place each summer in a wide variety of settings, from national parks and forests to inner-city neighborhoods and small towns. Projects are generally offered in Belarus, Belgium, Britain, Canada, Costa Rica, the Czech Republic, Denmark, Finland, France, Germany, Ghana, Greece, India, Ireland, Italy, Japan, Lithuania, Mexico, Morocco, Netherlands, Philippines, Poland, Russia, Slovakia, Spain, Tunisia, Turkey, Ukraine, and the United States.

Work/Learn Program Specifics: Help is needed worldwide on a variety of nature conservation, renovation, archaeological, agricultural, and social projects. You may choose to build a playground, plant trees, restore a castle, organize a festival, or implement a recreation program for at-risk children. You'll live the life of a local: drinking tea with Turkish villagers, riding bicycles to work in Holland, and carrying buckets of water on one's head to replenish the water supply in a Ghanaian village are typical tastes of local life experienced on a work-camp. As part of a group of volunteers from at least five or six different countries, you'll learn about yourself, the local area, and other cultures from many different perspectives. You'll have the chance to develop team-building and cross-cultural communication skills, learn firsthand about social and political conditions in other countries, and make friends from around the world.

Duration: Most projects take place from June through September and last two to four weeks. You'll work five to seven hours per day, five days a week, with evenings and weekends free to explore the surroundings with your fellow volunteers.

Compensation and Perks: There is a $295 placement fee for one two- to four-week project; $250 for each additional project. Room and board are provided, and volunteers live together with other volunteers in a school, church, hostel, or tents, preparing meals and organizing activities as a group. Some projects have additional fees of $50 to $400, depending on the local economic situation. Participants arrange and pay for their own travel and insurance.

The Ideal Candidate: Individuals aged eighteen and older who are self-motivated, open-minded, and flexible (the average age of participants is twenty-one to twenty-five). There is an upper age limit of thirty-five in Turkey and Tunisia, thirty in Spain, and twenty-six in Belgium, due to the requirements of the local youth ministries. No special skills are required, although conversational ability in French for North Africa and Spanish for Spain is necessary.

Making It Happen: To apply, you must first order the *Directory of International Volunteer Projects*. The $15 cost will be credited toward your placement fee. The directory comes out in late March, with placements beginning in April and continuing on a first-come, first-served basis until July, by which time most summer projects have been filled.

Contact Information: Program Director • International Volunteer Projects • CIEE • 205 E. 42nd St. • New York, NY 10017-5706 • Phone: (212) 661-1414 • Fax: (212) 972-3231 • E-mail: info@ciee.org • Web Site: www.ciee.org

Internship Programs/ Australia

REGION/HQ: Australia/California • **CATEGORY:** International Education • **POSITION TYPE:** Unique Experience • **DURATION:** Year-Round • **IDEAL CANDIDATE:** College Students, Career Changers, Retired Folks, Foreigners • **APPLICANT POOL:** 150/term • **APPLICANTS ACCEPTED:** 50/term

CUSTOM-DESIGNED professional-development internships are for advanced undergraduates, recent college graduates, or midcareer professionals who want international experience in a professional field to give them an edge when securing professional employment or further education. They represent Global Education Designs (GED), a highly respected firm in Australia that specializes in designing semester- and year-long academic programs for American colleges and universities. GED has been in business for more than ten years and has worked with scores of schools and hundreds of students from around the United States and around the world. They have been active in recruiting interns from the United States and abroad via campus visits, study-abroad fairs, and the Internet.

Work/Learn Program Specifics: Interns will be placed in Australia in various fields, including business (management, marketing, finance, and accounting), communications (radio, television, newspapers, and public relations), law, politics, the arts, social work, biology, farm studies, and ecotourism. Those with a clear idea as to the possibilities offered by an internship have an initial advantage. However, those willing to work toward developing an unusual program will also find satisfactory placements. Rotating internships are popular, especially those combining headquarters and field-placement opportunities within a single venue/business/agency/program.

Duration: Internships, typically, run six to sixteen or more weeks, and are offered year-round, with flexible start and end dates. Longer internships are possible and may be arranged.

Compensation and Perks: Fees for a typical twelve-week internship currently run $5,158 and include round-trip airfare from Los Angeles, airport transfers, accommodations (homestay with two meals or an apartment without meals), placement fee, help securing an occupational trainee visa, professional development supervisor, and on-call administration and welfare support service.

The Ideal Candidate: The program is designed for recent college graduates about to begin graduate studies, although it is open to advanced undergraduates as well. In addition, the program is suitable for practicing professionals wishing to benefit from international experience in the field.

Making It Happen: Call for an application. A three- to four-month lead time is best.

INSIDER TIPS: *We are seeking good people who wish to immerse themselves in a cost-effective and unique education/vocational experience Down Under. Party animals are discouraged from applying. Since each internship is custom designed, you need to have a clear idea about how your internship is to be structured. If you don't have an idea but want to pursue the possibility of designing an internship, please feel free to visit our Web site and then contact us via E-mail or phone to discuss the possibilities.*

Contact Information: Robert and Barbara Yoshioka, Managing Consultants • Internship Programs/Australia • 4361 Eastwood Dr. • Santa Maria, CA 93455-3917 • Phone: (805) 937-4880 • Fax: (800) 704-4880 • Toll Free: (800) 704-4880 • E-mail: rby2oz@terminus.com • Web Site: www.advc.com/internships

Japan Exchange and Teaching Programme

REGION/HQ: Japan/California • **CATEGORY:** Teaching • **POSITION TYPE:** Work/Learn Adventure • **DURATION:** Year Long • **IDEAL CANDIDATE:** Career Changers, Retired Folks • **APPLICANT POOL:** Varies • **APPLICANTS ACCEPTED:** Varies

THE JAPAN EXCHANGE and Teaching (JET) Programme seeks to enhance internationalization in Japan by promoting mutual understanding between Japan and other countries, including the United States. The program's aims are to intensify foreign language education in Japan and to promote international contacts at the local level by fostering ties between Japanese youth and young foreign college/university graduates. Over 5,000 participants are currently involved in the JET Program, approximately half of whom come from the United States.

Area and Working Environment: Program sites are in various cities, towns, and villages throughout Japan.

Work/Learn Program Specifics: Assistant language teacher participants are assigned to local schools and boards of education in Japan as team-teachers and engage in foreign language instruction. They may also be involved in language clubs, teachers' seminars, and judging speech contests. Coordinator for international relations participants engage in international activities carried out by local governments throughout Japan. These activities include receiving guests from abroad, editing and translating documents, interpreting during international events, assisting with the language instruction of government employees and local residents, assisting with international exchange programs, and various other activities.

Duration: The duration for an individual contract is one year, beginning in late July. JET contracts are generally renewable for up to three years, upon consent of both the participant and his or her employer.

Compensation and Perks: An annual salary of approximately $33,000 per year (3,600,000 yen per year at $1.00 = 110 yen) is provided to cover the cost of the participant's accommodations, living expenses, and mandatory health insurance. Round-trip airfare is provided, although only from designated points within the United States. The host institution in Japan will assist the participant in finding his or her accommodations.

The Ideal Candidate: Assistant language teacher applicants must have excellent English communication skills and have an interest in Japan. Neither Japanese language ability nor teaching experience is required. Applicants for the coordinator position must have a functional command of Japanese and excellent communication skills. In addition to the above, both positions require a bachelor's degree and U.S. citizenship.

Making It Happen: Applications for the following year's JET Program will be available beginning in late September. Call 1-800-INFO-JET for an application. Completed application packets must be received by the Japanese Embassy in Washington, D.C. by the first week of December (call for exact dates).

Contact Information: Andrew Lee, Education Coordinator • Japan Exchange and Teaching Programme • Japan Information Center • 50 Fremont St., Suite 2200 • San Francisco, CA 94105 • Phone: (415) 356-2462 • Toll Free: (800) 463-6538 • E-mail: cgj5@mail.mikuni.com • Web Site: www.infojapan.com/cgjsf

Teaching your way around the world will be as much an education for you as it will be for your students. You may be invited to their homes for dinner or perhaps taken to local sites and events that do not appear in the best of travel guides. You will not be a tourist, but you will be an integral and valued member of the community. You will experience other cultures, not just read about them. you can be sure that this is a big change from the nine-to-five world that is so prevalent around us. It's an education that goes beyond libraries and lecture halls, a way to travel that's as beneficial to you as to the people you meet along the way.

—JEFF DARLING, NEW WORLD TEACHERS

La Sabranenque

REGION/HQ: France/New York • **CATEGORY:** International Education • **POSITION TYPE:** Work/ Learn Adventure • **DURATION:** Year-Round • **IDEAL CANDIDATE:** College Students, Career Changers, Foreigners • **APPLICANT POOL:** 100/year • **APPLICANTS ACCEPTED:** Varies

LA SABRANENQUE PROGRAMS offer the chance to discover French village life, and/or the French language, "from the inside" through dynamic and genuine immersion in regional life and historic preservation. A grassroots, nonprofit organization created in 1969, La Sabranenque has won several national awards for its restoration work and its international cultural activities.

Area and Working Environment: All activities are based in the restored old quarter (full modern comfort) in the village of Saint Victor la Coste (near Avignon, southern France), listed as one of the "most beautiful villages in France."

Work/Learn Program Specifics: Summer Volunteer Restoration Projects: Volunteers have the opportunity to become actively and directly involved in preservation and reconstruction work on sites and monuments often dating back to the Middle Ages. The goal of the La Sabranenque is the preservation of rural architecture and habitat. Volunteers learn the traditional construction techniques on-the-job from experienced technicians and, in a short period, experience the satisfaction of making a lasting contribution to the preservation of the villages of southern France. Work is shared with a diverse multinational team and can include stone masonry or cutting, tile floor or roof restoration, dry-stone walling, or vault construction. French Language Session: This program offers a genuine experience of French village life, and daily classes provide an intensive study of the French language. An array of activities are designed to offer an in-depth discovery of the region for the twelve participants per session. Participants speak French at all times and very rapidly gain a facility in French comprehension and expression. Daily life in the restored old village is shared with the French members of the La Sabranenque team and meals are prepared family-style with fresh local produce.

Duration: Restoration project participants must commit to a minimum of two weeks during June, July, and/or August. The language sessions are offered in the spring (three months) and the fall (one- and three-month programs).

Compensation and Perks: For both programs, participants cover costs of room and board, and, in the case of the French language sessions, of language classes and other activities. Restoration projects: $535 for a two-week session. Language Program: $5,100 for a three-month program. Participants live in rooms in the restored stone houses. At least one day is spent during each two-week period exploring the region.

The Ideal Candidate: All programs require a minimum age of eighteen and good health. Restoration Project: No experience is necessary, and some knowledge of French is helpful, but not necessary. Language Program: intermediate French language level required.

Making It Happen: Write for application form. No formal deadline. Contact the director in France: Marc Simon, La Sabranenque, Centre International, Rue de la Tour de L'Oume, 30290 Saint Victor la Coste, France. Phone: 33 (0) 466 50 05 05; Fax: 33 (0) 466 50 12 48.

Contact Information: Jacqueline Simon, U.S. Correspondent • La Sabranenque • 217 High Park Blvd. • Buffalo, NY 14226 • Phone: (716) 836-8698

Latin American Art Resource Project

REGION/HQ: Honduras/Maryland • **CATEGORY:** Arts Administration • **POSITION TYPE:** Unique Experience • **DURATION:** Year-Round • **IDEAL CANDIDATE:** College Students, Career Changers, Foreigners • **APPLICANT POOL:** Varies • **APPLICANTS ACCEPTED:** Varies

• •

THE LATIN AMERICAN Art Resource Project (LAARP) is a development program that enables underprivileged artists and artisans to create work with low-cost, local resources. Directed by William Swetcharnik, an artist with extensive experience in traditional painting media of different cultures, the priority of this program is to provide opportunity through education. Working with school districts that cannot afford to buy expensive imported art supplies, the program team shows teachers how they can make art in the classroom with materials from their own environments. Reviving techniques native to their own history, the children also begin to discover and develop their individual talents. These local teacher-training workshops are also made available to local artists and artisans, as well as to community-based art and artisan projects, such as school murals, neighborhood beautification, vocational training and rehabilitation, and the formation of crafts cooperatives. The program also works with art schools and universities involved in teacher training, and provides additional teaching aids, such as manuals, curriculum guides, and videos.

Area and Working Environment: The home base in Honduras is a great point of departure for Mayan ruins, tropical rain forests, and coral-reef islands. When the team takes off for workshop tours in remote areas of the isthmus, there are usually weekend opportunities for exploring as well.

Work/Learn Program Specifics: These internships are excellent opportunities for anyone interested in a firsthand experience of what it takes to run a development project in a poor country, and it must be said that a great deal of this experience consists of learning to navigate within a culture that operates very differently, and not nearly as efficiently, as those of Europe and North America. Patience and love and creativity are required to make things work. Some aspects of the work fit the training profile for any arts or development program administrator: maintaining lines of communication, coordination of activities with collaborating institutions, public relations, photo files, publications, grant applications, presentations, and exhibitions. The fieldwork includes traveling to set up regional workshops, researching local materials and methods at each site, and, of course, helping with the workshops themselves. To help effectively with the workshops, interns need firsthand experience with materials and methods, which entails a fair amount of studio work, particularly in the production of demonstration pieces for art and artisanry. Depending on the time frame and the intern's circumstances, LAARP internships can take place either in the U.S. or in Honduras, the program's present base of operations. For more information on the artistic work of William Swetcharnik and studio intern opportunities with him and his wife Sara, please see the listing for Swetcharnik Studio.

Duration: Internships are normally arranged for a minimum stay of three months.

Compensation and Perks: Interns do not receive salaries or any other employment benefits. Structured weekly art classes are provided at no cost. Nearby room and board are available for $400 per month in Honduras and $700 per month in Maryland. Assistance is provided in seeking grants.

The Ideal Candidate: No special skills are required, only emotional maturity and eagerness to learn, attested through good school records, work history, and letters of reference.

Making It Happen: Send a cover letter and resume.

Contact Information: William and Sara Swetcharnik, Artists Latin American Art Resource Project • 7044 Woodville Rd. • Mt. Airy, MD 21771 • Phone: (301) 831-7286 • Fax: (301) 694-7653 • E-mail: wswetcharnik@nimue.hood.edu • Web Site: www.hood.edu/academic/art/laarp

Little Children of the World

REGION/HQ: Philippines/Tennessee • **CATEGORY:** Ministry • **POSITION TYPE:** Unique Experience • **DURATION:** Year-Round • **IDEAL CANDIDATE:** College Students, Career Changers, Retired Folks • **APPLICANT POOL:** 25/year • **APPLICANTS ACCEPTED:** 10/year

• •

LITTLE CHILDREN OF THE WORLD is a nonprofit Christian service agency dedicated to helping create caring communities for children who are victims of poverty or abuse. Work is also done with other service agencies, including the Alger Foundation, Habitat for Humanity, and Teen Missions International.

Area and Working Environment: At this point, their work is concentrated in the central Philippines. You'll work in Negros, a beautiful tropical island with sandy beaches and mountains climbing to 7,000 feet.

Work/Learn Program Specifics: Health workers assist in a special community-based health program; housing helpers assist in the construction of new houses and the repair of old ones; education helpers teach in a survival school, an informal program designed to help children, youth, and parents cope in a poverty culture; livelihood workers help with organic farming and biointensive gardening to promote self-reliance amongst indigent families; and peace workers help with the Sunday school, weekly Bible study groups, daily staff devotions, and training in the theory and practice of peaceful conflict resolution.

Duration: Most of the programs are ongoing, so you could "plug in" at almost any point. Most volunteers stay for at least three months for a full experience, but shorter terms are welcome.

Compensation and Perks: Volunteers receive free dorm-style housing, which includes cable TV, utilities, linens, and office space. Your food expenses will be minimal; cooked meals will cost you about $5 per day.

The Ideal Candidate: Candidates must have at least a high school diploma, but most are college students or recent graduates. Applicants with developed skills, such as computer knowledge or bookkeeping, are particularly desired.

Making It Happen: Call for an informational packet which includes brochures, a newsletter, and an application form. Rolling deadlines; however, it's best to apply a minimum of three months prior to your departure date.

Little Children of the World

INSIDER TIPS: *Adaptability, flexibility, and ability to work with people of a different race and culture, as well as a love of children and a willingness to work with poor families, are trademarks of the best candidates.*

Contact Information: Doug Elwood, Program Director • Little Children of the World • 361 County Rd., 475 • Etowah, TN 37331 • Phone: (423) 263-2303 • Fax: (423) 263-2303

Los Niños

REGION/HQ: Mexico/California • **CATEGORY:** Service Learning • **POSITION TYPE:** Unique Experience • **DURATION:** Summer • **IDEAL CANDIDATE:** College Students, Career Changers, Foreigners • **APPLICANT POOL:** Varies • **APPLICANTS ACCEPTED:** Varies

LOS NIÑOS IS A NONPROFIT, community development organization with projects along the Mexico/U.S. border. Los Niños is dedicated to improving the quality of life for Mexican children and their families and, simultaneously, to providing education on the benefits of community self-development through cultural interaction.

Work/Learn Program Specifics: The internship will familiarize students with Tijuana—its geography, people, and culture—and their specific work projects. Interns will also learn about long-term Los Niños projects in Tijuana and Mexicali. The interns' main focus will be teaching summer school in several low-income communities in Tijuana. They will plan and teach classes from 9 A.M. to early afternoon, five days a week, in cooperation with a Mexican teacher and other interns. Interns will also attend classes, seminars, and workshops where they will learn about Mexico and the border region.

Duration: The internship program will run from early July to mid-August, with an intensive orientation during the first week.

Compensation and Perks: Room and board and low-cost medical care are provided. Program cost for the summer is $900 per person. Scholarships are available, but limited.

The Ideal Candidate: Interested students need to enjoy working with children; understand and support the concepts of development and helping others to help themselves; have the ability to work independently and to contribute to a team effort; familiarity with the Spanish language, fluency preferred; cultural sensitivity;

and the ability to plan creative lessons. A valid United State's driver's license is required identification for crossing the border into the United States or Mexico.

Making It Happen: Call for application materials.

Contact Information: David Cox, Program Director • Los Niños • 287 G St. • Chula Vista, CA 91910-3927 • Phone: (619) 426-9110 • Fax: (619) 426-6664 • E-mail: losninos@electriciti.com • Web Site: www. electriciti. om/~losninos

Mobility International USA

REGION/HQ: Worldwide/Oregon • **CATEGORY:** Therapeutic Recreation • **POSITION TYPE:** Internship • **DURATION:** Year-Round • **IDEAL CANDIDATE:** College Students, Career Changers, Foreigners • **APPLICANT POOL:** 40–70/year • **APPLICANTS ACCEPTED:** 2–8/term

MOBILITY INTERNATIONAL USA (MIUSA), founded in 1981, is an innovative, dedicated, and respected organization that fosters and promotes international educational exchange for people with and without disabilities. MIUSA programs, both in the United States and overseas, focus on disability rights, leadership training, cultural awareness, diversity, and language learning. MIUSA has coordinated exchanges with China, Germany, England, Italy, Costa Rica, Russia, Bulgaria, Mexico, East Asia, Japan, and other countries. Programs change every year, so call for current information.

Work/Learn Program Specifics: Interns will work directly with staff volunteers and have the opportunity to develop skills and gain direct work experience in disability rights, international educational exchange, leadership, travel and recreational opportunities, research, article and grant writing, program development, public relations, computer graphics and layout, and the day-to-day operation of a nonprofit organization. Interns are encouraged to work independently on their own projects, as well as assigned and supervised projects.

Duration: Internship programs usually last between three and six months.

Compensation and Perks: For interns committed to six months or longer, a stipend of $125 per month is available to reimburse living expenses.

The Ideal Candidate: Interest in people with disabilities and promoting cross-cultural understanding is

necessary. Good writing skills and the ability to work independently and on a project basis are also important. Preference will be given to applicants with international exchange or travel experience or who have career or master's-project goals in conjunction with the goals of MIUSA. Persons with disabilities are especially encouraged to apply.

Making It Happen: Submit cover letter (with statement of goals and objectives), resume, and completed MIUSA questionnaire. Rolling deadlines.

PROGRAM NOTE: With adequate preparation and precautions, much of the world is accessible to a disabled traveler. If you have a disability and are about to travel, be sure to check out their quarterly newsletter, *Over the Rainbow* ($15), and the book *A World of Options* ($30, plus $5 postage), which provide useful information about both travel and study abroad.

Contact Information: Mary Ann Curulla, Program Director • Mobility International USA • P.O. Box 10767 • Eugene, OR 97440 • Phone: (541) 343-1284 • Fax: (541) 343-6812 • E-mail: miusa@igc.apc.org

New World Teachers

REGION/HQ: Worldwide/California • **CATEGORY:** Teaching • **POSITION TYPE:** Unique Experience • **DURATION:** Year-Round • **IDEAL CANDIDATE:** High School Students, College Students, Career Changers, Retired Folks, Foreigners • **APPLICANT POOL:** 1,000/year • **APPLICANTS ACCEPTED:** 700/year

NEW WORLD TEACHERS is the largest teacher-owned school in the United States. In San Francisco, they are right downtown and have their own guest house just off Union Square. In Boston, they are in the Back Bay, two blocks from Boston Common. In Puerto Vallarta, their school is at the new University of Guadalajara; trainees stay in the old town, less than a five-minute walk from the beach.

Area and Working Environment: English is fast becoming the international language of business and culture. People from all walks of life want to learn English or want their children to learn it. These developments drive the great demand for English instructors in most areas of the world, particularly in Southeast Asia, Latin America, and both Eastern and Western Europe.

Work/Learn Program Specifics: New World Teachers will train you in a one-month intensive TEFL (Teaching English as a Foreign Language) certificate course, so you will have the ability to teach English overseas. Their methodology is based on learning through doing. They'll train you in a fun, participatory way, in small workshop groups. In these groups, they show you how to create a dynamic classroom learning environment. Course components will also include grammar, drama, cross-cultural training, teaching children, video and computers, TOEFL, and business English. They have graduates teaching in fifty different countries around the world. Job-placement assistance is included, and you don't need a second language or previous teaching experience.

Duration: Most contracts are for one year, working twenty-five hours a week. Shorter assignments and flexible schedules are also possible.

Compensation and Perks: The TEFL Certificate course costs $2,200 (in San Francisco or Boston), or $2,750 (in Puerto Vallarta, Mexico). English teachers' pay overseas varies from a few hundred dollars a month to $3,000 a month, plus housing and airfare in some countries. A contract and airfare can often, in some countries, be secured before leaving the U.S. Teachers often further supplement their income by giving private lessons at rates up to $35 an hour, depending again on the country. The real perks and benefits are unlimited self-funded world travel and the opportunity to interact more closely and directly with other cultures than a tourist can ever do.

The Ideal Candidate: High school graduates are acceptable, but most course participants have college degrees. The key is fluency in English (employers overseas often expect native English speakers).

Making It Happen: Applicants are welcome to visit any of the New World schools, at any time, and sit in on classes if they so desire, or call for a free information packet and application forms. Send in the application form and a refundable deposit ($75 for most courses). They will then contact you to arrange an in-person or a telephone interview, which normally takes thirty to forty-five minutes. You may be offered a place on one of their programs immediately following the interview. Courses may sell out one to two months before start dates.

INSIDER TIPS: *We are all about adventurous people who can communicate well. That is what we are like, and those are the people who will benefit the most from our programs. Having said that, we are a trainee-centered organization in that once we accept you into one of our TEFL Certificate courses, we will pull out all the stops to help you be successful. Our pass rate is over 96 percent, and over 98 percent of our graduates who look for work overseas are offered jobs, usually within the first two weeks.*

Contact Information: Neville Fridge, President • Ne World Teachers • 605 Market St., Suite 800 • San Francisco, CA 94105 • Phone: (415) 546-5200 • Fax: (415) 546-4196 • Toll Free: (800) 644-5424 • E-mail: teachersSF@aol.com • Web Site: www.goteach.com

Operation Crossroads Africa

REGION/HQ: Africa/New York • **CATEGORY:** Global Development • **POSITION TYPE:** Unique Experience • **DURATION:** Summer • **IDEAL CANDIDATE:** College Students, Career Changers • **APPLICANT POOL:** Varies • **APPLICANTS ACCEPTED:** 150–200/year

SINCE OPERATION CROSSROADS AFRICA's founding in 1957, over 10,000 volunteers have made contributions to development in Africa, the Caribbean, and South America. President Kennedy paid special tribute to Crossroads for serving as the example and inspiration for the creation of the Peace Corps. Because of its highly successful organizational model, it continues to be a prototypical program for broadening the scope of international understanding and cooperation while making a tangible contribution to the process of development.

Area and Working Environment: Participating countries include, in Africa, Botswana, Gambia, Ghana, Eritrea, Ivory Coast, Kenya, Senegal, South Africa, Tanzania, Uganda, Zimbabwe, Namibia, Guinea Bissau, Ethiopia, Malawi, Mali, and Benin; and, in South America, Brazil.

Work/Learn Program Specifics: As a Crossroads volunteer, you will be a part of an international team of eight to ten women and men of various racial, cultural, and educational backgrounds living and working with your African or Brazilian hosts on a development project which they have initiated. On a Crossroads Africa project, everyone puts in several hours per day of manual labor and takes part in communal maintenance activities. You will be living a simple life with basic amenities, but you will also have the chance to enjoy meaningful exposure to the languages, music, history, and customs of your host country. Typical projects include community construction/community development, agricultural/ farming/reforestation, archaeology/ anthropology/art, primary medicine/public health projects, wildlife/fisheries management, computer literacy program, distance learning/electronic education, African/Brazilian music, and teaching/recreation programs/youth work.

We are here not to get all we can out of life for ourselves, but to try to make the lives of others happier. —WILLIAM OSLER

403

Duration: Volunteers generally work several hours a day for six weeks and will have one week of travel.

Compensation and Perks: There is a participation fee of $3,500, and volunteers must raise this through fund-raising efforts. Crossroads will provide you with sample letters of appeal on which you can model your own, an excellent guide for raising funds, and "donation collection vouchers" that you can distribute, making it easy for individuals and businesses to send in tax-deductible donations on your behalf.

The Ideal Candidate: All are encouraged to apply to their program. Fluency in French or Portuguese is a plus, since these are the main languages of the host countries.

Making It Happen: Call for application materials. Candidates for the program will be reviewed on a rolling basis. As soon as your completed application and references are received, they will inform you of your acceptance.

INSIDER TIPS: *You will experience Africa from the inside out...this is not an African tour.*

Contact Information: LaVerne Brown, Overseas Development Director • Operation Crossroads Africa • 475 Riverside Dr. • New York, NY 10015-0050 • Phone: (212) 870-2106 • Fax: (212) 870-2055 • E-mail: oca@igc.apc.org

Overseas Development Network

REGION/HQ: Pacific Northwest/California
• **CATEGORY:** Global Development • **POSITION TYPE:** Work/Learn Adventure • **DURATION:** Year-Round
• **IDEAL CANDIDATE:** High School Students, College Students, Career Changers, Foreigners • **APPLICANT POOL:** Varies • **APPLICANTS ACCEPTED:** 12/term

THE OVERSEAS DEVELOPMENT NETWORK is a national, student-based, nonprofit organization. Since its creation in 1983, it has been a forum for thousands of young people to address global issues such as hunger, poverty, and social injustice. Its mission is to involve students in addressing global problems through education, activism, and firsthand experience. ODN believes that people can meet their basic needs, strengthen communities, and contribute to global welfare through grassroots action. ODN campus groups directly support community development projects and organizations around the world that are using their own resources and ideas to improve their lives.

Work/Learn Program Specifics: International Opportunities Clearinghouse Intern: Manage and develop the ODN database of international internship opportunities. Assist organizations in filling their human resource needs and individuals in finding opportunities for volunteering abroad. Bike-Aid Environmental Education Coordinator: Set up environmental education outreach events and activities for Bike-Aid riders. Gain a working knowledge of environmental activism across the country. Educational Resource Coordinator: Research, write, edit, create, and design educational material that promotes community development and global education. Global Links Co-Editor: Build your media skills through the production of ODN's national newsletter, distributed to college campuses, students, and individuals across the country. Media Correspondent: Help coordinate Bike-Aid's national outreach program through college and national press. Webweaver: Assist with continued updating of ODN's Web site.

Duration: Time commitments for these positions are somewhat flexible. They range from sixteen to twenty-four hours per week; although, for summer positions, an eight-week commitment is required, from mid-June to mid-August.

Compensation and Perks: None. Their staff provides ongoing training and supervision, as needed, in basic Macintosh skills, nonprofit financing, publicity, event organizing, research, forming partnerships with Asia, Latin America, and Africa, student mobilizing, leadership skills, teamwork, and community education. In addition, ODN's Summer Internship Program offers weekly brown-bag seminars given by grassroots development workers from around the world and free participation in their Leadership Training Conference held in August.

The Ideal Candidate: Young adults interested in working in the international development or nonprofit field and being a part of a small, grassroots-oriented, nonprofit organization.

Making It Happen: Internships are arranged on an individual basis. To begin the process, send a resume and a cover letter indicating the position your interested in and interest in ODN. Rolling deadlines.

Contact Information: Wendy Phillips, Program Coordinator • Overseas Development Network • 333 Valencia St., Suite 330 • San Francisco, CA 94103 • Phone: (415) 431-4204 • Fax: (415) 431-5953 • E-mail: odn@igc.org • Web Site: www.igc.apc.org/odn

Partnership for Service-Learning

REGION/HQ: Worldwide/New York • **CATEGORY:** International Education • **POSITION TYPE:** Internship • **DURATION:** Year-Round • **IDEAL CANDIDATE:** College Students, Foreigners • **APPLICANT POOL:** 800–900/year • **APPLICANTS ACCEPTED:** 100–200/year

PARTNERSHIP FOR SERVICE-LEARNING, a consortium of colleges, universities, and service agencies, develops programs of service-learning which unite college-level academic students with volunteer service in international/intercultural settings.

Area and Working Environment: Czech Republic, Ecuador, England, France, India, Israel, Jamaica, Mexico, Philippines, Scotland, and South Dakota (U.S.).

Work/Learn Program Specifics: Community internship placements include teaching/tutoring at all levels, rehabilitation for mentally and/or physically handicapped, health care, counseling, recreation, community development, and teaching English as a second language. They also introduced a program leading to a British master's degree in international service. The purpose of this program is to prepare degree recipients for professional careers with international non-profit, private, and voluntary organizations, and in governmental and intergovernmental agencies in fields such as development, relief, international education, and social services.

Duration: Programs are offered during January intersession, summer, or the spring/fall semesters. Year-long programs are also available.

Compensation and Perks: Housing is arranged and varies from dorms to flats to boarding with families in their homes. There is a program fee which provides for room, board, orientation, field trips, instruction, placement, and administrative costs.

The Ideal Candidate: Applicants must be college students who show maturity, responsibility, and a willingness to learn from other cultures.

Making It Happen: Write or call for application form and program descriptions. Deadlines: spring—November 1; summer—May 1; and fall—June 15.

Contact Information: Howard Berry, President • Partnership for Service-Learning • 815 Second Ave., Suite 315 • New York, NY 10017-4594 • Phone: (212) 986-0989 • Fax: (212) 986-5039 • E-mail: pslny@aol.com • Web Site: www.studyabroad.com/psl

Peace Corps

REGION/HQ: Worldwide/Washington, D.C. • **CATEGORY:** Global Development • **POSITION TYPE:** Unique Experience • **DURATION:** Two or more years • **IDEAL CANDIDATE:** College Students, Career Changers, Retired Folks • **APPLICANT POOL:** Thousands • **APPLICANTS ACCEPTED:** Thousands

SINCE 1961, PEACE CORPS volunteers have been sharing their skills and energies with people in the developing world. They are helping these people learn new ways to fight hunger, disease, poverty, and lack of opportunity. In return, volunteers are seeing themselves, their country, and the world from a new perspective. The Peace Corps was created to promote world peace and friendship; more specifically, its goals are to help the people of interested countries meet their needs for trained men and women, to help promote a better understanding of the American people on the part of the people served, and to promote a better understanding of other people on the part of the American people.

Area and Working Environment: Positions are located worldwide, and volunteers live in both rural and urban settings in their host countries.

Work/Learn Program Specifics: Peace Corps offers men and women an unparalleled chance to gain impressive credentials, stretch themselves personally, and help solve the world's pressing problems. National and international employers in government and private enterprise regard highly the experience acquired by Peace Corps volunteers. Peace Corps assignments emphasize appropriate technology, cultural sensitivity, and lasting skill transference. Volunteers work in a variety of fields including small business and cooperative development, agriculture, forestry and environment, fish culture, health and nutrition, education, engineering, and industrial arts. Volunteers receive eight to twelve weeks of intensive language, cultural, and technical training. Periodic in-service workshops assist volunteers in project planning, reinforce skills, and teach new ones.

Duration: Most Peace Corps assignments are for two years and begin after the successful completion of training. Vacation time is accrued at two days per month and may be taken when the work situation permits.

Compensation and Perks: During service, volunteers receive a monthly allowance in the local currency to cover housing, food, clothing, and spending money. They

The best of all things is to learn. Money can be lost or stolen, health and strength may fail, but what you have committed to your mind is yours forever. —LOUIS L'AMOUR

405

also receive free medical and dental care, transportation to and from their overseas sites, and twenty-four vacation days a year. Most student loan payments are deferred for the duration of Peace Corps service. When service is completed, volunteers receive a $5,400 readjustment allowance and job-hunting assistance.

The Ideal Candidate: Any healthy U.S. citizen of eighteen years or older is eligible for consideration, with most assignments requiring at least a bachelor's degree or three to five years of substantive work experience. For many assignments, a language other than English is required. Previous knowledge of another language can be very helpful, but is not always required. Perseverance, adaptability, creativity in problem-solving, and sociability are traits important to volunteers.

Making It Happen: For more information call the toll-free number to locate the recruitment office nearest you.

Contact Information: Director • Peace Corps • Volunteer Recruitment and Selection • 1990 K St., NW, Room 8500 • Washington, DC 20526 • Phone: (202) 606-3454 • Toll Free: (800) 424-8580 • E-mail: info@ peacecorps.gov • Web Site: www.peacecorps.gov

Peacework

REGION/HQ: Worldwide/Virginia • **CATEGORY:** Workcamp • **POSITION TYPE:** Unique Experience • **DURATION:** Year-Round • **IDEAL CANDIDATE:** College Students, Career Changers, Retired Folks, Foreigners • **APPLICANT POOL:** Varies • **APPLICANTS ACCEPTED:** Varies

PEACEWORK BRINGS TOGETHER volunteers from different countries with experienced project leaders for short-term work on indigenous development projects. Projects are located in exciting countries: the former Soviet Union, Mexico, Nicaragua, Cuba, Vietnam, Honduras, and Costa Rica. Through volunteer interaction and cooperation, participants learn about the world's cultures, customs, politics, and problems while contributing their skills and interests to a positive process of international development.

Area and Working Environment: Peacework projects are located in some of the most interesting and exciting countries in the world. Sites change every year and have included projects in Mexico, the United States, Cuba, Honduras, Costa Rica, Nicaragua, Ghana, the Dominican Republic, Vietnam, and the former Soviet Union.

Work/Learn Program Specifics: Peacework sponsors short-term international volunteer projects in developing communities around the world. Volunteers from different countries learn about the dynamics of global hunger and poverty by working together on housing, health, and other development initiatives. Projects typically involve the construction or renovation of schools, houses, orphanages, or clinics, planned and implemented by leaders in the host community, along with the opportunity to participate in discussions and cultural programs in the host country. Group leaders are uniquely experienced in the host country, languages, and working with volunteer groups. Volunteers live and work in sometimes difficult and demanding conditions.

Duration: Projects are typically two to four weeks in length. The majority of the programs occur during the summer, spring break, or during other holiday seasons.

Compensation and Perks: Typical costs range from $300 to $800, plus airfare. Limited scholarship assistance is available. Volunteers get the opportunity for overseas travel, service learning, and the chance to live and work with people from different countries as well as indigenous community development groups. In-country arrangements (including housing), visas, supplemental international health insurance, and contributions toward project materials/program administration are included in the program cost.

The Ideal Candidate: Peacework seeks enthusiastic volunteers with a genuine interest in international development and overseas service. They encourage individuals of all ethnic, racial, and economic backgrounds to apply. Selection may be competitive with some projects because of local volunteer needs or limited resources. Foreign language skills are not required, but are very desirable and may be considered in the application process.

Making It Happen: Call for application materials. Rolling deadlines. Peacework also provides a four-page guide to scholarships and other assistance with fundraising for those who need additional support in order to participate in this kind of international experience.

INSIDER TIPS: *Acceptance is generally based on one's enthusiasm for international service, academic preparation, volunteer experience, or travel and references which indicate one's ability to work and live in a multicultural and often demanding environment.*

Contact Information: Stephen Darr, Program Director • Peacework • 305 Washington St., SW • Blacksburg, VA 24060 • Phone: (540) 953-1376 • Fax: (540) 552-0119 • Toll Free: (800) 272-5519 • E-mail: 75352. 261@compuserve.com

PGL Young Adventure Ltd.

REGION/HQ: Europe/England • **CATEGORY:** Outdoor Adventure • **POSITION TYPE:** Seasonal • **DURATION:** Year-Round • **IDEAL CANDIDATE:** College Students, Career Changers, Foreigners • **APPLICANT POOL:** Varies • **APPLICANTS ACCEPTED:** 3,000

PGL ADVENTURE, Europe's largest provider of activity courses for children, has been offering work in the outdoors to young people for nearly forty years.

Area and Working Environment: They have "Centres" located in Britain, France, and Spain.

Work/Learn Program Specifics: Instructor Positions: sailing, canoeing, rafting, surfing, safety boat driving, rowing, swimming and lifesaving, pony trekking, farm studies, environmental studies, archery and rifle shooting, fencing and judo, hill-walking, climbing, rappelling, caving, orienteering, initiative exercises, assault course, and raft building. Group Leaders: You will take responsibility of a group of children throughout their stay at the centre, playing the role of a friend, teacher, or parent. Support Staff: catering, nurses, administration assistants, housekeeping (they call them domestic assistants), store assistant, drivers, night security, and maintenance. Each participant will receive intensive in-house training from a highly qualified and experienced training and development team. Successful applicants will experience the satisfaction of working as part of a highly motivated and professionally trained team in the stimulating environment of a PGL Centre. They also have many other vacancies not listed above, including English/French tutors and ski instructors. Their application materials cover all the details.

Duration: Vacancies exist from February until October. You do not need to be available for this entire period, although priority will be given to applicants who can start in May, which is the beginning of their heaviest staffing period. Limited vacancies exist just for the summer holiday period. Seasonal staff are required to work for a minimum period of eight weeks.

Compensation and Perks: All posts are residential (indoors, tents, caravans, or chalets), with meals and accommodation provided free of charge. Pocket money rates range from £30 to £100 per week, depending on the position and experience. Ask about the "early starter bonus," if employed before mid-June. With many positions, PGL provides a staff T-shirt, sweatshirt, and/or breathable waterproof jacket.

The Ideal Candidate: Applicants need to be at least eighteen years old unless applying specifically to work in France or to work as a group leader, in which case the minimum age is twenty. PGL offers an unequaled experience for anyone wishing to pursue careers in teaching, outdoor pursuits, social/youth work, and catering.

Making It Happen: Write or call for a PGL application.

Contact Information: Steve Reynolds, Recruitment Officer • PGL Young Adventure Ltd. • Alton Court, Penyard Lane, Ross-on-Wye • Herefordshire, HR9 5NR • England • Phone: 989 767833 • Fax: (011) 989 765451

The School for Field Studies

REGION/HQ: Worldwide/Massachusetts • **CATEGORY:** Environmental Education • **POSITION TYPE:** Work/Learn Adventure • **DURATION:** Year-Round • **IDEAL CANDIDATE:** High School Students, College Students • **APPLICANT POOL:** 960/year • **APPLICANTS ACCEPTED:** 768/year

THE SCHOOL FOR FIELD STUDIES is the country's oldest and largest educational institution exclusively dedicated to teaching and engaging undergraduates in environmental problem solving. Since the school's founding in 1980, over 7,500 college and high school students, with a variety of academic interests, have conducted hands-on fieldwork in SFS programs around the world.

Work/Learn Program Specifics: SFS uses a case-study approach so that students may gain an interdisciplinary perspective of environmental issues. Lessons that are taught in classroom lectures are often complemented by work in the field. Students learn about environmental problems and work to solve them by actually living within the ecosystems and communities where they take place. For example, students at their Center for Rainforest Studies, in Australia, are engaged in rainforest restoration and have assisted the communities there in replanting over 20,000 trees. Other centers around the world include the Center for Wildlife Management in Kenya; the Center for Marine Resource Studies in the British West Indies; the Center for Wetland Studies, in Baja, Mexico; the Center for Coastal Studies in the Pacific Northwest Canada; and the Center of Sustainable Development Studies in Costa Rica.

Duration: SFS offers both a spring and fall semester program, as well as a thirty-day summer program at each center. Programs typically begin with a ten-day introductory module. Afternoons are filled with field trips and laboratory work, and on average, three to four weeks are spent off-campus with field trips.

Compensation and Perks: Fees for the summer range from $2,960 to $3,450, and the semester program ranges from $11,200 to $11,600. SFS also offers over $500,000 in financial aid to help students participate. Historically, one-third of their participants have been awarded aid.

The Ideal Candidate: Semester program participants must be eighteen years of age or older, have completed at least one college-level ecology or biology course and, preferably, one semester of college. Summer program participants must be at least sixteen years of age and have completed at least their junior year of high school.

Making It Happen: Call for application materials. Rolling admissions for all programs.

Contact Information: Andrea Walgren, Vice President • The School for Field Studies • 16 Broadway, Box B • Beverly, MA 01915 • Phone: (508) 927-7777 • Fax: (508) 927-5127 • E-mail: sfshome@igc.apc.org

SCI-International Voluntary Service USA

REGION/HQ: Worldwide/Virginia • **CATEGORY:** Workcamp • **POSITION TYPE:** Work/Learn Adventure • **DURATION:** Summer • **IDEAL CANDIDATE:** College Students, Career Changers, Retired Folks, Foreigners • **APPLICANT POOL:** Varies • **APPLICANTS ACCEPTED:** 50–100/year

SCI-International Voluntary Service is the U.S. branch of Service Civil International, celebrating over seventy-five years of promoting peace and international understanding through community service projects. The hallmark of SCI is the exchange of thousands of volunteers each year, who work at short-term community service projects around the world.

Area and Working Environment: Workcamps are offered in over fifty countries, including the United States and Canada, as well as Asia, Africa, Latin America, and Eastern Europe.

Work/Learn Program Specifics: Each workcamp has a local sponsor, such as an environmental group, children's playscheme, artists' cooperative, or biodynamic farm. People of all races, ideologies, and nationalities live together for two to four weeks on a project bene-

ficial to the local area. Each workcamp is made up of eight to fifteen volunteers who come together to share cooking and cleaning, to solve problems, to work together, and to have fun. The more diverse the group, the more opportunity there is for learning and sharing. They also have the need for part-time office workers (who will receive a stipend) in their Virginia office.

Duration: Most workcamps occur during the summer months.

Compensation and Perks: The application fee for residents of the United States and Canada is $50 for domestic workcamps and $100 for most overseas workcamps. For camps in Asia, Africa, Latin America, and Eastern Europe, the fees are higher and vary by location. For overseas camps, there is a nonrefundable fee of $10. For additional camps in the United States, the fee is $30; for additional overseas camps, $60. There is a limit of three camps per year. Your fee also pays for a year's membership in SCI-IVS. SCI covers room and board and a supplemental health and accident insurance. You must pay your own way to the workcamp site and cover pocket expenses.

The Ideal Candidate: U.S./Canadian volunteers must be sixteen and older for U.S. camps and eighteen and older for overseas camps. There are a few places each year for the Africa or Asia exchange for volunteers who are at least twenty-one and have workcamp experience. There is no upper age limit, and retirees are welcome. In general, there is no special experience required, except the ability to work in a team environment.

Making It Happen: Their *Directory of International Workcamps* (which is available in early April each year) costs $5 and includes registration/application information. Volunteers are placed in workcamps of their choice, beginning on May 1 on a first-come, first-served basis (after June 15, it becomes more difficult to get your first choice). Have patience, as applications are run by a small group of volunteer staff across the country.

Contact Information: Volunteer Exchange Coordinator • SCI-International Voluntary Service USA • 5474 Walnut Level Rd. • Crozet, VA 22932 • Phone: (804) 823-1826 • Fax: (804) 823-5027 • E-mail: sciivsusa@ igc.apc.org • Web Site: wworks.com/~sciivs

---

If you reject the food, ignore the customs, fear the religion, and avoid the people, you might better stay home. You are like a pebble thrown into water; you become wet on the surface but you are never part of the water.

—James Mitchener

What is "Service Learning" Travel? . . . . . .

Traveling as a volunteer departs from conventional adventure travel and cultural immersion experiences in one very important way. The purpose of "service learning" travel is foremost to serve, and thereby, to learn firsthand about the host community and its people. It is not simply an alternative to a standard vacation, but an opportunity to use your skills and interests in an unconventional setting. Increasingly, people are offering their services on work projects in places they would not ordinarily have the occasion to visit. It is a true exchange of ideas, cultures, and dreams to which most any open-minded individual can contribute.

—GLOBAL VOLUNTEERS

Sea Education Association

REGION/HQ: Worldwide/Massachusetts • **CATEGORY:** Educational Travel • **POSITION TYPE:** Unique Experience • **DURATION:** Year-Round • **IDEAL CANDIDATE:** College Students, Career Changers, Foreigners • **APPLICANT POOL:** Varies • **APPLICANTS ACCEPTED:** 49/term

FOR OVER 25 YEARS, Sea Education Association (SEA) has provided a challenging multidisciplinary academic program that educates individuals about the ocean's vital role in the earth's global system. SEA uses theoretical and practical studies, ashore and at sea, using sailing ships and marine research, to promote knowledge of the oceanic environment.

Area and Working Environment: The shore component begins on their campus in Woods Hole, and the sea component starts in Newfoundland then sails the Gulf Stream, to waters of Venezuela and the Lesser Antilles in the Caribbean on a sailing research vessel.

Work/Learn Program Specifics: On shore, students take classes in oceanography (chemical, physical, bio-

logical and geological), nautical science (navigation, meteorology and ship's operations), and maritime studies (art, history, literature, and international policy), and will design an individual project. At sea, students become active members of the ship's crew and conduct oceanographic research and gather data for research projects.

Duration: The semester program is a twelve-week program offered five times per year; the summer session is eight weeks, from early June to late July.

Compensation and Perks: The cost for a SEA semester is about the same as a semester at a private university, and financial aid is available. The program cost is $13,465 ($9,535 for the summer session) and includes tuition, lab, fees, housing on shore, and room and board at sea. Students will earn seventeen semester units for the SEA semester and twelve semester units for the SEA summer session; credits are awarded by Boston University.

The Ideal Candidate: Both programs are undergraduate programs for students majoring in all disciplines. To be eligible, students must have completed one college-level lab science course.

Making It Happen: Call for details. Send the completed application, a copy of both high school and college transcripts, and two references.

INSIDER TIPS: *Because there are only forty-nine spaces in each class, it's in the students' best interest to apply early.*

Contact Information: William McMurray, Jr., Dean of Admission • Sea Education Association • P.O. Box 6 • Woods Hole, MA 02543 • Phone: (508) 540-3954 • Fax: (508) 457-4673 • Toll Free: (800) 552-3633 • E-mail: admission@sea.edu • Web Site: www.sea.edu

Semester at Sea

REGION/HQ: Worldwide/Pennsylvania • **CATEGORY:** Adventure Travel • **POSITION TYPE:** Work/Learn Adventure • **DURATION:** Spring/Fall • **IDEAL CANDIDATE:** College Students, Career Changers, Retired Folks • **APPLICANT POOL:** Varies • **APPLICANTS ACCEPTED:** 25–30/voyage

WITH SEMESTER AT SEA, you'll live with Chinese students in a dorm at the University of Beijing, stay at an Untouchable village in India, watch 20-foot waves hit the bow of your "campus"—the S.S. Universe Explorer,—walk the crowded byways of Istanbul's 400-year-old covered markets, learn about the life of the

Masai while on safari in Kenya, or study tropical rain forests while canoeing down the Amazon River; all of which provides for a life-altering learning adventure.

Area and Working Environment: The spring voyage travels to the Bahamas, Venezuela, Brazil, South Africa, Kenya, India, Vietnam, Philippines, Hong Kong, Japan, and finishes in Seattle, Washington. The fall voyage travels to British Columbia, Japan, China, Hong Kong, Vietnam, India, Egypt, Turkey, Greece, Morocco, and finishes in Ft. Lauderdale, Florida.

Work/Learn Program Specifics: Staff positions are available as adult coordinator, assistant to the academic dean, assistant to the administrative dean, assistant field office coordinator, assistant librarian, assistant AV/media coordinator, AV/media coordinator, bursar, computer support specialist, director of student life, executive secretary, field activities advisor, field office coordinator, librarian, mental health professional, nurse, physician, resident director, and security officer. In addition to regularly assigned duties, you will be expected to be an integral part of the shipboard community. You will participate in all aspects of the Semester at Sea program as your shipboard work schedule permits. In addition, you will serve on a limited number of in-port duty assignments which may include serving as a trip leader for some of the field practicums.

Duration: Spring voyages depart in late January and return mid-May. Fall voyages depart in mid-September and return just before Christmas. Staff is hired on a nonpermanent basis for one term only.

Compensation and Perks: Staff will be paid a small stipend (usually $1,500 to $4,000), depending on the position. In addition, a $700 travel allowance is provided to help defray the cost of travel to/from the ports of embarkation/debarkation. Room and board on ship are provided.

The Ideal Candidate: Ideal applicants are those who support the concept of academic and personal enrichment through travel and education. Maximum flexibility, cooperation, and adaptability are essential traits of all applicants.

Making It Happen: Call for application packet. Send completed application, resume, two letters of reference, transcripts, photocopy of passport, and other specific materials related to each position. Due to the volume of applicants, telephone interviews are conducted to finalists. Deadlines: spring voyages—June 15 (April 1 for resident directors); fall voyages—April 1.

Contact Information: Staff Selection • Semester at Sea • University of Pittsburgh • 811 William Pitt Union • Pittsburgh, PA 15260 • Phone: (800) 854-0195 • Fax: (412) 648-2298 • E-mail: shipboard@sas.ise.pitt.edu

St. Vincent Pallotti Center

REGION/HQ: Worldwide/California • **CATEGORY:** Ministry • **POSITION TYPE:** Work/Learn Adventure • **DURATION:** Year-Round • **IDEAL CANDIDATE:** College Students, Career Changers, Retired Folks, Foreigners • **APPLICANT POOL:** Varies • **APPLICANTS ACCEPTED:** Varies

THE ST. VINCENT PALLOTTI CENTER promotes Catholic/Christian international and domestic volunteer programs. Their annual publication, *Connections*, lists over 100 social service volunteer programs. The St. Vincent Pallotti Center provides support for volunteers before, during, and after their term of service.

Area and Working Environment: Positions are available in the United States and throughout the world.

Work/Learn Program Specifics: The majority of their volunteer programs are Catholic-sponsored and offered to all Christians, as there is a spiritual dynamic to the service you do. The types of services available are extensive and include: tutoring, business, law, immigration, teaching, clerical work, youth/campus ministry, social services, agriculture, counseling, medical/dental, recreation/summer camps, social justice ministry, Native American/Hispanic ministry, and volunteer coordination.

Duration: Positions are available from one week up to three months to a year in the United States. Internationally, you must commit for one to three years.

Compensation and Perks: Volunteers receive an education stipend and will live within a community setting. Benefits include health insurance, transportation costs, severance pay, retreats, and spiritual direction and orientation.

The Ideal Candidate: The majority of programs require twenty-one years and older; some programs require at least eighteen years of age. You must have a desire and will to serve.

Making It Happen: Write or call for the *Connections* directory, which will provide you with all the details of each program and application. For those programs you are interested in, you will apply directly to the organization (each has its own application). There are no formal deadlines. After completing and sending back the application, you will be interviewed over the phone. If you're on the East Coast, call their Washington, D.C. office at (202) 529-3330.

INSIDER TIPS: *Always speak to a former volunteer, the work-site director, and a paid staff member to learn more about the program.*

Contact Information: Wendy Borchers, Program Director • St. Vincent Pallotti Center • 5890 Newman Ct. • Sacramento, CA 95819 • Phone: (916) 454-4320 • Fax: (916) 454-4320 • E-mail: Pallotti02@aol.com • Web Site: www.cua.edu/www/rel/pallotti

Third World Opportunities

REGION/HQ: Mexico/California • **CATEGORY:** Human Service • **POSITION TYPE:** Unique Experience • **DURATION:** Year-Round • **IDEAL CANDIDATE:** High School Students, College Students, Career Changers, Retired Folks, Foreigners • **APPLICANT POOL:** 25/program • **APPLICANTS ACCEPTED:** 250/year

THIRD WORLD OPPORTUNITIES is a hunger- and poverty-awareness program designed to provide opportunities for appropriate responses to human need. It seeks to encourage increased sensitivity to life in the Third World, intentional reflection on our relationships with Third World people, effective work projects that offer practical services to the hungry, the homeless, and the poor, and organized efforts to change existing conditions.

Area and Working Environment: Tecate, Mexico, is a small border community (population 40,000) that was formed by border bandits and Indian raiders in the early 1800s. It is bordered by a mountain considered sacred by the local Indians (*cuchuma*), and was made famous by its local, large brewery (Tecate beer) and nearby spa (Rancho La Puerta), once the largest health spa in North America.

Work/Learn Program Specifics: Become involved with a program that is both innovative and sensitive to the environment, utilizing straw bales, that would otherwise be burned for building material, for low-income housing. Straw-bale house building involves the construction of new homes under the direction of Mexican "maestros" who are skilled in various aspects of construction. Your group may be divided up into smaller work groups, each doing a different task. These tasks may include digging foundation, laying of the concrete slab, putting up the straw-bale walls, building roof tresses, or

stucco work on the walls. Tools and building materials are supplied. One of the highlights of this experience is the integration of work and worship, study, and play, growth and fellowship with one another and with new friends from another culture.

Duration: Volunteers work on six-day work projects.

Compensation and Perks: Participants are fed and housed at the house-building site. You will have the opportunity of interacting with a Third-World community, the chance to practice your Spanish language, and to be involved in an exciting sustainability project.

The Ideal Candidate: Minimum age requirement is fifteen, and knowledge of Spanish and building experience are helpful, but not necessary. Prospective participants are those who are interested in the Third World and who want to learn about the root causes of hunger and poverty. This program is also for those who want to become involved in a developmental response to need (not charity), enabling the poor to help themselves with dignity.

Making It Happen: Call for application materials. There is a $30 nonrefundable fee to reserve a work slot; a deductible $20-per-person preregistration fee, due six weeks prior to event; and a $200-per-person fee for the actual program.

Contact Information: M. Laurel Gray, Coordinator • Third World Opportunities • 1363 Somermont Dr. • El Cajon, CA 92021 • Phone: (619) 449-9381

Up With People

REGION/HQ: Worldwide/Colorado • **CATEGORY:** Educational Travel • **POSITION TYPE:** Unique Experience • **DURATION:** Year-Round • **IDEAL CANDIDATE:** High School Students, College Students, Career Changers • **APPLICANT POOL:** 6,000/year • **APPLICANTS ACCEPTED:** 2,400/year

UP WITH PEOPLE is an international educational program that provides personal and professional growth through the unique combination of international travel, performing arts, and community service. Since 1965, they have visited over 3,500 communities, lived with more than 750,000 host families, visited 58 countries, and alumni have represented almost 100 countries. The UWP show is an original production, and a new show is developed every two to three years. Major performances include (and have included) four Super Bowls, the Munich Olympics, World Youth Day, the Olympic Arena in Moscow, the Radio City Music Hall, Carnegie Hall, the Conservatory of Music in Beijing, the Royal Albert Hall in London, the Hollywood Bowl, several World Expos, Atlanta Olympics, Kennedy Center in Washington, D.C., Olympia Theater in Paris, several performances for the Pope in the Vatican City, a 771-city U.S. Bicentennial Tour, the Rugby League Grand Finals in Sydney, Australia, and many more.

Area and Working Environment: All students start their year at Up With People's world headquarters just outside of Denver, at the base of the Rocky Mountains. From there, 30,000 miles of foreign countries await.

Work/Learn Program Specifics: Though many experienced and talented performers and musicians refine their skills in the Up With People program, there's more to it than singing and dancing. In addition to onstage musical performance, the program also offers intercultural education, community service, and extensive world travel. You develop career skills, self-awareness, a sense of the world around you, and a commitment to others. You'll be living and working with students as you perform and stage the show, The Festival. There's music performance, singing, dancing, and stagecraft to be done. Through community service, you'll help people in places such as schools, nursing homes, and shelters. Service teaches you a lot about the world and your role in it. More importantly, you'll be helping people who really need it.

Duration: The UWP student program is a one-year commitment. There are two starting points every year—July and January. The year is broken into semesters, with a semester break in between.

Compensation and Perks: There is a tuition for the student program which covers most expenses while on tour, including the student program, meals, transportation, staff and administrative costs. Host families in the different countries will put you up for a few nights. This is your chance for an inside look at how others live, from their family structure to their furniture and the conversations you'll have.

The Ideal Candidate: Applicants must be seventeen to twenty-five years old, high school graduates (or equivalent), single, in good health, and willing to participate in all aspects of the program. The average participant is twenty years of age, with some college background.

Making It Happen: Call their toll-free number to get the information you need. Interviews are generally conducted during an Up With People cast's stay in the applicant's community. If a cast is not coming to the

region for a while, an interview may be set up with an Up With People alumnus. Rolling deadlines.

INSIDER TIPS: *Ideal applicants are school- or career-bound. They are adventuresome and have a desire to learn and an interest in other cultures. They want a unique travel experience.*

Contact Information: Inge De Mulder, Admissions Counselor • Up With People • One International Ct. • Broomfield, CO 80021 • Phone: (303) 438-7373 • Fax: (303) 438-7301 • Toll Free: (800) 596-7353 • E-mail: uwp-admissions@upwithpeople.org • Web Site: www.upwithpeople.org

Visions in Action

REGION/HQ: Worldwide/Washington, D.C. • **CATEGORY:** Service Learning • **POSITION TYPE:** Unique Experience • **DURATION:** Year Long • **IDEAL CANDIDATE:** College Students, Career Changers, Retired Folks, Foreigners • **APPLICANT POOL:** 100/year • **APPLICANTS ACCEPTED:** 60/year

VISIONS IN ACTION is an international nonprofit organization founded in 1988 out of the conviction that there is much that we can learn from and contribute to the developing world by working as part of a community of volunteers committed to social justice in the urban setting.

Area and Working Environment: Volunteer opportunities are available in primarily urban areas of Africa and Latin America, including Uganda, Zimbabwe, South Africa, Burkina Faso, and Mexico.

Work/Learn Program Specifics: Volunteers select positions according to their experience, skills, and interests. Positions may include project manager, program assistant, community development, health professional, public health educator, researcher, journalist, youth group coordinator, and positions in many other areas, including theatre, dance, art, fashion design, music, and folklore.

Duration: You must be able to commit to the entire length of the program, which is generally one year.

Compensation and Perks: The total estimated cost for the one-year program is $5,000 to $6,000. Total fees include airfare, housing, orientation and language training, medical insurance, overseas support, and all local expenses (food, transport, and entertainment). All volunteers receive a monthly stipend of $50 to $100 while overseas. All funds donated towards your program are tax-deductible, and Visions in Action will help you with fund-raising ideas once you have been accepted as a volunteer. Most interns do community fund-raising to cover the cost of the program, and student loans may be deferred.

The Ideal Candidate: Almost any background is welcome. The more specialized your skills, the more specialized your volunteer position will be. Applicants must have a college degree or equivalent work experience and must be responsible and adaptable individuals who recognize the challenges and opportunities of living and working in a developing country. Undergraduates without significant work experience are not eligible. You do not have to speak another language, except in Burkina Faso, where French is required, and in Mexico, where Spanish is required. The minimum age is twenty, the average, twenty-seven.

Making It Happen: Call for an application. Rolling deadlines, although you must submit your application ninety days prior to departure.

INSIDER TIPS: *Be serious about social justice and international development. Apply early so you have time to fund-raise before you go.*

Contact Information: Program Coordinator • Visions in Action • 2710 Ontario Rd., NW • Washington, DC 20009-2154 • Phone: (202) 625-7403 • Fax: (202) 625-2353 • E-mail: visions@igc.apc.org

Visions International

REGION/HQ: Nationwide/Pennsylvania • **CATEGORY:** Outdoor Adventure • **POSITION TYPE:** Unique Experience • **DURATION:** Spring-Summer • **IDEAL CANDIDATE:** College Students, Career Changers, Foreigners • **APPLICANT POOL:** 200/year • **APPLICANTS ACCEPTED:** 60/year
....

VISIONS INTERNATIONAL is a nonprofit which offers teens one-month summer experiences based in Alaska, Plains Indian reservations in Montana, South Carolina, the Dominican Republic, the British Virgin Islands, Dominica, and Guadeloupe. A Visions summer integrates community-service work, outdoor adventure, cross-cultural living, and learning in coed residential programs of up to twenty-four students and six staff. This group of students and staff lives in a school or other local buildings in the heart of each host community. Projects include ground-up construction of schools, medical clinics, playground structures, hurricane shelters, and many more.

Work/Learn Program Specifics: Staff positions include summer trip leaders and specialists, instructing climbing, backpacking, carpentry, and mentoring teenagers. Duties include supervision of teenagers in a residential living setting and during the community service program. You'll teach participants how to use tools and building techniques; outdoor activities like backpacking, rock climbing, and rafting; as well as cross-cultural activities and experiences.

Duration: Most programs run during the months of June through August.

Compensation and Perks: Stipends start at $200 per week (dependent on position/experience), including room and board. For those who wish to participate in the program, the fee is $2,300 to $3,300, not including airfare.

The Ideal Candidate: All applicants must be at least twenty-one years old, have strong interpersonal skills, a safe driving record, current wilderness first aid and CPR certification, experience leading or teaching teenagers, and flexibility and a sense of humor. It's also preferred that you have carpentry and masonry skills and/or advanced first aid certification. Spanish is required for the Dominican Republic and French for Guadeloupe.

Making It Happen: Send cover letter and resume. They start accepting applications in October for the following season.

Contact Information: Joanne Pinaire, Program Director • Visions International • P.O. Box 220 • Newport, PA 17074-0220 • Phone: (717) 567-7313 • Fax: (717) 567-7853 • Toll Free: (800) 813-9283 • E-mail: visions@pa.net • Web Site: www.visions-adventure.org

Volunteers for Peace, Inc.

REGION/HQ: Worldwide/Vermont • **CATEGORY:** Workcamp • **POSITION TYPE:** Unique Experience • **DURATION:** Year-Round • **IDEAL CANDIDATE:** High School Students, College Students, Career Changers, Retired Folks, Foreigners • **APPLICANT POOL:** Thousands • **APPLICANTS ACCEPTED:** Thousands
....

VOLUNTEERS FOR PEACE (VFP) is a nonprofit membership corporation that has, since 1981, been coordinating international workcamps in the USA and abroad. VFP is a part of a sizable international network of workcamp organizations operating under the aegis of UNESCO. The office staff and hundreds of field volunteers facilitate this program. Services include providing a consultation and placement service for workcamp hosts and volunteers, linking people with programs, thereby fostering the spirit of volunteerism, community service, and international education.

Area and Working Environment: Over 800 programs in over 60 countries are offered, including Africa, Asia, the Americas, Western/Eastern Europe, and Russia.

Work/Learn Program Specifics: Workcamps are an inexpensive and personal way to travel, live, and work in an international setting. As a fully internationalized short-term "Peace Corps," workcamps are a way you can respond positively to the challenges we face in our world. Focusing on cooperation, caring, and sharing, you'll have a fun-filled adventure, building bonds with people from diverse cultural backgrounds. Through the challenges of experiential work projects and group living, you can create a more positive vision for the future and help change the course of our planet in a personal way. Workcamps are sponsored by an organization in a host country but are coordinated by people in a local community. Generally ten to twelve people from four or more countries arrive on a given day in a host community, and the work involved is casual. Construction, restoration, environmental, social, agricultural, archaeological, and maintenance workcamps are common.

Duration: Workcamp programs vary as to their start dates and length, but generally run two to three weeks. About 95 percent of the programs are from mid-June to mid-October, although many are offered throughout the year. About 20 percent of the people they place abroad every year register for multiple workcamps in the same or different countries and spend several months abroad.

Compensation and Perks: Most programs cost $175, and room and meals are provided at all workcamps. Programs in Russia and Latin American range from $200 to $600. You may be housed in a school, church, private home, or community center. Living arrangements are generally cooperative, like a family, with workcampers coordinating and sharing the day-to-day activities, food preparation, work projects, and recreation. Travel expenses will be left up to the volunteer.

The Ideal Candidate: You must be at least eighteen years old (although there are some workcamps for sixteen- and seventeen-year-olds in France and Germany), and there is no upper age limit (they've placed several folks in their seventies). Volunteers need to bring a backpack, sleeping bag, pictures of home, musical instruments, and a cooperative spirit.

Making It Happen: Call for the *International Workcamp Directory* for complete listings (over 120 pages worth), registration information, and their free newsletter. The directory, which comes out April 1, is $12 postpaid, but the price is deductible from your program fees. Volunteers are placed on a first-come, first-served basis and are advised to register as soon as possible after receipt of the directory. Of their workcamp volunteers, 90 percent register between mid-April and mid-May.

Contact Information: Peter Coldwell, Director • Volunteers for Peace, Inc. • 43 Tiffany Rd. • Belmont, VT 05730-0202 • Phone: (802) 259-2759 • Fax: (802) 259-2922 • E-mail: vfp@vfp.org • Web Site: www.vfp.org/

Volunteers in Asia

REGION/HQ: Asia/California • **CATEGORY:** Teaching • **POSITION TYPE:** Work/Learn Adventure • **DURATION:** Year-Round • **IDEAL CANDIDATE:** College Students, Career Changers, Foreigners • **APPLICANT POOL:** 80/term • **APPLICANTS ACCEPTED:** 40/term

VOLUNTEERS IN ASIA (VIA) traces its origins to a 1963 group of Stanford students who saw volunteer work as an appropriate way to enter and better understand the non-Western world. Since its beginnings in the refugee settlements of Hong Kong, VIA has sent over a thousand volunteers to a wide range of assignments in Asia. Current programs in China, Indonesia, Laos, and Vietnam continue to reflect the organization's original goals: to immerse Americans directly into the workplaces and neighborhoods of contemporary Asia and to provide Asian organizations with volunteer assistance. The goal is to provide a service opportunity that develops volunteers' skills, stimulates a long-term interest in Asia, and commitment to improving our world; and to further the communication and understanding between the people of the United States and those of Asia.

Area and Working Environment: Volunteers work in China, Indonesia, Laos, and Vietnam.

Work/Learn Program Specifics: "Offering Americans cross-cultural learning and work experience in Asia." As a small organization with limited resources, VIA focuses its efforts on one skill Americans can offer Asian organizations without displacing Asian workers—native English-language assistance. Thus, most volunteers teach English at the college level or in community organizations such as the YMCA. Others act as

English resource volunteers, assisting community development, women's, and environmental groups with their translation and editing needs. All volunteers must attend the VIA cross-cultural training sessions offered at Stanford in March, April, and May.

Duration: Durations range from seven weeks in the summer to two years. Most participants depart in late June.

Compensation and Perks: While overseas, one to two year volunteers receive a monthly housing and living stipend. Summer and six-month volunteers contribute some of their living expenses. The program covers the cost of round-trip transportation, VIA's cross-cultural training, basic health insurance, and for most volunteers, an orientation program in Asia en route to their post. Living arrangements may be in guest houses, faculty apartment buildings, or dormitories. Participant fees: summer, six month, and one year—$1,350; two year—$950. This represents approximately 10 percent of the cost of sending a volunteer to the field. Scholarships are available.

The Ideal Candidate: Applicants must be mature, responsible, native English speakers, and college age or older. Students at semester schools and non-student applicants must be enrolled in TESL and language classes before interviews.

Making It Happen: Applications are available in November and are due at the end of January. They hold information meetings in this time frame and encourage prospective applicants to come to the office to talk with staff and returned volunteers, so you'll get a clearer picture of what VIA has to offer and whether this it your needs and interests. Acceptance to the VIA program will be announced in early March.

Contact Information: Volunteer Coordinator • Volunteers in Asia • P.O. Box 4543 • Stanford, CA 94309 • Phone: (415) 723-3228 • Fax: (415) 725-1805 • E-mail: via@igc.apc.org • Web Site: www.volasia.org

Washington Center

REGION/HQ: Washington, D.C./Washington, D.C. • **CATEGORY:** Clearinghouse • **POSITION TYPE:** Internship • **DURATION:** Year-Round • **IDEAL CANDIDATE:** College Students, Foreigners • **APPLICANT POOL:** Varies • **APPLICANTS ACCEPTED:** 200/term

THE WASHINGTON CENTER is the largest independent, nonprofit organization that enables students to earn college credit for internships and academic seminars in our nation's capital. Since it was founded in 1975, the center has provided more than 23,000 college students with real-world experiences that have helped them gain the critical knowledge and preparation they need to begin fulfilling careers.

Work/Learn Program Specifics: The Washington Center offers internships for every field of study, from nonprofit associations and government agencies to museums and advocacy organizations. You pick an area of interest, and a Washington Center staff member will find an internship that matches your request. You will work as an entry-level professional, with duties varying according to placement, participate in a weekly academic course, and attend a speaker series and at least two breakfasts with members of Congress.

Duration: The center offers ten- to fifteen-week programs, full-time, with openings year-round.

Compensation and Perks: There is a program fee of $2,330 or $2,670, depending on your length of stay. Some internships offer a stipend, and housing is provided by the center for an additional fee. Scholarship awards up to $2,000 are offered to help offset the program fees. More than 68 percent of the students receive some form of financial assistance.

The Ideal Candidate: You must be at least a second-semester sophomore from an accredited institution.

Making It Happen: Call for application form. Send completed application, transcripts, essays, and letters of recommendation. A nonrefundable application fee is required. Apply at least three months prior to your desired start date.

Contact Information: Student Services Coordinator • Washington Center • 1101 14th St., NW, Suite 500 • Washington, DC 20005-5622 • Phone: (202) 336-7600 • Fax: (202) 336-7609 • Toll Free: (800) 486-8921 • E-mail: info@twc.edu • Web Site: www.twc.edu

World Zionist Organization

REGION/HQ: Israel/New York • **CATEGORY:** Service Learning • **POSITION TYPE:** Unique Experience • **DURATION:** Varies • **IDEAL CANDIDATE:** College Students, Career Changers • **APPLICANT POOL:** Varies • **APPLICANTS ACCEPTED:** Varies

SHERUT LA'AM EXPERIENCE: This program, sponsored by the World Zionist Organization, enriches both the participants and the people of Israel. Since 1965 thousands of Sherut La'am participants from all over the world have contributed to the development of the Jewish state. Sherut La'am participants discover that Israel is a country of contrasts: 3,000 years of history intertwined with a modern nation close to 50 years old; tremendous industrial and agricultural progress during a time of difficult political circumstances; modern, bustling cities in contrast to rural development towns; the multicolored patchwork of immigrant groups, many newly arrived, from all over the world. The Sherut La'am participant is immersed in all of these contrasts while living, working, and socializing with Israelis from all walks of life.

Work/Learn Program Specifics: The Sherut La'am program offers a unique opportunity to experience Israel by combining Hebrew study, living on a kibbutz, and participating in a volunteer internship.

Duration: The participant has two options: The twelve-month program includes four months of Hebrew study and a minimum of six months professional placement, with the option to stay for eight months; the six-month program is appropriate for those who already know Hebrew and are able to begin a professional placement soon after their arrival in Israel.

Compensation and Perks: The cost of the program is $1,900 for one year and $1,650 for six months, excluding airfare. Upon the start of the program, participants will receive a monthly stipend of between $140 and $180, which covers basic food expenses.

The Ideal Candidate: The one-year program is open to those between the ages of twenty-two and twenty-five who hold a bachelor's degree. The six-month version is open to those between the ages of twenty and thirty who have conversational knowledge of Hebrew.

Making It Happen: Call for an application. There is a $50 nonrefundable registration fee.

Contact Information: Israel Program Center • World Zionist Organization • 110 E. 59th St. • New York, NY 10022 • Phone: (212) 339-6916 • Fax: (212) 755-4781 • Toll Free: (800) 274-7723 • E-mail: usd@netcom.com • Web Site: www.wzo.org.il

WorldTeach

REGION/HQ: Worldwide/Massachusetts • **CATEGORY:** Teaching • **POSITION TYPE:** Unique Experience • **DURATION:** 6 months to 1 year

• **IDEAL CANDIDATE:** College Students, Career Changers, Retired Folks, Foreigners • **APPLICANT POOL:** 850/year • **APPLICANTS ACCEPTED:** 300/year

WORLDTEACH IS A nonprofit project of Harvard University's social-service organization, with the goal of promoting cultural exchange and creating opportunities for Americans to work in the developing world while providing needed service overseas.

Area and Working Environment: Positions are available in Africa (Namibia/South Africa), Asia (China/Thailand/Vietnam), Europe (Lithuania/Poland), and Latin America (Costa Rica/Ecuador/Mexico/Paraguay).

Work/Learn Program Specifics: WorldTeach finds volunteers positions as teachers in developing countries. For the Mexico Nature Guide Training Program, you will develop and implement a curriculum combining English-as-a-foreign-language instruction and natural history to train local people for work in nature tourism and environmental education. Here you will volunteer either in Baja California Sur or the Yucatan Peninsula.

Duration: All WorldTeach volunteers commit to teach for a school year (ten to twelve months) except those volunteers participating in the six-month Mexico Nature Guide Training Program and the eight-week-long Shanghai Summer Teaching Program.

Compensation and Perks: To cover the cost, there's a fee of $3,600 to $4,700. In return, the volunteer receives round-trip airfare, health insurance, training, a teaching position, and field support. Housing and a small salary are also included. They publish a useful pamphlet, *Fundraising Suggestions for WorldTeach Volunteers.*

The Ideal Candidate: Candidates must have a bachelor's degree and have a sincere interest in education, international development, and/or cultural exchange. Candidates do not have to speak a foreign language or have any teaching experience.

Making It Happen: Call for application and current deadlines.

Contact Information: Internship Director • WorldTeach • Harvard Institute for International Development • One Eliot St. • Cambridge, MA 02138-5705 • Phone: (617) 495-5527 • Fax: (617) 495-1599 • Toll Free: (800) 483-2240 • E-mail: info@worldteach.org • Web Site: www.igc.org/worldteach

Worldwide Internships & Service Education

REGION/HQ: Europe/Pennsylvania • **CATEGORY:** Experiential Learning • **POSITION TYPE:** Work/Learn Adventure • **DURATION:** Year-Round • **IDEAL CANDIDATE:** College Students, Career Changers, Foreigners • **APPLICANT POOL:** Varies • **APPLICANTS ACCEPTED:** Varies

WORLDWIDE INTERNSHIPS and Service Education (WISE) is a nonprofit educational organization dedicated to increasing international and cross-cultural understanding through programs of experiential learning abroad.

Area and Working Environment: Positions are scattered all over Europe.

Work/Learn Program Specifics: Through its portfolio of affordable opportunities abroad, WISE tailors programs just for you, based on your interests, experience, and goals. Au pairs baby-sit, transport children to school and activities, help with homework, and assist the family with light housekeeping. Live as a member of a host family in Austria, France, Germany, the Netherlands, or Monaco. Community service volunteers help people while exploring careers in human services. Work alongside social-service professionals in England, Scotland, Wales, or Northern Ireland. Working farm guests live on a farm in Norway as a member of a family. London Internships are individually designed, with placements in all fields. The Language Immersion Program combines classroom learning with daily life in France, Germany, Italy, or Spain. WISE and its extensive professional resource network provides support before, during, and after your stay abroad.

Duration: Placements run from a minimum of two weeks to one year, available year-round.

Compensation and Perks: Most positions have a stipend paid in local currency. Housing or room and board is included in all program fees. WISE also includes a Go 25 International Youth ID Card for everyone under twenty-five years of age. Benefits include discounts on travel, accommodations, meals, and basic insurance coverage.

The Ideal Candidate: University students, graduates, and travelers from all academic backgrounds are encouraged to apply. Many of the programs have upper age limits of thirty-five.

Making It Happen: Write or call for more information and an application. Program fees range from $475 to $6,250, depending on choice of program, accommodations, and length of stay. Deadlines vary with each program.

Contact Information: Linda Greenberg, Executive Director • Worldwide Internships & Service Education • 303 South Craig St., Suite 202 • Pittsburgh, PA 15213 • Phone: (412) 681-8120 • Fax: (412) 681-8187 • E-mail: wise+@pitt.edu • Web Site: www.pitt.edu/~wise

YMCA of the USA

REGION/HQ: Taiwan/Illinois • **CATEGORY:** Teaching • **POSITION TYPE:** Unique Experience • **DURATION:** One Year • **IDEAL CANDIDATE:** College Students, Career Changers, Retired Folks, Foreigners • **APPLICANT POOL:** 150/year • **APPLICANTS ACCEPTED:** 25–30/year

THE YMCA OF THE USA assists the national council in Taiwan with their teaching program by identifying possible teacher candidates from the United States and Canada. This program offers a rich cross-cultural experience to people who want to teach English as a second language in community-based YMCAs. For many years, the YMCAs in Taiwan have offered English language programs, not only for the sake of improving language skills, but as a way of building international understanding and sharing cultures.

Work/Learn Program Specifics: The YMCA is looking for qualified teachers who want to teach conversational English to individuals of all ages and become involved in the life of the community, and who are willing to spend occasional evenings and weekends participating in bowling parties, barbecues, and other activities that strengthen personal relationships and a sense of community.

Duration: This is a one-year contract, in which you will classroom-teach up to twenty hours per week, with an additional ten to twenty hours of planning lessons, testing, developing texts, participating in English camp, speech contests, holiday festivals, and the like.

Compensation and Perks: Teachers earn $16,000 to $18,000 (NT) per month, plus housing. Medical insurance is provided in addition to return airfare, one week paid vacation, $12,000 (NT) bonus at end of contract, sponsorship for resident visa, predeparture orientation in the States, and orientation in Taiwan.

The Ideal Candidate: The minimum requirement is a bachelor's degree. Teaching experience and training are desirable. Motivation to teach, share cultures, and build international understanding is important. Teachers need to have a strong command of written and spoken English. In addition, it is important to be flexible in adapting to another culture.

Making It Happen: Request application materials. They must receive your completed application by April 15 for program starting October 1.

INSIDER TIPS: *Successful candidates have strong communication skills, both oral and written, are flexible and friendly, can deal with a variety of people, and are comfortable in adapting to unfamiliar situations.*

Contact Information: Jann Sterling, OSCY Program Administrator • YMCA of the USA • International Division • 101 N. Wacker Dr. • Chicago, IL 60606 • Phone: (800) 872-9622 • Fax: (312) 977-0884

• • • • • • • • • • • • • • • •

Short Listings

American Association of Overseas Studies

REGION/HQ: Worldwide/New York • **CATEGORY:** International Exchange • **POSITION TYPE:** Unique Experience • **DURATION:** Year-Round • **IDEAL CANDIDATE:** College Students, Career Changers, Foreigners • **APPLICANT POOL:** Varies • **APPLICANTS ACCEPTED:** 100/term

THE AMERICAN ASSOCIATION of Overseas Studies offers internships, travel, and study programs geared to meet an individual's academic, professional, and personal goals. Internships are available in their New York office. The AAOS International Internship Network places students in England, France, Germany, Italy, Spain, and Israel. London summer internships are designed to provide valuable career experience in London. Students may become part of the professions of law, journalism, business, theatre, publishing, government, politics, marketing, public relations, and museum curatorship. London acting, film, and video students can learn and participate in the production of an original feature film. They will earn internship

credit while working with an accomplished screenwriter and a leading BBC director.

Contact Information: Program Director • American Association of Overseas Studies • 158 West 81st St., #53 • New York, NY 10024 • Phone: (212) 724-0804 • Fax: (212) 724-0136 • Toll Free: (800) 338-2748

American-International Homestays, Inc.

REGION/HQ: Worldwide/Colorado • **CATEGORY:** Educational Travel • **POSITION TYPE:** Unique Experience • **DURATION:** Year-Round • **IDEAL CANDIDATE:** College Students, Career Changers, Retired Folks, Foreigners • **APPLICANT POOL:** Varies • **APPLICANTS ACCEPTED:** Varies

AMERICAN-INTERNATIONAL HOMESTAYS takes travelers to locales throughout the world and houses them in homes of local inhabitants. It is a unique, culturally rich travel experience that opens up doors of perception and allows you to totally immerse yourself in the customs and traditions of your chosen destination. Host families open their homes and their hearts to their guests with warmth, hospitality, and authentic home-cooked meals. As your personal guides and interpreters, your hosts take you off the beaten path, allowing you to discover your surroundings through the eyes of a native. Travelers range from college students to retired people in their eighties, as well as families with children. Rates start at $49 per night.

Contact Information: Joe Kinczel, Program Director • American-International Homestays, Inc. • P.O. Box 1754 • Nederland, CO 80466-1754 • Phone: (303) 642-3088 • Fax: (303) 642-3365 • Toll Free: (800) 876-2048 • E-mail: ash@igc.apc.org • Web Site: www.spectravel.com/homes

Au Pair in Europe

REGION/HQ: Worldwide/Canada • **CATEGORY:** Au Pair • **POSITION TYPE:** Unique Experience • **DURATION:** Year-Round • **IDEAL CANDIDATE:** High School Students, College Students, Foreigners • **APPLICANT POOL:** 500/year • **APPLICANTS ACCEPTED:** 500/year

AU PAIR IN EUROPE offers au pair positions in seventeen countries around the world. Contracts range from three months to one year. The pay is $75 to $100 per week, and room and board are offered. There is a program fee of 295 Canadian dollars for Canadian applicants; and for those outside Canada, 295 U.S. dollars.

Contact Information: Corinne and John Prince, Program Directors • Au Pair in Europe • P.O. Box 68056 • Blakely Postal Outlet • Hamilton, Ontario L8M 3M7 • Canada • Phone: (905) 545-6305 • Fax: (905) 544-4121 • E-mail: aupair@princeent.com • Web Site: www.princeent.com

Au Pair/Homestay Abroad

REGION/HQ: Europe/Washington, D.C. • **CATEGORY:** Au Pair • **POSITION TYPE:** Seasonal • **DURATION:** Year-Round • **IDEAL CANDIDATE:** College Students, Career Changers • **APPLICANT POOL:** 100/year • **APPLICANTS ACCEPTED:** 100/year

AU PAIRS PROVIDE CHILDCARE and help around the house for families for three to twelve months. You will also get a chance to spend time studying the language and culture of the host country, while sharing American culture and the English language with your host family. Au pairs receive room and board, approximately $300 per month in local currency, and other family "perks." Au Pair/Homestay Abroad can place you in Argentina, France, Germany, Great Britain, Iceland, Netherlands, Norway, Spain, and Switzerland. There is a nonrefundable application fee of $75, a program fee of $1,000, and a monthly insurance rate of $28.

Contact Information: Imelda Farrell, Program Specialist • Au Pair/Homestay Abroad • World Learning • 1015 15th St., NW, Suite 750 • Washington, DC 20005 • Phone: (202) 408-5380 • Fax: (202) 408-6597 • Toll Free: (800) 479-0907 • E-mail: Imelda.Farrell@worldlearning.org

Boston University International Programs

REGION/HQ: Worldwide/Massachusetts • **CATEGORY:** Global Development • **POSITION TYPE:** Unique Experience • **DURATION:** Year-Round • **IDEAL CANDIDATE:** College Students • **APPLICANT POOL:** Varies • **APPLICANTS ACCEPTED:** Varies

BOSTON UNIVERSITY INTERNATIONAL PROGRAMS offers internships and language/liberal arts programs in China, France, England, Spain, Italy, France, Australia, Niger, and Russia. You will complete intensive courses and then work for two months or more in a business, agency, or organization, directly involving yourself in the local work life. The program fee starts at $8,400, which generally includes tuition, room, board, internship, and round-trip airfare.

Contact Information: International Program Director • Boston University International Programs • 232 Bay State Rd., 5th Floor • Boston, MA 02215 • Phone: (617) 353-9888 • Fax: (617) 353-5402 • E-mail: abroad@bu. edu • Web Site: www.bu.edu/abroad

BUNAC USA

REGION/HQ: Europe/Connecticut • **CATEGORY:** Global Development • **POSITION TYPE:** Work/Learn Adventure • **DURATION:** Year-Round • **IDEAL CANDIDATE:** College Students • **APPLICANT POOL:** Varies • **APPLICANTS ACCEPTED:** Varies

WORKING IS THE BEST and most affordable way to really get to know Britain from the inside. It's a fun and educational way to learn those things they don't teach you in the classroom. Using program or personal contacts, Work in Britain participants have taken career-related or casual jobs ranging from waiter to banker, secretary to balloon bender. U.S. full-time students need work permits to take employment, and for a fee of $200 you can obtain a special working document called a Blue Card. You can work up to six months, anywhere in England, Scotland, Wales, and Northern Ireland.

Contact Information: Program Director • BUNAC USA • P.O. Box 49 • South Britain, CT 06487 • Phone: (203) 264-0901 • Alternate: (212) 316-5312

The Casa de Los Amigos

REGION/HQ: Mexico/Mexico City • **CATEGORY:** Social Service • **POSITION TYPE:** Internship • **DURATION:** Year-Round • **IDEAL CANDIDATE:** College Students, Retired Folks • **APPLICANT POOL:** Varies • **APPLICANTS ACCEPTED:** Varies

THE CASA DE LOS AMIGOS, a volunteer-operated Quaker guest house and service center in Mexico City, places volunteer interns for full-time work with Mexican social-service organizations at varying times of the year. Most organizations prefer commitments of six months or more, although the Casa also has arranged shorter-term opportunities. Placement organizations require Spanish proficiency of all interns. The

Casa provides support and guidance for all interns at their placement, as well as orientation in the city. They also organize social, recreational, and personal development activities.

There is an initial $50 fee, plus $25 per month to cover administrative costs. Interns should budget a minimum of an additional $150 to $275 per month for room, board, and personal expenses. The Casa offers a variety of housing options, and many offer room and/or board.

Contact Information: Service and Education Project • The Casa de Los Amigos • Ignacio Mariscal 132 • 06030 Mexico, DF • Phone: 52-5-705-0521 or 705-0646 • Fax: 705-0771 • E-mail: amigos@laneta.apc.org

Center for Education Abroad

REGION/HQ: United Kingdom/Pennsylvania • **CATEGORY:** International Exchange • **POSITION TYPE:** Internship • **DURATION:** Year-Round • **IDEAL CANDIDATE:** College Students • **APPLICANT POOL:** 150/year • **APPLICANTS ACCEPTED:** Varies

THE CENTER FOR EDUCATION Abroad at Beaver College arranges study-abroad/internships for college juniors in Ireland, Northern Ireland, England, and Wales. Internships are individually designed on the basis of a proposal written by the applicant and approved by the applicant's home college. All interns are supervised and evaluated by faculty from an appropriate department of the cooperating host institution. Positions are available in mathematics and computing, arts administration, communications, drama and theatre, business and finance, economics, marketing and advertising, human services, education, health services, psychology, social services, and public policy/government. There is a program fee of $8,500 for semester programs and $4,000 for summer programs, which cover full tuition, housing, and flight to London (from the East Coast).

Contact Information: Stephanie McNerney, Program Coordinator • Center for Education Abroad • Beaver College • 450 S. Easton Rd. • Glenside, PA 19038-3295 • Phone: (215) 572-2901 • Fax: (215) 572-2174 • Toll Free: (800) 755-5607 • Web Site: www.beaver.edu/cea

Center for INTERIM Programs

REGION/HQ: Worldwide/Massachusetts • **CATEGORY:** Clearinghouse • **POSITION TYPE:** Unique Experience • **DURATION:** Year-Round • **IDEAL CANDIDATE:** High School Students, College Students, Career Changers, Retired Folks, Foreigners • **APPLICANT POOL:** Varies • **APPLICANTS ACCEPTED:** Varies

FOUNDED IN 1980, The Center for INTERIM Programs is a service that enables people to pursue structured alternatives to formal education or work by matching client's interests with over 2,500 internships, volunteer positions, apprenticeships, and jobs worldwide, to create "time off" that can give new direction, sharpen hazy career goals, rejuvenate those on the verge of burnout, and give a much needed break. They have tailored creative time off for some 3,000 young people between the ages of fifteen and seventy. Their nonrefundable $1,500 flat fee entitles you to consultation and information over a continuous period of two years. They have opportunities in every region of the United States and in most countries around the world; most of which are either inexpensive or provide benefits such as room and board. Western Office address: Samuel Bull, Director, 45640 Highway 72, Ward, CO 80481; (303) 459-3552; SamuelBull@aol.com

Contact Information: Cornelius Bull, President • Center for INTERIM Programs • Home Office • P.O. Box 2347 • Cambridge, MA 02238 • Phone: (617) 547-0980 • Fax: (617) 661-2864 • E-mail: interim@thecia. net • Web Site: www.thecia.net/users/interim/index. html

Centre for International Mobility

REGION/HQ: Finland/Helsinki • **CATEGORY:** International Education • **POSITION TYPE:** Work/Learn Adventure • **DURATION:** Varies • **IDEAL CANDIDATE:** College Students, Career Changers, Foreigners • **APPLICANT POOL:** Varies • **APPLICANTS ACCEPTED:** Varies

THE CENTRE FOR International Mobility (CIMO) arranges temporary training opportunities for those aged eighteen to thirty. Work placements include agriculture, forestry, horticulture, hotels and restaurants, tourism, nursing, social and youth work, technical and commercial fields, language teaching by native speakers (mainly English, German, and French), and a teaching assistant and family program. The training period normally takes place during the summer months; however, it is possible to work for up to eighteen months. You can expect a reasonable wage for your work (about $800 to $1,000 per month) and your accommodations will be organized by either CIMO or your employer.

Contact Information: Program Director • Centre for International Mobility • P.O. Box 242 (Hakanieumenkatu 2) • FIN-00531, Helsinki • Finland • Phone: 358 0 7747 7033 • Fax: 358 0 7747 7064 • E-mail: cimoinfo@cimo.fi • Web Site: www.cimo.fi

Château de Jean d'Heurs

REGION/HQ: France/Lisle En Rigault • **CATEGORY:** Castle • **POSITION TYPE:** Seasonal • **DURATION:** Summer • **IDEAL CANDIDATE:** College Students, Career Changers, Retired Folks, Foreigners • **APPLICANT POOL:** Varies • **APPLICANTS ACCEPTED:** Varies

LIVE AND WORK IN A French castle! Château de Jean d'Heurs is a superb example of eighteenth-century French château architecture. Officially classified as a national historic monument, it is noted for its majestic staircases and monumental ironwork. The castle is about a two-hour train ride from Paris (which will cost you about US$30). Housekeeper/gardener and assistant art-restoration painter positions are available, each with a flexible thirty-six-hour-per-week work schedule that gives you plenty of time to explore this beautiful region. Although no wages are provided, pocket money will be given. Room and board will also be provided in double bedrooms with a shared bathroom. In addition, you'll have complete use of the castle's kitchen. The château is open May 1 to September 30, and start and finish dates are flexible.

Contact Information: Mezian F., Program Manager • Château de Jean d'Heurs • 55000, Lisle En Rigault • France • Phone: 33-329713177

Conservation International

REGION/HQ: Worldwide/Washington, D.C. • **CATEGORY:** Conservation • **POSITION TYPE:** Unique Experience • **DURATION:** Year-Round • **IDEAL CANDIDATE:** College Students, Career Changers, Retired Folks • **APPLICANT POOL:** Varies • **APPLICANTS ACCEPTED:** Varies

CONSERVATION INTERNATIONAL accepts volunteers to work with local people to conserve rain forests in Botswana, Brazil, Colombia, Costa Rica, Indonesia, and other countries.

Contact Information: Program Director • Conservation International • 1015 18th St., NW, Suite 1000 • Washington, DC 20036 • Phone: (202) 429-5660

Cross-Cultural Solutions

REGION/HQ: India/Colorado • **CATEGORY:** Service Learning • **POSITION TYPE:** Unique Experience • **DURATION:** Year-Round • **IDEAL CANDIDATE:** High School Students, College Students, Career Changers, Retired Folks, Foreigners • **APPLICANT POOL:** Varies • **APPLICANTS ACCEPTED:** Varies

CROSS-CULTURAL SOLUTIONS is a nonprofit organization dedicated to empowering the underprivileged, facilitating cross-cultural communications, and promoting international understanding through person-to-person contact. Their flagship program, Project India, allows volunteers to contribute to service projects while experiencing India in extremely rewarding environments.

Contact Information: Program Director • Cross-Cultural Solutions • P.O. Box 625 • Ophir, CO 81426 • Phone: (970) 728-5551 • E-mail: CCSmailbox@aol.com • Web Site: emol.org/emol/projectindia

Earthwatch

REGION/HQ: Worldwide/Massachusetts • **CATEGORY:** Expedition • **POSITION TYPE:** Unique Experience • **DURATION:** Year-Round • **IDEAL CANDIDATE:** College Students, Career Changers, Retired Folks • **APPLICANT POOL:** Varies • **APPLICANTS ACCEPTED:** Varies

EARTHWATCH, an international nonprofit founded in 1972, offers unique opportunities to work side-by-side with leading scientists on important two-week field research projects worldwide. Earthwatch offers over 150 expeditions in more than 30 U.S. states and in 60 countries. Project disciplines include archaeology, wildlife management, ecology, ornithology, and marine mammalogy. Participants support the research and cover food and lodging ranging from $600 to $2,400 (airfare is additional).

Contact Information: Program Director • Earthwatch • 680 Mt. Auburn St. • P.O. Box 403 • Watertown, MA 02272-9924 • Phone: (617) 926-8200 • Fax: (617) 926-8532 • Toll Free: (800) 776-0188 • E-mail: info@earthwatch.org • Web Site: www.earthwatch.org

Fédération Unie des Auberges de Jeunesse

REGION/HQ: Europe/England • **CATEGORY:** Hostel • **POSITION TYPE:** Seasonal • **DURATION:** Year-Round • **IDEAL CANDIDATE:** College Students, Career Changers, Foreigners • **APPLICANT POOL:** Varies • **APPLICANTS ACCEPTED:** Varies

PROVIDES SHORT-TERM WORK at youth hostels throughout France. Most work involves catering, receptions, sports, and instruction.

Contact Information: Programme Director • Fédération Unie des Auberges de Jeunesse • 27 Rue Pajol • Paris, 75018 • France

Hostelling ....

Suppose that the thoughtful young people of all countries could be provided with suitable meeting places where they could get to know each other. That could and must be the role of our youth hostels, not only in Germany, but throughout the world, building a bridge of peace from nation to nation.

—RICHARD SCHIRRMANN,

FATHER OF THE HOSTELLING MOVEMENT

Short of camping on the roadside, hostels are by far the cheapest place to rest your weary head for the night, with costs ranging from $5 to $30 per night. The 6,000 hostels scattered across the globe vary widely, from lighthouses, tree forts, and home hostels to ranch bunkhouses, Victorian buildings, mountain huts, and medieval castles—each of which has a personality and charm of its own.

One thing is certain about hostels: they are usually crammed with other budget-conscious folks who are looking for the same things that you are—adventure and excitement. They tend to be fun places to meet other happy wanderers. Many hostels are dormitory-style and separated by gender. Others offer private rooms (for a few dollars more) for those traveling together or if you want a good night's rest (especially after a few nights next to those sawin' logs, you'll want to spend the extra money). Hostels generally supply a bed and a blanket. You just need to bring your own sleepsack, and many provide do-it-yourself kitchens, lockers, laundry facilities, and common areas to discuss global events with people from the world over.

Hostelling is perhaps best described as traveling cheaply with an adventurous spirit. You see the world from a perspective that the average tourist will never see. You meet local people, learn customs, eat local food, and often have opportunities to do things you never imagined. Budget hotels, pensions (family-owned inns), university dorms, and bed and breakfasts provide alternatives to hostels for the same or slightly higher costs.

FINDING OUT MORE

Although there are plenty of super guidebooks on finding great sleeps around the world, an investment in a **Hostelling International membership** might be your ticket. Contact HI-AYH at (202) 783-6161; 733 15th St., NW, Suite 840, Washington, DC 20013; www.hiayh.org. A one-year membership card is $25, which includes a complimentary guide to HI-AYH hostels in Canada and the United States, plus newsletters from a regional office nearest you!

On the Web: visit the **Internet Guide to Hostelling.** Learn how numerous adventure travelers are using hostels to meet more people, have more fun, and extend their travel budget for trips up to a year long. www.hostels.com

Discovering Life's Trails: Adventures in Living by Tom Dennard. When Tom Dennard takes a vacation from his day-to-day life, he makes the best of it in adventures that address the testing of self and self-discovery. These stories and adventures show how he has managed to accommodate to the realities of everyday life, but still follow his dreams. His own extensive travel experience around the globe introduced him to hostelling and prompted his desire to build a hostel of his own—**A Hostel in the Forest,** where guests check in at a geodesic dome and can sleep in a bunkhouse or a private tree suite. To get your own copy of his book or to learn more about staying at the hostel, call (912) 264-9738 or check your local bookstore.

A must for information on all inexpensive accommodations in North America is Jim Williams's **The Hostel Handbook.** This guide provides contact information and prices for almost every hostel. The information is extremely fresh, and the newest edition is released every March. Available at independent hostels or by sending a check or money order for $4 to Jim Williams, 722 St. Nicholas Ave., New York, NY 10031; (212) 926-7030; infohostel@aol.com

The word hostel does not describe a place; it describes attitude, a philosophy, a coming together of culturally diverse people sharing the wonders, high and low, of the traveling adventure.

—JANET THOMAS,
AUTHOR OF AT HOME IN HOSTEL TERRITORY

For a moment we smile, striving to pull down barriers quickly. Strangers becoming friends, we only have a small amount of time. Tomorrow…you go north, I go south. Adventures in travel, seeking new experiences. This moment is special. Our lives were meant to touch, to share. My life is richer because I have met you. There have been so many people like you in the youth hostels of the world.

—FOUND IN A HOSTEL JOURNAL AT
REDWOOD NATIONAL PARK'S YOUTH HOSTEL

Friendly Hotels PLC

REGION/HQ: Europe/England • **CATEGORY:** Hotel • **POSITION TYPE:** Seasonal • **DURATION:** Year-Round • **IDEAL CANDIDATE:** High School Students, College Students, Career Changers, Foreigners • **APPLICANT POOL:** Varies • **APPLICANTS ACCEPTED:** 50/year

FRIENDLY HOTELS PLC is a hotel chain with 28 locations in England, Scotland, France, Germany, and Denmark. Seasonal positions are available in food and beverage, accommodation services, and front-of-house. Besides a weekly wage, benefits include free meals, uniforms, and opportunities for transfer/promotion around UK hotels. Housing provided in some hotels. Send resume and cover letter, requesting an application form. There is no formal deadline, but you should apply twelve weeks before desired start date.

Contact Information: Brian Worthington, Personnel Director • Friendly Hotels PLC • Premier House, 10 Greycoat Place • London, SW1P 1SB • England • Phone: 0171-222 8866 • Fax: 0171-233 0769. • E-mail: admin@friendly.u-net.com

Friends of World Teaching

REGION/HQ: Worldwide/California • **CATEGORY:** Teaching • **POSITION TYPE:** Unique Experience • **DURATION:** Year-Round • **IDEAL CANDIDATE:** College Students, Career Changers, Retired Folks, Foreigners • **APPLICANT POOL:** Varies • **APPLICANTS ACCEPTED:** Varies

FRIENDS OF WORLD TEACHING, since 1967, provides assistance and application information about overseas teaching opportunities to American and Canadian educators, graduating seniors, and retired folks. There are assignments which last anywhere from three months to two years; and most contracts are renewable. Prospective applicants may apply throughout the year. Most of the assignments are also paid. Currently they offer teaching and administrative employment opportunities with English-speaking schools and colleges in over 100 foreign countries, from kindergarten to the university level. Foreign language knowledge is not required. To receive an application packet, send a self-addressed stamped envelope.

Unless one says goodbye to what one loves and unless one travels to completely new territories, one can expect merely a long wearing away of oneself. —JEAN DUBUFFET

423

Contact Information: Louis Bajkai, Director • Friends of World Teaching • P.O. Box 1049 • San Diego, CA 92112-1049 • Phone: (619) 224-2365 • Fax: (619) 224-5363 • Toll Free: (800) 503-7436 • E-mail: bajkai@juno.com

Institute for Experiential Learning

REGION/HQ: England/Washington, D.C. • **CATEGORY:** Experiential Learning • **POSITION TYPE:** Internship • **DURATION:** Year-Round • **IDEAL CANDIDATE:** College Students, Career Changers • **APPLICANT POOL:** Varies • **APPLICANTS ACCEPTED:** Varies

THE INSTITUTE FOR EXPERIENTIAL LEARNING offers experiential learning programs in Washington, D.C. and throughout England.

Contact Information: Dr. Eugene Schmiel, Program Director • Institute for Experiential Learning • UK Centres for Experiential Learning • 1901 Pennsylvania Ave., NW, Suite 107 • Washington, DC 20006 • Phone: (202) 833-8580 • Fax: (202) 833-8581 • Toll Free: (800) 435-0770 • E-mail: gene@ielnet.org • Web Site: www.ielnet.org

Intercristo

REGION/HQ: Worldwide/Washington • **CATEGORY:** Ministry • **POSITION TYPE:** Unique Experience • **DURATION:** Year-Round • **IDEAL CANDIDATE:** High School Students, College Students, Career Changers, Retired Folks, Foreigners • **APPLICANT POOL:** Varies • **APPLICANTS ACCEPTED:** Varies

KNOWN AS THE "Christian Career Specialists," Intercristo is a nonprofit, interdenominational ministry dedicated to assisting Christians with their careers through career-building resources and a job-referral program. They list thousands of short-term and career openings with other nonprofit Christian organizations (all over the United States and overseas), and applicants receive personalized reports describing current openings appropriate to their interests, education, and experience. This is a very inexpensive way to launch a job search in the field of Christian service.

Contact Information: Program Director • Intercristo • P.O. Box 33487 • Seattle, WA 98133 • Phone: (202) 546-7330 • Fax: (206) 546-7375 • Toll Free: (800)

426-1342 • E-mail: aab@crista.org • Web Site: www.halcyon.com/ico

International Volunteer Expeditions

REGION/HQ: Worldwide/California • **CATEGORY:** Expedition • **POSITION TYPE:** Unique Experience • **DURATION:** Year-Round • **IDEAL CANDIDATE:** High School Students, College Students, Career Changers, Retired Folks, Foreigners • **APPLICANT POOL:** Varies • **APPLICANTS ACCEPTED:** Varies

INTERNATIONAL VOLUNTEER EXPEDITIONS (IVEX) conducts short-term volunteer projects in California, Africa, the Caribbean, and Latin America. Most work projects require unskilled manual labor, with an emphasis on the environment and outdoor activities. Many programs involve camping and extensive interaction among people of different nationalities. Accommodations range from camping to homestays to a self-contained house in the rain forest. Participants are recruited internationally and all ages are welcome. Costs range from $395 to $1,070, exclusive of airfare. The average project length is two weeks.

Contact Information: Dawn Moorhead, Executive Director • International Volunteer Expeditions • P.O. Box 189518 • Sacramento, CA 95818-9518 • Phone: (916) 444-6856 • Fax: (916) 448-6830 • E-mail: oakland2@ix.netcom.com

Interns for Peace

REGION/HQ: Israel/New York • **CATEGORY:** Community Service • **POSITION TYPE:** Internship • **DURATION:** Year-Round • **IDEAL CANDIDATE:** College Students • **APPLICANT POOL:** 100/year • **APPLICANTS ACCEPTED:** 5/year

INTERNS FOR PEACE is a training program of Jewish–Arab cooperation through community work and serves as a nonthreatening third-party social intervener. Guided by IFP's Jewish and Arab field staff, intern community workers carry out the bulk of the program while receiving in-depth work experience designed to help them become human-relations professionals. Interns are trained and placed to live and work in paired Arab and Jewish communities in Israel for two years. They develop cooperative, action-oriented projects in education, sports, health, the arts, community and workplace relations, and adult interest groups. A weekly stipend, room, and board are provided.

Contact Information: Karen Wald Cohen, National Director • Interns for Peace • 475 Riverside Dr., 16th Floor • New York, NY 10115-0109 • Phone: (212) 870-2226 • Fax: (212) 870-2119

INTERNships INTERNational

REGION/HQ: Worldwide/North Carolina • **CATEGORY:** Experiential Learning • **POSITION TYPE:** Internship • **DURATION:** Year-Round • **IDEAL CANDIDATE:** College Students, Career Changers, Foreigners • **APPLICANT POOL:** Varies • **APPLICANTS ACCEPTED:** Varies
••

INTERNSHIPS INTERNATIONAL, a program for college grads, offers the opportunity to add a foreign dimension to your college or graduate degree through carefully chosen placements in major international cities, including London, Paris, Dublin, Stuttgart, Florence, Madrid, Mexico City, Santiago, Budapest, and Melbourne. These quality internships, covering all disciplines and fields, provide valuable exposure to the foreign market. You will be placed in a nonpaying, full-time internship for a minimum duration of six weeks, and the $500 placement fee is well worth the cost. Many students have found ways to moonlight to bring in a little money. "You must be very specific about what you want in an internship. We help you to focus so that by the time you are through with your internship, you are viewed as a professional in your field."

Contact Information: Judy Tilson, Director • INTERNships INTERNational • 1116 Cowper Dr. • Raleigh, NC 27608 • Phone: (919) 832-1575 • Fax: (919) 832-1575 • E-mail: intintl@aol.com • Web Site: http://rtpnet.org/~intintl

Japan—America Student Conference, Inc.

REGION/HQ: Washington, D.C./Washington, D.C. • **CATEGORY:** International Education • **POSITION TYPE:** Internship • **DURATION:** Year-Round • **IDEAL CANDIDATE:** College Students, Career Changers, Foreigners • **APPLICANT POOL:** Varies • **APPLICANTS ACCEPTED:** 3–4/year
••

THE JAPAN—AMERICA STUDENT CONFERENCE is a non-profit educational and cultural exchange program for university students from the United States and Japan. Each year thirty American and thirty Japanese students spend an intense month living, studying, and traveling together. Internships are available in alumni activities, university relations, development, computer systems, Japanese language interpretation, and historical archives library assistant.

Contact Information: Akiko Clayton, Assistant Director • Japan—America Student Conference, Inc. • 606 18th St., NW, 2nd Floor • Washington, DC 20006 • Phone: (202) 289-4231 • Fax: (202) 789-8265 • E-mail: jascinc@access.digex.net • Web Site: www.twics.com/~jasc/home.en.html

Lost World Trading Company

REGION/HQ: Worldwide/California • **CATEGORY:** Expedition • **POSITION TYPE:** Unique Experience • **DURATION:** Year-Round • **IDEAL CANDIDATE:** High School Students, College Students, Career Changers, Retired Folks, Foreigners • **APPLICANT POOL:** Varies • **APPLICANTS ACCEPTED:** Varies
••

THIS IS AN OPPORTUNITY for anyone who is interested in being an archaeologist, marine biologist, or scientist who travels to the ends of the earth to make discoveries. Every project Lost World supports is chosen because of its needs and its desire for volunteer help. Past volunteers have ranged in age from fourteen to eighty-six, all with a sense of adventure. Each volunteer makes a contribution to make the project possible. Projects are operated around the globe, year-round, and vary from two days to one month in length. A quarterly newsletter announces the new projects.

Contact Information: Program Director • Lost World Trading Company • P.O. Box 365 • Oakdale, CA 95361 • Phone: (209) 847-5393 • Fax: (209) 847-6383

Malta Youth Hostels Association Workcamp

REGION/HQ: Malta/Malta • **CATEGORY:** Workcamp • **POSITION TYPE:** Unique Experience • **DURATION:** Year-Round • **IDEAL CANDIDATE:** High School Students, College Students, Career Changers, Retired Folks, Foreigners • **APPLICANT POOL:** Varies • **APPLICANTS ACCEPTED:** Varies
••

THE MALTA YOUTH HOSTELS ASSOCIATION operates a year-round workcamp where their main service is helping people who come in need of shelter. Volunteers, aged sixteen to thirty, may receive free bed and breakfast from two weeks to three months and will work three hours per day on various projects, which may include hostel maintenance and administration. To apply, send three international reply coupons (which you can get at a local post office), and you will receive detailed information and an application form. Where IRC's are unavailable, $2 in U.S. funds will suffice. The application form should be received at least three months before you plan on arriving. Also inquire about the Youth Accommodation Centres International (188, St. Lucia Street, Valletta, VLT 06, Malta; and use the E-mail address below). This group operates a workcamp program, for those aged sixteen to fifty, where workcamp/fund-raising tasks are performed in the home country (where you will distribute handbooks which have listings of low-priced accommodation centers around the world—currently in Italy, France, Morocco, Spain, Portugal, and Algeria), while appreciation is enjoyed in Malta (you'll receive free accommodations when you arrive).

"We are looking for people who have a generous nature and are ready to help others."

Contact Information: Workcamp Organizer • Malta Youth Hostels Association Workcamp • 17, Triq Tal-Borg • Pawla, PLA 06 • Malta • Phone/Fax: 356-693957 • E-mail: myha@keyworld.net

Mar de Jade

REGION/HQ: Mexico/Mexico • **CATEGORY:** Community Service • **POSITION TYPE:** Work/Learn Adventure • **DURATION:** Year-Round • **IDEAL CANDIDATE:** College Students, Career Changers, Retired Folks • **APPLICANT POOL:** Varies • **APPLICANTS ACCEPTED:** Varies

MAR DE JADE IS A tropical beachfront retreat center in a small fishing village 1¹/₂ hours north of Puerto Vallarta, surrounded by tropical forests, palms, and mango groves. This is a three-week work/study program, where you will participate in community health care, local construction, organic gardening, and teaching. You will also have the chance to study Spanish in small groups with native teachers. The $865 fee includes a shared room, board, twelve hours per week of Spanish, and fifteen hours per week of community work.

Contact Information: Laura Del Valle, Director • Mar de Jade • APDO 81 • Las Varas, Nayarit 63715 • Mexico • Phone/Fax: (011) 52-327-20184 • E-mail: Mardjade@ pvnet.com.mx

Mercy Ships

REGION/HQ: Worldwide/Texas • **CATEGORY:** Ministry • **POSITION TYPE:** Unique Experience • **DURATION:** Year-Round • **IDEAL CANDIDATE:** High School Students, College Students, Career Changers, Retired Folks, Foreigners • **APPLICANT POOL:** Varies • **APPLICANTS ACCEPTED:** Varies

MERCY SHIPS IS A NONPROFIT Christian humanitarian organization committed to a threefold purpose of mercy and relief, training, and ministry. Mercy Ships has served the poor in over seventy port cities by providing medical care, assisting through development projects, and fulfilling basic daily needs in order to demonstrate the message of hope through Jesus Christ. Whatever your interest or background, there could be a place for you in Mercy Ships—at sea, on land, even in your hometown. Join Mercy Ships for as little as two weeks and up to two years (although many make a lifetime commitment). As a volunteer short-term crew member you will have the opportunity to take a short-term look at missions as well as at Mercy Ships. Openings are available in a wide variety of positions, both skilled and nonskilled. Must be at least eighteen. You can make a difference.

Contact Information: Twink DeWitt, Program Director • Mercy Ships • P.O. Box 2020 • Lindale, TX 75771-2020 • Phone: (903) 963-8341 • Fax: (903) 963-7300 • Toll Free: (800) 772-7447 • E-mail: info@mercyships.org • Web Site: www.mercyships.org

National Future Farmers of America

REGION/HQ: Worldwide/Virginia • **CATEGORY:** Agriculture • **POSITION TYPE:** Unique Experience • **DURATION:** Year-Round • **IDEAL CANDIDATE:** High School Students, College Students, Career Changers, Foreigners • **APPLICANT POOL:** Varies • **APPLICANTS ACCEPTED:** Varies

NATIONAL FUTURE FARMERS OF AMERICA provides a cross-cultural experience combined with a practical, hands-on agriculture program. Participants, usually aged eighteen to twenty-four, observe, study, and participate in the agricultural operation of a host family they choose to visit. In exchange for the assistance provided at the host placement, participants usually receive room and board and a monthly stipend. Placements are available in over twenty countries for three, six, or twelve months.

Program fees range from $1,500 to $6,000, depending on the country and length of stay. Fees include international airfare, a two-day orientation, visa fee (if required), host arrangements, and health and accident insurance.

Contact Information: Student Services—International • National Future Farmers of America • P.O. Box 15160 • Alexandria, VA 22309-0160 • Phone: (703) 360-3600 • Fax: (703) 360-5524

People to People International

REGION/HQ: Worldwide/Missouri • **CATEGORY:** International Exchange • **POSITION TYPE:** Internship • **DURATION:** Year-Round • **IDEAL CANDIDATE:** College Students, Foreigners • **APPLICANT POOL:** 50/year • **APPLICANTS ACCEPTED:** Varies

PEOPLE TO PEOPLE INTERNATIONAL is a nonprofit educational and cultural exchange organization founded by President Eisenhower in 1954, with internships in these cities: Rockhampton (Australia), Brisbane, Buenos Aires, Copenhagen, Dublin, London, Moscow, Munich, Nairobi, Paris, Prague, Seville, Stockholm, Sydney, and many more. Interns engage in an eight-week, active, non-paid work assignment with a company, government organization, educational institution, or other appropriate association. Each internship is tailor-made to accommodate the student's specific academic/work experience and career goals. There is a program fee of $1,675 which covers tuition, advisor fees, placement, evaluation, orientation, housing for the first week, and ongoing program coordination. The student must cover room and board for two months. Approximate cost for the entire experience will run $3,000 to $4,000.

Contact Information: Dorel Drinkwine, Collegiate Internship Coordinator • People to People International • 501 E. Armour Blvd. • Kansas City, MO 64109-2200 • Phone: (816) 531-4701 • Fax: (816) 561-7502 • E-mail: ptpi@cctr.umkc.edu • Web Site: cei.haag.umkc.edu/ptp/

Sea Turtle Restoration Project

REGION/HQ: Costa Rica/California • **CATEGORY:** Ecotourism • **POSITION TYPE:** Unique Experience • **DURATION:** Year-Round • **IDEAL CANDIDATE:** College Students, Career Changers, Retired Folks • **APPLICANT POOL:** Varies • **APPLICANTS ACCEPTED:** Varies

VOLUNTEERS ARE NEEDED for beach patrols and sea turtle hatchery work from August to January at Punto Banco, on the Pacific coast of Costa Rica, not far from the Costa Rican/Panamanian border. The volunteers will work with a Costa Rican biologist and community members. Activities include walking the beaches at night searching for nesting turtles, moving turtle nests to the hatchery, and participating in environmental education programs in the community. Adult turtles will be tagged and measured, and data on hatching success will be recorded. Leisure activities include jungle hikes and snorkeling. Volunteers will stay in rustic cabins operated by the Tiskita Jungle Lodge. Each cabin accommodates one to six people and a two-week commitment is required. The program cost is $800 for two weeks and doesn't include transportation.

Contact Information: Ellen Purcell, Program Associate • Sea Turtle Restoration Project • Earth Island Institute • P.O. Box 400 • Forest Knolls, CA 94933 • Phone: (415) 488-0370 • Fax: (415) 488-0372 • Toll Free: (800) 859-7283 • E-mail: epurcell@ earthisland.org

University Research Expeditions Program

REGION/HQ: Worldwide/California • **CATEGORY:** Expedition • **POSITION TYPE:** Unique Experience • **DURATION:** Year-Round • **IDEAL CANDIDATE:** High School Students, College Students, Career Changers, Retired Folks, Foreigners • **APPLICANT POOL:** Varies • **APPLICANTS ACCEPTED:** Varies

THE UNIVERSITY RESEARCH Expeditions Program (UREP) invites you to join in the challenges and rewards of field research expeditions around the world. These research teams investigate everything from Costa Rican monkeys that use medicinal plants to excavating medieval castles of Ireland. Whether you choose to study archaeological sites to learn about the past or record the biodiversity of fragile environments, your participation will improve our understanding of the planet and help plan for the future. You don't need special training or experience to participate—your curiosity, adaptability, and willingness to share the costs and lend a helping hand are the most important qualifications. Each participant on a UREP expedition is a working member of the team and makes an equal contribution to cover the project's costs. More than just contributing to a worthy cause, you will have a unique opportunity to learn new skills, make new friends, and gain insights into other cultures in a way that ordinary travelers rarely experience. It's an adventure with a purpose.

Contact Information: Jean Colvin, Program Director • University Research Expeditions Program • UC, Berkeley • 2223 Fulton St. • Berkeley, CA 94720-7050 • Phone: (510) 642-6586 • Fax: (510) 642-6791 • E-mail: urep @uclink.berkeley.edu • Web Site: www.mip.berkeley.edu/urep

VENUSA

REGION/HQ: Venezuela/Florida • **CATEGORY:** Language • **POSITION TYPE:** Unique Experience • **DURATION:** Year-Round • **IDEAL CANDIDATE:** College Students, Career Changers, Retired Folks, Foreigners • **APPLICANT POOL:** Varies • **APPLICANTS ACCEPTED:** Varies

MÉRIDA IS THE principal city of the Venezuelan Andes—a clean, safe university town where the weather and people are always warm and the scenery is breathtaking. This intensive and highly individualized program offers four hours of instruction with a qualified teaching professional each weekday. Students and professors work together to tailor schedules, teaching styles, and course content to the specific needs of each student. Obtaining room and board with a Venezuelan family is optional, but is highly recommended. Program participants and Venezuelan students of English are invited to social events and activities. Some day trips or outings are available for a small additional cost. Programs start every Saturday, year-round. There is an instruction fee of $150 per week, and room and board cost $75 per week (with discounts if you stay longer than three weeks). Semester programs cost $3,000 to $5,500.

Contact Information: Rosa Corley, Coordinator • VENUSA • 6342 Forest Hill Blvd., Suite 287 • West Palm Beach, FL 33415 • Phone: (561) 753-3761 • Fax: (561) 753-3758 • E-mail: venusa@flinet.com • Web Site: www.flinet.com/~venusa

Wildlands Studies

REGION/HQ: Worldwide/California • **CATEGORY:** Wildlife • **POSITION TYPE:** Unique Experience • **DURATION:** Year-Round • **IDEAL CANDIDATE:** College Students, Career Changers, Foreigners • **APPLICANT POOL:** Varies • **APPLICANTS ACCEPTED:** Varies

WILDLANDS STUDIES IS sponsored by San Francisco State University. The Wildlands team searches for answers to important environmental problems in remote areas of the mountainous West, Alaska, Hawaii, Canada, Russia, Thailand, Nepal, or New Zealand, with its goal to protect wildlife and preserve our wild areas. Your research project occurs entirely in the field and involves extensive on-site wildlife, wildland management, or ecological research under the direction of experienced resource faculty. In backcountry settings, you will acquire and directly apply practical research skills while examining, firsthand, issues in environmental policy, resource management, and conservation ecology. There is a fee of $425 to $1,900.

Contact Information: Crandall Bay, Program Director • Wildlands Studies • 3 Mosswood Circle • Cazadero, CA 95421 • Phone: (707) 632-5665 • Fax: (707) 632-5665 • E-mail: wildlnds@sonic.net

World Trade Centers Association

REGION/HQ: Worldwide/New York • **CATEGORY:** Global Development • **POSITION TYPE:** Internship • **DURATION:** Year-Round • **IDEAL CANDIDATE:** College Students, Career Changers, Foreigners • **APPLICANT POOL:** Varies • **APPLICANTS ACCEPTED:** Varies

THE WORLD TRADE CENTERS ASSOCIATION stands outside of politics across national boundaries, in service to those who develop and facilitate international trade. Currently, there are over 250 World Trade Center member associations, located in cities across the globe, from Abidjan to Zurich. Very few WTCA internships offer monetary compensation; however, working as an intern may be the easiest and friendliest springboard to executives involved in the global marketplace.

Contact Information: Matthew Kleinknecht, Administrator • World Trade Centers Association • One World Trade Center, Suite 7701 • New York, NY 10048 • Phone: (212) 432-2648 • Fax: (212) 488-0064 • E-mail: matt@wtca.geis.com

Addresses

China Teaching Program

REGION/HQ: Asia/Washington
CATEGORY: Teaching
CONTACT INFORMATION:
Program Director
China Teaching Program
Western Washington University
Old Main 530
Bellingham, WA 98225-9047
Phone: (202) 650-3753

Chol Chol Foundation

REGION/HQ: Worldwide/Washington, D.C.
CATEGORY: Community Service
CONTACT INFORMATION:
James Mundell, Internship Coordinator
Chol Chol Foundation
4431 Garrison St., NW
Washington, DC 20016-4055
Phone: (202) 525-8844

Inca Floats

REGION/HQ: Worldwide/California
CATEGORY: Adventure Travel
CONTACT INFORMATION:
Bill Robertson, President
Inca Floats
1311 ATD 63rd St.
Emeryville, CA 94608
Phone: (510) 420-1550 • Fax: (510) 420-0947
• E-mail: incafloats@aol.com

Middlebury Language School

REGION/HQ: Northeast/Vermont
CATEGORY: Language
CONTACT INFORMATION:
Program Director
Middlebury Language School
Sunderland Language Center
Middlebury, VT 05753-6131
Phone: (802) 388-3711

Seniors Abroad

REGION/HQ: Worldwide/California
CATEGORY: Educational Travel
CONTACT INFORMATION:
Evelyn Zivetz, Director
Seniors Abroad
12533 Pacato Circle, North
San Diego, CA 92128
Phone: (619) 485-1696 • Fax: (619) 487-1492

YMCA International Program Services

REGION/HQ: Northeast/New York
CATEGORY: Global Development
CONTACT INFORMATION:
Program Director
YMCA International Program Services
71 W. 23rd St.
New York, NY 10010
Phone: (212) 727-8800 • Fax: (212) 727-8814

Each friend represents a world in us, a world possibly not born until they arrive, and it is only by this meeting that a new world is born. —ANAÏS NIN

Alternatives to the Peace Corps offers many other options for those who want to volunteer their time (almost anywhere in the world) for a good cause. This resource guide provides a listing of groups that work to support development as defined by the local people and stresses that learning the dynamics of a community will be your greatest challenge as a volunteer. A must for anyone dedicated to grassroots work in your own backyard and in the Third World. (Food First Books, $9.95); foodfirst@igc.apc.org; www.netspace.org/hungerweb/FoodFirst/index.htm; (510) 654-4400.

Around The World: A Postcard Adventure by Pam Terry. When Pam Terry travels, unexpected things happen to her at every turn. This humorous whirlwind chronicle of the author's round the world journey is uniquely written in postcard form. It appeals to the explorer in all of us, and you'll experience firsthand what it's like to get Pamela Terry's 400+ postcards and vicariously share her incredible travel adventures. (800) 590-7778; traveler@atwTraveler.com; www.atwTraveler.com (Quest Press, $12.95)

Instead of carting around a diary and a guidebook on your next journey, carry **Lucy Izon's Backpacker Journal.** Author (and travel writer) Lucy Izon has created the perfect two-in-one journal. It includes 122 pages to record your adventures, but also includes over 300 tips and helpful quotes throughout. How else would you know not to blow your nose in public in Japan, or not to pick up food with your left hand in Indonesia, or not to point your feet a certain way in Thailand? With your scintillating entries alongside the author's, you'll have more than just memories of your adventure. Call Christie Associates at (800) 263-1991 to order a copy ($9.95 plus $2.50 shipping and handling). Travelers can also visit Izon's Backpacker Journal web site at www.izon.com; izon@compuserve.com

The Big Book of Adventure Travel by James Simmons. From Boston to Borneo, California to Costa Rica, this guide features more than 400 great escapes around the globe for those seeking excitement. Although the book is geared more for the vacationer, this might be a great resource to get contact information and inquire about seasonal work. (John Muir Publications, $17.95)

Travel on the cheap and down-to-earth! **Big World,** an alternative bimonthly magazine, provides such inspiring destination articles, that you'll want to drop everything and travel to some unique locales. Subscriptions are $15 for one year, or pick up a single copy for $3. For more information (or if you'd like to submit a tale or tips from one of your journeys), contact Jim Fortney, **Big World,** P.O. Box 8743, Lancaster, PA 17604-8743; bigworld@PAonline.com; www.PAonline.com/bigworld

Club TELI (Travail-Études-Loisirs-Internationaux) is an association based in France, created in 1991 by traveler Dominique Girerd, who wanted to share his travel experiences with others. Each member (more than 1,000 now) receives a newsletter, five times per year, full of addresses, tips, testimonies, jobs, training courses, dwellings, and the like, all over the world. It is mainly for French, aged eighteen to thirty-five, who want to get information on how to prepare themselves for a foreign experience (job, training period, au pair, vacation) especially in North America, Australia, and Europe, or for international people who want to get French contacts. Club TELI, Dominque Girerd, Director, BP 21, Cran Gevrier Cedex, 74961, France; Phone: (33) 450 52 26 58; Fax: (33) 450 52 10 16; www.aussieworld.com/teli

Author Rick Steves takes a lighthearted, personal approach to sharing with you everything you need to know to have a great trip in Europe. *Europe Through the Back Door* is full of practical travel advice, from planning and packing tips to everyday survival skills for coping abroad, and is one of seventeen travel guides written by the author. His books help you discover a more intimate feel for the places that locals patronize, rather than hitting the main tourist stops. You can receive a free quarterly travel newsletter, which also explains and promotes ETBD's travel guidebooks, maps, videos, accessories, tours, and other great stuff. They're also known for having the best deals on Eurail passes. Contact Rick at (206) 771-8303; P.O. Box 2009, Edmonds, WA 98020-2009; ricksteves @aol.com; www.ricksteves.com ($18.95, John Muir Publications)

Adventures by bus? Try **Green Tortoise.** You'll travel in their beautiful green buses to all sorts of unique destinations. You'll sleep lying down on fitted sheets over thick foam on raised platforms and bunks. By day you'll swim, cook breakfast, explore caves, climb mountains, raft down streams, stand under waterfalls, walk through the forest, cook dinner, build campfires, visit towns, meet people, and generally take it easy. Some days you travel and some nights you camp. Even a short ride on the Tortoise is a vacation. The longer trips will become lifelong memories. Green Tortoise, 494 Broadway, San Francisco, CA; (800) 867-8647; tortoise@greentortoise.com; www.greentortoise.com

The International Employment Hotline (edited by Will Cantrell) provides monthly listings of overseas job openings, including information-packed articles on internships, programs recruiting for teaching English abroad, and more. For $39 you'll receive twelve issues. Worldwise Books, P.O. Box 3030, Oakton, VA 22124; (703) 620-1972

Are you a foreign student involved in educational activity in the United States? If so, contact the **International Students Organization,** a group established by international students to serve international students. The *International Spirit* newsletter is the main channel of communication between ISO and you. This newsletter brings you stories, information, scholarships and grants, and other great stuff to assist you while you are here in the States. The International Student Organization, P.O. Box 763, New York, NY 10150-0763; (800) 244-1180, iso@village.ios.com

A perfect companion for your travels is *Jim's Backpacker's Bible,* a handbook for backpackers, wanderers, college students in between semesters, latter-day hippies, and just about anyone who wants to see America on a bare-bones budget and doesn't mind sharing a room with

● ● ● ● ● ● ● ● ● ● ● ● ● ● ● ● ● ●

Travel reminds me that life is fundamentally about relationships with other living creatures and to the physical world. It renews my childlike wonder at our planet. In a completely new environment, the intensity of each moment is somehow heightened. I return to my daily life with a fresh perspective.

—LISA IKLE GIEGER

● ● ● ● ● ● ● ● ● ● ● ● ● ● ● ● ● ●

The little choices we must make will chart the course of life we take.
We either choose the path of light or wander off in darkest night.

another traveler. Over 1,000 hostels, motels, inns, and KOA "Kamping Kabins" are listed, all of which are $20 or less (with quite a few below $10). The book is loaded with photos and maps. A former backpacker and hitchhiker, the author operates his own hostel (Jim's at the Beach) in Venice Beach, California. To get your own copy of the *Backpacker's Bible,* send $7 if you're in the States or $8 if you're in Canada (which includes shipping and handling) to Jim de Cordova, P.O. Box 5650, Santa Monica, CA 90409; (800) 208-7226; dedecord@aol.com; www.hostels.com/guides/jbb

Journeywoman is a quarterly magazine offering a brash, unapologetically female take on travel. It is full of practical, money-saving tips that men would find useful as well. But the primary message is that women should boldly venture forth to see the world for themselves. Sample copies cost $6, or if you'd rather get a subscription, send $24.07 to JW, 50 Prince Arthur Ave., Suite 1703, Toronto, Ontario, M5R 1B5, Canada; (416) 929-7654; editor@journeywoman.com; www.journeywoman.com

The classic Europe handbook, *Let's Go,* has been the bible for a generation of student travelers. Over the years they have added in-depth regional and country guides to most of Europe and North America.

At 5 P.M. in most countries the museums close; but at the same time, most cafés, dance clubs, pubs, and late-night food spots are just opening their doors. *Let's Party!* (Vagabond Publishing) takes you neighborhood to neighborhood to see the mainstream and the obscure. If you like to meet the locals when you travel, these guidebooks will show you where they hang out. Call (800) 541-7323; party2max@aol.com (Vagabond Publishing)

Lonely Planet publishes down-to-earth, comprehensive, and practical guidebooks for independent travelers who "have an interest in things." There are over 200 books in print, all written in a straightforward, readable style with lots of firsthand tips and recommendations. You can also receive their free quarterly newsletter. (800) 275-8555; info@lonelyplanet.com; www.lonelyplanet.com

Make a Mil-¥en: Teaching English in Japan by Don Best. Can you teach without any experience? Author Don Best says you can. Most foreigners who teach conversational English in Japan's language schools start with little or no teaching experience. The language school that hires you will teach you everything it thinks you need to know to be a successful teacher. *Make a Mil-¥en* is a great starter guide for everything you need to know and do to get a good job teaching English in Japan. In addition, if you would like to deepen your knowledge of Japan and its culture, Stone Bridge Press hopes to acquaint you with Japan's customs through their books. (Stone Bridge Press, $14.95); www.stonebridge.com; (800) 947-7271.

For more than two decades, *Moon Travel Handbooks* have been guiding independent travelers to the world's best destinations. The guidebooks are adventures in themselves, providing coverage of off-the-beaten-path

> *The true traveler has in him something of the explorer's urge to discover. It does not matter that there is little scope left for original discovery. The important thing is that he should discover things that are new to him and be able to feel the same thrill and excitement as though they were equally unknown to everyone else.*
>
> —M.A. MICHAEL

destinations, fascinating accounts of the region's history and varied cultures, insight into political and environmental issues, street-savvy advice, language glossaries, accommodations and transportation information—everything travelers need for an extraordinary travel experience. Whether you are headed for the Hawaiian surf, the Colorado Rockies, or the streets of Tokyo, Moon has the guide to get you there. For U.S. travelers, a must is *Road Trip USA*, ($22.50), which covers eleven cross-country routes, providing practical information and entertaining sidebars. For more information on their handbooks or to receive a subscription to their free newsletter, *Travel Matters*, call (800) 345-5473; travel@moon.com; www.moon.com

For those interested in job listings on international educational exchange, **NAFSA (the Association of International Educators)** puts out the *NAFSA Job Registry*. For $30 per ($20 for members), you'll receive ten issues per year. NAFSA Job Registry,1875 Connecticut Ave. NW, Suite 1000, Washington, DC 20009-5728; (202) 939-3131

Check out these two web sites on learning the ins and out of becoming a nanny anywhere in the world: **Nanny Jobs USA** www.ilovemynanny.com/jobs; **Nannies Plus** www.nanniesplus.com or call (800) 752-0078

O-HAYO SENSEI, The Newsletter of English Teaching Jobs in Japan. Published twice each month, issues generally include new teaching positions, positions still available, writing/editing jobs, the classifieds, schools/employers, current exchange rates, and airfares, all related to Japan. Each issue runs $1, and you can have it delivered to your E-mailbox automatically. Questions, requests, and comments can be directed to: editor@ohayosensei.com; www.ohayosensei.com; 1032 Irving St., Suite 508, San Francisco, CA 94122.

The **Overseas Development Network** puts out a handful of publications. My favorites include ***Development Opportunities Catalog*** ($10), a guide to internships, volunteer work, and employment opportunities with development organizations, and ***A Handbook for Creating Your Own Internship in International Development*** ($7.95), written by experienced interns who provide practical advice on getting and financing your internship overseas, and returning home. Call to receive their publications brochure: (415) 431-5953; odn@igc.org; www.igc.apc. org/odn

The **Quaker Information Center** provides an information packet on a smorgasbord of opportunities ranging from weekend workcamps, volunteer service, internships, and alternatives to the Peace Corps programs, both domestic and international. More than 280 resources are listed. Updated periodically, this booklet is great for people of all ages. To defray the cost of putting this information together and postage, send $10 to Peggy Morscheck, Director, Quaker Information Center, 1501 Cherry St., Philadelphia, PA 19102; quakerinfo@afsc.org; (215) 241-7024.

Rough Guides are aimed squarely at independent-minded travelers of all kinds, on all budgets—whether vacationers, business travelers, or backpackers. Thoughtful writing, painstaking research, and conscientiously

Inexperience is a quality of the human condition. We are born one time only; we can never start a new life equipped with the experience we've gained from a previous one. We leave childhood without knowing what youth is; we marry without knowing what it is to be married; and even when we enter old age, we don't know what it is we're heading for: the old are innocent children of their old age. In that sense, man's world is the planet of inexperience.

prepared maps are fundamental to their commitment to provide you with the best possible guides. (212) 366-2348; www.roughguides.com

Volunteering can be a very worthwhile, constructive, and interesting way of exploring the world. It has the power to bring one much closer to a particular culture than through simple tourism. Besides the workcamps **SCI-International Voluntary Service** sponsors, they provide a comprehensive listing of other short-term volunteer programs throughout the world. wworks.com/~sciivs

STA Travel is the world's leading student travel organization offering a range of services to help you put your trip together. (800) 777-0112; www.sta-travel.com

Travel is not only a good way to gain exposure to the diversity of ideas and cultures, it also, at times, is the only way to go deep into a particular area of interest. Travel, properly pursued, is a form of learning, and learning can lead to interesting work opportunities.

Student Travels magazine is a bold and sassy information source on international study, work, and volunteer opportunities via the Council on International Educational Exchange. To get your free copy, call (888) COUNCIL or check out their web companion on-line at www.ciee. org/zone.htm. Travelers can post photos and stories from their journeys, ask the travel advisors at Council Travel for advice, and join in ongoing discussions on a variety of travel topics.

Study Abroad.com is the on-line study abroad information resource. Here you will find listings for thousands of study-abroad programs in more than 100 countries throughout the world. They have an experiential listings page which includes internships as well as opportunities to volunteer overseas, and you will also find hundreds of links to other study abroad program home pages. www.studyabroad.com

Transitions Abroad is a tool for anyone who desires to travel abroad, for whatever reason. Their *Alternative Travel Directory* and their bimonthly magazine's articles, columns, departments, and advertisements tell readers when to go, where to go, and—most importantly—how and why to go abroad. Travel for pleasure is certainly not ignored, but the emphasis in Transitions Abroad is on travel that is personally enriching and socially responsible. You can subscribe to their bimonthly magazine ($24.95 per year or $6.25 for a single issue) or get the latest edition of the *Alternative Travel Directory* for $19.95. To get a free catalog sent to you call (800) 293-0373; trabroad@aol.com; www.transabroad.com; Transitions Abroad, P.O. Box 1300, Amherst, MA 01004-1300.

Travel-Links is a full-service travel agency that emphasizes responsible tourism and seeks to promote understanding and cooperation among people through nonexploitive travel. Co-op American Travel-Links, 120 Beacon St., Somerville, MA 02143-4369; (800) 648-2667

Travel Smart publishes a monthly newsletter on unique travel ideas, merchandise, trips, and information on the best travel deals throughout the world; all with an emphasis on paying less and enjoying more. Call for a complimentary issue. Travel Smart, 40 Beechdale Rd., Dobbs Ferry, New York, NY 10522, (800) 327-3633

The **Travelers' Tales** series (O'Reilly and Associates) collects firsthand experiences of some of the world's best travel writers and blends a travel guidebook with contemporary travel literature. You won't find hotel and restaurant reviews, but short of living there yourself, there is no better way to get a feel for a country. Each volume collects travelers' tales that entertain, inform, and sometimes show the dark side of the country for the would-be traveler. Travelers' Tales/O'Reilly and Associates, 101 Morris St., Sebastopol, CA 95472; (800) 998-9938; ttales@ora.com; www.ora.com/ttales

TRIP is the magazine for those who travel with youthful vigor and occasional reckless abandon. This quarterly focuses on exciting, affordable, and doable adventures, ranging from rock climbing in Montana and teaching in Milan to surfing in Baja and trekking through the Himalayas. The glossy, professional design is bold and fresh, as is the content. A yearly subscription is a measly $10 (for six issues). (310) 454-1473; triptravel@tripmag.com; www.tripmag.com/tripmag

Walkabout Travel Gear supplies independent travelers with information, travel tips, and essential gear needed to enhance the journey. For a free catalog and/or newsletter (which you can also receive through E-mail each month), you can reach them at 732 Millcreek Dr., Moab, UT 84532; (800) 852-7085; www.walkabouttravelgear.com

Get the real scoop on working overseas through the eyes of author Susan Griffith. **Work Your Way Around the World** ($17.95), revised every other year, is a complete planning guide for the working traveler, with detailed country-by-country overviews, covering the best spots for job hunting, employment agencies, working conditions, accommodations, and more. **Teaching English Abroad** ($15.95) intertwines actual accounts of enjoyable and disappointing experiences by people who have taught abroad. You'll also find specific job vacancy information compiled from language schools from the south of Chile to Iceland, and from Korea to Córdoba, as well as insights on how to talk your way around the world. This book just might be your stepping-stone to a brilliant year abroad. Pick up these books through Vacation Work—England. They're distributed by Peterson's in the United States; (800) 338-3282; www.petersons.com

The World Awaits by Paul Otteson. Ever thought about grabbing your backpack and hitting the road? Author Paul Otteson provides you with the details and insights you'll need to plan a fulfilling journey, traveling only with what you can fit into your pack. (John Muir Publications, $16.95)

The Worldwide Guide to Cheap Airfares by Michael McColl. This book will help you learn how to beat the airlines at their own game. You don't have to be a travel agent or flight attendant to get amazing deals on airfares. You just need to know the right places to call. This is the best resource for budget air travel available. (Inside Publications, $14.95) To order your own book, call (800) 78-BOOKS; insider@sfnet.com

* * *

To awaken quite alone in a strange town is one of the pleasantest sensations in the world. You are surrounded by adventure. You have no idea of what is in store, but you will if you are wise and know the art of travel, let yourself go...and accept whatever comes in the spirit in which the gods may offer it.

—FREYA STARK

* * *

11

Alphabetical Index . . . . .

Indexes

Do not be too timid and squeamish about your actions. All life is an experiment.
—RALPH WALDO EMERSON

Poor is the man whose pleasures depend on the permission of another.
—MADONNA

There is no shortcut to life. To the end of our days, life is a lesson imperfectly learned.
—HARRISON E. SALISBURY

It is a good idea to obey all the rules when you're young, just so you'll have the strength to break them when you're old. —MARK TWAIN

I know when one door closes another one opens, but these hallways are really a pain!
—BARBARA EFIRD

Category Index . . . .

From Adventure Travel to Zoos (and everything in between), this index provides you with a "buzz word" associated with each program. And although each has been assigned a particular category, some of the programs cover such a wide spectrum of opportunities that they could be listed under each! For example, your focus might be on Grassroots programs; however you may find the information you're looking for in other areas—such as advocacy, global development, human service, public interest, research, or sustainable living! So become an explorer while perusing this index!

Idealists...foolish enough to throw caution to the winds...have advanced
mankind and have enriched the world. —EMMA GOLDMAN

If a man will begin with certainties, he shall end in doubts; but if he will be content to begin with doubts, he shall end in certainties. —FRANCIS BACON

Geographical Index · · · ·

A re you looking for a particular program in a specific locale? This index gives you the tools to narrow your search to a specific state, country, or region! The United States is broken down by each state, with the rest of the world grouped by country. You'll also find programs that are offered in more than one state grouped under the heading "Nationwide" and those offered in more than one country grouped under "Worldwide." The programs under these headings are not listed separately by their respective state or country, so you'll have to get the specifics by referring to each listing.

Of magic doors there is this—you do not see them even as you are passing through.
—MERLYN STORM

Colorado

The whole soul is composed into a kind of real harmony the instant
one sets oneself to work. —Thomas Carlyle

It's not what we have, but what we are that makes the poverty or richness of our life.
—Phillips Brooks

North Carolina

North Dakota

Ohio

Oregon

Either you let your life slip away by not doing the things you want to do,
or you get up and do them. —CARL ALLY

I don't go where the puck is. I go where the puck is going to be.
—WAYNE GRETZKY

The price of not following your dream is the same as paying for it.
—PAULO COELHO

Resource Directory . . . . .

Here's a look at all the books, magazines, journals, newletters, and other resources scattered throughout your guide (for Web sites, see the next section).

Once we believe in ourselves, we can risk curiosity, wonder, spontaneous delight, or any experience that reveals the human spirit. —E.E. CUMMINGS

469

The Back Door Guide to Short Term Job Adventures

Web Site
Quick Reference. . . . . . .

Here's a quick look at all the web sites contained in your guidebook!

Success isn't something you chase. It's something you have to put forth the effort for constantly. Then
maybe it'll come when you least expect it. Most people don't understand that. —MICHAEL JORDAN

12

Have you ever received a really fun piece of mail—say, a letter enclosed in an envelope created from a torn-out page of a magazine? I did. I also knew that when I opened this letter, I would find a unique individual.

Yes, this letter was from someone who turned out to be one of my very first *Back Door* readers. However, unlike most orders I received, this one also enclosed a two-page note explaining its writer's dreams and aspirations and her desire to make an impact on this world. A guidebook and a personal letter from me—providing, I hoped, the information and inspiration needed to fulfill this person's adventures and dreams—was sent off. "What would become of this person?" I wondered.

You see, the most frustrating part of being an author is that I rarely get to hear about the great things that come about from using this guide. This frustration got me thinking. Plenty of books have made an impact on my life. Have I ever taken the time to let the authors of the world know of the impact they made on my life? Well, who has the time to do that? And would these authors really care? The fact is, I think most authors do. And by becoming an author myself, I learned how important it is to tell others, to share with them how they've helped me along the way. Without their good works, I wouldn't be the person I am today.

Alona Jasik is one of the people who have helped me. Over the years, she has fed me with letters and postcards of her adventures. Secretly, over this period, I have lived vicariously through the adventurous life she leads. She is an explorer and an adventurer and has a deep passion for life. I thought I'd share her unique tale.

After graduating from college, Alona decided to take a back door approach to life, to feed her mind and soul with the things the world was beckoning her to do, things that also developed her innate abilities. "I believe it is so important to constantly feed yourself with experiences and ideas, and to practice personal growth on a daily basis…and digesting the experience is just as important. Find people who you resonate with and have them be your support."

Happy Ad

And support is what she got on her first adventure. She became part of the Bike-Aid "movement," cycling from Texas to Washington, D.C. with a group of other riders from around the world, doing environmental education along the route, and fund-raising over $2,000 for the Overseas Development Network. "Bike-Aid satisfied my quest for community. My interests lay in the cause, promoting environmental solutions, rather than in the physical challenge of the ride itself." To Alona, the group dynamics were more of a challenge than the actual pedaling through humidity. She learned that each of us is the solution: it takes too much wasted energy to blame others for things that don't work right in our world.

This experience gave Alona a new way of looking at her life. It was also a driving force in looking at each day as an opportunity. Soon after Bike-Aid, she applied for a work permit through the Council on International Educational Exchange, and off to New Zealand she went. Upon arrival, she traveled and worked her way around the country by working on organic farms (commonly known as WWOOFing), where the host would offer free room and board in exchange for a day's work. "It's the good, the bad, and the ugly: accommodations can range from a bike shop to a retreat center to a biodynamic farm in the hills."

Upon finishing her adventures Down Under, she returned to California. Working with the challenge of being spoiled by travel and living with her ideals while creating a livelihood, she's exploring various jobs. She truly believes that if you do what you love, the money will follow. She has focused her attention on Bay Area Action, an environmental action group in Palo Alto that grew out of the 1990 Earth Day campaign. At that time Alona participated in the campaign as a volunteer: now she's the volunteer coordinator. Funny how life happens!

venturing

Y̶ou finally did it. Your short-term adventure will bring you a wealth of experience, a firmer sense of who you are and where your career is going, a supportive network of friends and colleagues in the industry, and a trunkful of great memories. But, before you rush off, here are some final thoughts to help you make the most of your adventure.

Be prepared to work in areas not related to your main responsibility. Additionally, be willing and excited to chip in wherever needed. Look at every job you're given as an opportunity to learn more about the field you've chosen and a chance to contribute to the overall success of the program.

Make it a goal to acquire as many skills, in as many areas, as you can. Attend every class and seminar that is offered and immerse yourself in every aspect of the program.

Throughout the course of your adventure, talk to fellow staff members about their careers (and lives). You'll be surprised at how much your peers enjoy giving advice and sharing "their story" with you. It's also flattering (to most) to be asked one's opinion—insights which might help you make better decisions in your life.

Make as many friends as possible. You never know when this newfound alliance will be able to help you down the road.

And, finally, thank everybody that helps you along your path. People like to be appreciated, especially if they've taken time out to help you grow. In a world that is sometimes cold and indifferent, sending a thank-you letter or an uplifting note is not only a nice gesture, but can also make a difference in another's life. We all want to know we're doing good. Why not say so?

And don't forget to:

Be gentle with yourself.

Find your very own retreat (and use it often).

Give support, encouragement, and praise to others; and learn to accept it in return.

Remember that in the light of all the pain we see, we are bound to feel helpless at times. Admit it without shame. Caring and being there are sometimes more important than doing.

Work on your lists.

Change your routine often and your tasks when you can.

If you go around doing your thing without expectation, then you already have everything you need. If you receive something in return, you take it with open arms. It should always come as a surprise. But if you expect a response and it comes, it's a bore. Cease expecting and you have all things.

—LEO BUSCAGLIA

I expect to pass through this world but once; any good thing therefore that I can do, or any kindness that I can show to any fellow creature, let me do it now.

—ETIENNE DE GRELLET

Sometimes the road less traveled is less traveled for a reason.

—JERRY SEINFELD

Each night, focus on a good thing that occurred during your day.

Be creative and try new approaches.

Use the "buddy system" regularly as a source of support, assurance, and redirection.

Surprise someone with something.

Find the child inside.

Laugh, play, and smile.

Be yourself and do the best job you can do.

Follow those hunches, take risks, work and play hard, be flexible, and make plans—but also bend with life's flow.

Fill the pages of your life with wonder and imperfection and...

Have fun (in everything you do)!

AUTOBIOGRAPHY IN FIVE SHORT CHAPTERS
BY PORTIA NELSON

ONE
I walk down the street. There is a deep hole in the sidewalk. I fall in. I am lost. I am helpless. It isn't my fault. It takes forever to find a way out.

TWO
I walk down the same street. There is a deep hole in the sidewalk. I pretend I don't see it. I fall in again. I can't believe I am in the same place. But it isn't my fault. It still takes a long time to get out.

THREE
I walk down the same street. There is a deep hole in the sidewalk. I see it is there. I still fall in. It's a habit. My eyes are open. I know where I am. It is my fault. I get out immediately.

FOUR
I walk down the same street. There is a deep hole in the sidewalk. I walk around it.

FIVE
I walk down another street.

What I hear, I forget. What I see, I remember. What I do, I know.
—CHINESE PROVERB

Back Door Readers... . . . .

After reading your guide from cover to cover, hopefully it has become a short-term learning experience in itself, and has given you the confidence to set forth on the road to adventure, discovery, and growth. And if it has, I'd love to hear from you. Each year, I get a rather large handful of mail from readers who provide me with their feedback. In fact, the most rewarding part about creating this guidebook for you is receiving your letters, postcards, and E-mail notes! So keep letter writing alive—drop me a card in the mail and tell me what you thought (or where your journeys have taken you)!

Are you participating in a "Back Door" program?. . . . .

If you happen to be working/learning/living at one of the spots listed in this guide, get in touch with me. Each year, I try to experience as many programs listed in your guidebook as I can—and it's always a treat when an actual Back Door reader is on site! Your "insider information" can turn into great stories for future editions or for my Web site. So—drop me a line and let me know what you're up to!

New Programs and Resources. . .

Would you like me to consider your program or resource for future editions? Please send detailed information about your work/learn/travel program and/or a review copy of your unique resource to the address below and I will be in contact with you!

To get in touch with the author:

Michael Landes
Back Door Experiences
45 Pearl St., #3
Dorchester, MA 02125-1815
USA
(800) 552-PATH (US and Canada)
mlandes@backdoorjobs.com
www.backdoorjobs.com

About the Author. . . . .

MICHAEL LANDES has dedicated his life to living out the dream of his book (or he just can't seem to settle for one job…) and believes there is room for every person in our world to work at a job they love and to find meaning in their work. At age 32, Landes has worked in literally hundreds of short-term experiences over the course of his life, and fills his days plotting and experiencing new work adventures. Besides spending a great deal of his time developing and researching the BACK DOOR GUIDE, some of his most recent work stints include coordinating the internship program for California State University, Chico and short-term assignments with Apple Computer, MTV, Gallo Winery, Yellowstone National Park, the American Institute of Wine & Food, Harvard University, and many other places.

More Fun Stuff From Ten Speed Press . . . .

What Color Is Your Parachute?
A Practical Manual for Job Hunters & Career Changers
by Richard Nelson Bolles

The classic in the field for over 25 years, PARACHUTE is updated every year, with solid advice on every aspect of job-hunting, from figuring out what you really want to do to landing the job of your dreams. Millions of readers have used the sensible advice, helpful exercises, and bountiful resources to find career happiness. 6 x 9, 560 pages

Major in Success (Revised)
by Patrick Combs

A hip, fun-to-read guide to making college easier, beating the system while still enrolled, and getting a really cool job when you graduate. Covers how to get into the hot internships, mentorships, and study-abroad programs, lists classes that are worth their weight in gold in the work world, and demystifies academic success through a series of hot tips. 5 1/2 x 8 1/2, 176 pages, ISBN 0-89815-998-9

Running a One-Person Business (Revised)
by Claude Whitmyer and Salli Rasberry

Tom Peters, author of *In Search of Excellence*, has called this book "a fabulous testament to creating a rewarding lifestyle through your work, whether gardener, physicist, or dressmaker. It's also a no-nonsense, one step at a time primer to getting there from here." Enough said. 7 3/8 x 9 1/4, 224 pages, ISBN 0-89815-598-3

How to Be an Importer and Pay for Your World Travel (Revised)
by Mary Green and Stanley Gillmar

Completely revised and updated, here is all the information you'll need on where to go, what to buy, how to pay for it, how to get it home and how to sell it. 5 1/2 x 8 1/2, 160 pages, ISBN 0-89815-501-0

For more information, or to order, call the publisher at the number below or visit our website. We accept VISA, Mastercard, and American Express. You may also wish to write for our free catalog of over 500 books, posters, and audiotapes.

Ten Speed Press
P.O. Box 7123
Berkeley, CA 94707
www.tenspeed.com

800-841-BOOK